Anomaly Detection and Complex Event Processing Over IoT Data Streams

With Application to eHealth and Patient Data Monitoring

Anomaly Detection and Complex Event Processing Over IoT Data Streams

With Application to eHealth and Patient Data Monitoring

Patrick Schneider
Universitat Oberta de Catalunya (UOC)
Barcelona, Spain

Fatos Xhafa
Universitat Politècnica de Catalunya (UPC)
Barcelona, Spain

ACADEMIC PRESS
An imprint of Elsevier

Academic Press is an imprint of Elsevier
125 London Wall, London EC2Y 5AS, United Kingdom
525 B Street, Suite 1650, San Diego, CA 92101, United States
50 Hampshire Street, 5th Floor, Cambridge, MA 02139, United States
The Boulevard, Langford Lane, Kidlington, Oxford OX5 1GB, United Kingdom

Notices

Knowledge and best practice in this field are constantly changing. As new research and experience broaden our understanding, changes in research methods, professional practices, or medical treatment may become necessary.

Practitioners and researchers must always rely on their own experience and knowledge in evaluating and using any information, methods, compounds, or experiments described herein. In using such information or methods they should be mindful of their own safety and the safety of others, including parties for whom they have a professional responsibility.

To the fullest extent of the law, neither the Publisher nor the authors, contributors, or editors, assume any liability for any injury and/or damage to persons or property as a matter of products liability, negligence or otherwise, or from any use or operation of any methods, products, instructions, or ideas contained in the material herein.

Library of Congress Cataloging-in-Publication Data
A catalog record for this book is available from the Library of Congress

British Library Cataloguing-in-Publication Data
A catalogue record for this book is available from the British Library

ISBN: 978-0-12-823818-9

For information on all Academic Press publications
visit our website at https://www.elsevier.com/books-and-journals

Publisher: Mara Conner
Acquisitions Editor: Sonnini R. Yura
Editorial Project Manager: John Leonard
Production Project Manager: Selvaraj Raviraj
Designer: Victoria Pearson

Typeset by VTeX

Patrick dedicates this book to his family and friends, who gave him endless support in a long and exciting research and writing journey, as well as to you, the reader, who motivated him through this journey.

Fatos dedicates the book to his family and wishes readers enjoy it!

Contents

List of figures

List of tables

Biographies

Patrick Schneider holds a BSc in Business Informatics from the DHBW Mannheim, Germany, and an MSc in Master in Informatics Research Innovation-Data Science from the Faculty of Informatics of Barcelona at the Technical University of Catalonia (UPC). He is affiliate teaching staff at Open University of Catalonia. His areas of interest include -but are not limited to- Data Science, focusing on Real-World application of Machine Learning with specific emphasis in IoT, Big Data architectures, Process Optimization and Process Mining. He regularly participates in Program Committees of International Conferences.

Fatos Xhafa, PhD in Computer Science, is Full Professor at the Universitat Politècnica de Catalunya (UPC), Barcelona, Spain. He has held various tenured and visiting professorship positions. He was a Visiting Professor at the University of Surrey, UK (2019/2020), Visiting Professor at the Birkbeck College, University of London, UK (2009/2010) and a Research Associate at Drexel University, Philadelphia, USA (2004/2005). He was a Distinguished Guest Professor at Hubei University of Technology, China (2016-2019). Prof. Xhafa has widely published in peer reviewed international journals, conferences/workshops, book chapters, edited books and proceedings in the field (H-index 55). He is awarded teaching and research merits by Spanish Ministry of Science and Education, by IEEE conferences and best paper awards. Prof. Xhafa has an extensive editorial service. He is founder and Editor-In-Chief of Internet of Things - Journal - Elsevier (Scopus and Clarivate WoS Science Citation Index) and of International Journal of Grid and Utility Computing, (Emerging

Sources Citation Index) and AE/EB Member of several indexed Int'l Journals. He is founder and Editor-in-Chief of two books series: the Springer Book Series Lecture Notes in Data Engineering and Communication Technologies (SCOPUS, EI Compendex, ISI WoS) and the Elsevier Book Series Intelligent Data-Centric Systems (SCOPUS, EI Compendex). Prof. Xhafa is a member of IEEE Communications Society, IEEE Systems, Man & Cybernetics Society and Founder Member of Emerging Technical Subcommittee of Internet of Things. His research interests include IoT and Cloud-to-thing continuum computing, massive data processing and collective intelligence, optimization, security and trustworthy computing and machine learning, among others. He can be reached at fatos@cs.upc.edu and more information can be found at WEB: http://www.cs.upc.edu/~fatos/ Scopus Orcid: http://orcid.org/0000-0001-6569-5497.

Preface

Internet-of-Things (IoT) is being fast established as the new computing paradigm, which is bound to change the ways of our everyday working and living. With the ever-increasing number of connected devices, the IoT devices have become a primary source of data generation in the form of Big Data or Big Data streams. Few years following the introduction of the IoT concept, significant hype was generated as a result of the proliferating number of IoT-enabled devices, which are expected to amount to several billion in the next years. During recent years, this hype has been turning to reality, as a wave of IoT applications with significant social and economic has been emerging. In most cases, these applications rely on the processing of IoT data in order to optimize operations and facilitate decision making. IoT analytics applications will ensure the proper exploitation of huge volumes of IoT data for a variety of nontrivial purposes, involving not only the production of simple data-driven insights on operations but also the prediction of events and build the basis for prescriptive analytics.

Healthcare domain is one such field of activity where IoT computing is envisioned to play a revolutionary change. Indeed, healthcare is at its core driven by data. Research needs to conduct studies to get data for further inferences of reasons and treatments for illnesses. Based on this knowledge, a healthcare professional observes the patient (in other words gets information/data) and sets the diagnosis and treatment accordingly. Data gathering is an expensive process for researchers, doctors, and patients in terms of time, space, cost and staffing requirements. This is a constraint that finally leads to less insight which could be used to react quickly to critical situations, detect health issues or provide more accurate data for research on diagnosis and treatment. Due to the nonavailability of ready to access healthcare data, many health problems may remain undetected in conventional healthcare systems.

Over the past few decades, Information and Communication Technologies (ICT) lead the healthcare environment to the development of the Electronic Health Record (EHR) to make health-care access and delivery easier and more cost-effective. EHRs contain complete patient health history and can be easily shared among various actors and stakeholders. Digital health care applications have been developed to allow patients to connect with their provider, leading to, commonly referred to, as connected health. Connected health uses smartphones and mobile applications, together with wireless technologies to allow patients to connect with their providers without visiting them frequently. This shift allows further flexibility and convenience in health-care management. The most radical development that we might experience in healthcare builds around smart health wherein mobile, wearable-medical and IoT devices enable continuous patient monitoring and treatment. For example, wearable sensors (such as a temperature and the heartbeat sensors) can act as data collecting units, collecting the physiological signals from the patient's body. These devices work together to create a unified medical report that can be accessed by various providers.

This book presents data-centric approaches in healthcare and how IoT revolutionizes the fields of collection, studies, detection, classification, real-time processing, advanced analytics, and complex reasoning in eHealth domain. These concepts and approaches are developed along the following main pillars.

Large scale data gathering for eHealth systems

- IoT can gather patient data at scale on a continuous basis, where resources can be spared and, therefore, more extensive analysis and data gathering can be conducted, such as identification of disease patterns. Observational, prevention, epidemiological, supportive care and diagnostic trials can have a major benefit from large scale data gathering.
- As a game changer, IoT computing in eHealth will revolutionize the eHealth solutions to early detection and prediction at scale. This will make a significant shift of current diagnosis systems, in which early detection and predictions are limited and stay lags behind current needs.

Patient remote monitoring for healthcare and medical services

- Chronic care management based on remote and continuous health checkups and health evaluation of chronic disease patients is among largest burdens of current health systems. Remote patient monitoring simultaneously improves the quality of care through constant attention and reduces the cost of care by eliminating the need for a caregiver to actively engage in data collection and analysis. It helps the doctor to access real-time data of chronic disease patient and replaces the process of having a health professional come by at regular intervals to check the patient's vital signs. Smart wireless pill bottles provide tracking and analytics of medication usage of chronic care patients.
- IoT-based health systems can track a patient's health development to early detect health issues or critical health condition, through accessing both historical and real-time health data.
- Healthcare workers can monitor patient health condition and whenever anomalous events occur an alert can be sent to family members or caregivers.

Advanced eHealth analytics and decision support systems

- A real-time patient analysis that concludes in an event can be further integrated into complex event scenarios. While bio-signals are in the center of patient monitoring, information like the location of the patient can be used to further integrate into decision scenarios to dispatch the nearest health worker, volunteer or family member in case of an emergency.
- Machine Learning-based, self-learning and self-improvement enable accurate and timely treatments that can be made based on fast patient evaluation, and the development of rehabilitation procedures corresponding to the medical investigation. Many factors need to be considered to provide a precise treatment. Computer tools merely rely on data collected by sensors and past case studies, while self-learning techniques can adaptively analyze and recommend new treatment options. Using IoT computing, it is possible to integrate accurate medical data, analytics and automation into decision support systems to recommend or validate preferred actions taken in a critical situation.
- In a continuous monitoring scenario the patient's health development can be easily followed and issues can be early detected to alert medical actors before a critical condition manifests. Data analysis can provide useful insights into detecting anomalies and providing appropriate treatments to patients.

Challenges of eHealth IoT streams processing

- IoT data streams and IoT analytics pose a myriad of challenges including the heterogeneity of the IoT data sources, the typically high velocity of IoT data streams, the noisy and error-prone nature of IoT data, as well as the time and location-dependent nature of IoT data resources.

- As a result of these challenges, IoT analytics require sophisticated processing models and methods. The detection of an unexpected event, that might be hard to classify with current knowledge, represents a major challenge in stream analytics. Dealing with anomaly detection algorithms to detect unexpected events in data streams, as well as classifying anomalous events and further used in multiple events scenarios to infer correlated insight in complex event processing scenarios, is of paramount importance.

IoT technologies, eHealth and health industry

- IoT healthcare technology is set to revolutionize the healthcare industry to the next decade, as it has great potential and multiple potential applications, from remote monitoring to medical integration. Synergies between sensor-based info gathering, healthcare knowledge domain, and advanced analytics offer new possibilities to infer knowledge, diagnose and act at the moment an anomalous event is happening or evening preventing unfavorable situations.
- The dependency of healthcare on IoT is increasing day by day to enhance access to care and strengthen the quality of health service and finally reduce the cost of health system. The main purpose behind the IoT based healthcare system is to provide better healthcare services to all the people anywhere and at any time in the world.
- Devices and infrastructures are already here and are getting more sophisticated in monitoring as well as gathering massive amounts of data. While the health-care sector is increasingly interested in leveraging IoT and big data technologies to become more efficient, there are several challenges that need to be addressed before digital health care can become a widespread reality. The exponential increase in the volume of health-care data generated by IoT devices makes data processing and analysis very challenging. This is exemplified with the application of ECG data sets and evaluated in terms of accuracy, efficiency and scalability.

Multidisciplinarity, actors and stakeholders in eHealth

- Health is a field of many interdisciplinary domains working together, where the questions of how we process data and gain actionable insight will build the foundation for the proper action of actors and stakeholders in the field.
- In this context, IoT stakeholders, including researchers, architects, medical engineers, health professionals, researchers, data scientists, data engineers, solution integrators and service providers must be able to understand the vision and challenges associated with the design, development, deployment, and operation of advanced IoT analytics systems.
- The objective is to build a data science foundation for technologists, engineers, scientists, and clinicians to synergize their efforts in creating low-cost yet high performance, highly efficient, deployable IoT scenarios in healthcare systems, as well as to give access to practitioners in an interdisciplinary field of IoT stream analytics, Edge computing and complex event processing.

Towards supporting various actors and stakeholders in the eHealth domain, this book gives a comprehensive coverage of IoT data stream processing with a focus on real-time anomaly detection in eHealth domain. The full data cycle, from data collection, semantic enrichment, abnormal/anomaly detection to reasoning and decision making is addressed. A case study with real ECG data sets and data analysis is presented based on the theoretical foundation to give a practical vision to the theoretical foundation, which we believe will be useful to researchers, practitioners and developers in the field.

Emerging research issues and challenges such as ethics and privacy issues in patient data monitoring, data protection regulations, noninvasive and personalized solutions are also discussed in the book.

We hope the readers will find the book useful in their study, research and professional activities.

Patrick Schneider
Fatos Xhafa
Barcelona, Spain
August 6, 2021

Fundamental concepts, models and methods

IoT data streams: concepts and models

Introductory concepts and models

1.1 IoT streams in the context of Big Data

Data stream analytics' core utility is the recognition and extraction of meaningful patterns from raw data inputs. With that, a higher level of insight can be retrieved and used for event detection, complex event processing, reasoning, and decision making. Extracting knowledge from raw data is essential for many applications and businesses since it potentially enables competitive advantages. Several works have described Big Data characteristics from different points in terms of volume, velocity, and variety. A commonly used model to characterize IoT Big Data is that of the many "*Vs*"–the definition of up to 10 Vs can be found in current literature. Although originally defined for Big Data, the Vs model can be used also for identifying the main characteristics of data streams, as follows next, by distinguishing batch data collection versus online, real-time data streams.

Volume

Volume of data exponentially increases every day, based on the concept of Internet of Everything (IoE), where humans, machines and small devices interconnected in cyber-physical systems (CPS) are producing faster and larger amounts of new information, i.e., data. In the community, data of the order of Terabytes and bigger are considered as "big volume" as conventional software and hardware systems are unable to handle it in reasonable amount of time and space. The volume contributes to the challenging issue that traditional storage systems, such as traditional databases, could be no longer suitable to host and process vasts amounts of data. Data generated by IoT devices that surround most of our lives are collected and stored in a continuous mode. For instance, in the field of healthcare, diagnostic imaging, together with genomics information, represent a large part of data volume. Current figures show that in the 2019 year, one in ten persons in Europe has undergone imaging with computed tomography (CT), one in 13 undergoes magnetic resonance (MR), and one in 200 positron emission tomography (PET) [19]. A patient can generate hundreds to thousands of images using various protocols, modalities (e.g., CT, MRI, PET, X-ray), and multiple dimensions (e.g., volumetric 3D, time series, etc.). The size of medical images can be extremely large, for example, the whole-slide histopathological images can include more than 100,000×100,000 pixels, and thus each is usually split into millions of small patches for processing [39].

While Big Data is mainly understood as large amounts of data at still, gathered over time and processed in large batches in an unlimited access mode, Big Data streams refer to large amounts of data generated and processed in real-time in smaller batches, which can be accessed and seen only once. This characterization of Big Data vs. Big Data streams makes a significant impact on the applications sustained by such data types. The former supports applications of historical data processing, knowledge discovery and prediction at large, while the latter supports applications for detecting anomalies,

Anomaly Detection and Complex Event Processing Over IoT Data Streams. https://doi.org/10.1016/B978-0-12-823818-9.00011-0

patterns, event classification, prediction, etc., in real-time. Together, Big Data and Big Data streams are able to achieve a better understanding of the phenomenon under study. They are of paramount importance to a new generation of eHealth applications.

Velocity

Velocity is the speed in which new data is generated and arrives in input to the stream processing system. There is velocity in Big Data, however, it is different from velocity in Big Data streams. Researchers have tried to estimate data growth, in an attempt similar to Moore's rule, however, it is not possible to cast a data growth law due to its exponential nature. It should be noted however that in lack of a data growth law, data rate is very important to both Big Data and Big Data stream processing.

1. Data in motion and real-time Big Data analytics: Big data are produced in real-time and, most of the time, need to be analyzed in real-time. Therefore, an architecture for capturing and mining Big Data flows must support real-time turnaround.
2. Lifetime of data utility: The second dimension of data velocity is how long data will be valuable. Understanding this additional temporal dimension of velocity will allow discarding data that is no longer meaningful when new up-to-date and more detailed information has been produced. The period of data lifetime can be long, but in some cases short. For example, we might think that we only need the results from a recent lab test for a specific analysis (Big Data stream processing). However, we might want to trace the same measurements from the past for a more detailed analysis (Big Data processing).

Variety

Variety represents the different data types as well as different data sources that contribute to Big Data and Big Data streams.

1. Different data types: Traditionally, major sources of clinical data were databases or spreadsheets. Now data can come under the form of free text in the form of reports or electronic health records or images like CT scans. This type of data is usually characterized by structured, semistructured (e.g., databases with some missing values or inconsistencies) or unstructured data. Data types such as text, signals, sound, video, etc., can be found in just one Big Data stream.
2. Different data sources: Variety means that data can come from different sources. These sources do not necessarily belong to the same system and or in the context of IoT, the same IoT device(s).

Based on different sensor/IoT networks, the same application can have different data schemes. This affects both data collection and storage. Two major challenges must be faced:

1. Storing and retrieving this data efficiently and cost-effectively.
2. Aligning and normalizing data types from different sources, so that all the data is processed simultaneously.

There is also an additional complexity due to the interaction between variety and volume. Unstructured data usually grows much faster than structured data. Estimations indicate that unstructured data doubles around every three months [17]. Therefore, the complexity and fragmentation of data are far from being slowed down and applications will have to deal with much more unstructured data than expected.

Veracity

Veracity represents the accuracy as well as the trustworthiness of data. Data streams appear in many forms where quality and accuracy are hard to manage precisely. Unreliable devices could be a source of imprecise data, missing data, data errors, etc. Volumes often balance the lack of quality or accuracy, where the aspects of real-time analytics stay in a trade-off between volume-driven accuracy and fast analytics. On the other hand, veracity of sensitive data sources is an issue in many applications. Indeed, data tampering, which intentionally modifies and manipulates data through unauthorized channels, can cause malfunction of applications. The problem arises in both Big Data and Big Data streams. In the latter case, tampering can directly affect the data sources, i.e., tampered IoT devices, requiring techniques for detecting IoT Device tampering.

Value

Value results from the transformation of raw data to meaningful information and knowledge. It applies to both Big Data and Big Data streams, although in the former case, knowledge can be more wide and deep than in the latter case, where detecting events of interest is often the use case. The value highly depends on the underlying processes, services, and the way the data is processed. For example, an ECG signal monitoring may need all sensor data, as opposed to a weather forecast application, which may only need random samples of sensor data. In real-time analytics, the value of the data could decay with a slower processing. Indeed, as data can be seen only once and therefore the faster the processing the larger the data amounts generated in input can be processed.

Variability

Variability represents the different data flow rates. Depending on the field in which IoT devices are applied, inconsistent data flows can result. A data source can have different data load rates based on specific times. For example, in environmental monitoring, devices are required to maximize their battery life. This results in a need for efficient processing and low network overhead. The processing speed, however, is usually not as crucial in these cases. In a clinical environment, the power usage of the sensing devices and processing is not a concern, as power is readily available, and the usage is marginal compared to other power demands of a clinic. The data rates in these environments, however, can be very high, and there may be a need for instantaneous processing. If an error is not detected within seconds or even milliseconds may result in more significant issues.

To see the presented main four V's in action, consider the case of imaging data (e.g., patient's scans) collected and *streamed* within groups of experts in hospitals, medical centers, etc.:

1. Due to improvements in the hardware (e.g., scanning machines), a large number of images are produced within a short elapsed of time, which need to be stored and streamed (*Volume*).
2. Developments on hardware and, in general, in the imaging healthcare sector are designing machines able to produce many more images, combining different modalities at the same time yielding each time higher data rates (Velocity).
3. Different imaging modalities are combined (*Variety*).
4. Despite the existence of unified standards for storing and transmitting medical images (e.g., *DICOM - Digital Imaging and Communications in Medicine*), there is no agreement on associated metadata, such as medical annotations of patients scans. Metadata associated with imaging data can be of different formats, without a unique agreed data model. Additionally, scans can be of poor quality, errors can occur in patient identification information, etc. Tampering with scanning equipment

to produce false or manipulated images is possible by exploring security weaknesses in medical imaging equipment and transmission networks (*Veracity*).

1.2 Static *vs.* continuous data systems

The main objective of both Data Stream Management Systems (DSMS) and DataBase Management System (DBMS) is to provide generic data management for applications. Still, there are differences in how to manage data and evaluate queries. DSMSs have their origin in DBMSs but present substantial differences. DSMSs manage continuous data streams while DBMS manage static data. This impacts on how data queried are performed. DSMSs implement flexible query processing, where short latency is relevant, in a continuous query in the course of data arrival (data stream) at the system. Complex Event Processing (CEP) is also possible in DSMS through more complex queries.

We briefly evaluate next their different characteristics.

Query types

The first difference can be seen in the type of queries, where DBMS run one-time queries over persistently stored data, while DSMS system makes use of continuous queries over transient data. A DBMS query is executed and gives the output for the current state of the relations. DSMS, on the other side, are long-running queries and stay active in the system over a longer time window. Once a DSMS registered a continuous query, the results will be generated as output continuously over new arriving stream elements until it is unregistered.

Query answers

The query answer of a DBMS always produces exact answers for a given query. Continuous queries, on the other side, usually provide approximate query answers. The reasons for the approximate answers are:

1. Continuous queries might not be computed with a finite amount of memory. An example of this is the Cartesian product over two infinite streams, which lead in bounded computation to an approximate answer.
2. The group-by operator would block an infinite stream for exact answers, hence an approximate result over a finite space is obtained.
3. The accumulation of data can be faster than the system can process (higher data rate in input). It should be noted, however, that in the context of continuous streaming, high quality approximated data is accepted as an answer and newly arrived data are seen as more accurate and relevant in continuous data than in old data.
4. The nature of data streams, where data can be incomplete (missing data), with errors, imprecise event boundaries detection, etc., makes the query computation in DSMS approximate yet reasonable for real-time processing.

Processing methodology

DBMS can be seen as demand-driven computation models, where the processing of a query is issued. The tuples are read from the persistently stored data via scan or index-based access methods. In contrast, Continuous Query Processing (CQP) in a DSMS is a data-driven approach, where the answer is computed incrementally on the arrival of new stream elements. Without the use of buffering, DSMS can access the stream elements only in a sequential arriving order, where DBMS can access tuples randomly.

Query optimization

The query optimization in DBMS is done before the execution. The optimizer generates semantically equivalent query execution plans based on cost approximation, which contains different performance characteristics. The approximation of the cost is handled with statistical information of the tables, relations, and system information. The optimizer chooses the plan afterward with the lowest estimated cost. Continuous queries in DSMS require query optimization at run-time to adapt to changing stream characteristics and system conditions. Query workload can therefore change over time, as well as data distributions and arrival rates. To not degrade the stream application's performance, run-time optimization is a critical aspect to consider in DSMS.

1.3 Time variability in data streams

In continuous data streams, the validity and usefulness of stream elements have a lifespan. Latency in a network or out-of-date stream elements could degrade the value of the analysis. Also, the anticipated time variability of the data streams is necessary for later processing steps and reasoning. An example can be that of an alarm will be triggered over an average threshold of the last n data elements. The problem occurs if the time variability is not constant, and only $n - 1$ data elements arrived, and further elements are not generated in a constant time interval.

Throughout the book, data streams are generally described as:

- A data stream is a possible unbounded sequence of data items generated by a data source. A single data item is called a stream element.
- Stream elements usually arrive in a continuous mode at a system.
- The core system might not have control or knowledge over the sequence of the arriving elements as well as of their arrival rates. The stream rates and ordering can be unpredictable and may change over time.
- A data source sends the stream elements only once. As stream elements are accessed sequentially, a past arrived stream element cannot be retrieved unless stored. With the unbounded size of stream data, a full materialization is not possible in some cases.
- Data stream queries need to run continuously and return new results while new stream elements arrive. The ordering of stream elements may be implicit, which can be in the form of arrival time at the system, or explicit when the stream elements provide an application timestamp with their time of creation. In addition to raw stream data, some use cases need to enrich the data streams with stored data.

Data stream types

The variability of a data stream can be generally characterized into one of the following categories:

1. Time intervals between packages:

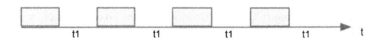

FIGURE 1.1

Illustration of data flow with fixed time intervals t_1.

FIGURE 1.2

Illustration of data flow with segments with periodic nature represented by t_2.

FIGURE 1.3

Illustration of data flow with no pattern of the time interval between tuples.

- Strongly periodic data stream
  - When the time intervals stay the same length between two tuples, the stream has a strongly periodic characteristic (see Fig. 1.1). In the optimal case, the jitter –the deviation from true periodicity– has the value zero.
  - Example: Pulse code modulation coded speech in classic telephone switching.

- Weakly periodic data stream
  - When the time interval between two tuples is not constant but periodical, then the stream has a weakly periodic characteristic (see Fig. 1.2).
  - Example: Segmented transmission.

- A-periodic data stream
  - When the sequence of time intervals is neither strongly nor weakly periodic, and the time period or time gap varies between tuples to tuples during the transmission, then such data stream is called an aperiodic data stream, as illustrated in Fig. 1.3.
  - Example: Instant messaging systems.

2. Variation of consecutive tuple amounts:

- Strongly regular data stream
  - When the amount of data is constant during the lifetime of a data stream. This feature is especially found in uncompressed digital or sensor data transmission. Fig. 1.4 illustrates this characteristic.
  - Example: Video stream of cameras in uncompressed form, audio stream or ECG sensors.

- Weakly regular data stream

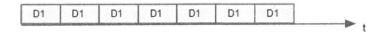

FIGURE 1.4

Illustration of a constant data size.

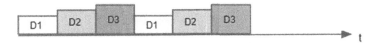

FIGURE 1.5

Illustration of a weakly regular data size stream.

FIGURE 1.6

Illustration of an irregular data size stream.

- When the size of the data stream items varies periodically then it is called weakly regular data stream, as shown in Fig. 1.5.
- Example: Compressed video stream.

3. Connection or continuity between consecutive tuples:

- Continuous data stream
  - If the packets are transmitted without intermediate gaps.
  - Example: Audio data.

- Unconnected data stream
  - A data stream with gaps between information items is called an unconnected data stream.
  - Example: Compressed video stream.

- Irregular data stream
  - If the amount of data is not constant or changes, then the data stream is called irregular. Transmission and processing of this type of stream are more complicated since the stream has a variable (bit) rate after applying compression methods. Fig. 1.6 illustrates this characteristic.
  - Example: Sentiment analysis on trending tweets.

Batch vs. real-time analytics

Data streaming analytics on high-performance computing systems or Cloud platforms is mainly based on data parallelism and incremental processing [37]. Through data parallelism, a large dataset is partitioned into several subsets, on which parallel analytics can be performed simultaneously. Incremental or serial processing refers to fetching a small sample of batch data to be processed quickly in a pipeline. Although these techniques reduce the response latency from the streaming analytics framework, they might not be the best solution for stream IoT applications. By bringing stream analytics closer to the source of IoT and edge devices (*Edge/Fog computing*), the need for central data parallelism and sequential processing is less sensible.

1.4 Dynamic data stream structure – the drift concept

In web mining, social networks, network monitoring, sensor networks, telecommunications, or financial forecasting, data samples arrive continuously through unbounded streams. The underlying phenomena generating these data streams may evolve, where the system's environment can be considered dynamic, evolving, or nonstationary.

The output of classification learning is a discrete class label, and in a regression learning, a numeric value of a variable. In both cases, the thing to be learned is called "concept". The learner's output is the description of this concept. As mentioned before, the data streams may evolve so that the mapping between the input space and the output space (classes) changes, leading to concept drift [22]. Thus, to deal with data stream classification, the classifier must be able to self-adapt online over time [11,30,10].

Drift can be defined according to how the new concept replaces the old one [42,67]. The criteria defining the drift give indications about drift period, speed, intensity, severity, and frequency. These characteristics support finding methods and tools suitable to handle the concept drift. Data streams' evolving nature poses another challenge that is rarely addressed in the literature and known as concept evolution. Concept evolution occurs when new classes emerge or existing classes vanish.

1.4.1 Drift speed

The drift duration, also called drifting time or drift width is the number of time steps for a new concept to replace the old one because no data samples of the old samples will occur. Speed is the inverse of the drifting time because a higher speed is related to a lower number of time steps and vice-versa. Therefore, the drift speed V_d is calculated by $V_d = \frac{1}{t_{de} - t_{ds}}$ where t_{ds} and t_{de} are, respectively, the time when the drift starts and ends. According to its speed, a drift can be either abrupt or gradual:

- An abrupt drift occurs when the new concept suddenly replaces the old one in a short drifting time. This kind of drift immediately deteriorates the classifier's performance, as the new concept quickly substitutes the old one (see Fig. 1.7).
- A gradual drift occurs when the drifting time is relatively large. This type of drift is hard to detect since it creates uncertainty due to both old and new concepts' active coexistence. Gradual drift can be either probabilistic or continuous:
  - Gradual probabilistic drift refers to a period where both old concepts generated by the source S_1 and new concepts generated by the source S_2 coexist. There is a weighted combination between data samples generated by S_1 (old concept) and the ones generated by S_2 (new concept). As time passes, the probability of sampling from S_1 decreases, whereas the probability of sampling from S_2 increases until the new concept replaces the old one (see Fig. 1.8).

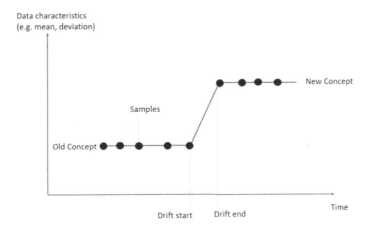

FIGURE 1.7

Abrupt drift.

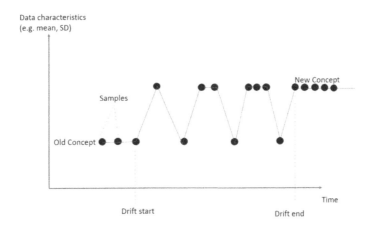

FIGURE 1.8

Gradual probabilistic drift.

- Gradual continuous or incremental drift defines the case where the concept itself continuously changes from the old to the new concept by small modifications at every time step. Therefore, during the continuous or incremental change, the new concept does not yet appear. These changes are so small that they are only noticed after a long period (see Fig. 1.9).

An example of probabilistic gradual drift

Let us assume that incoming data samples arrive within batches, each containing 100 data samples. A source S_1 generates the patterns or data samples in the first batch. In the second batch, 80 patterns were

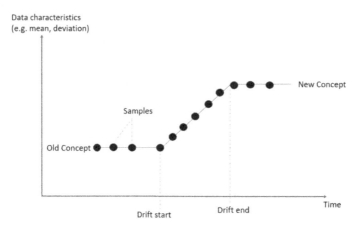

FIGURE 1.9

Gradual continuous drift.

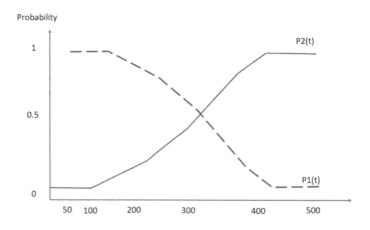

FIGURE 1.10

Probability P_1 of the occurrence of patterns from old concept and the probability P_2 of the occurrence of patterns from new concept for the case of probabilistic gradual drift.

generated by source S_1 (old concept), while 20 patterns by a new source S_2 (new concept). In the third batch, 50 patterns are generated by S_1 and 50 patterns by S_2. Finally, in the fourth and fifth batches, all the patterns are generated by the S_2. Therefore, this drift gradually replaced the old concept (S_1) with the new one (S_2).

Fig. 1.10 shows the probabilities of patterns belonging to the old and new concepts. Here, the probability P_1 of occurrence of patterns generated by S_1 decreases, while the probability P_2 of patterns generated by S_2 increases over time, resulting in P_1 equal to 0 and P_2 equal to 1, indicating that the new concept has completely replaced the old one.

1.4.2 Drift severity

Severity refers to the number of changes caused by the drift occurrence. The drift severity can be high or low. A high or global severity means that the old concept has been completely changed. Therefore, the whole region occupied by this old concept will be impacted by the drift. A low or partial severity refers to a change impacting only a part of the region occupied by the feature space's old concept. Therefore, patterns belonging to both old and new concepts will become indistinct.

For example, let us consider the user preferences in document retrieval where a complete change in search criteria for documents occurs. Therefore, the new documents do not share similarities with previous documents. At this point, no old document belongs to the user's actual preferences anymore. The user may also change only some of the search criteria for document search, where some old documents remain in the preferences.

1.4.3 Drift influence zones

Concept drift can be global or local according to the feature space's impact zone of the drift. Local concept drift is defined as change that occurs in partial regions of the feature space. Therefore, the time required to detect the local drifts can be arbitrary due to the rarity of data samples belonging to the new concept since both old and new concepts are coexisting. Data samples generated from the new concept can be considered noise, making the model unstable. To overcome the instability, the model has to differentiate between local changes and noises and deal with the scarcity of data samples representing the local drift to update the learner effectively. The global concept drift is more straightforward to detect since it affects the overall feature space. The difference between the old and the new concept is more significant, and the drift can be detected earlier since the old concept will not be confused anymore with the new concept.

1.4.4 Drift occurrence frequency and recurrence

A concept may suffer from several drifts over time. If drifts occur within regular time intervals, then they are called periodic drifts. Their occurrence frequency can be measured as the inverse number of time steps between two consecutive drift starts. Drifts occurring in random or irregular time intervals are called aperiodic drifts. A concept suffering from the same drift at different time instances is called recurrent drift. In this case, concepts previously active may reappear after some time. Recurrent drifts can be differentiated in cyclic or acyclic:

- Cyclic recurrent drift (see Fig. 1.11–above) occurs according to a certain periodicity or due to a seasonal trend. For instance, in the electricity market, the prices may increase in winter due to the increase of demand and then return to the previous level in the other seasons. The weather prevision is another example of cyclic recurrent drift where the prevision rules change cyclically according to the active season.
- Acyclic recurrent drift (see Fig. 1.11–below) occurs in aperiodic or random time intervals. For instance, the electricity prices may suddenly increase due to the increase in petrol prices (because of a political or economic crisis) and then return to the previous level when petrol prices decrease.

When an old concept reappears, it may not be completely similar to its initial state. For example, a machine with two classes representing normal and failure operation conditions, where the initial

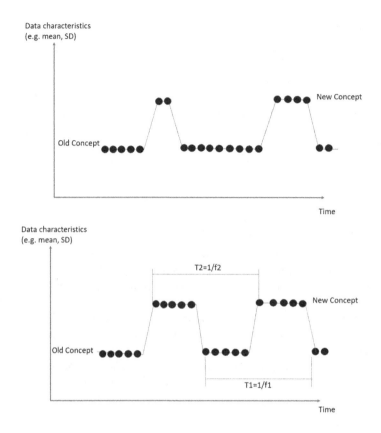

FIGURE 1.11

Cyclic (periodic) recurrent drift (above) and acyclic (aperiodic) recurrent drift (below). f_1 is the occurrence frequency of the old concept, while f_2 is the occurrence frequency of the new concept.

state only has the normal operation class. In the moment of failure, a new concept occurs, and the old concept disappears. When the machine is repaired, it returns to the normal class (old concept). However, according to the maintenance actions' efficiency and the machine degradation status, the machine may not return completely to the normal operating conditions.

1.4.5 Drift predictability

The predictability criterion was initially used in [42], to indicate whether the drift follows a pattern or completely at random. A drift is predictable if it follows a certain mechanism or set of rules like in weather forecasting. The change in the prediction rules is predictable according to the change in seasons. A drift is considered unpredictable when it occurs randomly and does not follow any mechanism or rule, like in faults. It is still possible, in some cases, to predict the occurrence of fault before its occurrence [40]. Faults can occur at any time and in different contexts. It is interesting to consider a drift's predictability to understand its origins and get a prognostic function.

1.4.6 Drift concept in real-world application

There are multiple application domains in which concept drift plays an essential role. For these applications, the machine learning and data mining methods used to build a prediction or classification model must consider the concept drift to maintain the model performance and accuracy. In real-life applications, the concept drift may be complex because it presents time-varying characteristics. As an example, a concept drift can be recurrent, gradual, and local at some time instances, and then abrupt and global at other time instances. In reality, a mixture of many drift characteristics can be observed during the transition phase of concept drift [22].

In [67,22], authors classify drift problem into four categories:

1. Monitoring adversary actions in intrusion detection [46] or in traffic control and traffic management [16]
2. Personal assistance and information as recommender systems [12], customer profiling [23], and spam filtering [51]
3. Predictions for decision making as evaluation of creditworthiness [57], electricity prices prediction, and sales prediction [3]
4. A wide spectrum of moving stationary systems which interact with changing environments like robots [47] and smart house appliances [49]
5. Detecting or identifying atypical characteristics when large amount of data streams are generated continuously in Cloud data centers.

Design of self-adaptive models

To design an efficient self-adaptive model, the following points need to be determined:

–Objective of the model in terms of classification or regression
–Sources of the drift: The environmental or isolated system itself
–Characteristics of the drift: Speed, severity, or predictability
–Learning speed and required amount of data (labeled)
–Required accuracy and costs of errors
–Data samples balanced or imbalanced

The above points define a drift phenomenon and guide the selection of suitable methods and tools to design an efficient self-adaptive learning scheme.

For example, fault diagnosis aims at deciding whether a system works in normal operating conditions or a failure has occurred or will occur. The occurrence of a fault involves a drift in the system's normal operating conditions. Such an application has the following characteristics:

–Objective is the classification of a new pattern, representing the current operation conditions, to a normal or failure state.
–Drift reasons are caused by the system environment, such as a cut of physical connection between two switches due to an external action or degradation of service quality due to wearing or accumulated pollution.

Characteristics of the drift

–Permanent or intermittent faults may occur, where permanent fault can be abrupt or gradual, where in an abrupt scenario, the drift is a shift in the operation conditions from normal to faulty.

In a gradual scenario, the drift is a continuous or incremental degeneration in the system performance. If the fault is intermittent, the drift is gradual probabilistic since patterns representing normal and faulty classes exist. Then the number of fault patterns increases over time until the failure takes over completely.

–The drift speed in gradual probabilistic and gradual continuous cases depends on external factors generating these degradations, like rate of pollution, moisture, or temperature.

–The drift is acyclic recurrent since the fault may occur at any time and can be eliminated via maintenance actions.

–The fault may be local (low severity) or global (high severity), impacting partially or completely the feature space. For example, a small degradation leads to a local drift since the system keeps an acceptable performance. An example of local drift is the case where a pump is partially failed off or failed on. In contrast, an abrupt and severe fault generates a global drift.

- Speed of learning must be fast since the decision about the system status must be taken online to limit the fault adversary impact.
- Required accuracy and costs of errors depending on the application and the impact of faults on the system performance. If the system is a part of a nuclear reactor, then the required accuracy of detecting faults is very high.
- Data samples are highly imbalanced since the data samples belonging to normal operating conditions are much bigger than those representing a fault.

Given the importance of the drift concepts, researchers are investigating ways to reduce its impact on classification algorithms. Authors in [1], proposed a drift detector approach that can be combined with an arbitrary classification algorithm. Other works in this direction can be found in the literature.

1.5 IoT data streams in healthcare

Before the advent of IoT and Cloud computing, doctor-patient interaction was limited to in-person visits, tele, and text communications. It was not possible for doctors to remotely monitor patients' health for timely treatment. However, IoT and cloud computing-based healthcare systems enable real-time healthcare applications that leverage IoT and cloud computing's full potential in healthcare and help physicians deliver excellent healthcare services. IoT and Cloud computing have increased patient confidence and satisfaction by making communication between patients and physicians more accessible and efficient. Also, remote monitoring shortens the length of hospital stay and avoids readmission to a hospital. These new technologies significantly impact reducing healthcare costs and improving patient outcomes. IoT and Cloud computing technologies improve healthcare by developing a new range of IoT-connected medical devices.

Healthcare applications can be divided into two main groups; the first group focuses on concepts arising from IoT and Cloud computing synergy, while the second group focuses on classifying healthcare applications into single parameter and multiparameter applications, where a parameter can be described as a single stream. A single parameter application treats one disease or condition, while a multiparameter application is used to treat multiple conditions as a whole. Fig. 1.12 shows concepts and trending applications in healthcare.

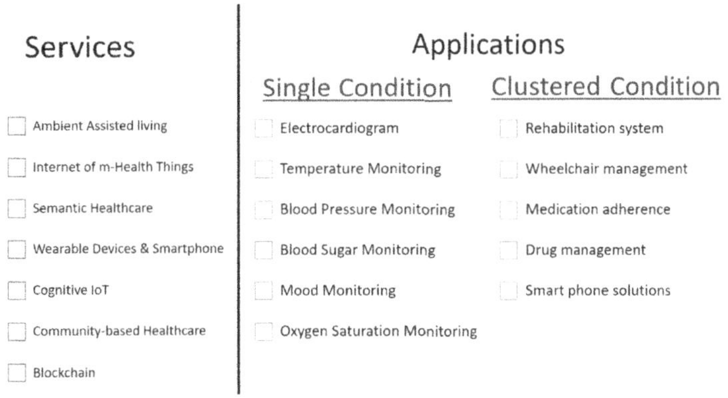

Services	Applications	
	Single Condition	**Clustered Condition**
☐ Ambient Assisted living	☐ Electrocardiogram	☐ Rehabilitation system
☐ Internet of m-Health Things	☐ Temperature Monitoring	☐ Wheelchair management
☐ Semantic Healthcare	☐ Blood Pressure Monitoring	☐ Medication adherence
☐ Wearable Devices & Smartphone	☐ Blood Sugar Monitoring	☐ Drug management
☐ Cognitive IoT	☐ Mood Monitoring	☐ Smart phone solutions
☐ Community-based Healthcare	☐ Oxygen Saturation Monitoring	
☐ Blockchain		

FIGURE 1.12

Illustration of the DBMS processing (left) vs. DSMS processing (right) paradigm.

Table 1.1 Ambient assisted living domains and their related sensors.

Domain	Sensor Type
Vital Monitoring	Temperature, Heart rate, glucose meter, electromyography
Activity Recognition	Force, ultrasonic, button, accelerometer, kinect
Surrounding environment	Air temperature, moistness, carbon, monoxide, carbon dioxide, glow

1.5.1 Healthcare concepts

Concepts are defined as trending methods or solutions that have the chance of being a foundation for different applications. The following section introduces several basic concepts of IoT and Cloud computing in healthcare.

Ambient Assisted Living (AAL)

AAL is a subarea of ambient intelligence. It is a relatively new discipline where smart objects are placed to support seniors live independently. Research on AAL has increased thanks to advances in data science, sensor technology, and smart health device availability. More and more AAL applications are using cloud computing [33,59] to manage and analyze the collected data and identify person-specific activities for real-time remote monitoring and emergency response. Table 1.1 summarizes common domains and related sensors in current studies on AAL. Three main areas of AAL are activity detection, vital monitoring, and environmental awareness. Among these, activity detection is of interest to many researchers as it is vital to the well-being of the elderly and identifies potential threats that may affect elderly.

Internet of Medical Things (IoMT)

IoMT refers to the use of mobile computing, medical sensors, and cloud computing to monitor patients' vital signs in real-time [20] and the use of communication technologies to relay data to a Cloud computing framework. The data can be accessed by physicians to monitor, diagnose, and treat patients effectively. A platform for a cloud computing-based m-health monitoring application was presented in [62]. The platform includes many important layers; in the data storage module, a multiple client access concept was introduced to ensure data privacy. A linked list was used in the annotation module to enhance Electronic Medical Records (EMRs) exchange semantically.

Semantic healthcare

The use of semantics and ontologies in healthcare has increased to store and manage large amounts of medical data in more efficient and effective ways [31,53]. Defining semantics and ontologies on top of the IoT enables semantic interoperability among multiple wearable devices. For example, a semantic Fog network model has been proposed to store and exchange health data about soldiers and weapon conditions between network components [53]. Through tactical and nontactical operations, the system ensured communication between soldiers and the control station. [31] presented an IoT-based Semantic Health framework that supports communication between heterogeneous IoT devices. The authors focused on designing a lightweight model for semantic annotation of data to make it semantically expressive. Other researches have addressed semantic medical issues using IoT, such as semantic modeling [50] and semantic interoperability for Big Data in a heterogeneous healthcare IoT infrastructure [58].

Wearable devices and smart phone

Wearable technology is a characteristic feature of modern IoT. In healthcare, wearable devices reduce overall costs and bring numerous benefits to medical staff and patients like mobility and constant monitoring capabilities. Sensors built into these smart devices allow them to sense the user's health status or environment and enable real-time processing data. These devices are supported by smartphones equipped with computing power to analyze the collected data or transmit it to further computing units to store, process, and analyze the data. A recent study presented an IoT framework for healthcare that included numerous wearable devices to collect and analyze bio-signals from sensors [32]. The framework is characterized by having two- or eight-channel electrodes for analyzing ECG and EMG signals at a fixed frequency of 1 kHz, an analog front-end (AFE) compliant with the IEEE 802.11 standard, including a micro-controller for data transmission and processing, and power management. The transceiver was combined with AES for real-time data encryption and had a high common-mode rejection ratio (CMRR).

Cognitive IoT (CIoT)

The impressive advances in sensor technology led to a significant reduction in sensors' price. Cognitive computing refers to an intelligent device that can mimic the human brain in solving problems. The CIoT applications support data analysis and identify hidden patterns in Big Data streams, which can improve sensor capabilities in processing and automatically adapting to the environment. Given IoT devices' challenging nature to continuously generate a large amount of data, CIoT becomes a critical part of handling and analyzing it. In a CIoT framework, it is a requirement that all sensors work together with each other and with other smart devices to monitor the patient's health status effectively. The IoT and Cloud computing framework for healthcare, based on a cognitive approach, it is intelligent enough to make appropriate decisions based on the collected data and provides the required healthcare services promptly.

The emerging vision on medical ontologies has attracted the attention of developers of IoT-based health applications. The idea of a cognitive IoT framework with semantic data representation and message-oriented middleware has been introduced in [65]. Semantic publishers (sources) have, over time, sent personalized data to semantic subscribers (consumers) for particular topics — a semantic message broker transfers the data from a publisher to a subscriber. A semantic representation is required for all exchanged data to support interoperability. A more comprehensive framework for managing semantic health data was demonstrated in [50]. It can derive valuable information from raw data sources and combine this information on the same topic. This framework can automatically perform inference and generalization, promote the data mining process, and expand healthcare IoT data.

Community-based healthcare

Community-based healthcare aims to establish a network covering different parts of a local community, which may involve IoT and Cloud computing in a healthcare facility serving a public clinic, a residential, or a rural area. In a community-based healthcare framework, different networks can be connected to build a collaborative network structure. Moreover, an exclusive benefit, community-based healthcare, is inevitable to meet the aggregate practical needs as a whole. [14] demonstrated an IoT bio-fluid analyzer, an electronic reader based on Bluetooth technology, for a biomedical examination framework. They demonstrate the potential of long-distance data transmission and an associated smartphone application to create a community-based platform for urinary tract infection (UTI) health screening. The proposed prototype transmitted data over a distance of up to 6 km and later upload it in a Cloud storage.

Data integrity, security and blockchain

A critical problem in preventing connected healthcare systems from different healthcare providers is data fragmentation. Stringent security requirements and trust must be addressed to realize the full potential of healthcare components. A radical breakthrough in solving data fragmentation has been achieved with the blockchain technology [35]. A key benefit of blockchain technology is that it helps healthcare organizations bridge traditional data repositories and facilitate the secure exchange of sensitive medical data. Blockchain technology increases transparency between patients and physicians and ensures efficient collaboration between healthcare providers and research institutions. Blockchain has an immutable "ledger" [66] that any involved actor of the system can view, verify, and control. It is guaranteed that once a record is entered into the ledger, it cannot be changed. Moreover, blockchain is built as a distributed technology operated by multiple units simultaneously, which means there is no single point of failure where digital assets or records could be compromised or hacked. Lastly, blockchain technology supports data exchange logic and contract rules through a flexible mechanism of smart contracts.

For example, a smart contract can manage identity and set different permissions for different EMRs stored on the blockchain. As another example, physicians are only allowed to access their assigned EMR profile. Many promising blockchain projects in healthcare use blockchain to manage EMRs, pharmaceutical supply chain, drug prescriptions, payment distribution, and clinical pathways. Yet another example is a system that triggered a smart contract when a handshake occurred between sensors and smart devices [26]. After that, all transactions were recorded in the blockchain. The proposed system supported real-time medical interventions and patient monitoring by automatically notifying the responsible healthcare worker when they needed urgent emergency services. All events were recorded in the blockchain, which addresses several security vulnerabilities associated with notification delivery remote patient monitoring for all stakeholders. Another three-tiered architecture for storing health data on a blockchain included medical professionals, healthcare facilities, and inpatients [9]. Data retrieval was strictly based on the individuals' role on the blockchain that ensured privacy and security and provided a promising way to avoid issues that prevented providers, researchers, and patients from taking full advantage of connected healthcare.

1.5.2 IoT in healthcare applications

By practicing the above mentioned concepts, various healthcare applications have been introduced at pace. It can be noted that concepts from the previous sections are applied to implement real-world applications, while applications refer to end-to-end products written to serve end-users. Consequently, concepts are proposed by researchers while developers create healthcare applications to serve patients and physicians. Wearable technology, wearable gadgets, healthcare sensors, and the latest medical devices have recently appeared in this section. These technologies are considered as an IoT breakthrough leading to potential solutions for various healthcare problems. Modern sensors can track a patient's vital signs and then transmit the data directly to a network or through mobile devices, which enable healthcare professionals to monitor a patient's health status in real-time and provide appropriate treatment. Sensors can also track a user's vital signs while exercising or monitor sleep quality. Many medical sensors evaluate blood sugar, heart rate, arterial oxygen, blood pressure, and emotions, where they can notify patients or doctors in time when abnormalities occur.

Next we describe some basic IoT healthcare applications, categorizing single and multiparameter scenarios, where the parameter can be described as single or multistream applications.

ECG monitoring

An ECG sensor records the heart's electrical activity at rest and provides information about heart rate and rhythm. The information is valuable for the early prediction of heart enlargement due to high blood pressure or myocardial infarction. ECG screening is necessary if a patient is at risk group for heart diseases and has symptoms like palpitations or chest pain. The integration of IoT with ECG monitoring has a high potential to alert users and caregivers of heart rate abnormalities, which are an important sign for the early detection of heart diseases. Several studies [64,52,7,54,28,5] have discussed ECG monitoring using IoT technology. In [56], the authors presented a low-power framework that performed ECG compression and QRS detection for wearable devices in real-time. They further proposed a mechanism to increase QRS detection with less computational power. In recent years, heart rate sensors developed into one of the most important features in smartwatches and fitness trackers. Optical heart rate sensors [6,34] are suitable to get measurements or resting heart rate data, which are essential indicators of current health status.

Temperature monitoring

Human body temperature is a critical variable that allows general practitioners to diagnose a patient's health status. In, e.g., sepsis and trauma, a change in core body temperature is an early warning sign. By measuring the body temperature, physicians can chart disease progression for many conditions. A common approach to measuring body temperature is a thermometer. With the development of IoT in healthcare, various replacement solutions have been proposed recently. For example, a smart 3D-printed audible gadget with an infrared sensor has been demonstrated [45], worn on the human ear to monitor ear temperature based on the eardrum. The device was equipped with a wireless module and data processing circuits for data processing functionality. The device served as a hearing aid as it was equipped with a microphone and amplifier. Several other studies summarized the stages of developing wearable core body temperature thermometry [29,38]. Experimental results proved that thermometry accurately captured variations in core body temperature.

Blood pressure monitoring

Blood pressure monitoring is a regular procedure in hospitals. This type of measurement can have a high cost on resources like paper and personal. In the move to a paperless EMR, many hospitals attempt to reduce this process's resource need. [61] presented a wearable device that relies on photo-sensors to monitor blood pressure and stores the data in a Cloud platform, resulting in accurate blood pressure data without errors in systolic and diastolic blood pressures. Another study demonstrated a blood pressure monitoring framework based on Deep Learning that could continuously monitor blood pressure [15]. Here they combined CNN with time-domain characteristics to evaluate systolic and diastolic blood pressures. A prototype monitoring system that evaluated blood pressure based on ECG and photo-plethysmogram (PPG) acquisition from fingertips was presented in [18]. The collected signals were transmitted and processed in a micro-controller where the blood pressure was calculated, displayed locally, and then sent to the Cloud platform for storage.

Blood Glucose (BG) monitoring

Diabetes is one of the largest epidemics and costly diseases to manage healthcare and occurs when blood sugar remains high for an extended time. There are three main types of diabetes: type 1 diabetes (juvenile diabetes), type 2 diabetes (noninsulin-dependent diabetes), and gestational diabetes. Based on the characteristic features of diabetes, three main tests are performed to identify diabetes and pre-diabetes, including a random plasma glucose test, an oral glucose tolerance test, and a fasting plasma glucose test. The results provide the required signs for diabetes diagnosis and treatment plan. A widely used blood sampling method for diabetes diagnosis is "finger-picking", and BG determination with a BG meter.

Blood collection from the patient's fingertip is an uncomfortable process, which can expose the patient to blood-borne disease with contaminated equipment. Wearable devices have been increasingly used to measure blood glucose levels with the benefit of being safer, more convenient, and more comfortable. For instance, a BG monitoring framework was presented in [25] where the authors selected a suitable sensor and designed a front-end interface to display glucose level, core body temperature, and environmental data in real-time. They also developed a communication protocol tailored to the BG test with low energy consumption characteristics. Lastly, various experiments were conducted, proving that the proposed framework included numerous structured design improvements for BG monitoring, such as push notifications to inform physicians when a patient's blood glucose level was out of the normal thresholds. Another proposal is based on a compact optical sensor in conservative management for glucose monitoring [55]. Here, the sensor circuit consisted of an infrared LED to measure the glucose level and a near-infrared photo-diode that detected the light reflected from the human body. The obtained light signals were used to calculate the glucose level quickly and accurately.

Asthma monitoring

Asthma is a long-lasting disease that affects the airways and causes breathing difficulties. When a patient has asthma, an airways' swelling occurs, causing temporary shrinkage of the airways and causing asthma signs such as coughing, shortness of breath, and chest pain. To immediately control an asthma attack, handheld inhalers are usually used. The most typical inhaler is a metered-dose inhaler, which releases a medication as a spray when compressed.

An IoT asthma monitoring system containing a heart pulse sensor was presented in [2], where the collected data was wireless sent to a micro-controller in real-time and transmitted to a remote server. On the server-side, a database was used to manage the data. Hospital staff can access a website to observe a live update of a patient's health status. In another study, a custom temperature sensor was used to calculate respiratory rate and displayed in a web browser which was very convenient for clinicians to monitor patients' health status from anywhere [48]. The monitoring data were used by an artificial intelligence system to automatically evaluate patients' health data and reduce medical staff burden.

Mood monitoring

Mood monitoring includes various psychological techniques that help individuals remain in healthy emotional states and assist them with mental illnesses such as bipolar disorder and depression. Self-monitoring of emotions improves the user's understanding and proactive management of their thoughts. The new smartphone apps support many health purposes to maintain a healthy lifestyle. Self-tracking is one of the most important health apps' features to monitor a user's physical and mental state continuously. A mood tracking approach based on a set of predefined rules was recently presented in [13], where collected data from sensors and smart cities had the aim to prevent frailty and mild cognitive impairment in elderly people.

Oxygen saturation monitoring

An important physiological parameter for cardiovascular monitoring is blood oxygen saturation. It is also an important measurement in other healthcare and medical treatments. Noninvasive methods in tracking oxygen saturation solve problems encountered in conventional approaches and show the potential of real-time monitoring. A noninvasive tissue oximeter was proposed to obtain information on oxygen saturation, heart rate, and pulse parameters in [21,60]. The obtained data were transmitted to a remote server and processed by an expert decision-making system.

Rehabilitation system

Rehabilitation includes procedures that help patients maintain and achieve their maximum physical, mental and social abilities. In [44], a walker-based physical therapy system using orientation, ultra-sound, and force sensors was proposed. The system consisted of edge, Cloud, and application layers. The smart walker continuously evaluates motion metrics and sends them to the Cloud. Then, data is analyzed and updated the results in the website and mobile application. An IoT-based stroke reha-bilitation system was also demonstrated that included a low-power IoT sensing device in a wearable wristband [63]. The device measures, computes, and transmits bio-potential signals to a robotic hand. A machine-learning algorithm then interprets the signals and provides feedback to the user on their muscle movements, while the robotic hand adjusts the patient's posture and walking behavior in real-time.

Wheelchair management

A wheelchair gives physical and psychological support to people with disabilities. The electric wheelchair was invented and introduced to make it easier for people with disabilities to become more independent in their daily activities. However, the wheelchair failed to support people whose mobil-ity was limited due to brain damage. Therefore, a smart wheelchair with an easier navigation system has been presented recently. An example of such a smart wheelchair can be controlled using an IoT-based steering system, and real-time obstacle detection and avoidance method [36]. The steering system was developed by recording real-time videos and image processing to examine possible obstacles. The m-health concept was applied to developing a smart wheelchair, using infrared and wearable device sensors connected to a Cloud computing system [24]. This system included software that allowed people with disabilities to interact with the wheelchair through a mobile app. The sensor data are analyzed and visualized for caregivers to monitor the patient remotely.

Medication adherence

Medication nonadherence is reaching epidemic proportions, leading to increased illness, complications, and premature death. Some people do not strictly follow doctor instructions, skip doses or take them less regularly. Active research in IoT healthcare development focuses on tracking patients' medication intake and reducing patients' time spent at a hospital to fill a prescription. A medication box system for managing medication compliance was proposed [8]. The system included glucometer, blood pressure, body temperature, and ECG sensors connected to a Raspberry Pi 3, where the raw data was transferred to a Cloud system for further analysis. The box contained three compartments, with each containing medications for a specific time of day. The authors developed an Android application to support communication between the patient and the physician. An intelligent medication compliance management system used fuzzy logic to analyze raw data collected by temperature sensors [41]. The system also treats fevers by constantly monitoring a patient's core body temperature in real-time to adjust the dose and time between doses automatically.

Medication management

Medication management is an important area of healthcare industry where IoT technology impacts the costly problems associated with new drug development, medication storage, and warehousing. RFID and IoT were combined to manage medicines in a smart drugstore system [27], where the study can be divided into three parts. The first part demonstrates the sensor and RFID device setup to collect environmental parameters efficiently. The second section describes the data stream and communication protocol for the data transmission to a Raspberry PI. The last section defines the user roles method of access. In another project, a system model was presented to solve sensitive temperature monitoring for drug storage, which uses RFID tags and sensors to set a suitable temperature for each drug type accordingly [43].

Smartphone solutions

The rapid development of mobile computing, including various compact devices such as smartphones, tablets, and personal digital assistants, has significantly impacted many fields, including healthcare. Mobile devices have essentially become handheld computers, thanks to larger memory, advanced computing, highly customized mobile OS, larger screen size, and higher screen resolution. In addition to text-only and voice capabilities, the mobile device has become smarter and offers more cutting-edge technologies, including video calling, multimedia messaging, web browsing, video recording, camera, and a significant number of apps. The rise of IoT in healthcare has led to the release of many clinical apps. The authors in [4] presented a systematic review of mobile health apps by categorizing each app into a specific class, such as BG and vital sign monitoring, as well as m-health apps. Critical challenges and issues that smartphone health apps are facing were highlighted.

Diagnostic apps match patients' symptoms with an extensive medical database of symptoms to recommend the most appropriate remedy. Drug reference apps typically contain a complete list of drug names, descriptions, side effects, interactions, dosages, and properties. Educational apps include instructions on medications and video tutorials on different procedures. Medical news apps provide the most recent medical news. Tele-medicine apps support patients receiving remote treatments from doctors via phone or video without visiting the clinic. Calculator apps provide various equations and formulas for the calculation of commonly used parameters. Finally, clinical communication apps provide a simple and effective communication interface between physicians.

Recently, smartwatches that can be paired with smartphones are being developed in the health space to help individuals set exercise goals, track their performance, and monitor important body functions. Currently, two major brands in the smartwatch market are Apple and Fitbit. Both have a clear goal to focus on the health industry. Apple's wearable smartwatch includes multiple sensors that can inform the user of an abnormal heart rhythm. On the other hand, Fitbit is conducting clinical trials to gain regulatory approval for its wearable devices to assess health conditions such as sleep disorders and abnormal heart rhythm. Apple and Fitbit are striving to lead the smart wearables industry by continuously developing their smart devices.

1.6 Key features

In this chapter we have introduced the basic IoT data stream concepts and models.

- ☑ Data stream definition is given to cast the most important characteristics.
- ☑ The various characteristics of data streams (the Vs) are analyzed in terms of their impact on efficiency and accuracy of processing.
- ☑ Data stream types that arise in various application scenarios are presented.
- ☑ Features of Data Stream Management Systems (DSMS) for continuous data streams are contrasted with Database Management Systems (DBMS) for data at rest.
- ☑ The drift concept for dynamic data streams is presented, and its main features are analyzed in terms of impact on efficiency and accuracy.
- ☑ A list of IoT healthcare applications with references and technologies used is compiled.

References

[1] Detecting concept drift in data streams using model explanation, Expert Systems with Applications 92 (2018) 546–559.

[2] T.G. AL-Jaf, E. Al-Hemiary, Internet of things based cloud smart monitoring for asthma patient, in: ICIT 2017, 2017.

[3] J. Armstrong, V. Morwitz, V. Kumar, Sales forecasts for existing consumer products and services: do purchase intentions contribute to accuracy?, International Journal of Forecasting 16 (3) (2000) 383–397.

[4] M. Baig, H. Gholamhosseini, M. Connolly, Mobile healthcare applications: system design review, critical issues and challenges, Australasian Physical & Engineering Sciences in Medicine 38 (2014) 23–38.

[5] M. Bansal, B. Gandhi, IoT based smart health care system using CNT electrodes (for continuous ECG monitoring), in: 2017 International Conference on Computing, Communication and Automation (ICCCA), 2017, pp. 1324–1329.

[6] J.B. Bathilde, Y.L. Then, R. Chameera, F.S. Tay, D.N.A. Zaidel, Continuous heart rate monitoring system as an IoT edge device, in: 2018 IEEE Sensors Applications Symposium (SAS), 2018, pp. 1–6.

[7] C. Beach, S. Krachunov, J. Pope, X. Fafoutis, R. Piechocki, I. Craddock, A. Casson, An ultra low power personalizable wrist worn ECG monitor integrated with IoT infrastructure, IEEE Access 6 (2018) 44010–44021.

[8] S. Bharadwaj, D. Yarravarapu, S.C.K. Reddy, T. Prudhvi, K. Sandeep, O.S.D. Reddy, Enhancing healthcare using m-care box (monitoring non-compliance of medication), in: 2017 International Conference on Innovative Mechanisms for Industry Applications (ICIMIA), 2017, pp. 167–171.

[9] M.Z.A. Bhuiyan, A. Zaman, T. Wang, G. Wang, H. Tao, M. Hassan, Blockchain and big data to transform the healthcare, in: ICDPA 2018, 2018.

[10] A. Bouchachia, Incremental learning with multi-level adaptation, Neurocomputing 74 (2011) 1785–1799.

[11] A. Bouchachia, C. Vanaret, GT2FC: an online growing interval type-2 self-learning fuzzy classifier, IEEE Transactions on Fuzzy Systems 22 (2014) 999–1018.

[12] R. Burke, Hybrid recommender systems: survey and experiments, User Modeling and User-Adapted Interaction 12 (2004) 331–370.

[13] A. Capodieci, P. Budner, J. Eirich, P. Gloor, L. Mainetti, Dynamically adapting the environment for elderly people through smartwatch-based mood detection, in: Collaborative Innovation Networks, 2018.

[14] P. Catherwood, D. Steele, M. Little, S. McComb, J. Mclaughlin, A community-based IoT personalized wireless healthcare solution trial, IEEE Journal of Translational Engineering in Health and Medicine 6 (2018) 1–13.

[15] P. Chao, T. Tu, Using the time-domain characterization for estimation continuous blood pressure via neural network method, in: ASME 2017 Conference on Information Storage and Processing Systems, 2017.

[16] F.A. Crespo, R. Weber, A methodology for dynamic data mining based on fuzzy clustering, Fuzzy Sets and Systems 150 (2005) 267–284.

[17] A. Dekker, Fundamentals of Clinical Data Science, 2019.

[18] A. Dinh, L. Luu, T. Cao, Blood pressure measurement using finger ECG and photoplethysmogram for IoT, in: 6th International Conference on the Development of Biomedical Engineering in Vietnam, 2017.

[19] I. Dinov, Volume and value of big healthcare data, Journal of Medical Statistics and Informatics 4 (2016).

[20] S.P. Erdeniz, I. Maglogiannis, A. Menychtas, A. Felfernig, T. Tran, Recommender systems for IoT enabled m-health applications, in: AIAI, 2018.

[21] Y. Fu, J. Liu, System design for wearable blood oxygen saturation and pulse measurement device, Procedia Manufacturing 3 (2015) 1187–1194.

[22] J. Gama, I. Žliobaitė, A. Bifet, M. Pechenizkiy, A. Bouchachia, A survey on concept drift adaptation, ACM Computing Surveys (CSUR) 46 (2014) 1–37.

[23] S. Gauch, M. Speretta, A. Chandramouli, A. Micarelli, User profiles for personalized information access, in: The Adaptive Web, 2007.

[24] A. Ghorbel, S. Bouguerra, N.B. Amor, M. Jallouli, Cloud based mobile application for remote control of intelligent wheelchair, in: 2018 14th International Wireless Communications & Mobile Computing Conference (IWCMC), 2018, pp. 1249–1254.

[25] T.N. Gia, M. Ali, I. Dhaou, A. Rahmani, T. Westerlund, P. Liljeberg, H. Tenhunen, IoT-based continuous glucose monitoring system: a feasibility study, in: ANT/SEIT, 2017.

[26] K.N. Griggs, O. Ossipova, C.P. Kohlios, A.N. Baccarini, E.A. Howson, T. Hayajneh, Healthcare blockchain system using smart contracts for secure automated remote patient monitoring, Journal of Medical Systems 42 (2018) 1–7.

[27] K. Gupta, N. Rakesh, N. Faujdar, M. Kumari, P. Kinger, R. Matam, IoT based automation and solution for medical drug storage: smart drug store, in: 2018 8th International Conference on Cloud Computing, Data Science & Engineering (Confluence), 2018, pp. 497–502.

[28] J. He, J. Rong, L. Sun, H. Wang, Y. Zhang, J. Ma, D-ECG: a dynamic framework for cardiac arrhythmia detection from IoT-based ECGs, in: WISE, 2018.

[29] M. Huang, T. Tamura, Z. Tang, W. Chen, S. Kanaya, A wearable thermometry for core body temperature measurement and its experimental verification, IEEE Journal of Biomedical and Health Informatics 21 (2017) 708–714.

[30] G. Hulten, L. Spencer, P.M. Domingos, Mining time-changing data streams, in: KDD'01, 2001.

[31] S. Jabbar, F. Ullah, S. Khalid, M. Khan, K. Han, Semantic interoperability in heterogeneous IoT infrastructure for healthcare, Wireless Communications and Mobile Computing 2017 (2017).

[32] A. Kelati, I. Dhaou, H. Tenhunen, Biosignal monitoring platform using wearable IoT, in: Proceedings of the 22nd Conference of Open Innovations Association FRUCT, 2018.

[33] E. Konstantinidis, P. Antoniou, G. Bamparopoulos, P. Bamidis, A lightweight framework for transparent cross platform communication of controller data in ambient assisted living environments, Information Sciences 300 (2015) 124–139.

[34] S. Krachunov, C. Beach, A. Casson, J. Pope, X. Fafoutis, R. Piechocki, I. Craddock, Energy efficient heart rate sensing using a painted electrode ECG wearable, in: 2017 Global Internet of Things Summit (GIoTS), 2017, pp. 1–6.

[35] T. Kumar, V. Ramani, I. Ahmad, A. Braeken, E. Harjula, M. Ylianttila, Blockchain utilization in healthcare: key requirements and challenges, in: 2018 IEEE 20th International Conference on e-Health Networking, Applications and Services (Healthcom), 2018, pp. 1–7.

[36] Y.-K. Lee, J. Lim, K.S. Eu, Y. Goh, Y. Tew, Real time image processing based obstacle avoidance and navigation system for autonomous wheelchair application, in: 2017 Asia-Pacific Signal and Information Processing Association Annual Summit and Conference (APSIPA ASC), 2017, pp. 380–385.

[37] B. Li, Y. Diao, P. Shenoy, Supporting scalable analytics with latency constraints, Proceedings of the VLDB Endowment 8 (07 2015) 1166–1177.

[38] Q. Li, L. Zhang, X. ming Tao, X. Ding, Review of flexible temperature sensing networks for wearable physiological monitoring, Advanced Healthcare Materials 6 (12) (2017).

[39] Z. Li, X. Zhang, H. Müller, S. Zhang, Large–scale retrieval for medical image analytics: a comprehensive review, Medical Image Analysis 43 (2018) 66–84.

[40] R. Malhotra, A systematic review of machine learning techniques for software fault prediction, Applied Soft Computing 27 (2015) 504–518.

[41] J. Medina, M. Espinilla, Á.L.G. Fernández, L. Martínez, Intelligent multi-dose medication controller for fever: from wearable devices to remote dispensers, Computers & Electrical Engineering 65 (2018) 400–412.

[42] L.L. Minku, A. White, X. Yao, The impact of diversity on online ensemble learning in the presence of concept drift, IEEE Transactions on Knowledge and Data Engineering 22 (2010) 730–742.

[43] S. Monteleone, M. Sampaio, R. Maia, A novel deployment of smart cold chain system using 2G-RFID-sys temperature monitoring in medicine cold chain based on internet of things, in: 2017 IEEE International Conference on Service Operations and Logistics, and Informatics (SOLI), 2017, pp. 205–210.

[44] C. Nave, O. Postolache, Smart walker based IoT physical rehabilitation system, in: 2018 International Symposium in Sensing and Instrumentation in IoT Era (ISSI), 2018, pp. 1–6.

[45] H. Ota, M. Chao, Y. Gao, E. Wu, L.-C. Tai, K. Chen, Y. Matsuoka, K. Iwai, H. Fahad, W. Gao, H. Nyein, L. Lin, A. Javey, 3d printed "earable" smart devices for real-time detection of core body temperature, ACS Sensors 2 (7) (2017) 990–997.

[46] A. Patcha, J. Park, An overview of anomaly detection techniques: existing solutions and latest technological trends, Computer Networks 51 (2007) 3448–3470.

[47] M. Procopio, J. Mulligan, G.Z. Grudic, Learning terrain segmentation with classifier ensembles for autonomous robot navigation in unstructured environments, Journal of Field Robotics 26 (2009) 145–175.

[48] A. Raji, P.K. Devi, P.G. Jeyaseeli, N. Balaganesh, Respiratory monitoring system for asthma patients based on IoT, in: 2016 Online International Conference on Green Engineering and Technologies (IC-GET), 2016, pp. 1–6.

[49] P. Rashidi, D. Cook, Keeping the resident in the loop: adapting the smart home to the user, IEEE Transactions on Systems, Man, and Cybernetics - Part A: Systems and Humans 39 (2009) 949–959.

[50] R. Reda, F. Piccinini, A. Carbonaro, Semantic modelling of smart healthcare data, in: IntelliSys, 2018.

[51] F.F. Riverola, E. Iglesias, F. Díaz, J. Méndez, J. Corchado, Applying lazy learning algorithms to tackle concept drift in spam filtering, Expert Systems with Applications 33 (2007) 36–48.

[52] U. Satija, B. Ramkumar, M.S. Manikandan, Real-time signal quality-aware ECG telemetry system for IoT-based health care monitoring, IEEE Internet of Things Journal 4 (2017) 815–823.

[53] D. Singh, G. Tripathi, A. Alberti, A. Jara, Semantic edge computing and IoT architecture for military health services in battlefield, in: 2017 14th IEEE Annual Consumer Communications & Networking Conference (CCNC), 2017, pp. 185–190.

[54] D. Sobya, S. Muruganandham, S. Nallusamy, P.S. Chakraborty, Wireless ECG monitoring system using IoT based signal conditioning module for real time signal acquisition, Indian Journal of Public Health Research and Development 9 (2018) 294–299.

[55] S. Sunny, S. Kumar, Optical based non invasive glucometer with IoT, in: 2018 International Conference on Power, Signals, Control and Computation (EPSCICON), 2018, pp. 1–3.

[56] T. Tekeste, H. Saleh, B. Mohammad, M. Ismail, Ultra-low power QRS detection and ECG compression architecture for IoT healthcare devices, IEEE Transactions on Circuits and Systems I: Regular Papers 66 (2019) 669–679.

[57] L. Thomas, Modelling the credit risk for portfolios of consumer loans: analogies with corporate loan models, Mathematics and Computers in Simulation 79 (2009) 2525–2534.

[58] F. Ullah, M.A. Habib, M. Farhan, S. Khalid, M.Y. Durrani, S. Jabbar, Semantic interoperability for big-data in heterogeneous IoT infrastructure for healthcare, Sustainable Cities and Society 34 (2017) 90–96.

[59] D. Venuto, V. Annese, A. Sangiovanni-Vincentelli, The ultimate IoT application: a cyber-physical system for ambient assisted living, in: 2016 IEEE International Symposium on Circuits and Systems (ISCAS), 2016, pp. 2042–2045.

[60] Y. Xie, Y. Gao, Y. Li, Y. Lu, W. Li, Development of wearable pulse oximeter based on internet of things and signal processing techniques, in: 2017 European Modelling Symposium (EMS), 2017, pp. 249–254.

[61] Q. Xin, J. Wu, A novel wearable device for continuous, non-invasion blood pressure measurement, Computational Biology and Chemistry 69 (2017) 134–137.

[62] B. Xu, L. Xu, H. Cai, L. Jiang, Y. Luo, Y. Gu, The design of an m-health monitoring system based on a cloud computing platform, Enterprise Information Systems 11 (2017) 17–36.

[63] G. Yang, J. Deng, G. Pang, H. Zhang, J. Li, B. Deng, Z. Pang, J. Xu, M. Jiang, P. Liljeberg, H. Xie, H. Yang, An IoT-enabled stroke rehabilitation system based on smart wearable armband and machine learning, IEEE Journal of Translational Engineering in Health and Medicine 6 (2018) 1–10.

[64] Z. Yang, Q. Zhou, L. Lei, K. Zheng, W. Xiang, An IoT-cloud based wearable ECG monitoring system for smart healthcare, Journal of Medical Systems 40 (2016) 1–11.

[65] R. Zgheib, E. Conchon, R. Bastide, Engineering IoT healthcare applications: towards a semantic data driven sustainable architecture, in: eHealth 360°, 2016.

[66] Z. Zheng, S. Xie, H. Dai, X. Chen, H. Wang, An overview of blockchain technology: architecture, consensus, and future trends, in: 2017 IEEE International Congress on Big Data (BigData Congress), 2017, pp. 557–564.

[67] I. Žliobaitė, Learning under concept drift: an overview, arXiv:1010.4784 [abs], 2010.

Data stream processing: models and methods

The complexity of data stream processing

2.1 Semantic primitives for stream processing

In this section, the main universal primitive functions of stream processing are explained in detail. To facilitate their understanding, the represented operators are explained with their requirements in a streaming scenario. The operators can be categorized into two categories, namely, nonblocking and blocking operators. *Nonblocking* operators can be applied to a constant stream without further requirements, while *blocking* operators are applicable to only finite sequences.

2.1.1 Nonblocking operations

Two most common nonblocking operations to a stream are filter and map. Both of them are stateless operations, that is, they do not maintain state information while moving from processing one stream element to the next one. Due to their stateless nature, such operations are convenient for stream processing in either sequential or parallel mode as stream elements are processed independently enabling thus independent processing of substreams. As a matter of fact, Big Data stream analytic platforms such as Spark, Storm, Kafka, Samza and others offer implementations of these operations to enable high performance parallel computing for stream analytics.

Filter

Filter operation is applied to a stream to either omit or include stream tuples based on a predicate (criteria). For example, values of the body temperature within normal limits of 36.5-37.5°C, can be omitted for processing while those that are out of the specified range are included, creating a new stream instance with the filtered values (stream tuples, in general). Filtering is done by defining a logical predicate, which is then used by the filter method.

Let P_T be the set of filter predicates over tuples of type T of a stream S_t. The filter

$$\sigma : S_T \times P_T \rightarrow S_T \qquad (2.1)$$

returns all stream elements of a stream S_t whose tuple satisfies a given filter predicate. A filter predicate $p \in P_T$ is a function

$$p : \Omega_T \rightarrow \{true, false\} \qquad (2.2)$$

The argument predicate is expressed as a subscript. The definition of σ_p indicates that the input and output stream have the same type.

Map

A map operation is used to transform each tuple in the input stream by applying to it a function that alters the stream tuples. For instance, a map operation can be applied to a stream to map the original values to values within a normalized interval. Mapping can produce tuples of the same type or of a different type.

Let F_{map} be the set of all mapping functions that map tuples of type T_1 to tuples of type T_2. The map operator

$$\mu : S_{T_1} \times F_{map} \to S_{T_2} \qquad (2.3)$$

applies a given mapping function $f \in F_{map}$ to the tuple component of every stream element. The argument function is expressed as a subscript.

The mapping function can be a higher-order function. It is, therefore, sufficient to have only a single mapping function. This definition of the map operator is more important than its relational counterpart as it allows to create tuples of an entirely different type as output. The projection operator of the extended relational algebra can only project to attributes and add new attributes by evaluating arithmetic expressions over the existing attributes.

Map operation usually comes with different forms such as *flatMap*, *mapValues*, etc. For concrete implementation of these stream operations the reader is referred to Java Stream API, Kafka Stream API, Spark Streaming API, Scala Stream API, Flink Stream API and other similar platforms.

2.1.2 Blocking operations

Differently from stateless operations, stateful operations make possible to memorize records or partial results over a data stream. Typically, window processing operates over input tuples and keep the state of computation which can the be accessed through designated APIs. For an example of implementation, readers are referred to Flink's DataStream API, which *"exposes interfaces to register, maintain, and access state in user-defined functions."*

We define next principal blocking operations over data streams.

Union

Union operation merges two logical streams of compatible types. The multiplicity of a tuple at time instant t in the output stream results from the sum of the corresponding multiplicities in both input streams. This operation is formally defined, in the usual way, over a stream S_T of tuples of type T, as follows:

$$U : S_T \times S_T \to S_T \qquad (2.4)$$

Cartesian product

The Cartesian product of two logical streams combines elements of both input streams whose tuples are valid at the same time instant. Letting T_3 denote the output type, then this operation is formally defined as:

$$X : S_{T_1} \times S_{T_2} \to S_{T_3} \qquad (2.5)$$

The auxiliary function:

$$\Omega T_1 \times \Omega T_2 \rightarrow \Omega T_3 \qquad (2.6)$$

creates an output tuple by concatenating the contributing tuples. The product of their multiplicities determines the multiplicity of the output tuple.

Duplicate elimination

The duplicate elimination operation, formally defined as:

$$\delta : S_T \rightarrow S_T \qquad (2.7)$$

eliminates duplicate tuples over a stream for every time instant. The multiplicities of all tuples are hence set to 1.

Difference

The difference operation:

$$\Delta : S_T \times S_T \rightarrow S_T \qquad (2.8)$$

subtracts elements of the second argument stream from the first argument stream. Value-equivalent elements valid at the same time instant are subtracted in terms of multiplicities. The types of both streams need to be compatible.

Grouping

Let F_{group} be the set of all grouping functions over a stream of type T. Let $k \in N, k > 0$, be the number of possible groups for a given input stream. A grouping function $f_{group} \in F_{group}$:

$$f_{group} : \Omega T \rightarrow 1, \ldots, k \qquad (2.9)$$

determines a group identifier for every tuple. The grouping partitions the input stream into k disjoint substreams according to the given grouping function (expressed as subscript).

Scalar aggregation

Aggregation consists of the aggregate values and grouping information. The latter is essential if a grouping is performed before the aggregation. An aggregate function should retain the portion of the tuples relevant to identify their group. For the relational case, this portion would correspond to the grouping attributes. We recall here that the scalar aggregation treats its input stream as a single group. Aggregate functions to a data stream are usually applied according to a user-defined time interval.

Let F_{agg} be the set of all aggregate functions over a stream of type T_1. An aggregate function $f_{agg} \in F_{agg}$

$$f_{agg} : \mathcal{P}(\Omega T_1 \times N) \rightarrow \Omega T_2 \qquad (2.10)$$

computes an aggregate of type T_2 from a set of elements of the form (tuple, multiplicity). The aggregate function is specified as subscript $\mathcal{P}$ denotes the power set.

The aggregation

$$\alpha : SlT_1 \times F_{agg} \to SlT_2 \tag{2.11}$$

evaluates the given aggregate function for every time instant on the nontemporal multiset of all tuples from the input stream being valid at this instant.

The aggregation implicitly eliminates duplicates for every time instant as it computes an aggregate value for all tuples valid at the same time instant weighted by the corresponding multiplicities. It should be noted that the aggregate function can be of higher-order function. As a result, it is possible to evaluate multiple aggregate functions over the input stream in parallel. The output type T_2 describes the aggregates returned by the aggregate function.

For examples of implementations, readers are referred to aggregation on streaming data in Spark, Kafka and Flink streaming aggregation.

2.2 Window-based methods

The continuous data stream model introduces new challenges for the implementation of queries. Algorithms only have sequential access and need to store some state information from stream elements that have been seen previously, e.g., the join, and aggregation, which must be computable within a limited amount of space on an unbounded stream. This requires approximation techniques that trade output accuracy for memory usage and opens up the question of which reliable guarantees can be given for the output. Like previously mentioned, some implementations of relational operators are blocking. Examples are the difference that computes results by subtracting the second input from the first input, or the aggregation with SUM, COUNT, or MAX.

Stateful/blocking operators (Cartesian product, join, union, set difference, or spatial aggregation) require the entire input sets to be completed. These blocking operators will produce no results until the data stream ends or over a user-defined interval. To output results continuously and not wait until the data streams end, blocking operators must be transformed into monotonic queries. A selection operator over a single stream is an example of a monotonic query at any point in time t' when a new tuple arrives, it either satisfies selection predicate, or it does not, and all the previously returned results (tuples) remain in $Q(t')$. Both standard and spatial aggregate operators always return a stream of length one - they are nonmonotonic and thus blocking.

A dominant technique to overcome transforming the blocking queries into their nonblocking counterpart is to restrict the operating range to a finite window over input streams. Windows limit and focus on an operator's scope or a query to a manageable portion of the data stream. A window is a stream-to-relation operator that specifies a snapshot of a finite portion of a stream at any time point as a temporary relation. In other words, a window transforms blocking operators and queries to compute in a nonblocking manner. Simultaneously, the most recent data is emphasized, which is more relevant than the older data in the majority of data stream applications. The following types are being extensively used in conventional DSMS: (logical) time-based windows and (physical) tuple based windows. By default, a time-based window is refreshed at every time tick, and tuple based window is refreshed when a new tuple arrives. The tuples enter and expire from the window in a first-in-first-expire pattern. Whenever a tuple becomes old enough, it is expired (deleted) from memory. These two window types are not useful in answering an important class of queries over the spatio-temporal data stream, and a predicate based window has been proposed in which an arbitrary logical predicate specifies the window content.

In the following subsections, the description of different windowing methods is given.

Time-based sliding window

Time-based sliding windows are characterized by two parameters: the window size and the window slide. The size is defined in terms of the time length and indicates that the window content at time t contains only the elements with timestamps bigger than $t-size$. The slide parameter, fixed as a time length, indicates how often the window is going to be computed or slid over time.

Time-based tumbling window

In this case, the size of the sliding window is equal to the window length. For instance, give the room number where person X has been within the last ten minutes; change results every ten minutes.

Triple-based windows

Triple-based windows were characterized by emulating tuple count windows in Contextual Query Language (CQL)-like data stream systems.

Count-based window for Basic Graph Pattern (BGP)

BGP count-based window is introduced to deal with the limitation of a triple-based window on RDF streams characterized as sequences of graphs [30]. Rather than counting single triples, this count-based window can count the groups of triples (subgraphs) that match a specific basic graph pattern.

Partitioned windows

This type of window deals with one input stream and several other output streams (i.e., partitions) over which the query is evaluated. Partitioned windows are based on knowing the underlying schema and deciding how to do the partition in an effective way for the query.

Predicate-based window

In predicate-based windows, qualified objects are a part of the window once they fulfill a particular query predicate. Objects expire if they no longer satisfy a particular predicate. Predicate-based windows can be seen as generalizations of tuple-count and time-based windows [30].

2.3 Feature domain processing

This section discusses fundamental time domain techniques and how time-domain oscillations can be transformed into a frequency-domain representation.

A signal can be described as raw time-series data, which is represented in the time domain. Time-domain processing operates on temporal relations between data points and provides a natural representation of these relationships. The techniques used in a time-domain follow the goal of identifying and detecting transient information's temporal morphology in time series. Repeating information over regular or semiregular intervals enable an information transformation from time to a frequency domain.

This transformation can isolate oscillatory information for comparison within and across oscillatory frequencies present in the time series.

2.3.1 Basic magnitude features and time-locked averaging

Peak-picking and integration are basic feature extraction methods. Peak-picking determines the minimum or maximum value of the data points in a time interval. Peaks are usually defined by a specific labeled event in the data and the value and occurrence point as features in a segment.

The time series can be averaged over the time interval or integrated in order to retrieve alternative features. Averaging and integration can be beneficial over simple peak-picking. A varying latency in the responses to the signal or noise in the time series could lead to an imprecise peak estimation. Averaging and integration methods can also be applied in the frequency domain to track transient amplitude peaks. A noisy time series with multiple observations can be time-aligned, typically to an event onset or a window operator, and averaged across observations. The average reduces uncorrelated noise and can represent the typical time series morphology across a series.

The signal-to-noise ratio (SNR) serves as an evaluation number for assessing the quality of a time series. The signal must be reliably identified from the background noise to extract information reliably so that the SNR is sufficiently large. As the SNR decreases, the error rate for digital transmissions increases. The SNR of the uncorrelated noise average increases by a factor of $\sqrt{N}$, where N is the number of observations. Therefore, the reliability of feature estimates can be increased with averaging.

Time-locked averaging assumes a stationary time series, meaning that the data distribution (e.g., mean and variance) stays unchanged over time. Additional considerations must be taken when dealing with nonstationary time series [6].

2.3.2 Template matching

A predefined template can be used to find similarities to parts of a time series. The similarity is generally computed inside a sliding window that correlates to the matched filter template with the time series.

A variation of this method can be considered Wavelet analysis. It is performed by a mathematical transform, which stands for a convolution between the analyzed time series and shifted to a position and dilated by scale patterns of the mother wavelet. This analysis method uses templates with specific properties to produce a frequency decomposition related to the Fourier analysis.

2.3.3 Weighted moving averages: frequency filtering

Frequency filtering of a time series begins by first exploring weighted moving averages to manipulate the time series. Fig. 2.1 shows the basic concept of feature filtering. Here, moving average filters (high- and low-pass) are computed over the sum of a high-frequency and low-frequency sinusoidal component of a time series. The low-pass filter follows the goal to preserve the low frequencies and suppresses the high-frequency oscillation. On the other hand, the high-pass filter preserves the low frequency and suppresses the high frequencies. The weighted moving average's characteristics (e.g., mean and variation) determine the degree of preservation/suppression.

In Fig. 2.1, the original (orange (mid gray in print version)) signal's high-frequency component is attenuated when using a uniform low-pass filter with a moving average (blue (dark gray in print version)). The filtering resulted in a slight phase shift. When using a high-pass filter with an alternating

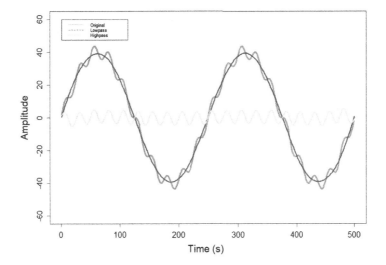

FIGURE 2.1

Moving average: frequency filtering.

moving average, lower frequency components in the original time series are attenuated (green (light gray in print version)), mainly the original time series' high-frequency component. The green (light gray in print version) time series shows that low-frequency vibrations are still present and may not be removed entirely by the filter. Filters can be designed in such a way that they increase the stop band attenuation by adjusting the filter coefficients or the filter length.

A uniform moving average represents the most basic type and takes the current data point, sums it with the prior $N - 1$ data points, and divides the sum by N. Equivalently, this can be described by multiplying the data point by $1/N$ and sum all the points. For each subsequent data point, this process is repeated.

The weighted moving average is the most basic form of a low-pass filter, which preserves the amplitude of low-frequency oscillations and reduces the higher frequency oscillation amplitude. In case of increasing observations, the preserved range of low-end frequencies decreases due to a longer covering average over more cycles of high-frequency oscillations, where the positive and negative half-cycles are canceled in the average. The opposite effect is observed by alternating the weight sign in the moving average. In this case, the lower frequencies' amplitudes are steady, and the higher frequencies are preserved.

Based on these two basic filter types, it can be assumed that the weight coefficients in the moving average and the filter length can be adjusted to preserve and smoothen arbitrary frequency ranges and create desired outputs with filtered frequencies.

Two other basic filters are the band-pass and band-reject filters. The bandpass filter smoothens a low and high-frequency oscillation range to preserve the center frequency range. The band-reject filter preserves low- and high-frequency ranges while smoothing an intermediate frequency range.

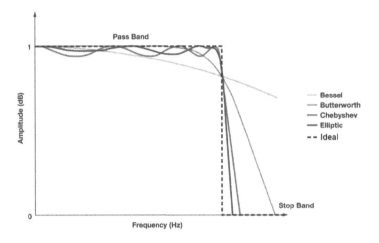

FIGURE 2.2

Magnitude response diagrams of IIR filters. The transition band slop and pass band and stop band ripple for the different filter types.

A frequency-domain plot can be used to visualize the effects of the filter response characteristic or smoothing and magnification factors. The time variable is removed in the plot and merely tracks the smoothing for each input oscillation frequency.

A perfect threshold between the frequencies requires an infinite length filter. That is why, in practice, the filter contains a finite slope to the transition band. Hence, the transition band's threshold needs to be defined in the frequency response characteristic as the point where the attenuation drops by 3 dB point (referred to as "cutoff frequency") from the pass-band.

Weighted moving averages with feedback

By taking a finite impulse response (FIR) filter structure and adding weighted values of the past output, an infinite impulse response (IIR) filter is formed. The added weighted output enables an infinite time series, even with a finite input signal. A finite impulse response (FIR) filter is a filter whose impulse response is finite duration because it decays to zero in finite time. The infinite impulse response (IIR) filters continue to respond indefinitely. IIR filters offer a better precision of frequency discrimination using fewer data points in the averaging, which leads to lower computing time.

On the other side, the IIR filter tends to distort the resulting time series due to differing computing delays of all the input frequencies, known as nonlinear phase response. Due to this behavior, the IIR Filter requires careful engineering to function stable. An unstable IIR filter could occur when a positive feedback loop continuously increases the output amplitude over time.

To achieve a practical frequency response characteristic with the IIR filter, four common design types (illustrated in Fig. 2.2) have been established to determine the filter weights:

- Butterworth: Provides a flat pass-band and stop-band with the smallest transition-band slope for a given filter order.

- Chebyshev I: Provides a flat pass-band and rippled stop-band with a higher transition-band slope for a given filter order than Butterworth.
- Chebyshev II: Provides a flat stop-band and rippled pass-band with a higher transition-band slope for a given filter order than Butterworth (equivalent to Chebyshev I).
- Elliptic: Provides a rippled pass-band and stop-band with the highest transition-band slope for a given filter.

A flat pass-band or stop-band represents a constant gain factor of the band's oscillation, while a rippled band represents a gain factor that varies with the frequency. A rippled band is generally undesired but can be improved by using design constraints.

If the filter application's primary goal is good frequency discrimination (e.g., sharp transition bands) and a ripple can be accepted in both bands, elliptic filters would be recommended. If the result requires a uniform frequency in both bands, the Butterworth approach provides a sharpness of the transition band.

With the previously illustrated features, the main selection criteria can be summarized in the following considerations:

Computational complexity – filter order
The order of the filter affects the output delay, which can be crucial for critical real-time applications. Ideal filters with, e.g., transition and stop-band smoothing, have higher orders leading to more computational requirements. A generally lower order for given constraints has an elliptic IIR but faces design challenges regarding other trade-offs like nonlinear phase and ripple effects.

Linear phase
It is a constant phase delay without distortion achieved by symmetric FIR, which can also be approximated with an IIR, particularly Butterworth.

Filter precision
Describes the sharpness of the transition band used to separate two neighboring oscillations. The elliptic IIR generally provides the sharpest transition for a given filter order, but other trade-offs must be analyzed like nonlinear phase and ripple.

Pass-band/stop-band smoothness
Describes the amplitude distortion degree in the pass-band and stop-bands. Chebyshev variants can have sharper transition bands if only one of the pass- or stop-band must be smooth, while the Butterworth IIR smoothens the pass-band and stop-band.

Stop-band attenuation
Describes the blocking degree of undesired oscillations in the stop-band. A fixed filter order has a trade-off between filter precision and stop-band attenuation.

2.3.4 Frequency-domain
The frequency-domain processing basis is built using weighted moving averages (i.e., FIR and IIR filters) to preserve or attenuate specific oscillatory frequencies over an input time series. Such a time

series can be represented with the sum of sinusoidal with different oscillation frequency, amplitude, and phase shift characteristics.

The Fourier Transform method identifies the frequencies with their characteristics by converting the time series from time-domain into the frequency domain. The specific oscillations of a time series can be compared in a time-domain visualization. Filter response characteristics for preservation or attenuation of specific oscillations can be better designed in the frequency domain. The introduced filters can operate on a mixture of oscillations so that the filter's frequency response characteristic defines the mixture of oscillations at the output. That is, if a time series is a simple sum of a low-frequency oscillation and a high-frequency oscillation, a low-pass filter would only retain the low-frequency oscillation at the output and sufficiently dampen the high-frequency oscillation.

Band power

One of the most intuitive methods of tracking amplitude modulations at a specific frequency is to isolate the frequency by filtering the signal with a band-pass filter. The result is a mostly sinusoidal signal. For estimating the positive amplitude envelope, the signal is next rectified by squaring the signal or calculating its absolute value. Finally, the neighboring peaks are smoothed together by integration or low-pass filtering.

The effects of each of these steps are illustrated in Fig. 2.3. In the figure, the original signal (blue (dark gray in print version) line) is band-pass filtered first. The filtered signal is then rectified to estimate the positive amplitude envelope. Adjacent peaks are smoothed using integration or low-pass filtering. The slight delay in the resulting instantaneous magnitude can be seen in the difference in the lower panel. Due to the smoothing step, the smoothed signal follows the magnitude envelope frequency of interest, but the resulting size estimate will be delayed. For the comparison and tracking of multiple frequency bands, it is recommended to use an FFT or AR-based technique rather than calculating the band power at multiple frequencies.

Spectral analysis

In spectral analysis, the calculation of waves or oscillations in a data stream is done, where the spatial or temporal observation interval is considered constant.

Fast Fourier Transform (FFT)

The Fast Fourier Transform (FFT) algorithm transforms a time series into a frequency domain representation. The frequency spectrum of a digital signal is represented as a frequency resolution of sampling rate/FFT points, where the FFT point is a chosen scalar that must be greater than or equal to the time series length. Because of its simplicity and effectiveness, FFT is often used as a base method against which other spectrum analysis methods are compared.

The FFT takes an N sample time series and produces N frequency samples evenly distributed over a frequency range of sample rate/2, making it a one-to-one transform that does not cause any loss of information.

The Nyquist frequency (folding frequency) is the maximum frequency of the sampling rate/2 in this transform, reconstructed with the FFT. The bins of the FFT magnitude spectrum track the sinusoidal amplitude of the signal at the corresponding frequency. The FFT produces several values that can be converted into size and phase. The FFT spectrum of a signal has a symmetry so that only half of the bins are unique, from zero to + sample rate / 2. The bins from zero to sample rate / 2 are a mirror image of the

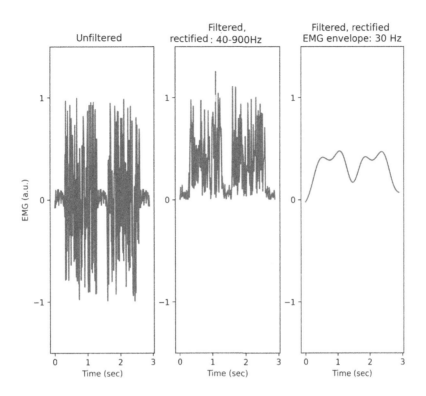

FIGURE 2.3

Extraction amplitude modulations in a specific frequency range.

positive bins around the origin (i.e., H, the frequency zero). Therefore, $N / 2$ unambiguous frequency ranges from zero to the sampling rate / 2 for a real N-sampling signal. By following this principle, the FFT can be applied and interpreted without the complicated mathematics associated with the concept of "negative Frequencies" necessary to be understood precisely.

Accurate frequency sampling can be achieved by appending M zeros to the N sample signal, thereby generating $(M + N)/2$ bins from zero to sampling rate/2. This is known as zero paddings. Padding with zero does not increase the spectral resolution, as no additional signal information is included in the calculation, but it does provide an interpolated spectrum with different bin frequencies. The magnitude spectrum is usually referred to as the power spectrum density PSD or power spectrum.

The signal power is proportional to the amplitude (or magnitude) squared. A power spectrum estimate can be obtained just by squaring the FFT amplitude. Variants of the periodogram can be used to obtain more robust FFT-based estimates of the power spectrum [12]. Fig. 2.4 illustrates the power spectral density using a squared FFT on a time series consisting of the sum of two sinusoids. Note that the sinusoid frequencies are resolved using the FFT. In the figure, the time-domain signal was sampled at a rate of 50 Hz resulting in a Nyquist-Frequency of 25 Hz. In the frequency-domain, it can be seen that the time-domain signal was created by a combination of a 5 Hz and a 10 Hz sinusoidal signal.

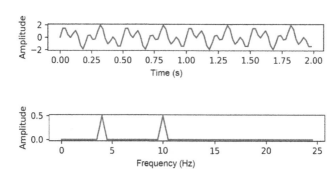

FIGURE 2.4

Signal represented in Time-Domain (top) and Frequency-Domain (bottom).

Tapering windowing of time series

Since N-sample signal windows can cut the signal abruptly to create false discontinuities at the edges of the block, there is a tendency to create artificial ripples around the spectrum's peaks. This can be mitigated by multiplying the sample window by tapering the samples at the sample window edges and ultimately reducing the spectrum ripples. Two of the most common tapered windows are Hamming and Hanning windows, which balance ripple attenuation and trade-offs in the windows' spectral resolution.

Auto-regressive modeling

Auto-regressive modeling (AR) is an alternative to Fourier-based methods for calculating a signal's frequency spectrum. AR modeling assumes that the signal was generated by passing white noise (a random signal having equal intensity at different frequencies) through an IIR (Infinite Impulse Response) filter. The IIR filter weights form the input with white noise to match the signal's properties. In AR modeling, the IIR filter structure uses no delayed input terms but a delayed output terms, which leads to more efficient computation of the filter weights. The power spectrum of white noise is flat, which means that it has the same power at all frequencies. The IIR filter weights fit the spectrum to achieve a matching to the actual spectrum of the signal.

With the IIR filter weights' property to fit the spectrum of the signal, AR modeling can resolve better the spectrum for shorter signal windows compared to FFT.

Short signal windows are desired for real-time applications. The IIR filter structure models spectra with sharp peaks, which can be used for biological signals such as ECG or EEG. Authors in [12] discuss the theory and various approaches for computing the IIR weights (i.e., AR model) from an observed signal. The main problem with AR modeling is that the spectral estimate's accuracy is highly dependent on the model order selected. Inadequate model order tends to blur the spectrum, while too large an order can create artificial peaks.

The complexity of time series should be taken into account for accurate spectral estimates, which often cannot be reliably achieved with small model orders. The model order is related to the sampling rate and the spectral content of the signal. The model order should be proportionally increased to an increased sampling rate. For more information on AR modeling, see [11,23].

2.3.5 Time-frequency domain

In conventional spectrum analysis techniques, the resulting estimates' temporal and spectral resolution depend on the time series length, model order, and other parameters. This is problematic if the time series contains transient oscillations localized in time. For example, for a given time series observation length, the amplitude of a specific high-frequency oscillation (concerning the observation length) can fluctuate significantly over each cycle within the observation. In contrast, the amplitude of a lower frequency oscillation will not do this because fewer cycles are within the window. For a specific observation length, the FFT and AR techniques only generate one frequency range bin, representing these variations at the particular frequency. It is impossible to determine when a transient oscillation occurs at that particular frequency within the observation by analyzing this bin in isolation.

Wavelet analysis solves this problem by creating a time-frequency representation of the signal. As predicted, according to Heisenberg's principle of uncertainty, there is always a compromise between time and frequency resolution in time series analysis, namely, it is impossible to precisely determine the instantaneous frequency and time of an event. This means that longer observation lengths produce spectral estimates with higher frequency resolution, while shorter time windows produce lower frequency resolution estimates.

Instead of displaying a time series as the sum of sinusoids as in the FFT, the wavelet analysis conceptually represents the time series as the sum of specific, time-limited oscillation pulses, which are referred to as wavelets. These impulses have an identical morphology known as the mother wavelet. The wavelets used to represent the time series are simply time-scaled and shifted versions of the mother wavelet.

The different time scales of the mother wavelet are roughly analogous to the sine frequencies of the FFT. Therefore, each sample of the wavelet set represents a specific oscillation frequency over a specific time interval, which leads to a time-frequency decomposition of the time series.

There is a variety of mother wavelets, each with specific time-frequency properties and mathematical properties. Application-specific mother wavelets can also be developed if general mother wavelet properties are known or desired. For theoretical details of wavelets, the reader is referred to [24,9].

2.4 Dimensionality reduction and analysis techniques

We illustrate here primitive processing in time series in more detail. With a high load of data and continuous streams, it can be of interest to reduce the data size. Representation methods deal with dimensionality reduction, data transformation, and keeping characteristic features rather than storing and processing long and complex time series. After retrieving representative features, subsequent stream analysis can be differentiated between three main categories:

1. Indexing: Given a database of stored time series, a query time series, and a similarity measure, indexing can help to efficiently extract the set of the most similar time series from a database.
2. Clustering: Clustering is a technique where data is positioned into homogeneous groups where no explicit definitions nor metainformation on the groups are known. Clustering can help to find groupings of time series data. With a similarity measure present, clusters are constructed by grouping time series with maximum similarity with other time series within the same group and minimum similarity with time series from the other groups. An example could be detecting anomalous behavior

in the data stream, where no previous knowledge exists of how such an anomalous behavior could look.

3. Classification: With a set of predefined classes present, a database of classified time series, and with the help of a specific similarity measure, an unlabeled time series, when going through the classification procedure, will be assigned a known class at the end. An example represents the classification of activities of a sensor streams attached to an athlete.

Besides these three main categories, several more terms are used in the research community, which can, general speaking, categorized into the categories as mentioned earlier. The following methods are some of them: subsequence matching, motif discovery, pattern identification, trend analysis, summarizing, and forecasting.

2.4.1 Dimensionality reduction

Dimensionality reduction is one of the main goals of data stream and time-series representation methods. By reducing the dimension, the number of data points that make up a time series will decrease. The challenge lies in preserving the semantic, character, and shape of the original time series. A basic example approach is to randomly sample over a time series, periodically, or follow different criteria to reduce the dimension. Depending on the use case, the global shape and general semantic can be lost if the sampling window is not specified precisely. Instead of taking sampled data points, other metrics can be of use like Piecewise Aggregate Approximation (PAA) to build averages with adaptive varying-length segments, the Segmented Sum of Variation (SSV) or Min-Max extraction of a segment.

One of the most used representation methods is the Piecewise Linear Representation (PLR), which averages time series into segments, leading to an approximation of the original shape. Linear regression can also be used to break a time series window down into segments with its best-fitting line. The Perceptually Important Points (PIPs) algorithm identifies points of interest. The idea is to preserve the most important and descriptive points within a time series and discard all other points in between. At the initialization of a window, the first data points are considered as PIPs. The following PIPs are identified by the max distance to the other preserved PIPs. Another method is to transform time series data into symbolic strings representing a pattern of the time series. This type of method can be used in combination with sampling methods like PAA, where an algorithm such as Symbolic Aggregate Approximation (SAX) can be used to represent the fixed window of the time series by a predefined alphabet.

The methods mentioned above keep the transformation in the time domains. Other methods convert time series into different representations in various domains. A paradigmatic example of those methods is the Discrete Fourier Transform (DFT) or Discrete Wavelet Transformation (DWT) and Haar Transform.

Shapelets is a recently introduced concept to represent a maximally discriminative subsequence of time series data. Shapelets identify short discriminative series segments. Modern methods discover shapelets by analyzing subsequences from all possible time-series segments [4,2] and follow by sorting the top-performing segments according to their target prediction quality. Distances between series and shapelets represent shapelet-transformed classification features for a series of segregation metrics, such as information gain [4,3], FStat [1] or Kruskal-Wallis.

2.4.2 Indexing

The aim of indexing is to put time series representations into indexing structures to reduce the processing overhead. Given a query time series, a set of the most similar time-series is retrieved and returned. The queries could be divided into two types: the e-range and k-nearest neighbors. E-range retrieves all time-series where the distances between them and the query time series are less or equal to e. k-nearest neighbors return to the query time series depending on a specific similarity measure. With that, the k-nearest neighbors' technique can deal with scaling, gaps, and faster rejection of irrelevant candidates [31,20].

2.4.3 Sequence matching

Similarity is only an approximation over a continuous time-series data stream. Two ways of measuring can be considered, namely whole sequence matching or subsequence matching. A popular method in the category of whole sequence matching is the dynamic time warping technique, which extracts patterns from time series for further matching analytics. In subsequence matching, two time series of different lengths are matched. The main task is to find subsequences that have the same length and are similar. The sliding window mechanism is an ideal support for this specific task [18]. Subsequence matching is computationally expensive, and it suffers from bottlenecks regarding the processing time and the disk access time because of redundant access to store and process resources for the postprocessing step that enhances the results [21].

2.4.4 Clustering

The distribution of time series over clusters should be carried out to maximize intercluster variance and minimize intra-cluster variance. Such grouping mechanisms could help to understand and analyze what knowledge is conveyed in data. Distance-based clustering is extensively used for motif discovery [29], anomaly detection [19,16] and finding discords [32]. One main challenge in clustering is to specify a correct number of clusters to capture the (dis)similarity of time series. Time-series clustering could be further divided into two parts, whole series, and subsequence.

Whole series clustering

Whole time-series are used to form a cluster. Partitioning, hierarchical, model-based clustering are relevant for time series data. Whole series clustering has proven to be very efficient for data streams [8, 7,25].

Subsequence clustering

Clusters for data streams are constructed from subsequences instead of the complete time series. Time series may vary in their structure over time, where subsequences belong in different clusters. An example could be to use DFT to analyze the periodicity of time series and, therefore, to slice them into nonoverlapping chunks. These chunks are tested for similarity and grouped into clusters. Here the questions lay in whether to use overlapping or nonoverlapping information to catch important structures and not produce meaningless results. Solutions to these inconsistencies start when not all subsequences were forced into the clustering procedure, but some of them were ignored all together [14,17].

2.4.5 Classification

The significant difference between classification and clustering is that classification is known in advance. The task is to learn distinctive features that characterize each class. Afterward, the unlabeled data can be assigned to the right class. An essential characteristic of the features should be nonoverlapping distinguishing and discriminating so that the classification can be done more precisely.

Whole series classification

Nearest neighbor classifiers are often used to, e.g., classify the unlabeled query with the same class as the most similar labeled time series. This technique can be beneficial if there may be discriminatory features that characterize the whole time series. Euclidean distance could be used in its simplest form, either on raw time series or transformed representations, like PLR, SAX, and others. However, this assumes that time series are perfectly aligned, which is often not the case in real-life situations. Therefore alternative elastic distance measures are usually employed like DTW. However, DTW suffers from some drawbacks when it comes to outliers and data imperfection. To boost classification accuracy, different approaches have enhanced this raw method. For instance, in [15], the authors added a multiplicative weight penalty to reduce warping effect.

Interval-based classification

In the case of noise and redundant shapes, whole series classifiers may get confused and deliver inaccurate results. This is where extracting features from intervals rather than the whole series could be desirable. The challenge to conduct such a technique is finding the best interval. Specifically, there is an undefined number of possible intervals, so how to select the best one and what to extract from each interval once selected? Authors in [28] proposed an approach where interval lengths were equal to powers of two, and binary features were extracted from each interval. Afterward, an SVM was trained on the extracted features. A popular interval-based classification approach is the Time Series Forest (TSF) [10]. It is a Random Forest approach. After specifying the number of desired decision trees, each tree is trained by dividing the time series into random intervals. Effectively the training is done on three features extracted from each interval; the mean, the standard deviation, and the slop. A majority voting determines the final classification result.

Dictionary-based classification

Dictionary-based classification methods are suitable approaches if motifs or frequent patterns characterize a given class. This technique counts the frequency of patterns. The main idea is to slide a window of a given length and then compute the distribution of words over the different training instances. Following this mechanism, the correlation between the frequency of specific patterns and particular classes' occurrence could be established. The Bag of Patterns (BoP) approach proposed in [22] computes a histogram of words for time series that are transformed with SAX. The same method is then followed to build a histogram for unlabeled time series, and finally, the new series is given the class of the most similar histogram.

Shapelet-based classification

In scenarios where discriminative patterns could characterize the time series class, shapelets are the most suitable technique. They are shapes (subsequences) that occur within the time series, independently from the phase (the placement at the beginning, middle, or end). E.g., ECG abnormality detection could be seen in fatal heartbeats in ECG data. Shapelets were devised in 2009 [33], and in their work, authors discover shapelets through testing all possible candidates between two given lengths. This approach is called brute force algorithm. It archives very accurate results but with a high computation cost. The time complexity is $O(n^2 m^4)$, where n is the number of time series, and m is the length. A more recent approach is the Fast Shapelets (FS) algorithm, which drastically improved the time complexity to find shapelets. In this context, the computing complexity results in $O(nm^2)$.

Other shapelet-based approaches [13,5] formulate the so called Shapelet Transform (ST). These approaches are more concerned with discovering discriminative shapelets rather than building a classifier to use them. Following the ST, the original time series is transformed into a vector of distances where each element represents the distance between a given time series and a specific shapelet. ST balances the trade-off between the number and quality of shapelets by counting on the information gain metric. In the end, the top k shapelets for each class are returned. Another interesting approach that learns shapelets is called Learning Shapelets (LS), which learns shapelets that characterize the available classes; however, the learning procedure is different from other algorithms like FS and ST. Traditionally, shapelets are defined as subsequences from the original time series, yet in LS, they are not limited to that. LS uses k-means clustering of candidates in the training data set to initialize k-shapelets. Then these shapelets are adjusted based on a regression model for each class.

Early classification

Early classification usually deals with online stream classification where the interest is to classify the currently streamed time series as early as possible without waiting for the complete time series to be read. Given the smallest possible subsequence of a time series, the main goal is to accurately predict its class. As mentioned, shapelets are shapes that characterize a specific class, and the class could be immediately predicted at any given point in the stream. Furthermore, if shapelet lengths are considered when attributing utility scores, earliness could be significantly boosted. Approaches such as [26,27] prove that shapelets perfectly fit for early classification and rule discovery.

2.5 Key features

In this chapter we have presented data stream processing models and methods.

- ☑ Semantic primitives for stream processing and their classification into nonblocking and blocking operations are defined and briefly analyzed.
- ☑ Window-based processing methods are detailed.
- ☑ Feature domain, frequency domain, and time-frequency domain processing methods are described.
- ☑ Dimensionality reduction methods and their importance to clustering and classification are discussed.
- ☑ The complexity of presented methods for data stream processing is highlighted.
- ☑ Big Data stream analytic platforms such as Spark, Storm, Kafka, Samza are referred to as software platforms for high-performance parallel processing of data streams.

References

[1] B. Babcock, S. Babu, M. Datar, R. Motwani, J. Widom, Models and issues in data stream systems, in: Proceedings of the Twenty-First ACM SIGACT-SIGMOD-SIGART Symposium on Principles of Database Systems, June 3–5, Madison, Wisconsin, USA, 2002, pp. 1–16.

[2] A. Bagnall, A run length transformation for discriminating between auto regressive time series, Journal of Classification 31 (07 2013).

[3] A.J. Bagnall, C. Ratanamahatana, E.J. Keogh, S. Lonardi, G.J. Janacek, A bit level representation for time series data mining with shape based similarity, Data Mining and Knowledge Discovery 13 (2005) 11–40.

[4] D. Berndt, J. Clifford, Finding patterns in time series in advances, 05 2019.

[5] M.S. Cetin, A. Mueen, V.D. Calhoun, Shapelet ensemble for multi-dimensional time series, in: Proceedings of the 2015 SIAM International Conference on Data Mining (SDM), 2015, pp. 307–315.

[6] C. Chatfield, Non-linear and non-stationary time series analysis: M.B. Priestley, (Academic Press, London, 1988), [UK pound]25.00, pp. 237, International Journal of Forecasting (1989).

[7] M. Corduas, D. Piccolo, Time series clustering and classification by the autoregressive metric, Computational Statistics & Data Analysis 52 (02 2008) 1860–1872.

[8] G. Cormode, S. Muthukrishnan, W. Zhuang, Conquering the divide: continuous clustering of distributed data streams, in: 2007 IEEE 23rd International Conference on Data Engineering, 05 2007, pp. 1036–1045.

[9] I. Daubechies, The wavelet transform, time-frequency localization and signal analysis, IEEE Transactions on Information Theory 36 (5) (1990) 961–1005.

[10] H. Deng, G.C. Runger, E. Tuv, V. Martyanov, A time series forest for classification and feature extraction, Information Sciences 239 (2013) 142–153.

[11] B.E. Hansen, Time series analysis James D. Hamilton Princeton University Press, 1994, Econometric Theory 11 (3) (1995) 625–630.

[12] M.H. Hayes, Statistical Digital Signal Processing and Modeling, 1996.

[13] J. Hills, J. Lines, E. Baranauskas, J. Mapp, A. Bagnall, Classification of time series by shapelet transformation, Data Mining and Knowledge Discovery 28 (4) (July 2014) 851–881.

[14] X. Huang, Y. Ye, L. Xiong, R. Lau, N. Jiang, S. Wang, Time series k-means: a new k-means type smooth subspace clustering for time series data, Information Sciences 367 (06 2016).

[15] Y. Jeong, M. Kee Jeong, O. Omitaomu, Weighted dynamic time warping for time series classification, Pattern Recognition 44 (09 2011) 2231–2240.

[16] M. Jones, D. Nikovski, M. Imamura, T. Hirata, Exemplar learning for extremely efficient anomaly detection in real-valued time series, Data Mining and Knowledge Discovery 30 (01 2016) 1–28.

[17] E. Keogh, C.A. Ratanamahatana, Exact indexing of dynamic time warping, Knowledge and Information Systems (2004).

[18] E.J. Keogh, M.J. Pazzani, Scaling up dynamic time warping for datamining applications, in: Proceedings of the Sixth ACM SIGKDD International Conference on Knowledge Discovery and Data Mining, KDD'00, ACM, New York, NY, USA, 2000, pp. 285–289.

[19] H. Lamba, T.J. Glazier, J. Cámara, B. Schmerl, D. Garlan, J. Pfeffer, Model-based cluster analysis for identifying suspicious activity sequences in software, in: Proceedings of the 3rd ACM on International Workshop on Security and Privacy Analytics, 03 2017, pp. 17–22.

[20] X. Lian, L. Chen, B. Wang, Approximate similarity search over multiple stream time series, in: Proceedings of the 12th International Conference on Database Systems for Advanced Applications, 04 2007, pp. 962–968.

[21] S.-H. Lim, H. Park, S.-W. Kim, Using multiple indexes for efficient subsequence matching in time-series databases 177 (01 2006) 65–79.

[22] J. Lin, R. Khade, Y. Li, K rotation-invariant similarity in time series using bag-of-patterns representation, Journal of Intelligent Information Systems 39 (10 2012).

[23] H. Madsen, Time Series Analysis, 10 2008.

[24] S. Mallat, Iii - discrete revolution, in: S. Mallat (Ed.), A Wavelet Tour of Signal Processing, second edition, Academic Press, San Diego, 1999, pp. 42–66.

[25] K.Ø. Mikalsen, F.M. Bianchi, C. Soguero-Ruíz, R. Jenssen, Time series cluster kernel for learning similarities between multivariate time series with missing data, Pattern Recognition 76 (2018) 569–581.

[26] R. Mousheimish, Y. Taher, K. Zeitouni, Automatic learning of predictive rules for complex event processing: doctoral symposium, in: Proceedings of the 10th ACM International Conference on Distributed and Event-Based Systems, 06 2016, pp. 414–417.

[27] R. Mousheimish, Y. Taher, K. Zeitouni, Complex event processing for the non-expert with autoCEP: demo, in: DEBS, 2016.

[28] J.J. Rodríguez, C.J. Alonso, J.A. Maestro, Support vector machines of interval-based features for time series classification, Knowledge-Based Systems 18 (4–5) (Aug. 2005) 171–178.

[29] J. Serrà, J.L. Arcos, Particle swarm optimization for time series motif discovery, Knowledge-Based Systems 92 (01 2015).

[30] W3C. RDF stream processing: requirements and design principles, http://streamreasoning.github.io/RSP-QL/RSP_Requirements_Design_Document/#count-based-window-based-on-basic-graph-pattern, 2016. (Accessed 26 March 2019).

[31] X. Xu, C. Gao, J. Pei, K. Wang, A. Al-Barakati, Continuous similarity search for evolving queries, Knowledge and Information Systems (10 2015).

[32] D. Yankov, E. Keogh, U. Rebbapragada, Disk aware discord discovery: finding unusual time series in terabyte sized datasets, Knowledge and Information Systems 17 (11 2008) 241–262.

[33] L. Ye, E.J. Keogh, Time series shapelets: a new primitive for data mining, in: Proceedings of the 15th ACM SIGKDD International Conference on Knowledge Discovery and Data Mining, 06 2009, pp. 947–956.

Anomaly detection

Concepts and methods

3.1 Introduction to anomaly detection

Data points that are inconsistent with the major data distribution are called anomalies [2]. Originally, the problem of anomaly analysis has been tackled by the statistics community and fundamental results have been published in the literature in the field [60,31,53].

According to Barnett and Lewis' definition [60], an anomaly is *"an observation (or subset of observations), which appears to be inconsistent with the remainder of that set of data"*. Hawkins [31] defined an anomaly as *"an observation which deviates so much from other observations as to arouse suspicions that it was generated by a different mechanism"*. Anomalies are also referred to as rare events, abnormalities, deviants, or outliers.

More recently, anomaly detection has received significant attention from many other research communities such as machine learning and data mining, networking, health, security, fraud detection, etc., due to the insights that rare events can provide for the phenomenon under study. Thus, outlier detection techniques can be used to monitor a wireless sensor network to identify faulty sensors or interesting behavior patterns. The availability of data used for the anomaly detection task depends on the properties of the data set. In static datasets, anomaly detection can be conducted over the whole data set in which all observations are available.

In continuous data stream scenarios, the observations may not be available at any moment and arrive sequentially. The observations in data streams can be seen only once and anomalies should be detected in real time. In environments where the distribution changes over time (nonstationary), traditional detection methods cannot be applied, and the models change. Therefore, adaptive models need to be considered to deal with dynamically changing characteristics to detect anomalies in the evolving time series.

In recent years, several algorithms have been proposed to detect anomalies in data sets or data streams. Some of them consider scenarios where a sequence with one or more characteristics unfolds over time. While others focus on more complex scenarios in which streaming elements with one or more characteristics have causal / noncausal relationships with each other.

Extensive research on the detection of outliers in static data related to various applications scenarios can be found in [4,8,13,14,30].

3.2 Challenges in anomaly detection

An anomaly in a dataset or data stream can be considered as a pattern that does not correspond to an expected normal behavior. A simple approach to detecting anomalies is therefore to define an area that represents normal behavior and identifies observations that do not belong to this area as an anomaly. This simple approach still faces major challenges:

1. It is challenging to define a normal realm that encompasses every possible normal behavior. Also, the frontier between normal and abnormal behavior is often imprecise. Thus, an anomalous observation that is close to the limit can be normal and vice versa.
2. Often, when anomalies are the result of malicious actions, the malicious adversaries adapt to make the abnormal observations appear normal, making it more difficult to define normal behavior and detect anomalies.
3. In many areas, normal behavior keeps evolving over time, and a current definition of normal behavior may not be representative in the future.
4. The exact concept of an anomaly is different for context areas of application. In the medical field, for instance, a small deviation from normal (e.g., fluctuations in body temperature) might be an anomaly, while a similar deviation in the stock market (e.g., fluctuations in the value of a stock) might be classified as normal. Therefore, applying a technique developed in one area to another one may not provide accurate results.
5. The availability of tagged data for training and validation of models used by anomaly detection techniques is usually a major problem.
6. Often, the data contains noise, which tends to be similar to the actual anomalies and hence it is difficult to distinguish and remove anomalies.
7. The exponential growth of data size, either in the form of Big Data or Big Data stream, makes the anomaly detection very challenging due to the need of more computing resources satisfy the demanding requirements of applications (popularly referred to as "big data haystack").

Because of the above challenges, anomaly detection in its general form is not straightforward to solve. Most of the anomaly detection methods solve a domain and application-specific type of the problem. The solution is influenced by various factors such as data type, availability of labeled data, or type of anomalies to be detected. Concepts from various disciplines such as statistics, machine learning, data mining, information theory, and spectral theory have been adapted to specific problems.

3.3 Anomaly types and detection techniques

3.3.1 Anomaly types

There are three common types of anomalies:

1. Point anomalies: A single data instance is abnormal to the rest of the data (e.g., a point is far from the rest). This is the simplest anomaly, and it is the focus of most research in anomaly detection [13].
2. Contextual or conditional anomalies: A data instance is anomalous only in a specific context [13].
3. Collective anomalies: A collection of related data points is anomalous, while individual instances within that collection may not be anomalous [13].

3.3.2 Anomaly detection mode

Depending on the availability of the labels, anomaly detection techniques can be performed in one of the following three modes:

Supervised anomaly detection

The supervised mode requires a training data set that has instances with normal and anomaly class labels. A common approach is to create a predictive classification model for normal and anomaly classes. Each unseen data instance is fed to the model to determine to which class it belongs. There are, however, two main problems with supervised anomaly detection. Commonly, the anomalous instances are far fewer than the normal instances in the training data. Problems arising from unbalanced class distributions have been addressed in the data mining and machine learning literature [34,15,44,58]. Furthermore, it is often difficult to obtain accurate and representative labels, especially for anomalies. New techniques propose the injection of artificial anomalies into the data set to balance the data set [57,1]. Aside from these two problems, the supervised anomaly detection problem is similar to building predictive models.

Semisupervised anomaly detection

Anomaly detection techniques that work in a semisupervised mode require that the training data have instances marked only for the normal class. Since the anomaly class does not require labels, it is more general than supervised techniques, for example, in detecting spacecraft fault [26], where an anomaly scenario would mean an accident that is not easy to model. The typical approach to such techniques is to build a class model that corresponds to normal data and uses the model to discriminates anomalies. Only a limited set of anomaly detection techniques assume that only the anomaly instances are available for training [21,20]. Such techniques are not widely used, mainly because of the difficulty of obtaining a training data set that will cover every possible normal behavior that may appear in the data.

Unsupervised anomaly detection

Anomaly detection methods operating in the unsupervised mode do not require training data and are, therefore, the most common. This category's techniques implicitly assume that normal instances will occur far more frequently than anomalies in the test data. If this assumption does not hold, such techniques could suffer from a high false-positive rate. Various semisupervised techniques can be adapted to operate in an unsupervised mode using an example of the unlabeled data set as training data.

3.3.3 Anomaly detection techniques

The main categories of anomaly detection are statistical, probabilistic, proximity-based, clustering-based, and prediction-based methods. As an example, anomaly detection in a sensor's time-series data belongs to such categories.

Statistical techniques

Statistical techniques use measurements to approximate a model. Whenever a new measurement is registered, it is compared to the model and, if the results are statistically incompatible with it, then it is marked as an anomaly [27]. Statistical methods can be applied to single elements or window segments.

An approximation over a window improves the approximation. However, a priori knowledge regarding the data distribution is required, which is often unavailable when data evolves over time.

Among the main advantages of statistical techniques we could distinguish:

1. If the assumptions of the data distribution hold, statistical techniques provide a statistically justifiable solution for anomaly detection.
2. The provided anomaly score is linked to a confidence interval that can be used as additional information while a decision is being made regarding a test instance.
3. If the estimation of the distribution is robust to anomalies, statistical techniques can operate in an unsupervised environment without the need for labeled training data.

There are, however, several limitations of statistical techniques:

1. The main drawback of statistical techniques is the assumption that data is generated from a specific distribution. This assumption often does not hold, particularly for high-dimensional real data.
2. Even if the statistical assumption could be reasonably justified, several hypothesis testing statistics can be used to detect anomalies. Choosing the best statistic is often not an easy task [42]. Constructing hypothesis tests for complex distributions to fit high dimensional data sets is in general a complicated task.
3. Histogram-based techniques are relatively easy to implement, but a major disadvantage for multivariate data is that they cannot capture the interactions between different attributes. An anomaly can have attribute values that are very common individually, but their combination could be unique, i.e., anomalous. A histogram-attribute-based technique might not be able to detect such anomalies.

Probabilistic techniques

These techniques describe probabilistic models in parametric or nonparametric nature, depending on the distribution. The classification of anomalies is performed by measuring the probability of an analyzed element or segment. If the probability of distribution falls below a threshold, an anomalous event is detected.

Proximity-based techniques

These techniques rely on distances between data measurements to distinguish between anomalous and correct readings. A popular proximity-based algorithm is the Local Outlier Factor (LOF)—a reading is considered as an outlier based on its local neighborhood. The algorithm assigns an outlier score to each element based k nearest neighbor density measurements [27]. Readings with high outlier scores are labeled as anomalies.

Nearest neighbor based techniques have the advantage:

1. A major advantage of nearest neighbor techniques is that they are unsupervised and make no assumptions about the distribution of the data. Instead, they are data-driven.
2. Semisupervised techniques are better than unsupervised techniques for missed anomalies because the likelihood that an anomaly will form a close neighborhood in the training data set is minimal.
3. Changing nearest neighbor based techniques to different data types is straightforward and primarily requires defining an appropriate distance measure for the specified data.

Disadvantages of nearest-neighbor based techniques are the following:

1. With unsupervised techniques, the data will not be flagged correctly if the normal instances do not have enough near neighbors or if the data contains anomalies that have close neighbors, resulting in not detecting anomalies.
2. In the case of semisupervised techniques, the false positive rate is high when the test data's normal instances do not have enough similar normal instances in the training data.
3. The computational complexity of these techniques can be a significant challenge since each test instance's distance is calculated with all instances that belong to the test and training data to calculate the closest neighbors.
4. The performance of nearest-neighbor-based techniques depends on a distance measure defined between a pair of data instances that can effectively differentiate between normal and anomalous instances. Defining distance measures can be difficult for complex data, like sequences.

Distance based techniques

In terms of streaming data in [6] and [63], sliding windows are used to detect global distance-based outliers in data streams. The authors in [38] have improved the time complexity and memory consumption compared to [6] and [63]. In [11], LEAP (LifEspan-Aware Probing operation) optimizes the search space for high volume high dimensional data streams. Since the outliers are calculated with the last n data points, the detected outliers are referred to as "global" outliers. Therefore, these approaches cannot detect outliers in heterogeneous densities.

Density based techniques

In contrast to distance-based "global" outliers, the distance-based "local" outliers (density-based outliers) are outliers related to their k nearest neighbors. LOF is a well-known algorithm for detecting outliers on a density-based algorithm [9].

LOF technique achieves good detection accuracy at heterogeneous densities without assuming the underlying distribution of the data. In practice, it has become a popular approach, and many variants of this technique have developed. Pokrajak *et al.* [45] proposed an incremental LOF technique (iLOF) that can be used for data streams. In all previous versions, the entire data set had to calculate LOF values for the data points. With the iLOF technique, the outlier score is computed for every incoming data point. The iLOF finds the k-nearest neighbors of the incoming data point, calculates the local outlier factor based on the k-NNs outlier factors, and updates the k-NNs with their local outlier factors. In this approach, only a few data points are needed to be updated. All past data points must be retained to calculate the outlier factor for each new data point, which leads to a high memory requirement and time complexity. A more memory efficient algorithm called MiLOF was proposed to tackle these limitations in density-based outlier detection problems [54].

Clustering-based techniques

These techniques create a measurement between different elements and cluster them based on their similarity. New measurements are assigned to similar clusters or labeled as anomalous with a high distance to existing clusters. Cluster methods and proximity-based methods are usually not the best choices for high dimensional data [27]. The typical approach is to find the right representation method of differentiating between normal and anomalous data.

These techniques can be divided into two groups:

- Techniques that assume that the anomalies fall within the clusters with a small number of data points or a low density.
- Techniques for which the distance from data points to their closest cluster centroids is used to detect anomalies.

BIRCH (Balanced Iterative Reducing and Clustering using Hierarchies) was proposed for large databases [64] and is categorized under the first group. It takes into account that memory requirements cannot support large databases. The method uses a landmark window operator and groups the data points incrementally and dynamically in a single scan of the data. Also, BIRCH is the first algorithm that processes noise and detects outliers in the data stream. It is based on a concept called the Cluster Feature (CF). It is a triplet made up of three values and contains useful information to describe a cluster.

An algorithm called CluStream was proposed in [3], which clusters unfolding data streams. This algorithm also uses the CF concept used in [64] but extends it by adding the temporal properties of clusters. This algorithm essentially consists of two steps: online and offline steps. In the online step, the microclusters are created, while in the offline step, macro clusters are generated by applying a k-means algorithm to microclusters. For each incoming data point, the microclusters are updated as follows:

1. the new data point is assigned to one of the microclusters, or
2. far away from the existing clusters, therefore, a new microcluster is created, and one of the previous microclusters becomes an outlier-microcluster identified and deleted based on the microcluster's timestamps points or merged with another microcluster.

Therefore, outliers are not identified by the size of the microclusters, but by the fact that they were not active in the last stream elements. DenStream [10] can be considered an improved CluStream algorithm that focuses explicitly on creating clusters of any shape.

Therefore, a density-based clustering approach (DBSCAN) [49] is used to create micro-clusters. DBSCAN can be used in noisy data sets and can create normal microclusters and outlier microclusters comparable to [3]. With a dampened window model, the current data points with higher values are weighted. In the next step, a grid-based density approach is proposed based on two online and offline steps, called DStream [16].

The online step assigns each data point to a grid cell, where low-density grid cells are identified as outliers and removed. The low-density grid cells refer to either the grid cells with a small number of data points or the grid cells with many data points, while a decay factor has reduced their effect.

The offline step clusters the grids using a density-based clustering algorithm, which is time and memory efficient and able to group clusters of any shape. While [10] and [16] are based on a dampened window model, SDstream [51] is recommended based on a sliding window model. Here, a two-step approach is used, except that only the last few data points are retained. The above approaches assume that outliers with a low number of data points or low density fall within the clusters.

Other techniques

In the remainder of this section, other approaches are described that work with the data points' distance to their closest cluster centroids of anomalies in data streams.

A new outlier detection algorithm, called AnyOut, was proposed to detect outliers in streaming data at any time [7]. Here, data streams have different arrival rates, and at a certain point in time t, the outlier score for the current data point pt should be calculated until the next data point arrives. AnyOut creates a specific tree structure called ClusTree [7], which is suitable for clustering at any time. Cluster Features (CFs) are stored in each node and a buffer for inserting clusters at any time is used. AnyOut examines the ClusTree from top to bottom and, at each level, finds the CF that comes closest to the point. As soon as the next data point arrives, an outlier score is calculated as the distance from p_t to its next cluster feature centroid.

In [24], the data stream is divided into data blocks and uses k-means for each data block. Then data points far enough away from cluster centroids are identified as outlier "candidate". Therefore, the outlier value of data points may change depending on the upcoming data blocks. Another approach proposes a hyperellipsoid clustering to model the system's normal behavior in which data points outside this clustering limit are classified as anomalies [41]. The hyperellipsoid parameters (mean and covariance matrix) are incrementally updated to track changes in data streams' underlying distributions.

The eTSAD method [43] is a new clustering algorithm that models data streams using a set of fuzzy elliptic rules. Similar to the previous approach, the fuzzy clustering model parameters are updated for each incoming data point to identify outliers and regime changes in data streams. Instead of modeling data streams just by a set of cluster profiles and updating them over time, [55] proposed an ensemble-based algorithm for developing data streams in which a pool of clusters models is generated. After that, an outlier value is calculated for each incoming data point based on a consensus decision, using only the relevant set of cluster models.

Similar to [41], a hyperellipsoidal clustering approach is used to model the expected behavior of the data streams in each data block. The distance between the cluster centroids is used to detect anomalies. In [17], a time/memory-efficient algorithm for detecting anomalies was proposed, in which the term active cluster is introduced. The input data streams are divided into different data blocks, and active clusters in the current data block are identified for each incoming data block. When there are new distributions, an update follows the model, which consists of a series of hyperellipsoidal clusters.

All of the previous mentioned algorithms detect anomalies by modeling data streams based on clustering, but none can identify anomalies in real-time. Authors in [18] propose a new approach to discover the temporal development of clusters and, at the same time, to detect anomalies in real-time.

The main advantages of clustering based techniques are as follows:

1. Clustering-based techniques can operate in an unsupervised mode
2. They can often be adapted to other complex data types simply by inserting a clustering algorithm to handle the particular data type.
3. The evaluation phase for cluster-based techniques is fast due to the small number of clusters that each test instance must be compared to.

There are, however, several disadvantages of clustering based techniques, as follows:

1. Many methods detect anomalies as a byproduct of clustering and are therefore not optimized for anomaly detection.
2. Performance of clustering-based techniques is highly dependent on the clustering algorithm's effectiveness in capturing the cluster structure of normal instances.
3. Multiple clustering algorithms force each instance to be assigned to a cluster. This can result in anomalies being assigned to a large cluster, making them normal instances by techniques that assume that anomalies do not belong to any cluster.
4. Multiple clustering-based techniques are effective only if the anomalies do not form significant clusters among them.

5. The computational complexity for clustering the data is often a bottleneck, especially when using $O(N^2 d)$ (N—number of data points to be categorized and d—dimensionality of each data point) clustering algorithms.

Prediction-based techniques

These techniques use past measurements to train a model that can predict the value of the next measurement of time-series data. If the actual data has no similarity with the predicted data, it will be labeled an anomalous element. The domain of prediction is increasing steadily with the rise of machine learning and Big Data and Big Data streams. Examples of such methods are SVM, Deep Neural Networks (DNN), Long Short-Term Memory (LSTM), or Hierarchical Temporal Memory (HTM) (which is applied later in this book in the case study).

The selection of the algorithm/model strongly depends on the characteristics of the data. The following questions can be taken as criteria for selecting a predictive model:

1. What kind of data is available for training the predictive models (online vs. offline training)?
2. Which format does the data have—are representative features for prediction given?
3. The properties may change over time, which is called concept drift. Will the learning algorithms be able to learn in presence of drifts?

The use of the HTM online learning algorithm is given in the case study by analyzing anomalous behavior in an ECG signal stream in Part 3 of this book.

Assumption

A prediction model that can distinguish between normal and anomalous classes can be learned in the existing feature space.

Based on the existing labels for the training phase, prediction-based anomaly detection techniques can be divided into multiclass and single-class anomaly detection techniques. Techniques for detecting anomalies based on classifying multiple classes require that the training data contain labeled instances for multiple classes. The classifier learns to distinguish between all normal classes. An instance is considered an anomaly if it is not classified as normal by any of the classifiers. Some techniques use a confidence value for each class prediction. If each confidence value of the normal classes is under a specified threshold, it is classified as an anomaly. Anomaly detection techniques based on the classification of one class assume that all training instances have only one class. Those techniques train a boundary of discrimination around the normal instances using a one-class classification algorithm. Everything outside this boundary is classified as an anomaly.

The advantages of prediction-based techniques can be listed as follows:

1. Prediction-based techniques can benefit from state-of-the-art algorithms in the field of machine learning.
2. The evaluation of new data is fast since each new observation will be compared against the pretrained model.

Several drawbacks of prediction-based techniques are identified as follows:

1. Multiclass prediction techniques rely on accurately labeled data for all normal classes, which can be difficult in practice.

2. Some classification techniques classify each test instance with a label and not with a probability. This can be a disadvantage if only a label is given and not a prediction confidence score to better ensure whether the instance is *clearly* or *maybe* an anomaly.

3.3.4 Anomaly detection in health domain

Detection of abnormalities in health domain usually requires operating with patient records. Reasons for anomalies can be due to an abnormal patient condition or recording errors. Various techniques have focused on detecting disease outbreaks [19], where the detection of anomalies is a critical problem and requires high accuracy. The record features have various characteristics, such as the patient's age, blood group, weight, or lifestyle. The data can have both temporal and spatial aspects. Most of the anomaly detection techniques in this domain try to detect anomalous records (anomaly data points). Typically, the data belong to healthy patients, so most techniques use a semisupervised approach. Another form of data processing in this domain is that of time-series data such as electrocardiograms (ECG) and electroencephalograms (EEG).

An individual data instance may not be an anomaly by itself, but it can be in an occurrence with other data classified as a real anomaly. Collective anomaly detection techniques are beneficial in this field for detecting anomalies and have been applied in the health domain [36]. A challenging aspect of anomaly detection in this domain can be the cost for wrong classifications, in case an anomaly is classified as normal and a possible unfavorable health condition not being identified.

3.4 Accuracy and prediction from anomaly detection

Accuracy and prediction are of paramount importance for anomaly detection in health domain. Various types of metrics that measure accuracy and prediction are analyzed in next subsections.

3.4.1 Classification and regression metrics

In a binary classification task, model evaluation during training can be done using a confusion matrix. In the confusion matrix, shown in Table 3.1, the predicted class's information is in the rows, and the actual class is in the columns. t_p and t_n denote the number of correctly classified positive and negative instances. f_p and f_n denote the number of misclassified negative and positive instances.

Table 3.1 Confusion Matrix to evaluate Binary Classification.

	Actual Positive Class	Actual Negative Class
Predicted Positive Class	True positive (t_p)	False negative (f_n)
Predicted Negative Class	False positive (f_p)	True negative (t_n)

Commonly used metrics generated from the results of a confusion matrix can be seen in Table 3.2, which summarizes more metrics for the evaluation of multiclass problems.

Previous studies [15,28,50] have shown that accuracy is the most commonly used evaluation metric in practice, either for binary or for multiclass classification problems. The quality of a generated solution is evaluated by accuracy, based on the percentage of correct predictions over all instances. The

Table 3.2 Overview of evaluation metrics for binary and multiclass classification. Note: t_{p_i}—true positive for C_i; f_{p_i}—false positive for C_i; f_{n_i}—false negative for C_i; t_{n_i}—true negative for C_i.

Metrics	Formula	Evaluation criteria
Accuracy (acc)	$\frac{t_p+t_n}{t_p+f_p+t_n+f_n}$	The accuracy metric measures the ratio of correct predictions over the total number of instances evaluated.
Error Rate (err)	$\frac{f_p+f_n}{t_p+f_p+t_n+f_n}$	Misclassification error measures the ratio of incorrect predictions over the total number of instances evaluated.
Sensitivity (sn)	$\frac{t_p}{t_p+f_n}$	Sensitivity used to measure the fraction of positive patterns that are correctly classified. True Positive Rate TPR
Specificity (sp)	$\frac{t_n}{t_n+f_p}$	Specificity measure the fraction of negative patterns that are correctly classified. True Negative Rate TNR
Precision (p)	$\frac{t_p}{t_p+f_p}$	Precision measures the correctly predicted positive patterns from the total predicted patterns in a positive class.
Recall (r)	$\frac{t_p}{t_p+t_n}$	Recall is used to measure the fraction of correctly classified positive patterns
F-Measure (FM)	$\frac{2*p*r}{p+r}$	F-Measure represents the harmonic mean between recall and precision
Geometric-mean (GM)	$\sqrt{t_p * t_n}$	Geometric-mean is used to maximize the tp and tn rate, while keeping both rates balanced
Averaged Accuracy	$\frac{\sum_{i=1}^{l} \frac{t_p+t_n}{t_{p_i}+f_{n_i}+f_{p_i}+t_{n_i}}}{l}$	The average effectiveness of all classes
Averaged Error Rate	$\frac{\sum_{i=1}^{l} \frac{f_p+f_n}{t_{p_i}+f_{n_i}+f_{p_i}+t_{n_i}}}{l}$	The average error rate of all classes
Averaged Precision	$\frac{\sum_{i=1}^{l} \frac{t_{p_i}}{t_{p_i}+f_{p_i}}}{l}$	The average precision per-class
Averaged Recall	$\frac{\sum_{i=1}^{l} \frac{t_{p_i}}{t_{p_i}+f_{n_i}}}{l}$	The average recall per-class
Averaged F-Measure	$\frac{2*p_M*\tau_M}{p_M+\tau_M}$	The average F-Measure over all classes. M—macro-averaging.

complementary metric to accuracy is the error rate, which assesses the solution based on the percentage of incorrect predictions. Researchers have widely used both metrics to select the optimal solution. The benefit of accuracy or error rate is that these metrics are easy to compute, have low complexity, apply to multiclass and multilabel problems, allow easy evaluation, and be easily understood by humans. As highlighted in many studies, the accuracy metric has limitations in evaluation and discrimination processes. A main limitation of accuracy is that it produces less discriminative and less discriminable scores [33,48]. Consequently, it leads to less discriminative power than accuracy in selecting and determining the optimal classifier. Accuracy is also powerless in terms of informativeness [39] and lower preference for minority class instances [15,61].

Alternatively to accuracy, F-measure (FM) and G-mean (GM) have shown good discriminative power and better performance than accuracy in classifier optimization for binary classification problems [35]. It should be noted that FM and GM have been used less to discriminate and select the optimal solution for multiclass classification problems in any previous work. In contrast, the other metrics in Table 3.2 are not ideal for determining and selecting the optimal solution based on a single evaluation task. The significance tradeoff between classes is important to ensure that the representative samples represent each class. The tradeoff between classes becomes even more important when an unbalanced data set is to be analyzed. The best-selected solution is useless if none of the minority class instances were not correctly predicted by the chosen representative(s).

Area under the ROC curve (AUC)

The AUC is a popular metric for ranking type. In [29,32,52], AUC was used to construct an optimized learning model and compare learning algorithms [48,47]. Unlike the threshold and likelihood metrics, the AUC value reflects the overall ranking performance of a classifier. For a two-class problem [29], the AUC value can be calculated as follows:

$$AUC = \frac{S_p - n_p(n_n + 1)/2}{n_p n_n} \tag{3.1}$$

where S_p is the sum of all ranked positive examples, while n_p and n_n denote the number of positive and negative instances, respectively. The AUC value has been theoretically and empirically shown to be better than the accuracy metric [32] to evaluate the classifier's performance and identify an optimal solution during classification training. Although the implementation of AUC was excellent for evaluation and discrimination processes, the computational cost of AUC is high, especially for discriminating a set of generated solutions of multiclass problems. To compute AUC for multiclass problems, the time complexity is $O(|C|n\log n)$ for the AUC model in [47] and $O(|C^2|n\log n)$ for the AUC model of [29].

Mean Square Error (MSE)

Supervised learning vector quantization (LVQ) [37] is a prototype selection classifier that allows to choose how many training instances to keep and learns what those instances should look like. During the learning process, the supervised LVQ uses the MSE to evaluate its performance in classification training. The MSE measures the difference between the predicted and the actual values, defined as follows:

$$MSE = \frac{1}{n} \sum_{j=1}^{n} (P_j - A_j)^2 \tag{3.2}$$

where P_j is the predicted value of instance j, A_j is the actual target value of instance j, and n the number of instances. Through the LVQ learning process, the solution with the lowest MSE value is used as the final model (best solution). Like accuracy, the main limitation of MSE is that this metric does not provide information about the tradeoff between the class data, which may cause the discrimination process to select the suboptimal solution. Also, this metric is highly dependent on the initialization of the weights. For an imbalanced class problem, if the initial weights are not properly selected (i.e., not representing the minority class), the discrimination process may end up with a suboptimal solution. While the MSE value is minimized, the solution could under- or over-fit due to a lack of information about the minority class.

Mean Absolute Error (MAE)

Mean absolute error (MAE) is a popular metric because, as with Root mean squared error (RMSE), see next subsection, the error value units match the predicted target value units. Unlike RMSE, the changes in MAE are linear and therefore intuitive. MSE and RMSE penalize larger errors more, inflating or increasing the mean error value due to the square of the error value. In MAE, different errors are not weighted more or less, but the scores increase linearly with the increase in errors. The MAE score is measured as the average of the absolute error values. The Absolute is a mathematical function that makes a number positive. Therefore, the difference between an expected value and a predicted value can be positive or negative and will necessarily be positive when calculating the MAE.

The MAE value can be calculated as follows:

$$MAE = \frac{1}{n}\sum_{i=1}^{n}|y_1 - \hat{y}_i|^2 \qquad (3.3)$$

Root Mean Square Error (RMSE)

The root mean squared error (RMSE) is an extension of the MSE. The error's square root is calculated, meaning that the units of the RMSE are the same as the original units of the predicted target value. Therefore, it may be common to use the MSE loss to train a regression prediction model and use the RMSE to evaluate and report its performance.

The RMSE can be calculated as follows:

$$RMSE = \sqrt{\frac{1}{n}\sum_{i=1}^{N}(\hat{y}_i - y_i)^2} \qquad (3.4)$$

3.4.2 Anomaly detection rules on data streams
Anomaly score with HTM algorithm

Because HTM is a continuous learning online system, it detects transient anomalies and learns when they are the new normal [5]. HTM works for both numeric and categorical input data. The two types of data can be mixed in an input stream to HTM as they are converted to a sparse distributed representation (SDR).

HTM computes an anomaly score for each new sample it receives [5]. If a received sample was predicted, the anomaly score equals zero. If the sample was not predicted at all, the score equals one. A partially predicted sample score is between 0 and 1. The anomaly score depends on the similarity between the received samples and the predicted samples. The sparse distributed representations of the samples determine the similarity. If none of the representation cells in a column were predicted, all cells are made active. This process is called bursting. It occurs when there is no context, i.e., when HTM learns a new transition. At each instance of time, the anomaly score is simply the fraction obtained by dividing the number of bursting columns by the total number of active columns. At the beginning of training, the anomaly score is high because most of the patterns are new. As HTM learns, the anomaly score decreases until there is a change in the pattern stream.

The reader is referred to [62] for an application of the HTM algorithm to car data streams (CAN bus data) for pothole detection in roads.

Detection rules

In some anomaly detection scenarios, only the anomaly score is needed, but there are also scenarios where the anomaly score gives too many false positives because the data is noisy. Detection rules can be applied to mitigate high false-positive rates by avoiding a simple threshold technique applied to a data point.

Two types of threshold techniques are described in more detail, the accumulator and the Gaussian probability rule. The accumulator method works by defining a metric to determine a local failure and then increments the numerator for each failure and decrements for each nonabnormal value. Based on Numenta's formulations, the statistical method works by comparing the short-term variance to the long-term variance [5]. A study conducted by [56] showed that both methods worked very similarly and triggered at almost the same points. Nevertheless, both offer a unique theoretical and practical advantage because the accumulator method is easily modified and controlled, while the statistical method gives a percentage chance of being an outlier. These properties can be used in combination for a more robust anomaly scoring.

Accumulator rule

The accumulator rule's goal is to seek several point anomalies in a given time before a persistent anomaly is reported. Two main rules can be distinguished here as to how a point anomaly is detected. The goal is to prevent the noise that a local anomaly detection algorithm would cause since multiple anomalies are required in a short time frame to reach each threshold for signaling. The main part of this rule is a counter that would grow or shrink. For each local anomaly, the counter grows by one, and for each nonanomalous value, it shrinks by two, and pure noise shrinks the counter.

- Threshold: This algorithm defines a local anomaly as any value where the actual value is less than the expected value by more than a specified δ if the actual value is greater than a hard-coded threshold that states that any value above it is not anomalous.
- Variance-based: A local variance to determine failures by defining a failure as any value that falls outside of the current forecast's rolling variance multiple times, so noisy areas would allow more noise in anomalies. However, this method proved to be somewhat less effective than the simple threshold [56].

Gaussian tail probability rule

Another anomaly detection rule is the Gaussian tail probability rule defined by Numenta. The aim is to detect changes in the anomaly score itself. Numenta's rule requires calculating a raw anomaly score between the inference value and the ground truth [5]. The calculation of the raw anomaly score is simply the difference between the inference and the ground truth. The anomaly probability is then determined by a window of previously calculated anomaly scores that computes estimates of the expected value and standard deviation of the scores, assuming normally distributed values.

Fig. 3.1 shows the right half of a normal distribution of possible anomaly scores. When a new anomalous value arrives, it will be estimated how likely the value is using the normal distribution based on the previous values' window. A new value on the x-axis below the central region of the curve in Fig. 3.1 is a typical value that frequently occurs. These typical values indicate that the system is operating as expected. The goal is to find values that belong to the calculated normal distribution's right tail to detect anomalies. Values that fall at the beginning of the tail in Fig. 3.1 are more likely to be anomalous, while values that fall further out in the tail represent anomalous behavior. Since the distribution of anomaly scores may change over time, the estimated value and standard deviation are recomputed as the window slides over the obtained scores.

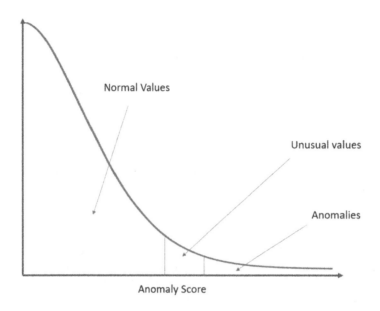

FIGURE 3.1

Gaussian normal distribution of anomaly scores divided in the areas of normal values, unexpected values, and anomalies.

3.4.3 Other metrics

As alternatives to the above metrics, graph-based metrics, have been proposed to evaluate classifiers' performance. As reported in [46], these metrics can represent the trade-offs between different evaluation perspectives, which allows a more comprehensive analysis of the results. Although these metrics have advantages over accuracy or error rate metric, their graph-based output limits the use of a metric such as Receiver Operating Curve (ROC) [25], Bayesian Receiver Operating Characteristic (B-ROC) [12], Precision-Recall Curve [22], Cost Curve [23], Lift and Chart Calibration Plot [59] as discriminators. Some other metrics are developed for specific classification algorithms. Information gain and entropy metrics are probability types that have been used to evaluate the utility of data attributes in building optimized decision tree classifiers [40]. Due to their specific purpose, these metrics are not suitable for discriminating and selecting the optimal solution.

Hybrid discriminant metrics

Optimized precision is a hybrid threshold metric and has been proposed as a discriminator for building an optimized heuristic classifier [50]. This metric is a combination of precision, sensitivity, and specificity metrics. The sensitivity and specificity metrics were used to stabilize and optimize the precision performance when dealing with unbalanced two-class problems.

The OP metric can be defined as follows:

$$OP = acc - \frac{|sp - sn|}{sp + sn} \tag{3.5}$$

where acc is the accuracy score, while sp and sn denote the specificity and sensitivity scores, respectively. As an example, in [50], the OR metric chose a better solution and increased the classification performance of ensemble learners and multiclassifier systems for solving human DNA sequence datasets.

3.5 Key features

In this chapter, anomaly types, concepts, and detection methods are presented.

☑ Anomaly detection in Big Data and Big Data streams is discussed.
☑ Challenges of anomaly detection are highlighted.
☑ Anomaly detection modes are presented for various data stream types (supervised, semisupervised, and unsupervised).
☑ Anomaly detection techniques are classified and detailed.
☑ Prediction techniques in anomaly detection and the most important metrics for accuracy and prediction are given.
☑ Finally, anomaly detection rules on data streams, such as anomaly score with HTM Algorithm, and detection rules are described.

References

[1] T. Abe, C. Kearns, S. Fujita, M. Sakamaki-Sunaga, Y. Sato, W. Brechue, Skeletal muscle size and strength are increased following walk training with restricted leg muscle blood flow: implications for training duration and frequency, International Journal of Kaatsu Training Research 5 (01 2009) 9–15.
[2] C. Aggarwal, Outlier Analysis, 11 2013.
[3] C. Aggarwal, J. Han, J. Wang, P. Yu, T. Watson, R. Ctr, A framework for clustering evolving data streams, in: Proceedings of the 29th International Conference on Very Large Data Bases, 06 2003.
[4] M. Agyemang, K. Barker, R. Alhajj, A comprehensive survey of numeric and symbolic outlier mining techniques, Intelligent Data Analysis 10 (11 2006) 521–538.
[5] S. Ahmad, A. Lavin, S. Purdy, Z. Agha, Unsupervised real-time anomaly detection for streaming data, Neurocomputing 262 (2017) 134–147.
[6] F. Angiulli, F. Fassetti, Detecting distance-based outliers in streams of data, in: Proceedings of the Sixteenth ACM Conference on Information and Knowledge Management, 11 2007, pp. 811–820.
[7] I. Assent, P. Kranen, C. Baldauf, T. Seidl Anyout, Anytime outlier detection on streaming data, in: DASFAA, 04 2012, pp. 228–242.
[8] R. Beckman, R. Cook, Outlier .. .. s, Technometrics 25 (03 2012) 119–149.
[9] M. Breunig, H.-P. Kriegel, R. Ng, J. Sander, LOF: identifying density-based local outliers, in: Proceedings of the 2000 ACM SIGMOD International Conference on Management of Data, vol. 29, 06 2000, pp. 93–104.
[10] F. Cao, M. Ester, W. Qian, A. Zhou, Density-based clustering over an evolving data stream with noise, in: Proceedings of the Sixth SIAM International Conference on Data Mining, vol. 2006, 04 2006.
[11] L. Cao, D. Yang, Q. Wang, Y. Yu, J. Wang, E. Rundensteiner, Scalable distance-based outlier detection over high-volume data streams, in: 2014 IEEE 30th International Conference on Data Engineering, 03 2014, pp. 76–87.
[12] A. Cárdenas, J. Baras, B-ROC curves for the assessment of classifiers over imbalanced data sets, in: AAAI, 2006.

[13] V. Chandola, A. Banerjee, V. Kumar, Anomaly detection: a survey, ACM Computing Surveys 41 (07 2009).

[14] V. Chandola, A. Banerjee, V. Kumar, Anomaly detection for discrete sequences: a survey, IEEE Transactions on Knowledge and Data Engineering 24 (05 2012) 1.

[15] N. Chawla, N. Japkowicz, A. Kotcz, Editorial: special issue on learning from imbalanced data sets, SIGKDD Explorations 6 (2004) 1–6.

[16] Y. Chen, L. Tu, Density-based clustering for real-time stream data, in: KDD'07, 2007.

[17] M. Chenaghlou, M. Moshtaghi, C. Leckie, M. Salehi, An efficient method for anomaly detection in nonstationary data streams, in: GLOBECOM 2017 - 2017 IEEE Global Communications Conference, 12 2017, pp. 1–6.

[18] M. Chenaghlou, M. Moshtaghi, C. Leckie, M. Salehi, Online clustering for evolving data streams with online anomaly detection, in: Advances in Knowledge Discovery and Data Mining, 06 2018, pp. 508–521.

[19] K. Cheong, E. Djunaedy, T. Poh, K. Tham, C. Sekhar, N.H. Wong, M. Ullah, Measurements and computations of contaminant's distribution in an office, Building and Environment 38 (01 2003) 135–145.

[20] D. Dasgupta, N.S. Majumdar, Anomaly detection in multidimensional data using negative selection algorithm, in: Proceedings of the 2002 Congress on Evolutionary Computation. CEC'02 (Cat. No. 02TH8600), vol. 2, 2002, pp. 1039–1044.

[21] D. Dasgupta, L.F. Nino, A comparison of negative and positive selection algorithms in novel pattern detection, in: 2000 IEEE International Conference on Systems, Man and Cybernetics, vol. 1, 02 2000, pp. 125–130.

[22] J. Davis, M. Goadrich, The relationship between precision-recall and ROC curves, in: ICML'06, 2006.

[23] C. Drummond, R. Holte, Cost curves: an improved method for visualizing classifier performance, Machine Learning 65 (2006) 95–130.

[24] M. Elahi, K. Li, M. Nisar, X. Lv, H. Wang, Efficient clustering-based outlier detection algorithm for dynamic data stream, in: 2008 Fifth International Conference on Fuzzy Systems and Knowledge Discovery, vol. 5, 10 2008, pp. 298–304.

[25] T. Fawcett, An introduction to ROC analysis, Pattern Recognition Letters 27 (2006) 861–874.

[26] H. Fujimaki, T. Shimano, M. Inoue, K. Nakane, Effect of a salt crust on evaporation from a bare saline soil, Vadose Zone Journal 5 (2006) 11.

[27] F. Giannoni, M. Mancini, F. Marinelli, Anomaly detection models for IoT time series data, 11 2018.

[28] Q. Gu, L. Zhu, Z. Cai, Evaluation measures of the classification performance of imbalanced data sets, in: Computational Intelligence and Intelligent Systems, vol. 51, 10 2009, pp. 461–471.

[29] D. Hand, R. Till, A simple generalisation of the area under the ROC curve for multiple class classification problems, Machine Learning 45 (2004) 171–186.

[30] A.Z. Hans-Peter Kriegel, Peer Kröger, Outlier detection techniques, 2010.

[31] D. Hawkins, Identification of Outliers, 1980.

[32] J. Huang, C. Ling, Using AUC and accuracy in evaluating learning algorithms, IEEE Transactions on Knowledge and Data Engineering 17 (2005) 299–310.

[33] J. Huang, C. Ling, Constructing new and better evaluation measures for machine learning, in: IJCAI, 2007.

[34] J. Joshi, B. Schmid, M.C. Caldeira, P.G. Dimitrakopoulos, J. Good, R. Harris, A. Hector, K. Huss-Danell, A. Jumpponen, A. Minns, C.P.H. Mulder, J.S. Pereira, A. Prinz, M. Scherer-Lorenzen, A.-S.D. Siamantziouras, A.C. Terry, A.Y. Troumbis, J.H. Lawton, Local adaptation enhances performance of common plant species, Ecology Letters 4 (6) (2001) 536–544.

[35] M. Joshi, On evaluating performance of classifiers for rare classes, in: 2002 IEEE International Conference on Data Mining, 2002. Proceedings, 2002, pp. 641–644.

[36] E. Keogh, J. Lin, A. Fu, H. van herle, Finding unusual medical time-series subsequences: algorithms and applications, IEEE Transactions on Information Technology in Biomedicine: a Publication of the IEEE Engineering in Medicine and Biology Society 10 (08 2006) 429–439.

[37] T. Kohonen, Self-organizing maps, in: Springer Series in Information Sciences, 1995.

[38] M. Kontaki, A. Gounaris, A. Papadopoulos, K. Tsichlas, Y. Manolopoulos, Continuous monitoring of distance-based outliers over data streams, in: 2011 IEEE 27th International Conference on Data Engineering, 04 2011, pp. 135–146.

[39] D. Mackay, Information theory, inference, and learning algorithms, IEEE Transactions on Information Theory 50 (2004) 2544–2545.

[40] T.M. Mitchell, Machine Learning, international edition, McGraw-Hill Series in Computer Science, 1997.

[41] M. Moshtaghi, J. Bezdek, T. Havens, C. Leckie, S. Karunasekera, S. Rajasegarar, M. Palaniswami, Streaming analysis in wireless sensor networks, Wireless Communications and Mobile Computing 14 (06 2014).

[42] H. Motulsky, Intuitive Biostatics, 01 1995.

[43] I. Noble, A. Gill, G. Bary, Mcarthur's fire-danger meters expressed as equations, Australian Journal of Ecology 5 (07 2006) 201–203.

[44] C. Phua, A comprehensive survey of data mining-based fraud detection research, in: Intelligent Computation Technology and Automation (ICICTA), 01 2010, pp. 50–53.

[45] D. Pokrajac, A. Lazarevic, L.J. Latecki, Incremental local outlier detection for data streams, in: 2007 IEEE Symposium on Computational Intelligence and Data Mining, 01 2007, pp. 504–515.

[46] R. Prati, G.E.A.P.A. Batista, M.C. Monard, A survey on graphical methods for classification predictive performance evaluation, IEEE Transactions on Knowledge and Data Engineering 23 (2011) 1601–1618.

[47] F. Provost, P.M. Domingos, Tree induction for probability-based ranking, Machine Learning 52 (2004) 199–215.

[48] A. Rakotomamonjy, Optimizing area under ROC curve with SVMs, in: ROCAI, 2004.

[49] A. Ram, J. Sunita, A. Jalal, K. Manoj, A density based algorithm for discovering density varied clusters in large spatial databases, International Journal of Computer Applications 3 (06 2010).

[50] R. Ranawana, V. Palade, Optimized precision - a new measure for classifier performance evaluation, in: 2006 IEEE International Conference on Evolutionary Computation, 2006, pp. 2254–2261.

[51] J. Ren, R. Ma, Density-based data streams clustering over sliding windows, in: 2009 Sixth International Conference on Fuzzy Systems and Knowledge Discovery, vol. 5, 01 2009, pp. 248–252.

[52] S. Rosset, Model selection via the AUC, in: Proceedings of the Twenty-First International Conference on Machine Learning, 2004.

[53] P.J. Rousseeuw, A.M. Leroy, Robust Regression and Outlier Detection, John Wiley & Sons, Inc., USA, 1987.

[54] M. Salehi, C. Leckie, J. Bezdek, T. Vaithianathan, X. Zhang, Fast memory efficient local outlier detection in data streams (extended abstract), in: 2017 IEEE 33rd International Conference on Data Engineering (ICDE), 04 2017, pp. 51–52.

[55] M. Salehi, C. Leckie, M. Moshtaghi, T. Vaithianathan, A relevance weighted ensemble model for anomaly detection in switching data streams, in: Advances in Knowledge Discovery and Data Mining, 05 2014, pp. 461–473.

[56] D.T. Shipmon, J.M. Gurevitch, P.M. Piselli, S.T. Edwards, Time series anomaly detection; detection of anomalous drops with limited features and sparse examples in noisy highly periodic data, arXiv:1708.03665 [abs], 2017.

[57] J. Theiler, M. Cai, Resampling approach for anomaly detection in multispectral images, Proceedings of SPIE 5093 (04 2003).

[58] R. Vilalta, Y. Drissi, A perspective view and survey of meta-learning, Artificial Intelligence Review 18 (09 2001).

[59] M. Vuk, ROC curve, lift chart and calibration plot, 2006.

[60] J. Wiley, S. Chichester, Outliers in statistical data, 3rd edition, 584 pp., International Journal of Forecasting 12 (1994).

[61] S. Wilson, Mining oblique data with XCS, in: IWLCS, 2000.

[62] F. Xhafa, B. Kilic, P. Krause, Evaluation of IoT stream processing at edge computing layer for semantic data enrichment, Future Generations Computer Systems 105 (2020) 730–736.

[63] L. Yu, N. Wang, X. Meng, Real-time forest fire detection with wireless sensor networks, in: Proceedings. 2005 International Conference on Wireless Communications, Networking and Mobile Computing, vol. 2, 10 2005, pp. 1214–1217.

[64] T. Zhang, R. Ramakrishnan, M. Livny, Birch: an efficient data clustering method for very large databases, in: SIGMOD'96, 1996.

Complex event processing

Building complex events from simple, atomic events

4

While the purpose of Data Stream Management Systems (DSMS) is to perform stream analytics over a local scope, for instance, at a geographically concentrated area, Complex Event Processing (CEP) aims to infer the global meaning of raw events to provide real-time decision support over multiple events.

Atomic events, that is, single events corresponding to a parameter, a simple predicate, or a concept, are detected directly from stream data tuples. They are defined as indivisible events or atomic events. Atomic events might have no special meaning but can get a higher meaning in correlation with other events or specific contexts. CEP analyses continuous streams of events, most notably from multistream data, to identify complex sequences of events (event patterns) or complex predicates over the data stream. A pattern match represents a relevant state of the phenomenon under study and is the base to trigger creating a new, more complex event or triggering an action in turn.

CEP can be considered a continuous intelligence application that improves situational awareness and provides decision support in real-time. Complex event patterns are inferred over multiple data sources to predict and manage events, situations, and potential anomalous situations, such as threats in the health condition of patients. CEP is a paradigm and technology to query data before storing it into a database, making it suitable for real-time decision-making. In stream analytics, CEP is used to track and analyze incoming data to identify cause and effect relationships between real-time events to conclude on specific complex events. Due to such features, CEP is often referred to as event stream processing.

CEP technologies have been used for situation awareness and decision-making for several years [13]. The increasing popularity of Big Data and the Internet of Things (IoT), coupled with the need for real-time analytics, has driven CEP technologies and tools to further developments to embrace and cope with new application scenarios. Event processing for healthcare applications, especially in real-time IoT-based applications with medical devices, has several benefits that reduce risk and improve patient care due to instant data analysis. Combining CEP and IoT with medical data opens the door to personalized analytics scenarios to predict and manage critical health situations and provide support.

A CEP engine analyzes events and related data drawn from several sources such as health sensors or environmental sensors in real-time and provides health care insights. An event object carries general metadata (event ID, timestamp) and event-specific information (sensor-id, measurements). Complex events can be built from personal sensors combined with smart home devices to provide insights that answer questions about the connection between personal health, food consumed, and lifestyle quality. Additionally, health changes can be correlated with environmental factors such as humidity, air quality, or temperature by connecting to events from environmental monitoring sensors (see [36] for a comprehensive coverage of Smart Sensors Networks).

Massive amounts of Big Data that are of no interest can be filtered using CEP as it is analyzed. A major challenge is defining these filters to detect critical situations and not drop useful information.

Anomaly Detection and Complex Event Processing Over IoT Data Streams. https://doi.org/10.1016/B978-0-12-823818-9.00014-6

4.1 **Fundamental concept of CEP**

The Event Processing Language (EPL) is a fundamental CEP concept that contains event processing rules defining event patterns, actions, and event processing engines to analyze events and match rules continuously [5]. CEP engines usually have the following basic characteristics:

- Continuous in-memory processing: Designed to handle a sequential input stream of events and in-memory processing enables real-time operations.
- Correlating Data: Enables the combination of different event types from heterogeneous sources. Event processing rules transform primitive events into complex events that represent a significant meaning for the application domain.
- Temporal Operators: Within event stream processing, timer functionalities and sliding time windows can be used to define event patterns representing temporal relationships.

CEP provides a rich set of concepts and operators for processing events, including the CQL like queries, rules, primitive functions (aggregation, filtering, or transformation), and production of derived events. The events are manipulated by CEP rules, called Event-Condition-Action (ECA) rules, inspired by the ECA approach in active databases, where ECA rules were developed to support reactions to different kinds of events occurring in active databases. An ECA rule is a combination of continuous query primitives with context operators. Context operators can contain temporal, logical, and quantifiable characteristics, where a positive correlation generates a complex event that summarizes the correlated input [11].

The following steps represent phase examples of a CEP processing flow:

1. Signaling: Detection of an event.
2. Triggering: Check an event against a defined set of rules.
3. Evaluation: Evaluate the condition of each checked rule.
4. Scheduling: Execution order of selected rules.
5. Execution: Execute all actions for the relevant selected rules.

Basic definitions

An event can be defined as a record of activity in a computer processing system or an occurrence of interest in time [34]. In general, events can be categorized into basic events and complex events (or composite events). We use upper case and lower case, such as E and e, to represent an event type and an event instance.

Primitive event – A basic event can be denoted as $E = E(id, a, t)$, where id is the unique ID of an event $a = a_1, a_2, \ldots, a_m$, $m > 0$ is a set of event attributes and t is the event occurrence time. A basic event is atomic, indivisible, and occurs at a point in time.

Complex event – A complex event is usually defined by applying event constructors to its constituent events, which are either primitive events or other complex events. The A complex event can be defined as $E = E(id, a, c, t_n, t_e)$, $t_e >= T_b$, where $c = e_1, e_2., \ldots, e_n$, $n > 0$ is the vector that contains the basic events and complex events that cause this event happen; t_b and t_e are the starting and ending times of this complex event, namely, it can happen over a period of time (i.e., from t_b to t_e).

A complex event is built by aggregating basic events or other complex events using a specific set of event constructors such as disjunction, conjunction, and sequence. It signifies or refers to other events to indicate a situation described in an application scenario. Complex events contain more semantic meaning and are more useful for all applications where decision-making is crucial, most notably in health applications.

Event querying

Unlike database queries, event queries are continuously evaluated as events occur. Databases often work with event-related data (e.g., historical listing of orders), where the queries are unique, spontaneous against a finite amount of data, not permanent. In contrast to CEP, where the queries stand against a (conceptually) infinite event stream, the following aspects can define the requirements for an event request language:

1. Extraction of data: Events contain data relevant to whether and how to respond. The data must be available for conditions in queries, possible reactions, enrichment with other data (for example, database tables), or constructing new events. Events are increasingly represented as XML messages; the data can then be structured in a complex way.
2. Composition: It must be possible to link several single events so that their common occurrence distributed over time yields to a complex event. This composition often has to be data-related (e.g., it only combines events that affect the same patient).
3. Temporal relationships: Event requests often contain temporal conditions that express that events must happen in a certain period or sequence. Other contexts, e.g., causal, can also play a role.
4. Accumulation: Requests with negation (absence of an event) or aggregation of event data make little sense on infinite data streams since they could only be answered correctly at the end. Such queries can only be made against certain finite sections (or "windows") of the data stream where their result is well defined.

Rule model

This model can be classified into two main classes of transforming rules and detecting rules.

- Transforming rules can be considered as a graph connecting primitive operators. The operators take multiple input flows and produce new elements forwarded to other operators or consumers. Transforming rules can usually be found with homogeneous information flows where the input and output structure can be anticipated [8].
- Detecting rules present a distinction between a condition and an action. The condition part represents a logical predicate that captures patterns in a sequence of elements. The action part defines how the information gets processed and aggregated.

Likewise, CEP language types can be divided into classes of transforming and detection based languages [8]:

- Transforming languages defines transforming rules on input streams by filtering, joining, and aggregating received information to produce new output flows [8]. Transforming rules can be divided into two subclasses:
    – Declarative languages express processing rules by specifying the expected results instead of the execution flow.
    – Imperative languages define rules that specify a plan of primitive operators. Each operator contains a transformation over its input.

- Detecting or pattern-based languages specify the trigger conditions and the actions to be taken when specific conditions hold. Conditions are represented by patterns over the input stream and constructed with logical operators, timing and content, and constraints. Actions define how the detected events have to be combined to produce new events. This type of language is a common language in CEP systems that can detect relevant information before the evaluation process is started.

Modern languages consolidate operators of different languages. An example of a declarative language is CQL [3].

4.2 Primitive functions for CEP

CQL defines three classes of operators [8]:

- Relation-to-relation operators define classical queries over database tables and are similar to SQL queries.
- Stream-to-relation operators create tables out of a bounded segment of a data stream. Relation-to-stream operators create a data flow out of fixed tables.
- Stream-to-stream operators are expressed using the other operators.

Stream-to-relation operators

These operators are based on sliding window operator concepts. The relation is obtained from a stream by extracting the set of tuples included in the current window.
CQL contains 3 relation-to-stream operators:

- ISTREAM(): whenever a tuple t is inserted into the input relation at time $\tau \rightarrow$ Outputs (τ, t)
- DSTREAM(): whenever a tuple t is deleted from the input relation at time $\tau \rightarrow$ Outputs (τ, t)
- RSTREAM(): whenever a tuple t is updated in the input relation at time $\tau \rightarrow$ Outputs (τ, t)

As an example, let us consider the following CQL query:

```
SELECT  ISTREAM(*)
FROM    S  [Rows 100]
WHERE   S.A -> 2
```

whose execution explanation is as follows:

1. The source of the query is the referenced stream S.
2. Stream-to-relation operator [Rows 100] converts the input stream of 100 entries into a relation.
3. Relation-to-relation filter SA $\rightarrow$ 2 selects the attributes with values higher than 2, which results in another relation.
4. ISTREAM relation-to-stream operator transforms the output back into a stream.

Pattern-based languages use selection operators to find items or events of a complex pattern. In a publish-subscribe system, they are the leading operators of choosing items to be forwarded to consumers [20]. The following logical and temporal event operators or event constructors are used in a CEP system to define event patterns that cast meaningful information from real-time data streams.

Event constructors or event operators express the relationships among events and correlate events to form complex events. The authors in [35] give a comprehensive set of event constructors and classify them into temporal and nontemporal constructors.

Logical (nontemporal):

- A conjunction of elements $E_1, E_2, \ldots, E_n$ is satisfied when all the elements $E_1, E_2, \ldots, E_n$ have been detected.
- A disjunction of elements $E_1, E_2, \ldots, E_n$ is satisfied when at least one of the elements $E_1, E_2, \ldots,$ E_n has been detected.
- A repetition of an element E of degree m, n is satisfied when E is detected at least m times and not more than n times.
- A negation of an element I is satisfied when E is not detected.
- Sequences are used to define the arrival of a set of elements where the order of arrival is considered. A sequence defines an ordered set of elements $E_1, E_2, \ldots, E_n$, which is satisfied when all the elements $E_1, E_2, \ldots, E_n$ have been detected in the same order.

An example – Conjunction: A patient stroke alarm is being notified when a sudden, severe headache and a sudden stumbling or loss of coordination happen.

Temporal operator:

- window - Event E_1 occurs n times
- within - Event E_1 occurs within an interval t or between the interval t_1 and t_2
- at - Event E_1 occurs at time t [system time]
- every - Every occurrence of E_1
- during - Event E_2 occurs during event E_1

Pattern-based vs. declarative and imperative language

These logic operators are present in pattern-based languages, where they combine different events. Declarative and imperative languages do not provide logic operators explicitly. They allow conjunctions, disjunctions, and negations using rules that transform the input stream.

- Declarative and imperative language approach: Joining two information flows, e.g., body vital signs (heart rate (HR), blood pressure (BP), respiration, temperature) with mobility signs (gait disturbances, loss of coordination) of a patient.
- Pattern-based language approach: Do not provide a join operator but use the conjunction operator to capture single events, e.g., body vital signs (heart rate, blood pressure, respiration, temperature) and mobility signs (gait disturbances, loss of coordination) of a patient via parametric filtering on the streams.

Parameterization

Parameterizations define the capability to filter data streams based on elements that are part of other streams.

Aggregates

Many CEP applications need to aggregate the content over multiple incoming streams to produce new insights.

Most languages have predefined aggregates, which include minimum, maximum, and average. In declarative and imperative languages, aggregates are usually combined with the use of windows. Pattern-based languages include detection aggregates to capture patterns over stored values.

CEP rules

CEP rules are defined to specify domain syntax and semantics based on the formalization of events and event constructors described above. A rule is the predefined inference logic or pattern for detecting complex events. Several studies [34,39] have described a different syntax for CEP rules. In [38], the authors used an ECA (Event–Condition–Action)-like rule expression language to describe event patterns. The generic syntax of such ECA rule can be expressed as follows:

```
BEGIN
Rule rule_id, rule_name, rule_group, priority
        ON event
        IF condition
        THEN action_1, action_2, ..., action_n
END
```

where rule_id and rule_name are unique for each rule, suggesting:

- id and name for a rule
- rule_group is a group of semantically related rules
- priority defines the priority of the rule
- the event specifies the event of interest
- condition is a boolean combination of user-defined functions
- action defines a user-defined procedure (e.g., to send out alarms) or an update in the database (e.g., update of patient status)

4.3 MultiIoT data stream in healthcare

Event processing offers numerous benefits to healthcare applications, especially IoT-based solutions that blend real-time data streams from various medical devices - some commonly used are listed next.

1. Physiological Sensors: Pulse, HR, ECG, EEG, BP, EMG, Pulsoxymetrie, PPG, ACC, Glucose, Gyroscope, motion tracker or Body temperature.
2. Environmental Sensors: RFID, Cameras, GPS, Ultrasonic, Microphone, Speakers, Humidity, Weight, Ambient or Light.

4.3.1 Chronically ill patient monitoring

The development of Cloud and IoT technologies has led to the effective development of remote patient monitoring platforms. The aim is to remotely monitor a chronically ill patient by remotely measuring relevant signs of the patient's health state (e.g., monitoring a patient with chronic heart disease for acute heart failure signs by measuring blood pressure changes, weight, and pulse). If the combination of the measurements, taken several times a day, changes by a predetermined percentage over a multiday period, an automatic alert is sent to a caregiver.

Remote patient monitoring has a clear positive impact on alleviating the burden to the health system of periodic controls of chronic disease patients.

It should be noted that remote patient monitoring can effectively serve not only to periodical checks but also to real-time detection and prediction of critical health situations of patients. For instance, to this example of aggregation-based event processing, the system also looks for other abnormal events, like sudden weight loss, indications of difficulty of standing and coordination, and, finally, triggering an alarm.

The following medical devices can be used:

- Weight Scale
- Blood Pressure Cuff
- Pulse Oximeter

Overview of a patient's scenario

The implementation is based on a schedule in which a remotely monitored patient is instructed to take health measurements four times a day. Every day, the system calculates each measurement's average and compares it to the patient's baseline or the average over time. This is a possible procedure:

- Patient's baseline measurements for medical devices are recorded and stored.
- Patient takes four readings each day with each device.
- The average of each day's readings is compared to the baseline readings.
- Each day's average of multiple measurements is compared to the previous two days' measurements.
- The average of the current day is compared to each measurement taken during the day.

The cumulative change over time is measured to analyze the data and look for trends (over two days). In the following event-processing example, the boolean logic formula is used to determine the potential for heart failure:

```
If WEIGHT increases by 3% over two days
 OR
If WEIGHT decreases by 10% over two days
 OR
(
 If AVERAGE BP increases by 2% over two days (8 readings)
   AND
 If AVERAGE WEIGHT increases 2% over two days (8 readings)
   AND
  If AVERAGE PULSE increases 2% over two days (8 readings)
)
Then
 Generate HEART FAILURE ALARM event
```

The illustrated scenario is a complex event processing scenario because it involves multiple event streams:

- Raw data events (WEIGHT, BP, and PULSE)
- Calculated events (AVERAGE WEIGHT)
- Aggregated events (the Boolean AND logic as described above)

The following measurements can be tracked:

- AVERAGE BP: the average of blood pressure readings (both systolic and diastolic) for one day
- AVERAGE WEIGHT: the average of all weight measurements for one day
- AVERAGE PULSE: the average of all pulse readings for one day

Inside the CEP queries

Recall that event processing systems work with streams of dynamic data instead of static data. Event data streams are sometimes described as channels, which are the streams that effectively handle the routing of events.

The stream types of ISTREAM (inserts data into the real-time stream) and DSTREAM (delete stream), which removes or withholds (delays) data from the real-time stream can be implemented with CQL queries.

To calculate a moving average over a defined period, the following insert stream is defined as:

```
ISTREAM(
 SELECT
    AVG(weight) AS averageWeight,
 FROM
   weightInputChannel [ROWS 4 SLIDE 4]
)
```

The average weight is computed for two days, with each day containing four measurements. This CQL query looks for current weight values above a certain value (180 kg) and only generates data if the criteria are met.

The AVG keyword calculates the average of all streamed values (in this case, weight values). The ROWS keyword tells the query how many values to use, while the SLIDE keyword tells how many times to calculate a result. In this case, the average is calculated using the last four values after all four values have been received. The result is a daily average value for each medical device.

Event processing network diagram

The data event streams and channels are visualized (see Fig. 4.1). The event data flows are described as channels, which are the streams that effectively handle the routing of events. Event processing begins with raw event data from the medical devices and ends on the right side, where complex event alerts are generated. The diagram contains the correlation of the heart-rate and stress measurement event composition.

The intermediate queries are shown below for each event processing step. This implementation is just a showcase, and in a real application, measurements and thresholds must be evaluated.

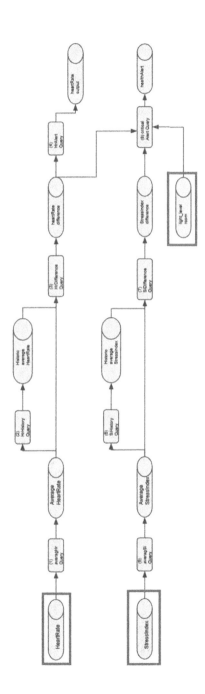

FIGURE 4.1

Event Processing Network Diagram of a complex event scenario for critical health status detection. The example contains the correlation of the heart-rate, stress measurement and light event composition. Inspired by [7].

(1) Average HeartRate query

```
ISTREAM(
SELECT
AVG(hr) As AverageHr
FROM
hrTopic[ROWS4 SLIDE4]
)
```

(2) HeartRate history query

```
DSTREAM(
SELECT averageHr AS averageHr
FROM averageHrTopic[ROWS 4]
)
```

(3) HeartRate difference query

```
ISTREAM(
SELECT
a.averageHr AS currentAverageHr,
h.averageHr AS historicAverageHr,
a.averageHr - h.averageHr AS hrDifference,
((a.averageHr-h.averageHr)/h.averageHr)*100 AS hrChangePercentage
FROM
averageHrTopic[now] AS a,
historicAverageHrTopic[ROWS 1] AS h
WHERE
a.averageHr>0 AND h.averageHr>0
)
```

(4) HeartRate alert query

```
SELECT
|'Hr increase of'||hrChangePercentage||'from'||
averageHr||'to'||  hr AS Alert
FROM
hrDifferenceTopic[now] AS d
WHERE
d.hrChangePercentage>5
```

Generating trends-based events

With incoming data, the average and delta (Δ) values are processed for trend analysis using event processing. We remind here that delta values express the amount of change in data stream values (when values are in chronological order we may have to subtract the larger value from the smaller one to preserve the order and this might result in a negative delta value).

There are basically two trends to watch for a sudden weight change (up or down) or a gradual increase in weight, pulse, and blood pressure that adds up over two days. Either trend may indicate imminent heart failure in a patient with chronic heart disease.

4.3.2 Dementia care, IoT data stream and CEP
A brief introduction to dementia care

We are witnessing rapid and significant demographic changes of the population world-wide, with the demographic pyramid shape including each time more elderly. These changes are currently having evident consequences and burden to current social healthcare systems. These consequences, however, are circumscribed in a broader scope of social, geopolitical, and financial implications not only for patients, health system and governmental bodies but also directly for individuals, caregivers, families and society.

The most relevant demographic change at present and in coming decades is a rapidly growing elderly population. Among elderly, the group of people with dementia and Alzheimer type conditions is an important part of the population, estimated in millions of people and projected to significantly increase by year 2050.

The syndrome of dementia causes a deterioration in memory, behavior and the ability to perform everyday activities. Most notably, this syndrome has a progressive nature where deterioration in cognitive functions of a person could scale up from a mild level (low level in which patients of dementia can still manage everyday life activities) to severe levels (in which condition patients of dementia show agitation and aggression and are fully dependent on health professionals and caregivers).

According to WHO (World Health Organization):

* Worldwide, around 50 million people have dementia, and there are nearly 10 million new cases every year.
* Alzheimer type conditions are the most common form of dementia and may contribute to 60–70% of cases.
* The total number of people with dementia is projected to reach 82 million in 2030 and 152 in 2050.

From a technological perspective and that of new generation of eHealth systems, effective ways of dealing with the long term care of dementia patients are being sought. Important progress is / will build upon achievements of IAL—Independent Assisted Living, based on intelligent context-aware decision-support systems. Indeed, the effective materialization of IAL systems for patients of dementia is an ambitious research endeavor involving a number of actors such as researchers from health domain, clinicians, IoT and networking, noninvasive sensor technologies, mobile technologies, caregivers, families and stakeholders.

The use of sensory devices to monitor daily living activities of early-stage dementia patients and subsequent analysis of sensory output to detect deviations from normal behavior patterns may indicate deterioration of the dementia state, such as agitation and wandering, and subsequently require intervention by caregivers or medical staff.

The aging population puts pressure on the resources of health and social systems. The care-giving of dementia patients by caregivers such as nurses, social workers is one of the main factors responsible for high costs associated with dementia care. The impact on those with the disease and their families is heavy. Dementia causes progressive deterioration in several functioning areas, including memory, reasoning, communication skills, and abilities needed to perform daily living activities. In addition to this deterioration, individuals may also develop behavioral and psychological symptoms such as depression, psychosis, aggression, and wandering, which complicate care-giving and occur at any stage of the disease.

Family caregivers of people with dementia are often elderly and frail themselves, have high levels of depression and physical illness, and suffer from a diminished quality of life. Although there is no treatment for dementia, a timely diagnosis allows those affected to access the emotional, practical, and financial support they need [29].

The reader is referred to [23,31,27,37] for state of the art in the field.

IoT and CEP

The IoT provides connectivity and intelligence to transform small devices into smart objects that enable the integration and transmission of enriched data from embedded sensors and wearables to provide people with disabilities with the help and support of living independently with a good quality of life. Wireless body area networks (WBANs) and smartphones have been recognized for their potential in rehabilitation, elderly support, and for obtaining information about elements such as patient movement, posture, and positioning [2]. Using assisting technology helps dementia patients to increase their safety by triggering automatic alarms when their health deteriorates. For those living alone, especially the elderly, there is often a fear of having an accident, which includes falls, accidents in the kitchen, and also general safety, such as leaving the house [30].

In [22], the application of CEP techniques via a wearable framework was proposed to identify patterns and causes suspected to be an impending fall or injury that help caregivers better monitor at-risk patients. Remote home monitoring combined with effective use of assisting technologies can help detect changes in health status and behavior in the home environment and enable successful adaptation to these changes.

Ontologies - knowledge base

Using background knowledge about events and their relationships to other concepts in the application domain can improve complex event processing systems' expressiveness and flexibility. Vast amounts of domain background knowledge stored in external knowledge bases, such as patient medical history, demographics, ethnicity, Genom info, can be used in combination with event processing to achieve more knowledgeable complex event processing. The value of decision support depends on the quantity and quality of knowledge of a domain. It is an important factor when complex event processing is used in environments that are rich in the domain and background knowledge, such as a nursing home or hospital.

The CEP architecture in [22] uses an ontology that helps formally model knowledge about a domain and enable reasoning over that knowledge. Ontologies are used to standardize terminology in a domain and facilitate knowledge sharing. This synergy of knowledge can be used to infer better decision making. An example can be found in Fig. 4.2.

Other uses of ontologies in medicine are as follows:

1. Disease Ontology (DO): human diseases for linking biomedical knowledge through disease data [15].
2. SNOMED-CT: advanced terminology and coding system for eHealth [10].

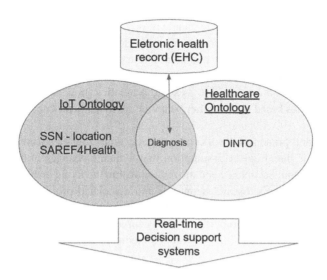

FIGURE 4.2

Illustration of a knowledge synergy between EHR, IoT CEP event inference and drug2drug interaction knowledge for possible real-time treatment recommendation.

3. OdIH-WS: Ontology-driven Interactive Healthcare with Wearable Sensors [14]. This ontology has the goal to retrieve in real-time context information in with ontological methods by integrating meteorological data in order to prevent disease.
4. ContoExam [6] is an ontology developed handle interoperability problems of sensor networks in the context of eHealth applications. This ontology contains specific expressions and specifications for medical uses as examination vocabulary and expressions.
5. MetaQ is an ontology-based framework for activity recognition in AAL environments that uses SPARQL queries and OWL 2 activity patterns [21].

Context-aware semantic modeling

Semantic technologies are used to manage background knowledge and join different data streams to perform inference. Therefore, combining event processing to handle data volumes and semantics to manage multiple data streams and background ontologies can improve timely detection of serious situations [1]. The main properties of ontologies can be summarized as:

- Structured: they facilitate interoperability between events published by different sources by providing a common understanding of the domain in question.
- Formal: an explicit representation by ontologies of the semantics of complex event patterns enables CEP to provide new services such as verification, gap analysis, and justification.
- Enabling inference: adds expressive power and inference capabilities.

Ontology rules provide a way to specify behavior for a system model and enable a shared conceptualization and understanding of a domain. Semantic ontology is used where CEP techniques have used application domain conceptualization to enable reasoning about events combined with other non-event concepts using formalized vocabularies/syntax and declarative rules. In the dementia example, the semantics repository is responsible for maintaining the contextual knowledge model that captures relevant information about the application's environment. In this example, the patient's home and the environment's physical layout are referred to as static semantics. In contrast, the patient's movement and engagement in activities based on his or her behavior are dynamically updated over time (dynamic semantics) [26].

For developing an appropriate framework for accurately analyzing data from assisted technologies, our modeling approach is based on the assumption that dynamic changes in the patient's situational conditions, such as. e.g., room occupancy and movement within the living environment, against semantic knowledge about the patient's disease symptoms and associated profile (medical history or age). Therefore, we can define our proposed framework as context-aware and knowledge-based. For example, context recognition can detect temporary room occupancy and wandering behaviors, which are analyzed based on agitation knowledge in the patient's medical history and inferred as deterioration of the patient's dementia state [33].

Wearable sensors in the form of a wearable device collect information about the patient's location and behavior. Patterns and the variation in the rate of change of these patterns are analyzed in real-time. Data streams are processed in real-time to detect variations in patient behavior using wearables sensor data. Data buffering will be achieved by storing data in message queues in message-oriented middleware that feeds the CEP engine. The data processing engine will provide the algorithms' implementation in the context of dementia patients, taking into account the background knowledge base and contextual semantics.

4.3.3 Other application scenarios
Event processing in health care management
Healthcare is a growing area for event processing scenarios. Information systems have been used to collect patient data in healthcare for many years. However, progress towards a unified health system has been slow. There are currently many different specialized systems in use, each containing only parts of a patient's medical record, rather than a centralized system with a patient's complete medical history. Much relevant information is existing in the evaluation of a diagnosis or treatment plan. In the past, these systems did not reduce the cost of medical care as expected.

A vision for the future would be a national medical information system, including all hospitals and patients, to analyze all diseases and conditions with diagnostic tests. A goal would be to automate the coordination and execution of individualized treatment of a patient over his medical history. Another primary goal of using CEP is to enable remote diagnosis and treatment by caregivers and specialists far from a patient's location. Relevant information concerning a patient's health should be immediately available to the medical staff who needs it to provide health care.

Event-driven processes in hospital operations
The types of events entered in a care management system vary from the events issued by medical devices monitoring a patient's vital signs, the results of medical tests, the availability status of operating rooms, and other critical hospital resources, location, and disposition on-duty medical staff.

An event processing management system is a synergy of smaller specialized systems. The system types include patient records, tests, radiology results, and events from hospital processes monitoring.

The long-term goal of developing such a system is to improve medical personnel and equipment allocation, reduce errors, prescribe nonoptimal medication treatment plans, reduce duplicate examinations, and ultimately reduce healthcare costs.

Patient monitoring

For the optimal dosage of medications or the early detection of health problems, more and more medical devices are either worn directly on the body as a so-called wearable (e.g., smartwatch, smart patch) implanted into a patient's body. Well-known examples of such analysis systems in predictive healthcare are sensors for measuring blood glucose levels in people with diabetes or implantable heart monitors for ECG measurement (electrocardiography).

CEP technology evaluates data collected automatically and in real-time from sensors and microchips located on or inside a body. When CEP software has identified a pattern in the data characteristic of a medical problem, it immediately initiates appropriate remedial action. The data can be analyzed in a small computer, such as a smartphone a Raspberry Pi (using the edge computing principle, i.e., decentralized at the site of the event), or it is transmitted via a wireless network to a cloud or directly into a computer at a central monitoring institution. The necessary actions can be taken by physicians, relatives, or patients themselves, or the software automatically initiates a response using implanted actuators. CEP's typical application monitors patients who, due to a disease such as early-stage dementia, reside in a nursing facility or are cared for at home by relatives. Not only data from the human body are relevant here, but also, for example, the exact location of the patient, the length of time the patient has not moved from the spot, the height of the water in the bathtub, the temperature and air pressure in the recreation room, and information on whether a particular medication was taken at the right time. All of this external data is collected with appropriate sensors and sent over a network (IoMT—Internet of Medical Things) to CEP software, which evaluates it together with the internal patient data promptly using medical background knowledge and initiates a response, if necessary. It should be noted that such use of CEP technology represents an additional support facility and cannot replace the necessary personal attention.

4.4 CEP and AI

Complex Event Processing can be considered as a metaframework of techniques consisting of event filtering, event pattern comparison, causal and time variate analysis, the hierarchical abstraction of events, construction of complex events, and specification of event hierarchies.

Artificial intelligence has experienced massive growth in its potential importance compared to its original conception propelled by Big Data, Big Data Streams, Cloud computing ecosystem, and other related technologies. A large array of AI methods are available nowadays at both algorithmic and software implementations in libraries of all major programming languages. With such huge available AI support, complex problems from the healthcare domain can be addressed. Therefore CEP can be considered as a technological component for an AI application and AI for complex event processing.

AI and CEP have therefore become indispensable in many application domains. They are intertwined, and the synergies between them exploited:

1. An AI system can use CEP-based stream processing frameworks or event stream processing platforms to process incoming events and forward insights to other components that use AI techniques like machine learning, rule engines, or control system logic. The CEP stream processing engine preprocesses the input data chronologically, allowing consecutive components to perform tasks on the insights. Such a scenario uses CEP to implement an AI Application.
2. CEP systems can use AI components on different levels. In modern CEP systems, the processing is usually a multistage pipeline where different stages can integrate AI implementations, such as evaluating incoming events' validity or assigning probabilities to complex events, aggregating low-level events, etc.

Big Data analytics, complex event processing, and IoT together have revolutionary potential to solve existing and future healthcare industry problems. With a renewed focus on better healthcare, population growth, and increasing prices, the healthcare industry has to embrace cutting-edge technologies. Such an application of technology should happen in an integrative manner in the form of an integral healthcare solution.

4.4.1 CEP video processing

In many application domains, including healthcare, data streams could be from video/camera sources. Such streams are usually Big Data streams due to a large amount of data to be processed. They can either single streams or part of multidata streams.

Existing event-driven systems allow interaction via structured queries in response to events. The Content-based Video Query Language (CVQL) is an extended version of existing query languages in that it allows querying of video databases [16]. It is designed to specify spatial and temporal relationships. Structure-based video query language (SVQL) is more expressive as it includes variable declaration, structure specification, feature specification, and Spatio-temporal specification [18]. Both CVQL and SVQL apply to video only, but they need to be extended and enhanced with more operators to handle complex multimedia events in real-time. In existing multimedia query languages, MPEG Query Format (MPQF) can be used as a standard interface for multimedia retrieval engines [9].

Authors in [28] present an event-based surveillance system that incorporates high-level image processing but is only applicable to unusual event detection for an airport environment. An event-driven smart city architecture is presented in [12] for the management and interaction of various sensors placed at multiple public locations. A neural image annotation generator that processes both text and images has also been proposed [32] to annotate the images and convert them into text. Thus, there is a need for a multipurpose system that can process generic multimedia events, which could be of particular use in health domain applications.

4.4.2 CEP video and audio processing in healthcare applications

Advanced health applications usually rely on multistreams from various sources. Typically, a multistream could be made up of a video stream or motion stream to capture patient moves, facial and corporal expressions, an audio stream to capture patients' voice or yells, and other streams such as from sensory sources measure vital signs. Obviously, all data streams are important to get full insights into the health status of the patient. In this context, CEP plays an important role in defining and implement events that need to correlate data from different streams.

For instance, in the context of a patient with dementia being monitored at home, a video stream would capture the patient's agitated moves, the audio stream would capture patient yells, and both events together would potentially define an agitation state of the patient, which could be mapped to an agitation level of the patient and the need for immediate support would be triggered. On the other hand, if the video streams show the patient without moving for hours during day-hours, not speaking at all, or patient losing weight (information provided by a stream of weight sensors on the floor), it would indicate another patient state, requiring another kind of support accordingly.

Current literature provides abundant examples of using video and audio processing in healthcare applications. However, full-fledged CEP-based applications are to be developed to cope with the complexity of the applications and nonfunctional requirements of real-time processing, reliability, security, privacy, and scalability. For achieving such demanding requirements, the new generation of multistream CEP applications in healthcare is poised to use Edge and Fog computing in the Cloud-to-thing continuum [17,19,4,25,24].

4.5 Key features

In this chapter, we have presented the fundamental concepts, definitions, operations, and methods used in Complex Event Processing (CEP).

☑ Basic definitions of primitive and complex events are formally given.
☑ Querying events, CEP language types, and primitive functions for CEP are listed, analyzed, and exemplified with queries to detect/extract patient health status.
☑ The application of CEP to multimodal data streams in healthcare is argued as an important means for complex and integral solutions in healthcare.
☑ The use of CEP and IoT multimodal data streams to develop dementia care applications is analyzed, and the benefits are highlighted.
☑ Several CEP examples illustrate application scenarios from healthcare.

References

[1] C. Aggarwal, Mining sensor data streams, in: Managing and Mining Sensor Data, 2013.

[2] H. Aloulou, M. Mokhtari, T. Tiberghien, J. Biswas, C. Phua, J. Lin, P. Yap, Deployment of assistive living technology in a nursing home environment: methods and lessons learned, BMC Medical Informatics and Decision Making 13 (2013) 42.

[3] A. Arasu, S. Babu, J. Widom, The CQL continuous query language: semantic foundations and query execution, The VLDB Journal 15 (2) (Jun 2006) 121–142.

[4] H.H. Attar, A.A. Solyman, A.-E.F. Mohamed, M.R. Khosravi, V.G. Menon, A.K. Bashir, P. Tavallali, Efficient equalisers for OFDM and DFrFT-OCDM multicarrier systems in mobile e-health video broadcasting with machine learning perspectives, Physical Communication 42 (2020) 101173.

[5] S. Beckstein, R. Bruns, J. Dunkel, L. Renners, Integrating semantic knowledge in data stream processing, in: CEUR Workshop Proceedings, vol. 1070, 01 2013, pp. 1–12.

[6] P. Brandt, T. Basten, S. Stuiik, V. Bui, P. de Clercq, L.F. Pires, M. van Sinderen, Semantic interoperability in sensor applications making sense of sensor data, in: 2013 IEEE Symposium on Computational Intelligence in Healthcare and e-Health (CICARE), IEEE, 2013, pp. 34–41.

[7] E. Bruno, Complex event processing in healthcare IoT solutions, LinkedIn 13 (2013) 42.

[8] G. Cugola, A. Margara, Processing flows of information: from data stream to complex event processing, ACM Computing Surveys 44 (06 2012).

[9] M. Döller, R. Tous, M. Gruhne, K. Yoon, M. Sano, I. Burnett, The MPEG query format: unifying access to multimedia retrieval systems, IEEE Multimedia 15 (2008).

[10] K. Donnelly, SNOMED-CT: the advanced terminology and coding system for eHealth, Studies in Health Technology and Informatics 121 (2006) 279.

[11] M. Endler, E. Haeusler, V. Pinheiro de Almeida, F. Silva, Towards real-time semantic reasoning for the internet of things, 10 2016.

[12] L. Filipponi, A. Vitaletti, G. Landi, V. Memeo, G. Laura, P. Pucci, Smart city: an event driven architecture for monitoring public spaces with heterogeneous sensors, in: 2010 Fourth International Conference on Sensor Technologies and Applications, 2010, pp. 281–286.

[13] S. Helmer, A. Poulovassilis, F. Xhafa, Reasoning in Event-Based Distributed Systems, vol. 347, 01 2011.

[14] J. Kim, J.-K. Kim, L. Daesung, K.-Y. Chung, Ontology driven interactive healthcare with wearable sensors, Multimedia Tools and Applications 71 (07 2014).

[15] J. Kim, J. Lee, OpenIoT: an open service framework for the internet of things, in: 2014 IEEE World Forum on Internet of Things (WF-IoT), March 2014, pp. 89–93.

[16] T.C.T. Kuo, A. Chen, Content-based query processing for video databases, IEEE Transactions on Multimedia 2 (2000) 1–13.

[17] Y. Liu, J. Liu, A. Argyriou, S. Ci, Cross-layer optimized authentication and error control for wireless 3D medical video streaming over LTE, Journal of Visual Communication and Image Representation 46 (2017) 208–218.

[18] C. Lu, M. Liu, Z. Wu, SVQL: a SQL extended query language for video databases, International Journal of Database Theory and Application 8 (2015) 235–248.

[19] A. Manocha, G. Kumar, M. Bhatia, A. Sharma, Video-assisted smart health monitoring for affliction determination based on fog analytics, Journal of Biomedical Informatics 109 (2020) 103513.

[20] A. Margara, G. Cugola, Processing flows of information: from data stream to complex event processing, in: DEBS, 01 2011, pp. 359–360.

[21] G. Meditskos, S. Dasiopoulou, I. Kompatsiaris, MetaQ: a knowledge-driven framework for context-aware activity recognition combining SPARQL and OWL 2 activity patterns, Pervasive and Mobile Computing 5 (02 2015).

[22] F. Mohamedali, N. Matoorian, Support dementia: using wearable assistive technology and analysing real-time data, in: 2016 International Conference on Interactive Technologies and Games (ITAG), 2016, pp. 50–54.

[23] P. Moore, A.M. Thomas, G. Tadros, F. Xhafa, L. Barolli, Detection of the onset of agitation in patients with dementia: real-time monitoring and the application of big-data solutions, International Journal of Space-Based and Situated Computing 3 (3) (2013) 136–154.

[24] T.P. Moreira, D. Menotti, H. Pedrini, Video action recognition based on visual rhythm representation, Journal of Visual Communication and Image Representation 71 (2020) 102771.

[25] S.R. Myers, M.K.F. Abbadessa, S. Gaines, J. Lavelle, J.M. Ercolani, C. Shotwell, M. Ainsley, K.W. Pettijohn, A.J. Donoghue, Repurposing video review infrastructure for clinical resuscitation care in the age of Covid-19, Annals of Emergency Medicine 77 (1) (2021) 110–116.

[26] T. Osman, A. Lotfi, C. Langensiepen, S. Chernbumroong, M. Saeed, Semantic-based decision support for remote care of dementia patients, in: 2014 IEEE Symposium on Intelligent Agents (IA), 2014, pp. 89–96.

[27] T. Qassem, G. Tadros, P. Moore, F. Xhafa, Emerging technologies for monitoring behavioural and psychological symptoms of dementia, in: 2014 Ninth International Conference on P2P, Parallel, Grid, Cloud and Internet Computing, Guangdong, China, November 8–10, 2014, IEEE Computer Society, 2014, pp. 308–315.

[28] C.-F. Shu, A. Hampapur, M. Lu, L. Brown, J. Connell, A. Senior, Y. Tian, IBM smart surveillance system (S3): a open and extensible framework for event based surveillance, in: IEEE Conference on Advanced Video and Signal Based Surveillance, 2005, 2005, pp. 318–323.

[29] C. Smyth, Rush to diagnose dementia is dismissed as pointless, The Times (2016).

[30] M. Strachan, J. Price, B. Frier, Diabetes, cognitive impairment, and dementia, BMJ: British Medical Journal 336 (2008) 6.

[31] A.M. Thomas, P. Moore, C. Evans, H. Shah, M. Sharma, S. Mount, F. Xhafa, H.V. Pham, L. Barolli, A. Patel, A.J. Wilcox, C. Chapman, P. Chima, Smart care spaces: pervasive sensing technologies for at-home care, International Journal of Ad Hoc and Ubiquitous Computing 16 (4) (2014) 268–282.

[32] O. Vinyals, A. Toshev, S. Bengio, D. Erhan, Show and tell: a neural image caption generator, in: 2015 IEEE Conference on Computer Vision and Pattern Recognition (CVPR), 2015, pp. 3156–3164.

[33] N. Vuong, S. Chan, C. Lau, K.M. Lau, Feasibility study of a real-time wandering detection algorithm for dementia patients, in: MobileHealth'11, 2011.

[34] F. Wang, S. Liu, P. Liu, Complex RFID event processing, The VLDB Journal 18 (2009) 913–931.

[35] F. Wang, S. Liu, P. Liu, Y. Bai, Bridging physical and virtual worlds: complex event processing for RFID data streams, in: EDBT, 2006.

[36] F. Xhafa, F.-Y. Leu, L.-L. Hung (Eds.), Intelligent Data-Centric Systems, Academic Press, 2017.

[37] F. Xhafa, P. Moore, G. Tadros (Eds.), Advanced Technological Solutions for e-Health and Dementia Patient Monitoring, IGI Global, 2015.

[38] W. Yao, C. Chu, Z. Li, Leveraging complex event processing for smart hospitals using RFID, Journal of Network and Computer Applications 34 (2011) 799–810.

[39] C. Zang, Y. Fan, R. Liu, Architecture, implementation and application of complex event processing in enterprise information systems based on RFID, Information Systems Frontiers 10 (2008) 543–553.

Rule-based decision support systems for eHealth

Supporting actors and stakeholders of health systems

5

5.1 Introductory concepts and background in expert systems and decision support systems

Medical and nursing professionals are trained to arrive at a diagnosis by exposure to numerous real-world cases and tutorials on the appropriate thinking processes. Fast thinking, sometimes referred to as Type 1 or intuitive reasoning, is often used by experienced clinicians to arrive at a diagnosis. In contrast, Type 2 reasoning involves a slower, deliberate process of forming a hypothesis based on the available indications or signs, using a series of well-documented if/then rules, and then retesting a tentative diagnosis as additional observations are made. Over time, with enough experience and exposure to enough cases, clinicians gradually build illness scripts that let them transition from Type 2 to Type 1 reasoning. The process is not all that different from the if/then rules used by DSSs, but as any clinician who has used a computerized diagnostic aid knows, even advanced software programs can reason wrong when dealing with human intricacies of pathophysiology.

In the past, physicians were limited by their physical senses to arrive at a diagnosis. One could palpate the chest, hear a wheezing child's lungs, observe a skin rash, or feel the skin's temperature. The microscope's invention enabled us to see a more detailed world of disease-causing microbes that were not previously on our list of potential causes. The discovery of X-rays lets us made the transition of physical senses to detecting pathology. Clinicians required a certain degree of humility to admit that their physical senses were not enough for a comprehensive analysis and need to embrace these technological tools.

Today, we are at a similar milestone, to recognize not only physical limitations but cognitive limitations as well. Everyone is subject to reasoning mistakes from time to time. If those cognitive errors influence a clinician's diagnostic judgment, they can end in life-threatening situations.

In cognitive science, this is called an affective error, which is the ability to convince ourselves that what we want to be true is true. If a patient comes into the office with a persistent headache but is healthy in all other regards, one may conclude that there is no serious underlying condition and that the symptom might be stress-related. Affective errors are often accompanied by confirmation bias, in which the clinician selectively picks clinical observations that confirm the suspicion. Clinicians may also fall victim to anchoring, a second cognitive mistake, by favoring a specific diagnosis because of a few initial clinical findings. Once the bias sets in, some might be unwilling to alter the tentative conclusion even in the light of new data. On the other hand, availability bias occurs if a physician sees numerous cases of a specific disorder. This exposure might tend to prejudice the clinician's judgment in the direction of the common disorder. That kind of reasoning reduces the odds of detecting a rare condition.

A healthy 20-year-old man with sudden, severe, sharp chest and back pain may be suspected of having a dissecting aneurysm of the thoracic aorta, as these clinical features are common in aortic dissection. The cognitive error does not account for the fact that aortic dissections are exceptionally rare in an otherwise healthy 20-year-old patient. This disorder might be rejected, and other more likely causes like pneumothorax should be considered. A display error can occur when a doctor fails to realize that positive test results are more likely to be falsely positive in a population where the disease being tested is rare as true positive.

There is a dilemma of many clinicians who still believe that even the most challenging diagnostic puzzles can be solved with astute cognitive skills, years of experience in diagnostic reasoning, and access to the medical literature [32]. The quantity of data now being generated on many patients is so massive that it is virtually impossible to decipher all the patterns and correlations needed to make an accurate diagnosis or plan the most effective therapeutic regimen. Often, the sheer volume of information in patient records alone makes it impossible for clinicians to read through all the relevant facts or make an in-depth analysis.

The quantity and quality of clinical data are increasing rapidly, including Electronic Health Records (EHRs), disease registries, patient surveys, and information sharing [42]. Big Data and digitization, however, do not automatically mean better patient care. Several studies have shown that just implementing an EHR and Computerized Order Entry for doctors (CPOE) reduced the frequency of specific errors but introducing many others [30,24,23].

Therefore, high-quality clinical decision support is essential if health organizations want to take full advantage of electronic health records and CPOE. In the current healthcare environment, healthcare providers often do not know that certain patient data is available in the EHR when making a decision. Furthermore, doctors do not always know how to access those data, do not have the time to search, or do not know about the latest medical findings. Healthcare providers often seem to drown in the sheer amount of information and insights [25].

The result of this massive amount of data was summarized in a report from the National Academies of Science, Engineering, and Medicine titled *"Improving Healthcare Diagnostics,"* which stated that it is estimated that each year 5 percent of adults in the US who seek treatment experience a diagnostic error. Decades of postmortem examinations have shown that diagnostic errors account for roughly 10 percent of patient deaths. Additionally, medical record reviews suggest that these errors account for 6 to 17 percent of adverse events in hospitals [29].

It would also be wrong to imply that all misdiagnoses are due to physicians not leveraging the advantages of big data analytics, machine learning, or other new technologies. There are several other reasons why clinicians infer the wrong conclusion when trying to identify the cause of a patient's condition:

1. Some patients are not aware of or lie about different signs and symptoms for various reasons.
2. Healthcare professionals are concluding through direct patient contacts, visits, or multidisciplinary meetings. Many decisions are made quickly and depend on having all of the patient's symptoms and medical knowledge available.
3. Changes in a patient's condition before admission to a hospital are often overlooked as doctors periodically perceive a patient in their current condition without considering changes.
4. Clinical laboratories can also make mistakes when analyzing patient samples.
5. Imaging test results might not reach in time for a clinician to make a time-sensitive decision.

6. Clinicians might miss a financial incentive to take the time to do a deep study of the patient data. A report of the US Institute of Medicine (IOM) describes the need to design a payment and care delivery environment that supports the diagnostic process. The payment is likely to affect the diagnostic process and the occurrence of diagnostic errors.
7. For example, when service fees are paid, there is a lack of consistent care incentives, and biases between procedural and cognitive care can divert attention from important diagnostic process tasks. A fundamental need for research is a better understanding of payment and care models' impact on a diagnosis. However, the human brain's limitations cannot be counted inherently as the reasons for the misdiagnosis dilemma. Emerging technology now removes these limitations and offers tools to improve diagnosis and treatment.

The structure of information for decision-making comes from various sources that are different in nature and structure. Managing all the data at a central point is highly complex. The data is about the patient, diseases, diagnosing reports, history of treatment applied to the patient, hospital history, medical devices used, and various resources. The medical industry always needs prior knowledge about the patient and treatment applied for the particular patient to precede further treatment and care. Hence, it is essential to extract relevant knowledge from the existing medical information to support medical industry processes. This extraction helps to save time, improve the accuracy in treatment, and reduce the cost. Data mining tools are applied that can extract the visible and hidden information to help the medical professionals get additional information for decision making.

5.2 Clinical Decision Support (CDS) basics

Typically, CDS' purpose is to help clinicians make more informed decisions at the point of care, enabling them to better analyze all the raw input they gather from a patient's family and medical history, physical examination, blood test results, or imaging studies. DSS's are usually divided into two broad categories: knowledge-based and nonknowledge based.

5.2.1 Knowledge-based DSS (KB-DSS)

KB-DSSs are systems that assist clinicians in decision-making by providing evidence-based knowledge related to patient data. This computer system consists of a language system, a knowledge system, and a problem processing system [5].

Knowledge base

A Knowledge Base contains rules and assignments of compiled data, mostly in the form of IF-THEN statements. Considering a system for drug interactions, a rule could be; when drug X is taken AND drug Y is taken, THEN alert the user. For example, if a patient consumes large doses of vitamin K while taking the anticoagulant warfarin, the drug will be less effective and might lead to a blood clot.

An interface allows an advanced user to edit the knowledge base to keep it up to date with new findings on new drugs or interactions. An inference engine retrieves deeper insights with the knowledge base rules in combination with the patient data. The communication mechanism enables the system to display the results to the user and enter inputs into the system [6].

An expression language is needed to express knowledge artifacts in a predictable way, such as GELLO or CQL (Clinical Quality Language). For example, a patient with diabetes, and the last hemoglobin A1c test result was less than 7%; it gets recommended to retest if the last test was more than six months ago. In case the last test result was greater than 7%, it gets recommended a retest if it has been more than three months.

Inference engine

An Inference Engine links the scientific knowledge and algorithms with the individual patient's data to help reach a diagnosis.

Communication tool

A Communication tool is used to share the recommendations with the user. Some CDS tools are primarily research repositories and collections of expert opinions and reviews, for example, UpToDate and ClinicalKey.

5.2.2 Nonknowledge based DSSs

Nonknowledge DSSs do not use a knowledge base but instead allow them to learn from previous experience or find clinical data patterns. Two of the main types of nonknowledge-based systems are machine learning and Genetic Algorithms.

1. Machine Learning analyzes the patterns found in patient data and infer associations between symptoms and diagnosis.
2. Genetic Algorithms are based on an evolutionary process using a directed selection of best-performing parameters. The selection algorithms evaluate components of random solution sets for a problem. The solutions that prevail are then recombined and mutated and iterate through the process again. This procedure will be repeated until a near-optimal solution is found. GA and ML are black boxes that try to derive knowledge from patient data [6]. Combinations and hybrid algorithms of GA and ML methods are sought to achieve higher accuracy in diagnosis and prediction [41,21,40,9].

It should be noted that in Nonknowledge based DSS's it is not required to write rules as needed in a knowledge base DSS. While this can be considered as an advantage, these systems often struggle in explaining the conclusions.

While ML and GA tools are in the past considered less useful for assisting in diagnosis and treatment, this view is gradually changing. Clinicians do not use them directly to aid decision-making for reasons of reliability and accountability. Nevertheless, they can be useful as postdiagnostic systems to suggest patterns that clinicians can dig deeper into. In some settings, ML tools are poised to replace the need for a physician's cognitive skills.

Numerous examples in literature and health systems show the advantages and improvement in the state of the art of ML for diagnosis. Thus, it was demonstrated that deep learning algorithms could be used to detect diabetic retinopathy more accurately than 54 licensed ophthalmologists and ophthalmologists. The machine learning system did this by reviewing over 11,000 images of the retinal fundus [17].

Similarly, with current software, it is now possible to accurately diagnose skin cancer. A deep convolutional neural network algorithm was tested on more than 129,000 clinical images [13] to differentiate between keratinocyte carcinoma and benign seborrheic keratosis and between malignant melanoma and benign nevi. The machine learning algorithms were just as effective as trained dermatologists in accurately identifying both types of cancer.

5.2.3 Hybrid -intelligent- DSS

A healthcare IDSS gathers and integrates health-related expertise and performs intelligent actions, including learning and inferring, while recommending clinical steps and justifying the results [43,4].

Clinical decisions that healthcare providers routinely make are often based on clinical guidelines and evidence-based rules derived from medicine. However, Intelligent Decision Support Systems (IDSS) enable doctors and nurses to quickly collect information and process it in various ways through the interpretive analysis of extensive patient data using intelligent and knowledge-based methods to facilitate diagnosis and treatment decision [14].

IDSS can be used in various healthcare areas, such as examining real-time data from various monitoring devices, analyzing patient and family histories for diagnosis purposes, reviewing common features or trends in medical records databases [14]. IDSS can identify meaning from complex data and extract patterns that are too complex to be perceived by humans or other traditional techniques. Specific domain knowledge is built from raw data by extracting patterns and making them understandable and usable for decision support. Unlike DSS, an IDSS supports a more comprehensive range of decisions, including uncertainties estimates in their recommendations [14]. The IDSS results are particularly important when clinical experts can validate the explanations provided by the IDSS [14].

Therefore, IDSS can aid in clinical decision-making in various ways, both at the individual patient level and at the population level. For example:

1. Diagnosis through regular analysis, interpretation, and monitoring of patient data. Rules and patterns can be implemented for individual patients based on clinical parameters and trigger warnings if a rule is violated and clinical interventions are recommended.
2. Help manage chronic illness by setting benchmarks and alerts. Any health issue or deterioration identified by an IDSS, such as based on a diabetic blood test, can lead to intervention before the patient gets serious problems.
3. Assistance in public health surveillance through pandemic disease detection or chronic disease surveillance. In the event of a pandemic, an IDSS can analyze data and predict the future spread of the disease.
4. IDSS performing regular clinical decisions such as preventing negative drug-drug interactions. If the prescribing physician does not notice a negative interaction, an IDSS can detect incompatibilities between prescribed drugs or dosages.

IBM Watson illustrates the previous shortcomings of IDSS. IBM Watson had an impressive history of defeating human champions in the game Jeopardize. That success encouraged IBM to venture into medical diagnosis and partner with the MD Anderson Cancer Center. However, these projects have not proven to be very successful.

Boston Globe Media reported that IBM Watson for Oncology struggled to understand the fundamental differences between different cancers. IBM Watson has collected doctors' notes, and patient records, entered clinical guidelines and analyzed that data in the assumption that it can supplement the diagnostic and treatment decisions made by oncologists. Experiences and reports showing how technology supports doctors and patients have been published in scientific literature [10,48,38]. Nevertheless, shortcomings have been exposed by doctors and researchers [3], and these should not turn clinicians away from the field of IDSS.

As discussed earlier, human limitations include cognitive errors and limited memory. Even clinicians with eidetic or photographic memory cannot keep up with the massive amount of research findings published every year. With this, IDSS have a large potential to be advanced and support doctors and practitioners in the health domain.

5.2.4 Examples of medication-related CDSS

Medication-related CDSS probably have the greatest potential benefit [15]. They assisted pharmacists in checking drug allergies, providing dose advice, checking drug interactions, and checking duplicate therapy. Drug-related CDSS took shape when they were directly linked to the Computer-Aided Order Entry for Doctors (CPOE) [22]. CPOE enables doctors to prescribe medication using electronic entries. The combination of CPOE and CDSS helps doctors choosing the right drug at the right dose and alert the doctor during the prescription if, for example, the patient is allergic. The combination of CPOE with CDSS represented a huge leap in the prescription of safe prescription of medications [31,45].

Another application for advanced CDSS follows decision tree-based models and can assist clinicians in drug dosing for patients with renal insufficiency, provide guidelines for drug-related laboratory testing, and perform drug-disease contraindication testing [22,35]. The parameters involved in drug-related CDSS have increased steadily over the past few decades, including pharmaco-genetics and other drug-disease interactions.

However, many current EHRs with built-in CDSS still do not provide guidance relevant to the specific patient receiving care, poorly presenting data, as well as causing alert fatigue for healthcare providers [1]. One of the main problems with these systems is that they consider only a few parameters for providing alerts, often leading to many false alters.

Hence, efforts need to be made to combine several parameters and clinical rules to provide proper advice. The parameters should incorporate all clinicians' efforts and combine patient characteristics and contexts at the same time.

5.3 Implementation challenges of a DSS

CDSS is an evolving technology with the potential for broad applicability to individualize and improve patient outcomes and resource use in healthcare [8,26]. However, making CDSS more useful requires careful design, implementation, and deep evaluation [37]. CDSSs exist since the 1960s. Simon *et al.* [36] found in 2008 that the vast majority of EHRs in the US implemented little or no decision support. A recent survey sent to all Dutch hospital pharmacies gave similar results, with only 48% using some advanced CDSS.[1] These alarming results were major reasons why the American Medical Informatics Association (AMIA) released the Roadmap for National Actions in Support of Clinical

---

[1] Workgroup Clinical Rules of the Dutch Association of Hospital Pharmacists (NVZA). Questionnaire on current state of clinical rule implementation in hospital pharmacy. 2015. http://www.nvza.nl.

Decision-Making [33]. Six strategic objectives were defined, broken down into three pillars, to achieve wide acceptance of the system's effective functions in support of clinical decisions.

In the following, we highlight these three pillars to provide an overview of the tasks and challenges ahead.

High adoption and effective use

- Remove policy/legal/financial obstacles, create additional support for a wide CDSS adoption.
- Enhance clinical adoption and use of CDSS interventions by helping clinical knowledge and information systems developers design easy to use and deploy CDSS systems that are easy to deploy and identify best practices for CDSS deployment.

Best knowledge available when needed

- Represent clinical knowledge and CDSS interventions in standardized formats for humans and machines so that a wide variety of knowledge contributors can create information in a way that users can easily understand, evaluate, and apply.
- Collect, organize, and distribute knowledge and interventions in one or more services that allow users to quickly find the material they need and integrate it into their information systems and processes.

Continuous improvement of knowledge and CDSS methods

- Assess and refine national experiences with CDSS by systematically recording, organizing, and exploring existing deployments. Share the lessons learned and use them in continuously improved implementation practices.
- Enhance nursing knowledge by taking full advantage of the data available in interoperable EHRs to improve clinical knowledge and improve health management.

5.3.1 Other challenges

Further general challenges include representing the knowledge base, reasoning under uncertainty, and systematic clinical evaluation. Many clinical diagnosis tasks involve reasoning under uncertainty. Researchers believe that intelligent behavior depends on the reasoning method and the knowledge used in the reasoning.

The growth of technological development in healthcare systems is forcing the knowledge corresponding to diagnosis and adjustment of treatment flow to be recorded using various methods such as clinical pathways or guideline-based DSS [27].

In order to fulfill the clinical expectations of CDSS, the next generation of rule-based CDSS will need to mature to:

1. Increase efficiency by allowing for scaling and portability through reuse of decision logic by separating the end-user application from the decision engine.
2. Accommodate increasing clinical complexity.
3. Respond to current patient status by incorporating real-time clinical information, including patient-reported data.

Complex algorithms can be called up via rule-based CDSS to promote evidence-based care in real-time at the point of patient contact. Current information provided by the patient is used to generate explicit, detailed, and patient-specific care instructions. This real-time information gathered from patients can inform the symptom management process and prioritize management interventions.

Adoption in practice remains a slow process, and many are still reinventing the wheel instead of supporting national initiatives. Decision support systems today mainly use the 'IF-THEN-ELSE' logic. Moreover, even using this method, validation is already very time-consuming and complex.

It is a promising perspective to make healthcare benefit more from Dig Data to draw conclusions that humans have not drawn themselves. However, validation, acceptance, and adaptation of "black box" systems will require a paradigm shift. Nevertheless, decision support keeps attracting health care professionals to work with these powerful and promising systems.

Folding the latest machine-learning technology into clinical decision support systems will undoubtedly improve the screening and diagnostic processes. However, these advances pale compared to what will eventually be achieved by incorporating systems biology findings into CDS.

5.3.2 Outlook on the precision medicine initiative

A future outlook could make a scenario on the "Precision Medicine Initiative's All of Us" project, which has been completed for many years, and the data collected on millions have been analyzed to yield new insights on health and disease. Furthermore, society has realized that if a little prevention is worth a great cure.

Although this has not yet been achieved, treatments that have been found safe and effective by the Food and Drug Administration (FDA) are usually covered by insurers regardless of their cost. However, preventive benefits have been kept at a higher level. They are often rated based on whether they have a positive return on investment and save money in the short term. This inequality leads to an oversupply of treatment, and an under-supply of prevention services, a trend that is exacerbated by high sales in many health insurance markets. Since insurance policies typically only last a year, insurers do not want to spend money trying to prevent illness in members that another insurer may cover in the near future [35].

Most medical hypothesis tests are based on a reductionist approach, a divide-and-conquer method based on the assumption that complex problems can be solved by breaking them down into smaller, simpler, and more manageable units [1]. As the name implies, systems biology looks at entire biological or pathological systems rather than deciphering the cause of a disorder by analyzing one variable at a time. Systems biology can also use sophisticated data analytics to tease out numerous interacting contributors rather than rely on traditional statistical methods that compare single causes for each phenomenon being studied. Using systems biology to inform clinical decision support in this futuristic scenario involves expanding the patient assessment process to include a long list of potential contributing causes and risk factors that in the past have not been fully understood or appreciated. The gathered patient information could include whole-genome sequencing, various lifestyle and behavioral measures, sensor-derived physiological data from mobile health apps, prescription, over-the-counter medication usage, psychosocial stress, or routine lab data. Equally important, it requires a DSS programmed to detect complex patterns that result from the interplay of contributing causes that only have clinical consequences when combined with other contributing causes. This DSS will also have the ability to detect each contributing cause's varying strengths and factor this into its recommendations.

For instance, the predictive analytics engine in future generations of DSS tools will likely send an alert to physicians recommending annual Prostate-Specific Antigen (PSA) testing. Although universal PSA screening is no longer recommended, that advice only applies to the general public, not individual patients at increased cancer risks.

Likewise, AI and Big Data are playing and will play a major role in precision medicine to bring treatments in various diseases that have been developed for the whole population to treatments that are tailored to patient's genetic information [18,16,39].

5.4 Rule base systems in practice and their limitations

Rule-based systems have been implemented and are in place in many application domains. Healthcare is not an exception, where various rule-based technologies are used for CDSS systems [28]. The authors in [11] highlight limitations in the development of CDSS systems and provide a guideline to support knowledge acquisition for rule-based CDSSs.

There are various rule-based frameworks used in the development of CDSSs systems in practice. Among them, Drools, a business rule management system (BRMS) that offers a forward and backward chaining inference-based rules engine, is a popular system thanks to its production rule engine, rule definition, and integration. With the support of Drools, conceptual models can be transformed into a prototypical implementation, achieve interoperability in the CDSS and create a knowledge base [46, 7].

Rule-based systems and Drools can be used to develop context-aware applications, which are relevant to health applications as well. Thus, authors in [34] proposed a toolkit, named JCOOLS, for generating context-aware applications with JCAF and DROOLS. Drools can also be used for developing complex event processing systems in health applications. Likewise, more broadly, semantic reasoners, such as Apache Jena framework,[2] have found applications as knowledge engines in practical health applications [12,44,2,19].

5.4.1 Semantic data enrichment and rule base systems

IoT data streams usually require data preprocessing to clean the data, detect errors, missing information, and give structure to data. The *new* data stream in output is then processed through single or complex event processing models. However, in health applications, once consumed, the data stream still needs to be stored and used to feed upper layers of the health system such as reasoning and rule-based layer, intelligent decision support systems, or Big Data analytics. To achieve this, it is often necessary to semantically enrich data tuples coming from the stream with context information (event information in context).

While semantic computing and technologies are well understood for web-based systems, they are more challenging for IoT data streams due to their nature of dynamic, spatio-temporal, and unbounded multimodal data [47].

---

[2] https://jena.apache.org/.

5.4.2 Limitations of rule base system for IoT stream processing

Despite their usefulness, rule-based systems come with various limitations, requiring careful analysis before their application in a health system. The most important limitations identified in the literature are as follows.

5.4.3 Limits of processing at scale

Rule-based systems do not scale well for complex event processing of IoT data streams as there would be needed a large number of rules to caption different event types and scenarios. Scaling properties are even more critical for real-time processing of heterogeneous and multimodal data streams, where every stream defines its events that need to be combined, and thus more rules be added. The more complex the application scenario, the larger is the number of rules needed and, therefore, the larger the impact on scalability.

5.4.4 Limits of processing unseen information from the stream

Data stream processing is characterized by processing unseen information in various forms such as single data, tuples, or data sequences. In many applications, the IoT data stream could be stochastic in nature, follow some nonstationary distribution, or has a drift concept with an unknown drift rate, and window-size may vary over time [20]. In all these cases, rule-based systems become complex and are therefore limited in handling such stream conditions.

5.4.5 Limits of processing multimodal data streams of continuous variables

Multimodal data streams comprising video, audio, sensory data, text, etc., are particularly more difficult to handle by rule-based systems due to the continuous nature of some of the parameters (variables) in the stream. To design the rule system, it would be necessary to make a mapping to discrete intervals and build rules on them, which *per se* is a challenging problem.

5.5 Key features

In this chapter, we have presented rule-based decision support systems in eHealth and their relation with event stream processing and complex event processing.

- ☑ Basic concepts and terminology of Decision Support Systems in the context of event processing and health applications.
- ☑ Particularization of DSS for Clinical Decision Support Systems in the forms of knowledge and nonknowledge-based DSS.
- ☑ The applicability of DSS for the case of medication is exemplified.
- ☑ Challenges of designing and building a new generation of DSS in healthcare are discussed.
- ☑ Examples of rule-based systems in practice are given, and their limitations for IoT data stream processing are discussed.

References

[1] A. Ahn, M. Tewari, C.-S. Poon, R. Phillips, The limits of reductionism in medicine: could systems biology offer an alternative?, PLoS Medicine 3 (06 2006) e208.

[2] F. Amato, G. De Pietro, M. Esposito, N. Mazzocca, An integrated framework for securing semi-structured health records, Knowledge-Based Systems 79 (2015) 99–117.

[3] I. Assent, P. Kranen, C. Baldauf, T. Seidl, Anyout: anytime outlier detection on streaming data, in: Database Systems for Advanced Applications, 04 2012, pp. 228–242.

[4] R. Basu, U. Fevrier-Thomas, K. Sartipi, Incorporating hybrid CDSS in primary care practice management, 2011.

[5] S. Begum, M. Ahmed, P. Funk, N. Xiong, M. Folke, Case-based reasoning systems in the health sciences: a survey of recent trends and developments, IEEE Transactions on Systems, Man and Cybernetics. Part C, Applications and Reviews 41 (08 2011) 421–434.

[6] E. Berner, Clinical Decision Support Systems: Theory and Practice, 01 2007.

[7] D. Calcaterra, G. Di Modica, O. Tomarchio, P. Romeo, A clinical decision support system to increase appropriateness of diagnostic imaging prescriptions, Journal of Network and Computer Applications 117 (2018) 17–29.

[8] Y. Chen, L. Tu, Density-based clustering for real-time stream data, in: KDD'07, 2007.

[9] Z. Chen, A. Huang, X. Qiang, Improved neural networks based on genetic algorithm for pulse recognition, Computational Biology and Chemistry 88 (2020) 107315.

[10] J. Choi, 375P - concordance study of between IBM Watson for oncology and real clinical practice for gastric, breast and ovarian cancer, Annals of Oncology 29 (2018) ix115, Abstract Book of ESMO Asia Congress 23–25 November 2018, Singapore.

[11] B. Cánovas-Segura, A. Morales, J.M. Juarez, M. Campos, F. Palacios, A lightweight acquisition of expert rules for interoperable clinical decision support systems, Knowledge-Based Systems 167 (2019) 98–113.

[12] H. Dong, F.K. Hussain, Semantic service matchmaking for digital health ecosystems, Knowledge-Based Systems 24 (6) (2011) 761–774.

[13] A. Esteva, B. Kuprel, R. Novoa, J. Ko, S. Swetter, H. Blau, S. Thrun, Dermatologist-level classification of skin cancer with deep neural networks, Nature 542 (01 2017).

[14] D. Foster, C. Mcgregor, S. El-Masri, A survey of agent-based intelligent decision support systems to support clinical management and research, in: Proc. of the First Int. Workshop on Multi-Agent Systems for Medicine, Computational Biology, and Bioinformatics, 01 2005, pp. 16–34.

[15] A. Garg, N. Adhikari, H. Mcdonald, M. Rosas Arellano, P. Devereaux, J. Beyene, J. Sam, B. Haynes, Effects of computerized clinical decision support systems on practitioner performance and patient outcomes: a systematic review, JAMA: Journal of the American Medical Association 293 (04 2005) 1223–1238.

[16] D. Grisafi, A. Ceschi, V.A. Clerici, F. Scaglione, The contribution of clinical pharmacologists in precision medicine: an opportunity for health care improvement, Current Therapeutic Research (2021) 100628.

[17] V. Gulshan, L. Peng, M. Coram, M. Stumpe, D. Wu, A. Narayanaswamy, S. Venugopalan, K. Widner, T. Madams, J. Cuadros, R. Kim, R. Raman, P. Nelson, J. Mega, D. Webster, Development and validation of a deep learning algorithm for detection of diabetic retinopathy in retinal fundus photographs, JAMA 316 (11 2016).

[18] I. Hajirasouliha, O. Elemento, Precision medicine and artificial intelligence: overview and relevance to reproductive medicine, Fertility and Sterility 114 (5) (2020) 908–913.

[19] N. Iglesias, J.M. Juarez, M. Campos, Comprehensive analysis of rule formalisms to represent clinical guidelines: selection criteria and case study on antibiotic clinical guidelines, Artificial Intelligence in Medicine 103 (2020) 101741.

[20] V. Khandekar, P. Srinath, Non-stationary data stream analysis: state-of-the-art challenges and solutions, in: Proceeding of International Conference on Computational Science and Applications, 01 2020, pp. 67–80.

[21] A. Kukker, R. Sharma, A genetic algorithm assisted fuzzy q-learning epileptic seizure classifier, Computers & Electrical Engineering 92 (2021) 107154.

[22] G. Kuperman, A. Bobb, T. Avery, T. Gandhi, G. Burns, D. Classen, D. Bates, Medication-related clinical decision support in computerized provider order entry systems: a review, Journal of the American Medical Informatics Association: JAMIA 14 (01 2007) 29–40.

[23] C. Lehmann, B. Séroussi, M.-C. Jaulent, Troubled waters: navigating unintended consequences of health information technology, in: IMIA Yearbook, 11 2016, pp. 5–6.

[24] F. Magrabi, E. Ammenwerth, H. Hyppönen, N. de Keizer, P. Nykänen, M. Rigby, P. Scott, J. Talmon, A. Georgiou, Improving evaluation to address the unintended consequences of health information technology: a position paper from the working group on technology assessment & quality development, in: IMIA Yearbook, 11 2016, pp. 61–69.

[25] B. Mamlin, W. Tierney, The promise of information and communication technology in healthcare: extracting value from the chaos, The American Journal of the Medical Sciences 351 (01 2016) 59–68.

[26] L. Moja, K. Kwag, T. Lytras, L. Bertizzolo, L. Brandt, V. Pecoraro, G. Rigon, A. Vaona, F. Ruggiero, M. Mangia, A. Iorio, I. Kunnamo, S. Bonovas, Effectiveness of computerized decision support systems linked to electronic health records: a systematic review and meta-analysis, American Journal of Public Health 104 (10 2014) e1–e11.

[27] T. Muthuraman, G. Sankaran, A framework for personalized decision support system for the healthcare application, Health Science Journal 8 (2014).

[28] K. Nammuni, C. Pickering, S. Modgil, A. Montgomery, P. Hammond, J. Wyatt, D. Altman, R. Dunlop, H. Potts, Design-a-trial: a rule-based decision support system for clinical trial design, Knowledge-Based Systems 17 (2) (2004) 121–129, AI 2003, the Twenty-third SGAI International Conference on Innovative Techniques and Applications of Artificial Intelligence.

[29] S. Nass, Improving Diagnosis in Health Care, 09 2015.

[30] J. Nebeker, J. Hoffman, C. Weir, C. Bennett, J. Hurdle, High rates of adverse drug events in a highly computerized hospital, Archives of Internal Medicine 165 (06 2005) 1111–1116.

[31] T. Nuckols, C. Smith-Spangler, S. Morton, S. Asch, V. Patel, L. Anderson, E. Deichsel, P. Shekelle, The effectiveness of computerized order entry at reducing preventable adverse drug events and medication errors in hospital settings: a systematic review and meta-analysis, Systematic Reviews 3 (06 2014).

[32] Z. Obermeyer, T. Lee, Lost in thought — the limits of the human mind and the future of medicine, The New England Journal of Medicine 377 (09 2017) 1209–1211.

[33] J. Osheroff, J. Teich, B. Middleton, E. Steen, A. Wright, D. Detmer, A roadmap for national action on clinical decision support, Journal of the American Medical Informatics Association: JAMIA 14 (01 2007) 141–145.

[34] J. Park, H.-C. Lee, M.-J. Lee Jcools, A toolkit for generating context-aware applications with JCAF and DROOLS, Journal of Systems Architecture 59 (9) (2013) 759–766.

[35] K. Pryor, K. Volpp, Deployment of preventive interventions — time for a paradigm shift, The New England Journal of Medicine 378 (05 2018) 1761–1763.

[36] S. Simon, M. McCarthy, R. Kaushal, C. Jenter, L. Volk, K. Yee, E. Orav, D. Williams, D. Bates, Electronic health records: which practices have them, and how are clinicians using them?, Journal of Evaluation in Clinical Practice 14 (03 2008) 43–47.

[37] D. Sittig, A. Wright, J. Osheroff, B. Middleton, J. Teich, J. Ash, E. Campbell, D. Bates, Grand challenges in clinical decision support, Journal of Biomedical Informatics 41 (05 2008) 387–392.

[38] S. Somashekhar, M.-J. Sepúlveda, S. Puglielli, A. Norden, E. Shortliffe, C. Rohit Kumar, A. Rauthan, N. Arun Kumar, P. Patil, K. Rhee, Y. Ramya, Watson for oncology and breast cancer treatment recommendations: agreement with an expert multidisciplinary tumor board, Annals of Oncology 29 (2) (2018) 418–423, Incorporating blood-based liquid biopsy information into cancer staging.

[39] C. Song, Y. Kong, L. Huang, H. Luo, X. Zhu, Big data-driven precision medicine: starting the custom-made era of iatrology, Biomedicine & Pharmacotherapy 129 (2020) 110445.

[40] Z. Soumaya, B. Drissi Taoufiq, N. Benayad, K. Yunus, A. Abdelkrim, The detection of Parkinson disease using the genetic algorithm and SVM classifier, Applied Acoustics 171 (2021) 107528.

[41] J.E. Sánchez Lasheras, F. Sánchez Lasheras, C. González Donquiles, A. Tardón, G. Castaño-Vinyals, C. Palazuelos, D. Salas, V. Martín Sánchez, F.J. de Cos Juez, Hybrid algorithm for the classification of prostate cancer patients of the MCC-Spain study based on support vector machines and genetic algorithms, Neurocomputing (2020).

[42] O. Terzo, P. Ruiu, E.M. Bucci, F. Xhafa, Data as a service (DaaS) for sharing and processing of large data collections in the cloud, in: L. Barolli, F. Xhafa, H. Chen, A.F. Gómez-Skarmeta, F. Hussain (Eds.), Seventh International Conference on Complex, Intelligent, and Software Intensive Systems, CISIS 2013, Taichung, Taiwan, July 3–5, 2013, IEEE Computer Society, 2013, pp. 475–480.

[43] S. Viademonte, F. Burstein, J. Gupta, G. Forgionne, M. T, From knowledge discovery to computational intelligence: a framework for intelligent decision support systems, in: Intelligent Decision-Making Support Systems, 01 2006, pp. 57–78.

[44] H.-Q. Wang, J.-S. Li, Y.-F. Zhang, M. Suzuki, K. Araki, Creating personalised clinical pathways by semantic interoperability with electronic health records, Artificial Intelligence in Medicine 58 (2) (2013) 81–89.

[45] J. Wolfstadt, J. Gurwitz, T. Field, M. Lee, S. Kalkar, W. Wu, P. Rochon, The effect of computerized physician order entry with clinical decision support on the rates of adverse drug events: a systematic review, Journal of General Internal Medicine 23 (04 2008) 451–458.

[46] A. Wulff, B. Haarbrandt, E. Tute, M. Marschollek, P. Beerbaum, T. Jack, An interoperable clinical decision-support system for early detection of sirs in pediatric intensive care using openEHR, Artificial Intelligence in Medicine 89 (2018) 10–23.

[47] F. Xhafa, B. Kilic, P. Krause, Evaluation of IoT stream processing at edge computing layer for semantic data enrichment, Future Generations Computer Systems 105 (2020) 730–736.

[48] N. Zhou, H. Lv, C. Zhang, T. Li, J. Zhu, M. Jiang, H. Hou, D. Liu, A. Li, G. Liu, K. Liu, G. Zhang, X. Zhang, P1.01-069 clinical experience with IBM Watson for oncology (WFO) cognitive system for lung cancer treatment in China, Journal of Thoracic Oncology 12 (11, Supplement 2) (2017) S1921, IASLC 18th World Conference on Lung Cancer.

Architectures and technological solutions for eHealth

Integrating technological solutions into innovative eHealth applications

At pace of advanced technology for eHealth

6

6.1 Telemedicine network architectures

The IoT-based telemedicine network is one of the most important elements to help society prevent diseases and provide accurate health services [96]. Telemedicine networks support IoT applications to access and transmit medical data between various layers of the Cloud ecosystem, comprising Edge, Fog, and Cloud layers, and enable health services, for various diseases, through tailored communication. The work presented in [3] can be considered a general foundation for developing insights into IoT telemedicine networks.

In the next subsections, we refer to three key building blocks in telemedicine networks: the topology, architecture, and technological platform.

A general view of a Cloud ecosystem also referred to as Cloud-to-thing-continuum, which serves as a basis for all modern IoT and Cloud platforms and applications, is depicted in Fig. 6.1.

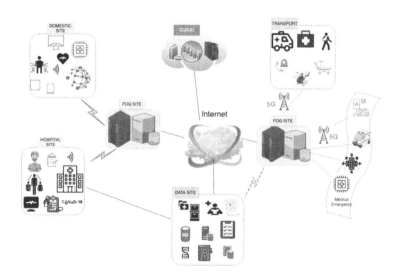

FIGURE 6.1

Cloud-to-thing-continuum for eHealth applications.

Anomaly Detection and Complex Event Processing Over IoT Data Streams. https://doi.org/10.1016/B978-0-12-823818-9.00017-1

Telemedicine network topology

The IoT telemedicine network topology demonstrates the compatibility of different layers in the telemedicine architecture and enables a workflow between components represented by Edge, Fog, and Cloud layers in an IoT-based healthcare network. An existing framework methodology aims to establish a service architecture topology using an open telemedicine interoperability (OTI) hub that enables bidirectional semantic interoperability between health information systems (HIS), telemedicine instruments (TI), and eHealth smart devices (eHSD) by establishing a Cloud-based system landscape based on the OTI hub and the Health Level Seven International interoperability standard [41]. An intelligent hybrid context-aware model named Intelligent Hybrid Context-Aware Model for Patients Under-Supervision in Home (IHCAM-PUSH) for elderly patients is used to facilitate the storage and processing of Big Data generated by Ambient Assisted Living (AAL) systems used to monitor chronic diseases of elderly people at home, based on the local components in case of Internet interruptions and Cloud-based components [50].

As another example of application, an autonomous health management system is using Fog computing technology, where the system is designed for autonomous fall detection using wearable IoT technologies [96]. The collected information is stored in a local database under the personal health record with a timestamp for continuous fall detection events. Similarly, there is the application of a remote monitoring and management architecture in Parkinson's disease patients suffering from Freezing of Gait (FoG) [101]. The collected information is stored in the local database through the app, which is later transferred to a central database when an internet connection exists. Given the limitations of IoT and Edge computing devices, there have been proposed IoT-based systems with four layers for a lightweight transmission algorithm based on Big Data visualization in telemedicine [141]. The goal was to increase transmission efficiency and achieve lossless transmission of the original data flow. Lastly, scalability and reliability are issues in a multilayer architecture of Cloud-to-thing computing for eHealth applications. A distributed and scalable computing framework to improve communication reliability for end-users of wearable IoT-based medical sensors is recently proposed in [39].

Telemedicine network architecture

A telemedicine architecture highlights the physical elements for the IoT telemedicine network and its functional organization, working techniques, and principles. The architecture is a multilayer one, where each level corresponds to a computing paradigm (IoT/Edge/Fog/Cloud variants and mobile and wireless technologies). We refer next to various layered eHealth applications for patient monitoring using different technological solutions.

Thus, a three-layer architecture was presented in [150] consisting of a community monitoring center, home monitoring nodes, and a hospital monitoring center, using IoT technology as the core to combine IoT technology with mobile technology to design a remote medical monitoring system. With the advent of new networking technologies and protocols such as 5G, LoRaWAN, etc., a new generation of eHealth applications is envisioned, and many such applications are currently under development. An architecture for an IoT device based on a Wireless Body Area Network (WBAN) application to ensure suitability for eHealth services through network caching and name-based routing instead of IP addresses can be found in [72]. The proposed protocol is for 5G Content-Centric Network (CCN) WBAN to ensure reliable, efficient, and secure application of eHealth services that meet existing IoT devices and IP protocol stack requirements. A four-layer architecture of an IoT-based health monitoring system, called IoT4HC, based on the LoRaWAN network is shown in [81]. It consists of the four main components of data collection, analysis, treatment plan generator, and treatment plan executor, which collect health parameters that are transmitted to a data analysis module via a LoRaWAN network.

Additionally, novel eHealth applications are built by combining various paradigms and technologies to overcome limitations of single technologies, such as limitations of Edge devices or centralized Cloud, and to increase the quality of services offered. Thus, authors in [90] proposed an intelligent eHealth system for chronic care through basic building blocks in designing a wireless connection between Android application and ECG blocks. In comparison, a smart Fog architecture was designed to improve analytics in wearable Internet of Medical Things [22]. The authors relied on unsupervised machine learning (ML) for Big Data analytics to discover patterns in physiological data from patient tele-monitoring, focusing on network bandwidth and resource constraints for IoT devices communicating with Fog nodes (see also Fig. 6.1).

A typical 4-layer architecture, from IoT end-devices to an application layer, is used in an IoT-based architecture to detect Cardiovascular diseases (CVDs) based on wearable 12-lead ECG SmartVest [76]. It consisted of the component of detection layer through a textile dry ECG electrode, followed by a network layer using Bluetooth, WiFi, and others, transmitting to a Cloud storage platform and server computation, and finally an application layer, which is responsible for signal analysis and decision making.

IoT-based architectures are being used for patient monitoring (and tracking) even for groups of patients with impairs or tend to not collaborate with the application, for instance, an architecture based on tracking and monitoring patients with mental disorders [53]. Based on IoT LoRa, the architecture functions consist of a client device attached to the patient for tracking followed by LoRa gateways, which are local servers and Cloud servers connected via cellular or WiFi in hospitals and public places [134]. A Lomb-Scargle periodogram (LOMB) algorithm –for efficient computation of a Fourier-like power spectrum estimator– for heart rate variability (HRV) analysis using a PPG sensor on a DSP processor at the node device uses the LoRaWAN IoT ecosystem.

The presence of various networking technologies coexisting in one application is the basis to achieve several advantages. However, issues also arise, and the QoS of the resulting architecture as a whole needs to be evaluated. In this context, authors in [144] presented a device developed to provide a QoS framework for evaluating wireless services in healthcare, where the services can be extended to support different networks, which can also determine the jitter size needed to avoid service failure to provide increased reliability ECG monitoring. The architecture of the 'ECG Android App' allows the end-user to visualize ECG waves with the functionality of recording data in the background [85]. The architecture includes various technologies such as micro-controllers for IoT, communication protocols, signal processing, efficient and secure mechanisms for large file transfer, a database management system, and a centralized Cloud. Scalable architecture with fault tolerance targeting healthcare covers various fault scenarios, such as a malfunction of sink node hardware, including the traffic bottleneck on a node resulting from the large data reception rate [46]. A heart rate sensor node for an embedded telemedicine system uses a body-area network and a multihopping structure [38]. The Medical Implant Communication Service (MICS) band can collect signals from sensors and WMTS. Such a method allows simultaneous remote monitoring of multiple patients. Ultimately, a cyber healthcare framework was built around the architecture of multilayer IoT.

Lastly, the myriad of technologies and open-access software and protocols are enabling the development of cost-effective, low-cost eHealth applications in the developing world [15]. IoT, Fog, and

Cloud servers can indeed be affordable for lightweight Cyber-Physical Health System (CPHS) infrastructures [103].

Telemedicine platforms

We present next several platforms in the IoT telemedicine domain, which are called a network and computing platform. In the study [142], a smart home platform called iHome Health-IoT was discussed, which enables seamless fusion between IoT devices and home telemedicine to improve patient experience and service efficiency. It includes an open platform-based smart iMedBox with enhanced connectivity and interchangeability to integrate devices and services, iMedPack, and Bio-Patch device [142]. In the same line, authors in [65] proposed a distributed coexistence IoT-based intelligent medical system in WBANs. The system includes the two phases of channel planning and the media access adaptation, which can dynamically avoid interference in a coexistence situation. In addition, the system guarantees reliable distributed communication.

Telemedicine platforms rely on collected data, for which various technologies can be used. Authors in [64] apply beacon data points after data processing inference using the variance rates used by Intel and Fitbit in the production network. It collects the sampled data via smartphone and provides the export for data processing when needed. Other location systems incorporate technologies such as Cloud, IoT, and 802.11 wireless technologies [80] aiming to provide a lower-cost alternative to traditional real-time monitoring systems. It integrates WiFi signals (802.11) with others, including embedded systems, Cloud computing platforms, and wireless networks, to implement an IoT-centric solution for a Real-time Location System (RTLS) in a healthcare environment.

The common recognition and identification platform (CRIP) design is a part of the CareStore project that provides sensor-based support for seamless identification of nonhealthcare device users [83]. By using various technologies, it enables seamless integration and interaction of sensors and patients. An optimization scheme for a large network of patients in a parallel distributed manner was developed to optimize the network into multiple processors for parallel computing [63]. Integration of Compressive Sensing into monitoring platforms based on the IoT, incorporating compressed sensing (CS)-based compression and recovery while detecting anomalies for each heartbeat using the random sensing matrix with entries drawn from the normal distribution to compress the data, with the Sparse Recovery Algorithms (SPA) provided for efficient ECG signal reconstruction [29]. A similar study quantifies the performance of a CS-based vital sign acquisition scheme for a networked health application over an IoT platform using multichannel EEG signals and a designed sparsifying basis to increase the sparsity of the EEG signal to improve the reconstruction quality and system efficiency [30].

In telemedicine platforms for patient monitoring, the energy-aware management of sensing nodes becomes an important aspect of dealing with. Particularly, in platforms using wireless and wearable ECG, the system could be embedded into an IoT platform and integrate heterogeneous nodes and applications [119]. The system achieves a long battery life while providing a high-quality ECG signal [40]. Amrita IoT Medical (AIM) was proposed, which is an IoT-based smart edge health tele-monitoring system [99]. The system contains wearable sensors that transmit vital data to two software engines to provides in the first engine a quick active summary responsible for effective prognosis (RASPRO), and the second a critical measure index (CMI) implemented for heart disease and acute hypotensive episodes.

Finally, IoT platforms for telemedicine can largely benefit from semantic data enrichment, which consists of complementing the sensing data with contextual information, such as Spatio-temporal data.

Authors in [105] developed a platform based on enriched tele-health data with contextual information by aggregating and preprocessing cross-domain inputs from multiple sources. The reader is also referred to the work [108,47] for an edge-stream computing infrastructure for real-time analysis of wearable sensors data, which uses semantic data enrichment and complex event processing techniques.

6.2 Telemedicine healthcare services

In healthcare, there is no standardized definition for IoT-based healthcare services. There have been some cases where a service cannot be objectively distinguished from a specific application or solution. A study by [7] suggests that health services in telemedicine technologies consist of two general types into which most sharing technologies tend to fall, namely asynchronous (store-and-forward) and synchronous (real-time) health services technologies [70,102].

6.2.1 Asynchronous healthcare services

Although asynchronous healthcare services are based on IoT perspectives, the concept does not involve live interaction with patient data as it is collected [70]. Instead, patient data, such as records, scans, and images, are collected and sent to medical centers or professionals, where the data can be analyzed. In an Edge and Cloud architecture that uses wearable IoT to provide Cloud-based clinical services such as alarms, phone calls, or text messages that leverage the transmission of human activity data for storage and analysis, where services are triggered when patients do not perform prescribed activities [70]. A model of micro-services in a web-of-objects platform that enables IoT services provides a development base of interoperable micro-services that support dynamic functions by leveraging streams of sensory data [10]. The development of intelligent mHealth services in telemedicine to introduce reference scenarios of personalized assistance focuses on emergencies was introduced [66]. It works by operating within a shared networked computing environment and interacts by sharing information and its semantics. Another service introduces a home health care system that makes patients feel that the system is responsible for their health care while meeting licensing requirements, legal requirements, and travel time constraints of medical personnel [75]. An IoT-based smart eHealth care system was developed that includes sensors, mobile apps, Bluetooth, and the cloud containing an offline collection of sensor data, which is automatically uploaded to the cloud as it becomes available [113].

6.2.2 Synchronous healthcare services

Real-time healthcare services are expected to have features such as immediacy and the ability to provide live access to healthcare providers remotely through video conferencing or live streaming of medical images and videos [25]. This feature enables an interactive experience where patients and physicians can make similar clinical assessments as they would do during in-person appointments. A simulation study within BoIT projects investigates the use of various IoT devices, such as a care phone, to establish a voice-over-IP (VOIP) connection with caregivers or family members [102]. IoT and decision support systems (DSS) aspects are used to provide both preventive and intelligent healthcare in the design of the IoT healthcare platform and DSS components [25]. Authors in [33] proposed medical IoT architectures based on LoRa and intended for home care and hospital services. The study analyzes and improves each component of the IoT architecture to develop reliable platforms to improve eHealth services in real-time. Multiple IoMT communication technologies were used in a remote health system for patients and doctors, by connecting multiple medical sensors to a server [2].

6.3 Telemedicine healthcare application

In addition to telemedicine health services, IoT telemedicine applications have attracted much attention. Telemedicine health services are used to develop telemedicine applications that can be used directly by patients. Therefore, health services and applications are closely related, and it is not easy to separate them. The applications in this category lead to various healthcare solutions in monitoring, detecting, and diagnosing. This category is further divided into sections dealing with various IoT-based telemedicine applications, including single-condition, multicondition, telemedicine rehabilitation, and AAL applications.

6.3.1 Physiological parameter monitoring

Monitoring of human physiological parameters of patients during life activities continuously is an important application domain. IoT technologies that adjust these parameters provide medical centers with instant knowledge of sudden changes in health status and can be integrated with other contributions such as disease monitoring, detection, and prevention [45]. The concept is established for patients' home use to prevent life-threatening situations and support their monitoring by family or remote physicians. The concept of these studies can effortlessly protect the lives of many patients from human diseases.

ECG monitoring

ECG-based data processing and analysis has been among the most fertile applications in the heart health monitoring domain. A revolutionary IoT-based ECG monitoring system called Tele-ECG that helps to monitor heart health within a telemedicine environment is discussed in [125]. Although the system is as competitive as an ECG from a specialist's office, the system provides basic monitoring by analyzing the patient's evolution over time. The ECG is among the most characteristic representatives of cardiac work, representing the recorded electrical activity of the heart from electrodes on the surface of the body [125]. The physiological parameters of ECG measure cardiac electrical vector variation and cardiac work rate [27].

It should be noted here that such monitoring frameworks for enabling IoT Health are based on both ECG data and other health data collected via mobile devices and sensors [55]. As in other health applications, securely transferring the data to the Cloud, enabling seamless access for medical personnel, etc., are issues that need to be addressed in such frameworks. An important objective in EEG applications is to make them easy to implement for practical purposes and reduce their cost. One such application example was proposed for 12-lead ECG, which is portable and shows effective results in ambulatory systems [27]. The system can also transmit the ECG to medical professionals from a remote location to anywhere globally. In the same line of cost-effective and low-cost IoT-based ECG health monitoring system, authors in [45] promote automatic analysis and notification, deal with energy-efficient wearable sensor devices through a Fog layer. The sensor nodes transmit vital signs to a smart gateway accessed by caregivers specializing in cardiovascular disease.

Providing reliable autonomous solutions with less intervention from medical staff is yet another objective in IoT architectures for monitoring ECG signals from a patient. The mobile Tele-ECG application, where health monitoring is possible without the involvement of a physician, was presented in [125,109]. Likewise, improving the accuracy and timely detection of symptoms are the foremost objectives. As another example, an implementation scheme for a health system using a Hidden Markov Model (HMM) chain and ECG sensors was discussed by [93] to provide improved monitoring and timely intervention for patients suffering from Cardio Vascular Diseases (CVDs). Another development of an ECG monitoring system was discussed, with the system being simultaneously accessible to different users for ECG signal media and data transmission [95]. From a practical perspective, a Tele-ECG and heart rate monitoring system should support both patients and medical staff for emergency requests, both with human intervention and automatic, and the ability to track multiple patients through smartphone, server-side, and website [97].

Human activity recognition, movement and falls

In the field of telemedicine applications, human activity detection and fall risk detection of patients are considered important and helpful to alert patients, exercise, or rest [123]. Human activity detection and fall risk, either indoor or outdoor, is even more important to the elderly due to their physical condition and impaired people and patients with disorders, Parkinson's, dementia, etc. Subsequently, many medical applications or frameworks based on IoT have been proposed to monitor human activity or physiological diseases that affect normal activity. The work of [104] discussed the use of an e-textile device as some glove-woven components, including Arduino, flex sensors, and laptop, to collect data from the gloves and transmit them to a patient app. The purpose was to monitor some of the motor symptoms of Parkinson's disease. Then a sensing system based on WiFi signals was introduced [123] to detect human indoor movements from the whole-body movements. The system uses Dopple, which describes an intrusive and pervasive IoT platform for home healthcare. A motor condition assessment system was developed by [71] for patients suffering from progressive neurodegenerative diseases. Achieving full nonintrusive systems is of utmost importance, especially for groups of people or patients who, due to their neuro-degenerative diseases, tend to not collaborate with the system, are reluctant to wearable sensors, etc.

Sleep disorder

Among sleep disorders, obstructive sleep apnea is the most common type of sleep disorder. The term "sleep-disordered breathing" is widely used to describe breathing problems during sleep in which insufficient air can enter the lungs [74]. Sleep-disordered breathing can increase the risk of cardiovascular disease, including other conditions such as hypertension, stroke, arrhythmia, and diabetes [74]. Implementing a sleep monitoring system using wireless polysomnography based on the IoT was discussed in [74]. The system uses a battery-powered and ambulatory bio-potential sensing unit and a user interface. Authors in [54] utilized IoT sensors for accurate classification of sleep patterns through data collection, as well as a hybrid of Deep Belief Network (DBN) and Long Short Memory (LSTM) network. A universal central monitoring system of IoT bio-signal technology has been described in [26]. The system is attached to a bed using a thin strip sensor, and then the user's sleep efficiency and breathing rate can be measured.

Blood pressure

Another physiological parameter describing cardiac work is blood pressure. The physiological pressure parameters measure systolic and diastolic blood pressure and heart rate [32]. A noninvasive optical fiber sensor architecture adaptable to a shoe sole was developed for remote monitoring of plantar pressure, integrated into an IoT eHealth solution for monitoring the well-being of individuals [32].

Pulse rate

Pulse is one of the most important physiological parameters defined by arterial blood oxygen content, which measures light absorption by blood [91]. The physiological parameters of pulse measure cardiac work rate [32]. An IoT monitoring system adapted into the lateral rotation mattress is used in bedridden patients through a pulse sensor to detect and alleviate discomfort in patients via an intelligent IoT system [91].

6.3.2 Chronic disease monitoring

Certain medical conditions require long-term monitoring of patients, especially in chronic diseases [100]. Therefore, continuous monitoring is essential for such cases. IoT applied to monitor patients via multiple sensors, parameters, and IoT devices provide limited and specific recommendations in case of change in patient's health status with emphasis on endocrine and metabolic disorders and diabetes, cardiac diseases, psychiatric diseases such as Alzheimer's disease, neurological diseases such as abnormal movement and gait disorder, epilepsy autonomic nervous system (ANS), and respiratory diseases. Monitoring blood glucose levels reveals changes in different patterns for individuals, and the latter helps in planning meals, medication times, and activities.

Monitoring vital parameters

Chronic Disease Monitoring is helpful and can be made available to medical staff, patients, and caregivers. In [44], a system architecture consisting of a sensor device was designed to present real-time data for body temperature and glucose and contextual data. These data should be displayed in graphical and human-readable form for end-users such as medical specialists and patients. A novel distributed software was presented in [100], which discussed a remote monitoring infrastructure for patients with chronic metabolic disorders. Some of the system activities included activity tracking, smart scales, pulse oximeters, blood pressure, and glucose meters. The system could perform analyses that would support the medical diagnostic process and promote bidirectional communication between patients and physicians.

Monitoring of diabetes

Diabetes, as one of the most commonplace chronic diseases, has also received much attention. Authors in [9] developed a telemedicine-based platform for diabetes management and control to help patients record and monitor their vital signs and diabetes and provide them with feedback. Other researchers discussed the digital innovations used in the IoT test beds and described the architectural solution underlying the diabetes digital coach platform [133].

An IoT-based management intervention approach for type 1 diabetes (T1D) was proposed that focused on various aspects, including functionality, structure, and development process of MyDay [146]. It is a solution tool for multifaceted self-management issues for pediatric T1D patients. Another approach to mHealth based on the IoT platform aims to support diabetes self-management to enable other dimensions of diabetes care. This goal will be achieved by collecting information and remotely monitoring patients, and providing individualized and personalized feedback on a smartphone platform [6]. A telecare system for diabetic patients and caregivers will be established. The system is interactive and can enhance the quality of self-care. This function is achieved by using IoT technology while enabling direct communication of patients' medical devices with their caregivers via smartphones [135].

Monitoring of chronic heart disease

An IoT-based human activity recognition (HAR) system aims to monitor patients' vital signs with chronic heart disease remotely. The system consists of a traditional HAR system and an eHealth application of any recognition or monitoring system, where both systems operate independently [23]. The IoT-based cardiac monitoring system, composed of data acquisition and data transmission, uses the patient's physical signs (blood pressure, ECG, SpO2, HR, pulse rate, blood glucose, blood lipids) and location [73]. The system is connected to remote medical applications in real-time and is designed to be sampled at different rates to detect the patient's risk conditions continuously.

A new approach called heart monitoring through perceptual computing (HMT Per-C) was introduced, in which a patient's health status is assessed to determine the risk of heart failure [49]. This approach works by processing the user's feedback in the form of "words" and providing a recommendation for needed medical attention. In the same vein, a system infrastructure, called pervasive patient health monitoring (PPHM), was introduced in [1]. The infrastructure was based on IoT technologies along with integrated cloud computing to monitor patients in real-time. Specifically, those suffering from congestive heart failure were monitored using ECG. ECG was used to demonstrate the suitability of the proposed PPHM. Efficient, low-cost, low-power IoT medical systems for ECG monitoring of cardiac patients based on IoT techniques but with greater memory autonomy were developed in various proposals [145,107,79].

Monitoring of Alzheimer and dementia disease

An IoT-based mobile tele-health infrastructure to monitor patients living at home and suffering from Alzheimer's disease using ECG and RFID for KFUPM Medical Centre in Saudi Arabia was proposed in [106]. In particular, in the case of Alzheimer's and dementia diseases, studying the cognitive state of patients is crucial. A novel cognitive stimulation therapy system was proposed in [92] assess cognitive impairment and emotional well-being of dementia patients from a social care perspective. In addition, the study discussed the provision of adaptive and computerized therapy to minimize therapist input during assessment and plan development.

Developing assistive solutions for patients with Alzheimer's and dementia is among the most challenging tasks. So, considerable efforts are devoted in this direction to increase the quality of assistance remotely and support Independent Assisted Living. Authors in [84] used assistive technology for dementia patients, where they developed a framework for monitoring assistive IoT devices along with wearable devices to address some of the barriers patients face in performing their daily activities while using data analytics, such as processing complex events in real-time, which in turn enables better monitoring.

Monitoring of movement disorders

An IoT-based system for remote patient monitoring used wireless inertial sensors with motion distur-bances to monitor dystonic tremors in patients with spasmodic torticollis [18]. An efficient algorithm was developed to successfully maintain the high scalability of the proposed solution in terms of mem-ory consumption, processing time, and energy consumption [114]. The approach can efficiently support data provisioning and parallelism by relying on the MapReduce platform to analyze large EEG data in real-time. This platform can help in epileptic seizure monitoring. A novel wearable ring sensor pro-vides continuous measurement of ANS with wearable biosensors in mobile health applications [77]. Seven patients were given electronic monitoring devices to monitor their inhaler use for one month via a SmartTrack device for asthma is one of the emerging technologies in IoT [56].

6.3.3 Disease detection

In clinical settings, the term "detection" often refers to the objective recognition of a problem or is-sue [112]. However, such a problem can also be subjective but credible at the same time, such as when a patient complains of an illness whose symptoms are not visible (e.g., back pain). There is an art or skill in detecting abnormalities outside the normal, acceptable range or threshold. The studies in this subsection refer to detection with an implicit medical orientation and are integrated with few other con-texts such as recognition, prediction, and prevention. A brief description of the detection process for each study described below explains how it is integrated with other medical contexts. We focus on heart disease, infectious diseases, such as influenza (H1N1), Ebola, and mosquito-borne, and Covid-19.

A live video stream was discussed to measure the heart rate (HR) of multiple people simultaneously by using face recognition in combination with object tracking to generate a set of face rectangles based on ML [89]. Certainly, in the case of cardiovascular disease, early warning systems are of paramount importance. Authors in [37] presented such a warning system for cardiovascular disease. Its main func-tions include context detection, anomaly detection, and risk prediction using knowledge engineering and data mining methods and personal situation knowledge discovery and refinement by the service center.

Other applications in this direction include alerting about arrhythmia and patient emergencies for chronic heart disease. Thus, an IoT system was developed that dealt with remotely collecting and pro-cessing patient readings from ECG sensors not attached to the human body to intelligently predict arrhythmia and immediately send an alert to the physician [94]. While, for patient emergencies for chronic heart disease, another approach constructed a triage algorithm called RLLT within a new frame-work (FTF-mHealth-IoT) in mHealth to detect patient emergencies for chronic heart disease and then identify the healthcare service package risk level [8]. A detection solution has been proposed for cere-bral stroke detection [42]. The detection solution uses cloud services for data analysis and storage to provide statistics for public institutions.

Detection, prediction, and prevention of virus spread such as H1N1 influenza and, most recently, Covid-19, are vital to early warning for pandemic situations. An architecture for intelligent H1N1 influenza surveillance, prediction, prevention, and detection using a random decision tree, cloud com-puting, and social network analysis is proposed [111]. A novel architecture for real-time Ebola detection was presented, where the IoT-based system was used in conjunction with cell phones, RFID, and cloud computing for early-stage prevention of the spreading infection [112]. A J48 decision tree was used to assess the level of infection depending on the user's symptoms. Likewise, an intelligent healthcare system based on wearables, IoT sensors, and Fog computing is used to analyze, categorize, and share medical information between the user and healthcare providers to distinguish the different mosquito-borne diseases (MBDs) based on the patient's symptoms [129]. Most recently, due to the global pandemic situation of Covid-19, there is a huge increasing interest and number of publications about detection, prediction, and prevention of Covid-19 virus [12,140,28].

6.3.4 Disease diagnostics

Diagnosing a problem intends to make sure that the specific medical condition is causing the problem [116]. The process of diagnostic application aims to determine what disease or condition explains a patient's symptoms and signs [35]. We consider various studies for diagnosis with an implicit medical orientation and are integrated with other contexts such as detection, recognition, prediction, treatment, and prevention. A brief description of the diagnostic process for each study described below explains how it is integrated with other medical contexts. We focus on infectious diseases such as communicable diseases, oncologic diseases such as lung cancer, ophthalmologic diseases, dermatologic diseases, psychiatric diseases such as mental illness, cardiac diseases, community medicine and general practice, renal diseases, gastrointestinal diseases such as ulcerative colitis, and rheumatologic diseases and rehabilitation.

A novel system [117] based on IoT sensors aims to monitor, classify, and distinguish patients infected by mosquito-borne disease (MBDs) at an early stage. The system aims to control MBD outbreak by calculating the similarity factor to distinguish MBDs and then using a J48 decision tree classifier to classify infectious categories for each user. The detection, diagnosis, and prevention of users infected with the Chikungunya virus (CHV) were also discussed. The Fog-based IoT system consists of three layers: IoT sensor, Fog, and Cloud layer. The decision tree is used to classify the user's infectious category depending on the health symptoms [116]. Moreover, a health system based on wearable IoT sensors is proposed to identify and control CHV outbreaks. Fuzzy C-means is used to diagnose potential users who may be infected and provide them with immediate diagnostic emergency alerts [115].

In another example, the authors in [24] explored the construction of segmentation regions within a small area to improve segmentation results using numerical modeling of IoT computer-aided image analysis. Segmentations of slices were generated by using volume data with a linear equation for thoracic CT images. ML and Deep Learning are also extensively used for developing IoT decision support systems with computer-assisted diagnosis [78]. The system uses a novel deep learning-based model for early classification and detection of lung cancer and diagnoses four stages of lung cancer. Metastasis information was obtained from the medical body area network. A wrist pulse signal processing method for diagnosis and treatment with insights from Jin pulse diagnosis (JPD) and enabled IoT cloud is proposed [147]. An iterative sliding window algorithm was developed to segment the denoised signal into individual periods for people with lung cancer. Other works proposed a hybrid architecture for IoT healthcare in which retinal images acquired with smartphone fundoscopy are processed with a superresolution (SR) algorithm and using multikernel support vector regression (SVR) to improve the quality of the images [59].

A deep neural network system, called dermatosis discrimination assistant (DDA), was proposed to classify images of dermatoses generated by confocal laser scanning microscopes [48]. The diagnosis of seborrheic keratosis (SK) and flat wart (FW) was used as examples. A multiagent system executed on commodity hardware such as Raspberry PI, smartphones, or Arduino for remote monitoring and detection of elderly patients with mental illness based on ontology-based diagnosis among sensors, symptoms, and diseases in the IoT paradigm is presented [58]. A telemedicine autodiagnosis application called My Kardio, based on M2M and kNN algorithm for cardiovascular patients to help the doctor perform diagnosis, uses a sphygmomanometer, heart rate, diagnosis, and ECG, and others, where the data is sent to the server over the internet along with the diagnosis [35].

A cloud and IoT-based mobile health application have been developed and implemented to predict and diagnose the severity of diabetes using a fuzzy rule-based neural classifier and IoT devices based on sensors [69]. A field-programmable gate array (FPGA)-based computer-aided diagnosis (CAD) algorithm was used to detect kidney abnormalities in an IoT-enabled ultrasound system based on a look-up table approach and a support vector machine (SVM) with multilayer perceptron classifier [68]. A novel IoT fog cloud-based cyber-physical system was proposed for diagnosing and staging ulcerative colitis [128]. A key point of this study is real-time alerting by the fog layer if the user needs emergency treatment when diagnosed with UC. A final example explores the application of IoT technology in medical systems for sports injuries and explains the application of telemedicine, mobile diagnosis, and user data management supported by IoT technology [143].

6.3.5 Disease prediction

Prediction of disease probability and intuition of preventive schemes are derived from the field of prediction to prevent diseases or minimize their impact on patients to a large extent (e.g., by preventing mortality or limiting morbidity). At the same time, developed applications for services, such as diagnosis and therapy, can potentially support the prediction of disease support conditions [87]. In addition, prediction within the system can assist in avoiding delays for timely medical treatment even before the person reaches a critical condition [131]. We refer next to studies that focus on heart disease, psychiatric conditions such as emotional disorders, kidney disease, endocrine, and metabolic disorders, and diabetes, as well as community medicine and general practice.

An ML-based prediction approach was proposed in [131] that uses heart rate variability (HRV) analysis along with ML-based monitoring through IoT. The approach uses a portable 3-lead ECG kit and focuses on performing real-time analysis to detect arrhythmia, thereby predicting cardiac risk. A stroke diagnosis and prediction system based on IoT and ML is proposed in [13], using a connected microcontroller for various wearable sensors and a cloud. The critical data is sent to the prediction system to test and predict whether the patient is at high risk of stroke or not, and the system then alerts the physician. In [118], an IoT-based healthcare system was introduced that continuously monitors and analyzes blood pressure statistics to predict the risk level of hypertension attack among users in remote locations.

An important family of applications in this domain is that of emotion-aware state that can help prediction. An emotion-aware smart system algorithm capable of launching a prediction for women with hypertension during pregnancy or postpartum depression is discussed in [87]. IoT sensors enable the collection of data in real-time, where ML algorithms are used in the analysis. This process takes place at the healthcare Cloud service provider to assess the current condition of a pregnant woman. For effective medical services, an online medical decision support system for chronic kidney disease prediction was introduced based on IoT and Cloud platforms [14]. Similarly, authors in [17] use a FreestyleFree sensor that enables continuous monitoring of blood glucose levels through integration between the patient and near-field communication sensors via an IoT card that sends the collected data for the LibreMonitor mobile application. A mHealth approach was discussed for detecting daily human activities recorded by an accelerometer using S-transform and supervised regularization-based robust subspace learning method.

6.3.6 Disease treatment

The cycle of disease detection, diagnosis, and prediction leads to disease treatment, which focuses on a patient's care to combat a disease or disorder [43]. For telemedicine applications, treatment may include the use of any device or system designed to treat any part of the body remotely. As an example, we could consider treatment related to ophthalmic conditions. An opto-electronic controller chip is developed that can be attached to a patient's head to control the micro-LED matrix that can help treat patients suffering from a retinal prosthesis that stimulates retinal ganglion cells that have been genetically modified to restore partial vision [43].

6.3.7 Multicondition application

General-condition applications address several diseases or conditions as a whole [121]. IoT telemedicine applications in this category are designed to help patients meet general requirements for form, fit and function based on various diseases. This section considers applications conducted in community medicine and general practice, psychiatric diseases such as emotional disorder and mental illness, geriatric medicine, and neurological diseases such as abnormal movement and gait disorder.

A context-aware IoT mobile application uses built-in sensors and other external sensors that gather the context of multidimensional health assessments are performed by the sick person, enabling him/her to monitor the activities and analyze the data to assess their functional status [19]. A new approach for the recognition and monitoring of real-time activity called basket-based sorting structure identifies the correlation between sensor events to identify the events of sensor (SEs) in concurrent activities and have the correlated SEs stored into the SE container instance (basket) for further prediction purposes [149].

6.4 Ambient Assisted Living (AAL)

In general, traditional IoT-based medical services and smart homes should, by default, provide the elderly with specialized services. That is, a separate IoT service is mandatory. AAL is an IoT platform that is enabled by artificial intelligence to address healthcare of the elderly and incapacitated individuals [4]. AAL aims to conveniently and safely extend elderly individuals' independent life in their homes [126]. AAL services can meet the expectations of individual elders, ensure greater autonomy, in addition to assisting similar to what is provided by a human caregiver when a problem arises [127]. Several studies combine ambient intelligence with telemedicine solutions based on the IoT, thereby improving the quality of life amongst the elderly. This section refers to studies that focus on psychiatric diseases such as sleep disorder and depressive disorder, geriatric medicine, community medicine, and general practice, and neurological diseases such as abnormal movement and gait disorder.

IoT-based unobtrusive sleep monitoring pillow [126] is capable of monitoring patterns of breathing and overall sleep quality of AAL, quantifying five variables whose thresholds can be varied among medical staff. An intelligent algorithm enabled by the system employs and processes decisions to enhance the AAL system. A system for the detection and treatment of elderly depression based on IoT, context awareness, and the concept of eHealth is proposed to determine the activities of daily living (ADL) through gesture recognition log events towards determining abnormality as a means to conclude the variations in the ADL [11]. Authors in [51] proposed a hybrid real-time remote monitoring framework based on IoT, which monitors the condition of elderly patients suffering from chronic disease and addresses the disadvantages of local and cloud AAL architecture to develop smart healthcare services that have great prediction capabilities.

An enhancement method for elderly assisted living is discussed in [122]. This process is done by incorporating an indoor positioning system (IPS) and nonvision-based motion tracking assisted living services, including emergency panic buttons and medical adherence system into the IoT platform [34]. Authors in [88] proposed a real-time health monitoring system of older adults living in geriatric residences to help caregivers monitoring their patients and have closer communication with their patients' family members. They proposed a scalable telemedicine system based on mobile IoT devices that can monitor thousands of older adults, detect falls and notify caregivers through the cloud and on edge. Multimodal sensing to detect existing situations and predict future situations is proposed using decision-tree and association analysis algorithms for activity recognition of the elderly in IoT–AAL smart homes environment; it allows for responses to accidents and emergency situations [4].

The application by [52], an eHealth system for monitoring elderly general health periodically in their homes, works in real-time with cloud-based on IoT and Fog computing using MySignals HW V2 platform and an Android app. An IoT CPS system integrates wireless, noninvasive devices in real-time algorithms to discern the volunteering of human movement through direct sensing of brain potentials combined with muscular action signal monitoring and to prevent falls for AAL affected by neurodegenerative diseases. Consequently, the system opens possibilities for mild cognitive impairment, Alzheimer's, and neurodegenerative disorders such as Parkinson's and Huntington's disease and multisystem atrophy [127].

A whole taxonomy results in telemedicine contexts such as monitoring, detection, diagnostics, prediction, and treatment can be built to support various human diseases and, therefore, an important direction for further research and development.

6.5 Telemedicine rehabilitation

Tele-rehabilitation is identified as a means of virtually delivering rehabilitation services to the patient's home; such methodology had demonstrated benefits when it was utilized to enhance and replace traditional means of therapy to overcome geographic, physical, and cognitive barriers [110]. The IoT can improve rehabilitation systems for addressing problems associated with the aging population and health expert's shortage within telemedicine applications [5,67]. In this section, we bring the views from various studies that focus on rheumatological disorder and rehabilitation, community medicine and general practice, and neurological diseases such as abnormal movement and gait disorder.

The system discussed by [130] is for tele-rehabilitation that utilizes a wearable muscle sensor and Kinect. Both are used to conduct interactive, personalized physical therapy, which can be done at home and allows for faster recovery for stroke patients using serious games. An application of wearable devices, video games, and IoT aims to facilitate the rehabilitation process of patients, while remote monitoring is enabled to allow rehabilitation of patients who suffer from disability in their upper limb as a result of stroke [5]. A sensor device and real-time therapist application are proposed based on three feedback systems. The latter employs IoT, wearables, big data analytics, cloud, and various cutting-edge technologies involved in the rehabilitation therapy evaluation of swimming exercises such as stroke time and stroke rotation angle symmetry [67].

As with other eHealth systems, assessing the accuracy, effectiveness, and reliability is an important issue. A rehabilitation assessment system was proposed by [60] based on IoT for stroke survivors based on different aspects, including a subsystem for sensing, data centers, Cloud computing, and Android-based software. A wearable IoT-based system for monitoring physical rehabilitation and characterization of the elbow can record movement data with a tri-axial accelerometer and gyroscope using sensors for movement characterization, which will, in turn, allow patients' state monitoring and estimation at all times [20].

Authors in [124] discuss a system for the rehabilitation of remote upper limbs aimed at poststroke patients. The system uses interactive digital media (IDM) and BSN for acquiring patterns of body motion. In addition, the system would be reconstructed in 3D activity recognition (AR) with gaming technologies that are interactive and immersive. To assist people's progress in physical rehabilitation tasks [110] a system that can enable the remote monitoring of telemedicine track movements was proposed. System components include modular electronics to act as matrix interface for 32 bendable force sensors assembled on a flexible PCB. In [36], produced an intelligent sports health vital sign acquisition system that explores the effects of wearable medical devices in vital sign monitoring, namely, ear temperature, pulse, blood oxygen saturation, and blood pressure, which is the key to telemedicine rehabilitation. A processing function for treatments, namely, AR and movement recognition, can use smartphones equipped with sensors, such as accelerometers and IoT elements, which are advantageous in detecting specialized movements needed in rehabilitation protocols for lower and upper limbs [21]. Lastly, a system for the long-term monitoring of children with movement disorders is proposed by [148]; the authors discussed that the movement disorder system comprises some subsystems in Malaysia. These subsystems will be responsible for collecting, detecting, transmission, and storing the different parameters of gait.

6.6 Patient-physician interactions

The authors of [138] consider many socio-political and technological developments in the area of Electronic Patient Records (EPR) and conclude that such collaboration is essential if EPR are ever to become a reality. Many socio-political and technological have been developed in the field of electronic health records (EPR). Technological aspects include EPR implemented via online transaction processing (OTP) using the Internet and Internet-based systems, more recently via cloud-based systems (CBS) using cloud service models (CSM). In addition, many socio-political considerations have included: (1) policy movements, including the UK government's policy to provide patients with 27/7 online access to their medical record; (2) ethical considerations and informed consent and acceptance by the public and nongovernmental organizations (NGOs); (3) technological considerations to identify appropriate CBS and data structures in distributed systems characterized by unstructured data; and (4) sharing and collaboration as a means to increase efficiency, security, privacy, etc. Overall, the goal is to provide medical professionals with advanced platforms for access and, more importantly, sharing and collaboration on a broad scale (e.g., national level). Addressing these aspects of EPR requires collaboration among all EPR stakeholders; this paper considers these and concludes that such a collaboration is vital if EPR is ever to become a reality.

In [138] authors advocate for collaboration through patient data access and sharing in the Cloud is an important research and development area to increase the interaction between patients and medical staff and thus improve the quality of health services as well as making them reach the mass of the population.

6.7 Complex event processing for remote patient monitoring

Kamel and George [62] have proposed a Remote Patient Tracking and Monitoring system (RPTM). In their system, medical sensors send health sensor data streams to an Android-based mobile device, which are then encrypted using the Advanced Encryption Standard (AES) encryption mechanism and forwarded to a General Packet Radio Services (GPRS) server for detecting complex events. Stipkovic *et al.* [120] developed a mobile CEP prototype system using an unofficial port of the Esper CEP engine on Android called Esper-Android. Banos *et al.* [16] have built a ubiquitous RPM system called PhysioDroid, which consists of wearable monitoring devices, a mobile device such as a smartphone, and a remote persistent storage system. The mobile device acts as an edge gateway to collect and upload sensor data to the remote persistent storage.

Pathak and Vaidehi [98] have developed a CEP-based Remote Health Monitoring System (CRHMS) that can receive various biological parameters such as heart rate, respiration rate, and blood pressure using Zephyr Bio Harness sensors. These sensor data streams are sent to an Android phone, which forwards them to JBoss Drools Fusion CEP Engine for complex event detection. Kakria *et al.* [61] have presented a server-based RPM system for monitoring cardiac issues such as Tachycardia and Bradycardia. They used a 3-tier architecture consisting of physiological sensors, an Android mobile device, and a web portal. An event forwarding application runs on the Android device, which receives sensor data using Bluetooth Low Energy (BLE) technology. This data is then transferred to a web server using the eXtensible Messaging and Presence Protocol (XMPP), and complex events are predicted using fuzzy logic.

Rodriguez *et al.* [82] have made a Complex Event Processing system for Heart Failure Prediction (CEP4HFP) system which uses predictive analytics on patient's historical database to predict a possible heart stroke. They used a 3-tier architecture consisting of monitoring, analysis, and visualization modules. The health data is collected using MySignals wearable sensors and sent to a RaspberryPi device, which forwards the data to a WSO2 Data Analytics Server (DAS) for historical analysis. Triggered alarms are sent to cardiologists using a web-based console and to caregivers using a mobile-based visualization module. The major limitation of these techniques mentioned above is that the mobile device is used as a forwarding agent while CEP is done on a remote server, and thus the techniques rely on the availability of network connectivity at all times. None of these existing works can raise the alarm notifying a health problem for the patient when the network becomes unavailable.

6.8 Other related issues to patient monitoring

6.8.1 NoSQL patient-electronic-record

Remote patient monitoring systems have to overcome the challenges of Big Data and Big Data streams. Indeed, data collected by sensors, which in many cases should be continuous (24/7), requires high performance and large capacity storage infrastructures to accommodate vast amounts of data and their fast, often in real-time, processing. Most notably, scalability and efficiency of processing become challenging issues. With the advent of NoSQL databases, a new generation of storage and processing of patient data arrived. NoSQL is of interest to store data that would be too large to fit into a relational database as well as to support distributed health record systems [86].

With NoSQL databases such as HBase, MongoDB, CouchDB, Dynamo, Cassandra and Google's BigTable, Neo4j, etc., built upon different data models (key-value, document, column-oriented, graph-based), applications can handle huge volumes of rapidly changing, unstructured data, which are typically generated in patient monitoring. NoSQL databases and their variants of NoSQL distributed databases can address three fundamental requirements in patient data monitoring: (1) the growing number of users that applications must support (along with growing user performance expectations, (2) the growth in the volume and scope and variety of data being processed by developers, and (3) the rise of cloud computing (which relies on a distributed, multitiered cloud-to-things-continuum architecture) [31].

6.8.2 Privacy and security

Health applications are among the most sensitive applications in terms of security and privacy. Indeed, any patient data breaches would be catastrophic for a correct functioning of a health system. All security and privacy techniques are faced with the demanding requirements of patient data, independently of their format, that are, data at still or in motion (data streams).

While encryption and cryptography, data anonymization, etc., can be successfully applied to patient data and enable data outsourcing, the main problem is data processing. Indeed, complex event processing, machine learning, and alike, to date, cannot be implemented successfully over encrypted data. Even there is progress in homomorphic computing, which addresses the design of primitives over encrypted data, there is not possible to achieve fast processing of encrypted data without prior decryption. In most cases, such primitives are reduced to searching and fine-grain access or attribute-based operations. The reader is referred to a series of publications covering security and privacy issues in this domain [137,136,139,57,132].

Audit policies and procedures for patient records are no less important. Audit trails for patient data are suitable for addressing and complementing security and privacy and anonymity and rights access to data. Although Cloud systems enable such procedures for single users, the current state of the art has not satisfactorily addressed access to sensitive data in a multiuser access (doctors or teams of doctors, nurses, caregivers, medical staff, stakeholders) in which patients should play an important role of patient-centric systems. Patients should be aware at any time who is accessing the data and eventually give consent to data access of involved actors. Audit trail defined as *"An audit trail (also called audit log) is a security-relevant chronological record, set of records, and/or destination and source of records that provide documentary"*, and enriched with other context information such as location access or medium access, are one important form of auditing patient data [138].

6.9 Key features

In this chapter, we have presented the state-of-the-art technological solutions and their integration into eHealth applications. We have carefully analyzed the main features and characteristics of the Cloud-to-thing ecosystem and the challenges of integrating current and future advances of technology into eHealth systems.

☑ About 150 references have been analyzed to distill the state-of-the-art of technological solutions in the field of eHealth systems.

☑ The IoT-based telemedicine network as a core component of eHealth applications is described and depicted in the full picture of the Cloud-to-ting continuum.

☑ Building blocs of telemedicine network, namely, topology, architecture, and technological platform, are identified and analyzed.

☑ A classification of telemedicine services is provided by focusing on synchronous and asynchronous health services.

☑ Various telemedicine healthcare applications, most notably remote patient monitoring and chronic disease monitoring, are given to exemplify the ideas in practical terms.

☑ The full cycle of patient monitoring, from IoT data collection to disease detection, disease diagnosis, disease prediction, and treatment is covered.

☑ Complex Event Processing is again presented as a building block of reasoning and intelligence in remote patient monitoring systems.

☑ Other issues such as NoSQL solutions to Patient-Electronic-Record, security, privacy, and auditing are also discussed.

References

[1] J. Abawajy, M. Hassan, Federated internet of things and cloud computing pervasive patient health monitoring system, IEEE Communications Magazine 55 (2017) 48–53.

[2] M. Abdellatif, W. Mohamed, Telemedicine: an IoT based remote healthcare system, International Journal of Online and Biomedical Engineering 16 (2020) 72–81.

[3] G. Acampora, D. Cook, P. Rashidi, A. Vasilakos, A survey on ambient intelligence in healthcare, Proceedings of the IEEE 101 (2013) 2470–2494.

[4] M. Al-khomsan, M.A. Hossain, S.M.M. Rahman, M. Masud, Situation awareness in ambient assisted living for smart healthcare, IEEE Access 5 (2017) 20716–20725.

[5] A. Al-Mahmood, M.O. Agyeman, On wearable devices for motivating patients with upper limb disability via gaming and home rehabilitation, in: 2018 Third International Conference on Fog and Mobile Edge Computing (FMEC), 2018, pp. 155–162.

[6] M. Al-Taee, W. Al-Nuaimy, A. Al-Ataby, Z. Muhsin, S.N. Abood, Mobile health platform for diabetes management based on the internet-of-things, in: 2015 IEEE Jordan Conference on Applied Electrical Engineering and Computing Technologies (AEECT), 2015, pp. 1–5.

[7] A. Albahri, J.k. Alwan, Z. Taha, S.F. Ismail, R.A. Hamid, A. Zaidan, O. Albahri, B. Zaidan, A. Alamoodi, M.A. Alsalem, IoT-based telemedicine for disease prevention and health promotion: state-of-the-art, Journal of Network and Computer Applications 173 (2021) 102873.

[8] O. Albahri, A. Albahri, A. Zaidan, B. Zaidan, M.A. Alsalem, A.H. Mohsin, K.I. Mohammed, A. Alamoodi, S. Nidhal, O. Enaizan, M.A. Chyad, K.H. Abdulkareem, E. Almahdi, G.A.A. Shafeey, M.J. Baqer, A.N.

Jasim, N.S. Jalood, A.H. Shareef, Fault-tolerant mHealth framework in the context of IoT-based real-time wearable health data sensors, IEEE Access 7 (2019) 50052–50080.

[9] S. Alelyani, A. Ibrahim, Internet-of-things in telemedicine for diabetes management, in: 2018 15th Learning and Technology Conference (L&T), 2018, pp. 20–23.

[10] S. Ali, M.G. Kibria, M. Jarwar, S. Kumar, I. Chong, Microservices model in woo based IoT platform for depressive disorder assistance, in: 2017 International Conference on Information and Communication Technology Convergence (ICTC), 2017, pp. 864–866.

[11] E. Almeida, M. Ferruzca, M. del Pilar Morales Tlapanco, Design of a system for early detection and treatment of depression in elderly case study, in: MindCare, 2014.

[12] M. Aminu, N.A. Ahmad, M.H. Mohd Noor, Covid-19 detection via deep neural network and occlusion sensitivity maps, Alexandria Engineering Journal 60 (5) (2021) 4829–4855.

[13] R. Ani, S. Krishna, N. Anju, M. Aslam, O. Deepa, IoT based patient monitoring and diagnostic prediction tool using ensemble classifier, in: 2017 International Conference on Advances in Computing, Communications and Informatics (ICACCI), 2017, pp. 1588–1593.

[14] P. Arulanthu, E. Perumal, An intelligent IoT with cloud centric medical decision support system for chronic kidney disease prediction, International Journal of Imaging Systems and Technology 30 (2020) 815–827.

[15] A. Bagula, M. Mandava, H. Bagula, A framework for healthcare support in the rural and low income areas of the developing world, Journal of Network and Computer Applications 120 (2018) 17–29.

[16] O. Baños, C. Villalonga, M. Damas, P. Gloesekoetter, H. Pomares, I. Rojas, PhysioDroid: combining wearable health sensors and mobile devices for a ubiquitous, continuous, and personal monitoring, The Scientific World Journal 2014 (2014).

[17] J.J.R. Barata, R. Muñoz, R.D.D.C. Silva, J. Rodrigues, V.H.C. de Albuquerque, Internet of things based on electronic and mobile health systems for blood glucose continuous monitoring and management, IEEE Access 7 (2019) 175116–175125.

[18] L. Berbakov, B. Pavkovic, V. Marković, M. Svetel, Architecture and partial implementation of the remote monitoring platform for patients with movement disorders, in: 2017 Zooming Innovation in Consumer Electronics International Conference (ZINC), 2017, pp. 22–25.

[19] J. Berrocal, J. García-Alonso, J.M. Murillo, D. Mendes, C. Fonseca, M. Lopes, Context-aware mobile app for the multidimensional assessment of the elderly, in: 2018 13th Iberian Conference on Information Systems and Technologies (CISTI), 2018, pp. 1–6.

[20] D. Bilic, T. Uzunovic, E. Golubovic, B.C. Ustundag, Internet of things-based system for physical rehabilitation monitoring, in: 2017 XXVI International Conference on Information, Communication and Automation Technologies (ICAT), 2017, pp. 1–6.

[21] I. Bisio, A. Delfino, F. Lavagetto, A. Sciarrone, Enabling IoT for in-home rehabilitation: accelerometer signals classification methods for activity and movement recognition, IEEE Internet of Things Journal 4 (2017) 135–146.

[22] D. Borthakur, H. Dubey, N. Constant, L. Mahler, K. Mankodiya, Smart fog: fog computing framework for unsupervised clustering analytics in wearable internet of things, in: 2017 IEEE Global Conference on Signal and Information Processing (GlobalSIP), 2017, pp. 472–476.

[23] D.M. Castro, W.C. Cuellar, C. Rodriguez, J. Cabra, J. Colorado, Wearable-based human activity recognition using an IoT approach, Journal of Sensor and Actuator Networks 6 (2017) 28.

[24] S.-H. Chae, D. Moon, D.-G. Lee, S. Pan, Medical image segmentation for mobile electronic patient charts using numerical modeling of IoT, Journal of Applied Mathematics 2014 (2014) 815039.

[25] P. Chatterjee, L. Cymberknop, R. Armentano, IoT-based decision support system for intelligent healthcare — applied to cardiovascular diseases, in: 2017 7th International Conference on Communication Systems and Network Technologies (CSNT), 2017, pp. 362–366.

[26] A. Choi, S. Noh, H. Shin, Internet-based unobtrusive tele-monitoring system for sleep and respiration, IEEE Access 8 (2020) 76700–76707.

[27] V. Choudhari, V. Dandge, N. Choudhary, R. Sutar, A portable and low-cost 12-lead ECG device for sustainable remote healthcare, in: 2018 International Conference on Communication Information and Computing Technology (ICCICT), 2018, pp. 1–6.

[28] C.E. Coltart, L. Collet-Fenson, Future developments in the prevention, diagnosis and treatment of Covid-19, in: Best Practice & Research Clinical Obstetrics & Gynaecology, 2021.

[29] H. Djelouat, H. Baali, A. Amira, F. Bensaali, IoT based compressive sensing for ECG monitoring, in: 2017 IEEE International Conference on Internet of Things (iThings) and IEEE Green Computing and Communications (GreenCom) and IEEE Cyber, Physical and Social Computing (CPSCom) and IEEE Smart Data (SmartData), 2017, pp. 183–189.

[30] H. Djelouat, H. Baali, A. Amira, F. Bensaali, Joint sparsity recovery for compressive sensing based EEG system, in: 2017 IEEE 17th International Conference on Ubiquitous Wireless Broadband (ICUWB), 2017, pp. 1–5.

[31] C. Dobre, F. Xhafa, NoSQL technologies for real time (patient) monitoring, in: Healthcare Ethics and Training: Concepts, Methodologies, Tools, and Applications, 03 2017, pp. 1112–1140.

[32] M. Domingues, N. Alberto, C. Leitão, C. Tavares, E.R. de Lima, A. Radwan, V. Sucasas, J. Rodriguez, P. André, P. Antunes, Insole optical fiber sensor architecture for remote gait analysis—an e-health solution, IEEE Internet of Things Journal 6 (2019) 207–214.

[33] A. Dragulinescu, A.F. Manea, O. Fratu, Lora-based medical IoT system architecture and testbed, Wireless Personal Communications (2020) 1–23.

[34] L.A. Durán-Vega, P.C. Santana-Mancilla, R. Buenrostro-Mariscal, J. Contreras-Castillo, L. Anido-Rifón, M.A. García-Ruiz, O. Montesinos-López, F. Estrada-González, An IoT system for remote health monitoring in elderly adults through a wearable device and mobile application, Geriatrics 4 (2019).

[35] I.K.A. Enriko, M. Suryanegara, D. Gunawan, My Kardio: a telemedicine system based on machine-to-machine (M2M) technology for cardiovascular patients in rural areas with auto-diagnosis feature using k-nearest neighbor algorithm, in: 2018 IEEE International Conference on Industrial Technology (ICIT), 2018, pp. 1775–1780.

[36] Y. Fan, P. Xu, H. Jin, J. Ma, L. Qin, Vital sign measurement in telemedicine rehabilitation based on intelligent wearable medical devices, IEEE Access 7 (2019) 54819–54823.

[37] Y. Fang, C. Li, L. Sun, Design of an early warning system for patients with cardiovascular diseases under mobile environment, in: KES, 2016.

[38] H. Fouad, H. Farouk, Heart rate sensor node analysis for designing internet of things telemedicine embedded system, Cogent Engineering 4 (2017).

[39] H. Fouad, N.M. Mahmoud, M.S.E. Issawi, H. Al-Feel, Distributed and scalable computing framework for improving request processing of wearable IoT assisted medical sensors on pervasive computing system, Computer Communications 151 (2020) 257–265.

[40] N. Fung, V. Jones, I. Widya, T.H.F. Broens, N. Larburu, R. Bults, E. Shalom, H. Hermens, The conceptual made framework for pervasive and knowledge-based decision support in telemedicine, International Journal of Knowledge and Systems Sciences 7 (2016) 25–39.

[41] A. Garai, I. Pentek, A. Adamkó, A. Nemeth, A clinical system integration methodology for bio-sensory technology with cloud architecture, Acta Cybernetica 23 (2017) 513–536.

[42] L. García, J. Tomás, L. Parra, J. Lloret, An m-health application for cerebral stroke detection and monitoring using cloud services, International Journal of Information Management 45 (2019) 319–327.

[43] A. Ghani, Healthcare electronics - a step closer to future smart cities, ICT Express 5 (2019) 256–260.

[44] T.N. Gia, M. Ali, I. Dhaou, A. Rahmani, T. Westerlund, P. Liljeberg, H. Tenhunen, IoT-based continuous glucose monitoring system: a feasibility study, in: ANT/SEIT, 2017.

[45] T.N. Gia, M. Jiang, V. Sarker, A. Rahmani, T. Westerlund, P. Liljeberg, H. Tenhunen, Low-cost fog-assisted health-care IoT system with energy-efficient sensor nodes, in: 2017 13th International Wireless Communications and Mobile Computing Conference (IWCMC), 2017, pp. 1765–1770.

[46] T.N. Gia, A. Rahmani, T. Westerlund, P. Liljeberg, H. Tenhunen, Fault tolerant and scalable IoT-based architecture for health monitoring, in: 2015 IEEE Sensors Applications Symposium (SAS), 2015, pp. 1–6.

[47] L. Greco, P. Ritrovato, F. Xhafa, An edge-stream computing infrastructure for real-time analysis of wearable sensors data, Future Generations Computer Systems 93 (2019) 515–528.

[48] K. Guo, T. Li, R. Huang, J. Kang, T. Chi, DDA: a deep neural network-based cognitive system for IoT-aided dermatosis discrimination, Ad Hoc Networks 80 (2018) 95–103.

[49] P.K. Gupta, P. Muhuri, A novel approach based on computing with words for monitoring the heart failure patients, Applied Soft Computing 72 (2018) 457–473.

[50] M.K. Hassan, A. El-Desouky, S.M. El-Ghamrawy, A. Sarhan, Intelligent hybrid remote patient-monitoring model with cloud-based framework for knowledge discovery, Computers & Electrical Engineering 70 (2018) 1034–1048.

[51] M.K. Hassan, A. El-Desouky, S.M. El-Ghamrawy, A. Sarhan, A hybrid real-time remote monitoring framework with NB-WOA algorithm for patients with chronic diseases, Future Generations Computer Systems 93 (2019) 77–95.

[52] H.B. Hassen, W. Dghais, B. Hamdi, An e-health system for monitoring elderly health based on internet of things and fog computing, Health Information Science and Systems 7 (2019) 1–9.

[53] N. Hayati, M. Suryanegara, The IoT LoRa system design for tracking and monitoring patient with mental disorder, in: 2017 IEEE International Conference on Communication, Networks and Satellite (Comnetsat), 2017, pp. 135–139.

[54] J. Hong, J. Yoon, Multivariate time-series classification of sleep patterns using a hybrid deep learning architecture, in: 2017 IEEE 19th International Conference on e-Health Networking, Applications and Services (Healthcom), 2017, pp. 1–6.

[55] M. Hossain, M. Ghulam, Cloud-assisted industrial internet of things (IIoT) - enabled framework for health monitoring, Computer Networks 101 (2016) 192–202.

[56] S. Howard, A. Lang, S. Sharples, D. Shaw, See I told you I was taking it! - Attitudes of adolescents with asthma towards a device monitoring their inhaler use: implications for future design, Applied Ergonomics 58 (2017) 224–237.

[57] C. Hsu, A. Inomata, S.M.M. Rahman, F. Xhafa, L.T. Yang, Security, privacy, and applications in mobile healthcare, International Journal of Distributed Sensor Networks 11 (2015) 675129.

[58] T. Ivascu, B. Manate, V. Negru, A multi-agent architecture for ontology-based diagnosis of mental disorders, in: 2015 17th International Symposium on Symbolic and Numeric Algorithms for Scientific Computing (SYNASC), 2015, pp. 423–430.

[59] J. Jebadurai, J. Peter, Super-resolution of retinal images using multi-kernel SVR for IoT healthcare applications, Future Generations Computer Systems 83 (2018) 338–346.

[60] Y. Jiang, Y. Qin, I. Kim, Y. Wang, Towards an IoT-based upper limb rehabilitation assessment system, in: Proceedings of the Annual International Conference of the IEEE Engineering in Medicine and Biology Society, 2017, pp. 2414–2417.

[61] P. Kakria, N. Tripathi, P. Kitipawang, A real-time health monitoring system for remote cardiac patients using smartphone and wearable sensors, International Journal of Telemedicine and Applications 2015 (2015).

[62] M. Kamel, L. George, Remote patient tracking and monitoring system, 2014.

[63] C. Kan, F. Leonelli, H. Yang, Map reduce for optimizing a large-scale dynamic network — the internet of hearts, in: 2016 38th Annual International Conference of the IEEE Engineering in Medicine and Biology Society (EMBC), 2016, pp. 2962–2965.

[64] J.J. Kang, T.H. Luan, H. Larkin, Enhancement of sensor data transmission by inference and efficient data processing, in: ATIS, 2016.

[65] B. Kim, A distributed coexistence mitigation scheme for IoT-based smart medical systems, Journal of Information Processing Systems 13 (2017) 1602–1612.

[66] D. Korzun, A. Borodin, I. Timofeev, I. Paramonov, S. Balandin, Digital assistance services for emergency situations in personalized mobile healthcare: smart space based approach, in: 2015 International Conference on Biomedical Engineering and Computational Technologies (SIBIRCON), 2015, pp. 62–67.

[67] A. Kos, A. Umek, Wearable sensor devices for prevention and rehabilitation in healthcare: swimming exercise with real-time therapist feedback, IEEE Internet of Things Journal 6 (2019) 1331–1341.

[68] K.D. Krishna, V. Akkala, R. Bharath, P. Rajalakshmi, A.M. Mohammed, S. Merchant, U. Desai, Computer aided abnormality detection for kidney on FPGA based IoT enabled portable ultrasound imaging system, IRBM 37 (2016) 189–197.

[69] P.M. Kumar, S. Lokesh, R. Varatharajan, G.C. Babu, P. Panchatcharam, Cloud and IoT based disease prediction and diagnosis system for healthcare using fuzzy neural classifier, Future Generations Computer Systems 86 (2018) 527–534.

[70] P. Kumari, M. López-Benítez, G. Lee, T.-S. Kim, A. Minhas, Wearable internet of things - from human activity tracking to clinical integration, in: 2017 39th Annual International Conference of the IEEE Engineering in Medicine and Biology Society (EMBC), 2017, pp. 2361–2364.

[71] A. Kuusik, M. Alam, T. Kask, K. Gross-Paju, Wearable m-assessment system for neurological disease patients, in: 2018 IEEE 4th World Forum on Internet of Things (WF-IoT), 2018, pp. 201–206.

[72] K.N. Lal, A. Kumar, E-health application over 5G using content-centric networking (CCN), in: 2017 International Conference on IoT and Application (ICIOT), 2017, pp. 1–5.

[73] C. Li, X. Hu, L. Zhang, The IoT-based heart disease monitoring system for pervasive healthcare service, in: KES, 2017.

[74] C.-T. Lin, M. Prasad, C.-H. Chung, D. Puthal, H. El-Sayed, S. Sankar, Y.-K. Wang, J. Singh, A.K. Sangaiah, IoT-based wireless polysomnography intelligent system for sleep monitoring, IEEE Access 6 (2018) 405–414.

[75] T. Lin, P. yu Liu, C. Lin, Home healthcare matching service system using the internet of things, Mobile Networks and Applications 24 (2019) 736–747.

[76] C. Liu, X. Zhang, L. Zhao, F. Liu, X. Chen, Y. Yao, J. Li, Signal quality assessment and lightweight QRS detection for wearable ECG smartvest system, IEEE Internet of Things Journal 6 (2019) 1363–1374.

[77] M. Mahmud, H. Fang, H. Wang, An integrated wearable sensor for unobtrusive continuous measurement of autonomic nervous system, IEEE Internet of Things Journal 6 (2019) 1104–1113.

[78] A. Masood, B. Sheng, P. Li, X. Hou, X. Wei, J. Qin, D. Feng, Computer-assisted decision support system in pulmonary cancer detection and stage classification on ct images, Journal of Biomedical Informatics 79 (2018) 117–128.

[79] Q.-U.-A. Mastoi, T.Y. Wah, R.G. Raj, A. Lakhan, A novel cost-efficient framework for critical heartbeat task scheduling using the internet of medical things in a fog cloud system, Sensors (Basel, Switzerland) 20 (2020).

[80] T. Mcallister, S. El-Tawab, M. Heydari, Localization of health center assets through an IoT environment (locate), in: 2017 Systems and Information Engineering Design Symposium (SIEDS), 2017, pp. 132–137.

[81] A. Mdhaffar, T. Chaari, K. Larbi, M. Jmaiel, B. Freisleben, IoT-based health monitoring via LoRaWAN, in: IEEE EUROCON 2017 - 17th International Conference on Smart Technologies, 2017, pp. 519–524.

[82] A. Mdhaffar, I.B. Rodriguez, K. Charfi, L. Abid, B. Freisleben, CEP4HFP: complex event processing for heart failure prediction, IEEE Transactions on Nanobioscience 16 (2017) 708–717.

[83] J. Miranda, J. Cabral, S. Wagner, C.F. Pedersen, B. Ravelo, M. Memon, M. Mathiesen, An open platform for seamless sensor support in healthcare for the internet of things, Sensors (Basel, Switzerland) 16 (2016).

[84] F. Mohamedali, N. Matoorian, Support dementia: using wearable assistive technology and analysing real-time data, in: 2016 International Conference on Interactive Technologies and Games (ITAG), 2016, pp. 50–54.

[85] J. Mohammed, C.-H. Lung, A. Ocneanu, A. Thakral, C. Jones, A. Adler, Internet of things: remote patient monitoring using web services and cloud computing, in: 2014 IEEE International Conference on Internet of

Things (iThings), and IEEE Green Computing and Communications (GreenCom) and IEEE Cyber, Physical and Social Computing (CPSCom), 2014, pp. 256–263.

[86] P. Moore, T. Qassem, F. Xhafa, 'NoSQL' and electronic patient record systems: opportunities and challenges, in: 2014 Ninth International Conference on P2P, Parallel, Grid, Cloud and Internet Computing, Guangdong, China, November 8–10, 2014, IEEE Computer Society, 2014, pp. 300–307.

[87] M.W.L. Moreira, J. Rodrigues, N. Kumar, K. Saleem, I.V. Illin, Postpartum depression prediction through pregnancy data analysis for emotion-aware smart systems, Information Fusion 47 (2019) 23–31.

[88] D. Mrozek, A. Koczur, B. Małysiak-Mrozek, Fall detection in older adults with mobile IoT devices and machine learning in the cloud and on the edge, Information Sciences 537 (2020) 132–147.

[89] C. Nadrag, V. Poenaru, G. Suciu, Heart rate measurement using face detection in video, in: 2018 International Conference on Communications (COMM), 2018, pp. 131–134.

[90] F. Nasri, N. Moussa, A. Mtibaa, Internet of things: intelligent system for healthcare based on WSN and Android, in: 2014 World Congress on Computer Applications and Information Systems (WCCAIS), 2014, pp. 1–6.

[91] S. Nataraja, P. Nataraja, IoT based application for e-health an improvisation for lateral rotation, in: 2017 2nd IEEE International Conference on Recent Trends in Electronics, Information & Communication Technology (RTEICT), 2017, pp. 1018–1021.

[92] J. Navarro, F. Doctor, V. Zamudio, R. Iqbal, A.K. Sangaiah, C. Lino, Fuzzy adaptive cognitive stimulation therapy generation for Alzheimer's sufferers: towards a pervasive dementia care monitoring platform, Future Generations Computer Systems 88 (2018) 479–490.

[93] M. Neyja, S. Mumtaz, K.M.S. Huq, S.A. Busari, J. Rodriguez, Z. Zhou, An IoT-based e-health monitoring system using ECG signal, in: GLOBECOM 2017 - 2017 IEEE Global Communications Conference, 2017, pp. 1–6.

[94] K.U. Nigam, A.A. Chavan, S.S. Ghatule, V. Barkade, IoT-beat: an intelligent nurse for the cardiac patient, in: 2016 International Conference on Communication and Signal Processing (ICCSP), 2016, pp. 0976–0982.

[95] M. Nurdin, S. Hadiyoso, A. Rizal, A low-cost internet of things (IoT) system for multi-patient ECG's monitoring, in: 2016 International Conference on Control, Electronics, Renewable Energy and Communications (ICCEREC), 2016, pp. 7–11.

[96] A.T. Özdemir, C. Tunc, S. Hariri, Autonomic fall detection system, in: 2017 IEEE 2nd International Workshops on Foundations and Applications of Self* Systems (FAS*W), 2017, pp. 166–170.

[97] H. Ozkan, O. Ozhan, Y. Karadana, M. Gulcu, S. Macit, F. Husain, A portable wearable tele-ECG monitoring system, IEEE Transactions on Instrumentation and Measurement 69 (2020) 173–182.

[98] R. Pathak, V. Vaidehi, Complex event processing based remote health monitoring system, in: 2014 3rd International Conference on Eco-Friendly Computing and Communication Systems, 2014, pp. 61–66.

[99] R.K. Pathinarupothi, P. Durga, E. Rangan, IoT-based smart edge for global health: remote monitoring with severity detection and alerts transmission, IEEE Internet of Things Journal 6 (2019) 2449–2462.

[100] E. Patti, M. Donatelli, E. Macii, A. Acquaviva, IoT software infrastructure for remote monitoring of patients with chronic metabolic disorders, in: 2018 IEEE 6th International Conference on Future Internet of Things and Cloud (FiCloud), 2018, pp. 311–317.

[101] L. Pepa, M. Capecci, F. Verdini, M. Ceravolo, L. Spalazzi, An architecture to manage motor disorders in Parkinson's disease, in: 2015 IEEE 2nd World Forum on Internet of Things (WF-IoT), 2015, pp. 615–620.

[102] D. Perez, S. Memeti, S. Pllana, A simulation study of a smart living IoT solution for remote elderly care, in: 2018 Third International Conference on Fog and Mobile Edge Computing (FMEC), 2018, pp. 227–232.

[103] N. Petrellis, M. Birbas, F. Gioulekas, On the design of low-cost IoT sensor node for e-health environments, Electronics 8 (2019) 178.

[104] L. Plant, B. Noriega, A. Sonti, N. Constant, K. Mankodiya, Smart e-textile gloves for quantified measurements in movement disorders, in: 2016 IEEE MIT Undergraduate Research Technology Conference (URTC), 2016, pp. 1–4.

[105] M. Pustisek, A system for multi-domain contextualization of personal health data, Journal of Medical Systems 41 (2016) 1–6.

[106] M. Raad, T. Sheltami, E. Shakshuki, Ubiquitous tele-health system for elderly patients with Alzheimer's, in: ANT/SEIT, 2015.

[107] S. Raj, An efficient IoT-based platform for remote real-time cardiac activity monitoring, IEEE Transactions on Consumer Electronics 66 (2020) 106–114.

[108] P. Ritrovato, F. Xhafa, A. Giordano, Edge and cluster computing as enabling infrastructure for internet of medical things, in: L. Barolli, M. Takizawa, T. Enokido, M.R. Ogiela, L. Ogiela, N. Javaid (Eds.), 32nd IEEE International Conference on Advanced Information Networking and Applications, AINA 2018, Krakow, Poland, May 16–18, 2018, IEEE Computer Society, 2018, pp. 717–723.

[109] M.I. Rizqyawan, M. Amri, R. Pratama, A. Turnip, Design and development of Android-based cloud ECG monitoring system, in: 2016 3rd International Conference on Information Technology, Computer, and Electrical Engineering (ICITACEE), 2016, pp. 1–5.

[110] M. Rossi, A. Rizzi, L. Lorenzelli, D. Brunelli, Remote rehabilitation monitoring with an IoT-enabled embedded system for precise progress tracking, in: 2016 IEEE International Conference on Electronics, Circuits and Systems (ICECS), 2016, pp. 384–387.

[111] R. Sandhu, H.K. Gill, S. Sood, Smart monitoring and controlling of pandemic influenza a (H1N1) using social network analysis and cloud computing, Journal of Computational Science 12 (2016) 11–22.

[112] S. Sareen, S. Sood, S. Gupta, IoT-based cloud framework to control Ebola virus outbreak, Journal of Ambient Intelligence and Humanized Computing 9 (2018) 459–476.

[113] N. Semwal, M. Mukherjee, C. Raj, W. Arif, An IoT based smart e-health care system, Journal of Information and Optimization Sciences 40 (2019) 1787–1800.

[114] M.A. Serhani, M. El-Menshawy, A. Benharref, S. Harous, A.N. Navaz, New algorithms for processing time-series big EEG data within mobile health monitoring systems, Computer Methods and Programs in Biomedicine 149 (2017) 79–94.

[115] S. Sood, I. Mahajan, Wearable IoT sensor based healthcare system for identifying and controlling Chikungunya virus, Computers in Industry 91 (2017) 33–44.

[116] S. Sood, I. Mahajan, A fog-based healthcare framework for Chikungunya, IEEE Internet of Things Journal 5 (2018) 794–801.

[117] S. Sood, I. Mahajan, Fog-cloud based cyber-physical system for distinguishing, detecting and preventing mosquito borne diseases, Future Generations Computer Systems 88 (2018) 764–775.

[118] S. Sood, I. Mahajan, IoT-fog-based healthcare framework to identify and control hypertension attack, IEEE Internet of Things Journal 6 (2019) 1920–1927.

[119] E. Spano, S.D. Pascoli, G. Iannaccone, Low-power wearable ECG monitoring system for multiple-patient remote monitoring, IEEE Sensors Journal 16 (2016) 5452–5462.

[120] S. Stipkovic, R. Bruns, J. Dunkel, Pervasive computing by mobile complex event processing, in: 2013 IEEE 10th International Conference on e-Business Engineering, 2013, pp. 318–323.

[121] A. Subasi, M. Radhwan, R. Kurdi, K. Khateeb, IoT based mobile healthcare system for human activity recognition, in: 2018 15th Learning and Technology Conference (L&T), 2018, pp. 29–34.

[122] N.E. Tabbakha, W. Tan, C. Ooi, Indoor location and motion tracking system for elderly assisted living home, in: 2017 International Conference on Robotics, Automation and Sciences (ICORAS), 2017, pp. 1–4.

[123] B. Tan, A. Burrows, R. Piechocki, I. Craddock, Q. Chen, K. Woodbridge, K. Chetty, Wi-fi based passive human motion sensing for in-home healthcare applications, in: 2015 IEEE 2nd World Forum on Internet of Things (WF-IoT), 2015, pp. 609–614.

[124] B. Tan, O. Tian, Short paper: using BSN for tele-health application in upper limb rehabilitation, in: 2014 IEEE World Forum on Internet of Things (WF-IoT), 2014, pp. 169–170.

[125] I. Ungurean, A. Brezulianu, An internet of things framework for remote monitoring of the healthcare parameters, Advances in Electrical and Computer Engineering 17 (2017) 11–16.

[126] A. Veiga, L. García, L. Parra, J. Lloret, V. Augele, An IoT-based smart pillow for sleep quality monitoring in AAL environments, in: 2018 Third International Conference on Fog and Mobile Edge Computing (FMEC), 2018, pp. 175–180.

[127] D. Venuto, V. Annese, A. Sangiovanni-Vincentelli, The ultimate IoT application: a cyber-physical system for ambient assisted living, in: 2016 IEEE International Symposium on Circuits and Systems (ISCAS), 2016, pp. 2042–2045.

[128] P. Verma, S. Sood, H. Kaur, A fog-cloud based cyber physical system for ulcerative colitis diagnosis and stage classification and management, Microprocessors and Microsystems 72 (2020).

[129] V. Vijayakumar, D. Malathi, V. Subramaniyaswamy, P. Saravanan, R. Logesh, Fog computing-based intelligent healthcare system for the detection and prevention of mosquito-borne diseases, Computers in Human Behavior 100 (2019) 275–285.

[130] S. Vukićević, Z. Stamenkovic, S. Murugesan, Z. Bogdanović, B. Radenkovic, A new telerehabilitation system based on internet of things, Facta Universitatis. Series: Electronics and Energetics 29 (2016) 395–405.

[131] A. Walinjkar, J. Woods, ECG classification and prognostic approach towards personalized healthcare, in: 2017 International Conference on Social Media, Wearable and Web Analytics (Social Media), 2017, pp. 1–8.

[132] X.A. Wang, J. Ma, F. Xhafa, M. Zhang, X. Luo, Cost-effective secure e-health cloud system using identity based cryptographic techniques, Future Generations Computer Systems 67 (2017) 242–254.

[133] A. Winterlich, I. Stevenson, A. Waldren, T. Dawson, Diabetes digital coach: developing an infrastructure for e-health self-management tools, in: 2016 9th International Conference on Developments in eSystems Engineering (DeSE), 2016, pp. 68–73.

[134] D.-Z. Wu, C.-C. Sun, K.-W. Chun, Y. Lin, Y. Lin, System integration of LOMB HRV analysis using PPG sensor based on LoRaWAN IoT, in: 2017 IEEE/SICE International Symposium on System Integration (SII), 2017, pp. 493–498.

[135] S.-J. Wu, R. Chiang, S. Chang, W.-T. Chang, An interactive telecare system enhanced with IoT technology, IEEE Pervasive Computing 16 (2017) 62–69.

[136] F. Xhafa, J. Feng, Y. Zhang, X. Chen, J. Li, Privacy-aware attribute-based PHR sharing with user accountability in cloud computing, Journal of Supercomputing 71 (5) (2015) 1607–1619.

[137] F. Xhafa, J. Li, G. Zhao, J. Li, X. Chen, D.S. Wong, Designing cloud-based electronic health record system with attribute-based encryption, Multimedia Tools and Applications 74 (10) (2015) 3441–3458.

[138] F. Xhafa, T. Qassem, P. Moore, Collaboration through patient data access and sharing in the cloud, in: F. Xhafa, L. Barolli, F. Palmieri, M. Koeppen, V. Loia (Eds.), 2014 International Conference on Intelligent Networking and Collaborative Systems, Salerno, Italy, September 10–12, 2014, IEEE, 2014, pp. 205–212.

[139] F. Xhafa, J. Wang, X. Chen, J.K. Liu, J. Li, P. Krause, An efficient PHR service system supporting fuzzy keyword search and fine-grained access control, Soft Computing 18 (9) (2014) 1795–1802.

[140] Y. Xiang, Y. Jia, L. Chen, L. Guo, B. Shu, E. Long, Covid-19 epidemic prediction and the impact of public health interventions: a review of Covid-19 epidemic models, Infectious Disease Modelling 6 (2021) 324–342.

[141] G. Xu, Y. Peng, W. Che, Y. Lan, W. Zhou, C. Huang, W. Li, W. Zhang, G. Zhang, E. Ng, Y. Cheng, An IoT-based framework of Webvr visualization for medical big data in connected health, IEEE Access 7 (2019) 173866–173874.

[142] G. Yang, L. Xie, M. Mäntysalo, X. Zhou, Z. Pang, L. Xu, S. Kao-Walter, Q. Chen, L. Zheng, A health-IoT platform based on the integration of intelligent packaging, unobtrusive bio-sensor, and intelligent medicine box, IEEE Transactions on Industrial Informatics 10 (2014) 2180–2191.

[143] H. Yu, Research and optimization of sports injury medical system under the background of internet of things, Transactions on Emerging Telecommunications Technologies 31 (2020).

[144] I. Zagan, V. Gaitan, N. Iuga, A. Brezulianu, m-GreenCARDIO embedded system designed for out-of-hospital cardiac patients, in: 2018 International Conference on Development and Application Systems (DAS), 2018, pp. 11–17.

[145] I. Zagan, V. Gaitan, A. Petrariu, A. Brezulianu, Healthcare IoT m-GreenCARDIO remote cardiac monitoring system - concept, theory of operation and implementation, Advances in Electrical and Computer Engineering 17 (2017) 23–30.

[146] P. Zhang, D. Schmidt, J. White, S. Mulvaney, Towards precision behavioral medicine with IoT: iterative design and optimization of a self-management tool for type 1 diabetes, in: 2018 IEEE International Conference on Healthcare Informatics (ICHI), 2018, pp. 64–74.

[147] Z. Zhang, Y. Zhang, L. Yao, H. Song, A. Kos, A sensor-based wrist pulse signal processing and lung cancer recognition, Journal of Biomedical Informatics 79 (2018) 107–116.

[148] C.Y. Zheng, J. Yunus, The accessibility, affordability, and availability of long-term monitoring system for children with movement disorders — proposed development the Malaysian context & opportunities, in: 2016 IEEE EMBS Conference on Biomedical Engineering and Sciences (IECBES), 2016, pp. 774–779.

[149] Z. Zhong, Z. Fan, F. Cao, Basket based sorting method for activity recognition in smart environments, in: 2018 IEEE 4th World Forum on Internet of Things (WF-IoT), 2018, pp. 161–166.

[150] X. Zou, Prototype design of a remote medical monitoring system based on the internet of things, International Journal of Online Engineering 12 (2016) 50–57.

IoT, edge, cloud architecture and communication protocols

7

Cloud digital ecosystem and protocols

7.1 IoT architecture

Current mobile network architectures already face challenges in managing the size and rate of generated data. In many implementations of Cloud-based applications, data is sent to Cloud data centers [42], which comes with several drawbacks.

Moving data from the IoT sources to the Cloud might not be efficient or even infeasible in many cases due to bandwidth limitations. Further, time-sensitive, or location-aware applications, have demanding requirements of ultra-low latency in which a distant Cloud processing will not offer an option [63] to cope with. Furthermore, privacy concerns over user-data generated at the edges of the Internet to Cloud services represent a significant challenge.

To address the issues of high-bandwidth, geographically-aware, ultra-low latency, and privacy-sensitive applications, a modern computing paradigm located closer to the source where data is generated, and thus, closer to the uses, has been proposed. Fog and Edge computing address some issues by enabling computing, storage, networking, and data management close to IoT devices [5]. Other emerging computing paradigms are mist computing or cloudlets, which also support addressing these challenges. A visualization of the different computing paradigms mentioned in this chapter can be seen in Fig. 7.1.

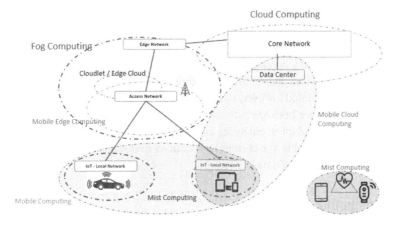

FIGURE 7.1

Overview of Cloud computing ecosystem paradigms. Reduced version of [62].

Anomaly Detection and Complex Event Processing Over IoT Data Streams. https://doi.org/10.1016/B978-0-12-823818-9.00018-3

Edge computing systems distinguish between "disposable data" and "critical data". IoT-capable devices produce large amounts of data with their sensors. With this, the Edge platform acts as a hyperresponsive mediator layer between cyber-physical systems and the data center. The prioritization of data transfer can occur on the spot, and therefore in real-time with minimal network load. The Fog platform is a system-level Edge-computing architectural pattern, with specialized gateways and other Fog nodes. The Edge computing model processes the data directly on the end devices themselves. Devices as small as Raspberry Pi or Arduino can handle data processing for a wide range of "smart" IoT endpoints-but their performance is barely scalable, and their availability is hardly guaranteed.

7.2 Decentralized architecture paradigms

In this section, we highlight the main architecture paradigms in Cloud digital ecosystem.

Fog computing

Fog Computing implements a decentralized Computing infrastructure based on Fog Computing Nodes (FCN) placed between end-devices and a central system. FCNs are heterogeneous and are based on different types of hardware, including routers, switches, and access points.

Mobile computing

The development of mobile computing, performed via mobile or portable devices, influences Fog and Cloud computing advancement. Mobile computing can be used to create context-aware applications, such as location-based reminders. Mobile computing holds the vision for adaptation in an environment of low processing power and sparse network connectivity. Using mobile computing solely is not suitable for many modern IoT use cases due to the evolving requirements of connected devices. Fog and Cloud computing enables computing outside of the local network and expands mobile computing's scope and scale. Mobile computing requires only mobile devices, which can be connected through WiFi, Bluetooth, and other cellular protocols.

Compared to Fog and cloud computing, mobile computing is more resource-constrained. Distributed applications benefit from the distributed mobile computing architecture because devices do not require a centralized location. However, mobile computing also has drawbacks, such as significant resource constraints, the balance between autonomy and interdependence, communication latency, and the need for mobile clients to adapt to changing environments efficiently [48]. These drawbacks often make mobile computing unsuitable for current applications that require low latency or robustness or the need to handle large amounts of data.

Mobile edge computing

Mobile Edge Computing (MEC) can be considered an Edge computing implementation that brings computational and storage to the edges of the network to improve context awareness and reduce latency. The MEC servers are often colocated within the Radio Network Controller or base stations. MEC offers real-time information on the network while providing information about connected devices, like location information.

Mobile Cloud Computing (MCC)

As Cloud computing technologies matured, MCC became a valuable complement to mobile computing. The data storage and data processing get offloaded outside of the mobile device [13]. MCC applications include healthcare and many other applications based on sensor data processing and task offloading [44, 47]. An important feature of mobile applications is that they can be partitioned at runtime to adaptively offload computationally intensive components of the application [53]. Resource-constrained mobile devices can leverage cloud resource services. MCC shifts computation from mobile devices to the Cloud, which can also increase the battery life of devices. However, this could introduce connectivity and latency challenges for delay-sensitive applications.

Mobile ad-hoc Cloud Computing (MACC)

The MCC computing paradigm is not always applicable for scenarios in which there is a deficit of infrastructure or a centralized Cloud. MACC consists of nodes that form a dynamic network and represent the most decentralized form of networks [27]. Mobile devices build a dynamic network topology, where the devices continuously join or leave. MACC can include use cases from healthcare and many others such as disaster management or unmanned vehicle systems.

Cloudlet computing

A Cloudlet can be defined as a trusted cluster of nodes with resources available to use for nearby mobile devices [4,49]. Cloudlet computing has similarities with MCC and MEC. Cloudlet nodes are mini clouds that are typically one hop away from mobile devices and provide resources for mobile device offloading mechanism [23]. Operators for cloudlet computing can be Cloud service providers who want their services available close to mobile devices to lower latency and energy consumption on mobile devices. MACC and cloudlet computing support mobility, while MACC is resource-constrained on mobile devices.

Mist computing

Mist computing aims to capture an endpoint edge of connected devices. This computing paradigm describes dispersed computing on the IoT devices and has been proposed with the idea of self-aware and autonomic systems [41]. Mist computing extends with the end device the compute, storage, and networking across the Fog. With these characteristics, mist computing can be considered a superset of MACC since networking may not necessarily be ad-hoc, and the devices may not be mobile devices. Authors in [34] introduced the idea of using mobile devices as a Cloud computing environment for storage and computing. Some advantages of Mist computing are to preserve the privacy of user data by local processing and analysis [46].

Micro data centers

Microsoft Research introduced micro Data Centers (MDC) as an alternative and complement to existing large Cloud data centers. They are similar to Cloudlets in that MDC offers computation, storage, and networking components. Also likewise, MCD supports an array of applications that require real-time data processing, low latency, and security.

A similar paradigm is Nano Data Centers, which improve the storage function of edge nodes and help to reduce the energy consumption [32,57,25].

Finally, readers can refer to Dew computing, yet another computing paradigm between end-devices and Edge computing aiming to provide more autonomy from upper layers of Cloud-to-thing ecosystem [22,59,36,43].

7.3 IoT architecture components

An IoT architecture can be generalized with the following components.

Sensing layer

It consists of sensors attached to physical devices. These sensors generate data continuously in a multi-data stream. The generated data from these multiple sensors can be heterogeneous. The sensing layer's primary goal is to identify any state in the device sensor and obtain data.

Ingestion layer

This component acts as a message queue for raw data streams that are pushed from the sensing layer. Multiple sources can continuously push data streams (e.g., sensor or social network data). Such a component must be able to deal with high throughput rates and scale according to the number of sources. One of the key responsibilities is to enable the ingestion of all incoming data. This component does not require any knowledge about the data or schema of incoming data streams. However, for each element, it must know its source and type. To assure fault-tolerance and durability of results in such a distributed environment, techniques such as write-ahead logging or the two-phase commit protocol are used, which impact data availability to the next components.

Stream processing

The Stream Processing component is responsible for performing One-Pass algorithms over the stream of elements. The presence of a summary is required as most of these algorithms leverage in-memory stateful data structures. Such data structures can be leveraged to maintain aggregates over a sliding window for a specific time period. Different processing strategies can be adopted, being the most popular tuple at-a-time and micro-batch processing, the former providing low latency while the latter providing high throughput.

Network layer

The network layer's role is a communication medium to transfer data from the sensing layer to other components. IoT devices use different communication technologies (e.g., WiFi, cellular network).

Processing and actuation layer

The data processing layer consists of the primary data processing unit. The processing layer takes collected data in the sensing layer and processes or analyses the data to make decisions based on the result.

In the following section are illustrated the most popular IoT stream processing infrastructures.

7.4 IoT stream processing infrastructures
Traditional cloud-based processing architecture

This architecture is based on the IoT devices and the upper cloud layer. In this architecture, the IoT devices communicate with the Cloud server via a local area network (LAN), mobile network, or wide area network (WAN). The energy consumption needs to be relatively high to enable uninterrupted performance. Due to this, these IoT devices are often stationary and connected to a continuous power supply. Static IoT sensor provides and consumes data occasionally, such as measuring temperature or controlling access to a door, a small quantity of data is exchanged between the cloud and the IoT device [21]. Issues arise with large quantities of data generated at high speed that need to be transferred to the cloud. Traditional Cloud-based architectures cannot cope with the increased demand for large data transfer. Likewise, this architecture might not support an energy-efficient solution, in the case of wireless IoT devices [21].

Vertical edge processing architecture

The previously presented architectural solution cannot cope with the situation when the Edge device cannot perform the required services, e.g., mobile edge devices with limited resources and wireless connectivity. To reduce or balance energy consumption on IoT devices, the Edge device can distribute/offload the processing task to other devices in the Edge. An architectural solution that supports such offloading is the vertical edge computing architecture. An edge server is on the next hop above the edge device and performs the data storage and complex operations. With this, the load on the edge device is reduced and balanced. This edge server can be in the form of a Raspberry Pi, mini-cloud, cloudlet server, or mobile computing clusters.

Horizontal edge processing architecture

A more promising solution is based on deviceless edge architecture. This architecture does not need the management of edge devices and servers, and offloading is realized horizontally to nearby edge devices [21].

7.5 Criteria for IoT architecture selection

To find the right architecture for an IoT application, several considerations about the environment limitations should be analyzed. A general selection survey could be considered under the following criteria [14]:

1. Proximity: Defines the logical- (how many hops) and physical-distance (actual distance to next layer). The lower proximity as a negative influence on the latency.
2. Access Medium: Access mechanisms are important to determine the bandwidth available to the end devices, the distance of connectivity, and support for different types of devices.
3. Context awareness: Further information about device and environment, like, e.g., the device location or network load.
4. Power consumption: The power consumption is a major contributing factor for resource-constrained end devices. The consumption with e.g., LTE and radio networks is higher than the energy consumption for WiFi [26]. The consumption by accessing Mobile Edge nodes is bigger than the consumption of accessing Cloudlets. On the other hand, Fog Computing allows access to its nodes through access mediums that consume lower energy like BLE.
5. Computation time: defines the required time at the Edge layer for performing the tasks and responding with the desired results. The computation time for MEC and Cloudlet Computing is beneficial due to the virtualized nature and dynamic resource provisioning. However, since the Fog devices are often legacy devices, the processing and storage capacities are lower, leading to higher computation time. In this vein, the RTT parameter (Round Trip Time) can also be considered.

For further reading, refer to the survey about IoT and Cloud computing in healthcare framework in [11].

7.6 Application protocols

In this section, we list the application protocols that are commonly used in different application scenarios.

7.6.1 Constrained Application Protocol (CoAP)

The IETF Constrained RESTful Environments (CoRE) have dealt with Constrained Application Protocol (CoAP), an application-level protocol for IoT applications [52,6].

The CoAP defines a web transfer protocol based on REPResentational State Transfer (REST) based on HTTP functions. REST offers an easier way to exchange data between clients and servers via HTTP. REST can be viewed as a cacheable connection protocol based on a stateless, client-server architecture paradigm and used in mobile and social networking applications. REST enables client and server applications to expose and consume web services with protocols like Simple Object Access Protocol (SOAP). REST does not require Extensible Markup Language (XML) for message exchanges. Unlike REST, CoAP is bound to User Datagram Protocol (UDP). UDP in CoAP makes it more suitable for IoT applications due to the reduced communication overhead and latency. CoAP meets the IoT requirements such as low power consumption and operation with lossy and noisy connections.

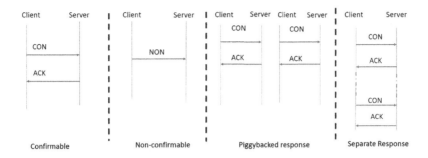

FIGURE 7.2

CoAP message model types.

Since CoAP was developed based on REST, the conversion between these two protocols in REST-CoAP proxies is uncomplicated. The overall functionality of CoAP is shown in 7.2. CoAP aims to enable mini devices with low power consumption, computing, and communication functionalities to utilize RESTful interactions. CoAP can be divided into the messaging and the request/response sublayer. The messaging sublayers function is detecting duplications and provides reliable communication over UDP using a schedule retransmission function called exponential backoff as an error recovery mechanism. The request/response sublayer is responsible for handling REST communication jobs. CoAP utilizes the four types of messages of confirmable, nonconfirmable, reset, and acknowledgment. CoAP realizes reliability with a combination of confirmable and nonconfirmable messages.

The response models can be classified into four models as illustrated in Fig. 7.2:

- Separate response mode: When the server needs to wait for a specific time before replying to the client.
- Nonconfirmable response mode: The client sends data without waiting for an ACK message. The message IDs are used to detect duplicates.
- Confirmable response mode: Server-side responds with a TCP reset message when message loss occurs.
- Piggybacked response mode: Utilizes GET, PUT, POST, and DELETE to achieve Create, Retrieve, Update, and Delete operations. For example, a GET method can be used by a server to inquire the specific client information using the piggybacked response mode. The client sends back the information if it exists; otherwise, it sends a status code containing the information that the requested data is not found.

CoAP uses a lightweight message format to encode messages, containing a fixed header with four bytes length, followed by a token value with a length between zero to eight bytes. The tokenizer is used for coordinating the request and response operations. The next optional fields are the options and payloads. CoAP message can range between 10 to 20 bytes [10].

Important features provided by CoAP include [6,33]:

- Resource observation: On-demand monitoring of resources using a publish-subscribe mechanism.
- Block-wise resource transport: Exchange transceiver data between the client and the server without updating the whole data to reduce the communication overhead.

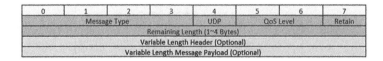

FIGURE 7.3

MQTT message format.

- Resource discovery: Utilization of URI paths based on the web link fields in CoRE link format client resource discovery.
- Interacting with HTTP: Flexible communicating with several devices. The REST architecture enables CoAP to interact with HTTP requests through proxies.
- Security: It is built on top of datagram transport layer security (DTLS) to guarantee exchanged messages' integrity and confidentiality.

7.6.2 Message Queue Telemetry Transport (MQTT)

MQTT is a messaging protocol to connect embedded devices and networks with applications and middleware. The connection operation provides different routing mechanisms (one-to-one, one-to-many, many-to-many). With these features, MQTT is considered an optimal connection protocol in IoT and M2M. MQTT uses the publish-subscribe paradigm to guarantee transition flexibility and a simple implementation and integration task. Due to its lightweight characteristics, MQTT is ideal for resource-constrained devices that have unreliable or low-bandwidth connections.

The two significant MQTT specifications are MQTT v3.1, and MQTT-SN [29] (formerly known as MQTT-S) V1.2. MQTT-SN was explicitly defined for sensor networks and provides a UDP mapping of MQTT and broker support for topic name indexing. The specification contains the three main elements of connection semantics, routing, and endpoint. The main actor components are broker and publisher, subscriber. A device registers as a subscriber for a topic informed by the broker when the topic publishers publish the messages. The publisher acts as a data source for specific topics and transmits the information to subscribers through the broker, where the broker also checks for authorization of the publisher and subscriber [29].

Application fields of MQTT are health care, smart home, remote, and many more, where it represents an ideal messaging protocol for everything related to IoT and M2M communication for routing of low power and low memory devices in uncertain low bandwidth networks.

Fig. 7.3 shows the message format used by the MQTT protocol. MQTT's message format consists of a 2-byte fixed header + a variable header, and a payload. This first 2-byte fixed header will always be present in all the packets, and the other two, variable header and payload, are not always present. The Message Type field indicates the specific message type being used, like CONNECT, CONNICK, PUBLISH, SUBSCRIBE, etc. The DUP flag indicated that the message is duplicated and that the receiver might have received it before. The level of QoS provides the assurance level of the message. The Retain Field: The information for the servers to retain the last received message and submit it to new subscribers as the first message. The Remaining Length contains the information over the remaining length of the variable header + the length of the payload. The Variable Length Header does not exist in

Annotated Message

Bare Message

FIGURE 7.4

AMQP message format.

all MQTT packets. This field is used for commands or messages to provide additional information and flags, and they vary on the packet type. The payload is optional and contains the data.

7.6.3 Extensible Messaging and Presence Protocol (XMPP)

XMPP is an IETF XML-based messaging standard used for multiparty chatting, voice and video calling, telepresence, and file transfer [45]. The Jabber community developed XMPP as a real-time XML streaming protocol. XMPP is a platform-independent communication protocol that gives IM applications the feature of authentication, privacy measurement, access control, hop-by-hop, end-to-end encryption, and compatibility with other protocols. XMPP runs decentralized, where it connects a client to a server using a stream of XML standards. An XML standard is divided into three components: message, presence, and IQ (info/query) [45]. The Message standard identifies the source and destination addresses, types, and IDs of XMPP entities over a push method to retrieve data. A message field fills the subject and body fields with the message title and contents. The presence standard shows and notifies clients of status updates: the IQ standard pairs message senders and receivers. XMPP has a high network overhead due to its text-based communication format, where a compression using EXI can mitigate it [50].

7.6.4 Advanced Message Queuing Protocol (AMQP)

AMQP [38] is an open standard protocol for the IoT application layer that focuses on message-oriented environments. Reliable message communication is provided via at-most-once, at-least-once, and exactly-once deliver, built on top of the TCP protocol. AMQP device implementations can interoperate with each other by defining a wire-level protocol where the communication is handled by the two main components of exchanges and message queues. Exchanges route the messages to the specific queues based on predefined rules and conditions. The messages are stored in the queues and sent to the receivers. Besides the point-to-point communication, AMQP also provides a publish-subscribe model through a messaging layer on top of its transport layer, where messaging capabilities are handled. AMQP differentiates the messaging types between "base messages" provided by the sender and "annotated messages" seen at the next receiver.

Fig. 7.4 illustrates the message format of AMQP from [38]. The header contains standard delivery details about the message transfer with durability, priority, time to live, first acquirer, and delivery count. The delivery-annotations section contains delivery-specific nonstandard properties at the head of the message. Delivery annotations convey information from the sending peer to the receiving peer.

The message-annotations section is used for message properties, which are for the infrastructure and should be propagated across all delivery steps.

7.6.5 Data Distribution Service (DDS)

Data Distribution Service (DDS) is used for real-time M2M communications and follows the publish-subscribe paradigm. It was developed by Object Management Group (OMG) [20]. DDS relies on architecture without brokers and uses multicasting to provide Quality of Service (QoS) and reliability to applications. Its publish-subscribe architecture is ideal for the real-time constraints for IoT and M2M application scenarios. DDS provides 23 QoS policies by which communication criteria like security, urgency, priority, durability, or reliability can be defined. DDS architecture contains the two layers of Data-Centric Publish-Subscribe (DCPS), responsible for delivering information to the subscriber, and Data-Local Reconstruction Layer (DLRL), which is an optional layer that serves as the interface to DCPS functionalities. The DCPS facilitates the sharing of distributed data between distributed objects [16].

The following five entities are parts of the data flow in the DCPS layer:

1. Publisher: Disseminates data.
2. DataWriter: Used by the application to interact with the publisher over the values and changes of data specific to a given type. DataWriter and publisher's association indicates that the application will publish the specified data in a provided context.
3. Subscriber: Receives published data and delivers them to the application.
4. DataReader: Employed by the subscriber to access the received data.
5. Topic: Relates DataWriter's to DataReader's. Data transmission is allowed inside a DDS domain, which is a virtual environment for connected publishing and subscribing applications.

Fig. 7.5 shows the conceptual architecture of the DDS protocol. Based on a study [55] comparing the performance of MQTT and CoAP, the results showed that MQTT delivers with a lower delay than CoAP when the packet loss rate is low. On the other side, when there is a high packet loss rate, CoAP outperforms MQTT. In the case of small-size messages and a loss rate under 25%, CoAP outperforms MQTT in generating less extra traffic. Another study [7] compared in a mobile device application environment concluded that bandwidth usage and round trip time of CoAP are smaller than those of MQTT. In another study, energy consumption and response time were compared between CoAP and HTTP [10].

Due to the small header and package size, CoAP was more efficient than HTTP energy consumption and transmission time. The authors in [31] evaluated XMPP applicability to real-time web communications scenarios in terms of XMPP performance over HTML5 WebSockets. The results showed that XMPP is an efficient option for real-time web applications communication scenarios. Another performance evaluation between AMQP and REST was conducted in [17], where the authors used the average number of exchange messages between clients and the server. Under a high volume of messages, AMQP demonstrated a better performance than RESTful web services. An experimental evaluation of two different implementations of DDS [16] showed that the DSS protocol scales well with an increasing number of nodes. Each of these protocols has there specific scenario and environment under which it performs well.

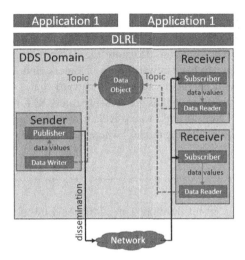

DDS architecture model.

7.7 Infrastructure protocols

7.7.1 Routing Protocol for Low Power and Lossy Networks (RPL)

The IETF routing standardized Routing Protocol for Low-Power and Lossy Networks (RPL) over low-power and lossy links (ROLL) working group, which is based on IPv6 for resource-constrained nodes [60,58]. RPL was created for minimal routing requirements by building a robust topology over lossy links. The RPL protocol supports simple and sophisticated traffic models like many-to-one, one-to-many, and point-to-point. A Destination Oriented Directed Acyclic Graph (DODAG) builds the core of RPL in the form of a routing diagram of nodes and refers to a single root graph. Each node is aware of its parent nodes but has no information about related child nodes. RPL keeps a minimum of one path for each node to the root and preferred parent to operate a fast path to increase performance. To maintain the routing topology and to keep routing information updated, RPL uses the following four types of control messages:

1. DODAG Information Object (DIO): Used to keep the current rank of the node, determines the distance of all nodes to the root based on specific metrics and chooses the preferred parent path.
2. Destination Advertisement Object (DAO): RPL provides upward traffic and downward traffic support using DAO messages with unicasts destination information towards the selected parents.
3. DODAG Information Solicitation (DIS): Used by a node to acquire DIO messages from a reachable adjacent node.
4. DAO Acknowledgment (DAO-ACk): Sent by a DAO recipient node (DAP parent or DODAG root) as a reply to a DAO message [8].

A DODAG is initially formed when the root, the only node in the DODAG, starts sending its location using DIO message to all Low-power Lossy Network (LLN) levels. The recipient routers register parent paths and participation paths for all nodes. They, in turn, propagate their DIO messages, and the whole DODAG is built gradually. After constructing the DODAG, a router's preferred parent stands as a default path towards the root. The root can also store the destination prefixes obtained by DIOs of other routers in its DIO messages to have upward routes. Routers emit and propagate DAO messages by unicasting to the root through parents to support downward routes. These messages identify the corresponding node of a route prefix as well as the crossing route. RPL routers work under one of two modes of operation (MOP) of "Nonstoring", where RPL routes messages move towards lower levels based on IP source routing, and the "Storing modes" whereas downward routing is based on destination IPv6 addresses [8].

7.7.2 6LowPAN

The IETF 6LoWPAN working group developed in 2007 the Low power Wireless Personal Area Networks (WPANs) standard. Many IoT communications rely on characteristics different from the former link-layer technologies like size constrained packet size, various address lengths, and low bandwidth [40,30,28]. 6LoWPAN is a mapping service required by IPv6 over Low power WPANs to maintain an IPv6 network [40]. Feature of this standard includes header compression for reduced transmission overhead, fragmentation to meet the IPv6 Maximum Transmission Unit (MTU) demand, and link-layer forwarding to support multihop delivery [28]. Datagrams enveloped by 6LoWPAN are followed by a combination of four types of headers, which are identified by two bits [40]:

- **(00) NO 6LoWPAN Header**: Packets that do not accord to the 6LoWPAN specification will be discarded.
- **(01) Dispatch Header**: Compression of IPv6 headers or multicasting is performed by specifying the Dispatch header.
- **(10) Mesh Addressing**: Mesh Addressing header identifies those IEEE 802.15.4 packets that have to be forwarded to the link-layer.
- **(11) Fragmentation**: For datagrams whose lengths exceed a single IEEE 802.15.4 frame, a Fragmentation header should be used.

With the IPv6 overhead reduction, a small datagram can be transferred over a single IEEE 802.15.4 hop in the best case.

7.7.3 IEEE 802.15.4

The IEEE 802.15.4 protocol specifies a sublayer for Medium Access Control (MAC) and a physical layer for low-rate wireless, private area networks (LRWPAN) [1]. With its low power consumption, low cost, low data rate, and high message throughput, it finds its application in the field of IoT, M2M, and WSNs. Features of IEEE 802.15.4 characterize reliable communication, platform interoperability, and handling a high number of nodes (65k) and provide a high level of security, encryption, and authentication services but do not provide QoS guarantees. IEEE 802.15.4 builds the base for the ZigBee protocol as they both are intended for low data rate services on power-constrained devices and build a complete network stack for WSNs. IEEE 802.15.4 can work on three frequency channel bands and uses the direct sequence spread spectrum (DSSS) method. The following data rates can be achieved depending on the used frequency channels: 20 kbps at 868 MHz, 40 kbps at 915 MHz, and 250 kbps at

2.4 GHz. High frequencies and wider bands lead to higher throughput and low latency, while low frequencies lead to better sensitivity and cover larger distances. By using the CSMA/CA protocol, IEEE 802.15.4 MAC reduced potential collisions.

A coordinator's job is to create, control, and maintain the network. A network mainly differentiates between two types of network nodes:

- Full Function Devices (FFD) can serve as a personal area network coordinator or just as a standard node. FFD can store a routing table in their memory and implement a full MAC. Furthermore, can they communicate with other devices using any available topology as seen in Fig. 7.6.
- Reduced function devices (RFD) are simple nodes with constrained resources that can only communicate with a coordinator. RFD are limited to a star topology.

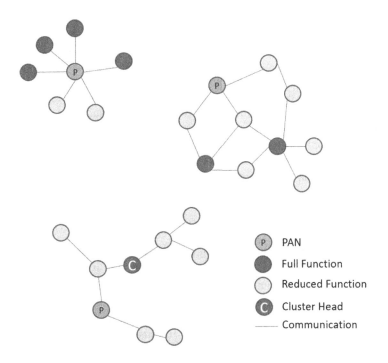

FIGURE 7.6

IEEE 802.15.4 network topologies [1]. (a) Star; (b) Peer-to-peer; (c) Cluster-tree.

Standard topologies to form IEEE 802.15.4 networks are star, peer-to-peer (mesh), and cluster-tree as shown in Fig. 7.6. The star topology contains at least one FFD and some RFDs. The FFD who works as a PAN coordinator should be located at the topology center and aims to manage and control the other nodes in the network. A peer-to-peer topology contains a PAN coordinator where other nodes communicate through intermediate nodes to other networks. The cluster-tree topology is a particular type of peer-to-peer topology that consists of a PAN coordinator, a cluster head, and standard nodes.

7.7.4 Bluetooth low energy

Bluetooth Low-Energy (BLE) or Bluetooth Smart uses a short-range radio with minimal power to operate longer (even for years) compared to previous versions.

The range (approx. 100 meters) is ten times as high as that of classic Bluetooth, while the latency is 15 times shorter [18]. BLE can be operated with a transmission power between 0.01 mW and 10 mW. With these properties, BLE is a technology candidate for IoT applications [12]. The BLE standard was developed by smartphone manufacturers and is available in most modern smartphones. The feasibility of using the BLE standard has been demonstrated in vehicle-to-vehicle communication. The BLE standard was rapidly developed by smartphone manufacturers and is now available in most smartphone models. Furthermore, this standard's feasibility was demonstrated in vehicle-to-vehicle communication [18], and wireless sensor networks [35].

BLE is more efficient than ZigBee in terms of energy consumption and the ratio of transmission energy per transmitted bit [54]. The BLE network stack is as follows: At the lowest level of the BLE, the stack is the physical layer that sends and receives bits. This layer provides link-layer services, including media access, connection establishment, error control, and flow control. Afterward, multiplexing for data channels, fragmentation, and assembly of larger packets is provided by Logical Link Control and Adaptation Protocol (L2CAP). The other upper layers are the Generic Attribute Protocol (GATT), which enables the efficient data collection from sensors, and the Generic Access Profile (GAP), which is used to configure and manage the application in different modes such as scanning and to promote as well as connection initiation and management [54]. Using BLE, devices can work as masters or slaves in a star topology. For the detection mechanism, slaves send advertisements through one or more dedicated advertising channels. In order to be discovered as a slave, these channels are scanned by the master. Except for the time that two devices are exchanging data, they are in sleep mode for the rest of the time.

7.7.5 EPCglobal

The electronic product code (EPC) is an identification number stored on an RFID tag and is mainly used in logistics and supply chain management to identify items. EPCglobal was the organization responsible for developing EPC and RFID technologies. The underlying architecture of EPC uses internet-based RFID technologies together with inexpensive RFID tags and reading devices to exchange product information [51]. This architecture is recognized as a promising technology for IoT's future due to supporting primary IoT requirements such as object IDs and service discovery [37] because of its openness, scalability, interoperability, and reliability.

EPCs number formats are divided into the types 64-bit, 96-bit, 204-bit. For example, the 96-bit type supports approximately 268 million companies with unique identities, 16 million product classes, and 68 billion serial numbers for each product class. The RFID system consists of the two components of radio signal transponder (tag) and tag reader. A tag consists of a chip that stores the unique identity number of the object and an antenna so that the chip can communicate with the tag reader. The tag reader creates a radio signal to identify objects through reflected radio waves from the tag. The reader can then forward the retrieved number to an application called Object-Naming Services (ONS) to identify the product behind the number further. An ONS searches a database for details of the tag.

The EPCglobal Network can be divided into five components: EPC, ID-System, EPC Middleware, Discovery Services, and EPC Information Services. The ID system links the EPC identities with a database via the middleware using an EPC reader. The discovery service is a mechanism from EPC-global to determine the required data based on the tags using the ONS. In 2006, the second generation of EPC tags was introduced and intended to cover various company products worldwide. A Gen 2 tag is known as passive RFID and provides features such as interoperability among heterogeneous objects, high performance for all requirements, high reliability, and inexpensive tags and readers.

7.7.6 LTE-A (Long Term Evolution – Advanced)

LTE-A includes a range of protocols for cellular communications that are well suited for Machine-to-Machine Communication and IoT infrastructures, especially in the field of smart cities where long-term infrastructure durability is expected [24]. LTE-A outperforms other cellular solutions in terms of cost of service and scalability. LTE-A operates on Orthogonal Frequency Division Multiple Access (OFDMA) and divides the channel bandwidth into smaller bands called Physical Resource Blocks (PRBs). LTE-A uses a multicomponent carrier spread spectrum (CC) technique that allows up to five 20 MHz bands. The architecture of the LTE-A network is based on two main parts. The first is the Core Network (CN), which controls the mobile devices and deals with data flow, while the Radio Access Network (RAN) manages wireless communications and radio access and establishes protocols for user planes and control planes. The RAN consists mainly of base stations (also referred to as evolved NodeBs) interconnected via the X2 interface. The RAN and the CN are connected via a so-called S1 interface. Mobile or MTC devices directly connect to a base station or through an MTC Gateway (MTCG). The LTE-A protocol has challenges in high network congestion when many devices access the network, or challenges in QoS, which can be compromised when MTC devices attempt to access the network via eNodeB MTCG selection. These issues were investigated in [24] and a solution based on advanced learning for eNodeB selection.

7.7.7 Z-Wave

Z-Wave has found widespread use in remote control applications in smart homes and small commercial settings [19]. It is a low-power wireless communication protocol for home automation networks (Hans) and was developed initially by ZenSys (now Sigma Designs) and further improved by the Z-Wave Alliance. Z-Wave covers approximately 30 meters' point-to-point communication and is specified for applications that require tiny data transmissions, such as lighting control, home appliance control, smart energy and HVAC systems, access control, healthcare wearables control, and fire detection. Z-Wave operates in the ISM band (around 900 MHz) and allows a transmission rate of up to 240 kbps. Its MAC layer uses a collision avoidance mechanism, where a Reliable transmission is possible through optional ACK messages. The architecture consists of a controller and nodes. Controllers manage the nodes by sending commands. For routing, a controller maintains a table of the entire network topology. Z-Wave performs source routing, where a controller transmits the path within a packet.

7.8 Comparison of infrastructure protocols

We discuss here the evaluation and comparison of some prominent infrastructure protocols needed to establish the underlying communication required by IoT applications. In [8], an evaluation of RPL for low-power and lossy networks was conducted; several issues were identified, including under-specification, incompatibility between saving, and nonsaving modes, and loops.

The performance analysis of RPL [2] showed RPL in fast network setup and limited communication delays as useful, while high overhead is a potential drawback. Unreliability issues were reported in [3] with RPL due to the lack of complete knowledge of link qualities. Since routing, reliability, scalability, and performance are critical components of IoT infrastructure, many fields rely heavily on RPL, and that is why there is a need for further research on improvements and optimizations of routing protocols to meet IoT requirements.

RTT (Round trip time) was evaluated in [9] using a point-to-point communication test, which showed an increase in round-trip delays when the ICMP payload size is increased. Other issues have been reported for a 6LoWPAN gateway, such as a high rate of packet loss and jamming [15].

Beyond the lower power consumption demonstrated by BLE compared to IEEE 802.15.4, the work in [39] investigated the performance of IEEE 802.15.4 against IEEE 802.11ah (candidate standard for IoT and M2M) in terms of throughput and power consumption. The results showed that IEEE 802.11ah achieves higher throughput than IEEE 802.15.4 in both idle and nonidle channels, while the energy consumption of IEEE 802.15.4 exceeds that of IEEE 802.11ah. Researchers proposed for EPC Gen-2 to use the code division multiple access (CDMA) technique instead of the dynamically framed slotted ALOHA technique to reduce collisions.

A performance evaluation of ALOHA techniques was performed in [56], where the average number of queries and the total number of transmitted bits required to identify all tags in the system as their measurement factors were used. Their results showed that the expected number of queries for tag identification using CDMA technology is lower due to decreased collisions. However, when comparing the number of transmitted bits and the time needed to identify all tags in the system, the standard EPC Gen-2 protocol performs better than the CDMA technique. Z-Wave has demonstrated acceptable performance, and despite being more expensive than ZigBee, it has been used widely in smart home applications. Furthermore, Z-Wave applications can benefit from the flexibility and security of this protocol. Its overall performance has been reported to be superior to ZigBee's performance [61].

7.9 Criteria for communication protocols selection

As there are many wireless technologies in the IoT network, each one has certain specifications and benefits. Thus, given the versatility of communication protocols and their performance, a guideline to select the right communication protocol is needed by researchers and developers in the field. Different criteria are used to benchmark the differences between communication protocols. Such criteria include standard, network, topology, power, range, cryptography, spreading, modulation type, coexistence mechanism, security, and power consumption shown in IoT IP coverage.

Security criteria

In terms of security, the considered communication protocols have encryption and authentication mechanisms. 6LoWPAN, ZigBee, BLE, NFC, Z-Wave use the Advanced Encryption Standard (AES) block cipher with counter mode, while Cellular and RFID use RC4. However, several serious weaknesses were identified. AES is exceptionally secure, while RC4 is not. RC4 is very fast compared to AES.

Power consumption criteria

In terms of power consumption, 6LoWPAN, ZigBee, BLE, Z-Wave, and NFC are designed for portable devices and limited battery power. Thus, it offers low power consumption. On the other hand, Cellular high power consumption is on the list.

Data rate

In terms of data rate, 6LoWPAN, ZigBee, BLE, NFC, SigFox, and Z-Wave have data rate ≤ 1 Mbps. However, RFID has the highest data rate of 4 Mbps. In terms of range, SigFox and Cellular are range longer than the coverage of several KM. However, 6LoWPAN, ZigBee, BLE, NFC, Z-Wave, and RFID are range shorter that cover less than KM. 6LoWPAN will be the future protocol because it is an IP-based WSN. It allows a vast number of smart devices to be deployed over the Internet easily by using the vast address space of IPv6 for data and information gathering through features and behaviors of various metrics, including low bandwidth, different topologies, and star or mesh, power consumption, low cost, scalable networks.

7.10 Key features

In this chapter, we have presented and analyzed existing IoT architecture models in which stream analytic scenarios can be deployed.

- ☑ Various paradigms within the Cloud digital ecosystem (Cloud-to-thing continuum) are considered and discussed in terms of their advantages and drawbacks.
- ☑ Demanding requirements of stream processing are identified and discussed, including low latency, round trip time, location-aware, context-aware, energy-aware, security, and privacy.
- ☑ Different communication protocols most commonly used in stream applications, focusing on the field of infrastructure and application protocols, are presented.
- ☑ Comparison results from various studies are referred to give insights on the suitability of different protocols according to application scenarios.
- ☑ Criteria about architecture and protocol selection are also discussed.

References

[1] IEEE standard for local and metropolitan area networks–part 15.4: low-rate wireless personal area networks (LR-WPANs), in: IEEE Std 802.15.4-2011 (Revision of IEEE Std 802.15.4-2006), 2011, pp. 1–314.

[2] N. Accettura, L.A. Grieco, G. Boggia, P. Camarda, Performance analysis of the RPL routing protocol, in: 2011 IEEE International Conference on Mechatronics, 2011, pp. 767–772.

[3] E. Ancillotti, R. Bruno, M. Conti, RPL routing protocol in advanced metering infrastructures: an analysis of the unreliability problems, in: 2012 Sustainable Internet and ICT for Sustainability, 01 2012, pp. 1–10.

[4] A.C. Baktir, A. Ozgovde, C. Ersoy, How can edge computing benefit from software-defined networking: a survey, use cases, and future directions, IEEE Communications Surveys and Tutorials 19 (4) (2017) 2359–2391.

[5] F. Bonomi, R. Milito, J. Zhu, S. Addepalli, Fog computing and its role in the internet of things, in: Proceedings of the First Edition of the MCC Workshop on Mobile Cloud Computing, MCC'12, ACM, New York, NY, USA, 2012, pp. 13–16.

[6] C. Bormann, A.P. Castellani, Z. Shelby, CoAP: an application protocol for billions of tiny internet nodes, IEEE Internet Computing 16 (2) (2012) 62–67.

[7] N.D. Caro, W. Colitti, K. Steenhaut, G. Mangino, G. Reali, Comparison of two lightweight protocols for smartphone-based sensing, in: SCVT, IEEE, 2013, pp. 1–6.

[8] T.H. Clausen, U. Herberg, M. Philipp, A critical evaluation of the IPv6 routing protocol for low power and lossy networks (RPL), in: WiMob, IEEE Computer Society, 2011, pp. 365–372.

[9] B. Cody-Kenny, D. Guerin, D. Ennis, R. Carbajo, M. Huggard, C. Mc Goldrick, Performance evaluation of the 6LoWPAN protocol on MICAz and TelosB motes, in: PM2HW2N'09: Proceedings of the 4th ACM Workshop on Performance Monitoring and Measurement of Heterogeneous Wireless and Wired Networks, 10 2009, pp. 25–30.

[10] W. Colitti, K. Steenhaut, N.D. Caro, B. Buta, V. Dobrota, Evaluation of constrained application protocol for wireless sensor networks, in: LANMAN, IEEE, 2011, pp. 1–6.

[11] L.M. Dang, M.J. Piran, D. Han, K. Min, H. Moon, A survey on internet of things and cloud computing for healthcare, Electronics 8 (7) (2019).

[12] J. DeCuir, Introducing bluetooth smart: Part 1: a look at both classic and new technologies, IEEE Consumer Electronics Magazine 3 (1) (2014) 12–18.

[13] H. Dinh Thai, C. Lee, D. Niyato, P. Wang, A survey of mobile cloud computing: architecture, applications, and approaches, Wireless Communications and Mobile Computing 13 (2013) 12.

[14] K. Dolui, S.K. Datta, Comparison of edge computing implementations: fog computing, cloudlet and mobile edge computing, in: 2017 Global Internet of Things Summit (GIoTS), June 2017, pp. 1–6.

[15] B. Enjian, Z. Xiaokui, Performance evaluation of 6LoWPAN gateway used in actual network environment, in: 2012 International Conference on Control Engineering and Communication Technology, 12 2012, pp. 1036–1039.

[16] C. Esposito, S. Russo, D.D. Crescenzo, Performance assessment of OMG compliant data distribution middleware, in: IPDPS, IEEE, 2008, pp. 1–8.

[17] J.L. Fernandes, I.M.C. Lopes, J. Rodrigues, S. Ullah, Performance evaluation of restful web services and AMQP protocol, in: 2013 Fifth International Conference on Ubiquitous and Future Networks (ICUFN), 2013, pp. 810–815.

[18] R. Frank, W. Bronzi, G. Castignani, T. Engel, Bluetooth low energy: an alternative technology for VANET applications, in: 2014 11th Annual Conference on Wireless On-Demand Network Systems and Services (WONS), 2014, pp. 104–107.

[19] C. Gomez, J. Paradells, Wireless home automation networks: a survey of architectures and technologies, IEEE Communications Magazine 48 (07 2010) 92–101.

[20] O.M. Group, About the data distribution service specification version 1.2, December.

[21] M. Gusev, B. Koteska, M. Kostoska, B. Jakimovski, S. Dustdar, O. Scekic, T. Rausch, S. Nastic, S. Ristov, T. Fahringer, A deviceless edge computing approach for streaming IoT applications, IEEE Internet Computing 23 (2019) 37–45.

[22] M. Gushev, Dew computing architecture for cyber-physical systems and IoT, Internet of Things 11 (2020) 100186.

[23] P. Hao, Y. Bai, X. Zhang, Y. Zhang, Edgecourier: an edge-hosted personal service for low-bandwidth document synchronization in mobile cloud storage services, in: SEC'17: Proceedings of the Second ACM/IEEE Symposium on Edge Computing, 10 2017, pp. 1–14.

[24] M. Hasan, E. Hossain, D. Niyato, Random access for machine-to-machine communication in LTE-advanced networks: issues and approaches, IEEE Communications Magazine 51 (6) (2013) 86–93.

[25] J. He, A. Chaintreau, C. Diot, A performance evaluation of scalable live video streaming with nano data centers, Computer Networks 53 (2) (2009) 153–167, QoS Aspects in Next-Generation Networks.

[26] J. Huang, F. Qian, A. Gerber, Z.M. Mao, S. Sen, O. Spatscheck, A close examination of performance and power characteristics of 4G LTE networks, in: MobiSys, 2012.

[27] J.-P. Hubaux, T.W. Gross, J.-Y.L. Boudec, M. Vetterli, Towards self-organized mobile ad hoc networks: the terminodes project, 2000.

[28] J.W. Hui, D.E. Culler, Extending IP to low-power, wireless personal area networks, IEEE Internet Computing 12 (4) (2008) 37–45.

[29] U. Hunkeler, H.L. Truong, A.J. Stanford-Clark, MQTT-S - a publish/subscribe protocol for wireless sensor networks, in: S. Choi, J. Kurose, K. Ramamritham (Eds.), COMSWARE, IEEE, 2008, pp. 791–798.

[30] J. Ko, A. Terzis, S. Dawson-Haggerty, D.E. Culler, J.W. Hui, P. Levis, Connecting low-power and lossy networks to the internet, IEEE Communications Magazine 49 (4) (2011) 96–101.

[31] M. Laine, Performance evaluation of XMPP on the web, 2012.

[32] N. Laoutaris, P. Rodriguez, L. Massoulie, Echos: edge capacity hosting overlays of nano data centers, SIGCOMM Computer Communication Review 38 (1) (Jan. 2008) 51–54.

[33] C. Lerche, K. Hartke, M. Kovatsch, Industry adoption of the internet of things: a constrained application protocol survey, in: ETFA, IEEE, 2012, pp. 1–6.

[34] P.M. Pinto Silva, J. Rodrigues, J. Silva, R. Martins, L. Lopes, F. Silva, Using edge-clouds to reduce load on traditional WiFi infrastructures and improve quality of experience, in: 2017 IEEE 1st International Conference on Fog and Edge Computing (ICFEC), 05 2017, pp. 61–67.

[35] E. Mackensen, M. Lai, T.M. Wendt, Bluetooth low energy (BLE) based wireless sensors, in: SENSORS, 2012 IEEE, 2012, pp. 1–4.

[36] A. Manocha, M. Bhatia, G. Kumar, Dew computing-inspired health-meteorological factor analysis for early prediction of bronchial asthma, Journal of Network and Computer Applications 179 (2021) 102995.

[37] D. Minoli, Building the Internet of Things with IPv6 and MIPv6: The Evolving World of M2M Communications, 06 2013.

[38] OASIS, Advanced message queuing protocol (AMQP) version 1.0, 2012.

[39] B.B. Olyaei, J. Pirskanen, O. Raeesi, A. Hazmi, M. Valkama, Performance comparison between slotted IEEE 802.15.4 and IEEE 802.1 lah in IoT based applications, in: WiMob, IEEE Computer Society, 2013, pp. 332–337.

[40] M.R. Palattella, N. Accettura, X. Vilajosana, T. Watteyne, L.A. Grieco, G. Boggia, M. Dohler, Standardized protocol stack for the internet of (important) things, IEEE Communications Surveys and Tutorials 15 (3) (2013) 1389–1406.

[41] J.S. Preden, K. Tammemäe, A. Jantsch, M. Leier, A. Riid, E. Calis, The benefits of self-awareness and attention in fog and mist computing, Computer 48 (7) (July 2015) 37–45.

[42] B. Ravandi, I. Papapanagiotou, A self-learning scheduling in cloud software defined block storage, in: 2017 IEEE 10th International Conference on Cloud Computing (CLOUD), June 2017, pp. 415–422.

[43] P.P. Ray, D. Dash, D. De, Internet of things-based real-time model study on e-healthcare: device, message service and dew computing, Computer Networks 149 (2019) 226–239.

[44] J. Ren, Y. Zhang, K. Zhang, X. Shen, Exploiting mobile crowdsourcing for pervasive cloud services: challenges and solutions, IEEE Communications Magazine 53 (3) (March 2015) 98–105.

[45] P. Saint-Andre, Extensible messaging and presence protocol (XMPP): instant messaging and presence. Internet RFC 3921, October 2004.

[46] A. Salem, T. Nadeem, LAMEN: leveraging resources on anonymous mobile edge nodes, in: S3@MobiCom, 2016.

[47] Z. Sanaei, S. Abolfazli, A. Gani, R. Buyya, Heterogeneity in mobile cloud computing: taxonomy and open challenges, IEEE Communications Surveys and Tutorials 16 (1) (First Quarter 2014) 369–392.

[48] M. Satyanarayanan, Fundamental challenges in mobile computing, in: Proceedings of the Fifteenth Annual ACM Symposium on Principles of Distributed Computing, PODC'96, ACM, New York, NY, USA, 1996, pp. 1–7.

[49] M. Satyanarayanan, P. Bahl, R. Caceres, N. Davies, The case for VM-based cloudlets in mobile computing, IEEE Pervasive Computing 8 (4) (Oct. 2009) 14–23.

[50] J. Schneider, T. Kamiya, Efficient XML interchange (EXI) format 1.0, Working Draft WD-exi-20080919, World Wide Web Consortium, September 2008.

[51] R. Sees, RFID and auto-ID in planning and logistics: a practical guide for military UID application (review), Transportation Journal 51 (01 2012) 258–259.

[52] Z. Shelby, K. Hartke, C. Bormann, The constrained application protocol (CoAP), RFC 7252 (June 2014) 1–112.

[53] M. Shiraz, A. Gani, R.H. Khokhar, R. Buyya, A review on distributed application processing frameworks in smart mobile devices for mobile cloud computing, Journal IEEE Communications Surveys Tutorials 15 (3) (Third Quarter 2013) 1294–1313.

[54] M. Siekkinen, M. Hiienkari, J. Nurminen, J. Nieminen, How low energy is bluetooth low energy? Comparative measurements with ZigBee/802.15.4, in: IEEE Wireless Communications and Networking Conference Workshops (WCNCW), Paris, France, 04 2012.

[55] D. Thangavel, X. Ma, A.C. Valera, H.-X. Tan, C.K.-Y. Tan, Performance evaluation of MQTT and CoAP via a common middleware, in: ISSNIP, IEEE, 2014, pp. 1–6.

[56] E. Vahedi, R. Ward, I. Blake, Performance analysis of RFID protocols: CDMA versus the standard EPC Gen-2, IEEE Transactions on Automation Science and Engineering 11 (2014) 1250–1261.

[57] V. Valancius, N. Laoutaris, L. Massoulié, C. Diot, P. Rodriguez, Greening the internet with nano data centers, in: CoNEXT'09: Proceedings of the 5th International Conference on Emerging Networking Experiments and Technologies, 01 2009, pp. 37–48.

[58] A.J. Vasseur, RPL: the IP routing protocol designed for low power and lossy networks internet protocol for smart objects (IPSO), 2011.

[59] Y. Wang, A blockchain system with lightweight full node based on dew computing, Internet of Things 11 (2020) 100184.

[60] T. Winter, P. Thubert, A. Brandt, J.W. Hui, R. Kelsey, P. Levis, K. Pister, R. Struik, J.-P. Vasseur, R.K. Alexander, RPL: IPv6 routing protocol for low-power and lossy networks, RFC 6550 (March 2012) 1–157.

[61] C. Withanage, R. Ashok, C. Yuen, K. Otto, A comparison of the popular home automation technologies, in: 2014 IEEE Innovative Smart Grid Technologies - Asia (ISGT ASIA), 05 2014, pp. 600–605.

[62] A. Yousefpour, C. Fung, T. Nguyen, K.P. Kadiyala, F. Jalali, A. Niakanlahiji, J. Kong, J.P. Jue, All one needs to know about fog computing and related edge computing paradigms: a complete survey, arXiv:1808.05283 [abs], 2019.

[63] B. Zhang, N. Mor, J. Kolb, D.S. Chan, K. Lutz, E. Allman, J. Wawrzynek, E.A. Lee, J. Kubiatowicz, The cloud is not enough: saving IoT from the cloud, in: HotCloud, 2015.

Machine learning

ML for eHealth systems

8

8.1 Learning models

Given that the focus of machine learning is "learning", there are 14 types of learning that can be differentiated into four main categories (see Fig. 8.1). Each type of learning describes a whole subfield of different concepts and algorithms. In the following, the different learning models are classified and described.

The main difference between the general learning problems is the level of availability of ground truth data, which is prior knowledge of the model's output for a given input.

8.1.1 Supervised learning

The methods that build the association between inputs and outputs using *labeled* training data are supervised learning methods. When the output is discrete, the task is called classification, while for a continuous value output, the task is called regression. Classic examples of supervised learning methods in healthcare are classification tasks of different lung disease types [88] and organ recognition from medical images [114]. There is, of course, a large body of literature on applications of supervised learning methods in healthcare.

Models are fitted to training data consisting of inputs and outputs and used to make predictions for test sets where only the inputs are provided, and the outputs of the model are compared to the retained target variables and used to estimate the quality of the model.

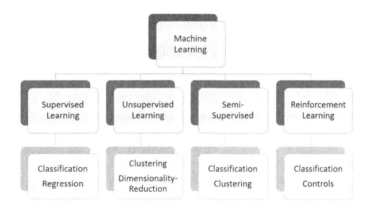

FIGURE 8.1

Illustration of different Machine Learning models with their corresponding application tasks.

Anomaly Detection and Complex Event Processing Over IoT Data Streams. https://doi.org/10.1016/B978-0-12-823818-9.00019-5

Supervised learning problems can be classified into two main types of classification, which involves the prediction of a class label, and regression, which involves the prediction of a numerical value.

Classification and regression problems can have one or more input variables of any data type, such as numeric or categorical. The most commonly used learning algorithms are: Support Vector Machines, Linear Regression, Logistic Regression, Naive Bayes, (Deep) Neural Networks and their variants and combinations.

As examples, the following use cases are identified as supervised learning problems in the healthcare domain:

- Deep similarity learning frameworks simultaneously learn patient representations and measure pairwise similarity via a convolutional neural network (CNN) to capture important local information in EHRs and then feed the learned representation into triplet loss or softmax cross-entropy loss. By utilizing the similarity information, it then performs disease predictions and patient clustering. Experimental results showed that CNN could better represent the longitudinal EHR sequences, and where proposed frameworks outperform state-of-the-art distance metric learning methods [99].
- In radiology, the automatic detection of a pulmonary nodule from a chest X-ray based on CNN models.
- In cardiology, automated interpretation of the ECG signals, where pattern recognition is performed to select from a limited set of diagnoses.
- The Framingham Risk Score [108] for coronary artery disease (CAD) is also an application of supervised learning. Such risk models exist throughout medicine to guide antithrombotic therapy for atrial fibrillation [67] and automated implantable defibrillators in hypertrophic cardiomyopathy [77].

In regression and classification, the goal is to find certain relationships or structures in the input data to produce correct output data effectively. The "correct" output is determined entirely from the training data. Thus, although having a ground truth that the model assumes to be true, this does not mean that data labels in real-world situations are always correct. Noisy or incorrect data labels reduce the effectiveness of the model.

To use a certain supervised learning model, one must perform the following steps:

1. Determine the type of training samples. Prior the user must decide what kind of data to use as a training set. For instance, in handwriting analysis, this could be a single handwritten character or an entire handwritten word.
2. Collect a training set. The training set must be representative of the real-world use of the function. Therefore, input objects are collected, and corresponding outputs are captured from human experts or measurements.
3. Define the input feature space of the underlying data distribution. The accuracy of the learned distribution depends on how the input object is represented. Normally, the input object is transformed into a feature vector that contains several descriptive features of the object. The number of features should not be too big due to the impact of dimensionality, but at the same time should contain enough information to predict the output accurately.
4. Determine the structure of the learned data distribution and the corresponding learning algorithm. For example, one may choose support vector machines or decision trees.
5. Evaluate the learning model. Run the learning algorithm with the training set. Many supervised learning algorithms do specify certain hyperparameters. These parameters can be adjusted by optimizing performance on a validation set of the training set or by cross-validation.

6. Evaluate the accuracy of the learned function. After parameter adjustment and learning, the resulting function's performance should be measured on a separate test set from the training set.

Achieving the right model for the problem at hand is not an easy task. Indeed, that model has to have acceptable accuracy, be efficient, and not so complex.

Bias-variance trade-off

The tradeoff between bias and variance also relates to model generalization. Usually, there is a balance between bias (constant error term) and variance, i.e., how the error can vary between different data sets. A high bias and low variance model could be consistently wrong 20% of the time, while a low bias and high variance model could be wrong 5%-50% of the time due to the data used to train.

The bias-variance tradeoff relates to model generalization. There is a balance between bias in any model, which is the constant error term, and variance, which is how the error may vary between different data sets. A high bias and low variance model might be consistently wrong 20% of the time, whereas with a low bias and high variance would be a model that can be wrong between 5%-50% of the time, depending on the data used to train.

Bias and variance often move in opposite directions; increasing bias will usually lead to lower variance and vice versa. When creating the model, the specific problem and the nature of the data should allow us to decide where to fall on the bias-variance spectrum.

Increasing bias and decreasing variance lead to a relatively stable baseline performance model, which may be critical in specific tasks. Additionally, to produce models that generalize well, the model's variance should scale with the training data size and complexity. Small and simple datasets should usually be learned with low-variance models, and large, complex datasets will often require higher-variance models to fully learn the structure of the data.

Complexity

The model complexity refers to the complexity of the function attempted to be learned –similar to a polynomial degree. The nature of the training data generally determines the proper level of model complexity. If a small amount of data or whole data is not uniformly spread throughout different possible scenarios, the model complexity should be decreased because a high-complexity model would overfit on a small number of data points.

Overfitting means training a model that fits the training data very well but does not generalize to other new data points. Here it is strictly learning to reproduce the training data without learning the actual distribution or structure in the data.

8.1.2 Unsupervised learning

The ML techniques that use *unlabeled* data are called unsupervised learning methods. Widely used examples of unsupervised learning methods include clustering data points using a similarity metric and dimensionality reduction to project high-dimensional data to lower subspaces. Unsupervised learning finds applications for anomaly detection, such as clustering [24]. Classic examples of unsupervised learning methods in healthcare include heart disease prediction using clustering [78] and hepatitis disease prediction using principal component analysis (PCA) –a dimensionality reduction technique [79].

Unsupervised learning describes a class of problems where a model is needed to describe or extract relationships in data. Compared to supervised learning, unsupervised learning works only with the input data without target variables. Therefore, there is no teacher to correct the model as there is in supervised learning.

Unsupervised learning can be found in many types, while two main issues can be faced. These are clustering, which involves finding groups in the data, and density estimation, which involves summarizing the data distribution. The goal is to learn the inherent structure of the data without using explicitly provided labels. Some basic algorithms are principal component analysis, k-means clustering, and autoencoders. Since the data is unlabeled, there is no specific way to compare model performance in most unsupervised learning methods.

Exploratory data analysis

Unsupervised learning is beneficial in exploratory data analysis by automatically detecting structure and relationships in data and provide initial insights used to test against individual hypotheses.

Dimensionality reduction

Dimensionality reduction refers to the methods used to represent data with fewer features and can be achieved through unsupervised methods. In representation learning, the aim is to learn relationships between features and represent the data using latent features that relate to the original features of the data. With fewer features, the sparse latent structure makes further data processing much less intensive and eliminates redundant features. In other contexts, dimensionality reduction can be used to convert data from one modality to another. For example, a recurrent autoencoder can be used to convert sequences to a fixed-length representation.

Other unsupervised methods can also be used, such as visualization, in which data is graphed or plotted in various ways, and projection methods, in which the dimensionality of the data is reduced. A visualization technique often used is a scatter plot matrix that creates a scatter plot for each variable pair in the data set. The principal component analysis can be used as a projection analysis to summarize a data set in terms of eigenvalues and eigenvectors, removing linear dependencies.

Perhaps the most compelling opportunity represents the "precision medicine" initiative [36]. Frustrated by the inherent heterogeneity of most common diseases, there are increasing efforts to redefine diseases according to pathophysiological mechanisms, which could uncover new therapy methods. However, identifying such mechanisms for complex multifactorial diseases is not trivial. As an example of where unsupervised learning could be applied to heart diseases, consider a heterogeneous disease such as myocarditis in a large group of apparently similar individuals with unexplained acute systolic heart failure. A myocardial biopsy could be performed and characterize the cellular composition of each sample using an immunostaining technique.

For example, one could determine the number of T lymphocytes, neutrophils, macrophages, or eosinophils and then see if there are recurring patterns in cellular composition, which could suggest mechanisms and guide therapies investigated. A similar approach focused on genomics identified an eosinophil subtype of asthma [109] that is uniquely responsive to a novel therapy targeting the cytokine IL-13 secreted by eosinophils [35]. The difference with supervised learning is to only focus on detecting patterns in the data. Treating such a scenario as a supervised learning problem, such as developing a mortality model in myocarditis and classifying patients according to risk, could miss such subgroups entirely, losing an opportunity to identify new disease mechanisms.

8.1.3 Reinforcement learning

Methods that learn a control function from a set of observations, actions, and rewards in response to actions performed over time fall into the class of reinforcement learning (RL) [100]. RL has great potential to transform many healthcare applications, and recently it has been used for context-aware symptom control for disease diagnosis [51]. In addition, the potential of using RL for healthcare applications can be seen through the recent example of the game of Go, where a computer using RL with the integration of supervised and unsupervised learning methods defeated a human master player [92].

Reinforcement learning describes a class of problems in which an agent acts in an environment and must learn using feedback. Environment means that there is no preexisting training data set. The training follows a goal or set for goals that an agent must achieve where allowed actions are performed, which results in performance feedback regarding achieving the goal.

It can sound similar to supervised learning in that the model trains based on a response, although in RL, the feedback may be delayed and statistically noisy, making it difficult for the agent to connect cause and effect.

An example of a reinforcement problem is a game in which the agent achieves a high score and can make moves in the game and receive feedback in the form of punishments or rewards. Recent results include reinforcement in Google's AlphaGo in outperforming the world's best Go player. Some famous examples of reinforcement learning algorithms are Q-learning, temporal-difference learning, and deep reinforcement learning. RL can be an attractive solution for constructing efficient policies in various healthcare domains, where the decision-making process is usually characterized by a long period of time or a sequential procedure [44].

A medical or clinical treatment regimen consists of a sequence of decisions to determine the course of treatment type, drug dosage, or retreatment timing at a given point in time according to an individual patient's current health status and prior treatment history to promote long-term patient benefit. Unlike the standard approach in traditional randomized controlled trials, where treatment regimens are derived from the average population response, RL can be tailored to provide precise treatment for individual patients, who may have high heterogeneity in treatment response due to variations in disease severity, personal characteristics, and drug sensitivity. In addition, RL can find optimal guidelines using only prior experience, without requiring prior knowledge of the mathematical model of the biological system. This makes RL more attractive than many existing control-based approaches in health domains. It might normally be difficult or even impossible to build an accurate model of the complex human body system and responses to administered treatments due to the nonlinear, varying, and delayed interaction between treatments and human bodies.

With the tremendous theoretical and technical achievements in generalization, representation, and efficiency in recent years, RL approaches have been successfully applied in many healthcare domains to date. These application domains can be categorized into three main types: dynamic treatment schemes in chronic diseases or critical care, automated medical diagnosis, and other general domains such as healthcare resource allocation and planning, optimal process control, drug discovery and development, and healthcare management. Fig. 8.2 provides a diagram outlining the application domains and illustrates how this overview is organized along with the three broad domains of the domain [117].

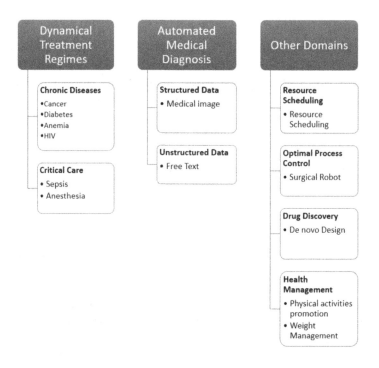

FIGURE 8.2

RL domain classification in Healthcare.

8.2 Hybrid learning models

The line between unsupervised and supervised learning is blurry, and many hybrid approaches draw from each field of study. This section looks at some more common hybrid fields of study, namely semisupervised, self-supervised, and multiinstance learning.

8.2.1 Semisupervised learning

Semisupervised learning is a hybrid model between supervised and unsupervised learning. Those kinds of models aim to use a small amount of labeled training data along with a large amount of unlabeled training data. This often occurs in real-world situations where labeling data is costly, and there may be a constant stream of data.

Indeed, many ML methods are neither supervised nor unsupervised in the real world, where the training data contains both labeled and unlabeled samples. Those kinds of methods are referred to as semisupervised learning methods. An overview and systematic review of supervised and unsupervised techniques can be found in [14].

Thus, semisupervised learning techniques are useful when labeled, and unlabeled samples are available for training, typically a small amount of labeled data and many unlabeled data. Semisupervised learning techniques can be beneficial to various healthcare applications, as it is difficult in healthcare to obtain a sufficient amount of labeled data for model training. Various facets of semisupervised learning with different learning techniques have been proposed in the literature. For example, a semisupervised clustering method for healthcare data is presented in [94] and a semisupervised ML approach for activity recognition with sensor data is presented in [118]. In [70] and [16], the authors applied a semisupervised learning method to medical image segmentation.

Semisupervised learning methods are supervised learning where the training data contains few labeled samples and a large number of unlabeled examples. Here the learning model aims to effectively use all available data, not just labeled data as in supervised learning. Effective use of unlabeled data may use unsupervised clustering or density estimation methods. Once the clusters or patterns are discovered, supervised methods can be used to label the samples or apply the labels to unlabeled representations later used for prediction tasks.

Many real-world supervised learning problems contain parts of semisupervised learning problems due to the overhead or computational cost of labeling the examples. For example, picture classification requires a dataset of pictures that human operators have already labeled. Many problems in computer vision, natural language processing, and automatic speech recognition fall into the semisupervised learning problem category and cannot be quickly solved using standard supervised learning methods.

Some standard semisupervised methods are transductive support vector machines and graph-based methods such as label propagation.

Assumptions

Semisupervised methods make assumptions about the data to justify using a small set of labeled data to make inferences about the unlabeled data points. These can be divided into three categories:

- Continuity Assumption: Assumes that data points that are "close" to each other are more likely to have a common label.
- Cluster Assumption: Assumes that data naturally form discrete clusters and that points in the same cluster are more likely to have a common label.
- Manifold Assumption: Assumes that the data lies roughly in a lower-dimensional space than the input space. This assumption is relevant in an unobservable or hard-to-observe system with a small number of parameters that produce a high-dimensional observable output.

8.2.2 Self-supervised learning

Self-supervised learning describes an unsupervised learning problem constructed as a supervised learning problem to apply supervised learning algorithms to solve an alternative task representing a model or representation that can be used to solve the original (actual) modeling problem.

An example of self-supervised learning can be found in computer vision where unlabeled images are used to train a supervised model, e.g., convert images to grayscale and have a model predict a color representation (colorization) or remove blocks of the image and have a model predict the missing parts (in-painting).

Another example of a self-supervised learning algorithm is autoencoders, a type of neural network used to model a compressed representation of an input sample. This is accomplished using a model with an encoder element and a decoder element separated by a bottleneck, the internal structure representing the input. The models are trained by samples provided both at the input and output, requiring the model to reproduce the input by first encoding it into a compressed representation and then decoding it back into the original at the output. After training, the decoder is discarded, and the encoder is used as needed to create compact representations of the input. Autoencoders are thus trained using supervised learning to solve an unsupervised learning problem, with a type of projection to reduce the dimensionality of the input data.

Another example of self-supervised learning is generative adversarial network (GAN). This kind of model is commonly used to create synthetic images using a collection of unlabeled examples from the same domain. GANs are trained indirectly using a discriminator model that classifies image examples from the domain as real or generated. The result is fed back to update the GAN model and encourage it to generate more realistic images in the next iteration.

8.2.3 Multiinstance learning

Multiinstance learning describes a supervised learning problem where individual examples are unlabeled, but groups or bags of samples are labeled. Modeling uses the knowledge that one or more of the instances in a bag are associated with a target label and predicts the label for new bags in the future if they consist of multiple unlabeled examples.

8.3 Statistical inference

Inferences are steps in reasoning, moving from premises to logical consequences.

In the context of machine learning, training a model and making a prediction are both types of inference. Different paradigms for inference can be used as a framework to understand how machine learning algorithms work or how learning problems can be addressed.

Examples of learning approaches are inductive, deductive, and transductive learning and inference. Between three types of inference can be differentiated in machine learning:

- Induction: Learning a general model from specific examples.
- Deduction: Using a model to make predictions.
- Transduction: Using specific examples to make predictions.

8.3.1 Inductive learning

While Inductive learning involves the use of evidence to determine the result, inductive reasoning refers to using specific cases to determine general outcomes (from specific to generalization). Most machine learning models train using inductive reasoning by learning general rules from specific historical samples.

The training data is used to create a model or hypothesis about the problem assumed to apply later to new, unseen data when the model is used.

8.3.2 Deductive learning

Deduction or deductive reasoning refers to the use of general rules to determine specific results. Induction can be better understood by contrasting it with deduction, where a deduction is the inverse of induction. If induction goes from the specific to the general, a deduction goes from the general to the specific. A deduction is a top-down type of reasoning where all premises must be satisfied before the conclusion is established. On the other side, induction is a bottom-up reasoning that uses available data as evidence.

In the context of machine learning, once the model has been fitted to a training data set using induction, it can be used to make predictions. The use of models is a type of deductive inference.

8.3.3 Transductive learning

Transduction or transductive learning is used in statistical learning to predict specific examples from a domain. Unlike induction, specific examples are used directly for reasoning, and no generalization is required. This can be a more specific problem to solve than induction. A classic example of a transductive algorithm is the k-nearest neighbor algorithm, which does not model the training data, but uses it directly each time of a prediction.

8.4 Learning techniques

Many learning techniques are described as specific learning types, like multitask, active, online, transfer, and ensemble learning. These are briefly described next.

8.4.1 Multitask learning

Multitask learning is a form of supervised learning in which a model is fit to a data set that addresses multiple related problems. The idea is to develop a model that can be trained on multiple related tasks, so the model performance is improved by training across multiple tasks compared to training on a single task. This approach can be useful to problems when there is a large amount of input data labeled for one task, which can be shared with another task with much less labeled data.

A multitask learning problem typically uses the same input pattern for multiple outputs or supervised learning problems. In this setup, each output can be predicted by a different part of the model, allowing the core of the model to generalize over each task for the same inputs.

A popular example of multitask learning is when the same word embedding is used to learn a distributed representation of words in the text used in multiple supervised natural language processing learning tasks.

8.4.2 Active learning

Active learning is supervised learning and attempts to achieve the same or better performance as so-called "passive" supervised learning, but through a more efficient selection of data collected or used by the model.

Active learning considers a model that can query a human operator during the learning process to resolve ambiguities during the learning process and is a useful approach when not much data is available or new data is expensive to label or collect. Active learning allows domain sampling to minimize the number of samples and maximize the effectiveness of the model.

8.4.3 Online learning

Online learning uses available data and updates the model directly before a prediction is required or after the last observation. It is suitable for problems where observations are provided over time and where the distribution of the observations is also expected to change over time. Therefore, the model is expected to change as frequently to capture and exploit these changes.

This approach is used by algorithms where there may be more observations than can reasonably fit in memory; therefore, learning is done incrementally over observations, such as a data stream.

An example of online learning is the so-called stochastic or online gradient descent used to fit an artificial neural network. More broadly, online learning is very useful to data stream processing, which has many applications in the health domain.

8.4.4 Transfer learning

Transfer learning is a type of learning in which a model is first trained for a task, and then part or all of the model is used as a starting point for a similar task. A useful approach can be found in training a task on a large existing data set and related the trained model to a similar task where only a few training samples exist.

It differs from multitask learning because, in transfer learning, the tasks are learned sequentially, whereas, in multitask learning, the goal is to achieve good performance on all considered tasks by a single model simultaneously. Transfer learning is beneficial for incrementally trained models, where an existing model can be used for further training, such as deep neural networks.

An example can be found in image classification, where a machine learning model can be trained on a large data set of available images, and the model weights are used for training a smaller, more specific data set, such as dogs and cats. The features that the model has already learned for the broader task, such as extracting lines and patterns, help with the new related task.

8.4.5 Ensemble learning

Ensemble learning is an approach in which two or more models are fitted to the same data, and the predictions of each model are combined. Ensemble learning aims to achieve better performance with the ensemble of models than with any individual model. This requires deciding how to create the models used in the ensemble and how best to combine the predictions of the ensemble members.

Ensemble learning is a useful approach to improving predictability and reducing the variance of stochastic learning algorithms, such as artificial neural networks. Some examples of popular ensemble learning algorithms are a weighted average, stacked generalization (stacking), and bootstrap aggregation (bagging); see also classification in Fig. 8.1.

8.5 Federated learning
8.5.1 Basic concepts

Artificial Intelligence (AI) research, and in particular advances in machine learning (ML) and deep learning (DL) [57], have led to breakthrough innovations in radiology, pathology, genomics, and other fields. Modern DL models have millions of parameters that must be learned from sufficiently large

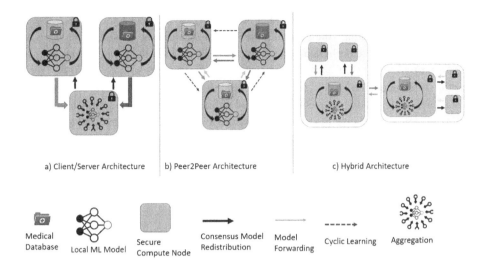

a) Client/Server Architecture   b) Peer2Peer Architecture   c) Hybrid Architecture

Medical Database   Local ML Model   Secure Compute Node   Consensus Model Redistribution   Model Forwarding   Cyclic Learning   Aggregation

FIGURE 8.3

Example federated learning (FL) workflows and difference to learning on a Centralized Data Lake.

curated datasets to achieve clinical-level accuracy while being safe, fair, equitable, and generalize well to unseen data [104,27,40,98].

For example, training an AI-based tumor detector requires a large database containing the full range of possible anatomies, pathologies, and input data types. Such data are difficult to obtain because health data are highly sensitive, and their use is strictly regulated [103]. Even if anonymizing data could circumvent these limitations, removing patient metadata such as name or birthday is often insufficient to preserve privacy [82]. Data sharing is not systematic in healthcare because collecting, curating, and maintaining a high-quality dataset requires significant time, effort, and cost. Consequently, such datasets may have significant commercial value, making it less likely that they will be shared freely. Instead, data collectors often retain fine-grained control over the data they collect.

Federated Learning (FL) [71,61,115] is a learning paradigm whose goal is to address data governance and data privacy by collaborative algorithm training without sharing the data itself. It was originally developed for various domains, e.g., mobile and edge-device scenarios [50], and has recently gained traction for healthcare applications [83,63,87,64,112,47,21,60]. FL enables collaborative learning, e.g., in the form of a consensus model, without taking patient data beyond the authority of the institutions it resides.

Instead, the ML process occurs locally at each participating institution, and only model characteristics (e.g., parameters, gradients) are transferred as depicted in Fig. 8.3. Recent research has shown that FL models can achieve performance levels comparable to ones trained on centrally hosted data sets and superior to models that only see isolated single-institutional data [63,87].

As can be seen from Fig. 8.3 a) an FL aggregation server –the typical FL workflow in which a federation of training nodes receive the global model, resubmit their partially trained models to a central server intermittently for aggregation and then continue training on the consensus model the server returns. In Fig. 8.3 b) an FL peer-to-peer –alternative formulation of FL in which each training node exchanges its partially trained models with some or all of its peers, and each does its aggregation. In Fig. 8.3 a), a centralized training –the general nonFL training workflow in which data were acquiring sites donate their data to a central Data Lake from which they and others can extract data for local, independent training.

Successful implementation of FL could thus hold significant potential for enabling precision medicine at a large scale, leading to models that yield unbiased decisions, optimally reflect an individual's physiology, and are sensitive to rare diseases while respecting governance and privacy concerns. However, FL still requires rigorous technical consideration to ensure that the algorithm is proceeding optimally without compromising safety or patient privacy. Nevertheless, it can overcome the limitations of approaches that require a single pool of centralized data.

8.5.2 Federated efforts in data-driven medicine

ML, and DL, in particular, are becoming the approach to knowledge discovery in many industries, but successful implementation of data-driven applications requires large and diverse datasets. However, medical datasets are difficult to obtain. FL addresses this problem by enabling collaborative learning without centralizing data and has already found its way into digital health applications. This new learning paradigm requires consideration of various stakeholders in healthcare.

The reliance on data

Data-driven approaches rely on data that represent the underlying data distribution of the problem. While this is a well-known requirement, modern algorithms are typically evaluated on carefully curated datasets, often from only a few sources. This can lead to biases where demographic or technical imbalances (e.g., acquisition protocol, different manufacturer) skew predictions and negatively impact the accuracy. However, to capture subtle relationships between disease patterns, socioeconomic and genetic factors, and complex and rare cases, it is critical to expose a model to different cases.

The need for large databases for AI training has spawned many initiatives that seek to pool data from multiple institutions. These data are often collected in data lakes. These have been built to exploit either the commercial value of the data like the IBM acquisition of Merge Healthcare [5], or as a resource for economic growth and scientific advancement, e.g., NHS Scotland's National Safe Haven [2], French Health Data Hub [39] and Health Data Research UK [4].

Major initiatives include the Human Connectome [96], the UK Biobank [97], the Cancer Imaging Archive (TCIA) [31], NIH CXR8 [105], NIH DeepLesion [113], the Cancer Genome Atlas (TCGA) [102], the Alzheimer's Disease Neuroimaging Initiative (ADNI) [48], and medical Grand Challenges such as the CAMELEON Challenge [68], the International multimodal Brain Tumor Segmentation (BraTS) Challenge [73,18,17] or the Medical Segmentation Decathlon [93]. Public medical data are usually task- or disease-specific and released with different licensing restrictions, which limits their use.

However, centralizing or releasing data brings regulatory, ethical, and legal challenges related to privacy, data protection, and technical aspects. Anonymization, access control, and secure transmission of health data is a nontrivial and sometimes impossible task. Anonymized electronic health record data may seem innocuous, and GDPR[1]/PHI compliant, but only a few data elements may allow patient re-identification [82]. The same is true for genomic data and medical images, which are as unique as a fingerprint [116]. Therefore, patient re-identification or information leakage cannot be ruled out unless the anonymization process destroys the fidelity of the data and likely renders it useless. Restricted access for approved users is often proposed as a putative solution to this problem. However, apart from limited data availability, this is only practical in cases where the consent of the data owners is unconditional, as recall of the data from those who may have had access to it is practically unenforceable.

The promise of federated efforts

The promise of FL is simple - addressing privacy and data governance challenges by enabling ML from nonlocal data. Each data steward defines their governance processes and associated privacy policies in an FL environment, controls data access, and can revoke it. This includes the training and validation phases. FL could create opportunities by enabling large-scale, intra-institutional validation or by enabling novel research on rare diseases where occurrence rates are low and datasets are too small at individual institutions. Moving the model to the data, rather than the other way around, has another significant advantage: high-dimensional, storage-intensive medical data do not have to be duplicated by local institutions into a central pool and duplicated again by each user who uses the local model training. When the model is transferred to local institutions, it can scale naturally with a potentially growing global dataset without disproportionately increasing data storage requirements.

An FL workflow can be implemented with different topologies and computational plans. The two most common applications in healthcare are via an aggregation server [63,87,64] and peer-to-peer approaches [83,26]. FL implicitly provides a degree of privacy because FL participants never directly access data from other institutions and only receive model parameters aggregated across multiple participants. In an FL workflow with an aggregation server, participating institutions may remain unknown to each other. It has been shown that the ML models can store information under certain conditions [91,85,119,23] and mechanisms such as differential privacy [10,90] or learning from encrypted data have been proposed to improve privacy in an FL environment. Overall, the potential of FL for healthcare applications has attracted community interest [56], and FL techniques are increasingly being explored in the field [50,112].

8.5.3 Current FL efforts for digital health

FL is a general learning paradigm that eliminates the need for data pooling for AI model development. With the ability to capture greater data variability and analyze patients across different demographics, FL can enable disruptive innovation for the future and can be used today.

In the context of electronic health records (EHRs), FL helps represent and find clinically similar patients [60,53] and predict hospitalizations based on cardiac events [21], mortality, and ICU length of stay [47]. The relevance and advantages of FL have also been demonstrated in medical imaging, e.g., whole-brain segmentation on MRI [83] and brain tumor segmentation [63,87]. Recently, FL has been used for fMRI classification (functional magnetic resonance imaging or functional MRI (fMRI)) to find

---

[1] GDPR –General Data Protection Regulation (EU) 2016/679– https://eur-lex.europa.eu/eli/reg/2016/679/oj.

reliable disease-related biomarkers [64], and a promising approach has been proposed in the context of COVID-19 [45].

FL efforts require agreements to define the target, scope, and technologies used, which can be challenging because it is still a novel approach. Today's large-scale initiatives are the foundation for tomorrow's standards for safe, fair, and innovative collaboration in healthcare applications. These include consortia aimed at advancing academic research, such as the Trustworthy Federated Data Analytics (TFDA) project [9] and the Joint Imaging Platform [6] of the German Cancer Consortium, which enables decentralized research between German medical imaging research institutions. Another example is an international research collaboration using FL to develop AI models for mammogram assessment [8]. The study showed that FL-generated models outperformed models trained on data from a single institute and were more generalizable, performing well on data from other institutes.

FL is not limited to academic settings, however. By linking healthcare institutions, not limited to research centers, FL can directly impact clinical outcomes. For example, the ongoing HealthChain project [1] aims to develop and deploy an FL framework for four hospitals in France. This solution generates standard models that can predict treatment response in breast cancer and melanoma patients. It helps oncologists determine the most effective treatment for each patient based on their histology or dermoscopy images. Another large-scale project is the Federated Tumor Segmentation (FeTS) initiative [3], an international consortium of 30 dedicated healthcare institutions using an open-source FL framework with a graphical user interface. The goal is to improve tumor boundary detection, including brain gliomas, breast tumors, liver tumors, and bone lesions from patients with multiple myeloma.

Another area of impact is industrial research and translation. FL enables collaborative research for, even competing, companies. In this context, one of the biggest initiatives is the Melody project [7], a project that aims to apply multitask FL to the datasets of 10 pharmaceutical companies. By training a basic predictive model that allows inferences about how chemical compounds bind to proteins, the partners intend to optimize the drug development process without revealing their extremely valuable internal data.

Impact on stakeholders

FL represents a paradigm shift from centralized data lakes, and it is critical to understand the implications for the various stakeholders in the FL ecosystem.

Clinicians typically deal with a subset of the population based on their location and demographics, leading to biased assumptions about the likelihood of certain diseases or their associations. Using ML-based systems, e.g., as second readers, they can supplement their expertise with expert knowledge from other institutions to ensure diagnosis that is not possible today. While this is true for ML-based systems in general, systems that have been trained in a network can potentially provide even less biased decisions and higher sensitivity to rare cases, as they have likely been exposed to a more complete distribution of data. However, this requires some upfront efforts, such as adherence to agreements regarding data structure, annotation, and reporting protocol, which are necessary to ensure that information is presented in a commonly understood format.

Patients are generally treated locally. Establishing FL in a global effort could ensure high-quality clinical decisions regardless of the treatment location. In particular, patients requiring medical care in remote areas could benefit from the same high-quality ML-based diagnoses that are available in hospitals with many cases. The same is true for rare or geographically uncommon diseases, which are likely to have milder outcomes under the premise of a faster and more accurate diagnosis. FL may also lower the barrier to becoming a data donor, as patients can be assured that their facility's data will be preserved and data access can be revoked.

Hospitals and practices

Hospitals and practices can retain full control and ownership of their patient data, with full traceability and transparency of data access, limiting the risk of misuse by third parties. Nevertheless, this requires investment in on-premises computing infrastructure or private cloud services and adherence to standardized data representations so that ML models can be trained and evaluated smoothly. The amount of computing capacity required depends on whether a site participates only in evaluation and testing or training. Even relatively small facilities can participate and will still benefit from the jointly created models.

Researchers and AI developers benefit from access to a potentially vast collection of real-world data, which significantly impacts smaller research labs and startups. This will allow resources to be directed toward solving clinical needs and related technical problems instead of relying on limited open datasets. It will be necessary to explore algorithmic strategies for federated training, e.g., how to efficiently combine models or updates, how to be robust to distribution shifts [115,50,112]. FL-based development also means that the researcher or AI developer cannot examine or visualize all data on which the model is trained; it is not possible to look at single failure cases to understand issues on the overall model performance.

In many countries, Healthcare providers face the issue of the ongoing paradigm shift from volume-based (fee-for-service) to value-based healthcare, which in turn is strongly linked to the successful establishment of precision medicine. This is not about promoting more expensive individualized therapies but about achieving better outcomes sooner through more targeted treatment, thereby reducing costs. FL can increase the accuracy and robustness of AI in healthcare while lowering costs and improving patient outcomes; it can be critical to precision medicine.

Healthcare software and hardware manufacturers could also benefit from FL, as combining learning from many devices and applications without revealing patient-specific information can facilitate continuous validation or improvement of their ML-based systems. However, realizing such a capability may require significant upgrades to local computing power, data storage, networking capabilities, and associated software.

8.5.4 Technical considerations

FL is perhaps famously known from the work of Konecny *et al.* [54], and since then, several other definitions have been proposed in the literature [71,115,50,112]. An FL workflow (see Fig. 8.3) can be implemented using different topologies and computational plans, but the goal remains the same, which is to combine knowledge learned from noncoordinated data. In this subsection, key challenges and technical considerations in applying FL to digital health are highlighted.

Federated learning definition

FL is the learning paradigm where multiple individuals train collaboratively without sharing or centralizing data sets. The general formulation of FL is as follows:

Let us denote by L a global loss function obtained by a weighted combination of K local losses $\{L_k\}_{k=1}^{K}$, processed from private data X_k residing at each individual involved and never exchanged between them:

$$\min_{\phi} L(X; \phi) \text{ with } L(X; \phi) = \sum_{k=1}^{K} w_k L_k(X_k; \phi) \tag{8.1}$$

where $w_k > 0$ means the respective weight coefficients.

In practice, each individual typically obtains and refines a global consensus model by performing a few rounds of optimization locally before sharing updates directly or through a parameter server. The more local training rounds are performed, the less the overall procedure guarantees minimization [71, 50]. The actual process for aggregating parameters depends on the network topology, as nodes may be split into subnetworks due to geographic or legal constraints. Aggregation strategies can rely on a single aggregation node (hub and spokes models) or on multiple nodes without any centralization. An example is peer-to-peer FL, where connections exist between all or a subset of the participants and model updates are exchanged only between directly connected sites [83,55]. Further to add, aggregation strategies do not necessarily need information about the full model update. Clients can choose to share only a subset of the model parameters to reduce communication overhead, provide better privacy preservation [61], or produce multitasking learning algorithms that have learned only a subset of their parameters in a federated manner.

A unifying framework that enables different training schemes can detach computational resources (data and servers) from the computational layer.

An example of an FL algorithm via Hub & Spoke (Centralized topology) with FedAvg aggregation is depicted in Algorithm 1.

Algorithm 1 FL Algorithm [63] in a client-server architecture with aggregation via FedAvg [72,81].

1: **Require**: *num_federated_rounds*, T
2: **procedure** AGGREGATING(*num_federated_rounds*, T)
3:      **Initialize** global model: $W^{(0)}$
4:      **for** $t = 1 \ldots T$ **do**
5:          **for** client $k = 1 \ldots K$ **do**   ▷ Run in parallel
6:              Send $W^{(t-1)}$ to client k
7:              Receive model updates and number of local training
                 $\hookrightarrow$ iterations $(\Delta W_k^{(t-1)}), N_k)$ from client's local
                 $\hookrightarrow$ training with $L_k(X_k; W^{(t-1)})$
8:          **end for**
9:          $W^{(t)} = W^{(t-1)} + \frac{1}{\sum_k N_k} \sum_k (N_k \cdot W_k^{(t-1)})$
10:     **end for**
           return $W^{(t)}$
11: **end procedure**

Challenges and considerations

Despite the benefits of FL, it does not solve all the inherent problems in learning on medical data. Successful model training still depends on factors such as data quality, bias, and standardization [104]. These issues need to be addressed for both federated and nonfederated learning efforts through suitable measures, such as careful study design, standard protocols for data collection, structured reporting, and sophisticated methods for detecting bias and hidden stratification.

Below, key aspects of FL are reviewed that are particularly relevant when applied to digital health and need to be considered when building an FL. Technical details and in-depth discussions can be found in recent studies [115,50,112].

Data heterogeneity

Medical data are diverse-not only because of the variety of modalities, dimensionality, and characteristics in general, but also within a given protocol due to factors such as acquisition differences, medical device brand, or local demographics. FL can help address specific sources of bias through potentially increased data source diversity, but heterogeneous data distribution presents a challenge for FL algorithms and strategies, as many assume independently and identically distributed (IID) data on participants. In general, strategies such as FedAvg [71] tend to fail under these conditions [71,62,120], which in part defeats the very purpose of collaborative learning strategies. However, recent results suggest that FL training is still feasible [65] even when medical data are not evenly distributed across institutions [63,87] or contain local bias [8]. Research addressing this problem includes, for example, FedProx [62], partial data sharing strategy [120], and FL with domain adaptation [64]. Another challenge is that data heterogeneity can lead to a situation where the optimal global solution is not optimal for a single local participant. Therefore, the definition of the optimality of the model training should be agreed upon by all participants prior to the training.

Privacy and security

Healthcare data is sensitive and must be protected accordingly, with appropriate confidentiality procedures. Therefore, some of the most important considerations are the trade-offs, strategies, and remaining risks regarding the privacy-friendly potential of FL.

Privacy vs. performance

FL does not solve all possible privacy issues, and, similar to ML algorithms in general, it will always introduce some risks. Privacy-preserving techniques for FL provide a level of protection that exceeds current commercially available ML models [50]. However, there is a trade-off in performance, and these techniques may affect the accuracy of the final model [61]. In addition, future techniques and auxiliary data could be used to compromise a model that was previously considered low risk.

Level of trust

Participating parties can enter into two types of FL collaboration:

Trusted - For FL consortia, where all parties are deemed trustworthy and bound by an enforceable collaboration agreement, we can rule out many of the more nefarious motivations, such as deliberate attempts to extract sensitive information or deliberate damage to the model. This reduces the need for sophisticated countermeasures and draws on the principles of standard collaboration research.

Untrusted - For FL systems operating at scale, it may be impractical to establish an enforceable collaboration agreement. Some clients may intentionally attempt to degrade performance, crash the system, or extract information from other parties. Therefore, security strategies are required to mitigate these risks, such as advanced encryption of model inputs, secure authentication of all parties, action traceability, differential privacy, verification systems, execution integrity, model confidentiality, and protection against adversarial attacks.

Information leakage

By definition, FL systems avoid sharing health data among participating institutions. However, the shared information may still indirectly reveal private data used for local training, such as the model inversion [111] of model updates, the gradients themselves [121], or adversarial attacks [106,46]. FL differs from traditional training because the training process is exposed to multiple parties, which increases the risk of leakage through reverse engineering. Leakage can occur when attackers can observe model changes over time, observe specific model updates (i.e., updating a single institution), or manipulate the model (e.g., additional memorization by others through gradient-ascent style attacks). Developing countermeasures, such as limiting the granularity of updates and adding noise [63,64] and ensuring adequate differential privacy [10], may be required and is still an active area of research [50].

Traceability and accountability

Required for all safety-critical applications, system reproducibility is critical for FL in healthcare. Unlike centralized training, FL requires computation with multiple participants in environments with a significant variety of hardware, software, and networks. Traceability of all system resources, including data access history, training configurations, and hyperparameter tuning throughout the training process, is imperative.

Especially for untrusted federations, traceability and accountability processes require integrity in execution. When the training process achieves the mutually agreed-upon model optimality criteria, it may be helpful to measure each participant's contribution, such as the computational resources consumed or the quality of data used for local training. These measurements could then determine appropriate compensation and establish a revenue model among participants [42]. One implication of FL is that researchers cannot examine which models are trained to understand unexpected outcomes. In addition, taking statistical measurements of their training data as part of the model development workflow must be approved by the collaborating parties as not to violate data privacy. Although each individual will have access to its raw data, the collaboratives may decide to provide some type of secure intra-node viewing capability to meet this need or provide another way to increase the explainability and interpretability of the global model.

System architecture

Unlike running FL on a large scale among consumer devices [71], healthcare participants have relatively powerful computational resources and reliable higher-throughput networks that enable larger models with many more local training steps that share more model information between nodes. These characteristics of FL in healthcare also carry challenges, such as ensuring data integrity in communications by using redundant nodes, designing secure encryption methods to prevent data leaks, or designing appropriate node schedulers to optimize distributed computing devices and reduce idle time.

The management of such a federation can be implemented in a variety of ways. In situations that require the strictest privacy between parties, training can be done through a type of "honest broker" system, where a trusted third party acts as an intermediary and facilitates access to the data. This setup requires an independent control entity of the overall system, which is not always feasible because it could involve additional costs and procedural implementations. However, it has the advantage of abstracting the exact internal mechanisms from the clients, making the system more agile and easier to update. In a peer-to-peer system, each site communicates directly with the other participants. There is no gatekeeper function, where all protocols must be agreed upon in advance, which requires significant agreement effort, and changes must be made by all participants in a synchronized manner to avoid problems.

8.5.5 The potential of federated learning

ML, especially DL, has led to a variety of innovations in digital health. Since all ML methods benefit significantly from data access that approximates the actual global distribution, FL is a promising approach to obtain accurate, secure, robust, and unbiased models. Because FL allows multiple parties to train collaboratively without sharing or centralizing datasets, it deftly addresses issues related to the leakage of sensitive medical data. As a result, it can open new directions in research and business and has the potential to improve patient care worldwide. FL is already impacting nearly all stakeholders and the entire care cycle, from improved medical image analysis that gives clinicians better diagnostic tools to true precision medicine by helping find similar patients, collaborative and accelerated drug development that reduces costs and time to market for pharmaceutical companies. Not all technical obstacles have been solved yet, but FL will undoubtedly be an active area of research in the next decade [50]. Nevertheless, the potential impact of FL on precision medicine and ultimately improving medical care is very promising.

8.6 Handling concept drifts

In [86], a general overview of the methods, tools and techniques for dealing with concept drift has been presented. Depending on the specific application, these methods have been classified according to predefined meaningful criteria to provide the reader with a guide for designing an efficient self-adaptive machine learning and data mining scheme. The different approaches to deal with concept drift have been classified into two main categories, depending on how they update the learner in response to the occurrence of a drift. The first category is the informed methods, where the learner is only updated when a drift is detected and confirmed. Therefore, the informed methods use a set of change indicators to trigger the updating of the learner. Depending on the availability of the true labels, these indicators are divided into supervised and unsupervised change indicators. Supervised change indicators assume that the true labels of the incoming patterns are immediately available, while unsupervised indicators monitor changes in the learner complexity or the properties of the data distribution in the feature space. The second category is the blind method, in which the learner is continuously updated on the incoming data patterns regardless of whether drift has occurred. The methods that deal with concept drift were also divided into two categories: Sequential and Window-based approaches. Sequential methods handle each data sample as soon as it arrives and then discard it, while window-based approaches process data samples within a time window.

The methods that handle concept drift can be based on either one learner or a set of learners. In the latter case, they are called ensemble methods. Single learners, or ensemble-based learners, can be managed in three techniques to handle concept drift:

- By exploiting the training set.

Table 8.1 Guidelines to select methods to handle concept drift according to the drift kind and characteristics [86].

Drift Type	Method
Abrupt	Sequential Methods + single learner + ensemble (fixed size)
Gradual Probabilistic	Window based (variable size) + ensemble (variable size)
Gradual Continuous	Window based (variable size) + ensemble (variable size)
Global	Sequential methods + single learner + ensemble (fixed size)
Local	Window based (variable size) + ensemble (variable size)
Real	Informed (supervised drift indicators)
Virtual	Informed (unsupervised drift indicators) + blind methods
Cyclic	Ensemble (fixed size)
Acyclic	Sequential Methods + single learner + ensemble (variable size)
Predictable	Informed methods
Unpredictable	Informed (unsupervised drift indicators) + blind methods

- By integrating a fixed or variable number of learners trained using the same learning method but with different parameter settings or using different learning methods.
- By managing the decisions of the ensemble's individual learners.

The final decision can be issued either by combining the individual learners' weighted decisions, selecting one of the individual learners, or combining the decisions of a subset of selected individual learners. Finally, in this chapter, the criteria that may indicate the evaluation outcome of the machine learning and data mining scheme to handle concept drift are defined. They allow evaluating the autonomy (involvement of a human being in the learning scheme), the reliability of drift detection and description, the independence and influence of parameter setting on the learning scheme performance, and the time and memory requirements for the decision computing. Table 8.1 summarizes the guidelines to help readers choose the methods suitable for handling concept drift according to its kind and characteristics.

For more information on drift concept for data streams, the reader is referred to Section 1.4 in Chapter 1.

8.7 ML frameworks

In the last 25 years, many frameworks for Data Mining have been developed using ML/DL techniques [49]. Their goal is to support the complex data analysis process and propose integrated environments based on standard programming languages. These tools are designed for purposes like analysis platforms, predictive systems, recommendation systems, and image/audio processors. Many of them are focused on fast processing and streaming large amounts of data, while others are specialized in implementing ML algorithms. There is no single tool that is appropriate for every problem, and often a combination of them is required to be successful. Authors in [76] provide a comprehensive grouped overview of ML frameworks and libraries. Fig. 8.4 depicts a comprehensive grouped overview of ML frameworks and libraries.

In the following subsections, we analyze the main ML frameworks in terms of their strength and weaknesses to help to understand their suitability.

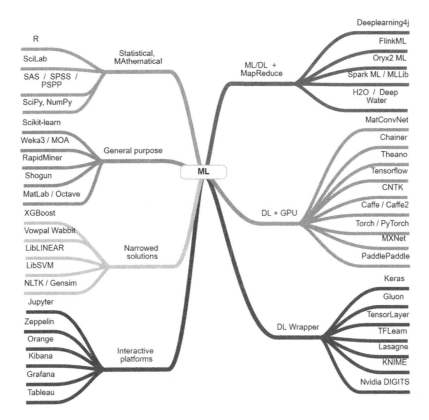

FIGURE 8.4

Overview of Machine Learning frameworks and libraries [76].

8.7.1 ML frameworks without special hardware support

Shogun

Shogun is an open-source general-purpose ML library that provides a wide range of efficient and ML methods [95] based on an architecture written in C++ and under GNU GPLv3 license.[2]

Strengths

- ML toolbox with many standard cutting-edge ML algorithms.
- Open-source, cross-platform API-oriented framework, implemented in C++.
- Links to many other ML libraries, programming interface in many languages.

Weaknesses

- Most of the code was written by researchers for their studies over a long time and is therefore not easy to maintain or extend.

---

[2] Shogun official web page https://www.shogun.ml/.

- Lack of documentation, mainly suitable for academic use.

RapidMiner

RapidMiner is a general-purpose data science software platform for data preparation, ML, text mining, and predictive analytics [74]. RapidMiner[3] (formerly YALE) was developed at the Chair of Artificial Intelligence at the Technical University of Dortmund in 2001. It is a cross-platform framework based on an open core model written in Java. Rapid-Miner supports GUI, command-line interface, and Java API.

Strengths
- Provides a comprehensive set of algorithms with learning schemes, models, and algorithms from Weka and R scripts.
- Support for add-ons with selected algorithms for big data.
- Platform independent framework with a strong community.

Weaknesses
- Proprietary product and not applicable for every large scale projects.

Weka3

Weka provides a collection of general-purpose ML algorithms implemented in Java and developed explicitly for Data Mining as a product of the University of Waikato in New Zealand under the GNU GPLv3 license for noncommercial purposes.[4]

Weka's functionality is extended with a package system that provides official and unofficial packages increasing the DM methods. The versions of Command Line Interface (CLI), Explorer, Experimenter, and KnowledgeFlow exist. In the most recent version, Weka can be used with Weka supports Hadoop due to many wrappers made for the latest versions of Weka3. It currently supports Map Reduce, but not yet Apache Spark.

Clojure[5] users can also leverage Weka over the Clj-ml library. The free, open-source software project Massive Online Analysis (MOA) can be used for data stream analytics and has a bi-directional interaction with Weka.

Strengths
- General purpose framework includes a wide range of algorithms with learning schemes, models, and algorithms.
- Provides a GUI and is API-oriented.
- Supports standard Analytics tasks including function selection, clustering, classification, regression, and visualization.
- Popular ML tool in the academic community.

Weaknesses
- Limited to big data, text mining, and semisupervised learning.
- Weak for sequence modeling like time-series problems.

---

[3] RapidMiner official web page https://rapidminer.com/.

[4] Weka official web page http://www.cs.waikato.ac.nz/ml/weka/.

[5] Clojure official web page https://clojure.org/.

Scikit-Learn

Scikit-Learn is a popular open-source Python tool containing a comprehensive Data Mining library.[6] The functionality of NumPy and SciPy is extended with numerous Data Mining algorithms and offer functions for classification, regression, clustering, dimension reduction, model selection, and preprocessing. Since April 2016, Scikit-Learn has been offered a joint development with Anaconda with Cloudera project on Hadoop clusters (Anaconda Cloudera). In addition to Scikit-Learn, Anaconda includes several popular mathematics, science, and engineering packages such as NumPy, SciPy, and Pandas.

Strengths

- General purpose, open source, commercially usable Python Data Mining tool.
- Supported by INRIA, Telecom Paristech, Google, and others.
- Well maintained and comprehensive algorithms.
- Part of many ecosystems and closely related to statistical and scientific Python packages.

Weaknesses

- API oriented only.
- Does not support GPUs.

LibSVM

LibSVM is a library for the famous Support Vector Machine Algorithm.[7] The development began in 2000 at the National Taiwan University [25] and is written in C/C++, and has parts in Java source code. Learning tasks can be categorized in the tasks of classification, regression, and distribution estimation. Supported problem formulations are: C-SVC, ν-SVC, distribution estimation (one-class SVM), ϵ-SVR, and ν-SVR. All formulations are quadratic minimization problems and are solved by the sequential minimal optimization algorithm. LibSVM provides configurations for unbalanced data using different penalty parameters and has been used in bioinformatics, computer vision, NLP, and neuroimaging. LibSVM provides interfaces for many programming languages like Python, R, MATLAB®, Perl, Ruby, Weka, or PHP. The base code was also reused in DM tools like Weka, RapidMiner, and KNIME. Scikit-Learn states to utilize LibSVM with modifications and improvements.

Strengths

- The LibSVM has a specific data format that is well accepted in other frameworks and libraries. The representation is dense and suitable for describing and processing big data, especially because it allows sparse representation.
- Special open-source tool that is very popular in the open-source ML community.

Weaknesses

- Compared to LibLinear or Vowpal Wabbit, the LibSVM training algorithm cannot scale well for large amounts of data [122]. In the worst case it takes $O(n^3)$ [12], and in typical cases $O(n^2))$ with n the number of data points.
- Limited to problems where SVM performs well.

---

[6] Scikit-Learn official web page https://scikit-learn.org/stable/.

[7] LibSVM official web page https://www.csie.ntu.edu.tw/~cjlin/libsvm/.

LibLinear

LibLinear is a library for solving large linear classification problems developed at National Taiwan University from 2007 [41] and written in C/C ++.[8] Logistic regression and linear SVM are supported tasks, with the problem formulations of L2-regulated logistic regression, linear SVMs with L2 loss and L1 loss. L1-SVM and L2-SVM are a coordinate descent method. For linear regression and L2-SVM, LibLinear implements a Newton method for confidence intervals. If there are problems with multiple classes, LibLinear implements the One-vs-Rest strategy and the Crammer & Singer method [37,38].

LibLinear offers interfaces for MatLab, Octave, Java, Python, and Ruby. The code is reused in DM tools like Weka and KNIME. Scikit-Learn states to use LibLinear to do calculations internally, but with changes and optimization. At National Taiwan University, the ML group work on MPI LibLinear, an extension of LibLinear for distributed environments, and Spark LibLinear, a LibLinear-based Spark implementation that integrates with the Hadoop distributed file system.

Strengths
- Designed to solve large-scale linear classification problems.
- Open source tool popular in the open-source ML community.

Weaknesses
- Limited to Logistic Regression and linear SVM.

VowpalWabbit

Vowpal Wabbit is an efficiently scalable implementation of online ML and supports various incremental ML methods.[9] VW is offered in Microsoft Azure and includes reduction functions, importance weighting, selection of various loss functions, and optimization algorithms. VW has proven to learn a data set with (10^{12}) features on 1000 nodes in one hour.

Strengths
- Open source, efficient, scalable, and fast out-of-core online learning supported by Microsoft and previously Yahoo.
- Feature identities are hash converted into a weighted index using a 32-bit MurmurHash3. Feature hashing or the hashing trick [107], is a fast and space-saving method of vectorizing features that enables fast online learning.
- The use of multicore CPUs in the Hadoop cluster through its own MPI-All Reduce library. The parsing of inputs and learning are carried out in separate threads.
- Allows the use of nonlinear features, such as n-grams.
- Produces a code compiled C++.
- One of the ML options offered in Microsoft Azure.
- Designed to solve linear classification problems.
- Open source tool popular in the open-source ML community.
- Runs properly in a single machine, Hadoop or HPC cluster [11].

Weaknesses
- The available ML methods are sufficient but limited.

---

[8] LibLinear official web page https://www.csie.ntu.edu.tw/~cjlin/liblinear/.
[9] Vowpal Wabbit official web page https://vowpalwabbit.org//.

XGBoost

XGBoost[10] is an open-source library for optimized distributed gradient tree boosting [28] that gained popularity lately as it has been the algorithm of choice for many winning teams from several ML competitions. This gradient boosting framework provides parallel tree augmentation to solve many data science problems quickly. XGBoost runs in a distributed environment (Hadoop, SGE, MPI) and can solve big data problems. The term gradient boosting originates in the idea of enhancing or improving a single weak model by combining it with several other weak models to produce a collectively robust model. The weak learning models are reinforced through iterative learning.

Strengths
- Interfaces for C ++, Java, Python, R, and Julia and works on Linux, Windows, and Mac OS.
- Supports the Apache Hadoop/Spark/Flink, and DataFlow distributed processing frameworks.
- High performance in model training and execution speed.
- Parallelization of the tree construction using all CPU cores during the training.
- Distributed computing for training large models with the help of a machine cluster.
- Out-of-core computing for huge amounts of data that do not fit in memory.
- Cache optimized data structures for optimal use of the hardware.

Weaknesses
- Boosting library designed for tabular data, hence, won't work for other tasks like NLP or Computer Vision.

8.7.2 Interactive data analytic and visualization tools

There are many data visualization packages on different abstraction levels in R or Python, like Matplotlib, Ggplot, Seaborn, Plotly, and Bokeh.

Web-based notebooks integrated with data analytic environments have gained popularity. The following are examples of those notebooks.

- Jupyter Notebook is an open-source application that supports the creation and sharing of documents, code execution, visualization, as well as an interface for more complex infrastructure automation or application interaction.[11]
- Zeppelin is a notebook for processing, analyzing, and visualizing large amounts of data that has native support for Apache Spark and can be expanded by using various interpreters like Spark, SparkSQL, Scala, Python, and Apache Spark Shell.[12]

Among open-source tools for data analysis integrated into platforms, we can distinguish:

- Kibana is the visualization front end for the Elastic Stack and complements the rest of the stack, including Beats, Logstash, and Elasticsearch, including Timelion for interactive time series diagrams.[13]

---

[10] XGBoost official web page https://xgboost.ai/.
[11] Project Jupyter official web page https://jupyter.org/.
[12] Zeppelin official web page https://zeppelin.apache.org/.
[13] Kibana official web page https://www.elastic.co/kibana.

- Grafana is a DevOps tool for real-time monitoring dashboard and supports backend data sources including InfluxDB, Graphite, Elasticsearch, and others.[14]
- Tableau is a universal analytics tool that can be used to extract data from various data sources such as CSV, Excel, SQL, or to connect frameworks and cloud-based sources.[15]

8.7.3 Other data analytic frameworks and libraries

- MatLab is a computing environment that uses a proprietary programming language developed by MathWorks. MatLab is very popular with over 2 million users in industry and science. The more popular free alternatives to MatLab are GNU Octave and SciLab.[16]
- SAS (Statistical Analysis System) is a proprietary software package written in C for advanced data analysis.[17] SPSS (Statistical Package for the Social Sciences) is another similar proprietary software package.[18] An open-source alternative of SPSS is GNU PSPP.
- R is a free environment for statistical calculations and graphics, including linear and nonlinear modeling, classical statistical tests, classification, clustering, and time series analysis. It compiles and runs on under Windows and Unix.[19] The R archive network has more than 10,000 packages, and the list is growing. Many frameworks have wrappers for R.
- Python is a programming language created by Guido van Rossum.[20] Python is well established in thousands of real-world business applications worldwide, such as Google and YouTube. The main reason for introducing Python for ML is because it is a universal programming language for research, development, and production on a small and large scale. Python has a dynamic type system and automatic memory management with extensive and comprehensive libraries for scientific calculations and data analysis. In addition to R, many frameworks have bindings for Python.
- SciPy is an open-source Python library for scientific and technical computing that is built on NumPy array objects and part of the NumPy stack, including tools like Pandas and SymPy.[21]
- Pandas is a Python package that provides fast, flexible, and expressive data structures that make working with relational or labeled data easier.[22] The two primary data structures of Series (one-dimensional) and DataFrame (two-dimensional) handle most use cases in finance, statistics, social sciences, and many technical areas.
- NLTK[23] and Gensim[24] are two leading toolkits for working with data in human language. NLTK contains a comprehensive list of word processing libraries for classification, tokenization, stemming, tagging, parsing, and semantic thinking. Gensim is an open-source vector space and topic modeling toolkit for large text collections via data streaming and incremental algorithms.

---

[14] Grafana official web page https://grafana.com.
[15] Tableau official web page https://www.tableau.com/.
[16] Matlab official web page https://mathworks.com/products/matlab.htm.
[17] SAS official web page https://www.sas.com/.
[18] SPSS official web page https://www.ibm.com/analytics/spss-statistics-software.
[19] R-Project official web page https://www.r-project.org.
[20] Python official web page https://www.python.org.
[21] SciPy official web page https://www.scipy.org.
[22] Pandas official web page https://pandas.pydata.org.
[23] NLTK official web page www.nltk.org.
[24] Gensim official web page https://gensim.org/home.

8.7.4 Deep learning frameworks and libraries

Modern ML frameworks already offer the ability to use GPU accelerators to speed up model training. Some of them enable optimized libraries like CUDA (cuDNN) or OpenCL to improve performance further. Multicore accelerators enable massively parallel architectures to accelerate matrix-based operations in computing tasks.

TensorFlow

TensorFlow is an open-source library for numerical calculation using data flow graphs.[25] It was created by the Google Brain team and is currently released under the Apache 2.0 open source license. TensorFlow is designed for distributed model training and inference on a large scale. Graph nodes represent mathematical operations, while the graph edges represent multidimensional arrays of data called tensors. The distributed TensorFlow architecture includes distributed master and worker services with kernel implementations, including 200 standard operations, including math, array manipulation, control flow, and state management operations, written in C ++. TensorFlow runs on single CPU/GPU, mobile device, and large distributed systems. TensorFlow Lite a lightweight solution for mobile and embedded devices.

It was created and is maintained by the Google Brain team within Google's Machine Intelligence research organization for ML and DL. It is currently released under the Apache 2.0 open-source license. TensorFlow is designed for large-scale distributed training and inference. Nodes in the graph represent mathematical operations, while the graph edges represent the multidimensional data arrays (tensors) communicated between them. The distributed TensorFlow architecture contains distributed master and worker services with kernel implementations. These include 200 standard operations, including mathematical, array manipulation, control flow, and state management. It can run on single CPU systems, GPUs, mobile devices, and large-scale distributed systems of hundreds of nodes. TensorFlow Lite is the lightweight version for mobile and embedded devices.[26] It allows ML model execution on device level with low latency and limited resources. The TensorFlow includes APIs for Python, C++, Java, Go, Haskell, and R. TensorFlow is also supported in Google and Amazon cloud environments.

Strengths

- By far the most popular open-source DL tool that is fast-evolving and supported by Google.
- Numerical library for dataflow programming that provides the basis for DL research and development.
- Efficient mathematical multidimensional array computation.
- Efficient in multiGPU and mobile computing,
- High-scale computing across machines and huge data sets.

Weaknesses

- Compared to other libraries, difficult to use for creating DL models.
- Each computational flow must be created as a static graph, although the TensorFlow Fold package tries to fix this problem.

---

[25] TensorFlow official web page https://www.tensorflow.org.
[26] TensorFlow Lite official web page https://www.tensorflow.org/lite/.

TensorFlow 2.0 focused on the ease of using a more robust integration with high-level APIs like Keras, Eager, and Estimators and eager execution of distributed training across multiple GPUs, multiple TPUs, and multiple machines.

Keras

Keras is a Python wrapper library that provides wrappers to other DL libraries such as TensorFlow, CNTK, Theano, MXNet, and Deeplearning4.[27] It was developed with the goal of rapid experimentation released under the MIT license. Keras runs under Python 2.7 to 3.6 and provides GPUs and CPUs support. Keras is developed and maintained according to four guiding principles:

Strengths
- Open source, quick evolving library with backend tools supported by strong industrial companies like Google and Microsoft.
- Popular API for DL with big community and comprehensive documentation.
- Convenient and straightforward way to define DL models in backends like Tensor-Flow, CNTK, or Theano.

Weaknesses
- Less flexible due to the trade-off with modularity and simplicity. Not ideal for researching new architectures.
- The multiGPU still does not work with 100% efficiency and simplicity, as shown by several benchmarks it used with a TensorFlow backend [76].

Microsoft CNTK

Microsoft Cognitive Toolkit (CNTK) is a commercial distributed DL framework with extensive data sets from Microsoft Research.[28] It implements efficient DNN training for speech, image, handwriting, and text data. Its network is given as a symbolic graph of vector operations, such as Matrix add, multiplication, or convolution with building block operators. CNTK runs on Linux and Windows systems with Python, C#, C++, and BrainScript API.

Strengths
- Open source, quick evolving library supported by Microsoft.
- Supports the Open Neural Network Exchange (ONNX) format, which has a universal representation schema to easily transform models between CNTK, Caffe2, PyTorch, and MXNet.

Weaknesses
- Limited functionality on mobile devices.

Caffe

Caffe is a DL framework developed by Yangqing Jia at BAIR (Berkeley Artificial Intelligence Research) and community contributors.[29] Data is entered via data layers in Caffe, where possible data sources are efficient databases (LevelDB or LMDB), the hierarchical data format (HDF5), or image

---

[27] Keras Lite official web page https://keras.io.

[28] CNTK Lite official web page https://docs.microsoft.com/cognitive-toolkit/.

[29] Caffe official web page https://caffe.berkeleyvision.org.

formats. Common layers and normalization layers provide various data vector processing and normalization operations, while custom layers need to be written in C++ or Python.

Strengths
- Great for image processing with CNNs.
- Pretrained models are available for fine-tuning in the Caffe Model Zoo.
- API/CLI interface for Python and MatLab.

Weaknesses
- Development is not as active anymore.
- Definition of a static model graph does not suit many RNN applications that require variable size input.
- Model definition in Caffe Prototxt files is too heavy for modular DNN models such as GoogleLeNet or ResNet compared to other frameworks.
- Custom levels must be written in C ++.

Several custom distributions are also currently available, like Intel Caffe (multimode and Intel Xeon processor-optimized), OpenCL Caffe (version with OpenCL backend and additional layers for image segmentation), Windows Caffe (version for Windows and Visual Studio).

Caffe2

Caffe2 is a lightweight, modular and scalable deep learning framework developed at Facebook.[30] Caffe2 is used at the production level on Facebook, while development is done in PyTorch. Caffe2 differs from Caffe in performance by adding mobile deployment and new hardware support in addition to CPU and CUDA. It is geared towards industrial-grade applications, with an emphasis on mobile devices. The basic arithmetic unit in Caffe2 is the Operator. It is expected that more than 400 different operators will be implemented in Caffe2 and more by the community. Caffe2 provides command-line Python scripts that can be used to translate existing Caffe models into Caffe2. It is possible to convert Torch models into Caffe2 models via Caffe.

Strengths
- Cross-platform framework with a focus on mobile, edge device inference framework of choice for Facebook.
- Intel, Qualcomm, NVIDIA officially support Caffe2 due to its robust, scalable deployment.
- Supports the Open Neural Network Exchange (ONNX) format, which has a universal representation schema to easily transform models between CNTK, Caffe2, PyTorch, and MXNet.

Weaknesses
- Not trivial for DL beginners in comparison with PyTorch.
- Does not provide dynamic graph computation.

Caffe2 is available for macOS, Ubuntu, Windows, iOS, CentOS, Android, and Raspbian. Caffe2 will be merged with PyTorch to combine the flexible user experience of PyTorch with the scaling, provisioning, and embedding capabilities of the Caffe2 backend. Caffe2 was merged with PyTorch to combine the PyTorch usability with the scaling, deployment, and embedding capabilities of the Caffe2 backend.

---

[30] Caffe2 official web page https://caffe2.ai/.

Torch

Torch is a scientific computing framework based on the Lua programming language, which has been under active development since 2002 [32].[31] Torch is supported and deployed by big companies like Facebook, Google, DeepMind, and Twitter and freely available under the BSD license. Torch is implemented in C++ and follows an object-oriented paradigm, and has an API used as a wrapper for C/C++ and CUDA. The core Tensor library supports CPU and GPU backends and many classical operations efficiently implemented in C, using SSE instructions on Intel platforms, and the possibility to bind linear algebra operations to existing BLAS/Lapack implementations like IntelMKL [33]. This framework provides parallel computation CPUs via OpenMP and GPUs via CUDA. Torch is mainly deployed for large-scale training in speech, image, video applications and supervised learning, unsupervised learning, reinforcement learning, optimization, graph models, and image processing.

Strengths
- Flexibility, readability, mid-level code, and high level (Lua) with efficient code reusability.
- Fast and modular coding structure.
- Convenient for research.

Weaknesses
- Smaller proportion of reference projects than Caffe. Compared to other frameworks, little resources and developers on the market.
- Lia is not popular and not further under development.

Apache MXNet

Apache MXNet is an efficient and flexible DL framework developed by Pedro Domingos and a team of researchers at the University of Washington and part of the Distributed (Deep) Machine Learning Common (DMLC) group.[32] MXNet enables the mixing of symbolic with imperative programming to speed up efficiency and productivity. The core contains a dynamic dependency scheduler that can automatically parallelize symbolic and imperative operations. An overlying graph optimization layer makes symbolic execution fast and memory efficient. MXNet is portable and lightweight and scales effectively to multiple GPUs and machines. It also supports efficient deployment of trained models in low-end devices over Amalgamation (mobile), AWSGreengrass (IoT), AWS Lambda (serverless), or containers. MXNet is licensed under an Apache 2.0 license and has broad API language support for R, Python, Julia, and other languages [29]. Major hyperscalers support MXNet.

Strengths
- Dynamic dependency scheduler for auto parallelism.
- Excellent computational scalability with multiple GPUs and CPUs.
- flexible programming model with multiple languages like C++, Python, Julia, R, Scala, Matlab, JavaScript, Go, Perl, and Wolfram.
- Supports the Open Neural Network Exchange (ONNX) format, which has a universal representation schema to transform models between CNTK easily, Caffe2, PyTorch, and MXNet.

Weaknesses
- APIs might not be always user-friendly.

---

[31] Torch official web page http://torch.ch/.
[32] Apache MXNet official web page https://mxnet.apache.org.

Chainer

Chainer is a standalone open-source framework for DL models.[33] The core team of Chainer developers works at Preferred Networks, an ML startup with engineers mainly from the University of Tokyo. Chainer offers a full range of DL models, including CNN, RNN, reinforcement learning (RL), and variational autoencoders [101]. It implements automatic differentiation APIs based on the define-by-run approach (dynamic computational graph (DCG)) and high-level object-oriented APIs for constructing and training models. Chainer constructs neural networks dynamically (on-the-fly), while other frameworks such as TensorFlow or Caffe build their graph initially and remain fixed (define-and-run). Chainer supports CUDA/cuDNN with CuPy, high-performance training and inference, and IntelMKL-DNN to accelerate DL frameworks on Intel-based architectures. Chainer includes libraries for industrial applications like ChainerCV (computer vision), ChainerRL (reinforcement learning), and ChainerMN (distributed DL). In one benchmark study [13], ChainerMN recorded the best performance in a multinode setting against MXNet, CNTK, and TensorFlow for ImageNet classification on the ResNet-50 model.

Strengths

- Dynamic computational graph (define-by-run principle).
- Industrial-grade application libraries.
- Strong support by companies like Toyota, FANUC, and NTT.

Weaknesses

- No higher order gradients (multidimension tensor) support.
- Even for fixed networks the DCG is generated every time.

Theano

Theano is an open-source DL tool supporting GPU computation developed in 2007 and released under the BSD license.[34] It is no longer developed but actively maintained by the LISA group at the University of Montreal. Theanos core consists of a python compiler for mathematical expressions using NumPy, BLAS, and native code to run fast on CPUs or GPUs. It supports multiGPU data parallelism and has a distributed framework model training.

Strengths

- Open-source, cross-platform framework.
- Powerful numerical library for DL research and development.
- The symbolic API supports loop control, which makes the implementation of RNNs efficient.

Weaknesses

- Wrappers like Lasagne or Keras exist, but lower-level API can be difficult to use for building DL models.
- Lack for mobile platform and other programming APIs.
- No longer actively developed.

---

[33] Chainer official web page https://chainer.org.
[34] Theano official GitHub https://github.com/Theano/Theano.

Performance-wise classification

Under the premise of the same datasets, methods, and hardware, the model performance (accuracy) and runtime performance (speed of training and inference) are metrics to evaluate DL frameworks and libraries' performance. Model performance is considered the main interest, while the DL community has made significant efforts to benchmark and evaluate runtime performances. The following list shows some of the DL framework benchmarks:

- Benchmark evaluation of the most famous DL frameworks [15,89,12,52,69] (TensorFlow, CNTK, PyTorch, Caffe2, Chainer, Theano, MXNet), in addition in the setup with wrappers like Keras or Gluon.
- Testing Keras back-ends [110,59,19] (e.g. TensorFlow, Theano, CNTK and MXNet).
- Comparison of Keras and PyTorch [75].
- Benchmarking methods, like CNNs [30] or LSTMs [20] in different DL framework setups.
- Evaluating CNN's in distributed DL frameworks (like Caffe, Chainer, CNTK, MXNet, and TensorFlow) for different characteristics like code conversion, functional features, GitHub popularity, performance, scalability, and memory utilization [12,69].

The most commonly used datasets for benchmarking are the IMDb review dataset for NLP and sentiment analysis, the MNIST [58], CIFAR-10, and ImageNet [84] datasets for image classification.

High complex datasets used in science benchmarks are, e.g., Microsoft COCO for image recognition, segmentation, and keypoints [66], or Cityscape for urban scene understanding and image recognition for autonomous driving [34]. Famously used DL architectures for benchmarking are CNNs (e.g., ResNet, GoogleNet, AlexNet, and VGGNet), multilayer perceptrons, RNNs autoencoders. Most of the scientific benchmarks showed similar accuracy for most frameworks, while runtime performance can often vary. As an example, Chainer outperforms MXNet, CNTK, and TensorFlow in the ResNet-50 [12] benchmark. In the field of RNNs, CNTK and PyTorch often outperform other libraries. There should not be a big runtime performance difference in theory since most frameworks use the same underlying cuDNN primitives. There is no overall winner for all use cases, as they are sensitive to different choices and problem sets [69]. The results show comparisons across specific cases across different frameworks and hardware and may change over time with new hardware and library updates.

Deep learning wrapper libraries

Besides of Keras, there are other wrapper libraries for DL libraries designed to hide low-level implementations:

- Tensor Flow has many wrappers under which are Keras, TensorLayer,[35] and TFLearn.[36] Wrappers for Google Deepmind are Sonnet[37] and PrettyTensor.[38] Native TensorFlow wrappers like TF-Slim.[39]

---

[35] TensorLayer web page https://tensorlayer.readthedocs.io/en/latest/.
[36] TFLean web page http://tflearn.org/.
[37] Sonnet (Deepmind) github https://github.com/deepmind/sonnet.
[38] Pretty tensor github https://github.com/google/prettytensor.
[39] TF-Slim–Tensorflow-Slim github https://github.com/tensorflow/tensorflow/tree/master/tensorflow/contrib/slim.

- A wrapper for MXNet is Gluon.[40] The Gluon API specification attempts to improve DL's speed, flexibility, and accessibility, regardless of their choice of DL framework. Gluon is delivered as a product by Amazon Web Services and Microsoft AI and released under the Apache 2.0 license.
- NVIDIA Digits[41] is a web application for training DNNs for image classification, segmentation, and object recognition using backends like Caffe, Torch, and TensorFlow. It simplifies tasks like managing data, designing and training on multiGPU systems, real-time performance monitoring with advanced visualizations, and model selection. Digits are released under the BSD 3 clause license.
- Lasagne is a lightweight library for building and training NNs in Theano base on the six principles of Simplicity, Transparency, Modularity, Pragmatism, Restraint, and Focus.[42] Other Theano wrappers are Blocks and Pylearn2.

DL frameworks and libraries' evolution is very dynamic, making it difficult to predict a leader in this rapidly changing ecosystem. Two main trends DL frameworks can be identified:

1. Using Keras for fast prototyping and TensorFlow for production. Furthermore, this trend is backed by Google.
2. Using PyTorch for prototyping and Caffe2 for production. Furthermore, this trend is backed by Facebook.

8.7.5 Machine learning and deep learning frameworks and libraries with MapReduce

Distributed frameworks address the scalability question of Big Data analytics using the MapReduce processing framework. The most famous frameworks are Apache Hadoop and Apache Spark. The main advantages of distributed systems are elasticity, reliability, and transparent scalability. Those fault-tolerant systems are designed to automatically distribute workloads without considering the cluster's hardware's specific details. These distributed computing frameworks share similar component technologies, although they have different scaling goals [22].

Deeplearning4j

Deeplearning4j (DL4J) is an open-source distributed DL library implemented in Java and targets the industrial Java development and Big Data processing ecosystem. The DL4J framework has built-in GPU support, which is an essential feature for the training process, and supports Hadoop and Spark.[43] DL4J consists of several subprojects:

- Raw data transformation into feature vectors (DataVec).
- NN configuration Tools (DeepLearning4j).
- Model import from Python and Keras models.
- Scala wrapper running on multiGPU with Spark (ScalNet).
- Native libraries support matrix data CPU and GPU processing (ND4J).

---

40 Gluon API GitHub https://github.com/gluon-api/gluon-api.
41 NVIDEA official webpage https://developer.nvidia.com/digits.
42 Lasagne Github https://github.com/Lasagne/Lasagne.
43 Deeplearning4j official webpage https://deeplearning4j.org.

– Reinforcement learning algorithms (RL4J).

– NN hyperparameter optimization and working examples (DL4J-Examples).

– Core NLP tools for feeding text piece by piece into a natural language processor (SentenceIterator), for segmenting text at the level of individual words or n-grams (Tokenizer), a cache for storing metadata (Vocab).

Strengths

- It uses the full potential of the Java ecosystem to perform efficient DL and can be implemented on popular Big Data tools like Apache Hadoop, Spark, Kafka with any number of GPUs or CPUs.
- Proven as commercial industry-focused distributed DL platforms where the Java ecosystem is predominant.
- Provides pretrained DL models with weights for various data sets.

Weaknesses

- Java and Scala are not as popular in DL research as Python.
- Gained less overall interest than H2O in Big Data and Spark communities.

Apache spark MLlib and spark ML

Apache introduced Mahout, which was built on top of MapReduce and also included many ML algorithms. However, ML algorithms require many iterations, making Mahout very slow to run. The solution of Apache Spark was MLlib and SparkML, which are built on the Spark ecosystem.[44]

Spark MLlib includes a legacy RDD-based API (Resilient Distributed Dataset). RDD is the core concept of Spark data, representing an immutable, partitioned collection of elements that operate parallel with a low-level API providing transformations and actions. SparkML includes a DataFrame-based API and ML pipelines and is currently the primary ML API for Spark. A DataFrame is a data set organized into named columns. A transformation or action over a DataFrame can be defined as an SQL query.

Spark SQL provides comprehensive information about the data structure and the computation performed than the Spark RDD API. Spark ML contains the concept of pipelines that help users to create and tune ML workflow pipelines so that multiple ML algorithms can be combined into a single pipeline or workflow. The main machine learning API for Spark is the ML library. Spark MLib/ML includes:

– Machine learning algorithms like regression, classification, clustering, or collaborative filtering.

– Tools for SparkML provide featurization tools for feature extraction, transformation, dimensionality reduction, and feature selection

– Pipeline tools for creating, evaluating, and tuning ML pipelines,

– Persistence utilities for storing and loading algorithms, models, and pipelines.

– Tools for linear algebra, statistics, and data processing.

MLlib can be easily used together with data streams with linear regression or k-means over continuous data streams. Some other streaming problems consider the model's training offline and then apply the model online to streaming data. Implementing a simple algorithm (e.g., distributed multilabel KNN) for large-scale data mining is not trivial [80,43] and requires knowledge of the underlying distributed

---

[44] MLlib https://spark.apache.org/docs/latest/mlguide.html.

environment, data and processing management, and programming skills. Therefore, ML algorithms for large-scale data mining differ in complexity and implementation from those for general purposes.

Strengths

- ML toolbox for large-scale data, already integrated into Apache Spark ecosystem and convenient for development and production.
- Optimized algorithms with optimized implementations for Hadoop.
- Pipelines for BigData processing with a set of feature engineering functions for data analytics over data streams.
- Scalability with SQL support and in-memory processing support.

Weaknesses

- High memory usage with the in-memory processing.
- Spark MLlib/ML are still in an early state compared to other DL frameworks.

H2O

H2O developed by H2O.ai in 2011[45] is a Hadoop-compatible framework for analytics over Big Data and Big Data Streams.

To access data, models, and objects across all nodes and machines, H2O uses a distributed key-value store. H2O's algorithms are implemented on the MapReduce framework and use the Java Fork/Join framework for multithreading. H2O can interact independently with HDFS storage via YARN or MapReduce. Java can be used to interact with H2O and a REST API over HTTP vis JSON and wrappers for Python (H2O-Python), R (H2O-R), and Scala. Besides the REST API and wrapping for common programming languages, H2O is accessible via CLI and offers various options for controlling the cluster's use, like how many are starting nodes, node memory allocation, and more. H2O offers a web-based notebook called Flow. DL in H2O is based on models trained with stochastic gradient descent (SGD) using backpropagation. The global model is built over the local models using averaging. Sparkling Water contains the same features and functions as H2O but offers a way to use H2O with Spark. It is ideal for managing large data processing clusters, especially when transferring data from Spark to H2O. Deep Water is H2O DL with native DL models for GPU-optimized backends such as TensorFlow, MXNet, and Caffe. These backends are accessible from Deep Water via connectors.

Strengths

- Industrial use and high popularity for companies in financial, insurance, and healthcare.
- Optimization algorithms for Big Data processing.
- Provides a generic set of ML algorithms that leverages Hadoop/Spark engines for large-scale processing.

Weaknesses

- The web-based UI for H2O does not support direct execution with Spark.
- H2O is more general-purpose and aims at a different problem than DL libraries like TensorFlow or DL4j.

---

[45] H2O official website https://www.h2o.ai/.

Other frameworks with MapReduce

Of the other frameworks and libraries that work with MapReduce, the following are considered as important to know:

- FlinkML is part of Apache Flink, an open-source framework for distributed stream and batch processing.[46] Flink ML provides scalable ML algorithms and APIs that have been adopted for the Flink distributed framework. It includes algorithms for supervised-, unsupervised learning, preprocessing, and other utilities. Flink focuses on working with a massive amount of data with low latency and high fault tolerance on distributed systems. The primary feature of Flink is the ability to process real-time streams. The significant difference between Flink and Spark is the way the frameworks handle data streams. Flink is a native stream processing framework able to process batch data, while Spark was designed to handle static data through its RDDs. The stream processing method of Spark enables the micro-batching functionality.
- Cloudera's Oryx 2 also has an ML layer. Oryx 2 follows the Lambda architecture builds on top of Apache Spark and Apache Kafka for large-scale real-time ML.[47] Oryx 2 is designed for building applications and includes end-to-end collaborative filtering, classification, regression, and clustering. Oryx 2 comprises the levels of
    - General lambda architecture for batch, speed, and serving layers, not specific to ML.
    - ML abstraction for selecting hyperparameters.
    - End-to-end implementation of the same standard ML algorithms as an application like k-means, random decision forests, alternating least squares.
- KNIME (Konstanz Information Miner) is the data analysis, reporting, and integration platform of Knime AG.[48]

  It integrates various ML and DM components in its modular data pipelining and enables the assembly of nodes for preprocessing, modeling, data analysis, and visualization. The platform is published under GNU GPLv3 open source license with more than 1500 modules, many integrated tools, and a large selection of advanced algorithms. KNIME is implemented in Java and allows wrappers for Java, Python, Perl, and others. It is integrated with Python, R, Keras, Weka, DL4J, and H2O.

8.8 Key features

Machine and deep learning are research areas in multidisciplinary fields that constantly evolve due to the advances in data analytics research in the age of Big Data, Cloud digital ecosystem, etc. The effects of new computing resources and technologies combined with increasing data sets are changing many research, health, and industrial areas. As technology advances, novel solutions are sought in many areas to address complex problems, presenting data mining projects with a significant challenge in deciding which tools to choose.

[46] Apache Flink official website https://flink.apache.org/.
[47] Oryx official website http://oryx.io/.
[48] KNIME official website https://www.knime.com/.

☑ A compendium of ML methods is presented with examples and references to application in health domain.

☑ Federated Learning and its potential to health applications is explored.

☑ Most of the deep learning frameworks are developed by the software companies like Google, Facebook, and Microsoft. These companies have huge amounts of data, high-performance infrastructures, human intelligence, and investment resources. Tools include TensorFlow, Torch, PyTorch, MXNet, Microsoft CNTK, Caffe, Caffe2. Other companies and research institutions support other frameworks and libraries like Chainer, Theano, H2O, and Deeplearning4J. Many high-level deep learning wrapper libraries build on top of the deep learning frameworks such as Keras, Tensor Layer, and Gluon.

☑ Big Data ecosystems like Apache Spark, Apache Flink, and Cloudera Oryx 2 contain integrated ML libraries for large-scale data mining. These libraries are currently evolving, but the performance of the entire ecosystem is significant.

☑ Vertical scalability for large-scale DL is limited due to the GPU storage capacity. Horizontal scalability is limited due to the latency of network communication between nodes.

☑ As of 2021, Python is the most popular programming language for data mining, Machine Learning, and Deep Learning applications. It is used as a general-purpose language for research and production for small and large-scale applications.

☑ ML tools provide a way to process large-scale data. The trend shows many interactive data analysis and data visualization tools that support decision-makers.

References

[1] AI on clinical data: Healthchain consortium, https://www.substra.ai/en/healthchain-project, 2020. (Accessed 11 January 2021).
[2] Charter for safe havens in Scotland: handling unconsented data from national health service patient records to support research and statistics, https://www.gov.scot/publications/charter-safe-havens-scotland-handling-unconsented-data-national-health-service-patient-records-support-research-statistics/pages/4/, 2015. (Accessed 11 January 2021).
[3] The federated tumor segmentation (FeTS) initiative, https://www.med.upenn.edu/cbica/fets/, 2020. (Accessed 11 January 2021).
[4] Health data research UK, https://www.hdruk.ac.uk/, 2020. (Accessed 11 January 2021).
[5] IBM to buy merge healthcare in $1 billion deal, https://www.reuters.com/article/us-merge-healthcare-m-a-ibm/ibm-to-buy-merge-healthcare-in-1-billion-deal-idUSKCN0QB1ML20150806, 2015. (Accessed 11 January 2021).
[6] Joint imaging platform, https://jip.dktk.dkfz.de/jiphomepage/, 2020. (Accessed 11 January 2021).
[7] Machine learning ledger orchestration for drug discovery, https://cordis.europa.eu/project/id/831472, 2020. (Accessed 11 January 2021).
[8] Medical institutions collaborate to improve mammogram assessment AI with NVIDIA Clara federated learning, https://blogs.nvidia.com/blog/2020/04/15/federated-learning-mammogram-assessment/, 2020. (Accessed 11 January 2021).
[9] Trustworthy federated data analytics, https://tfda.hmsp.center/, 2020. (Accessed 11 January 2021).
[10] M. Abadi, A. Chu, I. Goodfellow, H.B. McMahan, I. Mironov, K. Talwar, L. Zhang, Deep learning with differential privacy, in: Proceedings of the 2016 ACM SIGSAC Conference on Computer and Communications Security, 2016, pp. 308–318.

[11] A. Agarwal, O. Chapelle, M. Dudík, J. Langford, A reliable effective terascale linear learning system, Journal of Machine Learning Research 15 (1) (2014) 1111–1133.

[12] T. Akiba, Performance of distributed deep learning using ChainerMN, https://chainer.org/general/2017/02/08/Performance-of-Distributed-Deep-Learning-Using-ChainerMN.html, 2018.

[13] T. Akiba, S. Suzuki, K. Fukuda, Extremely large minibatch SGD: training resnet-50 on imagenet in 15 minutes, arXiv preprint, arXiv:1711.04325, 2017.

[14] M. Alloghani, D. Al-Jumeily, J. Mustafina, A. Hussain, A.J. Aljaaf, A systematic review on supervised and unsupervised machine learning algorithms for data science, in: Supervised and Unsupervised Learning for Data Science, Springer, 2020, pp. 3–21.

[15] S. Bahrampour, N. Ramakrishnan, L. Schott, M. Shah, Comparative study of deep learning software frameworks, arXiv preprint, arXiv:1511.06435, 2015.

[16] W. Bai, O. Oktay, M. Sinclair, H. Suzuki, M. Rajchl, G. Tarroni, B. Glocker, A. King, P.M. Matthews, D. Rueckert, Semi-supervised learning for network-based cardiac MR image segmentation, in: International Conference on Medical Image Computing and Computer-Assisted Intervention, Springer, 2017, pp. 253–260.

[17] S. Bakas, H. Akbari, A. Sotiras, M. Bilello, M. Rozycki, J.S. Kirby, J.B. Freymann, K. Farahani, C. Davatzikos, Advancing the cancer genome atlas glioma MRI collections with expert segmentation labels and radiomic features, Scientific Data 4 (2017) 170117.

[18] S. Bakas, M. Reyes, A. Jakab, S. Bauer, M. Rempfler, A. Crimi, R.T. Shinohara, C. Berger, S.M. Ha, M. Rozycki, et al., Identifying the best machine learning algorithms for brain tumor segmentation, progression assessment, and overall survival prediction in the brats challenge, arXiv preprint, arXiv:1811.02629, 2018.

[19] J. Bhatia, Search for the fastest deep learning framework supported by Keras, 2018.

[20] S. Braun, LSTM benchmarks for deep learning frameworks, arXiv preprint, arXiv:1806.01818, 2018.

[21] T.S. Brisimi, R. Chen, T. Mela, A. Olshevsky, I.C. Paschalidis, W. Shi, Federated learning of predictive models from federated electronic health records, International Journal of Medical Informatics 112 (2018) 59–67.

[22] A. Cano, A survey on graphic processing unit computing for large-scale data mining, Wiley Interdisciplinary Reviews: Data Mining and Knowledge Discovery 8 (1) (2018) e1232.

[23] N. Carlini, C. Liu, Ú. Erlingsson, J. Kos, D. Song, The secret sharer: evaluating and testing unintended memorization in neural networks, in: 28th {USENIX} Security Symposium ({USENIX} Security 19), 2019, pp. 267–284.

[24] V. Chandola, A. Banerjee, V. Kumar, Anomaly detection: a survey, ACM Computing Surveys (CSUR) 41 (3) (2009) 1–58.

[25] C.-C. Chang, C.-J. Lin, LIBSVM: a library for support vector machines, ACM Transactions on Intelligent Systems and Technology (TIST) 2 (3) (2011) 1–27.

[26] K. Chang, N. Balachandar, C. Lam, D. Yi, J. Brown, A. Beers, B. Rosen, D.L. Rubin, J. Kalpathy-Cramer, Distributed deep learning networks among institutions for medical imaging, Journal of the American Medical Informatics Association 25 (8) (2018) 945–954.

[27] G. Chartrand, P.M. Cheng, E. Vorontsov, M. Drozdzal, S. Turcotte, C.J. Pal, S. Kadoury, A. Tang, Deep learning: a primer for radiologists, Radiographics 37 (7) (2017) 2113–2131, PMID: 29131760.

[28] T. Chen, C. Guestrin, XGBoost: a scalable tree boosting system, in: Proceedings of the 22nd ACM SIGKDD International Conference on Knowledge Discovery and Data Mining, 2016, pp. 785–794.

[29] T. Chen, M. Li, Y. Li, M. Lin, N. Wang, M. Wang, T. Xiao, B. Xu, C. Zhang, Z. Zhang, MXNet: a flexible and efficient machine learning library for heterogeneous distributed systems, arXiv preprint, arXiv:1512.01274, 2015.

[30] S. Chintala, Easy benchmarking of all publicly accessible implementations of convnets, https://github.com/soumith/convnet-benchmarks, 2018.

[31] K. Clark, B. Vendt, K. Smith, J. Freymann, J. Kirby, P. Koppel, S. Moore, S. Phillips, D. Maffitt, M. Pringle, et al., The cancer imaging archive (TCIA): maintaining and operating a public information repository, Journal of Digital Imaging 26 (6) (2013) 1045–1057.

[32] R. Collobert, S. Bengio, J. Mariéthoz, Torch: a modular machine learning software library, Technical report, Idiap, 2002.

[33] R. Collobert, K. Kavukcuoglu, C. Farabet, Torch7: a Matlab-like environment for machine learning, in: BigLearn, NIPS Workshop, Number CONF, 2011.

[34] M. Cordts, M. Omran, S. Ramos, T. Rehfeld, M. Enzweiler, R. Benenson, U. Franke, S. Roth, B. Schiele, The cityscapes dataset for semantic urban scene understanding, in: Proceedings of the IEEE Conference on Computer Vision and Pattern Recognition, 2016, pp. 3213–3223.

[35] J. Corren, R.F. Lemanske Jr, N.A. Hanania, P.E. Korenblat, M.V. Parsey, J.R. Arron, J.M. Harris, H. Scheerens, L.C. Wu, Z. Su, et al., Lebrikizumab treatment in adults with asthma, The New England Journal of Medicine 365 (12) (2011) 1088–1098.

[36] N.R. Council, et al., Toward Precision Medicine: Building a Knowledge Network for Biomedical Research and a New Taxonomy of Disease, National Academies Press, 2011.

[37] K. Crammer, Y. Singer, On the algorithmic implementation of multiclass kernel-based vector machines, Journal of Machine Learning Research 2 (Dec) (2001) 265–292.

[38] K. Crammer, Y. Singer, On the learnability and design of output codes for multiclass problems, Machine Learning 47 (2) (2002) 201–233.

[39] M. Cuggia, S. Combes, The French health data hub and the German medical informatics initiatives: two national projects to promote data sharing in healthcare, Yearbook of Medical Informatics 28 (1) (2019) 195.

[40] J. De Fauw, J.R. Ledsam, B. Romera-Paredes, S. Nikolov, N. Tomasev, S. Blackwell, H. Askham, X. Glorot, B. O'Donoghue, D. Visentin, et al., Clinically applicable deep learning for diagnosis and referral in retinal disease, Nature Medicine 24 (9) (2018) 1342–1350.

[41] R.-E. Fan, K.-W. Chang, C.-J. Hsieh, X.-R. Wang, C.-J. Lin, Liblinear: a library for large linear classification, Journal of Machine Learning Research 9 (2008) 1871–1874.

[42] A. Ghorbani, J. Zou, Data Shapley: equitable valuation of data for machine learning, arXiv preprint, arXiv: 1904.02868, 2019.

[43] J. Gonzalez-Lopez, S. Ventura, A. Cano, Distributed nearest neighbor classification for large-scale multi-label data on spark, Future Generations Computer Systems 87 (2018) 66–82.

[44] O. Gottesman, F.D. Johansson, M. Komorowski, A.A. Faisal, D. Sontag, F. Doshi-Velez, L. Celi, Guidelines for reinforcement learning in healthcare, Nature Medicine 25 (2019) 16–18.

[45] C. He, M. Annavaram, S. Avestimehr, FedNAS: federated deep learning via neural architecture search, arXiv preprint, arXiv:2004.08546, 2020.

[46] B. Hitaj, G. Ateniese, F. Perez-Cruz, Deep models under the GAN: information leakage from collaborative deep learning, in: Proceedings of the 2017 ACM SIGSAC Conference on Computer and Communications Security, 2017, pp. 603–618.

[47] L. Huang, A.L. Shea, H. Qian, A. Masurkar, H. Deng, D. Liu, Patient clustering improves efficiency of federated machine learning to predict mortality and hospital stay time using distributed electronic medical records, Journal of Biomedical Informatics 99 (2019) 103291.

[48] C.R. Jack Jr, M.A. Bernstein, N.C. Fox, P. Thompson, G. Alexander, D. Harvey, B. Borowski, P.J. Britson, J.L. Whitwell, C. Ward, et al., The Alzheimer's disease neuroimaging initiative (ADNI): MRI methods, Journal of Magnetic Resonance Imaging: an Official Journal of the International Society for Magnetic Resonance in Medicine 27 (4) (2008) 685–691.

[49] A. Jovic, K. Brkic, N. Bogunovic, An overview of free software tools for general data mining, in: 2014 37th International Convention on Information and Communication Technology, Electronics and Microelectronics (MIPRO), IEEE, 2014, pp. 1112–1117.

[50] P. Kairouz, H.B. McMahan, B. Avent, A. Bellet, M. Bennis, A.N. Bhagoji, K. Bonawitz, Z. Charles, G. Cormode, R. Cummings, et al., Advances and open problems in federated learning, arXiv preprint, arXiv: 1912.04977, 2019.

[51] H.-C. Kao, K.-F. Tang, E. Chang, Context-aware symptom checking for disease diagnosis using hierarchical reinforcement learning, in: Proceedings of the AAAI Conference on Artificial Intelligence, vol. 32, 2018.

[52] I. Karmanov, M. Salvaris, M. Fierro, D. Dean, Comparing deep learning frameworks: a Rosetta stone approach, in: Machine Learning Blog, 2018.

[53] Y. Kim, J. Sun, H. Yu, X. Jiang, Federated tensor factorization for computational phenotyping, in: Proceedings of the 23rd ACM SIGKDD International Conference on Knowledge Discovery and Data Mining, 2017, pp. 887–895.

[54] J. Konečný, H.B. McMahan, D. Ramage, P. Richtárik, Federated optimization: distributed machine learning for on-device intelligence, arXiv preprint, arXiv:1610.02527, 2016.

[55] A. Lalitha, O.C. Kilinc, T. Javidi, F. Koushanfar, Peer-to-peer federated learning on graphs, arXiv preprint, arXiv:1901.11173, 2019.

[56] C.P. Langlotz, B. Allen, B.J. Erickson, J. Kalpathy-Cramer, K. Bigelow, T.S. Cook, A.E. Flanders, M.P. Lungren, D.S. Mendelson, J.D. Rudie, et al., A roadmap for foundational research on artificial intelligence in medical imaging: from the 2018 NIH/RSNA/ACR/the academy workshop, Radiology 291 (3) (2019) 781–791.

[57] Y. LeCun, Y. Bengio, G. Hinton, Deep learning, Nature 521 (7553) (May 2015) 436–444.

[58] Y. LeCun, B. Boser, J.S. Denker, D. Henderson, R.E. Howard, W. Hubbard, L.D. Jackel, Backpropagation applied to handwritten zip code recognition, Neural Computation 1 (4) (1989) 541–551.

[59] J. Lee, Keras backend benchmark: Theano vs tensorflow vs CNTK, 2018.

[60] J. Lee, J. Sun, F. Wang, S. Wang, C.-H. Jun, X. Jiang, Privacy-preserving patient similarity learning in a federated environment: development and analysis, JMIR Medical Informatics 6 (2) (2018) e20.

[61] T. Li, A.K. Sahu, A. Talwalkar, V. Smith, Federated learning: challenges, methods, and future directions, IEEE Signal Processing Magazine 37 (3) (2020) 50–60.

[62] T. Li, A.K. Sahu, M. Zaheer, M. Sanjabi, A. Talwalkar, V. Smith, Federated optimization in heterogeneous networks, arXiv preprint, arXiv:1812.06127, 2018.

[63] W. Li, F. Milletarì, D. Xu, N. Rieke, J. Hancox, W. Zhu, M. Baust, Y. Cheng, S. Ourselin, M.J. Cardoso, et al., Privacy-preserving federated brain tumour segmentation, in: International Workshop on Machine Learning in Medical Imaging, Springer, 2019, pp. 133–141.

[64] X. Li, Y. Gu, N. Dvornek, L. Staib, P. Ventola, J.S. Duncan, Multi-site fMRI analysis using privacy-preserving federated learning and domain adaptation: abide results, arXiv preprint, arXiv:2001.05647, 2020.

[65] X. Li, K. Huang, W. Yang, S. Wang, Z. Zhang, On the convergence of FedAvg on non-IID data, arXiv preprint, arXiv:1907.02189, 2019.

[66] T.-Y. Lin, M. Maire, S. Belongie, J. Hays, P. Perona, D. Ramanan, P. Dollár, C.L. Zitnick, Microsoft coco: common objects in context, in: European Conference on Computer Vision, Springer, 2014, pp. 740–755.

[67] G.Y. Lip, R. Nieuwlaat, R. Pisters, D.A. Lane, H.J. Crijns, Refining clinical risk stratification for predicting stroke and thromboembolism in atrial fibrillation using a novel risk factor-based approach: the euro heart survey on atrial fibrillation, Chest 137 (2) (2010) 263–272.

[68] G. Litjens, P. Bandi, B. Ehteshami Bejnordi, O. Geessink, M. Balkenhol, P. Bult, A. Halilovic, M. Hermsen, R. van de Loo, R. Vogels, et al., 1399 H&E-stained sentinel lymph node sections of breast cancer patients: the CAMELYON dataset, GigaScience 7 (6) (2018) giy065.

[69] J. Liu, J. Dutta, N. Li, U. Kurup, M. Shah, Usability study of distributed deep learning frameworks for convolutional neural networks, in: Proceedings of the Deep Learning Day at SIGKDD Conference on Knowledge Discovery and Data Mining (KDD'18), 2018.

[70] D. Mahapatra, Semi-supervised learning and graph cuts for consensus based medical image segmentation, Pattern Recognition 63 (2017) 700–709.

[71] B. McMahan, E. Moore, D. Ramage, S. Hampson, B.A. y Arcas, Communication-efficient learning of deep networks from decentralized data, in: Artificial Intelligence and Statistics, PMLR, 2017, pp. 1273–1282.

[72] H.B. McMahan, D. Ramage, K. Talwar, L. Zhang, Learning differentially private recurrent language models, in: 6th International Conference on Learning Representations, ICLR 2018, Vancouver, BC, Canada, April 30 - May 3, 2018, Conference Track Proceedings, OpenReview.net, 2018.

[73] B.H. Menze, A. Jakab, S. Bauer, J. Kalpathy-Cramer, K. Farahani, J. Kirby, Y. Burren, N. Porz, J. Slotboom, R. Wiest, et al., The multimodal brain tumor image segmentation benchmark (brats), IEEE Transactions on Medical Imaging 34 (10) (2014) 1993–2024.

[74] I. Mierswa, R. Klinkenberg, S. Fischer, O. Ritthoff, A flexible platform for knowledge discovery experiments: YALE–yet another learning environment, in: LLWA 03-Tagungsband der GI-Workshop-Woche Lernen-Lehren-Wissen-Adaptivität, 2003.

[75] P. Migdal, R. Jakubanis, Keras vs Pytorch: Keras or Pytorch as your first deep learning framework, 2018.

[76] G. Nguyen, S. Dlugolinsky, M. Bobák, V. Tran, Á.L. García, I. Heredia, P. Malík, L. Hluchỳ, Machine learning and deep learning frameworks and libraries for large-scale data mining: a survey, Artificial Intelligence Review 52 (1) (2019) 77–124.

[77] C. O'Mahony, F. Jichi, M. Pavlou, L. Monserrat, A. Anastasakis, C. Rapezzi, E. Biagini, J.R. Gimeno, G. Limongelli, W.J. McKenna, et al., A novel clinical risk prediction model for sudden cardiac death in hypertrophic cardiomyopathy (HCM risk-SCD), European Heart Journal 35 (30) (2014) 2010–2020.

[78] A.K. Pandey, P. Pandey, K. Jaiswal, A.K. Sen, Data mining clustering techniques in the prediction of heart disease using attribute selection method, International Journal of Science, Engineering and Technology Research (IJSETR) (2013) (ISSN 2277798).

[79] K. Polat, S. Güneş, Prediction of hepatitis disease based on principal component analysis and artificial immune recognition system, Applied Mathematics and Computation 189 (2) (2007) 1282–1291.

[80] S. Ramírez-Gallego, B. Krawczyk, S. García, M. Woźniak, J.M. Benítez, F. Herrera, Nearest neighbor classification for high-speed big data streams using spark, IEEE Transactions on Systems, Man, and Cybernetics: Systems 47 (10) (2017) 2727–2739.

[81] N. Rieke, J. Hancox, W. Li, F. Milletari, H. Roth, S. Albarqouni, S. Bakas, M.N. Galtier, B.A. Landman, K.H. Maier-Hein, S. Ourselin, M.J. Sheller, R.M. Summers, A. Trask, D. Xu, M. Baust, M.J. Cardoso, The future of digital health with federated learning, CoRR, arXiv:2003.08119 [abs], 2020.

[82] L. Rocher, J.M. Hendrickx, Y.-A. De Montjoye, Estimating the success of re-identifications in incomplete datasets using generative models, Nature Communications 10 (1) (2019) 1–9.

[83] A.G. Roy, S. Siddiqui, S. Pölsterl, N. Navab, C. Wachinger, Braintorrent: a peer-to-peer environment for decentralized federated learning, arXiv preprint, arXiv:1905.06731, 2019.

[84] O. Russakovsky, J. Deng, H. Su, J. Krause, S. Satheesh, S. Ma, Z. Huang, A. Karpathy, A. Khosla, M. Bernstein, et al., Imagenet large scale visual recognition challenge, International Journal of Computer Vision 115 (3) (2015) 211–252.

[85] A. Sablayrolles, M. Douze, C. Schmid, Y. Ollivier, H. Jégou, White-box vs black-box: Bayes optimal strategies for membership inference, in: International Conference on Machine Learning, PMLR, 2019, pp. 5558–5567.

[86] M. Sayed-Mouchaweh, Learning from data streams in dynamic environments, 2015.

[87] M.J. Sheller, G.A. Reina, B. Edwards, J. Martin, S. Bakas, Multi-institutional deep learning modeling without sharing patient data: a feasibility study on brain tumor segmentation, in: International MICCAI Brainlesion Workshop, Springer, 2018, pp. 92–104.

[88] W. Shen, M. Zhou, F. Yang, C. Yang, J. Tian, Multi-scale convolutional neural networks for lung nodule classification, in: International Conference on Information Processing in Medical Imaging, Springer, 2015, pp. 588–599.

[89] S. Shi, Q. Wang, P. Xu, X. Chu, Benchmarking state-of-the-art deep learning software tools, in: 2016 7th International Conference on Cloud Computing and Big Data (CCBD), IEEE, 2016, pp. 99–104.

[90] R. Shokri, V. Shmatikov, Privacy-preserving deep learning, in: Proceedings of the 22nd ACM SIGSAC Conference on Computer and Communications Security, 2015, pp. 1310–1321.

[91] R. Shokri, M. Stronati, C. Song, V. Shmatikov, Membership inference attacks against machine learning models, in: 2017 IEEE Symposium on Security and Privacy (SP), IEEE, 2017, pp. 3–18.

[92] D. Silver, A. Huang, C.J. Maddison, A. Guez, L. Sifre, G. Van Den Driessche, J. Schrittwieser, I. Antonoglou, V. Panneershelvam, M. Lanctot, et al., Mastering the game of go with deep neural networks and tree search, Nature 529 (7587) (2016) 484–489.

[93] A.L. Simpson, M. Antonelli, S. Bakas, M. Bilello, K. Farahani, B. Van Ginneken, A. Kopp-Schneider, B.A. Landman, G. Litjens, B. Menze, et al., A large annotated medical image dataset for the development and evaluation of segmentation algorithms, arXiv preprint, arXiv:1902.09063, 2019.

[94] M.N. Sohail, J. Ren, M. Uba Muhammad, A Euclidean group assessment on semi-supervised clustering for healthcare clinical implications based on real-life data, International Journal of Environmental Research and Public Health 16 (9) (2019) 1581.

[95] S. Sonnenburg, G. Rätsch, S. Henschel, C. Widmer, J. Behr, A. Zien, F. d. Bona, A. Binder, C. Gehl, V. Franc, The shogun machine learning toolbox, Journal of Machine Learning Research 11 (2010) 1799–1802.

[96] O. Sporns, G. Tononi, R. Kötter, The human connectome: a structural description of the human brain, PLoS Computational Biology 1 (4) (2005) e42.

[97] C. Sudlow, J. Gallacher, N. Allen, V. Beral, P. Burton, J. Danesh, P. Downey, P. Elliott, J. Green, M. Landray, et al., UK biobank: an open access resource for identifying the causes of a wide range of complex diseases of middle and old age, PLoS Medicine 12 (3) (2015) e1001779.

[98] C. Sun, A. Shrivastava, S. Singh, A. Gupta, Revisiting unreasonable effectiveness of data in deep learning era, in: Proceedings of the IEEE International Conference on Computer Vision, 2017, pp. 843–852.

[99] Q. Suo, F. Ma, Y. Yuan, M. Huai, W. Zhong, A. Zhang, Deep patient similarity learning for personalized healthcare, IEEE Transactions on Nanobioscience (05 2018) 1.

[100] R.S. Sutton, A.G. Barto, et al., Introduction to Reinforcement Learning, vol. 135, MIT Press, Cambridge, 1998.

[101] S. Tokui, K. Oono, S. Hido, J. Clayton, Chainer: a next-generation open source framework for deep learning, in: Proceedings of Workshop on Machine Learning Systems (LearningSys) in the Twenty-Ninth Annual Conference on Neural Information Processing Systems (NIPS), vol. 5, 2015, pp. 1–6.

[102] K. Tomczak, P. Czerwińska, M. Wiznerowicz, The cancer genome atlas (TCGA): an immeasurable source of knowledge, Contemporary Oncology 19 (1A) (2015) A68.

[103] W.G. Van Panhuis, P. Paul, C. Emerson, J. Grefenstette, R. Wilder, A.J. Herbst, D. Heymann, D.S. Burke, A systematic review of barriers to data sharing in public health, BMC Public Health 14 (1) (2014) 1–9.

[104] F. Wang, L.P. Casalino, D. Khullar, Deep learning in medicine—promise, progress, and challenges, JAMA Internal Medicine 179 (3) (2019) 293–294.

[105] X. Wang, Y. Peng, L. Lu, Z. Lu, M. Bagheri, R.M. Summers, ChestX-ray8: hospital-scale chest x-ray database and benchmarks on weakly-supervised classification and localization of common thorax diseases, in: 2017 IEEE Conference on Computer Vision and Pattern Recognition (CVPR), 2017, pp. 3462–3471.

[106] Z. Wang, M. Song, Z. Zhang, Y. Song, Q. Wang, H. Qi, Beyond inferring class representatives: user-level privacy leakage from federated learning, in: IEEE INFOCOM 2019-IEEE Conference on Computer Communications, IEEE, 2019, pp. 2512–2520.

[107] K. Weinberger, A. Dasgupta, J. Langford, A. Smola, J. Attenberg, Feature hashing for large scale multi-task learning, in: Proceedings of the 26th Annual International Conference on Machine Learning, 2009, pp. 1113–1120.

[108] P. Wilson, R. D'Agostino, D. Levy, A.M. Bélanger, H. Silbershatz, W. Kannel, Prediction of coronary heart disease using risk factor categories, Circulation 97 (18) (1998) 1837–1847.

[109] P.G. Woodruff, B. Modrek, D.F. Choy, G. Jia, A.R. Abbas, A. Ellwanger, J.R. Arron, L.L. Koth, J.V. Fahy, T-helper type 2–driven inflammation defines major subphenotypes of asthma, American Journal of Respiratory and Critical Care Medicine 180 (5) (2009) 388–395.

[110] M. Woolf, Benchmarking CNTK on Keras: is it better at deep learning than tensorflow, 2018.

[111] B. Wu, S. Zhao, G. Sun, X. Zhang, Z. Su, C. Zeng, Z. Liu, P3SGD: patient privacy preserving SGD for regularizing deep CNNs in pathological image classification, in: Proceedings of the IEEE Conference on Computer Vision and Pattern Recognition, 2019, pp. 2099–2108.

[112] J. Xu, B.S. Glicksberg, C. Su, P. Walker, J. Bian, F. Wang, Federated learning for healthcare informatics, Journal of Healthcare Informatics Research (2020) 1–19.

[113] K. Yan, X. Wang, L. Lu, R. Summers, Deeplesion: automated mining of large-scale lesion annotations and universal lesion detection with deep learning, Journal of Medical Imaging 5 (07 2018) 1.

[114] Z. Yan, Y. Zhan, Z. Peng, S. Liao, Y. Shinagawa, S. Zhang, D.N. Metaxas, X.S. Zhou, Multi-instance deep learning: discover discriminative local anatomies for bodypart recognition, IEEE Transactions on Medical Imaging 35 (5) (2016) 1332–1343.

[115] Q. Yang, Y. Liu, T. Chen, Y. Tong, Federated machine learning: concept and applications, ACM Transactions on Intelligent Systems and Technology (TIST) 10 (2) (2019) 1–19.

[116] F.-C. Yeh, J.M. Vettel, A. Singh, B. Poczos, S.T. Grafton, K.I. Erickson, W.-Y.I. Tseng, T.D. Verstynen, Quantifying differences and similarities in whole-brain white matter architecture using local connectome fingerprints, PLoS Computational Biology 12 (11) (11 2016) 1–17.

[117] C. Yu, J. Liu, S. Nemati, Reinforcement learning in healthcare: a survey, arXiv preprint, arXiv:1908.08796 [abs], 2019.

[118] A. Zahin, R.Q. Hu, et al., Sensor-based human activity recognition for smart healthcare: a semi-supervised machine learning, in: International Conference on Artificial Intelligence for Communications and Networks, Springer, 2019, pp. 450–472.

[119] C. Zhang, S. Bengio, M. Hardt, B. Recht, O. Vinyals, Understanding deep learning requires rethinking generalization, arXiv preprint, arXiv:1611.03530, 2016.

[120] Y. Zhao, M. Li, L. Lai, N. Suda, D. Civin, V. Chandra, Federated learning with non-IID data, arXiv preprint, arXiv:1806.00582, 2018.

[121] L. Zhu, Z. Liu, S. Han, Deep leakage from gradients, in: Advances in Neural Information Processing Systems, 2019, pp. 14774–14784.

[122] Z. Zygmunt, Vowpal wabbit, liblinear/SBM and streamSVM compared, 2018.

Anomaly detection, classification and CEP with ML methods
Machine learning pipeline for medicine

9.1 Anomaly detection by deep learning methods

Anomaly detection is an active research area, as it has applications in many important areas such as compliance, security, health and medical risk, and AI safety. Although it is a problem that has been widely studied with modern techniques, including data mining, machine learning, computer vision, there are still unique challenges that require advanced methods. In recent years, Deep-Learning-based anomaly detection has emerged as a critical component to address these challenges. These challenges can be summarized due to the unique and complex nature of anomalies such as:

- Unknowingness - they remain unknown until they occur
- Heterogeneity - different anomalies demonstrate completely different abnormal characteristics
- Rareness - anomalies that rarely occurred
- Diverse type of anomalies - point anomaly, contextual anomaly, and group anomaly

Based on the nature of anomalies, the following challenges were expressed [114]:

- **Challenge 1**: One of the biggest challenges is achieving a high recall rate for anomaly detection. Since anomalies are very rare and heterogeneous, it is difficult to identify all anomalies. Many normal instances are falsely reported as anomalies. Challenging anomalies are overlooked.
- **Challenge 2**: Detecting anomalies in high-dimensional or nonindependent data is a major challenge. Anomalies often show abnormal properties in a low-dimensional space but are hidden and unnoticed in a high-dimensional space. Detecting high-dimensional anomalies is a long-existing problem. A simple solution can be subspace/feature selection-based methods. However, identifying complex (e.g., high-order, heterogeneous, nonlinear) feature relations can be essential in high-dimensional data and remains a major challenge for anomaly detection.
- **Challenge 3**: Large-scale data collection of labeled anomaly data is difficult and costly, where it is important to learn normality/abnormality in a data-efficient manner. Two major challenges are learning meaningful normality/abnormality representations with a small amount of labeled anomaly data and learning detection models that generalize to unknown anomalies revealed by the given labeled anomaly data.
- **Challenge 4**: Many semisupervised anomaly detection methods assume that the given labeled training data is without anomalies, which can give vulnerability to noisy instances that are incorrectly labeled as an opposite class label. A major challenge here is to develop noise-resistant anomaly detection.
- **Challenge 5**: Most existing methods tackle the challenge of detecting point anomalies, which cannot be used for conditional anomalies and group anomalies because they have a different behavior com-

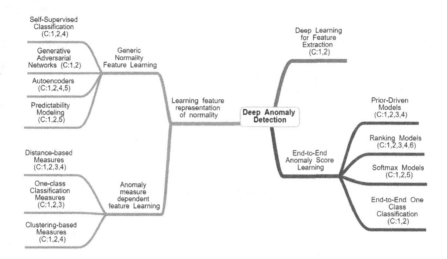

FIGURE 9.1

Current Deep Anomaly Detection Techniques [114]. The "C:1,2" represents the challenges this specific methods addresses.

pared to point anomalies. The main challenge here is to incorporate conditional/group anomalies into anomaly measures/models to detect these complex anomalies.

- **Challenge 6**: In many critical areas, major risks exist when anomaly detection models are used directly as black-box models. For example, rare data instances reported as anomalies can lead to possible algorithmic bias against underrepresented groups in the data. An effective approach to mitigating this risk is to provide anomaly explanation algorithms that provide clear guidance as to why a particular data instance is identified as an anomaly. Providing such an explanation may be as important as detection accuracy in some applications. Deriving anomaly explanations within a specific detection method is still an unsolved challenge. Developing interpretable anomaly detection models is critical, but balancing model interpretability and effectiveness remains a challenge.

In short, deep anomaly detection aims to learn feature representations or anomaly scores via neural networks to detect anomalies. In recent years, many deep anomaly detection methods have been introduced that show significantly better performance than conventional anomaly detection in addressing challenging detection problems in various real-world applications. The following section provides an overview of current deep anomaly detection methods and their capabilities in addressing these challenges.

To understand the domain of anomaly detection, existing deep anomaly detection methods were classified into three main categories. An overview of the taxonomy of methods along with the challenges they address is shown in Fig. 9.1. Deep Anomaly Detection consists of the major categories of Learning Feature Representations of Normality, Deep Learning for Feature Extraction and End-to-End Anomaly Score Learning.

In the first main category, Deep Learning for Feature Extraction, deep learning and anomaly detection are completely divided. Deep learning techniques are used only as independent feature extractors.

In the second main category Learning Feature Representations of Normality, the two modules are interdependent in some way to learn meaningful representations of normality. This category of methods can be further broken into two subcategories based on whether traditional anomaly measures are included in their objective functions. These two subcategories take a different approach to formulate the objective function.

In the third main category, End-to-End Anomaly Score Learning, deep learning and anomaly detection fully unify deep learning with anomaly detection, where the aim of the method is to learning anomaly scores based on neural networks in an end-to-end manner.

The detailed methodology and algorithms will be discussed for each category of methods, including objective functions, key intuitions, assumptions, advantages, and disadvantages. More details about anomaly detection in the context of DL/ML can also be found in the papers of [114,111].

9.1.1 Deep learning based feature extraction

Deep learning is able to extract low-dimensional representations from high-dimensional and nonlinearly separable spaces for anomaly detection. Feature extraction and anomaly detection are completely separate and independent of each other. The deep learning components thus only act as a dimension reducer.

Formally, the approach can be represented as

$$z = \phi(x; \theta) \tag{9.1}$$

where $z = \phi : X \mapsto Z$ is a deep neural network-based feature mapping function, with $X \in R^D$, $Z \in R^{(K)}$ typically $D >> K$. An anomaly scoring method f, which has no connection to feature mapping, is then applied to the new space to compute anomaly scores. Compared to popular dimensionality reduction methods in anomaly detection, such as principal component analysis (PCA) [22,135,184] and random projection [78,113,121], Deep learning techniques have shown much better ability in extracting semantically rich features and nonlinear feature relations [14,51].

9.1.2 Working principles of learning methods

Features extracted by deep learning models preserve the discriminative information used for separating anomalies from normal instances. One approach includes the use of the popular pretrained deep learning models such as AlexNet [73], VGG [139], and ResNet [49] to extract low-dimensional features. This direction is explored in anomaly detection in complex high-dimensional data such as image data and video data. Interesting work has been done for unmasking frameworks for online anomaly detection [150]. The idea is to iteratively train a binary classifier to separate a set of video images from subsequent video images in a sliding window, removing the most discriminative features at each iteration step. The framework assumes the first set of frames to be normal and evaluates its separability from subsequent video frames. Therefore, the training classification accuracy is expected to be high if the subsequent video frames are abnormal and low otherwise. The performance of the unmasking framework depends heavily on the quality of the features. Therefore, the video images must be represented by high-quality features. The VGG model trained with the ILSVRC benchmark [128] effectively produces expressive appearance features for this purpose [150].

Authors in [88] formulated the masking framework as a two-sample test task to understand its theoretical basis. The paper showed that using features extracted from a dynamically updated sampling pool of video images improves the framework's performance. Furthermore, similar to many other tasks, feature representations extracted from deep models trained on a source dataset can be transferred to fine-tune anomaly detectors on a target dataset. As shown in [9], one-class support vector machines (SVMs) can first be initialized with the VGG models pretrained on ILSVRC and then fine-tuned to improve anomaly classification on the MNIST data [76]. Similarly, ResNet models pretrained on MNIST can support the detection of abnormal events in various video surveillance datasets [117,181].

Another research direction in this category is to explicitly train a deep feature extraction model instead of a pretrained model for downstream anomaly assessment [41,62,162,171]. Specifically, in [162] three separate autoencoder networks are trained to learn low-dimensional features for the respective appearance, motion, and appearance-motion community representations for video anomaly detection. An ensemble of three one-class SVMs is trained independently on each of these learned feature representations to perform anomaly evaluation. Similar to [162], a linear one-class SVM is used to perform anomaly detection on low-dimensional representations of high-dimensional tabular data obtained from Deep Belief Networks (DBNs) [41]. Instead of single-class SVM, unsupervised classification approaches are used in [62] to enable anomaly detection in the projected space. First, the video frames' low-dimensional features provided by convolutional autoencoders are clustered, and then the cluster labels are treated as pseudo-class labels to perform one-versus-rest classification. The classification probabilities are used to define frame-wise anomaly scores.

Similar approaches are also found in graph anomaly detection [171], where unsupervised cluster-based anomaly measures in the latent representation space are used to compute the anomaly of graph vertices or edges. To retrieve meaningful graph vertex representation, vertex representations are optimized by minimizing autoencoder-based reconstruction loss and pairwise distances of adjacent graph vertices, using the one-hot encoding of graph vertices as input.

Advantages

- Many state-of-the-art (pretrained) deep models and off-the-shelf anomaly detectors are readily available.
- Deep feature extraction provides more powerful dimensionality reduction than linear methods.
- It is easy-to-implement given the public availability of the detection methods and deep models.

Disadvantages

- The disjointed anomaly scoring and feature extraction often lead to suboptimal anomaly scores.
- Pretrained deep models are normally limited to specific data types.

Deep learning methods project high-dimensional or nonindependent data on a lower-dimensional space, allowing existing anomaly detection methods to operate on a simpler data space. The lower space often helps uncover hidden anomalies and reduces false positives. However, these methods may not always preserve enough information for anomaly detection since the data projection is completely decoupled from the anomaly detection. Moreover, this approach allows us to use multiple types of features and learn semantically rich detection models (e.g., different predefined image/video features in [62,150,162]), which also helps to reduce false positives.

9.1.3 Learning feature representations of normality

This learning category combines feature learning with anomaly assessment. Methods can be divided into generic feature learning and anomaly measure dependent feature learning.

Generic normality feature learning

This method learns the data representations by optimizing a generic learning function for learning features, which is not primarily designed to detect anomalies. However, the representations learned can still detect anomalies as they are forced to capture some important underlying data regularities. Formally, this approach can be represented as:

$$\{\theta^*, W^*\} = \underset{\theta, W}{\operatorname{argmin}} \sum_{x \in X} \iota(\psi(\phi(x; \theta); W)) \tag{9.2}$$

$$s_x = f(x, \phi_\theta^*, \psi_{w^*}) \tag{9.3}$$

where ϕ maps the original data onto the representation space Z; ψ parameterized by W is a surrogate learning task that operates onto the Z space and is dedicated to enforcing the learning of underlying data regularities, ι is a loss function relative to the underlying modeling approach, and f is a scoring function that utilizes ϕ and ψ to calculate the anomaly score s. Methods are driven by several perspectives, including data reconstruction, generative modeling, predictability modeling, and self-supervised classification. Both predictability modeling and self-supervised classification are built upon self-supervised learning approaches, but they have different assumptions, advantages, and flaws, and thus they are reviewed separately.

Autoencoders

Autoencoders aim to learn a low-dimensional feature representation space on which the given data instances can be reconstructed. This is a widely used technique for dimensionality reduction or data compression [58,65,147]. The heuristic for using this technique in anomaly detection is that the learned feature representations are forced to learn important regularities in the data to minimize reconstruction error. Anomalies are difficult to reconstruct from the resulting representations and therefore increase reconstruction error.

Autoencoder working principle

Normal instances are restructured from compressed spatial anomalies. Autoencoder (AE) networks are famous techniques in this category. An AE consists of an encoding network and a decoding network, where the encoder maps the original data to a low-dimensional feature space, and the decoder tries to recover the data from a low-dimensional space. The parameters of the two networks are trained using the designed loss function. To conserve the low-dimensional representations of the original data, a bottleneck network architecture is used, where the model preserves the information that is important for reconstructing the data samples. To minimize the reconstruction error, the preserved information for the dominant instances is needed to represent the dominant classes (normal classes). Data instances that deviate from the dominant class are poorly reconstructed. The reconstruction error can be used directly as an anomaly score. The formulation of this approach is given as:

$$z = \phi_d(x; \theta_e), \quad x = \phi_d(z; \theta_d) \tag{9.4}$$

$$\{\theta_e^*, \theta_d^*\} = \underset{\Theta_e, \Theta_d}{\mathrm{argmin}} \sum_{x \in X} \|x - \phi_d(\phi_e(x; \theta_e); \theta_d)\|^2 \tag{9.5}$$

$$s_x = \|x - \phi_d(\phi_e(x; \theta_e^*); \theta_d^*)\|^2 \tag{9.6}$$

where ϕ_e represents the encoding network with parameters θ_e and ϕ_d the decoding network with parameters θ_d.

Encoder and Decoder can use the same weighting parameters to reduce parameters and regularize learning. s_x is the reconstruction error based anomaly score of x. Different types of regulated autoencoders have been introduced to learn more expressive feature representations [37,97,124,152].

Sparse AE

Sparse AE is trained to promote sparsity in the activation units of the hidden layer by keeping the top-K most active units [97].

Denoising AE

Denoising AE [152] aims to learn representations that are robust to small deviations by learning to reconstruct data from predefined altered data instances instead of original data. Contractive AE [124] tries to learn feature representations of instances that are robust to small deviations from their neighbors, which is accomplished by adding a penalty term to the encoder's activation functions.

Variational AE

Variational AE [37] introduces regularization into the representation space by encoding data instances using a priority distribution over the latent space, which prevents overfitting and ensures good characteristics of the learned space to enable the generation of meaningful data instances.

AEs for anomaly detection

AEs are easy to implement and have a clear intuition in anomaly detection. The Replicator Network explores the idea of data reconstruction for anomaly detection, with experiments focusing on static multidimensional data. The replicator network is a feedforward multilayer perceptron with three hidden layers that uses parameterized hyperbolic tangent activation functions to obtain different activation levels for different input values. This approach discretizes the intermediate representations into predefined bins. The resulting data instances from the hidden layers are naturally clustered into several groups, which enables clustered anomaly detection. Several studies addressed further improving the performance of this approach, such as RandNet [26] by learning an ensemble of different AEs. The set of independent AEs is trained with different initial random network setups. In another paper, the idea of autoencoder ensembling was extended to time series data [66].

Robust Deep Autoencoders (RDA) [180] aims to increase the robustness of AEs by decomposing the original data into the two subsets of normal and the anomaly set. This is accomplished by inserting a sparsity penalty l_1 or a grouped penalty l_2, l_1 into the objective function to regularize the coefficients of the anomaly set.

AEs are additionally used to detect anomalies in sequence data [90], image/video data [162] and graph data [36]. AEs can be categorized into two types of AE adaptations for complex data. The simple type is using AEs by adapting the network architecture to the input data type, such as CNN-AE [56,176],

LSTM-AE [97], Conv-LSTM-AE [92], and GCN (graph convolutional network)-AE [36]. For this type of AE, the encoder-decoder scheme is the entire procedure of these methods.

Other types of AE-based approaches use AEs to learn low-dimensional representations of the complex data and next learn to predict these learned representations. Learning and predicting the representations are often two separate steps, where these approaches differ from the first type in that the prediction of the representations is wrapped around the low-dimensional representations obtained by AEs. In another paper [90], denoising AEs are coupled with RNNs to learn normal patterns from multivariate sequence data, using a denoising AE with two hidden layers to learn representations from multidimensional data inputs at each time step, and then training an RNN with a single hidden layer to predict the representations provided by the denoising AE. A similar approach is used for acoustic anomaly detection [98] via a more complex RNN, bidirectional LSTMs.

Advantages - reconstruction-based methods:

- The idea of AEs is simple and generic for different types of data.
- Different types of AE variants can be used for anomaly detection.

Disadvantages - reconstruction-based methods:

- The learned feature representations may be biased by rare regularities and outliers or anomalies in the training data.
- The objective function of data reconstruction is designed for dimensionality reduction or data compression, not anomaly detection.

The resulting representations are a generic summary of the underlying regularities that are not optimized for anomaly detection. Different layers and architectures can be used to detect anomalies in high-dimensional data, and nonindependent data such as attributed graph data [36] and multivariate sequence data [90,98]. These methods can reduce false positives compared to traditional methods based on hand-crafted features when the learned representations are more informative. AEs are generally sensitive to data noise in the training data because they can be trained to remember this noise, leading to severe overfitting and small reconstruction errors of anomalies. The idea of Robust Principal Component Analysis (RPCA) can be used in AEs to train more robust detection models.

Generative adversarial networks

GAN-based anomaly detection generally aims to learn a latent feature space of a generative network G so that the latent space captures well the underlying normality of the data distribution. A form of residual between the real instance and the generated instance can be defined as an anomaly score. In GANs, normal data instances are considered to be better generated from the latent feature space of the generative network than anomalies.

One of the early methods is AnoGAN [132], that follows the intuition given a data instance x, an instance z is searched in the learned feature space of the generative network G such that the generated instance $G(z)$ and x are almost similar. As the latent space captures the underlying distribution of the data, anomalies are not supposed to have very similar generated counterparts to normal instances. A GAN is first trained with the following objective function:

$$\min_G \max_D V(D, G) =) E_{x \sim px}\left[\log D(x)\right] + E_{z \sim pz}\left[\log(1 - D(g(z)))\right] \tag{9.7}$$

where G and D are the generator and discriminator networks, respectively, parameterized by θ_G and θ_D, and V is the value function of the two-player minimax objectives. For each x, to find the best z, two loss functions (residual and discrimination loss) are used to supervise the search. The residual loss is defined as:

$$l_R(x, z_\gamma) = ||x - G(z_\gamma)||_1 \tag{9.8}$$

The discrimination loss is defined by a feature matching technique [130]:

$$l_{fm}(x, z_\gamma) = ||h(x) - h(G(z_\gamma))||_1 \tag{9.9}$$

where γ is the index of the search iteration and h is a feature mapping from a discriminator layer. The search starts with a randomly sampled z, followed by an update of z based on the gradients obtained from the total loss $(1 - \alpha)l_R(x, z_\gamma) + \alpha l_{fm}(x, z_\gamma)$, where α is a hyperparameter.

During the search, the trained GAN parameters are fixed, and the loss is used to update the coefficients of z over each iteration. Therefore, the anomaly score is defined by the similarity between x and z received in the final γ^* step:

$$s_x = (1 - \alpha)l_R(x, z_{\gamma^*}) + \alpha l_{fm}(x, z_{\gamma^*}) \tag{9.10}$$

The main problem with AnoGAN is computationally inefficient iterative search for z, which can be solved by adding a network that learns to map data instances to a latent space. An example of this is an inversion of the generator, leading to methods such as EBGAN [173] and fastAnoGAN [131]. Here, we focus on EBGAN based on bidirectional GAN (BiGAN) [38]. In particular, BiGAN has additionally an encoder E to map x to z in latent space while learning the parameters of G, D, and E. Instead of discriminating x and $G(z)$, BiGAN aims to discriminate the instance pairs $(x, E(x))$ from the pairs $(G(z), z)$:

$$\min_{G,E} \max_D E_{x \sim p_x} \left[E_{z \sim p_E(\cdot|x)} log\left[D(x, z) \right] \right] + E_{z \sim p_z} \left[E_{x \sim p_G(\cdot|z)} \left[log(1 - D(x, z)) \right] \right] \tag{9.11}$$

After training, EBGAN, inspired by Eq. (9.7) in AnoGAN, defines the anomaly score as:

$$s_x = (1 - \alpha)l_G(x) + \alpha l_D(x) \tag{9.12}$$

where $l_G(x) = ||x - G(E(x))||_1$ and $l_D(x) = ||h(x, E(x)) - h(G(E(x)), E(x))||_1$.

This eliminates the need to search z in AnoGAN iteratively. Adversarial Learned Anomaly Detection (ALAD) [174] is an extension of EBGAN and is designed by adding two additional discriminators, where one discriminator attempts to distinguish (x, x) from $(x, E(G(x)))$. GANomaly [3] further enhances the generator by changing the generator architecture to an encoder-decoder-encoder network and adding two additional loss functions. The generator can be formalized as:

$$\overset{G_E}{\rightarrow} z \overset{G_D}{\rightarrow} \hat{x} \overset{E}{\rightarrow} \hat{z}$$

where G is a composition of encoder G_E and decoder G_D. Additionally to the used feature matching loss:

$$l_{fm} = E_{x \sim p_x} ||h(x) - h(G(x))||_2 \tag{9.13}$$

the generator includes a context loss and an encoding loss to create realistic instances:

$$l_{con} = E_{x \sim p_x} ||x - G(x)||_1 \tag{9.14}$$
$$l_{enc} = E_{x \sim p_x} ||G_E(x) - E(G(x))||_2 \tag{9.15}$$

The contextual loss in Eq. (9.14) forces the generator to consider the contextual information of the input x when generating $\hat{x}$. The coding loss in Eq. (9.15) helps the generator learn how to encode the functions of the generated instances. The total loss is then defined as:

$$l = \alpha l_{fm} + \beta l_{con} + \gamma l_{enc} \tag{9.16}$$

where α, β and γ are the hyperparameters used to determine the weight of each loss. Since the training data contains mainly normal instances, the encoders G and E are optimized for encoding normal instances, and therefore the anomaly score can be defined as follows.

$$s_x = ||G_E(x) - E(G(X))||_1 \tag{9.17}$$

in which s_x is large as expected when x is an anomaly. Several other GANs have been introduced over the years, such as Wasserstein GAN [99] and Cycle GAN [182]. They can be used to further improve the anomaly detection performance of the above methods, e.g., to replace the standard GAN with Wasserstein-GAN [154]. Another relevant line of research is the adversarial learning of end-to-end one-class classification models, which can be categorized into the end-to-end learning framework for anomaly assessment.

Advantages
- GANs showed excellent abilities in generating realistic instances and enabled the detection of anomalous instances that can hardly be reconstructed from latent space.
- It exists a large variety of existing GAN-based models and theories that can be adapted to anomaly detection [30].

Disadvantages
- Training GANs can suffer from issues such as nonconvergence and mode collapse [103], leading to difficulties in training GAN-based anomaly detection models.
- The generator network may be tempted to generate data instances outside the distribution of normal instances. Even more so if the true distribution of the data set is complex or if the training data includes unexpected outliers.
- GAN-based anomaly scores can be suboptimal due to their establishment on top of the generator network, whose goal is data synthesis, not anomaly detection.

Like AEs, GAN-based anomaly detection can identify high-dimensional anomalies by analyzing the reconstruction from the learned low-dimensional latent space. When the latent space preserves important information to distinguish anomalies, it helps improve the accuracy of the detection over the original space.

Predictability modeling

Predictive modeling learns feature representations by predicting the current data instance based on previous instances using the representation in a temporal window. Data instances are considered as individual elements in a sequence, e.g., ECG sampling sequence or image frames of a video sequence. This technique is used to learn and predict sequence representations [59,100,80]. Feature representations are forced to capture temporal, sequential, and recurrent dependencies within a sequence to achieve accurate predictions. Normal instances usually retain such dependencies for prediction tasks, while anomalies often violate these dependencies and are difficult to predict. In this case, the prediction errors can be used to define the anomaly scores and identify anomalies.

Normal instances are more predictable over time than anomalies. This research area is popular in video anomaly detection [1,86,165]. Video sequences contain complex high-dimensional spatio-temporal features. To ensure accurate prediction of video images, various constraints on appearance and motion features are required in the prediction target. This deep anomaly detection approach was first explored in [86]. Given a sequence of consecutive t samples $x_1, x_2, \cdots, x_t$, the learning task is to generate a future sample $\hat{x}_{t+1}$ from all these samples such that $\hat{x}_{t+1}$ is as close as possible to the ground truth x_{t+1}.

The general objective function can be formulated as:

$$\alpha l_{pred}(\hat{x}_{t+1}, x_{t+1}) + \beta l_{adv}(\hat{x}_{t+1}) \tag{9.18}$$

where $\hat{x}_{t+1} = \psi(\phi(x_1, x_2, \cdots, x_t; \theta); W)$, l_{pred} is the sample prediction loss measured by the mean square error, l_{adv} is an adversarial loss.

A famous network architecture called U-Net [1] is used to instantiate the ψ function for sample generation. l_{pred} consists of three separate losses, each enforcing the closeness between $\hat{x}(t+1)$, such that $x(t+1)$ are three important sample feature descriptors, namely intensity, gradient, and optical flow. l_{adv} represents the use of adversarial training to improve sample generation. After training, for a given sample x, a normalized peak-to-noise ratio [100] based on the prediction difference $||x_i - \hat{x}_i||_2$ defines the anomaly score. In [165], an additional autoencoder-based reconstruction network is used to refine further the predicted sample quality, which helps to increase the anomaly score difference between normal and anomalous samples.

Another research direction is based on autoregressive models [52], which assume that each element in a sequence is a linear dependency on the previous elements. The autoregressive models are used in [1] to estimate the density of training samples in a latent space, which avoids assuming a particular class of distributions. In more detail, given x and its latent representation space $z = \phi(x; \theta)$, the autoregressive model factorizes $p(z)$ as:

$$p(z) = \prod_{j=1}^{K} p(z_j|z_{1:j-1}) \tag{9.19}$$

where $z_{1:j-1} = \{z_1, z_2, ..., z_{j-1}\}$, $p(z_j|z_{1:j-1})$ represents the probability mass function of z_j trained on all previous instances $z_{1:j-1}$ and K is the dimensionality size parameter of the latent space.

In [1], the goal is to learn an autoencoder and a density estimation network $\psi(z; W)$ with autoregressive network layers. The total loss can be represented as:

$$L = E_x \left[||x - \phi_d(\phi_e(x; \Theta_e); \Theta_d||_2 - \lambda \log(\psi(z; W)) \right] \tag{9.20}$$

The first part denotes the reconstruction error (MSE), the second is an autoregressive loss (log-likelihood). Minimizing the losses allows to learn the features that are frequent and easy to predict. In the evaluation phase, the reconstruction error and the autoregressive loss are combined to define the anomaly score.

Advantages
- Numerous sequence learning techniques can be adapted and integrated into this approach.
- This approach allows learning of different types of temporal and spatial dependencies.

Disadvantages
- This approach is limited to detecting anomalies in sequence data.
- Sequential predictions can be computationally intensive.
- The learned representations may be suboptimal for anomaly detection because the underlying goal is sequential prediction, not anomaly detection.

This approach is mainly designed to learn time-dependent low-dimensional representations, which helps to avoid false positive detection of anomalies in high-dimensional and temporal data. The prediction is bound to some expired temporal instances to detect temporal context-based conditional anomalies.

Self-supervised classification
These methods learn normality representations by building self-supervised classification models to identify instances that do not conform to the models as anomalies. The origins of this method are based on traditional cross-feature analyses and feature models [61,110,146]. These methods evaluate the normality of data instances based on their consistency to a set of predictive models, where each model learns to predict a feature based on the other features. The consistency of test instances can be measured using log loss-based *surprisal* [110], average prediction score [61], or majority voting of binary decisions [146]. Deep consistency-based anomaly detection focuses on image data and builds prediction models using feature transformation-based augmented data. The classification models are forced to learn relevant features to describe the underlying distribution of the training instances in order to distinguish the transformed instances. As a result, normal instances tend to have stronger matches to the classification models.

Self-supervised classification follows the assumption that normal instances are more regular than anomalies for self-supervised classifiers.

This approach was explored in [49]. Various compositions of geometric transformation operations, including horizontal flipping, translations, and rotations, are first applied to training images to build the predictive models. Then, a deep multiclass classification model is trained on the data, which treats data instances with a particular transformation operation from the same class (like a synthetic class). During inference, test instances are augmented with each of the transformation compositions, and the normality score is defined by aggregating all softmax classification results onto the augmented test instance. The loss function is defined as:

$$L_{cons} = CE(\psi(z_{T_j}; W), y_{T_j}) \tag{9.21}$$

where $z_{T_j} = \phi(T_j(x); \Theta)$ is a low-dimensional feature representation of instance x extended by transformation operation type T_j, ψ is a multiclass classifier parameterized by W, y_{T_j} is a one-hot encoding of the synthetic class for instances augmented with transformation operation T_j, CE is a cross-entropy loss function.

By minimizing the loss function in Eq. (9.21), it results the optimized representations for the classifier ψ. Next, the feature learner can be applied $\psi(\cdot, \Theta^*)$ and the classifier $\phi(\cdot, W^*)$ to obtain a classification score for the test instances augmented with a transformation T_j. The classification scores of each test instance for different T_j are aggregated next to calculate the anomaly score. The classification scores trained on each T_j are expected to follow a Dirichlet distribution to estimate the test instance's fit to the classification model ψ; a simple average of the classification scores associated with different T_j can also be used.

In [49], a semisupervised setting is assumed where the training data contains only normal instances. A similar approach is explored in [156], where the transformation sets include the four transformation operations of rotate, flip, move, and path reorder. In [156], two important findings showed that the gradient magnitude caused by normal instances is usually much larger than outliers when training self-supervised multiclass classification models. The other finding was that the direction of network update is biased toward normal instances. Therefore, normal instances often have a stronger fit to the classification model than anomalies. The studies evaluated three strategies for retrieving an anomaly score: maximum prediction probability, average prediction probability, and negative entropy over all prediction probabilities [156]. The anomaly scores with negative entropy generally perform better than the other two strategies.

Advantages
- They work well in unsupervised and semisupervised settings.
- Anomaly scoring is based on some intrinsic properties of the gradient size and its update.

Disadvantages
- Feature transform operations can be data-dependent. The described transformation operations are only applicable to image data.
- Although classification models are trained end-to-end process, the consistency-based anomaly scores are obtained from the classification scores and are not an integrated building block in the optimization and may be suboptimal.

The low-dimensional representation of normality learning supports anomaly detection better than in the original high-dimensional space. This approach can work in an unsupervised environment [156] and is robust to anomaly contamination in the training data in terms of the differences between anomalies and normal instances represented in the classifiers.

9.1.4 Anomaly measure-dependent feature learning

The aim of anomaly measure-dependent feature learning is to learn specifically optimized feature representations for a given existing anomaly measure. Instead of the general feature learning approach that computes anomaly scores based on heuristics after the learned representations are obtained, this field incorporates an existing anomaly measure into the objective function to optimize the feature representations. There are three types of common anomaly measures: One-class classification, distance-based measure, and cluster-based measure.

Distance-based measure

Deep distance-based anomaly detection aims to learn optimized feature representations for a particular type of distance-based anomaly measure. Distance-based methods are straightforward and easy to implement. Effective distance-based anomaly measures have been introduced, like DB outlier [68,69], average k-nearest neighbor distance [10], k-nearest neighbor distance [123], relative distance [177], and random nearest-neighbor distance [143,116]. A limitation of these traditional distance-based measures is that they are not effective in high-dimensional data due to the curse of dimensionality. Since deep distance-based anomaly detection methods project data onto a low-dimensional space before applying the distance measures, this limitation can be overcome.

This approach assumes that anomalies are far distributed from their nearest neighbors, while normal instances are in dense neighborhoods. Distance-based measures are explored in [113], in which the random neighborhood distance-based anomaly measure [143,116] is used to supervise the learning of low-dimensional representations from high-dimensional data. The representations are optimized so that the nearest neighbor distances of pseudo-labeled anomalies are larger than those of pseudo-labeled normal instances in random subsamples. Some commercially available anomaly detectors produce pseudo-labels.

Let the subset of data instances $S \in X$ be randomly selected from the data set X, A and N be the pseudo-labeled anomalous and normal instances, respectively, with $X = A \cap N$ and $\emptyset = A \cap N$, whose loss function is built on the hinge loss function [125]:

$$L_{query} = \frac{1}{|X|} \sum_{x \in A, x' \in N} \max \left\{ 0, m + f(x', S; \Theta) - f(x, S; \Theta) \right\}, \tag{9.22}$$

where m is a constant for the distance separating two distances by $f(x, S; \Theta)$, i.e., a random nearest neighbor distance function operating in the representation space:

$$f(x, S; \Theta) = \min_{x' \in S} \left\| \phi(x; \Theta), \phi(x'; \Theta) \right\|_2 \tag{9.23}$$

L_{query} is a hinge loss function augmented by the random nearest neighbor distance-based anomaly measure defined in Eq. (9.23). Minimizing the loss in Eq. (9.22) ensures that the random nearest neighbor distances of anomalies are m greater than that of normal instances in the ϕ-based representation space. In the evaluation phase, the random distance in Eq. (9.23) is directly used to obtain the anomaly score for each test instance. Following this approach, a similar representation learning for other distance-based measures can be derived by using Eq. (9.23) and replacing it with other measures, such as the k-nearest neighbor distance [123] or the average $k-$nearest neighbor distance [10].

Nevertheless, these measures are more computationally expensive. The authors of the paper in [113] required to query distances between nearest neighbors in random data subsets (inspired by [19]). A simpler idea of [154] uses the distance between optimized representations to randomly project representations of the same instances and guide representation learning. The objective of the method is as follows:

$$\Theta* = \underset{\Theta}{\operatorname{argmin}} \sum x \in X f(\phi(x; \Theta), \phi'(x)) \tag{9.24}$$

where ϕ' is a random mapping function instantiated from the neural network used in ϕ with initial weights set randomly, f is a measure of the distance between the two representations of the same instance. As shown in [19], solving the objective function is comparable to knowledge distillation from a neural network and helps learn the frequency of different patterns in the data. However, the objective function ignores the relative proximity between instances and is sensitive to anomalies in the data. As shown in [154], the approximation information can be learned by a task that involves predicting the distance between random pairs of instances. A boosting procedure can be used to filter potential anomalies and iteratively build robust detection models.

In the evaluation phase, $f(\phi(x; \theta*), \phi'(x))$ is used to compute the anomaly scores.

Advantages

- Distance-based anomalies are simple to apply, well-defined and have a comprehensive theoretical foundation in the literature.
- Works in low-dimensional representation spaces. Can effectively deal with high-dimensional data where traditional distance-based anomaly measures usually fail.
- Able to learn tailored representations.

Disadvantages

- Large computations associated with distance-based anomaly measures can limit distance-based anomaly measures in the representation learning process.
- The weaknesses of distance-based anomaly measures limit their capabilities.

This approach learns low-dimensional representations for distance-based anomaly measures, addressing the curse of dimensionality in distance-based detection [183]. As shown in [113], an adapted triplet loss can be developed to use some labeled anomaly samples to learn more effective normality representations. Thanks to pseudo-anomaly labeling, the methods [113,154] are more robust to possible anomaly contamination and work effectively in a fully unsupervised environment.

One-class classification-based measure

These methods aim to learn feature representations tailored for subsequent anomaly detection based on one-class classification. One-class classification learns a description of a set of data instances to detect whether or not new instances match the training data. One-class classification is a famously known approaches to anomaly detection [126,134,145,107]. Support Vector Machines (SVM) strongly inspired one-class classification models [29]. Two widely used one-class models are one-class SVM (or $\upsilon-SVC$) [134] and Support Vector Data Description (SVDD) [145]. An area of research is learning representations specifically optimized for these traditional one-class classification models.

One-class classification-based measurement assumes that all normal instances come from a single (abstract) class and are summarized by a model to which anomalies do not match.

Advantages

1. Representation learning and one-class classification models can be combined to learn tailored and more optimal representations.
2. One-class classification-based anomalies are thoroughly studied in the literature and provide a solid foundation for deep one-class classification-based methods.

Disadvantages

1. The one-class models may perform ineffectively in datasets with complex data distributions within the normal class.
2. Detection performance depends on anomaly measures based on one-class classification.

This category of methods improves detection accuracy by learning a low-dimensional representation space optimized for one-class classification models. A small amount of labeled normal and abnormal data can be used by these methods to learn more effective one-class description models that can detect known anomalies and novel classes of anomalies.

Clustering-based measure

Deep clustering-based anomaly detection goal is to learn representations such that anomalies differ from clusters in the newly learned representation space. The task of clustering and anomaly detection are naturally related. Thus, there are several studies that use clustering results to define anomalies via cluster size [63], distance between cluster centers [64], distance to cluster centers [57], and cluster membership [136]. Gaussian mixture model-based anomaly detection [95,40] is an example of this category due to its relationships with clustering via likelihood optimization in the Gaussian mixture model (GMM) compared to aggregation of data instance distances to Gaussian cluster centers [2].

This approach follows the assumption that normal instances have a larger membership in clusters than anomalies. Deep clustering aims to learn feature representations tailored to a particular clustering algorithm. Several studies have investigated the deep clustering problem in recent years [164,163,161, 148,48,36,24]. The motivation is that the effectiveness of the clustering method is highly dependent on the input data. Learning feature representations explicitly tailored to a clustering algorithm can provide good performance on different datasets [6]. The two key intuitions behind this method are:

- Good representations enable good clustering. Good clustering results can provide useful supervisory signals for representation learning.
- Representations optimized for one clustering algorithm are not always useful for other clustering algorithms because of the different underlying assumptions.

Methods for deep clustering typically consist of two modules. One to perform forward pass clustering and the other to learn representations using the cluster mapping as pseudo-class labels in the backward pass. The loss function is often the most critical part, which can be generally formulated as follows

$$\alpha l_{clu}(f(\phi(x;\Theta);W),y_x) + \beta l_{aux}(X) \tag{9.25}$$

where l_{clu} is a clustering loss function in which ϕ is the feature learner parameterized by Θ, f is a clustering assignment function parameterized by W, and y_x represents the pseudo-class labels obtained by clustering, l_{aux} is a nonclustering loss function used to enforce additional constraints on the learned representations, and α and β are two hyperparameters to control the significance of the two losses. l_{clu} can be used with a k-mean loss [24,161], a spectral clustering loss [148,164], an agglomerative clustering loss [163], or a GMM loss [35] that provides representation learning for the individual clustering algorithm. l_{aux} is often initiated with an autoencoder-based reconstruction loss [48,164] to learn robust and structure-preserving representations.

After deep clustering, the cluster assignments in the resulting function f can then be used to calculate anomaly scores based on [63,64,136,57]. However, anomalies can bias deep clustering if the training data contains anomalies. These methods can be used in semisupervised training where the data consists only of normal instances. In unsupervised training, additional constraints in l_{clu} or l_{aux} are required to eliminate the influence of potential anomalies.

These deep clustering methods focus on learning optimal clustering results. Although their clustering results are suitable for anomaly detection, the learned representations may not entirely capture anomalies. It is important to use clustering techniques to learn representations such that anomalies have weaker membership in clusters than normal instances. In [81,183], promising results for this type of approach are shown. The representations for a GMM-based model are learned using the representations optimized for anomaly detection. The two-loss functions are similar to Eq. 9.25, where l_{clu} and l_{aux} are given as GMM loss and autoencoder-based reconstruction loss, respectively. However, to learn different representations of anomalies, they concatenate hand-crafted features. The features are based on the reconstruction errors with the trained features of the autoencoder to optimize the combined features. Since the hand-crafted features (based on reconstruction errors) capture the normality of the data, the representations are more suited for anomaly detection than those provided by other deep clustering methods.

Advantages

- Several deep clustering methods and theories can boost the effectiveness and theoretical basis of anomaly detection.
- Unlike traditional clustering-based methods, deep clustering-based methods learn specially optimized representations to detect the anomalies more easily than on the original data, especially for complex datasets.

Disadvantages

- The performance of anomaly detection is highly dependent on the clustering results.
- The clustering process can be biased by contaminated anomalies in the training data, resulting in less effective representations.

The general clustering-based anomaly measures are used over newly learned low-dimensional representations of the input data. If the new representation space holds enough discriminative information, the deep methods can better detect accuracy than those in the original data space. Many clustering algorithms are sensitive to outliers, where deep clustering and following anomaly detection can be misled if anomalies contaminate the given data. Deep clustering with hand-crafted features from autoencoder reconstruction errors [183] can support learning more robustly concerning contamination.

9.1.5 End-to-end anomaly score learning

This research direction aims to learn scalar anomaly scores in an end-to-end process. Opposed to learning features that depend on anomaly measures, anomaly scoring in this type of approach does not depend on existing anomaly measures. A neural network is used that learns the anomaly scores directly. Novel loss functions often require to drive the anomaly scoring network. The goal of this approach is to train an end-to-end learning network for anomaly scores: $\tau(\cdot; \theta) : X \mapsto R$.

The framework can be formulated as:

$$\Theta^* = \underset{\Theta}{\arg\min} \sum_{x \in X} l(\tau(x; \Theta)), \tag{9.26}$$

$$s_x = \tau(x; \Theta^*) \tag{9.27}$$

These methods simultaneously learn the feature representations and anomaly scores, which greatly optimizes the anomaly scores and anomaly ranking. Therefore, they have similarities with anomaly-dependent feature methods.

Nevertheless, anomaly measure-dependent feature learning is limited by the built-in anomaly measures, while the end-to-end anomaly score learning category does not have this weakness. They represent two different directions of model design, one focusing on synthesizing existing anomaly measures and neural network models, while the other aims at developing novel loss functions for direct anomaly score learning. The four main approaches in this category are ranking models, priority-driven models, softmax likelihood models, and end-to-end one-class classification models. The key to end-to-end anomaly score learning is the inclusion of order or discrimination information into the anomaly scoring network.

Ranking models

This method aims to learn a ranking model directly so that instances can be sorted over an ordinal variable associated with the anomaly's absolute/relative order relation. The observable ordinal variable drives the scoring of the anomaly over the neural network.

Assumptions

An observable ordinal variable exists that captures an anomaly. One research direction in this approach is to develop ordinal regression-based loss functions to drive the neural network for anomaly scoring [115]. In [117], a self-trained deep ordinal regression model is presented to optimize anomaly scoring for unsupervised video anomaly detection. Formally, an observable ordinal variable $y = c_1, c_2$ with $c_1 < c_2$, where $\tau(x; \Theta) = \eta(\phi(x; \Theta_t); \Theta_s)$, A and N are pseudoanomalous and normal instances, respectively, and $G = A \uplus N$, then the objective function is formulated as follows:

$$\underset{\Theta}{\arg\min} \sum_{x \in G} l(\tau(x; \Theta), y_x), \tag{9.28}$$

where $l(\cdot, \cdot)$ is a loss function (MSE/MAE) and $y_x = c_1, \forall x \in A$ and $y_x = c_2, \forall x \in N$. Since y takes two scalar ordinal values, this is a two-class ordinal regression.

The end-to-end anomaly scoring network has A and N as inputs to optimize the anomaly scores such that the data inputs with similar behavior as in $A(N)$ receive large scores as close as possible to $c_1(c_2)$, resulting in anomalous samples being assigned larger anomaly scores than normal samples. ResNet-50 is used to specify the feature network ϕ due to its great ability for feature detection capability, followed by the anomaly scoring network η, which is constructed with a fully connected neural network, where η consists of a hidden layer with 100 neurons and an output layer with a single linear neuron. Similar to [113], A and N are initialized by existing anomaly measures, where the anomaly scoring model is iteratively updated and improved by self-training. The loss function (MAE) is used in the objective function in Eq. 9.28 to reduce the negative effects caused by incorrect pseudo-labels in A and N.

Unlike [117], which deals with an unsupervised environment, the work in [115,144] assumes a weakly supervised environment. In [115], a small number of labeled anomalies are expected to be available during training along with extensive unlabeled data. The anomaly detection problem is formalized as pairwise relation prediction to utilize the known anomalies. A two-stream ordinal regression network is developed to learn the relationship of randomly selected pairs of data instances to distinguish whether the instances contain only unlabeled data instances, a labeled anomaly, or two labeled anomalies.

Notation

a is considered as the small labeled anomaly set, U the big unlabeled dataset, and $X = A \cup A$, $P = \{\{x_i, x_j, y_{x_i x_j}\} | x_i, x_j \in X \text{ and } y_{x_i x_j} \in\}$ is generated. P are random instance pairs with synthetic ordinal class labels, and $y = \{y_{x_{a_i} x_{a_j}}, y_{x_{a_i} x_{u_i}}, y_{x_{u_i} x_{u_j}}\}$ is an ordinal variable. The synthetic label $y_{x_{a_i} x_{u_i}}$ is an ordinal value for any pairs of instances with instances x_{a_i} and x_{u_i} from A and U, respectively. $y_{x_{a_i} x_{a_j}} > y_{x_{a_i} x_{u_i}} > y_{x_{a_i} x_{u_j}}$ is predefined, so the pairwise prediction is equivalent to anomaly score learning. The method can be formulated as:

$$\Theta* = \underset{\Theta}{\text{argmin}} \frac{1}{|P|} \sum_{x_i, x_j, x_{ij} \in P} \left| y_{x_i x_j} - \tau((x_i, x_j); \Theta) \right| \tag{9.29}$$

It is optimized to train for larger anomaly scores for the pairs with two anomalies instead of the pairs with one or no anomaly by minimizing this function. In the inference phase, each instance is paired with instances from A or U to obtain the anomaly scores. The weakly supervised setting in [144] handles video anomaly detection at the image level. Nevertheless, only video-level class labels are available during training. For example, a video is normal or contains anomalous frames somewhere in the sequence, although we do not know the exact frames. In [144], a multiinstance learning (MIL) based ranking model is introduced to use high-level class labels for direct anomaly score learning over video segments. The goal is that the maximum anomaly score of the video segments containing anomalies is larger than that in a normal video sequence. In MIL, each video is considered a bag of instances, where the video segments with anomalies are considered positive bags, while the normal segments are treated as negative bags. The order of anomaly scores is enforced as a relative pairwise ranking using the hinge loss function. The overall objective function is defined as:

$$\underset{\Theta}{\text{argmin}} \sum_{B_p, B_n \in X} \max \left\{ 0, 1 - \max_{x \in B_p} \tau(x; \Theta) + \max_{x \in B_n} \tau(x; \Theta) \right\}$$

$$+ \lambda_1 \sum_{i=1}^{|B_p|} (\tau(x_i; \Theta) - \tau(x_{i+1}; \Theta))^2 + \lambda_2 \sum_{x \in B_p} \tau(x; \Theta) \tag{9.30}$$

where x being a video segment, B a bag of video segments, and B_p and B_n represent positive and negative bags, respectively. The first term guarantees the relative order of anomaly score (e.g., the anomaly score of the most anomalous video segment in the bag of the positive instance is larger than that in the bag of the negative instance). The last two terms are optimization constraints, where the first term enforces the uniformity of the score between successive video segments, while the second term enforces the sparseness of the anomalies (e.g., each video contains only a few anomalous segments).

Advantages

- The anomaly scores can be optimized with a adapted loss function.
- They are generally free of the definitions of anomalies by imposing a weak assumption of ordinal order among anomalous and normal instances.
- This approach can build on proven ranking techniques and theories from areas such as learning to rank [87,157,85].

Disadvantages

- Requires at least some form of labeled anomaly, which may not apply to applications where labeled anomalies are not available. In [117], the method is completely unsupervised and achieves promising performance, though there is still a large gap compared to semisupervised methods.
- Because the models are trained to detect the few labeled anomalies, they may not generalize to unseen anomalies with features other than the labeled anomalies.

The use of weak supervision such as pseudo-labels or noisy class labels provides important knowledge about suspicious anomalies and enables more meaningful training of the low-dimensional representation and better detection performance. The MIL scheme [144] and pairwise relation prediction [115] provide a way to incorporate coarse-grained anomaly labels into model training. End-to-end anomaly score learning is a simple explanation of anomaly by backpropagating gradients of anomaly scores to find the features responsible for large anomaly scores [117]. The methods in [115,117] work well with anomalous contamination or data noise.

Prior-driven models

This method applies a prior distribution to encode and control the learning of the anomaly scores. The prior can be forced on the internal module or the learning output (anomaly scores) of the score learning function τ, as the anomaly scores are learned in an end-to-end approach.

The methods of this category assume that the prior captures the (ab)normality pattern of the dataset. The inclusion of the prior in the anomaly scoring function is illustrated by a study using the Bayesian inverse reinforcement learning (IRL)-based method [112]. An agent takes a set of sequence data as input where its latent reward function can understand the agent's normal behavior, and therefore a test sequence is identified as an anomaly if a sequence is assigned to a low reward. IRL approaches [108] are used to determine the reward function. A sample-based IRL approach can be used to learn the reward function more efficiently. The IRL problem is formulated as a posterior optimization problem:

$$\max_{\Theta} E_{s \sim S} \left[log\, p(s|\Theta) + log\, p(\Theta) \right] \tag{9.31}$$

where $p(s|\Theta) = \frac{1}{Z} exp(\sum_{(0,a) \in s} \tau_{\Theta}(0, a))$, $\tau_{\Theta}(0, a)$ is a latent reward function configured by $\Theta, (0,a)$ is a pair of state-action in sequences s, Z represents the partition function, that is the integral of $exp(\sum_{(0,a) \in s} \tau_{\Theta}(0, a))$ over the sequences consistent with the underlying Markov decision process dynamics, $p(\Theta)$ is a prior distribution of Θ, and S a set of observed sequences. The inverse of the reward of τ is used as anomaly score. In the training stage, a Gaussian prior distribution is assumed over the weight parameters of the reward function, (e.g. $\Theta\ N(0, \Theta^2)$). The partition function Z is computed via a sequence set generated by a sample generation policy π:

$$Z = E_{s \sim \pi} \left[\sum_{(0,a) \in s} \tau_\theta(0, a) \right] \tag{9.32}$$

Policy π is represented as a neural network. τ and π are optimized alternatively (e.g., reward function τ is optimized with fixed policy π; π is optimized with updated reward function τ). τ is initiated in [112] using a multiple-output neural network. The idea of imposing a prior for anomaly scores is explored in [115]. In [72], the author showed that anomaly scores fit well to a Gaussian distribution in various real data sets. The work applies a Gaussian prior to encode the anomaly scores and allow direct optimization of the scores. Anomaly scores of normal instances are assumed to cluster together, while anomalies are assumed to deviate widely from this cluster. The prior is used to define a loss function called deviation loss built on the known contrastive loss.

$$L_{dev} = (1 - y_x)|dev(x)| + y_x \max\{0, m - dev(x)\}; \ dev(x) = \frac{\tau(x;\Theta) - \mu_b}{\sigma_b} \tag{9.33}$$

where μ_b and σ_b are the estimated mean and standard deviation, respectively, of the Gaussian prior $N(\mu, \sigma)$, $y_x = 1$ if x is an anomaly and $y_x = 0$ a normal individual, and m corresponds to a Z-score confidence interval parameter. μ_b and σ_b are estimated with a set of values $\{r_1, r_2, ..., r_l\}$ drawn from $N(\mu, \sigma)$ for each instance batch to learn a robust representation of (ab)normality. The detection model is controlled with the deviation loss to drive the anomaly scores of normal instances close to μ, while ensuring at least m standard deviations between σ and the anomaly scores of anomalies. If x is an anomaly and has a negative $dev(x)$, the loss would be large, resulting in large positive deviations for all anomalies. Consequently, the deviation loss is equivalent to forcing the score of the anomalies to be statistically significantly different from the normal instances in the upper tail. In addition to the end-to-end anomaly score learning, the Gaussian prior-driven loss leads to readily interpretable anomaly scores (e.g., given any anomaly score $\tau(x)$, the Z-score confidence interval $\mu \pm z_p \sigma$ can be used to explain the anomaly of instance x). This is a very practical feature that existing methods are not providing.

Advantages

- Anomaly scores can be optimized for a given prior.
- It provides a framework for including different prior distributions when learning the anomaly scores. Various Bayesian deep learning techniques [155] can be adapted for anomaly detection. It provides a framework for incorporating different prior distributions in learning the anomaly scores. Various Bayesian deep learning techniques can be adapted for anomaly detection.
- The prior can lead to more interpretable anomaly scores compared to other methods.

Disadvantages

- In some cases, it is difficult to design a universally effective prior for different anomaly detection scenarios.
- The model's performance may be less effective if the prior does not fit the underlying distribution.

The prior allows models to learn informed low-dimensional representations of complex data, such as high-dimensional data and sequential data. By requiring a prior over anomaly scores, the deviation network method [115] presents a promising performance in using a limited set of labeled anomaly data to improve its normality and anomaly representations, significantly increasing detection recall. Here, the detection models are driven by a prior distribution for the anomaly scoring function and work well on data with anomaly contamination in the training set.

Softmax likelihood models

This approach aims to learn anomaly scores by maximizing the probability of events in the training data. Since anomalous and normal instances correspond to rare or frequent patterns, it is assumed that normal instances are high probability events, while anomalies tend to be low probability events. Consequently, the negative of the event probability can be defined as an anomaly score. Softmax likelihood models are efficient and effective in achieving this goal using Noise Contrastive Estimation (NCE) [54].

Softmax likelihood models assume that anomalies and normal instances are low and high probability events, respectively. [27] presented the approach of learning anomaly scores by directly modeling the event likelihood. The problem is formulated as follows:

$$\Theta^* = \underset{\Theta}{\operatorname{argmax}} \sum_{x \in X} \log p(x; \Theta) \tag{9.34}$$

where $p(x; \Theta)$ is the probability of instance x (e.g., an event in the event space) with parameters Θ to be learned. To facilitate optimization, $p(x; \Theta)$ is modeled with a softmax function:

$$p(x; \Theta) = \frac{\exp(\tau(x; \Theta))}{\sum_{x \in X} \exp(\tau(x; \Theta))} \tag{9.35}$$

where $\tau(x; \Theta)$ is an anomaly scoring function intended to capture pairwise feature interactions:

$$\tau(x; \Theta) = \sum_{i,j \in \{1,2,\dots,K\}} w_{ij} z_i z_j \tag{9.36}$$

where z_i is a low-dimensional embedding of the i-th feature value of x into the representation space Z; w_{ij} the trainable weight parameter added to the interaction. Learning the likelihood function p is equivalent to optimizing the anomaly weighting function τ, since $\sum_{x \in X} \exp(\tau(x; \Theta))$ is a normalization term. Since computing this normalization term is costly, NCE is used in [27] to train the following approximated likelihood:

$$\log p(d = 1|x; \Theta) + \log \sum_{j=1}^{k} p(d = 0|x'_j; \Theta), \tag{9.37}$$

where

$$p(d = 1|x; \Theta) = \frac{exp(\tau(x; \Theta)}{exp(\tau(x; \Theta)) + kQ(x')}$$

and

$$p(d = 0|x'; \Theta) = \frac{kQ(x')}{exp(\tau(x; \Theta)) + kQ(x')}$$

for each instance x, k noise samples are generated $x'_{1,...,k} \sim Q$ from a synthetic known noise distribution Q. In another paper, a context-dependent method is applied to generate k negative samples over a univariate extrapolation of the observed instance x [27].

The method is primarily designed for anomaly detection in categorical data [27]. In other works, a comparable objective function is adapted to detect anomalous events in heterogeneous attributed bipartite graphs [44]. In [44], the problem is to detect anomalous paths that span over both partitions of the bipartite graph. For this, x in Eq. 9.36, is a graph path holding a set of heterogeneous graph nodes, with z_i and z_j be the representations of the pairs of the nodes in the path. Multilayer perceptron networks and autoencoders are applied to the node features and graph topology to map attributed nodes into the representation space Z.

Advantages
- Different types of interactions can be included in the learning process of the anomaly score.
- The anomaly scores are optimized for the specific anomalous interactions that should be captured.

Disadvantages
- Computing the interactions can be costly if the set of features in each data instance is large (e.g., $O(D^n)$ time complexity per instance of n-th order interactions of D features).
- Learning the anomaly score depends on the quality of the generation of negative samples.

These methods provide a good way to learn low-dimensional representations with heterogeneous data sources. The learned representations can capture more (ab)normality information from different data sources.

End-to-end one-class classification

This method aims to train a one-class classifier that learns to distinguish between normal and abnormal consistently. This approach does not rely on existing one-class classifiers such as one-class SVM or SVDD. This approach comes from the combination of GANs and the concept of one-class classification (e.g., adversarial learned one-class classification). The concept is to train a one-class discriminator of the normal instances to distinguish these instances from the adversarially generated pseudo-anomalies. This method differs from the GAN-based approach in that the GAN-based methods aim to learn a generative distribution to maximally approximate the data distribution to achieve a generative model that captures well the behavior of the normal training instances. Moreover, the GAN-based methods determine the anomaly scores based on residuals between the real instances and the corresponding generated instances, while the methods directly use the discriminator to classify anomalies (e.g., discriminator D acts as τ).

This type of method assumes that data instances that are approximated as anomalies can be effectively synthesized, as well as that a discriminative one-class model can summarize all normal instances. The concept of adversarially learned one-class classification (ALOCC) was first explored in [129]. The idea is to train two deep neural networks, where one network is trained as a one-class model to classify normal instances of anomalies, and the other network improves the normal instances and generates biased outliers. The two networks are instantiated and optimized by the GAN approach. The one-class model is based on the discriminator network, and the generator network is based on a denoising-AE [152]. The goal of the AE-empowered GAN is defined as:

$$\min_{AE} \max_{D} V(D, G) = E_{x \sim px} \left[\log D(x) \right] + E_{\hat{x} \sim p_{\hat{x}}} \left[\log(1 - D(AE(\hat{x}))) \right] \qquad (9.38)$$

where $p_{\hat{x}}$ stands for a data distribution of X manipulated by a Gaussian noise, (e.g. $\hat{x} = x + n$ with $n \sim N(0, \sigma^2 I)$. The objective is optimized along with the following data construction error in AE.

$$l_{ae} = \left| \left| x - AE(\hat{x}) \right| \right|^2 \qquad (9.39)$$

The intuition of Eq. 9.39 is that AE can reconstruct and improve normal instances, yet it can be confused by input outliers to further produces biased outliers. The discriminator D learns through minimax optimization to distinguish normal instances from outliers better than using the original instances. Therefore, $D(AE(has x))$ can be used directly to detect anomalies. The outliers in the work of [129], are randomly drawn from classes other than the normal instance classes. Nevertheless, obtaining reference outliers outside the given training data as in [129] may not be available in many domains.

In [179], one-class adversarial networks (OCAN) are introduced to exploit the concept of bad GANs [32] to generate edge instances based on the distribution of normal training data. Instead of traditional generators in GANs, the generator network in bad GANs is trained to generate instances that are complementary and do not match the training data. The formulation of the complement generator is:

$$\min_{G} -H(p_z) + E_{\hat{z} \sim p_z} \log p_x(\hat{z}) I[p_x \hat{z} > \epsilon] + \left| \left| E_{\hat{z} \sim p_z} h(\hat{z}) - E_{\hat{z} \sim p_x} h(z) \right| \right|_2 \qquad (9.40)$$

where $H(\cdot)$ is entropy; $I[\cdot]$ is an indicator function; ϵ a threshold hyperparameter; and h a feature map from an intermediate layer of the discriminator. The first two terms are used to generate low-density samples in the original feature space. However, it is computationally infeasible to obtain the probability distribution of the training data. Instead, the density estimate $p_x(\hat{z})$ is approximated via the discriminator of a regular GAN. The last term is the feature matching loss, which helps to generate data instances within the original space. An additional, conditional entropy term extends the discriminator target in OCAN to enable a high confidence detection:

$$\max_{D} E_{x \sim p_x}[log D(z)] + E_{\hat{z} \sim p_z}[log(1 - D(\hat{z}))] + E_{x \sim p_x}[D(x)log D(x)] \qquad (9.41)$$

In [109], Fence GAN generates data instances that lie closely along the boundary of the training data distribution. This is done by adding two loss functions to the generator that force the generated instances to be uniformly distributed along the spherical boundary of the training data. Formally, the goal of the generator is defined as follows:

$$\min_{G} E_{z \sim p_z}[log [|\alpha - D(G(z))|]] + \beta \frac{1}{E_{z \sim p_z} ||G(z) - \mu||_2} \qquad (9.42)$$

$\alpha \in (0, 1)$ is a hyperparameter used as a discrimination reference value for the generator to create the edge instances, and μ is the midpoint of the generated data instances. The first term is called enclosure loss, which enforces that the generated instances have the same discrimination value, resulting in a tight enclosure of the training data. The second term is called dispersion loss, which enforces that the generated instances cover the entire perimeter uniformly. Other methods have been introduced to generate the reference instances effectively. For example, uniformly distributed instances are generated to enforce that the normal instances are uniformly distributed over the latent space [120]. An ensemble of generators is used in [89], where each generator synthesizes edge instances for a given cluster of normal instances.

Advantages
- Its anomaly classification model is adversarial optimized in an end-to-end approach.
- It can be developed and supported by the rich techniques and theories of adversarial learning and one-class classification.

Disadvantages
- It is difficult to guarantee that the generated reference instances resemble the unknown anomalies well.
- The instability of GANs may lead to generated instances with different quality and consequently unstable classification performance of the anomalies. This problem was investigated in [172], where it was shown that the performance of this type of anomaly detector could vary in different training steps.
- The application is limited to semisupervised anomaly detection scenarios.

   The adversarially learned one-class classifiers learn to generate realistic edge/boundary instances, which enables the learning of meaningful low-dimensional normality representations.

9.1.6 End-to-end machine learning pipeline for medicine

The end-to-end machine learning pipeline includes the three phases: (1) data preprocessing, (2) model training, and (3) model interpretation. Most machine learning research focuses on the model training phase using supervised learning frameworks. Phase (1) and phase (3) are not widely researched, although they are critical in medicine.

Missing data attribution

Missing data is a pervasive problem. Data can be missing for many reasons, such as in the medical field when a patient's respiratory rate was not measured (it may have been deemed unnecessary), was accidentally not recorded [167,5], or certain information is difficult or even dangerous to obtain (e.g., information from a biopsy). The critical part of preprocessing medical data is dealing with missing values, so accurate estimation of missing data is important for diagnosis, prognosis, and treatment. Modern machine learning models work better when the input data is largely complete. Without proper handling of missing data, training of machine learning models cannot be successful.

Types of missing data

Missing data can be classified into the types of:

- MCAR: Data is missing completely at random, when the missing occurs completely at random (there is no dependence on any of the variables)

- MAR: Data is missing at random, when the missing depends only on the observed variables
- MNAR: Data are missing nonrandomly when the missing depends on both the observed variables and the unobserved variables. Therefore, the missing cannot be fully explained by the observed variables (when the missing is neither MCAR nor MAR).

Data attribution or imputation can be used to estimate missing values based on existing data, like a patient's systolic blood pressure and heart rate [169]. Research has been done to the development of imputation algorithms for medical data [122,142,94,12]. Imputation algorithms are also used in complex applications, such as data compression, image error concealment, and counterfactual estimation [127,71,168].

Modern imputation methods can be categorized as discriminative or generative, where discriminative methods include MissForest [141], MICE [159,21], Matrix Completion [23,133,170], Generative algorithms based on Expectation Maximization [47], algorithms based on Deep Learning like Denoising Autoencoders (DAE) and Generative Adversarial Nets [7,50,151].

Current generative imputation methods have several drawbacks like the approach of [47] that makes assumptions about the underlying distribution and does not generalize well when the dataset contains mixed categorical and continuous data. In contrast, DAE-based approaches [151] have shown to work well in practice but require complete data sets for the training. In many cases, missing values are part of the problem's inherent structure, making it impossible to obtain a complete data set. Another approach allows the DAE [50] to use an incomplete data set. However, it uses only the observed features to learn the data's representations. Thus, in [7] authors used Deep Convolutional GANs for image reconstruction but required complete data to train the discriminator.

Estimating missing data in temporal data streams

The problem is particularly challenging in medical environments where time-series exist containing many streams of measurements sampled at different and irregular times [169]. It is important because accurate estimation of missing measurements is often critical for accurate diagnosis, prognosis [4], and treatment, as well as for accurate modeling and statistical analyses [166].

Most standard methods for estimating missing data take three approaches, commonly referred to as interpolation, imputation, and matrix completion. Interpolation methods, such as shown in [106], use the correlation between measurements at different times within each stream but ignore the correlation between multiple streams. Imputation methods such as shown in [127,47,159,141] use correlation between measurements at the same time across streams but ignore correlation within streams. Medical measurements are often correlated within streams and across streams (e.g., blood pressure at one time is correlated with blood pressure at other times and with heart rate). Potentially important information is lost with these approaches. Matrix completion methods as shown in [23,133,170] exploit correlations within and between data streams. However, they assume that the data are static and therefore ignore the temporal component of the data or that the data are perfectly synchronized (an assumption that is routinely violated for medical time series data).

Other methods use modeling assumptions about the nature of the data-generating processor of the missing data patterns. Those methods are explicitly designed to take advantage of both correlation within data streams and the correlation between data streams and account for the data's temporal and nonsynchronous behavior and make no modeling assumptions about the data-generating process the pattern of missing data.

An aspect of medical data is that there is often tremendous uncertainty in the measurement. Simple imputation (SI) methods can provide the most probable estimate for each point of missing data but do not capture the imputed data's uncertainty. Multiple imputation (MI) methods estimate this uncertainty by sampling imputed values multiple times to create multiple complete imputed data sets, analyzing each imputed data set separately, and combining the results via Rubin's rule [119,20,127]. Detecting uncertainty in the data set is especially important in the medical setting, where diagnostic, prognostic, and treatment decisions are based on imputed values [142,94]. As shown in [102], a desirable aspect of imputation methods is congenial, which means it should produce imputed values that preserve the original relationships between features and labels.

A large body of literature uses recurrent neural networks (RNNs) for prediction based on time series with missing data. For example, [15] replaces all missing values with an average and follows with the use of a feedback loop from the hidden states to update the imputed values and use the reconstructed data streams as inputs for an RNN for prediction. Authors in [149] use the Expectation-Maximization (EM) algorithm to impute missing values to get reconstructed data streams as input for an RNN for prediction. In [118] is used a linear model to estimate missing values from the last observation over the hidden state within each data stream, followed by an RNN for prediction tasks. The first two papers use only the synchronous relationships between data streams for imputation and not the temporal relationships within streams. The third paper interpolates over the temporal relationships within each stream and not the relationships between streams. Further literature extended these methods to deal with missing data and irregularly sampled data [82,67,25] where they use sampling times to obtain information over missing data and time interval to deal with irregular sampling, using observation, sampling information, and time intervals as inputs of an RNN. These methods differ in the imputation for missing values. The work in [82,67] replaces the missing values with 0, mean, or the last observation, which is all independent of the intra-stream or interstream relationships while [25] imputes the missing values using only the last observation, the mean of each stream, and the time interval.

Time-series generative adversarial networks

The temporal setup presents a challenge for generative modeling. The model is not simply tasked with capturing each time point's distributions but also capturing the possible complex characteristics of these variables over time. When modeling multivariate sequential data $x_1 : T = (x_1, \ldots, x_T)$, the goal is to accurately capture the conditional distribution $(x_t | x_1 : t - 1)$ of temporal transitions. Much work has focused on improving the temporal dynamics of auto-regressive models for sequence forecasting. These methods address the problem of compound errors during multilevel sampling by introducing modifications for the training time to accurately display the testing-time conditions [11,74,13]. Auto-regressive models factor the distribution of sequences into a product of conditionals $\Pi t_p(x_t | x_1 : t - 1)$. While this approach is useful for prediction, it is deterministic and not truly generative so that new sequences can be randomly created without external conditioning.

A separate research direction has focused on applying the generative adversarial network (GAN) directly to sequential data by instantiating recurrent networks for the role of the generator and discriminator [42,77,105]. Although simple, the adversarial objective attempts to model $p(x1 : T)$ directly without using an auto-regressive prior. Simply summing the standard GAN loss over sequences might not be sufficient to ensure that the network efficiently captures the stepwise dependencies in the training data.

Auto-regressive recurrent networks trained using the maximum likelihood principle are prone to large prediction errors while performing multistage sampling due to discrepancy between closed-loop training (e.g., conditioned on ground truths) and open-loop inference (e.g., conditioned on prior estimation). Based on curriculum learning [16], scheduled sampling was proposed, where models are trained to produce an output based on a mixture of prior guesses and ground truth data [13]. Inspired by adversarial domain adaptation [46], the extension of Professor Forcing involves training an auxiliary discriminator to distinguish between free-running and teacher-forced hidden states to encourage the network's training and sample dynamics to converge [74]. Actor-critique methods [70] have been proposed that introduce a critic conditioned on target outputs, which are trained to estimate value functions for the next token that guide the free-running predictions of the actor [11].

These methods account for stepwise transition dynamics, but they are inherently deterministic and do not allow direct sampling from a learned distribution. Several studies have adopted the GAN framework directly in the temporal setting. The first C-RNN-GAN [105] applied the GAN architecture directly to sequential data via an LSTM as generator and discriminator. Here, the data is generated recurrently using a noise vector and the data from the previous time step. Recurrent Conditional GAN (RCGAN) [42] introduced minor architectural differences, such as ignoring dependence on the previous output while conditioning on additional input [104]. Several applied studies have used these frameworks to generate synthetic sequences in domains like text [178], finance [138] biosignals [55], sensor [8], smart grid data [175], and renewable scenarios [28]. Recent work [77] has proposed conditioning on timestamp information to handle irregular sampling. However, these approaches rely only on binary adversarial feedback for learning, which alone may not be sufficient to guarantee that the network efficiently captures temporal dynamics in the training data. Representation learning in a time series environment is primarily concerned with the benefits of learning compact encoding for the benefit of downstream tasks such as forecasting [93], prediction [31], and classification [140]. Other research works have explored the utility of learning latent representations for pretraining [43], interpretability [60], and disentanglement [79]. Several studies in the static setting have explored the benefits of combining autoencoders with adversarial training for learning similarity measures [75], enabling efficient inference [39], and improving generative ability [96].

9.1.7 Deep complex anomaly detection

Most deep anomaly detection methods focus on point anomalies and show better performance compared to traditional methods. However, deep models for conditional or group anomalies have been explored to this extend. Deep learning has excellent capabilities in capturing complex temporal or spatial dependencies and learning representations of sets containing unordered data points. The important aspect is to investigate if deep learning can achieve similar success in detecting complex anomalies. Like traditional approaches, Deep Anomaly Detection focuses largely on single data sources. Anomaly detection over multimodal data sources is a largely unexplored research area. For traditional approaches, it is difficult to bridge the gap created by multimodal data. Deep learning has shown success in learning feature representations from different types of raw data for anomaly detection [129,113,90,62,36]. Representations from different data sources can also be concatenated to learn unified representations [51]. That is why deep approaches provide an important and promising outlook for multimodal anomaly detection capabilities.

PATTERN

SEQ (Washing w, Recycle r,

      !SEQ(Sharpening s, Disinfection d, Checking c, s.id=d.id=c.id=o.id),

      Operating o, r.id=w.id=o.id and o.ins-type="surgery")

    WITHIN   1 hour

FIGURE 9.2

Query pattern example for RFID based surgical tool control.

9.2 Complex event processing

Complex Event Processing (CEP) is becoming increasingly relevant in modern applications. CEP requires support for sophisticated pattern matching on real-time event streams. CEP can be found in healthcare scenarios such as a hygiene control system equipped with sensors that monitor and regulates hygiene throughout the hospital facility by performing pattern queries on continuous sensor data. Services range from reporting contaminated medical equipment in hospitals [17] to tracking hygiene violations by healthcare workers [153]. In a real-world scenario running such a system, every healthcare worker wears an RFID badge. Surgical and nonsurgical devices are tagged. Sensors are located in every patient room, emergency room, intensive care unit, operating room, and near sanitary facilities. All of the sensors continuously capture the environment and send the collected events to a central system. Not only can the total number of events per second be high, but the pattern retrieval complexity also. Running pattern queries over such systems with high input rates in real-time is challenging and needs an efficient underlying IT ecosystem.

In the scenario that medical operations tools are RFID tagged, a central system monitors the equipment's history (e.g., washing, records of surgical use, sharpening, or disinfecting). If a health care worker places a box of surgical tools in an operation room table equipped with RFID readers, a warning will be generated like "tool with ID ="5" needs to be discarded".

Query Q1 (Fig. 9.2) expresses this critical condition of a surgical tool being returned to use after being recycled and washed without first being sharpened, disinfected, and then inspected for quality assurance.

An important feature of a query language is the flexible nesting of query expressions. Nested CEP queries provide users with an intuitive way to express different requirements. Without this capability, users are severely limited in forming complex patterns conveniently and concisely [137]. Some nested queries cannot be expressed as flat queries or result in an exponential number of flat queries. Current CEP systems like SASE [160], ZStream [101], and Cayuga [34] do not support nested CEP queries with negation.

Traditionally, an iterative execution strategy is used for processing nested queries [83]. First, all matching component events of the outer query are identified. Then, for each outer match, such as in Fig. 9.2 – SEQ(Recycle, Washing, Operating), the results for the nested inner subsequences would be iteratively computed. In this case, the subsequence of AND(Sharpening, Disinfection, Checking). Finally, any outer candidate sequence result would be constrained by the nonexistence of the inner subsequence match between the event pairs of Washing and Operating. In [84], the classical process of first constructing the outer sequences and then iteratively constructing the inner sequences showed prohibitively inefficient and missed crucial opportunities for optimization.

9.2.1 Three-level data fusion model

The paper [33] addresses the issue of data fusion in the Smart Healthcare domain in the context of IoT. Here the network consisting of edge devices, network, and communications units, a central Cloud platform. The paper proposed a distributed hierarchical data fusion architecture consisting of three levels to combine different sources to combine timely and accurate results.

The three-level data fusion model can be classified into the following parts:

1. The low level includes data fusion functions that are typically applied to raw data from sources that implement the initial processing or low abstraction level and perform local operations over temporal domain aimed at building a knowledge base or cooperate with other nodes in complementary activities.
2. The middle level includes higher-level functions performed on preprocessed information, as results of previous processing stages, local computations, or at a higher level of abstraction. Tasks can be obtaining parameter estimates in a spatial domain, perform feature extraction, pattern matching, or ML tasks.
3. The high-Level implements the final processing level for complex reasoning, decision making on data coming from lower layers, or implements temporal-spatial fusion.

One potentially promising data fusion approach applied in the smart healthcare context is Complex Event Processing (CEP) [91]. CEP goes beyond simple data retrieval/transformation and aims to recognize complex event patterns composed of simpler atomic events within a data stream. Continuously arriving tuples can be considered as notifications of events in the real world (e.g., rise in body temperature or a sudden drop in blood pressure). CEP focuses on detecting the occurrence of lower-level event patterns that build higher-level events. In practice, a CEP query fetches results if a corresponding lower-level event pattern is detected. For example, CEP systems' common task is detecting situational patterns in which one atomic event occurs strictly after another. To accomplish this, CEP systems rely on event timestamps and extend existing query languages with sequential operators, allowing them to specify the chronological order of events.

CEP's capabilities to facilitate data fusion over incoming data streams have been applied in scenarios of continuously distributed data flow networks for dynamic monitoring as of arrival of events. Several network intrusion detection systems (IDSs) have been realized with CEP to collect and correlate all network events in a central system to detect critical situations. It exists a motivation to enable runtime monitoring and data fusion in the context of distributed IoT networks [158,53,45,18]. There are similar challenges in the smart healthcare domain related to timely detection and response to collected data. Nevertheless, two main issues have not been broadly addressed in the literature:

- Existing approaches often implement CEP only at the highest level of cloud computing, dismissing the possibility of introducing intermediary data fusion at the fog and edge levels.
- Existing approaches focus on data collection and do not consider lower-level devices' coordination by changing data fusion policies in a top-down way.

Table 9.1 Three-tier data fusion pattern.

Category	Edge	Fog	Cloud
Processing Stage	Low	Intermediate	High
Levels of abstraction	Low	Medium	High
Data granularity	Raw data processing	Feature level	Decision level
Operation domains	Temporal	Spatial	Temporal & Spatial
Semantics	Knowledge-base construction	Pattern matching	Inference
Source relationships	Complementary	Redundant	Cooperative
User requirements	Local node	Region	Global network

Fusion architecture in healthcare

IoT infrastructure capabilities within healthcare organizations provide a foundation for a smart health-care data fusion architecture. A three-tier data fusion model matches the classification of IoT processing elements, where the low tier is considered as edge computing, the medium tier as fog computing, and the high tier as cloud computing. It is natural to consider how the edge and fog layer can be leveraged to enable data fusion tasks. A hierarchical, multilevel data fusion architecture in IoT healthcare is relevant, given different types of devices, event locations within the network topology, and data fusion patterns. Edge computing follows the principle to offload processing as close as possible to the source, where data should first be processed onboard (locally on edge objects) or moved to fog units and finally to central cloud centers, according to the three-tier data fusion pattern in Table 9.1.

The architecture includes three conceptual tiers, which can be aligned with geographic areas from where IoT health data is collected:

Low-level data fusion (LDF)   takes place on smart objects that collect incoming edge device data via gateways or on smart devices themselves. The data amount is small, so that data fusion can still be performed onboard. LDF aims to detect unfavorable health conditions of individual patients. The fusion of stream data with patients' health data enables detecting potentially critical health conditions, sending an alert or short report to a higher level, and informing appropriate experts. For example, when generally normal sensor measurements are collected, the LDF engine can match them with patient-specific records/knowledge and conclude that the observed readings for that particular patient may indicate a deterioration in health. In this way, data fusion, with integrating sensor readings with static background information, happens close at the data source so that only filtered/aggregated values are transmitted to a higher-level processing node.

Middle-level data fusion (MDF)   describes the act of performing deeper analysis on retrieved data from a larger network of devices. MDF is usually performed on communication and processing units that follow Fog computing principles and performs data fusion over a bigger field (e.g., clinic or hospital) to detect or even prevent possible disease outbreaks by mapping critical values originating from bed sensing devices to physical locations. Furthermore, by mapping rooms and floors within the hospital in a case of increased need for medical care (e.g., epidemic disease), MDF enables a better organization and staff management (e.g., nurse or expert assigned to particular floors or rooms where a need is observed). Background knowledge needs to be associated with each sensor device to rooms or floors to enable such a scenario.

High-Level Data Fusion (HDF)   builds the highest data fusion level, providing a global view of the entire managed system of edge devices and fog nodes. HDF involves processing large amounts of

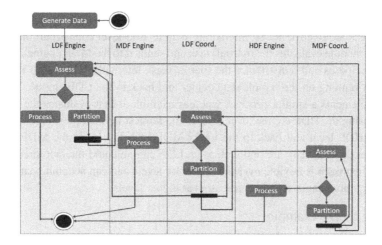

FIGURE 9.3

Hierarchical IoT Data Fusion. Illustration of the general data fusion workflow, starting with data generated with low-level processing and transformed when forwarded to higher levels [33].

data and is often expected to be implemented in a remote data center or cloud. The collection on this level can consider all hospitals within a city and provides a data fusion across the entire managed area. The HDF engine can provide a (near) real-time global view of individual hospitals and other healthcare facilities' current utilization to manage emergency vehicles or other shared services. Hospitals' streaming information and current GPS positions of emergency vehicles can be fused with static information about traffic routes and hospital locations nearby. An emergency vehicle can be directed to a hospital providing the best health offering (distance, available personal). Given the recent outbreak of Covid 19, incoming information from multiple hospitals can be correlated to timely detection and prevention of epidemic disease outbreaks on a regional scale. Furthermore, location-based dispatching over HDF provides a better assignment of medical expert knowledge to individual patients.

IoT systems in the context of smart healthcare tend to go beyond the notion of "bottom-up" monitoring where raw data is collected from edge devices and transmitted over the network but go further as to implement "top-down" feedback communication between managed and control devices (e.g., for triggering commands). For such a bidirectional communication, the architecture introduces coordination to receive data from lower-layer devices, collects, and forwards them to the higher layer's data fusion processors when needed.

All three levels are equipped with dedicated data fusion engine (DF) instances (i.e., low-level DF-LDF, middle-level DF-MDF, and High-Level DF HDF engines, respectively). The upper two levels contain coordination components (LDF and MDF coordinators) responsible for bi-directional communication between the lower and upper-level nodes and managing the offloading requests coming in from the lower level nodes.

Fig. 9.3 illustrates the interactions between these components. First, the data generated by a smart object is collected and sent to the LDF engine, which first evaluates whether the associated data fusion task can be processed onboard. If not, it splits the task into $n \geq 1$ subtasks that can then be redistributed internally and forwarded to edge nodes, interacting with its mid-level counterpart, the LDF Coordinator. Similarly, this module evaluates the (partial) task and sends it to the MDF engine if it is processable. Otherwise, it decomposes and redistributes the (partial) task internally or forwards it to the high-level MDF Coordinator running on the remote data center and back to the LDF engine. The MDF coordinator, in turn, implements a similar process, whereas example it first evaluates the incoming request and processes it using the HDF engine, or it divides the request into simpler requests, which are then forwarded to the HDF level and back to the lower MDF/LDF levels via the MDF coordinator. The two upper levels in the hierarchy are optional, as an LDF engine could interact directly with an MDF coordinator. This approach is flexible over the hierarchy levels and can accommodate more than three levels by deploying more engines and coordinators at higher levels.

Data fusion healthcare example

Some key objectives for automated data fusion in smart healthcare are:

- Perform situational awareness and minimize uncertainty by merging multiple data sources.
- Support timely automated decision making.
- Reduce security risks associated with remotely transmitting data over a public network.

One promising solution to address these requirements is to leverage smart objects' processing capabilities in IoT networks. Data fusion in IoT networks is a complex problem that needs to be considered from multiple perspectives. Using the taxonomy in Table 9.1, the following three types of data fusion occurring in a smart health domain can be addressed with CEP.

Temporal data fusion

Temporal data fusion refers to the aggregation of data from the same data source but at different times. It examines the temporal order of different values and attempts to find a temporal correlation between them, usually within a given time frame. For example, temporal fusion must be applied to readings from body temperature sensors to detect rapid increases within a short time that are highly likely to indicate fever or similar health deteriorations. With CEP, temporal data fusion can be implemented sequentially (i.e., detecting precise timing of events) and iteratively (i.e., detecting changes over previous values) operators. Sequential operators can detect critical situations when an increase in body temperature strictly follows a decrease in blood pressure, and iterative operators can detect fever symptoms such as sudden increases and decreases in body temperature.

Spatial data fusion

Spatial data fusion refers to the aggregation of multiple physically and logically distributed sources into a single representation. In Smart Healthcare, it may be necessary to perform spatial data fusion for data coming from sensors placed in different rooms to detect an epidemic pattern. CEP supports spatial data fusion by applying constraints to individual patterns to check whether events come from the same location. In this way, it is possible to group incoming sensor observations for the hospital rooms or floors they originate from or extract a subset of values that originate from a specific region of interest (matching).

Semantic data fusion

Semantic data fusion refers to heterogeneous data sources (i.e., physical and virtual sensors) in IoT healthcare that need to be represented and aggregated in a unified way to enable further analysis and pattern recognition. An example of semantic data fusion is detecting and diagnosing a disease based on multiple body indicator measurements, such as temperature, blood pressure, or heart rate. CEP alone cannot solve the heterogeneity of multiple data sources. This task is delegated to an actual CEP implementation that enables shared data representation and formatting as part of its programming model. To handle blood pressure, body temperature, or heart rate within a single CEP pattern, it is necessary to define them as classes (possibly as subclasses of the same superclass) with corresponding property sets. Once the corresponding sensor readings arrive in the system (possibly as a semistructured form such as JSON or XML), they are classified into the appropriate CEP classes and streamed to the actual CEP engine for processing.

9.3 Key features

Anomaly Detection, Classification and Complex Event Processing are a research area in multidisciplinary fields that constantly evolve due to the advances in data mining, machine learning, computer vision, big data, etc. The era of advanced data science enabled new solutions for long-existing challenges. As technology advances, novel solutions are needed in many areas to address complex problems. The inference of knowledge over a single data instance or complex situation requires a foundation to find the right technology and methods to use.

- ☑ Current challenges of Anomaly Detection and Methods addressing these challenges are presented.
- ☑ The detailed methodology and algorithms are discussed for each category of methods, including objective functions, key intuitions, assumptions, advantages, and disadvantages.
- ☑ In the context of AI/ML models in the context of healthcare, the pervasive problem with missing data was discussed as well as modern methods of addressing these problems.
- ☑ Complex Event processing is exemplified in the context of healthcare.
- ☑ A data fusion architecture for Complex Event Processing was described to enable spatial, temporal and semantic reasoning in the context of IoT-Healthcare.

References

[1] D. Abati, A. Porrello, S. Calderara, R. Cucchiara, Latent space autoregression for novelty detection, in: Proceedings of the IEEE Conference on Computer Vision and Pattern Recognition, 2019, pp. 481–490.

[2] C.C. Aggarwal, Outlier analysis, in: Data Mining, Springer, 2015, pp. 237–263.

[3] S. Akcay, A. Atapour-Abarghouei, T.P. Breckon, GANomaly: semi-supervised anomaly detection via adversarial training, in: Asian Conference on Computer Vision, Springer, 2018, pp. 622–637.

[4] A.M. Alaa, M. Van Der Schaar, A hidden absorbing semi-Markov model for informatively censored temporal data: learning and inference, Journal of Machine Learning Research 19 (1) (2018) 108–169.

[5] A.M. Alaa, J. Yoon, S. Hu, M. Van der Schaar, Personalized risk scoring for critical care prognosis using mixtures of Gaussian processes, IEEE Transactions on Biomedical Engineering 65 (1) (2017) 207–218.

[6] E. Aljalbout, V. Golkov, Y. Siddiqui, M. Strobel, D. Cremers, Clustering with deep learning: taxonomy and new methods, arXiv preprint, arXiv:1801.07648, 2018.

[7] A. Allen, W. Li, Generative adversarial denoising autoencoder for face completion, https://www.cc.gatech.edu/~hays/7476/projects/Avery_Wenchen/, 2016.

[8] M. Alzantot, S. Chakraborty, M. Srivastava, Sensegen: a deep learning architecture for synthetic sensor data generation, in: 2017 IEEE International Conference on Pervasive Computing and Communications Workshops (PerCom Workshops), IEEE, 2017, pp. 188–193.

[9] J. Andrews, T. Tanay, E.J. Morton, L.D. Griffin, Transfer representation-learning for anomaly detection, in: JMLR, 2016.

[10] F. Angiulli, C. Pizzuti, Fast outlier detection in high dimensional spaces, in: European Conference on Principles of Data Mining and Knowledge Discovery, Springer, 2002, pp. 15–27.

[11] D. Bahdanau, P. Brakel, K. Xu, A. Goyal, R. Lowe, J. Pineau, A. Courville, Y. Bengio, An actor-critic algorithm for sequence prediction, arXiv preprint, arXiv:1607.07086, 2016.

[12] J. Barnard, X.-L. Meng, Applications of multiple imputation in medical studies: from AIDS to NHANES, Statistical Methods in Medical Research 8 (1) (1999) 17–36.

[13] S. Bengio, O. Vinyals, N. Jaitly, N. Shazeer, Scheduled sampling for sequence prediction with recurrent neural networks, Advances in Neural Information Processing Systems 28 (2015) 1171–1179.

[14] Y. Bengio, A. Courville, P. Vincent, Representation learning: a review and new perspectives, IEEE Transactions on Pattern Analysis and Machine Intelligence 35 (8) (2013) 1798–1828.

[15] Y. Bengio, F. Gingras, Recurrent neural networks for missing or asynchronous data, in: Advances in Neural Information Processing Systems, 1996, pp. 395–401.

[16] Y. Bengio, J. Louradour, R. Collobert, J. Weston, Curriculum learning, in: Proceedings of the 26th Annual International Conference on Machine Learning, 2009, pp. 41–48.

[17] J.M. Boyce, D. Pittet, Guideline for hand hygiene in health-care settings: recommendations of the healthcare infection control practices advisory committee and the HICPAC/SHEA/APIC/IDSA hand hygiene task force, American Journal of Infection Control 30 (8) (2002) S1–S46.

[18] D. Brunelli, G. Gallo, L. Benini, Sensormind: virtual sensing and complex event detection for internet of things, in: International Conference on Applications in Electronics Pervading Industry, Environment and Society, Springer, 2016, pp. 75–83.

[19] Y. Burda, H. Edwards, A. Storkey, O. Klimov, Exploration by random network distillation, arXiv preprint, arXiv:1810.12894, 2018.

[20] S. Burgess, I.R. White, M. Resche-Rigon, A.M. Wood, Combining multiple imputation and meta-analysis with individual participant data, Statistics in Medicine 32 (26) (2013) 4499–4514.

[21] S.v. Buuren, K. Groothuis-Oudshoorn, mice: multivariate imputation by chained equations in R, Journal of Statistical Software (2010) 1–68.

[22] E.J. Candès, X. Li, Y. Ma, J. Wright, Robust principal component analysis?, Journal of the ACM (JACM) 58 (3) (2011) 1–37.

[23] E.J. Candès, B. Recht, Exact matrix completion via convex optimization, Foundations of Computational Mathematics 9 (6) (2009) 717.

[24] M. Caron, P. Bojanowski, A. Joulin, M. Douze, Deep clustering for unsupervised learning of visual features, in: Proceedings of the European Conference on Computer Vision (ECCV), 2018, pp. 132–149.

[25] Z. Che, S. Purushotham, K. Cho, D. Sontag, Y. Liu, Recurrent neural networks for multivariate time series with missing values, Scientific Reports 8 (1) (2018) 1–12.

[26] J. Chen, S. Sathe, C. Aggarwal, D. Turaga, Outlier detection with autoencoder ensembles, in: Proceedings of the 2017 SIAM International Conference on Data Mining, SIAM, 2017, pp. 90–98.

[27] T. Chen, L.-A. Tang, Y. Sun, Z. Chen, K. Zhang, Entity embedding-based anomaly detection for heterogeneous categorical events, arXiv preprint, arXiv:1608.07502, 2016.

[28] Y. Chen, Y. Wang, D. Kirschen, B. Zhang, Model-free renewable scenario generation using generative adversarial networks, IEEE Transactions on Power Systems 33 (3) (2018) 3265–3275.

[29] C. Cortes, V. Vapnik, Support-vector networks, Machine Learning 20 (3) (1995) 273–297.

[30] A. Creswell, T. White, V. Dumoulin, K. Arulkumaran, B. Sengupta, A.A. Bharath, Generative adversarial networks: an overview, IEEE Signal Processing Magazine 35 (1) (2018) 53–65.

[31] A.M. Dai, Q.V. Le, Semi-supervised sequence learning, Advances in Neural Information Processing Systems 28 (2015) 3079–3087.

[32] Z. Dai, Z. Yang, F. Yang, W.W. Cohen, R.R. Salakhutdinov, Good semi-supervised learning that requires a bad GAN, in: Advances in Neural Information Processing Systems, 2017, pp. 6510–6520.

[33] R. Dautov, S. Distefano, R. Buyya, Hierarchical data fusion for smart healthcare, Journal of Big Data 6 (1) (2019) 1–23.

[34] A.J. Demers, J. Gehrke, B. Panda, M. Riedewald, V. Sharma, W.M. White, et al., Cayuga: a general purpose event monitoring system, in: Cidr, vol. 7, 2007, pp. 412–422.

[35] N. Dilokthanakul, P.A. Mediano, M. Garnelo, M.C. Lee, H. Salimbeni, K. Arulkumaran, M. Shanahan, Deep unsupervised clustering with Gaussian mixture variational autoencoders, arXiv preprint, arXiv:1611.02648, 2016.

[36] K. Ding, J. Li, R. Bhanushali, H. Liu, Deep anomaly detection on attributed networks, in: Proceedings of the 2019 SIAM International Conference on Data Mining, SIAM, 2019, pp. 594–602.

[37] C. Doersch, Tutorial on variational autoencoders, arXiv preprint, arXiv:1606.05908, 2016.

[38] J. Donahue, P. Krähenbühl, T. Darrell, Adversarial feature learning, arXiv preprint, arXiv:1605.09782, 2016.

[39] V. Dumoulin, I. Belghazi, B. Poole, O. Mastropietro, A. Lamb, M. Arjovsky, A. Courville, Adversarially learned inference, arXiv preprint, arXiv:1606.00704, 2016.

[40] A.F. Emmott, S. Das, T. Dietterich, A. Fern, W.-K. Wong, Systematic construction of anomaly detection benchmarks from real data, in: Proceedings of the ACM SIGKDD Workshop on Outlier Detection and Description, 2013, pp. 16–21.

[41] S.M. Erfani, S. Rajasegarar, S. Karunasekera, C. Leckie, High-dimensional and large-scale anomaly detection using a linear one-class SVM with deep learning, Pattern Recognition 58 (2016) 121–134.

[42] C. Esteban, S.L. Hyland, G. Rätsch, Real-valued (medical) time series generation with recurrent conditional GANs, arXiv preprint, arXiv:1706.02633, 2017.

[43] O. Fabius, J.R. van Amersfoort, Variational recurrent auto-encoders, arXiv preprint, arXiv:1412.6581, 2014.

[44] S. Fan, C. Shi, X. Wang, Abnormal event detection via heterogeneous information network embedding, in: Proceedings of the 27th ACM International Conference on Information and Knowledge Management, 2018, pp. 1483–1486.

[45] J. Fonseca, C. Ferraz, K. Gama, A policy-based coordination architecture for distributed complex event processing in the internet of things: doctoral symposium, in: Proceedings of the 10th ACM International Conference on Distributed and Event-Based Systems, 2016, pp. 418–421.

[46] Y. Ganin, E. Ustinova, H. Ajakan, P. Germain, H. Larochelle, F. Laviolette, M. Marchand, V. Lempitsky, Domain-adversarial training of neural networks, Journal of Machine Learning Research 17 (1) (2016) 1–35.

[47] P.J. García-Laencina, J.-L. Sancho-Gómez, A.R. Figueiras-Vidal, Pattern classification with missing data: a review, Neural Computing and Applications 19 (2) (2010) 263–282.

[48] K. Ghasedi Dizaji, A. Herandi, C. Deng, W. Cai, H. Huang, Deep clustering via joint convolutional autoencoder embedding and relative entropy minimization, in: Proceedings of the IEEE International Conference on Computer Vision, 2017, pp. 5736–5745.

[49] I. Golan, R. El-Yaniv, Deep anomaly detection using geometric transformations, in: Advances in Neural Information Processing Systems, 2018, pp. 9758–9769.

[50] L. Gondara, K. Wang, MIDA: multiple imputation using denoising autoencoders, in: Pacific-Asia Conference on Knowledge Discovery and Data Mining, Springer, 2018, pp. 260–272.

[51] I. Goodfellow, Y. Bengio, A. Courville, Y. Bengio, Deep Learning, vol. 1, MIT Press, Cambridge, 2016.

[52] K. Gregor, I. Danihelka, A. Mnih, C. Blundell, D. Wierstra, Deep autoregressive networks, in: International Conference on Machine Learning, PMLR, 2014, pp. 1242–1250.

[53] Q. Guo, J. Huang, A complex event processing based approach of multi-sensor data fusion in IoT sensing systems, in: 2015 4th International Conference on Computer Science and Network Technology (ICCSNT), vol. 1, IEEE, 2015, pp. 548–551.

[54] M. Gutmann, A. Hyvärinen, Noise-contrastive estimation: a new estimation principle for unnormalized statistical models, in: Proceedings of the Thirteenth International Conference on Artificial Intelligence and Statistics, 2010, pp. 297–304.

[55] S. Haradal, H. Hayashi, S. Uchida, Biosignal data augmentation based on generative adversarial networks, in: 2018 40th Annual International Conference of the IEEE Engineering in Medicine and Biology Society (EMBC), IEEE, 2018, pp. 368–371.

[56] M. Hasan, J. Choi, J. Neumann, A.K. Roy-Chowdhury, L.S. Davis, Learning temporal regularity in video sequences, in: Proceedings of the IEEE Conference on Computer Vision and Pattern Recognition, 2016, pp. 733–742.

[57] Z. He, X. Xu, S. Deng, Discovering cluster-based local outliers, Pattern Recognition Letters 24 (9–10) (2003) 1641–1650.

[58] G.E. Hinton, R.R. Salakhutdinov, Reducing the dimensionality of data with neural networks, Science 313 (5786) (2006) 504–507.

[59] J.-T. Hsieh, B. Liu, D.-A. Huang, L.F. Fei-Fei, J.C. Niebles, Learning to decompose and disentangle representations for video prediction, in: Advances in Neural Information Processing Systems, 2018, pp. 517–526.

[60] W.-N. Hsu, Y. Zhang, J. Glass, Unsupervised learning of disentangled and interpretable representations from sequential data, in: Advances in Neural Information Processing Systems, 2017, pp. 1878–1889.

[61] Y.-a. Huang, W. Fan, W. Lee, P.S. Yu, Cross-feature analysis for detecting ad-hoc routing anomalies, in: 23rd International Conference on Distributed Computing Systems, 2003. Proceedings, IEEE, 2003, pp. 478–487.

[62] R.T. Ionescu, F.S. Khan, M.-I. Georgescu, L. Shao, Object-centric auto-encoders and dummy anomalies for abnormal event detection in video, in: Proceedings of the IEEE Conference on Computer Vision and Pattern Recognition, 2019, pp. 7842–7851.

[63] M.-F. Jiang, S.-S. Tseng, C.-M. Su, Two-phase clustering process for outliers detection, Pattern Recognition Letters 22 (6–7) (2001) 691–700.

[64] S. Jiang, X. Song, H. Wang, J.-J. Han, Q.-H. Li, A clustering-based method for unsupervised intrusion detections, Pattern Recognition Letters 27 (7) (2006) 802–810.

[65] X. Jiang, J. Gao, X. Hong, Z. Cai, Gaussian processes autoencoder for dimensionality reduction, in: Pacific-Asia Conference on Knowledge Discovery and Data Mining, Springer, 2014, pp. 62–73.

[66] T. Kieu, B. Yang, C. Guo, C.S. Jensen, Outlier detection for time series with recurrent autoencoder ensembles, in: IJCAI, 2019, pp. 2725–2732.

[67] H.-G. Kim, G.-J. Jang, H.-J. Choi, M. Kim, Y.-W. Kim, J. Choi, Recurrent neural networks with missing information imputation for medical examination data prediction, in: 2017 IEEE International Conference on Big Data and Smart Computing (BigComp), IEEE, 2017, pp. 317–323.

[68] E.M. Knorr, R.T. Ng, Finding intensional knowledge of distance-based outliers, in: VLDB, vol. 99, 1999, pp. 211–222.

[69] E.M. Knorr, R.T. Ng, V. Tucakov, Distance-based outliers: algorithms and applications, The VLDB Journal 8 (3–4) (2000) 237–253.

[70] V.R. Konda, J.N. Tsitsiklis, Actor-critic algorithms, in: Advances in Neural Information Processing Systems, 2000, pp. 1008–1014.

[71] D.M. Kreindler, C.J. Lumsden, The effects of the irregular sample and missing data in time series analysis, in: Nonlinear Dynamics, Psychology, and Life Sciences, 2006.

[72] H.-P. Kriegel, P. Kroger, E. Schubert, A. Zimek, Interpreting and unifying outlier scores, in: Proceedings of the 2011 SIAM International Conference on Data Mining, SIAM, 2011, pp. 13–24.

[73] A. Krizhevsky, I. Sutskever, G.E. Hinton, Imagenet classification with deep convolutional neural networks, Communications of the ACM 60 (6) (2017) 84–90.

[74] A.M. Lamb, A.G.A.P. Goyal, Y. Zhang, S. Zhang, A.C. Courville, Y. Bengio, Professor forcing: a new algorithm for training recurrent networks, in: Advances in Neural Information Processing Systems, 2016, pp. 4601–4609.

[75] A.B.L. Larsen, S.K. Sønderby, H. Larochelle, O. Winther, Autoencoding beyond pixels using a learned similarity metric, in: International Conference on Machine Learning, PMLR, 2016, pp. 1558–1566.

[76] Y. LeCun, L. Bottou, Y. Bengio, P. Haffner, Gradient-based learning applied to document recognition, Proceedings of the IEEE 86 (11) (1998) 2278–2324.

[77] M.B. Lee, Y.H. Kim, K.R. Park, Conditional generative adversarial network-based data augmentation for enhancement of iris recognition accuracy, IEEE Access 7 (2019) 122134–122152.

[78] P. Li, T.J. Hastie, K.W. Church, Very sparse random projections, in: Proceedings of the 12th ACM SIGKDD International Conference on Knowledge Discovery and Data Mining, 2006, pp. 287–296.

[79] Y. Li, S. Mandt, Disentangled sequential autoencoder, arXiv preprint, arXiv:1803.02991, 2018.

[80] B. Liao, J. Zhang, C. Wu, D. McIlwraith, T. Chen, S. Yang, Y. Guo, F. Wu, Deep sequence learning with auxiliary information for traffic prediction, in: Proceedings of the 24th ACM SIGKDD International Conference on Knowledge Discovery & Data Mining, 2018, pp. 537–546.

[81] W. Liao, Y. Guo, X. Chen, P. Li, A unified unsupervised Gaussian mixture variational autoencoder for high dimensional outlier detection, in: 2018 IEEE International Conference on Big Data (Big Data), IEEE, 2018, pp. 1208–1217.

[82] Z.C. Lipton, D. Kale, R. Wetzel, Directly modeling missing data in sequences with RNNs: improved classification of clinical time series, in: Machine Learning for Healthcare Conference, 2016, pp. 253–270.

[83] M. Liu, M. Ray, E.A. Rundensteiner, D.J. Dougherty, C. Gupta, S. Wang, I. Ari, A. Mehta, Processing nested complex sequence pattern queries over event streams, in: Proceedings of the Seventh International Workshop on Data Management for Sensor Networks, 2010, pp. 14–19.

[84] M. Liu, E. Rundensteiner, D. Dougherty, C. Gupta, S. Wang, I. Ari, A. Mehta, High-performance nested CEP query processing over event streams, in: 2011 IEEE 27th International Conference on Data Engineering, IEEE, 2011, pp. 123–134.

[85] T.-Y. Liu, Learning to Rank for Information Retrieval, Springer Science & Business Media, 2011.

[86] W. Liu, W. Luo, D. Lian, S. Gao, Future frame prediction for anomaly detection–a new baseline, in: Proceedings of the IEEE Conference on Computer Vision and Pattern Recognition, 2018, pp. 6536–6545.

[87] X. Liu, J. Van De Weijer, A.D. Bagdanov, Leveraging unlabeled data for crowd counting by learning to rank, in: Proceedings of the IEEE Conference on Computer Vision and Pattern Recognition, 2018, pp. 7661–7669.

[88] Y. Liu, C.-L. Li, B. Póczos, Classifier two sample test for video anomaly detections, in: BMVC, 2018, p. 71.

[89] Y. Liu, Z. Li, C. Zhou, Y. Jiang, J. Sun, M. Wang, X. He, Generative adversarial active learning for unsupervised outlier detection, IEEE Transactions on Knowledge and Data Engineering (2019).

[90] W. Lu, Y. Cheng, C. Xiao, S. Chang, S. Huang, B. Liang, T. Huang, Unsupervised sequential outlier detection with deep architectures, IEEE Transactions on Image Processing 26 (9) (2017) 4321–4330.

[91] D. Luckham, The Power of Events, vol. 204, Addison-Wesley Reading, 2002.

[92] W. Luo, W. Liu, S. Gao, Remembering history with convolutional LSTM for anomaly detection, in: 2017 IEEE International Conference on Multimedia and Expo (ICME), IEEE, 2017, pp. 439–444.

[93] X. Lyu, M. Hueser, S.L. Hyland, G. Zerveas, G. Rätsch, Improving clinical predictions through unsupervised time series representation learning, arXiv preprint, arXiv:1812.00490, 2018.

[94] A. Mackinnon, The use and reporting of multiple imputation in medical research–a review, Journal of Internal Medicine 268 (6) (2010) 586–593.

[95] V. Mahadevan, W. Li, V. Bhalodia, N. Vasconcelos, Anomaly detection in crowded scenes, in: 2010 IEEE Computer Society Conference on Computer Vision and Pattern Recognition, IEEE, 2010, pp. 1975–1981.

[96] A. Makhzani, J. Shlens, N. Jaitly, I. Goodfellow, B. Frey, Adversarial autoencoders, arXiv preprint, arXiv:1511.05644, 2015.

[97] P. Malhotra, A. Ramakrishnan, G. Anand, L. Vig, P. Agarwal, G. Shroff, LSTM-based encoder-decoder for multi-sensor anomaly detection, arXiv preprint, arXiv:1607.00148, 2016.

[98] E. Marchi, F. Vesperini, F. Weninger, F. Eyben, S. Squartini, B. Schuller, Non-linear prediction with LSTM recurrent neural networks for acoustic novelty detection, in: 2015 International Joint Conference on Neural Networks (IJCNN), IEEE, 2015, pp. 1–7.

[99] S. Martin Arjovsky, L. Bottou, Wasserstein generative adversarial networks, in: Proceedings of the 34th International Conference on Machine Learning, Sydney, Australia, 2017.

[100] M. Mathieu, C. Couprie, Y. LeCun, Deep multi-scale video prediction beyond mean square error, arXiv preprint, arXiv:1511.05440, 2015.

[101] Y. Mei, S. Madden, ZStream: a cost-based query processor for adaptively detecting composite events, in: Proceedings of the 2009 ACM SIGMOD International Conference on Management of Data, 2009, pp. 193–206.

[102] X.-L. Meng, Multiple-imputation inferences with uncongenial sources of input, Statistical Science (1994) 538–558.

[103] L. Metz, B. Poole, D. Pfau, J. Sohl-Dickstein, Unrolled generative adversarial networks, arXiv preprint, arXiv:1611.02163, 2016.

[104] M. Mirza, S. Osindero, Conditional generative adversarial nets, arXiv preprint, arXiv:1411.1784, 2014.

[105] O. Mogren, C-RNN-GAN: continuous recurrent neural networks with adversarial training, arXiv preprint, arXiv:1611.09904, 2016.

[106] D. Mondal, D.B. Percival, Wavelet variance analysis for gappy time series, Annals of the Institute of Statistical Mathematics 62 (5) (2010) 943–966.

[107] M.M. Moya, M.W. Koch, L.D. Hostetler, One-class classifier networks for target recognition applications, STIN 93 (1993) 24043.

[108] A.Y. Ng, S.J. Russell, et al., Algorithms for inverse reinforcement learning, in: ICML, vol. 1, 2000, p. 2.

[109] P.C. Ngo, A.A. Winarto, C.K.L. Kou, S. Park, F. Akram, H.K. Lee, Fence GAN: towards better anomaly detection, in: 2019 IEEE 31st International Conference on Tools with Artificial Intelligence (ICTAI), IEEE, 2019, pp. 141–148.

[110] K. Noto, C. Brodley, D. Slonim, FRaC: a feature-modeling approach for semi-supervised and unsupervised anomaly detection, Data Mining and Knowledge Discovery 25 (1) (2012) 109–133.

[111] R. C. U. of Sydney, C. M. C. R. Centre, S. C. Q. C. R. Institute, and Hbku, Deep learning for anomaly detection: a survey, 2019.

[112] M.-h. Oh, G. Iyengar, Sequential anomaly detection using inverse reinforcement learning, in: Proceedings of the 25th ACM SIGKDD International Conference on Knowledge Discovery & Data Mining, 2019, pp. 1480–1490.

[113] G. Pang, L. Cao, L. Chen, H. Liu, Learning representations of ultrahigh-dimensional data for random distance-based outlier detection, in: Proceedings of the 24th ACM SIGKDD International Conference on Knowledge Discovery & Data Mining, 2018, pp. 2041–2050.

[114] G. Pang, C. Shen, L. Cao, A.V. Hengel, Deep learning for anomaly detection, ACM Computing Surveys (CSUR) 54 (2021) 1–38.

[115] G. Pang, C. Shen, H. Jin, A. van den Hengel, Deep weakly-supervised anomaly detection, arXiv preprint, arXiv:1910.13601, 2019.

[116] G. Pang, K.M. Ting, D. Albrecht, Lesinn: detecting anomalies by identifying least similar nearest neighbours, in: 2015 IEEE International Conference on Data Mining Workshop (ICDMW), IEEE, 2015, pp. 623–630.

[117] G. Pang, C. Yan, C. Shen, A.v.d. Hengel, X. Bai, Self-trained deep ordinal regression for end-to-end video anomaly detection, in: Proceedings of the IEEE/CVF Conference on Computer Vision and Pattern Recognition, 2020, pp. 12173–12182.

[118] S. Parveen, P. Green, Speech recognition with missing data using recurrent neural nets, in: Advances in Neural Information Processing Systems, 2002, pp. 1189–1195.

[119] P.A. Patrician, Multiple imputation for missing data, Research in Nursing & Health 25 (1) (2002) 76–84.

[120] P. Perera, R. Nallapati, B. Xiang, OCGAN: one-class novelty detection using GANs with constrained latent representations, in: Proceedings of the IEEE Conference on Computer Vision and Pattern Recognition, 2019, pp. 2898–2906.

[121] T. Pevný, Loda: lightweight on-line detector of anomalies, Machine Learning 102 (2) (2016) 275–304.

[122] A. Purwar, S.K. Singh, Hybrid prediction model with missing value imputation for medical data, Expert Systems with Applications 42 (13) (2015) 5621–5631.

[123] S. Ramaswamy, R. Rastogi, K. Shim, Efficient algorithms for mining outliers from large data sets, in: Proceedings of the 2000 ACM SIGMOD International Conference on Management of Data, 2000, pp. 427–438.

[124] S. Rifai, P. Vincent, X. Muller, X. Glorot, Y. Bengio, Contractive auto-encoders: explicit invariance during feature extraction, in: ICML, 2011.

[125] L. Rosasco, E.D. Vito, A. Caponnetto, M. Piana, A. Verri, Are loss functions all the same?, Neural Computation 16 (5) (2004) 1063–1076.

[126] V. Roth, Outlier detection with one-class kernel Fisher discriminants, Advances in Neural Information Processing Systems 17 (2004) 1169–1176.

[127] D.B. Rubin, Multiple Imputation for Nonresponse in Surveys, vol. 81, John Wiley & Sons, 2004.

[128] O. Russakovsky, J. Deng, H. Su, J. Krause, S. Satheesh, S. Ma, Z. Huang, A. Karpathy, A. Khosla, M. Bernstein, et al., Imagenet large scale visual recognition challenge, International Journal of Computer Vision 115 (3) (2015) 211–252.

[129] M. Sabokrou, M. Khalooei, M. Fathy, E. Adeli, Adversarially learned one-class classifier for novelty detection, in: Proceedings of the IEEE Conference on Computer Vision and Pattern Recognition, 2018, pp. 3379–3388.

[130] T. Salimans, I. Goodfellow, W. Zaremba, V. Cheung, A. Radford, X. Chen, Improved techniques for training GANs, arXiv preprint, arXiv:1606.03498, 2016.

[131] T. Schlegl, P. Seeböck, S.M. Waldstein, G. Langs, U. Schmidt-Erfurth, f-AnoGAN: fast unsupervised anomaly detection with generative adversarial networks, Medical Image Analysis 54 (2019) 30–44.

[132] T. Schlegl, P. Seeböck, S.M. Waldstein, U. Schmidt-Erfurth, G. Langs, Unsupervised anomaly detection with generative adversarial networks to guide marker discovery, in: International Conference on Information Processing in Medical Imaging, Springer, 2017, pp. 146–157.

[133] T. Schnabel, A. Swaminathan, A. Singh, N. Chandak, T. Joachims, Recommendations as treatments: debiasing learning and evaluation, arXiv preprint, arXiv:1602.05352, 2016.

[134] B. Schölkopf, J.C. Platt, J. Shawe-Taylor, A.J. Smola, R.C. Williamson, Estimating the support of a high-dimensional distribution, Neural Computation 13 (7) (2001) 1443–1471.

[135] B. Schölkopf, A. Smola, K.-R. Müller, Kernel principal component analysis, in: International Conference on Artificial Neural Networks, Springer, 1997, pp. 583–588.

[136] E. Schubert, J. Sander, M. Ester, H.P. Kriegel, X. Xu, DBSCAN revisited, revisited: why and how you should (still) use DBSCAN, ACM Transactions on Database Systems (TODS) 42 (3) (2017) 1–21.

[137] P. Seshadri, H. Pirahesh, T.C. Leung, Complex query decorrelation, in: Proceedings of the Twelfth International Conference on Data Engineering, IEEE, 1996, pp. 450–458.

[138] L. Simonetto, Generating spiking time series with generative adversarial networks: an application on banking transactions, 2018.

[139] K. Simonyan, A. Zisserman, Very deep convolutional networks for large-scale image recognition, arXiv preprint, arXiv:1409.1556, 2014.

[140] N. Srivastava, E. Mansimov, R. Salakhudinov, Unsupervised learning of video representations using LSTMs, in: International Conference on Machine Learning, 2015, pp. 843–852.

[141] D.J. Stekhoven, P. Bühlmann, Missforest—non-parametric missing value imputation for mixed-type data, Bioinformatics 28 (1) (2012) 112–118.

[142] J.A. Sterne, I.R. White, J.B. Carlin, M. Spratt, P. Royston, M.G. Kenward, A.M. Wood, J.R. Carpenter, Multiple imputation for missing data in epidemiological and clinical research: potential and pitfalls, BMJ 338 (2009).

[143] M. Sugiyama, K. Borgwardt, Rapid distance-based outlier detection via sampling, Advances in Neural Information Processing Systems 26 (2013) 467–475.

[144] W. Sultani, C. Chen, M. Shah, Real-world anomaly detection in surveillance videos, in: Proceedings of the IEEE Conference on Computer Vision and Pattern Recognition, 2018, pp. 6479–6488.

[145] D.M. Tax, R.P. Duin, Support vector data description, Machine Learning 54 (1) (2004) 45–66.

[146] L. Tenenboim-Chekina, L. Rokach, B. Shapira, Ensemble of feature chains for anomaly detection, in: International Workshop on Multiple Classifier Systems, Springer, 2013, pp. 295–306.

[147] L. Theis, W. Shi, A. Cunningham, F. Huszár, Lossy image compression with compressive autoencoders, arXiv preprint, arXiv:1703.00395, 2017.

[148] F. Tian, B. Gao, Q. Cui, E. Chen, T.-Y. Liu, Learning deep representations for graph clustering, in: Proceedings of the AAAI Conference on Artificial Intelligence, vol. 28, 2014.

[149] V. Tresp, T. Briegel, A solution for missing data in recurrent neural networks with an application to blood glucose prediction, Advances in Neural Information Processing Systems 10 (1997) 971–977.

[150] R. Tudor Ionescu, S. Smeureanu, B. Alexe, M. Popescu, Unmasking the abnormal events in video, in: Proceedings of the IEEE International Conference on Computer Vision, 2017, pp. 2895–2903.

[151] P. Vincent, H. Larochelle, Y. Bengio, P.-A. Manzagol, Extracting and composing robust features with denoising autoencoders, in: Proceedings of the 25th International Conference on Machine Learning, 2008, pp. 1096–1103.

[152] P. Vincent, H. Larochelle, I. Lajoie, Y. Bengio, P.-A. Manzagol, L. Bottou, Stacked denoising autoencoders: learning useful representations in a deep network with a local denoising criterion, Journal of Machine Learning Research 11 (12) (2010).

[153] D. Wang, E.A. Rundensteiner, H. Wang, R.T. Ellison III, Active complex event processing: applications in real-time health care, Proceedings of the VLDB Endowment 3 (1–2) (2010) 1545–1548.

[154] H. Wang, M. Li, F. Ma, S.-L. Huang, L. Zhang, Unsupervised anomaly detection via generative adversarial networks, in: 2019 18th ACM/IEEE International Conference on Information Processing in Sensor Networks (IPSN), IEEE, 2019, pp. 313–314.

[155] H. Wang, D.-Y. Yeung, Towards Bayesian deep learning: a framework and some existing methods, IEEE Transactions on Knowledge and Data Engineering 28 (12) (2016) 3395–3408.

[156] S. Wang, Y. Zeng, X. Liu, E. Zhu, J. Yin, C. Xu, M. Kloft, Effective end-to-end unsupervised outlier detection via inlier priority of discriminative network, in: Advances in Neural Information Processing Systems, 2019, pp. 5962–5975.

[157] X. Wang, N. Golbandi, M. Bendersky, D. Metzler, M. Najork, Position bias estimation for unbiased learning to rank in personal search, in: Proceedings of the Eleventh ACM International Conference on Web Search and Data Mining, 2018, pp. 610–618.

[158] Y. Wang, K. Cao, A proactive complex event processing method for large-scale transportation internet of things, International Journal of Distributed Sensor Networks 10 (3) (2014) 159052.

[159] I.R. White, P. Royston, A.M. Wood, Multiple imputation using chained equations: issues and guidance for practice, Statistics in Medicine 30 (4) (2011) 377–399.

[160] E. Wu, Y. Diao, S. Rizvi, High-performance complex event processing over streams, in: Proceedings of the 2006 ACM SIGMOD International Conference on Management of Data, 2006, pp. 407–418.

[161] J. Xie, R. Girshick, A. Farhadi, Unsupervised deep embedding for clustering analysis, in: International Conference on Machine Learning, 2016, pp. 478–487.

[162] D. Xu, E. Ricci, Y. Yan, J. Song, N. Sebe, Learning deep representations of appearance and motion for anomalous event detection, arXiv preprint, arXiv:1510.01553, 2015.

[163] J. Yang, D. Parikh, D. Batra, Joint unsupervised learning of deep representations and image clusters, in: Proceedings of the IEEE Conference on Computer Vision and Pattern Recognition, 2016, pp. 5147–5156.

[164] X. Yang, C. Deng, F. Zheng, J. Yan, W. Liu, Deep spectral clustering using dual autoencoder network, in: Proceedings of the IEEE Conference on Computer Vision and Pattern Recognition, 2019, pp. 4066–4075.

[165] M. Ye, X. Peng, W. Gan, W. Wu, Y. Qiao, AnoPCN: video anomaly detection via deep predictive coding network, in: Proceedings of the 27th ACM International Conference on Multimedia, 2019, pp. 1805–1813.

[166] J. Yoon, A. Alaa, S. Hu, M. Schaar, ForecastICU: a prognostic decision support system for timely prediction of intensive care unit admission, in: International Conference on Machine Learning, 2016, pp. 1680–1689.

[167] J. Yoon, C. Davtyan, M. van der Schaar, Discovery and clinical decision support for personalized healthcare, IEEE Journal of Biomedical and Health Informatics 21 (4) (2016) 1133–1145.

[168] J. Yoon, J. Jordon, M. van der Schaar, GANITE: estimation of individualized treatment effects using generative adversarial nets, in: International Conference on Learning Representations, 2018.

[169] J. Yoon, W.R. Zame, M. van der Schaar, Deep sensing: active sensing using multi-directional recurrent neural networks, in: International Conference on Learning Representations, 2018.

[170] H.-F. Yu, N. Rao, I.S. Dhillon, Temporal regularized matrix factorization for high-dimensional time series prediction, Advances in Neural Information Processing Systems 29 (2016) 847–855.

[171] W. Yu, W. Cheng, C.C. Aggarwal, K. Zhang, H. Chen, W. Wang, Netwalk: a flexible deep embedding approach for anomaly detection in dynamic networks, in: Proceedings of the 24th ACM SIGKDD International Conference on Knowledge Discovery & Data Mining, 2018, pp. 2672–2681.

[172] M.Z. Zaheer, J.-h. Lee, M. Astrid, S.-I. Lee, Old is gold: redefining the adversarially learned one-class classifier training paradigm, in: Proceedings of the IEEE/CVF Conference on Computer Vision and Pattern Recognition, 2020, pp. 14183–14193.

[173] H. Zenati, C.S. Foo, B. Lecouat, G. Manek, V.R. Chandrasekhar, Efficient GAN-based anomaly detection, arXiv preprint, arXiv:1802.06222, 2018.

[174] H. Zenati, M. Romain, C.-S. Foo, B. Lecouat, V. Chandrasekhar, Adversarially learned anomaly detection, in: 2018 IEEE International Conference on Data Mining (ICDM), IEEE, 2018, pp. 727–736.

[175] C. Zhang, S.R. Kuppannagari, R. Kannan, V.K. Prasanna, Generative adversarial network for synthetic time series data generation in smart grids, in: 2018 IEEE International Conference on Communications, Control, and Computing Technologies for Smart Grids (SmartGridComm), IEEE, 2018, pp. 1–6.

[176] C. Zhang, D. Song, Y. Chen, X. Feng, C. Lumezanu, W. Cheng, J. Ni, B. Zong, H. Chen, N.V. Chawla, A deep neural network for unsupervised anomaly detection and diagnosis in multivariate time series data, in: Proceedings of the AAAI Conference on Artificial Intelligence, vol. 33, 2019, pp. 1409–1416.

[177] K. Zhang, M. Hutter, H. Jin, A new local distance-based outlier detection approach for scattered real-world data, in: Pacific-Asia Conference on Knowledge Discovery and Data Mining, Springer, 2009, pp. 813–822.

[178] Y. Zhang, Z. Gan, L. Carin, Generating text via adversarial training, in: NIPS Workshop on Adversarial Training, vol. 21, 2016.

[179] P. Zheng, S. Yuan, X. Wu, J. Li, A. Lu, One-class adversarial nets for fraud detection, in: Proceedings of the AAAI Conference on Artificial Intelligence, vol. 33, 2019, pp. 1286–1293.

[180] C. Zhou, R.C. Paffenroth, Anomaly detection with robust deep autoencoders, in: Proceedings of the 23rd ACM SIGKDD International Conference on Knowledge Discovery and Data Mining, 2017, pp. 665–674.

[181] J.T. Zhou, J. Du, H. Zhu, X. Peng, Y. Liu, R.S.M. Goh, Anomalynet: an anomaly detection network for video surveillance, IEEE Transactions on Information Forensics and Security 14 (10) (2019) 2537–2550.

[182] J.-Y. Zhu, T. Park, P. Isola, A.A. Efros, Unpaired image-to-image translation using cycle-consistent adversarial networks, in: Proceedings of the IEEE International Conference on Computer Vision, 2017, pp. 2223–2232.

[183] B. Zong, Q. Song, M.R. Min, W. Cheng, C. Lumezanu, D. Cho, H. Chen, Deep autoencoding Gaussian mixture model for unsupervised anomaly detection, in: International Conference on Learning Representations, 2018.

[184] H. Zou, T. Hastie, R. Tibshirani, Sparse principal component analysis, Journal of Computational and Graphical Statistics 15 (2) (2006) 265–286.

Case study: scalable IoT data processing and reasoning

3

Architectures and technologies for stream processing

HPC stream processing platforms

10.1 Introduction case study

ECG-stream processing

Patients with chronic diseases such as heart conditions or other medical conditions, usually need to frequently pay visits to physicians or are possibly hospitalized for monitoring. This care service can be very impractical for the patient and expensive for hospitals. In some cases, chronically ill patients receive home-based healthcare service from caregiver and doctors. These services are more and more improved with health-monitoring devices which deliver individual analytics results to the care service. The review of this data can help to improved care or alert of acute health conditions. Waiting for a batch analysis of the patient data or a manual review can leave the patient at risk in critical situations.

Personalized real-time analytics

Fusing Complex Event Processing (CEP) with medical data enables advanced and personalized analytics for each patient in real-time. The reasoning over composite events with the integration in existing health care knowledge bases, offers many use cases to support real-time decision making in emergency situations. Slight differences in a patient's blood pressure or heart rate might not raise any alarm. In a correlated analysis, this can indicate possible heart failure or other critical situations, where a fast prescriptive analysis could recommend specific medications or interventions. A caregiver could be alerted with the specific information and recommendation for medication based on the patient's situation and historical data, eliminating the need for additional extensive manual review. The inference can be retrieved out of a knowledge base to give information about the best suitable treatment method for a specific patient.

A particular focus in this case study will be held on the monitoring and the integration process of the detection of Cardiovascular disease (CVD). According to the World Health Organization, a significant number of deaths are caused by CVD [5]. Arrhythmia is a type of CVD that relates to any irregular change of the heart rhythms. Although a single arrhythmia heartbeat may not have a severe effect on life, continuous arrhythmia beats can indicate an incoming fatal situation. Prolonged premature ventricular contraction beats can turn into ventricular tachycardia or ventricular fibrillation beats, which can immediately lead to heart failure. Due to that, it is essential to periodically monitor the heart rhythms to prevent and interfere with the CVDs.

Methodology

The result of this case study will be a proposal of practical course of action to process IoT health data in a scalable IoT architecture by evaluating different implementation decisions based on the research fields

Anomaly Detection and Complex Event Processing Over IoT Data Streams. https://doi.org/10.1016/B978-0-12-823818-9.00022-5

of data processing, data enrichment and (semantic-) CEP. The methodology of exploratory research will be followed, which aims to explore and evaluate the identified theoretical background by applying a complex IoT use case in the field of eHealth.

The case study of an IoT use case is generalized in the following components:

1. Define a processing pipeline for IoT-based communication systems, semantic data acquisition, continuous query processing, complex reasoning, and detailing the implementation of each component.
2. Provide a semantic information model for the representation of IoT data, patient data, and medical domain knowledge in a scenario, by reusing existing semantic models.
3. Define an stream reasoning component as part of the eco-system, based on continuous query processing.

The proposed IoT stream architecture will have generalized requirements expected to be the minimum standard in a healthcare domain scenario. It is important to mention that the defined requirements are not based on a factual requirement analysis with healthcare domain experts. The proof of concept contains generalized requirements for the full integration of semantic enrichment and complex event processing over IoT data streams. The following generalized requirements were defined for the proof of concept:

1. **Requirement 1 - IoT integration in central analytics infrastructure**: Many traditional health monitoring devices have integrated and isolated monitoring functionalities, where an integration outside of the device itself is often not possible. This is shifting with modern IoT devices, that can be integrated into other services. A central analytics environment should be able to collect and correlate IoT data stream events.
2. **Requirement 2 - Real-time alarming system**: A fast reaction time should be made available on detected issues as soon as possible close to the source. With more powerful devices, the architecture design should be flexible enough to offer edge computing to decrease the latency of primitive reasoning over single event streams and forward events to the central complex event processing system if needed.
3. **Requirement 3 - Integrate device analytics in more complex analytics scenarios**: This requirement contains complex event processing over several stream elements to offer an in-depth analysis of a diagnosis that consists of composite events, as well as the integration of CEP inferences on patient data and knowledge base expert systems.
4. **Requirement 4 - Scalable and secure infrastructure**: A scalable and reliable messaging architecture is of utmost importance in the field of healthcare.

Conceptual design is the initial design step, in which the general outlines of function and the Eco-system was articulated. The main components are explained in the following subsections, where Fig. 10.1 shows the overview of the proposed Eco-system.

10.2 Ingestion and communication system - Kafka
The first component to be analyzed was the stream ingestion layer.

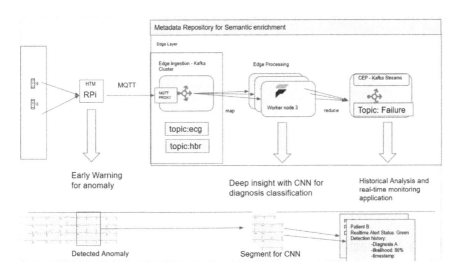

FIGURE 10.1

Complete processing architecture starting from the IoT data generation, the Kafka ingestion, the following processing via the Faust workers to the event classification.

Kafka is a high throughput, distributed log that can be used as a message queue system. Any number of producers and consumers can be handled by Kafka. With this principle, Kafka provides persistency for the messages and offers the following characteristics [1]:

- Reliability is the highest requirement
- Some messages should be kept a copy of, even after consumption
- Data loss is not acceptable
- Speed is not the biggest concern
- High data size

The main requirement for a health care system is reliability and data loss prevention, which made Kafka the choice for the implementation of this case study.

Apache Kafka is a streaming platform that allows users to publish data and subscribe to different stream topics. Kafka stores the streams in a fault-tolerant way. A Kafka system runs as a cluster and follows the concept of a topic in which data is published. In this system abstraction, every raw data stream type is published to a topic. This enables to structure streams by different topics, e.g., ECG, Heart Rate, light sensors. Each topic records all the messages for a specified retention period. This capability can be used not only for real-time singles stream analytics but also for health condition analytics in complex event compositions that require using historical patient data.

Different IoT devices act as data producers. Devices publish the raw and early preprocessed data in the specific Kafka cluster, where Kafka consumer can publish back the results of their processing or analytics into the cluster. Kafka manages the scalability of the system as the general load on the architecture may change with an increase in patients. Kafka serves as data retention, storage, and forwarding interface, where several consumers can consume the data.

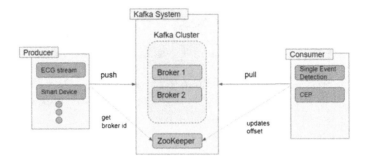

FIGURE 10.2

Overview of Kafka architecture for this case study. Illustrating the producer, cluster and consumer architecture.

10.2.1 Kafka architecture

The Kafka architecture is a cluster consisting of several components. Fig. 10.2 illustrates the different Kafka components, which are described in this section.

Kafka broker

A Kafka cluster consists of multiple brokers that enable load balancing. Kafka brokers are stateless, where the ZooKeeper maintains the cluster state. A Kafka cluster always has a leading broker, which will be elected by the ZooKeeper.

Kafka ZooKeeper

The ZooKeeper is the central management and coordination unit in the cluster. If a new broker enters the cluster or if a broker fails, the ZooKeeper notifies the producers and consumers. This notification allows producer and consumer on how to act and start communicating with other available brokers in the cluster.

Kafka producers

Producers push the data to the brokers. The Kafka Producer passes data to partitions in the Kafka topic based on the partition strategy that has been predefined. The Kafka producer takes care that the data rate can be handled by the broker.

Kafka consumers

The Kafka brokers are stateless, while the consumers maintain the number of messages that have been consumed. This is achieved by using a partition offset. A consumer confirms each message offset which is proof that all messages before were consumed.

10.2.2 Kafka-concepts

Kafka topics

A Kafka topic is a logical message channel to distinguish between different message types. Kafka topics are divided into several partitions. Partitions allow parallelizing a topic by splitting the data into

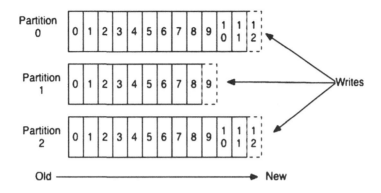

FIGURE 10.3

Showcase of a Kafka topic with 3 partitions. New entries are written with the offset number in the top of a queue.

a specific topic across multiple brokers. A partition writing process of a topic is illustrated in Fig. 10.3. Each partition can be assigned on a separate machine to allow multiple consumers to read from a topic in parallel. Further, can the message processing throughput of a consumer be increased by the parallel reading of multiple partitions.

Each message within a partition has the previously mentioned offset. The offset represents the ordering of messages as an immutable sequence. The consumer has different options to start reading from any offset point, which allows the consumers to join the cluster at any time.

With the offset info, each specific message in a Kafka cluster can be uniquely identified with the information of the message topic, partition and offset within the partition.

Partitions in Kafka

Each broker holds several partitions that can be either a leader or a replica for a topic. A leader coordinates all writes and reads to a topic, and coordinates updates in the replicas with new data. If a leader fails, a replica takes over as the new leader.

Topic replication factor

Topic replication helps to prevent system failure in case of broker failure. In case of a broker failure, the topic replicas of other brokers can secure the system stability. A replication factor determines how many backups are created for a topic.

10.3 Communication protocol between producer devices and the Kafka ingestion system - MQTT

MQTT is an ISO messaging protocol [3]. MQTT is famously used for IoT scenarios and uses a publish/subscribe architecture in contrast to HTTP with its request/response paradigm. The publish and subscribe concept is an event-driven paradigm and allows messages to be pushed to a client. The central communication point is an MQTT broker. A broker dispatches the messages between the senders and

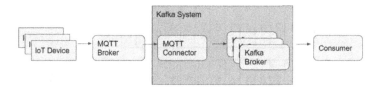

FIGURE 10.4

MQTT Broker ingestion.

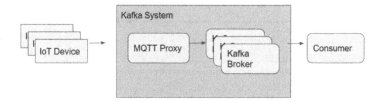

FIGURE 10.5

MQTT Proxy ingestion.

consumers. Clients publish the messages specified on a topic to a broker. This provides bi-directional communication between the devices over an MQTT broker.

MQTT and Apache Kafka are a good combination of end-to-end IoT integration from the edge to the processing nodes and back. In this case-study, the bidirectional and interdevice communication was not needed for the goal of having a monitoring and processing pipeline along with the IoT architecture with a centralized deep analytics engine. Nevertheless, the MQTT characteristics of being bandwidth and battery-efficient on IoT devices are considered a valuable component for this architectural concept. By evaluating different implementation recommendations of MQTT device integrations, the following two integration scenarios were evaluated.

Scenario 1 - MQTT Broker:

In this first scenario (Fig. 10.4), the data gets pulled from the MQTT Broker via the Kafka MQTT Connector to the Kafka Broker.

Scenario 2 - MQTT Proxy:

To reduce complexity and simplify the management of the infrastructure, in Scenario 2 (Fig. 10.5), an MQTT proxy can be used to get rid of the MQTT broker cluster that would be required to be managed in Scenario 1. In case, no additional broker cluster is needed, more reliable and performant processing can be guaranteed by having fewer components along the processing pipeline.

10.4 Stream processing and single-stream event detection - Faust

Faust is a high performance stream processing library, which adapts the idea of Kafka Streams in Python and for this chosen for the case-study. Faust has the following characteristics:

```
@app.agent()
async def myagent(stream):
    async for event in stream:
```

FIGURE 10.6

Faust agent basic code example.

1. Kafka Consumer: Faust worker can act as a consumer of a Kafka cluster and process events based on their assigned topics.
2. Scalability: Faust can be vertically scaled by assigning multiple workers to a topic.
3. No DSL: It is written in python. The whole range of python libraries is available for processing an event, which includes, e.g., Tensorflow for more sophisticated AI-based analytics.
4. Asynchronicity: With Python 3 and the *AsyncIO* module, Faust offers high-performance asynchronous processing. With *AsyncIO* and the *async/await* keywords in Python 3.6+, multiple stream processors can be run in the same process.
5. Stateful: Faust can persist in states and act as a database. Tables are named distributed key/value stores which are implemented as regular Python dictionary.
6. Stream Windows Processing: Tumbling, hopping and sliding windows are available. Windows can be subject to time constraints in which old windows can expire to stop loading data.
7. High Reliability: For reliability, Kafka topics possess a write-ahead-log. In case a key is changed, the information gets published to the changelog. Standby nodes consume the changelog info to keep a replica of the data. In the case of a node failure, this replica enables an instant recovery.
8. Persistence: Tables can be stored locally on each machine using RocksDB [4], a high performance embedded database for key-value data.

The core components are described in the next 5 paragraphs.

Agents
Agents process infinite streams using asynchronous generators. The agent concept comes from the actor model, where the stream processor executes concurrently on many CPU cores. An actual code example can be seen in Fig. 10.6

Tables
Tables are dictionaries that give stream processors states with persistent data. Sharding and partitioning are an essential part of stateful stream processing and need to be planned strategically for the right processing in a Faust cluster. Streams can be processed in a round-robin principle where Faust acts as a simple event processing and as a task queue.

Distribution
Faust relies on Kafka's consumer management principle, to identify whether any partition or topic is not being served to and launches an agent in an instance where the application is reporting as functioning.

Fig. 10.7 represents a single Kafka topic that has six partitions. Three Faust workers are running on the same application name. The left illustration shows a working cluster with an elected leader and

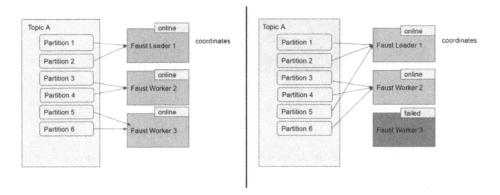

FIGURE 10.7

Faust topic replication example in case of a worker failure. Left side - All worker healthy; Right side - one worker fails and partitions are redistributed.

two further worker nodes. The elected topic leader will coordinate which partition will be fed to which worker. The node failure detection is based on a timeout value, after which a consumer group will inform the leader that one of the nodes is down and trigger a re-distribution of topics and partition assignments.

Table sharding

Tables shards in Kafka are organized using a disjoint distribution of keys. Any computation for a subset of keys happens together in the same worker. The following example illustrates an incorrect usage of key subsets assignments of worker processes: If we have patient and location information, depending on the use case and goal, we want to partition by a key on location or patient-ID. Should we partition on a patient-ID and process aggregated information on location information, most likely we run into a risk of incomplete data, where location information might be spread across different partitions. Such an issue can be solved with Faust by using two distinct agents and repartition the stream by location when populating the table.

The changelog

The changelog is used to recover from system failure, were every modification to a table has a changelog entry. The changelog is registered in the Kafka Cluster as its topic and only keeps the most recent values of a key in the log. The RocksDB storage allows the recovery of tables, where a worker retrieves missed updates since the last time the instance was running.

10.5 Complex event processing - Kafka Streams with KSQL

Faust acts in this Kafka infrastructure as a consumer for processing the data streams as well as producer of event streams. With this architecture design, CEP Engines can now be attached to the Kafka cluster as a consumer and can access those event streams in the Kafka architecture. In the implementation of the case study, the focus will be held on the "simple" CEP integration. This integration will not have the benefit of integrating complex reasoning over ontologies but explains the composite event behavior reasoning.

Based on the underlying Kafka ecosystem, the decision was made in favor of Kafka Streams. Kafka Streams is the Apache Kafka library for writing streaming applications and microservices in Java and Scala.

10.5.1 Kafka stream concept

Kafka Streams has following characteristics [2]:

1. Lightweight client library, that can be embedded in Java application.
2. Kafka is the only dependency as an internal messaging layer. Kafka Streams uses Kafka's partitioning principles to scale while maintaining ordering guarantees horizontally.
3. Fault-tolerant local state which enables stateful operations (windowed joins and aggregations).
4. Exactly-once processing is guaranteed, where each record will be processed once, even in case of a failure.
5. One-record-at-a-time processing for lower processing latency.
6. Event-time based windowing operations.
7. Includes stream processing primitives with a high-level DSL and low-level Processor API.

The core components are described in the next paragraphs.

Kafka stream processing topology

A stream processing application defines its logics through one or more processor topologies. A processor topology represents a graph of processor nodes that are connected by their streams. A stream processor represents a processing step of a stream input and applies operations to produce one or more outputs, which are sent to downstream processors in the topology.

There are two types of processors in the topology:

1. Source processor: A source processor produces an input stream from one or multiple Kafka topics and acts as a consumer of topics to forward them to downstream processors.
2. Sink processor: A sink processor does not have downstream processors. It received records from its upstream processors and sends the output to a specified Kafka topic.

Processed results can be forwarded to Kafka or to external systems.

Time dimension

Common notions of time in streams are:

- **Event-time**: When an event or data record occurred. In this case study, e.g., the record of the ECG signal at the device.
- **Processing-time**: When the event or data record is being processed. This can be the time of consumption and later than the event time.
- **Ingestion time**: When the event or message is stored inside a topic partition by the Kafka broker.

Kafka automatically embeds the timestamps into a message, where timestamps can represent event-time or ingestion-time. The corresponding Kafka configuration setting can be specified on the broker level or per topic.

Aggregation

Aggregations take one input stream or also table and create a new table by combining multiple records into a single output. An example is the computation of a sum.

Windowing & states

Kafka Streams offers windowing and lets group records that have the same key for stateful operations such as aggregations or joins. Windows can be specified with a retention period and are tracked per record key. Kafka streams state management enables joins over input streams, grouping and aggregation over records.

Processing guarantee and out-of-order-handling

Stream processing applications usually make use of a lambda architecture, which enables the infrastructure for real-time and batch processing in parallel. The goal is often to have real-time alerts and a batch layer that guarantees that no data-loss or data duplicates occur. Newer Kafka versions allow its producers to send messages to different topic partitions in a transactional and idempotent manner. With this characteristic, Kafka Streams offers the end-to-end exactly-once processing semantics without the need of adding a batch layer [1]. For stateless operations, out-of-order data will not impact the processing logics since only one record is considered at a time for stateful operations such as aggregations and joins. For the handling of out-of-order data, a longer wait time should be considered, where the state needs to be tracked. This will lead to a trade-off between latency, cost, and correctness.

Some of the out-of-order data cannot be handled by increasing the latency and cost in Streams:

1. Stream-Stream joins: All three types (inner, outer, left) handle out-of-order records correctly. The only problem can occur in the resulting stream, where left and outer joins contain unnecessary 1: null records.
2. Stream-Table joins: Out-of-order records are not handled and may result in unpredictable results.

10.5.2 Kafka stream architecture

Stream partitions and tasks

Kafka partitions data for storing and transporting, while Kafka streams partitions for further processing. In Kafka, partitioning enables data locality, scalability, high performance, and fault tolerance. With partitions and tasks as a logical unit, a parallel processing model can be realized.

Following similarity can be found between Kafka streams and Kafka:

- A stream partition is an ordered sequence of data records assigned to a Kafka topic partition.
- The keys of a topic element determine the data partitioning in Kafka and Kafka Streams.

The processor topology can be scaled by using multiple tasks, where a task is a fixed unit of parallelism for a topic. The instantiation of a processor topology is done by a task, where the task also maintains a buffer for each of the assigned partitions and process messages one-at-a-time from the record

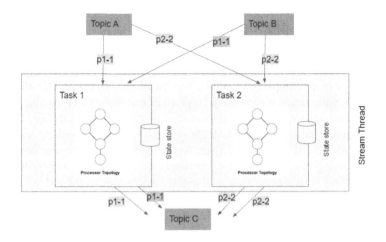

FIGURE 10.8

Illustration of a task assignment inside a Kafka Stream thread.

buffers. This characteristic gives the Kafka stream architecture the independent and parallel processing paradigm.

Kafka Streams can be run on a single machine or spread across multiple machines, where tasks are automatically distributed to the application instances. The diagram in Fig. 10.8 exemplifies how a task assignment structure could look.

Two tasks, where each one is assigned with one partition of the relevant topic, which in return enables a fault tolerance characteristic for processing. In case an application instance fails, all affected partitions will be automatically restarted on another instance and fed with the same stream partitions.

Threads

While the partitions, in combination with a task, enable fault tolerance, the threads enable parallel processing inside an application instance. With creating more threads, a different subset of partitions is used to enable parallelized processing. The threads run independently and can not communicate with each other. Kafka Streams takes care of distributing the partitions among the tasks.

Local state store

State stores enable to store and query data inside a task, which is essential for stateful operations (e.g., aggregation over a time window or join). The state stores are secured of failure by a changelog topic with each update, similar to the changelog of Faust. A changelog topic is partitioned so that each task state store has its partition.

10.5.3 KSQL

KSQL is built on Kafka Streams as a streaming SQL engine. Based on the simplicity of use and high expressiveness, KSQL was used as the (semi)CEP for detecting composite stream events in this work.

10.6 Other processing platform

10.6.1 Batch processing

Batch processing is responsible for scheduling and executing iterative batch algorithms, such as sorting, searching, indexing, or more complex algorithms like PageRank, Bayesian classification, or genetic algorithms. The MapReduce programming model represents mainly batch processing. Its disadvantages are apparent when processing large amounts of batch data, multiple jobs usually need to be concatenated to perform more complex processing than a single one, as well as intermediate results from Map to Reduce phases are physically stored on hard disks, which compromises response latency. Great efforts are being made to develop new solutions that overcome the problems of MapReduce. For example, by natively incorporating other atomic relational algebra operations connected via a directed acyclic graph or by keeping intermediate results in main memory [16,22]. In the following sections, the most common tools based on batch processing are discussed.

Hadoop/MapReduce

Apache Hadoop[1] is a well-known example of a batch processing framework to support distributed storage and processing of big data on clusters. It is an open-source Java-based framework that is widely used by large companies such as Facebook, Yahoo! Twitter to store and process Big Data workloads. Hadoop consists of a Hadoop Distributed File System (HDFS), in which storage of data is distributed across nodes in a cluster, and the Hadoop MapReduce engine assigns processing jobs to the node on which it resides. Hadoop implements the MapReduce programming model for processing large amounts of data, structured as in a database or unstructured as in a file system, using parallel and distributed algorithms on a cluster of nodes consisting of a master node multiple worker nodes. The master node takes input, divides the input into smaller subproblems, and distributes these smaller subproblems to the worker nodes, where a worker node can perform the subprocess, resulting in a multilevel tree structure. The worker node returns the response to its master node, where all answers are combined to form the output of the answer to the original problem [13,20]. Hadoop builds the framework of Apache Mahout, which provides machine learning algorithms to support dimensionality reduction, recommendation mining, frequent itemset mining, classification, and clustering. Newer versions of Mahout include new implementations that run on Spark. For example, implementations of Spark item similarity enable next-generation cooccurrence recommender, where user clickstreams and contexts are used in recommendation generation. However, Hadoop provides authentication, load balancing, high availability, flexible access, scalability, tunable replication, fault tolerance and security for Big Data applications, including financial analysis, machine learning, natural language processing, genetic algorithms, simulation and signal processing, etc. The second version of Hadoop was developed using Yet Another Resource Negotiator (YARN). YARN is a resource management framework that splits job tracker and task tracker responsibilities in MapReduce so that multiple applications can run in parallel while sharing a common cluster resource management. Hadoop clusters in new engines can scale to a much larger configuration while supporting iterative processing, stream processing, graph processing and general cluster computing. HBase and Hive are a part of the Hadoop framework, where HBase is a scalable distributed storage system and Hive a robust data warehouse platform for managing and

---

[1] Apache Hadoop official website https://hadoop.apache.org/.

querying the distributed Big Data sets. Hive comes with an SQL-like query language called HiveQL, can handle any data type without restriction and is not sufficient to handle real-time queries but outperforms its competitors on append-only type Big Data batch jobs [25].

Apache Pig

Apache Pig[2] is an integral part of the Hadoop ecosystem to reduce data analysis issues by running data streams in parallel on Hadoop. Pig is a structured query language (SQL) used by large organizations like LinkedIn, Twitter, Yahoo, etc. The scripting language for this platform is called Pig Latin, which abstracts the programming complexity in MapReduce from other languages like Java into high-level notations. Pig is a complete platform because it can call code in many languages such as JavaScript, Java, Jython, and JRuby by directly calling User Defined Functions (UDF). Therefore, developers can perform all required data manipulations in Hadoop using Pig. Pig can be used as a component with significant parallelization to build complex and heavy applications that address real business problems with their Big Data sets. Pig works with data from files, streams, structured and unstructured data using UDFs and performs the operations like select, transform or iterate and finally stores the results in HDFS [25,26].

10.6.2 Stream processing

Parallel processing of a huge amount of data can be solved via Hadoop, which can be considered a general-purpose engine. However, it is not a real-time, high-performance engine due to latency. Some streaming applications such as log file processing, machine-to-machine, sensory industry, and telematics require real-time responses to process large data streams. Streaming Big Data requires real-time analytics because Big Data has high velocity, high volume, and complex data types that must be developed. In applications that involve real-time processing, there are challenges for the Map/Reduce framework regarding the time dimension and high speed. Therefore, real-time Big Data platforms such as Spark, Storm, Flink, Kafka, Samza or Heron have been developed as the second generation for stream processing in real-time data analysis [15,36]. Real-time processing means that continuous data processing requires extremely low response latency to a large extent. This is due to the small amount of data collected in the time dimension of processing. In general, Big Data can be collected and stored in a dispersed environment, not in a single data center. Normally, in the Map/Reduce framework, the Reduce phase starts working after the Map phase. Therefore, the intermediate data generated in the Map phase is stored on disk before being passed to the Reduce. All of these results in a significant hindrance to processing. The high latency characteristics of Hadoop make it almost impossible for real-time analytics. The most common tools based on stream processing are explained in the following sections:

Spark

A more current alternative to Hadoop is Apache Spark.[3] It includes an additional component called MLlib; a library focused on machine learning algorithms like clustering, classification, regression, and even data preprocessing. Because of Spark's technological foundation, batch and streaming analytics can be

---

[2] Apache Pig official website https://pig.apache.org/.
[3] Apache Spark official website https://spark.apache.org/.

performed on the same platform. Spark was designed to overcome Hadoop's weakness of not being optimized for iterative algorithms and interactive data analytics where multiple operations are performed on the same data set. Spark is defined as the next generation distributed computing framework that can process large datasets in memory with a fast response time due to its memory-intensive scheme [30,37]. Also, it performs query processing and evaluation of Big Data, which is useful in optimizing workflows for managing huge data by developing a high-level application programming interface that significantly impacts application development productivity. Applications can request distributed processing operations such as map, reduce, and filter by passing specific closures (i.e., functions) to the Spark runtime framework. At the heart of Spark are Resilient Distributed Datasets (RDDs), which control the distribution and transformation of data across the cluster. Users define the high-level functions or additional operations over the data without strictly adhering to Map and Reduce functions. RDDs consist of a collection of data partitions distributed across multiple data nodes [33,29]. Various operations are available for transforming RDDs, such as filtering, grouping, and mapping operations. In addition, RDDs are highly customizable, allowing users to adjust partitioning for optimized data placement or preserve data in different formats and contexts. RDDs can be considered lazy because they only compute an action when they are invoked. Therefore, an application is needed to overcome this weakness. The application can be implemented as a set of actions on the RDDs. This is because when an action is executed on RDDs, a job is triggered. RDDs are a set of elements that can be run in parallel on the nodes of a cluster using two types of operations, namely transformations (Map, Filter, Union, etc.) and actions (Reduce, Collect, Count, etc.). Spark's unique features are that it is a high-level programming model for parallel processing, it has graph processing, machine learning algorithms, an API for multiple programming languages, it can run on multiple systems (Mesos, standalone, Hadoop, cluster), and it can do streaming processing. Spark is gaining popularity and replacing MapReduce as the dominant technology for Big Data application development. To solve fault tolerance in Spark, operations are interpreted in a structure called lineage. The transformations annotated in the lineage are executed only when I/O operations occur in the log. If an error occurs, Spark recalculates the affected one in the lineage log. Spark allows data to be swapped out to a local disk if storage capacity is insufficient. Spark's developers have released another high-level abstraction called data-frames, which leads to the concept of formal schema in RDDs. Moreover, the relational query plan developed by data-frames is optimized by Spark's Catalyst optimizer over the defined schema, which has led Spark to understand the data and remove the expensive Java serialization actions [33,28].

Advantages

1. Loads data once and keeps it in memory for iterative computation processes.
2. Enables distributed and parallel computations and makes computations practical and efficient by performing in-memory computations.
3. Hides complexity from developers in terms of fault tolerance, parallelism and cluster setting.
4. Suitable for SQL queries, streaming data, graph processing, machine learning (MLlib).
5. Runs on existing Hadoop clusters and can coordinate seamlessly with HDFS and HBase for data access.
6. Optimized I/O access, higher performance (up to a hundred times) and more flexible than Hadoop by utilizing main memory instead of disk.

Disadvantages

1. The reduction of computing time comes with higher compute costs than Storm.
2. Developing a stable and efficient machine learning algorithm on Spark is difficult and not easy.

Storm

Storm[4] is one of the most popular programs for stream processing in real-time analytics, focusing on assured message processing. Storm is a free and open-source distributed streaming processing environment for developing and running distributed programs that process a constant data stream. Thus, it can be said that Storm is an open-source, general-purpose, distributed, scalable, and partially fault-tolerant platform that reliably processes unlimited streams of data for real-time processing. One advantage of developing Storm is that it allows developers to focus on using a stable distributed process while delegating the complexity of distributed/parallel processing and technical challenges such as constructing a sophisticated recovery mechanism to the framework. Storm, a complex event processor and distributed computation framework, is fundamentally written in the Clojure programming language and consisting of Nimbus, Supervisor and Zookeeper. The Storm cluster mainly consists of master and worker nodes, with coordination provided by Zookeeper [38,39,34,6]. First, Nimbus in Storm distributes codes to perform parallel processing, delegates tasks to Supervisor and handles errors. Second, Supervisor assumes the role of initiating a work process to handle the topology created to process multiple events. Topology nodes fall into two categories called Spout and Bolt. The spout is an event receiver that collects streaming data or events from many sources and delivers to multiple bolts. The bolts then perform the tasks of unit logic event processors such as filtering, collecting, and merging for the event flow in the event processing network. Finally, as a coordination service for distributed applications, Zookeeper is responsible for synchronizing nodes and acts as a distributed coordinator to coordinate the system and record all situations from Nimbus and Supervisors on local disks. It supports a resurgence device against failures to ensure the fault tolerance of the framework [19,24]. The main abstraction structure of Storm is the topology. It is a top-level abstraction that describes the processing node that each message passes through. The topology is represented as a graph in which nodes represent processing components while edges represent message channels. Topology nodes are spout and bolt nodes. Spout nodes are entry points of the topology and the source of the first messages to be processed. Bolt nodes are the actual processing units that receive, process, and forward an incoming topic to the next stage in the topology. Multiple instances of a node in the topology can provide the actual parallel processing, with the storm data model represented using tuples. Each bolt node in the topology consumes and produces tuples. The tuple abstraction is universal so that any data in the topology can be passed around. In Storm, each node in the topology can exist on a different physical machine. Nimbus, the Storm controller, is responsible for distributing the tuples to the different machines and ensures that each message passes through all nodes in the topology. Nimbus also performs automatic rebalancing to balance the processing load between nodes. Storm integrates with queuing and database technologies already in use. A Storm topology consumes data streams and processes those streams in arbitrarily complex ways. However, reallocation of data streams between computation stages is required.

---

[4] Storm official website https://storm.apache.org/.

Advantages

1. Fault-tolerant, parallel, and distributed real-time computer system for very fast processing of unbounded data streams.
2. Easy to use graphical user interface.
3. Is scalable, easy to set up and operate, fault-tolerant, can be used with any programming language.
4. Guarantees processing of data prevents message loss and supports horizontal scalability.

Disadvantages

1. Does not explicitly assign different parts of the application to different physical nodes, typically required for real-time applications.
2. Lack the notion of scheduling parameters enforced in different compute nodes.

Flink

Flink[5] is a distributed processing component focused on streaming processing designed to solve problems arising from micro-batch models (e.g., Spark Streaming). Flink also supports batch data processing with programming abstractions in Scala and Java, although it is treated as a special case of streaming processing. In Flink, each job is run as a stream computation, and each task is run as a cyclic data flow with multiple iterations. Flink provides two operators for iterations, namely the standard iterator and the delta iterator. Flink works with only a single partial solution in the standard iterator, while the delta iterator uses two working sets: the next input set to be processed and the solution set. Among the advantages of iterators is the reduction of data to be computed and sent between nodes. New iterators have been developed specifically for machine learning and data mining problems. In addition to the iterators, Flink influences an optimizer that analyzes the code and data access conflicts to reorder operators and create semantically equivalent execution plans. Physical optimization is then applied to the plans to improve data transport and operator execution on the nodes. Finally, the optimizer selects the most resource-efficient plan in terms of network and memory. In addition, Flink also provides a complex fault tolerance mechanism to recover the state of data streaming applications consistently. This mechanism creates consistent snapshots of the distributed data stream and operator state. In the event of a failure, the system can fall back on these snapshots. FlinkML aims to provide Flink users with a set of scalable machine learning algorithms and an intuitive API. FlinkML has several alternatives such as Multiple Linear Regression or SVM for supervised learning, k-NN join for unsupervised learning, scalers and polynomial features for preprocessing, Alternating Least Squares for recommendation models, and other tools for validation and outlier selection in some areas of machine learning. FlinkML also allows users to build complex analysis pipelines via chaining operations (as in MLlib from Apache Spark).

Advantages

1. Support batch, stream, iterative, interactive, and graph processing in-memory computations with high-performance and low-latency data flow architecture.

---

[5] Flink official website https://flink.apache.org/.

Disadvantages

1. Flink can be difficult to understand as a beginner, as there are not many active communities and forums to share problems and doubts about Flink features.

Samza

Apache Samza[6] uses a publish/subscribe approach that observes the data stream, processes messages, and outputs its results to other streams. Samza can split a stream into multiple partitions and create a replica of the task for each partition. Apache Samza leverages the Apache Kafka messaging system, architecture, and guarantees to provide buffering, fault tolerance and state storage. Nevertheless, a Hadoop cluster is required (at least HDFS and YARN). Samza has a callback-based process messaging API and works with YARN to provide fault tolerance and migrates tasks to other machines if a node in the cluster fails. Samza processes messages in the order in which they were written and ensures that no message is lost. It is also scalable because it is partitioned and distributed at all levels.

Advantages

1. Provides replicated storage that offers reliable persistence with low latency.
2. Simple and cost-effective multisubscriber model.
3. Can eliminate backpressure so data can be persisted and processed later.

Disadvantages

1. Supports only JVM languages.
2. Does not support very low latency.
3. Does not support exact-once semantics.

Heron

Heron is a distributed stream processing framework developed at Twitter and now available as an open-source project in the Apache Incubator.[7]

Heron is similar to Apache Storm in its API, with many differences in the underlying engine architecture. Applications written in Storm can be implemented with no or minimal code changes. The goals of developing Heron are to handle petabytes of data, improve developer productivity, simplify debugging, and improve efficiency [21]. Heron consists of three main components:

1. Topology Master: It is responsible for managing a topology from submission to termination.
2. Stream Manager: It is responsible for managing the routing of tuples between topology components.
3. Heron instance: It performs a single task and allows easy debugging and profiling.

Advantages

1. Compared to Storm, Heron instance is an independent JVM process that is concise and easy to debug. Each task runs in isolation at the process level, making it easy to understand its behavior, performance, and profile. Each part can fail independently of other parts, making it easy to track,

---

[6] Apache Samza official website https://samza.apache.org/.
[7] Heron official GitHub https://github.com/twitter/heron.

isolate, and debug errors. Heron's API compatibility with Storm is good for Storm users migrating to the new system.

2. It increases performance predictability, improves developer productivity and simplifies administration. The topology in Twitter Heron uses only the distributed resources, which means it never goes over the resource limit.

3. The new implementation allows Heron to operate with higher throughput and lower latency than Storm.

4. Heron's selling point is its stability. It has been running on Twitter's processing requirements for more than a year, so it has a proven track record of reliability. Other top tech companies and other enterprises have also put Heron to the test, including numerous Fortune 500 companies.

5. One of the key differences with Heron is that the code is written in Java or Scala and the web-based user interface components are written in Python, while the code that manages topologies and network communications are written in C++.

Disadvantages

1. Although increasing throughput and reducing latency are attractive selling points for Heron; it relies on Mesos. Here, a Mesos infrastructure must first be built before Heron's benefits can be realized.

2. The downside is that Heron is not compared to anything other than Storm. Replacing Storm is good for Twitter, but there are few demonstrations of how it compares to other similar systems.

3. The current version of Heron does not implement exactly-once semantics that is critical for real-time analytics.

Kafka

Kafka[8] is an open-source distributed streaming framework that LinkedIn initially developed in 2010. It is a flexible publish-subscribe messaging system designed to be fast, scalable, and commonly used for log collection. Kafka is written in Scala and Java. It has a multiproducers management system that can salvage messages from multiple sources. For testing purposes, the streaming was emulated through a bash program by injecting transactions in Kafka at the desired rate per second. Generally, Kafka's data partitioning and retention make it a useful tool for fault-tolerant transaction collection; that is why applications can develop and subscribe to streams of records, with fault tolerance guarantees and the possibility of processing streams as they occur. Since Kafka does not use HTTP for ingestion, it delivers better performance and scale. Like other publish-subscribe messaging systems, Kafka stores streams of records in categories called topics, and each record is made up of a key-value pair with a timestamp. Kafka is a tool to cope with streaming and operational data via in-memory analytical techniques to obtain real-time decision-making. As a distributed messaging system, Kafka has four main attributes: high-throughput, persistent messaging, support for distributed processing, and parallel data load into Hadoop. It already has wide practices in several various companies as messaging tools and data pipelines. In recent years, activities and operational data play a crucial role in extracting features of websites. Activity data records different people's activities, such as webpage content, click-list, copy content, and search keywords. It is meaningful to log these activities and aggregate them for subsequent analysis. Operational data describes servers' performance, for example, CPU and IO

---

[8] Kafka official website https://kafka.apache.org/.

usage, service logs, request times, etc. The knowledge detection of operational data is beneficial for real-time operation management. Kafka combines offline and online processing to develop real-time computation and provide solutions for these two kinds of data. Kafka uses Zookeeper as a distributed coordinator and Topic consumer offset manager to keep a parallel distributed coordinated file structure for parallel low latency data access, with single write operations directed to a 'leader node'. Zookeeper is responsible for forcing data propagation down to the available nodes for distribution [11,31].

Advantages
1. Low latency, high throughput message handling and immutable activity data
2. Support very long and fast stream of data due to fast communication and distribution by using low latency techniques
3. Realize message brokers and the publish-subscribe communication

Disadvantages
1. Require a full set of coordination and management in messaging system
2. In delivering messages to the consumer, the broker in Kafka employs certain system calls, but if the messages need some tweaking, this decreases the performance of Kafka

10.7 Frameworks used in healthcare
The following frameworks were identified of using big data techniques in the context of healthcare:

MapReduce programming model on Hadoop
- Cloud computing for healthcare applications Zhang et al. (2015) [40], Lin et al. (2015) [23]
- Statistical analysis (Linear regression) for health and medical care Batarseh and Latif (2016) [10]
- ML (C-means clustering, fuzzy clustering) for health and government sector Tripathy and Mittal (2016) [32]
- ML (Sequential learning) for health and economic sector Wang et al. (2015) [35]
- ML (item-set mining algorithm) for health and government sector Apiletti et al. (2017) [7]
- ML (Sequential learning) on health and economic data Huang et al. (2016) [18]
- ML (support vector machine) on health and economic data Kumar and Rath [22] (2015)

Hadoop (HBase, Hive) + Pig
- ML (Stochastic gradient descent algorithm + logistic regression) for health and medical care Manogaran et al. (2017) [26]

Spark
- ML (Fuzzy rule-based classifiers) for health and economic sector Ferranti et al. (2017) [15]
- ML (Decision tree algorithm) for health and medical care Nair et al. (2017) [27]
- ML (Bayesian Network Classifiers) + Cloud Computing for health and economic sector Arias et al. (2017) [8]
- ML (Kernel function) for health and medical care Nguyen et al. (2017) [29]

- Semantic network analysis for social networking and internet + health and medical care Guo et al. (2017) [17], Chen et al. (2017) [12]

Storm
- Semantic network analysis for government and public sector + social networking and internet Basanta-Val et al. (2017) [9], Um et al. (2016) [34], Agerri et al. (2015) [6]

Hadoop + Spark
- ML (New functional networks classifier) for health and medical care Elsebakhi et al. (2015) [14]

10.8 Key features

In this chapter we have presented and analyzed state of the art, open source platforms for Big Data stream processing. These platforms (Kafka, Flink, Storm and others) have shown their usefulness for data stream processing and address the demanding requirements of stream processing.

- ☑ Proposal of practical course of action to process IoT health data in a scalable IoT architecture by evaluating different implementation decisions based on the research fields of data processing, data enrichment and (semantic-) CEP.
- ☑ Definition of requirements to the proposed IoT stream architecture.
- ☑ Overview of other processing frameworks in the fields of Batch and Stream processing with their special characteristics, advantages and disadvantages.
- ☑ In-depth introduction to Kafka Processing Architecture in combination with the Kafka Streams CEP Engine.
- ☑ Other similar platforms are analyzed in terms of advantages and limitations.

References

[1] Kafka 2.3 documentation, https://kafka.apache.org/documentation/. (Accessed 5 September 2019).
[2] Kafka streams, https://kafka.apache.org/documentation/streams/. (Accessed 5 September 2019).
[3] MQTT org website, http://mqtt.org/.
[4] Rocksdb website, https://rocksdb.org/.
[5] World health organisation cardiovascular diseases (CVDs), https://www.who.int/news-room/fact-sheets/detail/cardiovascular-diseases-(cvds). (Accessed 2 September 2019).
[6] R. Agerri, X. Artola, Z. Beloki, G. Rigau, A. Soroa, Big data for natural language processing: a streaming approach, Knowledge-Based Systems 79 (2015) 36–42.
[7] D. Apiletti, E. Baralis, T. Cerquitelli, P. Garza, F. Pulvirenti, P. Michiardi, A parallel mapreduce algorithm to efficiently support itemset mining on high dimensional data, Big Data Research 10 (2017) 53–69.
[8] J. Arias, J.A. Gámez, J.M. Puerta, Learning distributed discrete Bayesian network classifiers under mapreduce with apache spark, Knowledge-Based Systems 117 (2017) 16–26.
[9] P. Basanta-Val, N.F. García, A. Wellings, N. Audsley, Improving the predictability of distributed stream processors, Future Generations Computer Systems 52 (2015) 22–36.
[10] F.A. Batarseh, E.A. Latif, Assessing the quality of service using big data analytics: with application to healthcare, Big Data Research 4 (2016) 13–24.

[11] A. Castiglione, F. Colace, V. Moscato, F. Palmieri, CHIS: a big data infrastructure to manage digital cultural items, Future Generations Computer Systems 86 (2018) 1134–1145.

[12] Y. Chen, N. Crespi, A.M. Ortiz, L. Shu, Reality mining: a prediction algorithm for disease dynamics based on mobile big data, Information Sciences 379 (2017) 82–93.

[13] M. Elkano, M. Galar, J. Sanz, H. Bustince, CHI-BD: a fuzzy rule-based classification system for big data classification problems, Fuzzy Sets and Systems 348 (2018) 75–101.

[14] E. Elsebakhi, F. Lee, E.R. Schendel, A. Haque, N. Kathiresan, T. Pathare, N. Syed, R. Al-Ali, Large-scale machine learning based on functional networks for biomedical big data with high performance computing platforms, Journal of Computational Science 11 (2015) 69–81.

[15] A. Ferranti, F. Marcelloni, A. Segatori, M. Antonelli, P. Ducange, A distributed approach to multi-objective evolutionary generation of fuzzy rule-based classifiers from big data, Information Sciences 415 (2017) 319–340.

[16] R. Genuer, J.-M. Poggi, C. Tuleau-Malot, N. Villa-Vialaneix, Random forests for big data, Big Data Research 9 (2017) 28–46.

[17] J. Guo, B. Song, F. Yu, Z. Yan, L.T. Yang, Object detection among multimedia big data in the compressive measurement domain under mobile distributed architecture, Future Generations Computer Systems 76 (2017) 519–527.

[18] S. Huang, B. Wang, J. Qiu, J. Yao, G. Wang, G. Yu, Parallel ensemble of online sequential extreme learning machine based on mapreduce, Neurocomputing 174 (2016) 352–367.

[19] P. Karunaratne, S. Karunasekera, A. Harwood, Distributed stream clustering using micro-clusters on apache storm, Journal of Parallel and Distributed Computing 108 (2017) 74–84.

[20] J. Kranjc, R. Orac, V. Podpecan, N. Lavrac, M. Robnik-Sikonja, ClowdFlows: online workflows for distributed big data mining, Future Generations Computer Systems 68 (2017) 38–58.

[21] S. Kulkarni, N. Bhagat, M. Fu, V. Kedigehalli, C. Kellogg, S. Mittal, J. Patel, K. Ramasamy, S. Taneja, Twitter heron: stream processing at scale, in: Proceedings of the 2015 ACM SIGMOD International Conference on Management of Data, 2015.

[22] M. Kumar, S.K. Rath, Classification of microarray using mapreduce based proximal support vector machine classifier, Knowledge-Based Systems 89 (2015) 584–602.

[23] W. Lin, W. Dou, Z. Zhou, C. Liu, A cloud-based framework for home-diagnosis service over big medical data, The Journal of Systems and Software 102 (2015) 192–206.

[24] C.D. Maio, G. Fenza, V. Loia, F. Orciuoli, Distributed online temporal fuzzy concept analysis for stream processing in smart cities, Journal of Parallel and Distributed Computing 110 (2017) 31–41.

[25] G. Manco, E. Ritacco, P. Rullo, L. Gallucci, W. Astill, D. Kimber, M. Antonelli, Fault detection and explanation through big data analysis on sensor streams, Expert Systems with Applications 87 (2017) 141–156.

[26] G. Manogaran, R. Varatharajan, D. Lopez, P.M. Kumar, R. Sundarasekar, C. Thota, A new architecture of internet of things and big data ecosystem for secured smart healthcare monitoring and alerting system, Future Generations Computer Systems 82 (2018) 375–387.

[27] L.R. Nair, S. Shetty, S.D. Shetty, Applying spark based machine learning model on streaming big data for health status prediction, Computers & Electrical Engineering 65 (2018) 393–399.

[28] P. Nghiem, S. Figueira, Towards efficient resource provisioning in mapreduce, Journal of Parallel and Distributed Computing 95 (2016) 29–41.

[29] T. Nguyen, M. Larsen, B. O'Dea, D. Nguyen, J. Yearwood, D.Q. Phung, S. Venkatesh, H. Christensen, Kernel-based features for predicting population health indices from geocoded social media data, Decision Support Systems 102 (2017) 22–31.

[30] L. Oneto, E. Fumeo, G. Clerico, R. Canepa, F. Papa, C. Dambra, N. Mazzino, D. Anguita, Train delay prediction systems: a big data analytics perspective, Big Data Research 11 (2018) 54–64.

[31] M. Tennant, F. Stahl, O. Rana, J. Gomes, Scalable real-time classification of data streams with concept drift, Future Generations Computer Systems 75 (2017) 187–199.

[32] B. Tripathy, D. Mittal, Hadoop based uncertain possibilistic kernelized c-means algorithms for image segmentation and a comparative analysis, Applied Soft Computing 46 (2016) 886–923.

[33] C.-W. Tsai, S. Liu, Y. Wang, A parallel metaheuristic data clustering framework for cloud, Journal of Parallel and Distributed Computing 116 (2018) 39–49.

[34] J.-H. Um, S. Lee, T. Kim, C.-H. Jeong, S.-K. Song, H. Jung, Semantic complex event processing model for reasoning research activities, Neurocomputing 209 (2016) 39–45.

[35] B. Wang, S. Huang, J. Qiu, Y. Liu, G. Wang, Parallel online sequential extreme learning machine based on mapreduce, Neurocomputing 149 (2015) 224–232.

[36] H. Wang, A. Belhassena, Parallel trajectory search based on distributed index, Information Sciences 388 (2017) 62–83.

[37] H. Wang, Z. Xu, H. Fujita, S. Liu, Towards felicitous decision making: an overview on challenges and trends of big data, Information Sciences 367–368 (2016) 747–765.

[38] J. Wang, C. He, Y. Liu, G. Tian, I. Peng, J. Xing, X. Ruan, H. Xie, F.L. Wang, Efficient alarm behavior analytics for telecom networks, Information Sciences 402 (2017) 1–14.

[39] Y. Wang, S. Geng, H. Gao, A proactive decision support method based on deep reinforcement learning and state partition, Knowledge-Based Systems 143 (2018) 248–258.

[40] F. Zhang, J. Cao, S. Khan, K. Li, K. Hwang, A task-level adaptive mapreduce framework for real-time streaming data in healthcare applications, Future Generations Computer Systems 43–44 (2015) 149–160.

Technical design: data processing pipeline in eHealth

The case of ECG data sets

11.1 Medical background of ECG data

This section gives an overview of heart diseases that can be commonly detected from the ECG signal. The ECG morphology reflects the heart status [51]. In general, ECG provides two primary types of information. First, by measuring time intervals on ECG, a cardiologist can determine how long the electrical wave takes to pass through the heart's electrical conduction system. This information helps to find out if the electrical activity is regular or irregular, fast or slow. Second, by measuring the strength of electrical activity, a cardiologist can find out if parts of the heart are too large or are overworked. A normal ECG heartbeat includes three important waves of atrial depolarization (P-wave), ventral depolarization (QRS complex wave), and repolarization (T-wave). Any disorder in the electrical activity of neural heart cells affects ECG signals, known as arrhythmia. The most common types of arrhythmia are briefly described in the following sequels:

Atrial Fibrillation (AF)

AF occurs when action potentials fire rapidly within the atrium, resulting in a rapid atrial rate (roughly 400–600 beats/minute).

Right Bundle Branch Block (RBBB) and Left Bundle Branch Block (LBBB)

Bundle Branch Block is an interruption in the regular conduction system that leads to abnormal QRS morphology. Typically, the right bundle depolarizes the Right Ventricle (RV). In an RBBB, the right bundle does not activate. The right ventricle is instead depolarized by spreading the impulse from the left bundle through the Left Ventricle (LV) and then to the RV. This pattern of electrical spread creates an aberrant QRS morphology. Typically, the left bundle depolarizes the LV. In an LBBB, the left bundle does not activate. The LV is instead depolarized by the spread of impulse from the right bundle through the RV and then to the LV. This pattern of electrical spread creates an aberrant QRS morphology [75].

Premature Atrial Contraction (PAC) and Premature Ventricular Contraction (PVC)

PAC and PVC occur when the heart's regular rhythm is interrupted by a premature or early beat. If the premature beat arises from the atria, it is called a PAC, while if it arises from the ventricles, it is called PVC.

Ectopic beats

Ectopic atrial rhythms happen when a site outside of the sinus node within the atria creates action potentials faster than the sinus node (with an atrial rate of fewer than 100 beats/minute). Since this electrical activity does not originate from the sinus node, the P wave would not have its normal sinus appearance. Ectopic beats are also frequent during periods of stress or exercise, and they may happen by consuming specific foods such as alcohol.

Myocardial Infarction (MI)

MI happens when blood flow decreases or stops in a part of the heart, causing permanent damage to the heart muscle or arteries. Some of the MI patterns include the two below groups:

- ST segment elevation or new RBBB/LBBB.
- ST segment depression or T-wave inversion.

Fusion beat

A fusion beat happens when electrical impulses from different sources simultaneously act upon the same region of the heart. For example, it is called a Ventricular Fusion Beats (VFB) if it acts upon the ventricular chambers, whereas colliding currents in the atrial chambers produce Atrial Fusion Beats (AFB) [27,43].

Sinus bradycardia

Sinus bradycardia is a sinus rhythm with a lower than normal rate (fewer than 60 beats per minute). The decreased heart rate causes decreased cardiac output, resulting in light-headedness, dizziness, hypotension, vertigo, and syncope [94].

Tachycardia

Tachycardia happens when the heart rate exceeds the normal resting rate (so-called tachyarrhythmia). Generally, a resting heart rate over 100 beats per minute in adults is accepted as tachycardia [13]. Types of tachycardias are including:

- Atrial or Supraventricular Tachycardia (SVT): A fast heart rate staring in the upper heart chambers.
- Sinus Tachycardia: happens when the heart sends out electrical signals faster than usual, leading to a normal increase in the heart rate.
- Ventricular Tachycardia (VT): is a series of more than three abnormal consecutive QRS complex heart rhythms with a duration beyond 120 ms and the ST-T vector that points opposite the QRS deflection [16].

Atrial Flutter (AFL)

AFL is a prevalent abnormal heart rhythm that starts in the atrial chambers of the heart [64,86]. When it first occurs, it is usually associated with a fast heart rate and is classified as a type of SVT.

Ventricular Flutter (VF)

It is an unstable arrhythmia in which a tachycardia affecting the ventricles with a rate of over 150–300 beats per minute. VF is a possible transition stage between VT and fibrillation that can cause sudden cardiac death [16]. A sinusoidal waveform characterizes it without a clear definition of the T-waves and QRS.

Ventricular fibrillation

VFib is a cardiac arrhythmia in which the heart quivers instead of pumping due to disorganized electrical activity in the ventricles characterized by showing irregular unformed QRS complexes without any clear P-waves [14]. VFib results in cardiac arrest with loss of consciousness followed by death in the absence of treatment [14].

Idioventricular rhythm

An idioventricular rhythm is highly similar to VT but with a ventricular rate of fewer than 60 beats per minute. Therefore, the idioventricular rhythm is referred to as a slow ventricular tachycardia.

Ventricular bigeminy

Ventricular Bigeminy is an abnormal cardiac rhythm problem in which there are repeated rhythms heartbeats that each sinus beat is followed by an ectopic beat and pause frequently.

Pacemaker rhythm

Pacemaker clinical syndrome representing the consequences of pacemaker implantation, regardless of the pacing mode, due to suboptimal atrioventricular synchrony or dyssynchrony [20]. It is an iatrogenic disease resulting from medical treatment [33]. Individuals with a low heart rate before pacemaker implantation are more at risk of developing pacemaker syndrome. Patients who develop pacemaker syndrome may require pacemaker adjustment or fitting of another lead for better coordinating the timing of atrial and ventricular contraction.

11.2 ECG data sets

Given the importance of ECG data, there have been conducted numerous experiments and studies to build and use such data sets for medical purposes of heart diseases. There is a variety of data sets presented in the literature, from diverse research groups, and in different data formats, making ECG data sets one of most used in medicine. It should be also noted that the availability of ECG data sets in the literature has set benchmarking and state of the art results that allow researchers to advance the state of the art in the field.

In the following Table 11.1, we summarize the most relevant ECG data sets together with a brief information on number of recordings, data sampling and diseases targeted by each case.

11.3 Dataset used in the case study

For the purpose of showing the working principles of designing a data processing pipeline, we have selected the PhysioNet MIT-BIH arrhythmia dataset, which consists of labeled ECG recordings [72]. The MIT-BIH dataset comprises ECG recordings from 47 different subjects, each containing two-channel 30-minute ECG recordings. The original recordings were digitized at a frequency of 360 per channel and a resolution of 11 bits over a range of 10 mV. Each beat was annotated by at least two cardiologists.

Table 11.1 Popular ECG databases.

Database Name	Number of Recordings	Data Sampling Information	Included Disease
ECG Images dataset of Cardiac and COVID-19 Patients [52]	250 COVID-19 Patients; 859 Normal Person ECG Images; 77 Myocardial Infarction Patient; 203 Patients with Previous History of Myocardial Infarction; 548 Patients with Abnormal Heartbeat	12 Leads based ECG Images Data is collected from EDAN SERIES - 3 devices of 500 Hz sampling rate.	COVID-19, Abnormal Heartbeat, Myocardial Infarction (MI), Previous History of MI, and Normal Person
PhysioNet/ Computing in Cardiology Challenge [36]	Length: between 30 s and 60 s, total of 12,186 ECGs were used: 8528 in the public training set and 3658 in the private hidden test set	Digitized in real-time at 44.1 kHz and 24-bit resolution	NSR AF
The DNNIH Arrhythmia Database (MITDB) (Obtained between 1975 and 1979) [36]	48 half-hour excerpts of two-channel ambulatory ECG recordings, obtained from 47 subjects. The subjects were 25 men aged 32 to 89 years, and 22 women aged 23 to 89 years, Twenty-three recordings were chosen at random from a set of 4000 24-hour ambulatory ECG recordings collected from a mixed population of inpatients (about 60%) and outpatients (about 40%)	Digitized at 360 samples per second per channel with 11-bit resolution over a 10 mV range	Complex Ventricular, Supraventricular Arrhythmias Conduction Abnormalities
Physikalisch-Technische Bundesanstalt (PTB) [36]	549 records from 290 subjects (aged 17 to 87, mean 57.2; 209 men, mean age 55.5, and 81 women, mean age 61.6)	Digitized at 1000 samples per second, with 16 bit resolution over a range of $\pm$ 16.384 mV. Resolution: 16 bit with 0.5 V/LSB (2000 A/D units per mV)	MI
MIT-BIH Supraventricular Arrhythmia Database (SVDB) [36]	78 two-lead recordings of approximately 30 minutes	Digitized at 128 Hz	VEB SVEB
PhysioNet, the ECG-ID Database [36]	310 ECG recordings, obtained from 90 persons	20 seconds, digitized at 500 Hz with 12-bit resolution over a nominal $\pm$ 10 mV range	NSR AF
The MIT-BIH Atrial Fibrillation Database (MIT-BIHAF) [36]	25 long-term ECG recordings of human subjects with atrial fibrillation (mostly paroxysmal)	ECG signals each sampled at 250 samples per second with 12-bit resolution over a range of $\pm$ 10 millivolts.	NSR AF
Creighton University VT Database (CUDB) [36]	35 eight-minute ECG recordings of human subjects	Digitized at 250 Hz with 12-bit resolution over a 10 V range (10 mV nominal relative to the unamplified signals). Each record contains 127,232 samples (slightly less than 8.5 minutes).	Sustained VT VFVFib

continued on next page

Table 11.1 (*continued*)

Database Name	Number of Recordings	Data Sampling Information	Included Disease
The MIT-BIH Malignant Ventricular Arrhythmia Database (VFDB) [36]	22 half-hour ECG recordings	Digitized at 250 Hz	Sustained VT VF VFib
The UCI cardiac arrhythmia [12]	Number of Instances: 452 Number of Attributes:279	-	NSR Old Inferior MI Sinus Bradycardia RBBB
Long Term ST Database (LTSTDB).	Contains 86 lengthy ECG recordings of 80 human subjects	Digitized at 250 samples per second with 12-bit resolution over a range of $\pm$ 10 millivolts.	NSR SVEB VEB
CinC Challenge 2000 Datasets [36]	70 records	16 bits per sample, least significant byte first in each pair, 100 samples per second, nominally 200 A/D units per mV	Sleep Apnea NSR
E-HOL-03-0202-003 (Intercity Digital Electrocardiogram Alliance'IDEAL) Database [36]	202 healthy subjects 24 h Holter recordings	Sampling Frequency: 200 Hz Amplitude Resolution: 10 microV	Healthy ECG signal
The PAF Prediction Challenge Database [36]	50 record sets come from 48 different subjects	Digitized ECGs (16 bits per sample, 128 samples per signal per second, samples from each channel alternating, nominally 200 A/D units per mV).	PAF
St.-Petersburg Institute of Cardiological Technics 12-lead Arrhythmia Database (NCART) [36]	75 annotated recordings extracted from 32 Holter records. Each record is 30 minutes long and contains 12 standard leads	Each sampled at 257 Hz, with gains varying from 250 to 1100 analog-to-digital converter units per mV.	Acute MI Prior MI Coronary Artery Disease with Hypertension Sinus Node Dysfunction Supraventricular ectopy WPW AF Bundle Branch Block
Fantasia Database-PhysioBank [36]	20 young (21 - 34 years old) and 20 elderly (68 - 85 years old) rigorously-screened healthy subjects underwent 120 minutes of continuous supine resting	Digitized at 250 Hz. Each heartbeat was annotated using an automated arrhythmia detection algorithm	Normal Sinus Rhythm while watching a Fantasia movie
The MIT-BIH Normal Sinus Rhythm (NSR) Database [36]	18 long-term ECG recordings of subjects, 5 men, aged 26 to 45, and 13 women, aged 20 to 50	-	Normal Sinus Rhythm (NSR)
BIDMC PPG and Respiration Dataset [36]	The 53 recordings within the dataset, each of 8-minute duration	Sampled at 125 Hz	-

The annotations in this dataset are structured into five different beat categories following the Association for the Advancement of Medical Instrumentation (AAMI) EC57 standard. The following overview shows the AAMI class with the associated MIT-BIH heartbeat types:

- N: Normal beat (N), Left bundle branch block beat (L), Right bundle branch block beat (R), Atrial escape beat (e), Nodal (junctional) escape beat (j)
- S: Atrial premature beat (A), Aberrated atrial premature beat (a), Nodal (junctional) premature beat (J), Supraventricular premature beat (S)
- V: Premature ventricular contraction (V), Ventricular escape beat (E)
- F: Fusion of ventricular and normal beat (F)
- Q: Paced beat (/), Fusion of paced and normal beat (f), Unclassified beat (Q)

For the data set used in this case study, each signal should be labeled as one of the classes ("Normal," "Premature atrial," "Premature ventricular contraction," "Fusion of ventricular and normal," "Fusion of paced and normal").

11.3.1 Class imbalance

Class imbalance refers to the nonuniformity in the class distribution, which means that there are many examples in one class and few in other classes [46]. The problem of class imbalance is an important one that occurs in many domains, e.g., medical diagnosis [23], bioinformatics [83], text classification [96] and others. It affects the performance of standard learning algorithms, which require a balanced distribution of classes [46].

There are several approaches to dealing with the class imbalance problem: data-level (modify the distribution of training set to restore balance by adding or removing instances from the training dataset), algorithm-level (change the objective function of the classifier to increase the importance of the minority class), and hybrid methods (combine algorithm level methods with data level approaches).

In the following, five different methods are briefly explained:

1. Re-sampling (data-level)
2. Synthetic minority oversampling technique (SMOTE) (data-level)
3. Distribution based data sampling (data-level)
4. AdaBoost ensemble classifier (hybrid-level)
5. GAN-Synthesis (hybrid-level)

Re-sampling

Re-sampling is a widely used method for balancing class distributions. It modifies class distributions by two well-known strategies called random oversampling and random under-sampling [81]. Re-sampling is a widely used method for balancing class distributions. It changes the class distributions by using two well-known strategies called random oversampling and random under-sampling [81].

- Random oversampling - It increases the number of instances in the minority class by randomly replicating the instances of the same class.
- Random under-sampling - It generates a random subsample of instances of the majority class.

SMOTE

SMOTE is a popular oversampling method [21]. The main goal of this approach is to create "synthetic" minority samples instead of duplicating samples. SMOTE synthetically creates new minority instances between existing instances. The newly created instances are not simply a copy of the existing minority instances, but the algorithm takes a sample of the feature space for each target class and its neighbors

Table 11.2 GAN-synthesis results over each beat type of the MIT-BIH data set used for training and evaluating the classification model.

Beat Type	Unbalanced	Balanced
N	90,589	90,589
S	2779	**5121**
V	7236	7236
F	803	**2237**
Q	8039	8039

and then creates new instances that combine the features of the target instances with the features of their neighbors.

Distribution based data sampling

Imbalanced datasets suffer greatly from class oversampling and disjunctions. This problem is referred to as "interclass imbalance". This problem is addressed by preprocessing using distribution-based balancing [15]. The steps are:

1. Find the prior probability distribution of all features of the given class labels.
2. Sample new instances of each class with the prior probability distribution knowledge.

AdaBoost ensemble classifier

Ensemble classifiers have played a predominant role in machine learning algorithms. In particular, these classifiers are used to address the problem of class imbalance in various applications [76,34]. The main goal of an ensemble classifier is to reduce the misclassification rate (error rate) of a weak classifier by aggregating multiple classifiers. The basic idea is to obtain predictions of multiple classifiers on the original data and combine the different predictions to make a strong classifier. The main strategies in ensemble classifiers are bootstrap aggregation (bagging) [17] and boosting [87]. The decision tree-based learners are widely used. The Ada-Bost algorithm was developed by Freund [32].

GAN synthesis

Using GANs can increase the sample size for training instances for labeled data and solve privacy issues. Access to medical data is severely limited due to its sensitive nature, which prevents communities from using these data for research or clinical training. Other research [29,35] explored the ability of generative adversarial networks (GANs) to produce realistic medical time-series data that can be used without privacy concerns and what can also be used to solve class imbalance issues. The goal is to generate synthetic ECG signals that are representative of ECG waveforms. GANs have been successfully used to generate synthetic time series of good quality and have been shown to prevent the re-identification of individual datasets.

The balancing result on the data set used in this case study had the results shown in Table 11.2. As can be seen, the synthetic instances are created of the minority classes, which later helps improve the classifier performance.

11.4 Pipeline: preprocessing module

For the design of pipeline for the processing the ECG data, and of any other health data stream, the following issues need to be addressed:

1. Where to process data and how to make it scale: If the data processing step has the output result of reducing the overhead over the digital eco-system, the goal should be to put that processing step as close as possible to the source. Possible limitations in such a scenario can be the computing power or memory resources on the IoT device or edge computing nodes. Reliability could be affected by putting too high and fluctuating loads on devices, leading to an overload in the processing. In some scenarios, the battery life optimization is critical, where the processing power should be kept as low as possible.

2. Some processing steps might be based on semantically enriched data inference, which contains the linking of static data that can be subject to specific data protection laws. As a result, personal data cannot be shared with end devices or the end device data can not be shared with a cloud system.

3. In a scalable processing architecture with parallel worker nodes, stream elements could be processed on different worker nodes, and time-series correlation could be lost. A possible solution is to assign data streams on dedicated worker nodes. Another way would be to structure the processing so that it would be decoupled from the time series.

4. There are limitations on message size along the processing pipeline. For example, MQTT has the limitations of the length of the actual topic string at most 65,536 bytes, and the payload of the message is limited to 268,435,456 bytes [1]. The message size needs to be evaluated so that the message processing can be handled at later processing nodes of the following systems (Kafka, Faust), or a reduction of the data size needs to be considered.

As an initial edge preprocessing step, the standardization and normalization of the ECG data stream were conducted. Only standardized data was feed into the Kafka message broker and guaranteed consumers that the data contain identical data and semantic structure.

The heterogeneity of IoT devices is a primary challenge in IoT systems. Different ECG devices can be clocked on different frequencies. The initial step was to sample the raw data streams on 180-hertz frequency, which contains downsampling for higher and upsampling for lower frequencies. The high-frequency noise filter is the second computation step to retrieve a smooth ECG stream. As a final processing step, the data has been normalized on a scale of 0-1. The resulting standardized data stream can now be processed in the pipeline with different heterogeneous IoT devices.

11.4.1 Denoising approaches review

ECG signals can be distorted by many other artifacts that have nothing to do with cardiac functions. ECG artifacts take various and uncertain forms. Some physiological artifacts could mimic true cardiac arrhythmias, leading to incorrect diagnoses [38]. Hence, noise removal is a necessary step for abnormality detection in ECGs.

These noise artifacts can be of the type of nonphysiological or physiological. The first group is caused by equipment problems, such as network disturbances, and the other group is caused by muscle activity, skin disturbances, or body motion, electromyogram, and motion artifacts. Among all artifacts, motion artifacts are the most difficult noise to remove because the noise spectrum overlaps the ECG signal [91].

Conventional methods used for noise removal in ECG signals comprise the following.

Digital low-pass, high-pass, band-pass, and notch filters

A first approach is to use digital low-pass, high-pass, band-pass, and notch filters to remove noise. Many studies, such as [25,22,93,89,79] use a mix of low-pass and high-pass filters to remove the noise in an ECG signal. The low-pass filter's cutoff frequency ranges from 11 Hz to 45 Hz and mainly suppresses the high-frequency noise. The high-pass filter's cutoff frequency ranges from 1 Hz to 2.2 Hz and focuses on removing baseline wander in the signal.

In [25], notch filters are in the range of 50 Hz to 60 Hz and are used to remove power line noise. Band-pass filters with cutoff frequencies from 0.1 to 100 Hz are used by [54] to remove the noisy components of electronic noise. The advantage of using a fixed digital filter is that it is easy to implement and very efficient.

Discrete Wavelet Transform (DWT)

A second approach uses a discrete wavelet transform (DWT) to remove the noise components from a signal. The wavelet transform is a powerful method for analyzing nonstationary signals, such as ECGs [95]. The DWT noise removal method is used in [66,85,2]. In this method, the signal is decomposed into the approximation and detail coefficients using a wavelet function. The selection of the wavelet function is the most important task, which depends on the nature of the signal [84]. The most commonly used mother wavelet basis functions are Daubechies filter (Db), Symmlet filter (Sym), Coiflet filter (C), Battle-Lemarie filter (Bt), Beylkin filter (Bl), and Vaidyanathan filter (Vd) [88].

According to other studies [84,88,63], the 4th and 8th order Daubechies filters and 5th and 6th order Symmlet filters are the best wavelet functions for ECG signal analysis due to their similar signal structure to the QRS complex. After decomposing the ECG signal, a thresholding method is applied to the DWT coefficients. A clean ECG signal can be reconstructed from the thresholded DWT coefficients.

11.5 Pipeline: core-processing module

For this case study, the Hierarchical Temporal Memory (HTM) algorithm was used to find anomalous segments on the standardized ECG data stream. Anomalous segments are forwarded for storage inside the Kafka cluster for further processing by consumers. Topic-specific worker nodes will now be able to process the anomalous segments.

A recent study [57] applying a set of real-time anomaly detection methods (Twitter ADVec, Etsy Skyline, Random, and HTM) showed that HTM achieves the best overall results. Another study in the same line [6] showed that HTM leads in reducing false positives and true negatives. Therefore, HTM anomaly detection algorithm proves to be a promising real-time anomaly detection algorithm [5]. The complexity of the HTM anomaly detection algorithm is equal to $O(n \log n)$, where n is the number of records, so HTM is an efficient algorithm. The execution time depends on the number of columns, cells per column, and segments per cell for Temporal Memory and the potential pool size for Spatial Pooling. Regardless of the parameters, the time-per-record converges to a constant value when the algorithm reaches the upper bounds.

Evaluation of HTM and other unsupervised online algorithms

We summarize in Table 11.3 comparison of different unsupervised online algorithms according to various criteria.

The HTM has slightly higher detection latency compared to other algorithms (except Random Cut Forest). The reason behind this is that the HTM has a slightly higher time complexity (as can be seen from Table 11.3) than others because of its sequence learning capability in the complex sequential memory.

Table 11.3 Comparison among state-of-the-art real-time anomaly detection algorithms. The presented algorithms all are executed in an online unsupervised manner and are able to detect spatial anomalies. Notation: n = set size; w = sparsity; D = dimension; L1 = Manhattan distance; (u, v)⊂n.

Methods	Noise Immunity	Multistep prediction	Temporal Anomaly	Nonparametric	Time Complexity
HTM	yes	yes	yes	yes	$O(n \log n)$
Random Cut Forest	-	-	-	-	$D \log \frac{|x|}{L_1(u,v)}$
Bayesian Changepoint	yes	-	-	-	$O(n)$
Relative Entropy	yes	-	yes	yes	$O(n^2), a < 3$
EXPosE	yes	-	yes	yes	$O(n)$

From the anomalous segment to the extracted signal

The signal extraction in this study was based on the following step-wise approach:

1. Splitting the continuous ECG signal to 5 s windows and select a 5 s window from an ECG signal.
2. Amplitude normalization between the range between 0 and 1.
3. Determine the set of local maximums based on zero-crossings of the first derivative.
4. Determine the set of R-peaks candidates by applying a threshold of 0.9 on the normalized value of the local maximums. Experiments showed that the threshold could be between 0.85-0.92 for the R-peak detection.
5. Determine the median of R-R time intervals as the nominal heartbeat period of that window (T).
6. For each R-peak, selecting a signal part with a length equal to 1.2T. With this value, it should be assured that all beats are completely extracted.
7. Padding each selected part with zeros to m.
8. Send signal for classification.

Signal extraction algorithm

The algorithm is outlines as follows.

```
Input: is (Input segment received by anomaly detection)
Output: Signals (n signals extracted of input-segment
Initialize
previous=0

while worker online:
```

```
is_norm=(is_s-min(is_s))/(max(is_s)-min(is_s))
is_grad=gradient(is_norm)
    zero_crossing=zero_crossing(is_grad)
    peaks_index=is_norm[zero_crossing]>=0.9
    for peak in peaks_index
        peak_distances<-(peak-previous)
        previous=peak
    median_length=median(peak_distances)
    segment_length=median_length*1.2
    for signal in peaks_distances
        signal=is_norm[signal_index:(signal + median_length)]
        signal=fillup_zeros(signal, segment_length)
```

This approach is a very basic method to extract signals. More advanced methods are already proposed by other researchers and were not considered here.

Other segmentation methods

Measurements used by cardiologists to detect pathological beats and heart disease are based on features such as heart rate variability and different intervals or segments between waves of successive beats. For this purpose, it is imperative to accurately determine the onset/offset of a beat and the peak positions of the P, Q, R, S, and T waves of each ECG. However, ECG segmentation and finding the onset and offset of ECG waves are difficult tasks because there is no precise definition for the onset and offset of some ECG waves.

Traditional arrhythmia detection methods extract hand-crafted features from ECG data, such as R-R intervals [28,71], ECG morphology [28], or frequency [69]. These features are used for beat segmentation and classifiers such as linear discriminant analysis models [28], support vector machines [71], and random forests [8] are then built on these features. Beat segment detection also helps create individual beat images used as input to algorithms such as Convolutional Neural Network (CNN), as in this case study.

The following methods describe common segmentation approaches for providing information for detecting the onset of a heartbeat:

I. Christov

Christov [24] proposes an algorithm for detecting the QRS complex via the following steps:

1. Handling of powerline interference by applying a moving average filter
2. Moving average filter for suppression of electromyogram noise
3. complex lead synthesis (built with all lead)
4. complex lead signal is sampled, and each sample is evaluated with an adaptive threshold value
5. Detection occurs when the threshold is exceeded

The adaptive threshold is a linear combination of a steep-slope threshold (M), an integrating threshold (F), and a beat expectation threshold (R). Details on the various filters, complex lead, and threshold formulas can be found in [24].

Engelse and Zeelenberg

The algorithm of Engelse and Zeelenberg [67] (EZEEMod), has the following steps:

1. A differentiator is used on the original signal (X)
2. Low-pass filter the resulting differentiated signal in order to retrieve the signal Y
3. Scan Y and evaluate whether an adaptive threshold (A) is exceeded: if yes, step 4 is executed; otherwise, continue with step 5
4. Define a 160 ms window to the right of the intersection of the Y signal with Threshold A. Check if condition Y smaller than Threshold B holds for at least 10 consecutive milliseconds. If yes, an R peak was found, and it corresponds to the maximum value of the original X signal within the defined window
5. Update the thresholds
6. Move back to step 3 and look for a new intersection

The thresholds are adaptively updated each time and are a function of the maximum signal amplitude. In addition, the algorithm ignores peaks within a 200 ms interval of the previously detected R-peak.

P. Hamilton

In [37], Hamilton proposed an algorithm for detecting the QRS complex that works by scanning the ECG signal and evaluating the following set of rules:

1. ignore peaks that precede or succeed large r-peaks by less than 200 ms
2. if the peak is higher than the detection threshold, it is a QRS complex, otherwise noise
3. If a window equal to 1.5 times the average R-to-R interval has passed since the last detection, a peak greater than half the detection threshold occurred within that interval, and the peak being at least 360 ms after the previous detection, classify that peak as a QRS complex
4. The detection threshold is a function of average noise and average QRS peak values
5. The average noise peak, average QRS peak, and average R-to-R interval estimates are computed as the mean/average of the last eight values

H. Gamboa

H. Gamboa [65] proposed an algorithm that includes signal normalization and derivative calculation. It follows these steps:

1. ECG signal normalization via histogram calculation and threshold setting
2. R-peak detection via ECG signal derivation and threshold crossing
3. Validation of detected R-peaks considering heart rate in the range of 20-200 beats per minute

ECG slope sum function

The Slope Sum Function (SSF) is a weighted moving average function that enhances the slope of the ECG signal to facilitate R-peak detection. It was applied to the Blood Volume Pulse (BVP) signal in [97]. Similar to the ECG signal, the BVP signal also contains cardiovascular-derived information. The work of [18] adapted the SSF for the ECG signal. The following steps characterize this function:

1. Calculation of the 1st order derivative of the ECG signal.
2. Positive half-wave rectification.

3. Computing a 250 ms window moving average.

4. Onset detection.

5. Detection of R-peaks via searching for the ECG signal maximum in a 100 ms window after each onset.

6. Validation of detected R-peaks over the heart rate in the range of 20-200 beats per minute.

ECG segmentation

Following the ECG preprocessing, an ECG segmentation was performed by evaluating each QRS complex and truncating the ECG signal in an interval from 200 ms to the left of the R peak to 400 ms to the right (values based on the typical duration of the P-Q and S-T complexes). This way, information from the QRS complex and the P and T waves were secured, and an ECG pattern was generated for each heartbeat.

It should be noted that compression in the ECG signal may occur if the heart rate increases sharply, and the fixed interval of -200 ms to +400 ms would not be the most appropriate as it may contain information from 2 heartbeats.

Conclusion segmentation

An approach to segmentation widely used because of its simplicity and promising results is based on digital filters for attenuating noise and removing the fluctuating baseline, nonlinear translations that amplify the R peak, and adaptive detection thresholds were proposed by Pan and Tompkins [78]. More advanced methods have also been used, such as methods based on neural networks [42], genetic algorithms [80], wavelet transform [49,58,68,31], filter banks [4], quad level vector [53], Low Pass Differentiation (LPD) [56], Hidden Markov Models [26,44,10,55,9,92,60,11,59], partially collapsed Gibbs sampler (PCGS) [62,61], correlation analysis [41,50], support vector machine (SVM) [70], empirical mode decomposition (EMD) [77] and extended Kalman filter (EKF) [90,7].

Since Deep Learning methods can generate feature maps from raw data, heartbeat segmentation can be performed together with classification. Beat-by-beat classification uses separated heartbeats, which risks losing contextual information between heartbeats that can increase classification performance.

11.6 Pipeline: anomaly detection, classification and complex event processing

11.6.1 Anomaly detection

ECG monitoring can be classified into the applications of short-term and long-term monitoring. For example, an ECG signal in a long-term monitoring scenario will create data with a frequency of 360 hertz on a two signal stream with a timestamp, resulting in ~632 MB/day. An ECG signal stream usually contains a high amount of data that is considered normal. Periodical deviations are considered anomalous signals. Those signals need to be analyzed and classified for specific diagnoses. Based on these characteristics, the next processing step is to identify and extract those anomalous signals.

An implementation was tested to detect anomalous signals following the idea of an edge event detection close to the source. The detected anomalous signals are extracted and forwarded to the Kafka

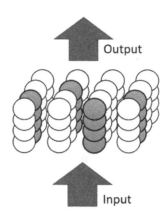

FIGURE 11.1

HTM contains columns with multiple cells, where active cells are colored in blue (mid gray in print version). If there is no previous state, all or none of the cells are active in a column [40].

infrastructure. A modern approach for online detection of anomalies in time series data presents the HTM algorithm.

Hierarchical temporal memory

HTM was inspired by the learning behavior of the neocortex, where the signals from the body's sensory organs are processed in one algorithm [73].

HTM is a self-learning and memory system to store invariant representations of physical structures and abstract concepts. Self-learning is described as the ability that no offline data set for pretraining is needed, and the learning is done in real-time on the incoming data. Furthermore, HTM is highly adaptive and can learn changing representations in real-time and forgets outdated representations, allowing HTM to learn with invariant representations of common patterns. By observing those patterns in a sequence, HTM can predict future patterns.

HTM structure

The HTM learning algorithm models how learning takes place in a single layer of the cortex. HTM creates sparse representations of time series patterns. When the HTM algorithm observes a new pattern, it will try to match it to stored patterns. Because inputs never repeat in the same way, invariance of the stored sequences is vital to recognize inputs. The HTM algorithm only knows what patterns are probably following a particular observed pattern. HTM's general learning principles are to train on every input. If a pattern is repeated, then strengthen it and if the pattern is not repeated, then forget it. HTM carries out at each time step three steps on the observed input.

Step 1 - Create a sparse distributed representation (SDR) of the input by activating whole columns

The first step contains the determination of the active columns of cells in the HTM (see Fig. 11.1). Each column has a connection to a subset of input bits via synapses at a proximal dendrite. Subsets for different columns may overlap but are not the same. Different input patterns result in different activation levels - the columns with the strongest activation levels block columns with weaker activations. The size of the inhibition region around a column is adjustable and can range from very small to the entire region. Thus, the inhibition mechanism provides a sparse representation of the input vector. If only a few input bits change, some columns will get a few more or a few less active inputs, but the set of active columns is unlikely to change much. Therefore, similar input patterns are associated with a relatively stable set of active columns.

HTM learns by forming/rebuilding connections between cells, learning by updating the values of synapses. Only active columns increase the permanence value of synapses connected to active bits and decrease otherwise. Therefore, columns that do not become active for a long time do not learn anything. To avoid wasting columns, the overlap values of these columns are "boosted" to ensure that all columns participate in pattern learning.

Step 2 - Place the input in context by selecting among cells in active columns. The cells can be in one of three different states:

1. If a cell is active due to feedforward input, it is assigned the active state.
2. If the cell is active due to lateral connections with nearby cells, it is in the predictive state.
3. Otherwise, it is in the inactive state.

In the second step, the column representation of the input is converted into a new representation containing the past context. This new representation is formed by activating a subset of cells within each column (usually only one cell per column). The rule for activating cells is as follows:

- When a column becomes active, HTM checks all cells in the column.
- If one or more cells within the column are in the predictive state; only those cells receive the active state.
- If no cells in the column are in the predictive state, then all cells become active.

In other words, if an input pattern is expected, then HTM approves the pattern by activating only the cells in the predictive state. If an unexpected input pattern follows, then HTM activates all cells in the column.

HTM can represent the same input differently in a different context by selecting different active cells in each active column. For example, Fig. 11.2 shows how HTM can represent a sequence AB as part of two longer sequences SABH and KABU. While the same columns have active cells in both cases, the specific active cells differ. If there is no previous state and thus no prediction, the cells in a column are activated when the column is set to active.

Step 3 - Predict future patterns from learned transitions between SDRs

In the third and final step, the probable new input is predicted. The prediction is based on the representation produced in the second step, which contains the context from the previous input patterns. While HTM makes a prediction, all cells that can become active based on the future feedforward input are changed to the prediction state. Due to the sparse representation, multiple predictions can be made at the same moment. The cells in the predictive state represent the HTM prediction for the next input.

The predictive state of each cell in HTM is determined by its distal segments. A segment connects to cells via synapses at distal dendrites. When enough of these cells are active, the segment becomes active (see Fig. 11.3). A cell changes to the predictive state when it has at least one active segment. However, a cell that is active from the second step does not change to the predictive state. The actual "learning" occurs by adjusting the permanence values of synapses on active segments at each time step.

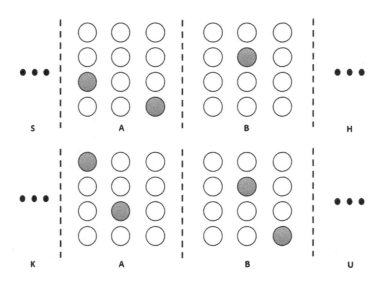

FIGURE 11.2

Representation of specific sequences in larger sequences. The sequence AB is part of two larger sequences. The same active columns with different active cells represent AB [40].

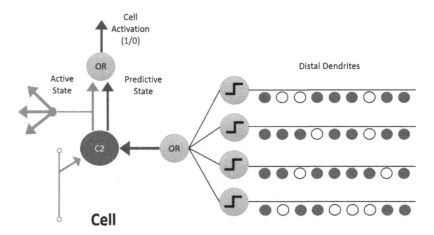

FIGURE 11.3

Each distal dendrite cell segment has synaptic connections to other cells within the neighborhood. A blue (dark gray in print version) circle represents a valid synaptic connection to another cell, and an empty circle represents a potential synaptic connection. The cell enters a predictive state when at least one of its dendrite segments is connected to enough active cells. The binary-valued predictive state of a cell is not propagated. Column activation due to feedforward input via the proximal dendrite is shown in orange (mid gray in print version) in the lower left. The binary-valued active state is the feedforward output of the cell and is also propagated to other cells via the lateral connections shown in the top left corner [82].

The permanence of a synapse is updated only when a predicted cell becomes active during the next time instance. Thus, the permanence of a synapse connected to an active cell is increased and to an inactive cell decreased. An abnormality score is determined for each sample. In a sliding window over the ECG current, the moving average of the anomaly score is determined and related to a patient-specific anomaly threshold.

The HTM result can trigger two functions:

- Early warning signal for a local caretaker on IoT devices or edge nodes like a raspberry pi.
- Forward the segment to the Kafka infrastructure, where it will be ingested for further in-depth processing over the anomalous segment.

The threshold can be configured depending on the clinical risk of the patient. The threshold represents the trade-off between detection accuracy and the data load on the ecosystem. To catch all anomalous signals, a very low threshold needs to be selected, which increases the amount of data falsely classified as anomalous. On the other hand, a high threshold will reduce the data load on extreme cases only, leading to overlook unhealthy beats.

HTM anomaly score

Anomaly detection in HTM is done by calculating the anomaly score. The anomaly score allows HTM to provide a metric for representing the degree of predictability of each data set, where each data set can have an anomaly score between "0" and "1", where "0" represents a fully predicted value, while a "1" represents a fully anomalous value. The anomaly score function in HTM is implemented on the core of the SP and TM algorithms and does not require any modifications to them.

Temporal Anomaly Model

This model is currently an approved and recommended model for anomaly detection and anomaly score reporting. To calculate the anomaly score, it uses temporal memory to detect new points in sequences, and it calculates the anomaly score based on the correctness of the previous prediction. This is done by calculating the percentage of active spatial pooler columns incorrectly predicted by temporal memory. The algorithm for the anomaly score is as described below. It describes that the raw anomaly score is the function of the active columns that were not predicted:

$$anomaly\,Score = \frac{\left| A_t - (P_{t-1} \cap A_t) \right|}{|A_t|}$$

where P_{t-1} = Predicted Columns at time t; A_t = Active Columns at time t.

HTM anomaly likelihood

Anomaly scores are used and postprocessed to generate anomaly likelihood values (Fig. 11.4), x_t is a data stream encoded into a sparse high-dimensional vector a (x_t), and a sparse vector π (x_t) represents a prediction of an input by HTM in the next timestamp (x_{t+1}).

When the anomaly score (S_t) is calculated, the anomaly likelihood distributions are analyzed by the anomaly likelihood. The likelihood estimates the historical distribution of anomaly scores and the likelihood of the current prediction rate by testing whether recent scores are very different.

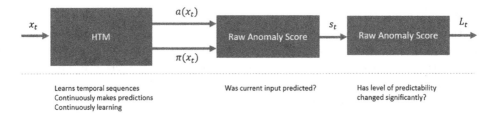

FIGURE 11.4

The primary function steps for Anomaly Score and Anomaly Likelihood Process [82].

Individual anomaly score window example pseudocode

A simpler anomaly evaluation technique was used in the case study, which only considers the average anomaly score over a predefined window.

Input: `incoming-data-t(ecg-signals as unbounded stream in time-step t), flag-send = anomaly based trigger for sending data, Queue-size = size of data queue, segment-size = size of anomalous segment for further analysis`

Output: `Anomalous segment for further processing`

initialize

```
data_queue(size=queue_size)     #FIFO Queue
moving_average_queue(size=segment_size) #FIFO queue

while device_is_online do:
    data_queue(insert=incoming_data_t)
    anomaly_score_t=HTM_anomaly_test(incoming_data_t)
    moving_average_queue(insert=anomaly_score_t)
    if moving_average_queue>=threshold
      flag_send=True
    if flag_send==true && length(data_queue)>=segment_size
      send_to_mqtt_broker(data_queue_dequeue(size=segment_size)
        falg_send=False
```

11.7 Pipeline: classification and prediction

This section describes the classification and prediction task, which follows after the anomaly detection and signal extraction.

11.7.1 Challenges ECG classification

The main difficulties of (Compute Aided Diagnosis Systems) CADS in arrhythmia classification can be summarized as follows:

- Arrhythmia symptoms may not be seen during ECG signal recording [19].
- ECG signal characteristics (such as period and amplitude) vary from person to person and depend on various factors such as age, sex, lifestyle, and physical conditions. Therefore, it is problematic to find a generalized framework along with the associated standards that are functional for the general population [19,47].
- The morphology of the ECG signal is often nonstationary, even in a test subject, due to physical conditions such as running, walking, and sleeping.
- The amount of data to be considered for ECG signal analysis is large. Therefore, there is a higher probability of misdiagnosis of cardiac arrhythmias.
- The noise, artifacts, and interference can lead to morphological variations, and discrepancies in the acquired ECG signal [3,30].

11.7.2 Types of ECG classifications

In the domain of ECG classification, three main approaches have been identified:

1. **Feature-based**: It aims to find a set of relevant features of ECG data that can attain a good classification accuracy.

   In ECG signals (see Fig. 11.5), one cardiac cycle includes the P-QRS-T waves. This feature extraction technique determines the amplitudes and intervals in the ECG signal for subsequent analysis.

2. **1-Dimensional ECG signal classification based on CNN**: An adaptive implementation of 1-D convolutional neural networks (CNNs) fuses the two significant blocks of the ECG classification into a single learning body: feature extraction and classification.

3. **2-dimensional ECG image classification based on CNN**: One-dimensional ECG signals can be transformed into two-dimensional ECG images, where noise filter and feature extraction are not required. Using ECG images as input also benefits in robustness. Traditional ECG arrhythmia detection methods are sensitive to noise. However, when the ECG signal is converted to a two-dimensional image, the proposed CNN model can automatically ignore the noise data while extracting the relevant feature map throughout the convolutional and pooling layer. Thus, the proposed CNN model can be applied to the ECG signals from the various ECG devices with different sampling rates and amplitudes. Furthermore, detecting ECG arrhythmia with ECG images resembles how medical experts diagnose arrhythmia since they observe an ECG graph from the patients throughout the monitor, which shows a series of ECG images [48].

11.7.3 Selected model for the case study

A 1D CNN classification was considered to keep the complexity of the classification as low as possible. However, improvement by the current state-of-the-art 2D CNN approach should be considered.

All convolutional layers apply 1-D convolution, where each consists of five residual blocks, followed by two fully linked layers of 32 neurons each, and a softmax layer to predict the output class. The residual block contains two convolutional layers each, two ReLU nonlinearities [74], a residual skip connection [39], and a pooling layer. The complete network consists of 13 weighting layers.

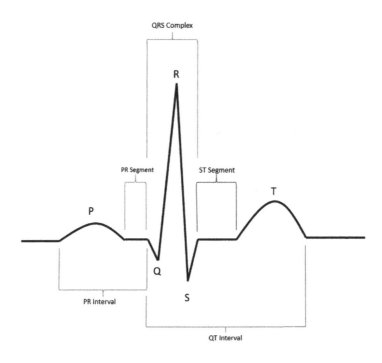

FIGURE 11.5

Example visualization of an ECG signal and its feature definitions.

Train-test protocol

Two approaches were identified in literature handling ECG classification:

- Intra-patient: Heartbeats of the same patients probably appear in the training as well as the testing dataset;
- Interpatient: Construct and evaluate the classification using heartbeats from different patients, following the protocol proposed by [28].

Papers that do not fit into the interpatient category do not allow fair comparisons with results in the literature once a large majority of authors did not follow the same protocol for the evaluations. It is also difficult to assess which technique contributes to heartbeat classification because methods with different approaches achieve very high (>98%) accuracies. Therefore, the reported results cannot be considered from a clinical point of view, as the values reported by these papers are likely to be different in terms of accuracy in a real scenario.

Unfortunately, the vast majority of publications in the literature do not take into account the classification defined in [28] or any other interpatient protocol, which dictates the nonuse of heartbeats from the same patient in training and testing [45].

For this case study, each dataset is split into two subsets, for training (DS1) and testing (DS2). The subsets are chosen to balance the different types of heartbeats and the number of subjects in each data set. In addition, the split between patients is taken into account, i.e., the subjects used for constructing or optimizing the classifier (DS1) are different from the subjects used for evaluating the classifier (DS2).

For the MIT-BIH AR database, the same set division as in Chazal et al. [28] was adopted for comparative purposes of the results.

11.8 Key features

In this chapter we have presented the technical design of a data processing pipeline in eHealth as a practical guide to data stream processing.

- ☑ The design is guided by the building blocks we have identified in previous chapters of the book, namely, *preprocessing – core-processing – anomaly detection – classification & prediction*.
- ☑ The ECG data set is used to exemplify the pipeline design for anomaly detection, classification and prediction in heart diseases.
- ☑ A compendium of the most relevant ECG data sets in the literature is presented.
- ☑ Throughout the chapter, we have shown the building blocks of the pipeline.
- ☑ Various challenges related to imbalanced data sets, denoising, segmentation are discussed.
- ☑ Although exemplified for the case of the ECG data set, the presented pipeline design applies to any data stream application.

References

[1] MQTT org website, http://mqtt.org/.
[2] U. Acharya, H. Fujita, S.L. Oh, Y. Hagiwara, J. Tan, M. Adam, Automated detection of arrhythmias using different intervals of tachycardia ECG segments with convolutional neural network, Information Sciences 405 (2017) 81–90.
[3] E.R. Adams, A. Choi, Using neural networks to predict cardiac arrhythmias, in: 2012 IEEE International Conference on Systems, Man, and Cybernetics (SMC), IEEE, 2012, pp. 402–407.
[4] V. Afonso, W.J. Tompkins, T. Nguyen, S. Luo, ECG beat detection using filter banks, IEEE Transactions on Biomedical Engineering 46 (1999) 192–202.
[5] S. Ahmad, A. Lavin, S. Purdy, Z. Agha, Unsupervised real-time anomaly detection for streaming data, Neurocomputing 262 (2017) 134–147.
[6] S. Ahmad, S. Purdy, Real-time anomaly detection for streaming analytics, arXiv:1607.02480 [abs], 2016.
[7] M. Akhbari, M. Shamsollahi, C. Jutten, ECG fiducial points extraction by extended Kalman filtering, in: 2013 36th International Conference on Telecommunications and Signal Processing (TSP), 2013, pp. 628–632.
[8] E. Alickovic, A. Subasi, Medical decision support system for diagnosis of heart arrhythmia using DWT and random forests classifier, Journal of Medical Systems 40 (4) (2016) 108.
[9] R.V. Andreão, J. Boudy, Combining wavelet transform and hidden Markov models for ECG segmentation, EURASIP Journal on Advances in Signal Processing 2007 (2007) 1–8.
[10] R.V. Andreão, B. Dorizzi, J. Boudy, ECG signal analysis through hidden Markov models, IEEE Transactions on Biomedical Engineering 53 (2006) 1541–1549.
[11] R.V. Andreão, S. Muller, J. Boudy, B. Dorizzi, T. Filho, M.S. Filho, Incremental HMM training applied to ECG signal analysis, Computers in Biology and Medicine 38 (6) (2008) 659–667.

[12] A. Asuncion, UCI machine learning repository, University of California, Irvine, School of Information and Computer Sciences, 2007.

[13] E. Awtry, C. Jeon, M.G. Ware, Blueprints Cardiology, Lippincott Williams & Wilkins, 2006.

[14] A. Baldzizhar, E. Manuylova, R. Marchenko, Y. Kryvalap, M.G. Carey, Ventricular tachycardias: characteristics and management, Critical Care Nursing Clinics 28 (3) (2016) 317–329.

[15] P. Bermejo, J.A. Gámez, J.M. Puerta, Improving the performance of naive Bayes multinomial in e-mail foldering by introducing distribution-based balance of datasets, Expert Systems with Applications 38 (2011) 2072–2080.

[16] R.O. Bonow, D.L. Mann, D.P. Zipes, P. Libby, Braunwald's Heart Disease e-Book: A Textbook of Cardiovascular Medicine, Elsevier Health Sciences, 2011.

[17] L. Breiman, Bagging predictors, Machine Learning 24 (1996) 123–140.

[18] F. Canento, A. Lourenço, H. Silva, A. Fred, Review and comparison of real time electrocardiogram segmentation algorithms for biometric applications, 2012.

[19] R. Ceylan, Y. Özbay, Comparison of FCM, PCA and WT techniques for classification ECG arrhythmias using artificial neural network, Expert Systems with Applications 33 (2) (2007) 286–295.

[20] T. Chalvidan, J. Deharo, P. Djiane, Pacemaker syndromes, in: Annales de Cardiologie et D'angeiologie, vol. 49, 2000, pp. 224–229.

[21] N. Chawla, K. Bowyer, L. Hall, W.P. Kegelmeyer, SMOTE: synthetic minority over-sampling technique, Journal of Artificial Intelligence Research 16 (2002) 321–357.

[22] P. Chazal, R. Reilly, A patient-adapting heartbeat classifier using ECG morphology and heartbeat interval features, IEEE Transactions on Biomedical Engineering 53 (2006) 2535–2543.

[23] Y.-S. Chen, An empirical study of a hybrid imbalanced-class DT-RST classification procedure to elucidate therapeutic effects in uremia patients, Medical & Biological Engineering & Computing 54 (2016) 983–1001.

[24] I. Christov, Real time electrocardiogram QRS detection using combined adaptive threshold, BioMedical Engineering OnLine 3 (2004) 28.

[25] I. Christov, G. Gómez-Herrero, V. Krasteva, I. Jekova, A. Gotchev, K. Egiazarian, Comparative study of morphological and time-frequency ECG descriptors for heartbeat classification, Medical Engineering & Physics 28 (9) (2006) 876–887.

[26] D. Coast, R. Stern, G.G. Cano, S. Briller, An approach to cardiac arrhythmia analysis using hidden Markov models, IEEE Transactions on Biomedical Engineering 37 (1990) 826–836.

[27] M.B. Conover, Understanding Electrocardiography, Elsevier Health Sciences, 2002.

[28] P. De Chazal, M. O'Dwyer, R.B. Reilly, Automatic classification of heartbeats using ECG morphology and heartbeat interval features, IEEE Transactions on Bio-Medical Engineering 51 (7) (2004) 1196–1206.

[29] A.M. Delaney, E. Brophy, T. Ward, Synthesis of realistic ECG using generative adversarial networks, arXiv:1909.09150 [abs], 2019.

[30] S.M.P. Dinakarrao, A. Jantsch, M. Shafique, Computer-aided arrhythmia diagnosis with bio-signal processing: a survey of trends and techniques, ACM Computing Surveys (CSUR) 52 (2) (2019) 1–37.

[31] J. Dumont, A. Hernández, G. Carrault, Improving ECG beats delineation with an evolutionary optimization process, IEEE Transactions on Biomedical Engineering 57 (2010) 607–615.

[32] Y. Freund, An adaptive version of the boost by majority algorithm, Machine Learning 43 (1999) 293–318.

[33] J. Frielingsdorf, A. Gerber, O. Hess, Importance of maintained atrio-ventricular synchrony in patients with pacemarkers, European Heart Journal 15 (10) (1994) 1431–1440.

[34] M. Galar, A. Fernández, E. Tartas, H. Bustince, F. Herrera, A review on ensembles for the class imbalance problem: bagging-, boosting-, and hybrid-based approaches, IEEE Transactions on Systems, Man, and Cybernetics, Part C (Applications and Reviews) 42 (2012) 463–484.

[35] T. Golany, G. Lavee, S.T. Yarden, K. Radinsky, Improving ECG classification using generative adversarial networks, in: AAAI, 2020.

[36] A. Goldberger, L. Amaral, L. Glass, J.M. Hausdorff, P. Ivanov, R. Mark, J. Mietus, G. Moody, C. Peng, H. Stanley, PhysioBank, PhysioToolkit, and PhysioNet: components of a new research resource for complex physiologic signals, Circulation 101 (23) (2000) E215–E220.

[37] P. Hamilton, Open source ECG analysis, in: Computers in Cardiology, 2002, pp. 101–104.

[38] R. Harrigan, T. Chan, W. Brady, Electrocardiographic electrode misplacement, misconnection, and artifact, The Journal of Emergency Medicine 43 (6) (2012) 1038–1044.

[39] K. He, X. Zhang, S. Ren, J. Sun, Deep residual learning for image recognition, in: 2016 IEEE Conference on Computer Vision and Pattern Recognition (CVPR), 2016, pp. 770–778.

[40] K.J. Hole, The HTM Learning Algorithm, Springer International Publishing, Cham, 2016, pp. 113–124.

[41] M. Homaeinezhad, M. ErfanianMoshiri-Nejad, H. Naseri, A correlation analysis-based detection and delineation of ECG characteristic events using template waveforms extracted by ensemble averaging of clustered heart cycles, Computers in Biology and Medicine 44 (2014) 66–75.

[42] Y. Hu, W.J. Tompkins, J. Urrusti, V. Afonso, Applications of artificial neural networks for ECG signal detection and classification, Journal of Electrocardiology 26 (Suppl) (1993) 66–73.

[43] J. Huff, ECG Workout: Exercises in Arrhythmia Interpretation, Lippincott Williams & Wilkins, 2006.

[44] N. Hughes, H. Term, Probabilistic models for automated ECG interval analysis, 2006.

[45] T. Ince, S. Kiranyaz, M. Gabbouj, A generic and patient-specific electrocardiogram signal classification system, in: ECG Signal Processing, Classification and Interpretation, Springer, 2012, pp. 79–98.

[46] N. Japkowicz, The class imbalance problem: significance and strategies, in: Proc. of the Int'l Conf. on Artificial Intelligence, vol. 56, Citeseer, 2000.

[47] A.J. Joshi, S. Chandran, V.K. Jayaraman, B.D. Kulkarni, Hybrid SVM for multiclass arrhythmia classification, in: 2009 IEEE International Conference on Bioinformatics and Biomedicine, IEEE, 2009, pp. 287–290.

[48] T.J. Jun, M.H. Nguyen, D. Kang, D. Kim, D. Kim, Y.-H. Kim, ECG arrhythmia classification using a 2-d convolutional neural network, arXiv:1804.06812 [abs], 2018.

[49] S. Kadambe, R. Murray, G. Boudreaux-Bartels, Wavelet transform-based QRS complex detector, IEEE Transactions on Biomedical Engineering 46 (1999) 838–848.

[50] A. Karimipour, M. Homaeinezhad, Real-time electrocardiogram P-QRS-T detection-delineation algorithm based on quality-supported analysis of characteristic templates, Computers in Biology and Medicine 52 (2014) 153–165.

[51] D. Kasper, A. Fauci, S. Hauser, D. Longo, J. Jameson, J. Loscalzo, Harrison's Principles of Internal Medicine, 19e, vol. 1, Mcgraw-Hill, 2015.

[52] A.H. Khan, M. Hussain, M.K. Malik, ECG images dataset of cardiac and Covid-19 patients, Data in Brief 34 (2021).

[53] H. Kim, R. Yazicioglu, P. Merken, C. Hoof, H. Yoo, ECG signal compression and classification algorithm with quad level vector for ECG holter system, IEEE Transactions on Information Technology in Biomedicine 14 (2010) 93–100.

[54] S. Kiranyaz, T. Ince, M. Gabbouj, Real-time patient-specific ECG classification by 1-D convolutional neural networks, IEEE Transactions on Biomedical Engineering 63 (2016) 664–675.

[55] S. Krimi, K. Ouni, N. Ellouze, An approach combining wavelet transform and hidden Markov models for ECG segmentation, in: 2008 3rd International Conference on Information and Communication Technologies: From Theory to Applications, 2008, pp. 1–6.

[56] P. Laguna, R. Jané, P. Caminal, Automatic detection of wave boundaries in multilead ECG signals: validation with the CSE database, Computers and Biomedical Research, an International Journal 27 (1) (1994) 45–60.

[57] A. Lavin, S. Ahmad, Evaluating real-time anomaly detection algorithms – the Numenta anomaly benchmark, in: 2015 IEEE 14th International Conference on Machine Learning and Applications (ICMLA), 2015, pp. 38–44.

[58] C. Li, C. Zheng, C. Tai, Detection of ECG characteristic points using wavelet transforms, IEEE Transactions on Bio-Medical Engineering 42 (1) (1995) 21–28.

[59] H. Li, J. Tan, ECG segmentation in a body sensor network using hidden Markov models, in: 2008 5th International Summer School and Symposium on Medical Devices and Biosensors, 2008, pp. 285–288.

[60] W. Liang, Y. Zhang, J. Tan, Y. Li, A novel approach to ECG classification based upon two-layered HMMs in body sensor networks, Sensors (Basel, Switzerland) 14 (2014) 5994–6011.

[61] C. Lin, G. Kail, J. Tourneret, C. Mailhes, F. Hlawatsch, P and T wave delineation and waveform estimation in ECG signals using a block Gibbs sampler, in: 2011 IEEE International Conference on Acoustics, Speech and Signal Processing (ICASSP), 2011, pp. 537–540.

[62] C. Lin, C. Mailhes, J. Tourneret, P- and t-wave delineation in ECG signals using a Bayesian approach and a partially collapsed Gibbs sampler, IEEE Transactions on Biomedical Engineering 57 (2010) 2840–2849.

[63] H. Lin, S. Liang, Y. Ho, Y.-H. Lin, H.-P. Ma, Discrete-wavelet-transform-based noise removal and feature extraction for ECG signals, IRBM 35 (2014) 351–361.

[64] M.S. Link, Evaluation and initial treatment of supraventricular tachycardia, The New England Journal of Medicine 367 (15) (2012) 1438–1448.

[65] E.D. Lisboa, Multi-modal behavioral biometrics based on HCI and electrophysiology, 2008.

[66] M. Llamedo, J.P. Martínez, Heartbeat classification using feature selection driven by database generalization criteria, IEEE Transactions on Biomedical Engineering 58 (2011) 616–625.

[67] A. Lourenço, H. Silva, P. Leite, R. Lourenço, A. Fred, Real time electrocardiogram segmentation for finger based ECG biometrics, in: BIOSIGNALS, 2012.

[68] J.P. Martínez, R. Almeida, S. Olmos, A.P. Rocha, P. Laguna, A wavelet-based ECG delineator: evaluation on standard databases, IEEE Transactions on Biomedical Engineering 51 (2004) 570–581.

[69] R.J. Martis, U. Acharya, C.M. Lim, ECG beat classification using PCA, LDA, ICA and discrete wavelet transform, Biomedical Signal Processing and Control 8 (2013) 437–448.

[70] S. Mehta, N.S. Lingayat, Combined entropy based method for detection of QRS complexes in 12-lead electrocardiogram using SVM, Computers in Biology and Medicine 38 (1) (2008) 138–145.

[71] F. Melgani, Y. Bazi, Classification of electrocardiogram signals with support vector machines and particle swarm optimization, IEEE Transactions on Information Technology in Biomedicine 12 (5) (2008) 667–677.

[72] G. Moody, R. Mark, The impact of the MIT-BIH arrhythmia database, IEEE Engineering in Medicine and Biology Magazine: the Quarterly Magazine of the Engineering in Medicine & Biology Society 20 (06 2001) 45–50.

[73] V. Mountcastle, An organizing principle for cerebral function: the unit module and the distributed system, in: The Mindful Brain, 1978.

[74] V. Nair, G.E. Hinton, Rectified linear units improve restricted Boltzmann machines, in: ICML, 2010.

[75] E.J. Otten, Cecil textbook of medicine, The Journal of Emergency Medicine 28 (1) (2005) 113.

[76] N. Oza, K. Tumer, Classifier ensembles: select real-world applications, Information Fusion 9 (2008) 4–20.

[77] S. Pal, M. Mitra, Empirical mode decomposition based ECG enhancement and QRS detection, Computers in Biology and Medicine 42 (1) (2012) 83–92.

[78] J. Pan, W.J. Tompkins, A real-time QRS detection algorithm, IEEE Transactions on Biomedical Engineering BME-32 (3) (1985) 230–236.

[79] A. Patel, P. Gakare, A. Cheeran, Real time ECG feature extraction and arrhythmia detection on a mobile platform, International Journal of Computer Applications 44 (2012) 40–45.

[80] R. Poli, S. Cagnoni, G. Valli, Genetic design of optimum linear and nonlinear QRS detectors, IEEE Transactions on Biomedical Engineering 42 (1995) 1137–1141.

[81] R. Prati, G.E.A.P.A. Batista, M.C. Monard, A study with class imbalance and random sampling for a decision tree learning system, in: IFIP AI, 2008.

[82] R. Price, Hierarchical temporal memory cortical learning algorithm for pattern recognition on multi-core architectures, 2011.

[83] P. Radivojac, N. Chawla, A. Dunker, Z. Obradovic, Classification and knowledge discovery in protein databases, Journal of Biomedical Informatics 37 (4) (2004) 224–239.

[84] H.M. Rai, A. Trivedi, De-noising of ECG waveforms based on multi-resolution wavelet transform, International Journal of Computer Applications 45 (2012) 25–30.

[85] H.M. Rai, A. Trivedi, S. Shukla, ECG signal processing for abnormalities detection using multi-resolution wavelet transform and artificial neural network classifier, Measurement 46 (2013) 3238–3246.

[86] N.S. Sawhney, G.K. Feld, Diagnosis and management of typical atrial flutter, Medical Clinics of North America 92 (1) (2008) 65–85.

[87] R. Schapire, The strength of weak learnability, Machine Learning 5 (2005) 197–227.

[88] B. Singh, A. Tiwari, Optimal selection of wavelet basis function applied to ECG signal denoising, Digital Signal Processing 16 (2006) 275–287.

[89] H. Sivaraks, C. Ratanamahatana, Robust and accurate anomaly detection in ECG artifacts using time series motif discovery, Computational & Mathematical Methods in Medicine (2015) 2015.

[90] A. Su, ECG noise filtering using online model-based Bayesian filtering techniques, 2013.

[91] N. Thakor, Y. Zhu, Applications of adaptive filtering to ECG analysis: noise cancellation and arrhythmia detection, IEEE Transactions on Biomedical Engineering 38 (1991) 785–794.

[92] J. Thomas, C. Rose, F. Charpillet, A multi-HMM approach to ECG segmentation, in: 2006 18th IEEE International Conference on Tools with Artificial Intelligence, ICTAI'06, 2006, pp. 609–616.

[93] M. Thomas, M.K. Das, S. Ari, Automatic ECG arrhythmia classification using dual tree complex wavelet based features, AEÜ. International Journal of Electronics and Communications 69 (2015) 715–721.

[94] S. Thornton, P. Hochachka, Oxygen and the diving seal, Undersea Hyperbaric Medicine 31 (1) (2004) 81–95.

[95] A. Velayudhan, S. Peter, Noise analysis and different denoising techniques of ECG signal - a survey, 2016.

[96] Z. Zheng, X. Wu, R. Srihari, Feature selection for text categorization on imbalanced data, SIGKDD Explorations 6 (2004) 80–89.

[97] W. Zong, T. Heldt, G. Moody, R. Mark, An open-source algorithm to detect onset of arterial blood pressure pulses, Computers in Cardiology 2003 (2003) 259–262.

Working procedure and analysis for an ECG dataset

Data stream processing in practice

12.1 Processing and analysis of an ECG dataset by Faust cluster computing

This section studies the effects of applying the Hierarchical Temporary Memory (HTM) algorithm as a prefilter step to identify anomalous segments for further analysis by the Faust classification cluster. Faust is a platform that enables porting Kafka stream to Python for building real-time data pipelines. The study will focus on the trade-off factors of the implementation configuration over different threshold values. A second evaluation was conducted on the Faust worker extraction and classification task, where time measurements were taken for different arrival rates of incoming anomalous segments. The final part of the result evaluation shows the total throughput time of the signal sample generation till the finished classification of the Faust worker.

12.1.1 Trade-off 1: HTM anomaly threshold vs. data size vs. detection rate

The evaluation presented here was conducted on the labeled MIT-BIH Arrhythmia Database [1]. This data set contains approximately 110,000 beats that have been annotated by two or more cardiologists independently. Each patient has a recording of 30 minutes in a frequency of 360 Hz, which results in 648,000 samples. The annotations were mapped by the cardiologist to a single sample, were an example can be seen in Fig. 12.1:

Time	Sample	Class
...		
0:05.025	1809	N
0:05.678	2044	A
0:06.672	2402	N
...		

FIGURE 12.1

Snippet of the ECG annotation set. The first column marks the time of a signal. The class expresses if the signal was marked as healthy or unhealthy.

The HTM algorithm, as well as the implementation, contains a complex setup of parameters. The following parameters are used in the experimental setup and can be seen in Fig. 12.2.

- Minimum and maximum queue window size.
- Hopping window size: Represents the overlapping interval.

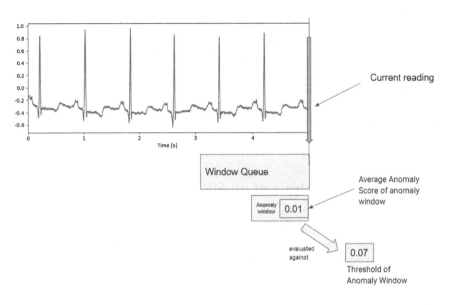

FIGURE 12.2

The model of the parameter setup for identifying and extracting anomalous segments with the HTM algorithm.

- Anomaly window size: Length of the moving average of the anomaly score.
- Threshold of moving average of anomalies: The factor of tolerance over detected anomalous segments.

In this experiment, the frequency was downsampled to 180 Hz to reduce the experiment duration (for different frequencies of an ECG stream, the implementation parameters need to be optimized and reconfigured). The raw data stream was not preprocessed and contains noisy samples.

For the evaluation on a 180 hz frequency, following settings were chosen:

- Minimum and Maximum queue window size: 200-450
- Anomaly window size: 20
- Hopping window size: 100

The major goal of the HTM algorithm was to detect unhealthy signals and reduce as much as possible the data rate on the infrastructure. For this, the detection rate of an unhealthy signal (True Positive Rate—TPR) was evaluated, as well as the rate of healthy signals that were considered as anomalous (False Positive Rate—FPR). The results can be seen in Fig. 12.3. With a low threshold of 0.06, 93% (TPR) of all the unhealthy signals and 42% (FPR) of healthy signals were forwarded to the Kafka system to be further classified by the CNN model. With a threshold of 0.10, it can be observed that the TPR is at 89%, while the FPR shrinks to 24%.

For the same setup and threshold ranges, the data volume was evaluated and can be seen in Fig. 12.5. The initially measured generated data of one ECG sensor over 24 hours is at ~480 MB. With an acceptable anomaly threshold of 0.08, the volume was reduced by 24% to a volume of 355 MB. All results of the threshold test can be viewed in Fig. 12.4.

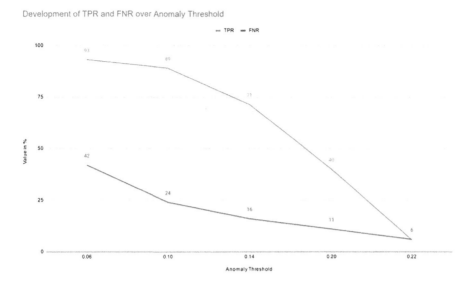

FIGURE 12.3

Evaluation of TPR and FPR over different anomaly thresholds.

Considering that the HTM algorithm had no optimization of the hyperparameters and that we used raw noisy data stream, the results are reasonably good. The HTM algorithm should be in a future outlook investigated on a preprocessed and clean ECG stream (e.g., noise filter, feature extraction, representation schemes).

Anomaly Threshold	TPR (recall) in %	FPR (fall-out) in %	Precision in %	Accuracy in %	Volume reduction in %	MB/24h	TP	TN	FP	FN
0.00	100	100	1,5	2	0	480	35	0	2239	0
0.06	93	42	3,3	59	57	275	33	1299	940	2
0.10	89	24	5,5	76	75	206	31	1702	537	4
0.14	71	16	6,5	84	83	171	25	1881	358	10
0.20	40	11	5,4	88	89	152	14	1993	246	21
0.22	6	6	1,5	93	94	143	2	2105	134	33

FIGURE 12.4

Evaluation table of binary classification analysis of the HTM anomaly detection over the raw data stream of patient-100.

12.1.2 HTM anomaly detection and segmentation Python script
htm_p27_sensor.py

```
"""
Description:    Execution code for the sensor data generation and HTM algorithm for sensor data anomaly
↪    detection.
```

Development of Sample reduction over Anomaly Threshold

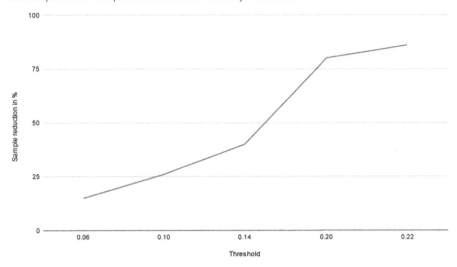

FIGURE 12.5

Example of Anomaly Threshold effects on stream volume of one ECG sensor over a 24 hours duration, where a raw generated volume was estimated with 480 MB every 24 hours.

```
Important note: File needs to be run in a python 2.7 environment due to the nupic library currently only
⤷   available in 2.7

Dataset can be retrieved at: https://physionet.org/physiobank/database/mitdb/

Input: Sensor Raw Stream
    {
      Timestamp: [time_1...time_n]
      Signal: [signal_1...signal_n]
      Frequency: 180 #downsampled at initialization
      Sensor_id: 6581
    }

Output: Sensor Segment Stream with Anomaly Score
    {
      Timestamp: Begin Timestamp
      Signal: [signal_1...signal_n]
      Anomaly_score: [score_1..score_n]
      Frequency: 180
      Sensor_id: 6581
    }

"""

#general libraries
```

```python
import os
import csv
import numpy as np
from json import loads
import datetime
import sys
import pprint
import numpy as np
import json
import time


#queue
from collections import deque
#requirement for nupic algorithm
from nupic.frameworks.opf.model_factory import ModelFactory
from nupic.encoders.adaptive_scalar import AdaptiveScalarEncoder
#load the parameter setup
import htm.model_params.single_signal188 as model_params
#mqtt setup
import paho.mqtt.client as mqtt #import the client1
import paho.mqtt.client as mqtt

#load file for patients
def find_csv_filenames(path_to_dir, suffix=".csv"):
    filenames = listdir(path_to_dir)
    return [ filename for filename in filenames if filename.endswith( suffix ) ]
#calculate the mean values
def mean(nums):
    return float(sum(nums)) / max(len(nums), 1)
#Main execution
def main(args):
  # extracting the argument input of selected input file and HTM threshold
  #selected_file_index, analytics_level=args
  # moving_average_threshold=analytics_level
  moving_average_threshold=0.06 #anomaly threshold
  selected_file_index=1 #number of patient 1 stand for the file 100.csv
  dir_path="/home/kafka/Documents/python" #general path of root directory of project
  data_path = "/data/raw_stream/" #sub root directory path, where the data is located
  output_path = "/output/" # sub root directory path for output data
  patient_files=dir_path+data_path # concat the patient file location

  #load input file
  filenames = find_csv_filenames(patient_files) #0-44 index for patient_files
  selected_input=str(filenames[selected_file_index])
  #initial setup
  downsampling_rate=2 # downsampling of 360hz to 180hz
  frequency=360/downsampling_rate
  DATE_FORMAT = "%Y-%m-%d %H:%M:%S.%f" # use for unified time standard for json sequentialisation
  verbose=None

  #initializing temporary arrays for the processing
```

```
signals_segment=[]
anomaly_score=[]
timestamp_segment=[]
moving_average_anomaly=0

#setup of mqtt connection
broker_url = "127.0.0.1" # localhost in case the MQTT broker/proxy is on the same machine, else choose
↪  here the external IP
broker_port = 1883 # MQTT port, this is the standard port, but it depends on the configuration of the
↪  MQTT broker server
topic="ECG" #MQTT and Kafka topic
#MQTT configuration
MQTT_HOST = "127.0.0.1" # localhost in case the MQTT broker/proxy is on the same machine, else choose
↪  here the external IP
MQTT_PORT = 1883 # MQTT port, this is the standard port, but it depends on the configuration of the MQTT
↪  broker server
MQTT_KEEPALIVE_INTERVAL = 45 #message connection keep alive value
MQTT_TOPIC = "temperature" #MQTT and Kafka topic

# window configuration
queue_size=500  #Size of whole queue
batch_size=300   #Size of extracted segment (minimum window size)

#moving average
max_samples = 20 # Anomaly evaluation on here 20 samples, which result in the storage in the moving
↪  average readings array below
moving_average_readings=[]
send_flag=False # flag that indicates an anomalous segment evaluation
flag_ma_valid=False # flag to indicate that the minimum window size is satisfied

#creating the moving window class
class Queue():
    def __init__(self,queue_size=queue_size):
        self._queue = deque(maxlen=queue_size)

    def enqueue(self, items):
        ''' Appending the items to the queue'''
        self._queue.append(items)

    def dequeue(self):
        '''remove the items from the top if the queue becomes full '''
        return self._queue.pop()
#START OF ACTUAL EXECUTION
#Load the sensor data in numpy array
mitbih_train=np.genfromtxt(dir_path+data_path+selected_input, usecols=(1,), skip_header=2,
↪  delimiter=".")
mitbih_train=mitbih_train[::downsampling_rate] # here the downsampling happens if selected
#create window object
q = Queue(queue_size=queue_size)
#create the scalar encoder for the HTM parameter input configuration
def addScalarEncoders(params, vector_length):
  for i in range(vector_length):
```

```python
        sensor_name = "f" + str(i)
        params["modelParams"]["sensorParams"]["encoders"].update({
            sensor_name: {
              'clipInput': True,
              'fieldname': sensor_name,
              'n': 491,
              'name': sensor_name,
              'type': 'AdaptiveScalarEncoder',
              'w': 21}
        })
    return params
#definition of the HTM model
def createModel(verbose):
    params = model_params.MODEL_PARAMS #load parameter
    # loop and add scalarencoders of n-dimension
    #params = addScalarEncoders(params, 1)
    if verbose:
        print ("Model parameters:")
        pprint.pprint(params)
    #create the model based on setup parameter
    model = ModelFactory.create(params)
    model.enableInference({"predictedField": "signal"}) # prediction based on field signal
    return model


## mqtt connect and send functions
def on_publish(client, userdata, mid):
    print ("Message Published...")
def on_connect(client, userdata, flags, rc):
    client.subscribe(MQTT_TOPIC)
    client.publish(MQTT_TOPIC, MQTT_MSG)
def on_message(client, userdata, msg):
    payload = json.loads(msg.payload) # use json.loads to convert string to json for mqtt
    ↪  sequentialization
    client.disconnect() # Got message then disconnect



model = createModel(verbose)  #Create HTMModel object

#timestamp configuration. Here an artificial was used.
timestamp_string=datetime.datetime.now().strftime(DATE_FORMAT)
timestamp_object= datetime.datetime.strptime(timestamp_string, DATE_FORMAT)

#Simulate for incoming samples of the mitbih_train set
for signal in mitbih_train:
    signal=round(signal, 3) #reduce float length for later processing and sending
    #create model input with timestamp and signal
    modelInput = {
        "timestamp": timestamp_object,
        "signal" : signal
    }
    #run online anomaly detection
    result = model.run(modelInput)
```

```python
#retrieve score of anomaly evaluation
result_anomalyscore=round(result.inferences["anomalyScore"], 2)
#add resulting anomaly score to json file
modelInput.update({
    "anomaly_score": result_anomalyscore,
    "patient_id": str(selected_input),
    "timestamp": timestamp_string
    })
if verbose:
    print ("Anomaly score: {}.".format(modelInput))
#add score to evaluation window
anomaly_score.append(result_anomalyscore)
#add signal to helping array
signals_segment.append(signal)
#add timestamp to helping array
timestamp_segment.append(timestamp_string)
#add signal and anomaly score to window operator
q.enqueue([signal, result_anomalyscore])
moving_average_readings.append(result_anomalyscore)
##If anomaly sampling window is at 20 samples, follow FIFO principles and delete first entry in
↪    array
if (len(moving_average_readings) == max_samples+1):
    moving_average_readings.pop(0)
    flag_ma_valid=True #set flag true to say that the minimum window for the anomaly score is
        ↪    fullfilled
#calculate score of moving average over anomalies and say if threshold is triggered
avg = mean(moving_average_readings)
if (avg>=moving_average_threshold):
    send_flag=True


#If moving average is above threshold, and minimum queue size is valid
if (len(q._queue)>=batch_size and send_flag):
    segment_extracted=[q.dequeue() for _i in range(batch_size)]
    send_flag=False #reset anomaly evaluation flag
    #SEND anomaly segment via MQTT to kafka ecosystem
    sendInput= {
    "timestamp": [str(timestamp_segment[0]), str(timestamp_segment[-1])],
    "signal" : [i[0] for i in segment_extracted],
    "anomaly_score" : [i[1] for i in segment_extracted],
    "frequency" : frequency,
    "sensor_id": str(selected_input)
    }
    #reset arrays
    moving_average_readings=[]
    anomaly_score=[]
    timestamp_segment=[]

    #create a local copy for evaluation
    with open(dir_path+output_path+'jsontestsensor'+str(selected_input)+'.json', 'w') as f:
        json.dump(sendInput, f)
    #create a json dump for the serial transmition
    MQTT_MSG=json.dumps(sendInput)
```

```
#initialize the mqtt object (might be better to be initialized earlier)
mqttc = mqtt.Client()
# Register publish callback function
mqttc.on_publish = on_publish
mqttc.on_connect = on_connect
mqttc.on_message = on_message

# Connect with MQTT Broker and send message
mqttc.connect(MQTT_HOST, MQTT_PORT, MQTT_KEEPALIVE_INTERVAL)

# Define on_publish event function
if __name__ == '__main__':
    main()
```

Computing infrastructure: AWS instance type

The processing was evaluated on an AWS instance type t2.medium with 2 vCPUs (3.3 GHz) and 4 GiB RAM. As indicated by the Amazon EC2 details page, T2 instances are low-cost, general purpose instance type that are designed to provide a baseline level of CPU performance with the ability to burst above the baseline. T2 instances are ideal, in particular, for developer environments. T2 instances are for workloads that don't use the full CPU often or consistently, but occasionally need to burst to higher CPU performance. T2 instances are engineered specifically for these use cases.

Processing time

It is highly depending on sample frequency and was tested with 180 hz:

- HTM algorithm: $\sim \leq 0.01$ seconds per sample.
- Queue segment evaluation: $\sim \leq 2$ seconds (mainly depending on window size configuration).

12.1.3 Faust signal extraction and classification evaluation

In this experimental study, the extraction and classification of anomalous signals were evaluated on a Faust worker node. A single Faust worker was deployed where the test consisted of measuring the time of extracting a signal and classifying it. Fig. 12.6 shows the evaluation results, where different event rate scenarios were tested. The worker was able to handle $\sim$245 events per second and showed a linear behavior for increased data rates. The experiment showed that the classification step took slightly more time than the signal extraction process.

12.1.4 Processing time along various layers of the architecture

This section contains the throughput time of a generated event at the sensor until the final event classification at the Faust worker node. Several measurements were taken at the HTM algorithm, MQTT connection, Kafka cluster, and Faust worker node, which can be seen in Fig. 12.7.

The HTM algorithm processed the raw ECG samples on a frequency of 180 Hz, where the analysis time was between 0.4 and 2 seconds of a single signal, which is due to the window operator configuration. Depending on the window size, the processing time will be affected. The HTM algorithm gives an anomaly score on a single signal in a fraction of a second. To establish a mechanism to prevent a

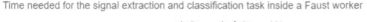

Time needed for the signal extraction and classification task inside a Faust worker

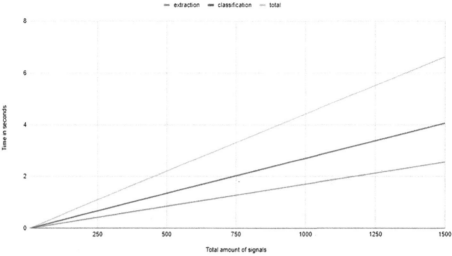

FIGURE 12.6

Processing time of a Faust worker over anomalous segments. The task consisted of signal extraction and classification.

system flooding based on noise elements inside the raw data stream, the evaluation was delayed until an clear decision can be made based on the followup samples of the time series of an ECG.

The network communication latency between the IoT device, Kafka ecosystem and Faust worker node are essential measurements to be considered for a real application. In this case study they were not considered for an in-depth investigation. Basic measurements were taken and showed a communication time of under 0.2 seconds of a sensor deployment in Barcelona area to the AWS availability zone 3 in Frankfurt.

Two measurements were taken at the Faust worker node for the anomalous segment task to extract signals and classifying. The total time of a segment classification was at under 0.006 seconds (note: an anomalous segment was consisting of 3 signals in the test based on the anomalous segment window configuration).

The maximum throughput time starting at the generation of an event until the classification of probable unhealthy signals was at 2.1 seconds plus the network latency characteristics in the deployed environment for MQTT and between the Kafka and Faust worker.

12.1.5 Classification

The model was implemented in a basic 1D-CNN to test the overall functionality. The signal preprocessing step follows the idea of [11]. By having the same input structure, the model can be replaced with the model of Jun et al. [11] proposed 2D-CNN model architecture that showed the following result for the classification of the same ECG data with the same setup:

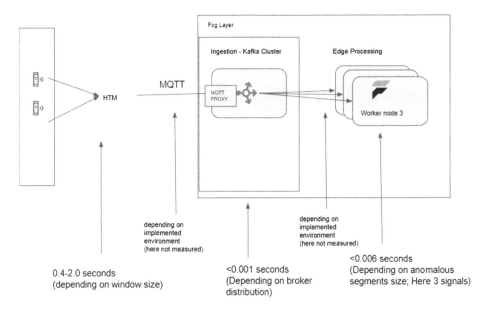

FIGURE 12.7

Visualization of the total throughput time of one ECG signal.

Precision over different heart beat types (%):

- N = 0.97
- S = 0.89
- V = 0.96
- F = 0.86
- Q = 0.98

The recreated model had a precision over different heart beat types (%) on the validation set of:

- N = 0.992
- S = 0.886
- V = 0.978
- F = 0.968
- Q = 0.990

A probable reason for the better result stems from the training data. By generating heartbeats via the GAN Synthesis explain in the previous chapter, more class samples were available for the minority class.

In a real world application, the implemented model can be simply replaced in the Faust worker node, whereas the remaining data pipeline can stay unchanged, as long as the input format stays the same of the model.

Model training script

```python
import math
import random
import pickle
import itertools

import numpy as np
import pandas as pd

from sklearn.metrics import accuracy_score, classification_report, confusion_matrix,
    label_ranking_average_precision_score, label_ranking_loss, coverage_error

from sklearn.utils import shuffle

from scipy.signal import resample

import matplotlib.pyplot as plt

np.random.seed(1)

import pickle
from sklearn.preprocessing import OneHotEncoder

from keras.models import Model
from keras.layers import Input, Dense, Conv1D, MaxPooling1D, Softmax, Add, Flatten, Activation# , Dropout
from keras import backend as K
from keras.optimizers import Adam
from keras.callbacks import LearningRateScheduler, ModelCheckpoint

import os
print(os.listdir("..data/input"))

df = pd.read_csv("../input/mitbih_train_gan.csv", header=None)
df2 = pd.read_csv("../input/mitbih_test_gan.csv", header=None)
df = pd.concat([df, df2], axis=0)

M = df.values
X = M[:, :-1]
y = M[:, -1].astype(int)

del df
del df2
del M

##Augmentation of data set - method used by original paper
def stretch(x):
    l = int(187 * (1 + (random.random()-0.5)/3))
    y = resample(x, l)
    if l < 187:
        y_ = np.zeros(shape=(187, ))
        y_[:l] = y
    else:
```

```python
        y_ = y[:187]
    return y_


def amplify(x):
    alpha = (random.random()-0.5)
    factor = -alpha*x + (1+alpha)
    return x*factor


def augment(x):
    result = np.zeros(shape= (4, 187))
    for i in range(len(result)):
        tmp = random.random()
        if tmp < 0.33:
            new_y = stretch(x)
        elif tmp < 0.66:
            new_y = amplify(x)
        else:
            new_y = stretch(x)
            new_y = amplify(new_y)
        result[i, :] = new_y
    return result

result = np.apply_along_axis(augment, axis=1, arr=X[C3]).reshape(-1, 187)
classe = np.ones(shape=(result.shape[0],), dtype=int)*3
X = np.vstack([X, result])
y = np.hstack([y, classe])


### Data set preparation
setsize=  #size of your whole dataset
testsize=  #size of test set

## Similar sized clusters
C0_subset = np.random.choice(C0, testsize)
C1_subset = np.random.choice(C1, testsize)
C2_subset = np.random.choice(C2, testsize)
C3_subset = np.random.choice(C3, testsize)
C4_subset = np.random.choice(C4, testsize)

## Train Test Split
X_test = np.vstack([X[C0_subset], X[C1_subset], X[C2_subset], X[C3_subset], X[C4_subset]])
y_test = np.hstack([y[C0_subset], y[C1_subset], y[C2_subset], y[C3_subset], y[C4_subset]])

X_train = np.delete(X, [C0_subset, C1_subset, C2_subset, C3_subset, C4_subset], axis=0)
y_train = np.delete(y, [C0_subset, C1_subset, C2_subset, C3_subset, C4_subset], axis=0)

X_train, y_train = shuffle(X_train, y_train, random_state=0)
X_test, y_test = shuffle(X_test, y_test, random_state=0)

# Arrange input shape
X_train = np.expand_dims(X_train, 2)
X_test = np.expand_dims(X_test, 2)
```

```
## One Hot Encoding of Heartbeat type
ohe = OneHotEncoder()
y_train = ohe.fit_transform(y_train.reshape(-1,1))
y_test = ohe.transform(y_test.reshape(-1,1))

### CNN Model
num_obs, feature, depth = X_train.shape
batch_size = 300
K.clear_session()

## Model Definition
input = Input(shape=(feature, depth))
C = Conv1D(filters=32, kernel_size=5, strides=1)(input)

# Layer1
Conv11 = Conv1D(filters=32, kernel_size=5, strides=1, padding='same')(C)
Acti11 = Activation("relu")(Conv11)
Conv12 = Conv1D(filters=32, kernel_size=5, strides=1, padding='same')(Acti11)
S1 = Add()([Conv12, C])
Acti12 = Activation("relu")(S1)
MaxP1 = MaxPooling1D(pool_size=5, strides=2)(Acti12)

# Layer2
Conv21 = Conv1D(filters=32, kernel_size=5, strides=1, padding='same')(MaxP1)
Acti21 = Activation("relu")(Conv21)
Conv22 = Conv1D(filters=32, kernel_size=5, strides=1, padding='same')(Acti21)
S2 = Add()([Conv22, MaxP1])
Acti22 = Activation("relu")(S2)
MaxP2 = MaxPooling1D(pool_size=5, strides=2)(Acti22)

# Layer3
Conv31 = Conv1D(filters=32, kernel_size=5, strides=1, padding='same')(MaxP2)
Acti31 = Activation("relu")(Conv31)
Conv32 = Conv1D(filters=32, kernel_size=5, strides=1, padding='same')(Acti31)
S3 = Add()([Conv32, MaxP2])
Acti32 = Activation("relu")(S3)
MaxP3 = MaxPooling1D(pool_size=5, strides=2)(Acti32)

# Layer4
Conv41 = Conv1D(filters=32, kernel_size=5, strides=1, padding='same')(MaxP3)
Acti41 = Activation("relu")(Conv41)
Conv42 = Conv1D(filters=32, kernel_size=5, strides=1, padding='same')(Acti41)
S4 = Add()([Conv42, MaxP3])
Acti42 = Activation("relu")(S4)
MaxP4 = MaxPooling1D(pool_size=5, strides=2)(Acti42)

# Layer5
Conv51 = Conv1D(filters=32, kernel_size=5, strides=1, padding='same')(MaxP4)
Acti51 = Activation("relu")(Conv51)
Conv52 = Conv1D(filters=32, kernel_size=5, strides=1, padding='same')(Acti51)
S5 = Add()([Conv52, MaxP4])
Acti52 = Activation("relu")(S5)
```

```
MaxP5 = MaxPooling1D(pool_size=5, strides=2)(Acti52)

Flat1 = Flatten()(MaxP5)
Dens1 = Dense(32)(Flat1)
Acti6 = Activation("relu")(Dens1)
Dens2 = Dense(32)(Acti6)
Dens3 = Dense(5)(Dens2)
Acti7 = Softmax()(Dens3)

# Compile
model = Model(inputs=input, outputs=Acti7)

## Learning rate definition
def exp_decay(epoch):
    initial_lrate = 0.001
    k = 0.75
    t = num_obs//(10000 * batch_size)  # every epoch we do num_obs/batch_size iteration
    learning_rate = initial_lrate * math.exp(-k*t)
    return learning_rate

learning_rate = LearningRateScheduler(exp_decay)

## Optimizer definition
adam = Adam(lr = 0.001, beta_1 = 0.9, beta_2 = 0.999)

## Compile Model
model.compile(loss='categorical_crossentropy', optimizer=adam, metrics=['accuracy'])

## Train model
history = model.fit(X_train, y_train,
                    epochs=75,
                    batch_size=batch_size,
                    verbose=2,
                    validation_data=(X_test, y_test),
                    callbacks=[learning_rate])

## Predict on Test Set
y_pred = model.predict(X_test, batch_size=32)

## Evaluation of Test Set
print(classification_report(y_test.argmax(axis=1), y_pred.argmax(axis=1)))

## Final Notes
#Safe model as json format, the model weights as .h5 file and include it in the code directory so that the
↪   model can be loaded by the faust worker node.
```

12.1.6 Faust worker Python script for signal extraction and classification
cnn_model.py

```
"""
Description:    Extracted signals are evaluated by the pre-trained cnn model. This script loads the
↪   pre-trained model parameter and weights at initialization.
```

```
                    The predict function is called for each signal.
    Important note: File needs to be run in a python 3.6+ environment.

    """
    # CNN Model setup
    # general libraries
    import math
    import random
    import pickle
    import numpy as np
    import pandas as pd
    import json

    np.random.seed(42)

    #keras models
    from keras.models import Model
    from keras import backend as K
    from keras.models import load_model
    from keras.models import model_from_json


    class CNN:
        def __init__(self):
        #load trained model parameter and model weight
            ospath="model/"
            with open(ospath+"model_in_json.json",'r') as f:
                model_json = json.load(f)

            self.model2 = model_from_json(model_json)
            self.model2.load_weights(ospath+"model_weights.h5")

        #prediction
        def predict(self, signal):
            X_test = np.expand_dims(signal, 2)
            y_pred = self.model2.predict(np.array( [X_test,]), batch_size=1)
            return y_pred
```

signal_extraction_faust_p36.py

```
    """
    Execution code for the signal extraction and classification(CNN) inside the Faust worker.

    Input:
    Output: Sensor Segment Stream with Anomaly Score
        {
         Timestamp: Begin Timestamp
         Signal: [signal_1...signal_n]
         Anomaly_score: [score_1..score_n]
         Frequency: 180
         Sensor_id: 6581
        }
```

```
Output: json: {timestamp:[XXXX.XX.XX,]
                signal:[21,123,512,13,5,1,2] #'MLII' normalized
                classification:{
                                N:85%
                                S:10%
                                V:5%
                                F:0%
                                Q:0%
                                }
                }
"""
np.random.seed(42)
#general libraries
import csv
import datetime
import numpy as np # linear algebra
import matplotlib.pyplot as plt
import json
import os
#faut worker import
import faust
#import the cnn model configurations
from model.cnn_test import CNN

#initialize CNN model on start of worker execution
model=CNN()

path=""#root folder
downsampling_rate=0#

#signal extraction of anomalous segment
def extract(data_batch):
    data_batch_signal=np.array(data_batch['signal'])

    #1. normalize the signal data on a 0-1 range
    print("load json",data_batch_signal)
    data_normalized =
    ↪ (data_batch_signal-min(data_batch_signal))/(max(data_batch_signal)-min(data_batch_signal))
    data_batch_normalized=np.column_stack((data_batch_signal, data_normalized))

    #2.& 3. calculate the gradient of the normalized signal and find local maxima based on zerocrossings
    ↪ of the first derivative
    zero_crossing=np.where(np.diff(np.sign(np.gradient(data_batch_normalized[:,1]))))

    #4. Find set of ECG R/peak candidates by applying a threshold of 0.9 on the normalized value of the
    ↪ local maxima
    data_batch_np=data_batch_normalized[:,1]
    detected_peaks=np.where(data_batch_np[zero_crossing]>=0.8)
    peak_indices=zero_crossing[0][detected_peaks]

    #5. Find median of R-R time intervals as the nominal heartbeat period of the window T
    previous=0
```

```python
peak_distances=[]
for peak in peak_indices:
    peak_distances.append(peak-previous)
    previous=peak
peak_distances=np.array(peak_distances)
median_length=int(np.median(peak_distances))
signal_save=0
#6. & 7. For each R-peak, selecting a signal part with the length equal to 1.2T. Padding each selected
↪   part with zeros to m
for model_inputs in peak_distances:
    signal_save+=1
    # create cnn input data for each signal
    plot_Data=np.append(
        data_batch_normalized[int(model_inputs):(int(model_inputs)+median_length),1],
        np.zeros((187-
        ↪   len(data_batch_normalized[int(model_inputs):(int(model_inputs)+median_length),1]),1)))

    # print("sendinput to prediction",plot_Data.tolist())
    # calculate heatbeat frequence for other use cases
    heartbeat_freq=data_batch['frequency']/median_length*60
    # classify signal
    results=model.predict(plot_Data.tolist())
    #create output schema for probability of all classification labels
    fields=[str(datetime.datetime.now()),'patient:',data_batch["sensor_id"],'room:
    ↪   A2',data_batch["sensor_id"],".Normal",results[0][0],"S",results[0][1],"V",results[0][2],
    "F",results[0][3],"Q",results[0][4],'heartbeat',heartbeat_freq]
    fields2=[str(datetime.date-
    ↪   time.now()),data_batch["sensor_id"],data_batch["sensor_id"],results[0][0],results[0][1],
    results[0][2],results[0][3],results[0][4],heartbeat_freq]

    #local save of results based on sensor_id(represents the patient)
    #append mode for each patient
    with open(path+'/result/result'+data_batch["sensor_id"]+'.csv','a') as f:
        writer = csv.writer(f)
        writer.writerow(fields)
#labeled classes are
#1 N
#2 S
#3 V
#4 F
#5 Q


#FAUST SETUP
app = faust.App(
    #Faust worker app name
    'ECG',
    #ip of the kafka broker and listening port. In this example the Faust worker is on the same node
    broker='kafka://localhost:9092',
    value_serializer='raw',
)
#topic name to listen on. ECG was defined as the topic list where the anomalous segments are stored
greetings_topic = app.topic('ECG')
```

```
#subscribe to topic(here ECG) and receive the signals(anomalous segments)
@app.agent(greetings_topic)
async def greet(signals):
    #of all anomalous segments, only take one at a time
    async for signal_input in signals:
        #load the anomalous segment which was send in json format
        data_json=json.loads(signal_input)
        #start the extraction and classification
        extract(data_json)
```

12.1.7 Directory tree explanation and execution instructions
Directory tree

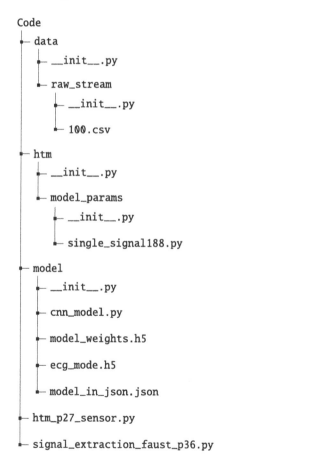

```
Code
├── data
│   ├── __init__.py
│   ├── raw_stream
│       ├── __init__.py
│       ├── 100.csv
├── htm
│   ├── __init__.py
│   ├── model_params
│       ├── __init__.py
│       ├── single_signal188.py
├── model
│   ├── __init__.py
│   ├── cnn_model.py
│   ├── model_weights.h5
│   ├── ecg_mode.h5
│   ├── model_in_json.json
├── htm_p27_sensor.py
├── signal_extraction_faust_p36.py
```

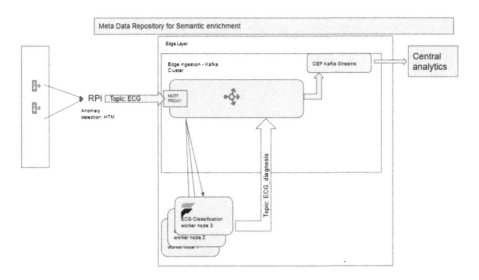

FIGURE 12.8

Complete processing architecture starting from the IoT data generation, the Kafka ingestion, the following processing via the Faust workers.

1 General information

We describe here the setup of the ecosystem for the demonstration of the anomaly detection and signal classification scenario over an ECG data stream.

2 System summary

System Summary section provides a general overview of the system (shown in Fig. 12.8). The summary outlines the software requirements and system's configuration. Three major components are required to execute the real-time analytics over anomalous ECG segments in this case study:

2.1 Anomaly detection prerequisites

The Numenta Platform for Intelligent Computing (NuPIC) is a machine intelligence platform that implements the HTM learning algorithms. NuPIC HTM is available for:

- Linux x86 64bit
- OS X 10.9
- OS X 10.10
- Windows 64bit

The following dependencies are required to install NuPIC on all operating systems.

- Python 2.7
- pip>=8.1.2
- setuptools>=25.2.0

- wheel>=0.29.0
- numpy
- C++ 11 compiler like gcc (4.8+) or clang

In this project the implementation was done in ubuntu.
Further was the MQTT connector library paho used.

2.2 ECG classification prerequisites

The following dependencies are required to execute the Keras ECG classifier:

- Python 3+
- Keras
- numpy
- Faust 1.8.0

Keras is a high-level neural networks API, written in Python and capable of running on top of TensorFlow. Faust is the worker node that executes the CNN model.

2.3 Kafka ecosystem prerequisites

The recommended OS is linux. It was tested to setup worker nodes on a window machine, were a successful execution was not possible.

With the focus of this manual to keep the complexity as low as possible, the basic requirements of the Confluent platform are given with:
CPU: Quad core 2 GHz+ CPU RAM: 6 GB Minimum database space: 10 GB

3.0 Getting started

Getting Started section explains how to get the proposed infrastructure installed in a step by step guide.

3.1 Eco-system setup

Kafka middleware and Kafka Streams (KSQL)
The setup was conducted on Ubuntu version 14.04.6 LTS. While Kafka and Kafka Streams were initially implemented manually, a setup can be done with the Confluent self managed Kafka service and stream processing platform. Due to the complexity of the configuration of all the components, the guide will follow the implementation with confluent.

Step 1: Setup confluent
The firewall needs to be configured based on the communication ports of the ecosystem. MQTT, distant workers or consumers might need to communicate with the kafka middleware component. Depending on the deployment, different ports of the firewall need to be configured.
Java 1.7+ is a prerequisite and was installed with the command:

```
sudo apt-get install openjdk-8-jre
```

The self managed confluent version 5.2.2 can be downloaded at
https://www.confluent.io/download/ and installed with:

```
sudo apt-get install curl
cd /opt/
```

```
sudo cp -r Downloads/confluent-5.2.2
chown -R /opt/confluent-5.2.2
```

Step 2: Test connection of MQTT with the Kafka eco-system

For the connection test with MQTT, the tool mosquitto was used. Mosquitto is an open source message broker that implements the MQTT protocol. With occurring problems in the setup and testing of the infrastructure, the communication ports of the producer can be tested as well as messages/events sent to the different ecosystem components. Following installation command was used in this project:

```
sudo apt-get update
sudo apt-get install mosquitto
sudo apt-get install mosquitto-clients
sudo apt install kafkacat
sudo apt install linuxbrew-wrapper
```

After the installation, the mqtt connection can be tested with the following example:

```
mosquitto_sub -h 127.0.0.1 -t dummy
mosquitto_pub -h 127.0.0.1 -t dummy -m "Test successful"
```

A positive test shows that the local MQTT communication is working. Remote connection to the MQTT Proxy should be tested in the same way with mosquito or similar tools to make sure that the identified ECG anomaly segments are retrieved by kafka.

The confluent environment variables need to be set in the following way. The instructions were retrieved at https://docs.confluent.io/current/cli/installing.html and modified for this project:

```
export PATH=/opt/confluent-5.2.2/bin:${PATH};
sudo apt-get install jq

export CONFLUENT_CURRENT=/opt/confluent-5.2.2/var
export CONFLUENT_HOME=/opt/confluent-5.2.2
export PATH=${CONFLUENT_HOME}/bin:${PATH};
```

After the right setup of the confluent framework, the following components need to be initialized in this project: Zookeeper, kafka cluster and kafka connectors (+ optional for CEP: Kafka streams and KSQL). The following command automatically starts the needed components:

```
confluent start ksql-server
kafka-mqtt-start /home/kafka/kafka-mqtt-quickstart.properties
```

To test the MQTT proxy, a consumer can be started to look for incoming messages (in this case on the topic "ECG").

```
kafka-console-consumer --bootstrap-server localhost: 9092
--topic ECG from-beginning
```

4.0 Using the system

The following section explains how to run the case study in the ecosystem.

4.1 Executing the ECG analytics in the ecosystem

To execute the ECG anomaly classification, first the Kafka infrastructure needs to be initialized. Afterwards the faust consumer for the classification tasks need to be started. As soon as eco-system is running, the ECG anomaly detection can be initialized, where incoming ECG data is analyzed with the HTM algorithm, and anomalous segments are sent over the Kafka infrastructure to the Faust workers that are assigned to the topic ECG.

STEP 1: Setup Kafka Infrastructure

The Kafka infrastructure is initialized with ksql and the mqtt proxy. To note, for this use case, KSQL is not needed but also started. The default MQTT proxy is 1883 and should be not blocked by other services.

```
export CONFLUENT_HOME=/opt/confluent-5.2.2
export PATH=${CONFLUENT_HOME}/bin:${PATH};
confluent start ksql-server
service mosquitto stop
kafka-mqtt-start /home/kafka/kafka-mqtt-quickstart.properties
```

STEP 2: Start Faust worker for ECG classification

The faust consumer is initialized with the command:

```
faust -A signal_extraction worker -l info
```

STEP 3: Execution of the anomaly detection over an incoming ECG stream

As soon as the Kafka system and Faust worker are running, the ECG anomaly detection can be tested with the file htm_p27.py. This file contains the setup with the connection configuration of the MQTT proxy. The configuration needs to be set on the IP address of the kafka system when run externally.

```
python htm_p27_sensor.py
```

Optional for analytics: Viewing the processed events and classification The anomalous events inside the Kafka architecture can be viewed with the command:

```
kafka-console-consumer --bootstrap-server localhost:9092
--topic ECG from-beginning
```

The classified signals inside the Kafka architecture can be viewed with the command:

```
kafka-console-consumer --bootstrap-server localhost: 9092
--topic ECG_classified from-beginning
```

This is the end of the user manual. An experimental step could be to track in a real-time analytics dashboard the aggregated probability of a heart condition of different users.

12.2 **Event processing network diagram**

In this section, the data event topics and channels are visualized (see Fig. 12.9). The event data flows are described as channels, which are the streams that effectively handle the routing of events. Event processing begins with raw event data from the medical devices and then ends on the right side, where complex event alerts are generated.

The intermediate queries are shown below for each event processing step. This implementation is just a showcase and in a real application, measurements and thresholds must be evaluated.

(1) Average HeartRate query

```
SELECT
AVG(hr) As AverageHr
FROM
hrTopic[ROWS4 SLIDE4]
```

(2) HeartRate history query

```
SELECT averageHr AS averageHr
FROM averageHrTopic[ROWS 4]
```

(3) HeartRate difference query

```
SELECT
a.averageHr AS currentAverageHr,
h.averageHr AS historicAverageHr,
a.averageHr - h.averageHr AS hrDifference,
((a.averageHr-h.averageHr)/h.averageHr)*100 AS hrChangePercentage
FROM
averageHrTopic[now] AS a,
historicAverageHrTopic[ROWS 1] AS h
WHERE
a.averageHr>0 AND h.averageHr>0
```

(4) HeartRate alert query

```
SELECT
|'Hr increase of'||hrChangePercentage||'from'||
averageHr||'to'||  hr AS Alert
FROM
hrDifferenceTopic[now] AS d
WHERE
d.hrChangePercentage>5
```

12.3 Data representation and enrichment

To achieve IoT semantic interoperability, data representation will be a fusion of already existing healthcare ontologies and IoT sensor stream representations. The existing healthcare ontologies will be not

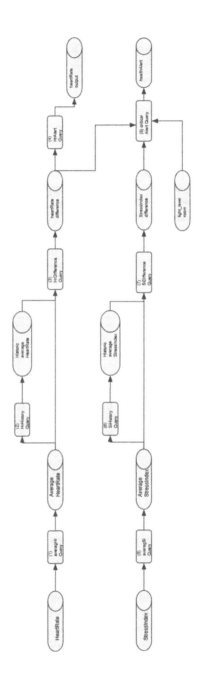

FIGURE 12.9

Event Processing Network Diagram of a complex event scenario for critical health status detection. The example contains the correlation of the heart rate and stress measurement event composition.

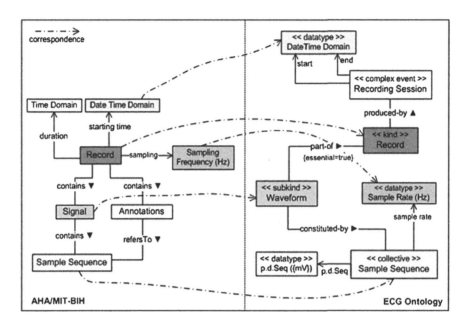

FIGURE 12.10

PhysioNet ECG data ontology representation [17].

defined in this work, and the focus held on the IoT stream representation and the possible option of linking the data. The IoT stream ontology decision factor will be the trade-off between expressiveness versus the complexity of the representation, with the goal of not unnecessarily increasing the complexity and message payload. The linking between existing healthcare ontologies and the IoT stream ontology will mainly be designed by the stream reasoning results and location-based information of patients and assisting personal. The final representation should enable complex inferences over treatments of an individual patient based on existing patient information and real-time diagnosis results.

12.3.1 Linked data and ontologies for healthcare applications

The used ECG data set is available as part of one of the databases at PhysioBank [15]. The databases comprehend ECG records containing a continuous recording from a single subject. In MIT-BIH, a signal is defined more restrictively as a finite sequence of integer samples. These are usually obtained by digitizing a continuous observed function of time at a fixed sampling frequency. All sample intervals for a given signal are equal. MIT DB records are each 30 min in duration and are annotated. This means that a label called an annotation describes each beat. The conceptual model resulting from this standard is depicted in the left-hand of Fig. 12.10. The figure illustrates a possible linking of the MIT-BIH dataset with the ECG ontology [7]. The annotation structure of the MIT-BIH ontology can be of importance in future ML training approaches.

To explicitly describe sensor measurements uniformly, there are proposals to enrich them with semantic web technologies. With an increasing amount of domain-specific IoT applications, the amount of specified domain knowledge-bases is increasing too. Domain applications use ontologies and semantic descriptions as a way to define types, properties, and relationships of entities that exist for a specific domain. In healthcare, many ontologies have been proposed to describe assisted living applications [17]. The following ontologies have been identified as being of relevance for a cross-domain correlation in this case study:

Medical applications

1. Disease Ontology (DO): human diseases for linking biomedical knowledge through disease data [13].
2. SNOMED-CT: advanced terminology and coding system for eHealth [6].
3. OdIH-WS: Ontology-driven Interactive Healthcare with Wearable Sensors [12]. This ontology has the goal to retrieve in real-time context information in with ontological methods by integrating meteorological data in order to prevent disease.
4. ContoExam [4] is an ontology developed handle interoperability problems of sensor networks in the context of eHealth applications. This ontology contains specific expressions and specifications for medical uses as examination vocabulary and expressions.
5. MetaQ is an ontology-based framework for activity recognition in AAL environments that uses SPARQL queries and OWL 2 activity patterns [14].

Ambient Assisted Living (AAL) applications

By definition, AAL refers to the integration of all kind of computerized and networking devices into a home environment aiming to improve the quality of life, especially, to elderly, for a well ageing in a digital world.

There are still issues and challenges in the field of AAL to tackle, such as defining an ontology that describes actions, activities with uncertainty, concurrent, and overlapping activities [10].

The Semantic Sensor Network Ontology (SSN) [5] is a suitable ontology for sensors description in IoT and can generate data in RDF format. Representing data using RDF or OWL enhances the interoperability between IoT systems [17]. Several healthcare ontologies have been proposed to describe diseases and activities of daily living.

The European project OpenIoT [13] is an open-source middleware platform. OpenIoT represents a on-demand access to cloud-based IoT services for connected objects [17]. OpenIoT architecture uses the CUPUS middleware as a cloud-based publish and subscribe processing engine for sensing as a service of sensors and relies on SSN sensors description. The stream data is stored as linked data and processed by SPARQL queries. OpenIoT can be viewed as a federation of several interconnected middleware projects in the field of smart cities or the campus and agriculture domain. OpenIoT could have been excellent for IoT health applications, but its complexity due to the variety of middleware solutions can be a significant drawback for the developer [17].

12.3.2 Proposed semantic representation along the data pipeline

For this thesis, the proposed RDF-schemas for the semantic representation of the data can be seen in Fig. 12.11. The representation followed the minimum requirements of the data processing pipeline and can be extended and mapped to different concepts in the field of healthcare and ECG representations.

```
Sensor Observations Example of ECG observation
PREF qu: <http://purl.oclc.org/NET/ssnx/qu/qu>
PREF ssn: <http://www.w3.org/ns/ssn/>
PREF ecg: <http://bioportal.bioontology.org/ontologies/1146>
PREF prov: <https://www.w3.org/TR/prov-o/>

:ecg_obs1 a ecg:Observation ;
        ssn:observedProperty ecg:ecg_waveform ;
        ssn:observedBy : ECG_device1 ;
        ssn:observationResult :ecg_obsvalue_1 ;
        time:inXSDDateTime "2019-07-21T16:20:00"^^xsd:datetime .

:ecg_obsvalue_1 a ecg:Sample ;
        qu:numericalValue "345.00"^^xsd:float ;
        qu:unit :millivolt .
```

FIGURE 12.11

Example of a semantic representation of sensor data.

```
@prefix s4h: <https://w3id.org/def/saref4health# > .
@prefix rdf: <http://www.w3.org/1999/02/22-rdf-syntax-ns# > .
@prefix rdfs: <http://www.w3.org/2000/01/rdf-schema# > .
@prefix saref: <https://w3id.org/saref# > .
@prefix saref4envi: <https://w3id.org/def/saref4envi# > .
@prefix sarefInst: <https://w3id.org/saref/instances# > .
@prefix om: <http://www.wurvoc.org/vocabularies/om-1.8/ > .
@prefix owl: <http://www.w3.org/2002/07/owl# > .

Session1_patient100 a s4h::TimeSeriesMeasurements;
        rdfs:label "Time series measurements patient 100";

Anomaly_observation_1 a s4h::ECGSampleSequence;
        rdfs:subClassOf: Session1_patient100 ;
        saref:isMeasuredIn = ElectricPotential_MilliVolts;
        saref:relatesToProperty(): only HeartElectricalActivity;
        saref:hasTimestap= "2018-04-22T22:15:30"^^xsd:dateTime ;

Anomaly_segment_1 asarefinst::ECGMeasurementsSeries_Example;
        rdf:type: Anomaly_observation_1 ;
        rdfs:label "sequence 001 -Patient 100 - ECG measurements series " ;
        saref4envi:hasFrequencyMeasurement sarefInst:FrequencyOf256Hertz ;
        saref:hasTimestamp= "2018-04-22T22:15:30"^^xsd:dateTime ;
        saref:hasValues =1002,1432,1222 (...);
```

FIGURE 12.12

Example of a semantic representation of anomalous segment.

Anomaly segment

It has turned out that the definition of an extracted anomalous time-series of an ECG stream can be hardly defined by ontologies in healthcare. In this scenario, the SAREF4Health ontology [2] offered a

```
Monitoring Result
:classified_events_patient100_2019-07-21 a prov:Entity;
        prov:wasGeneratedBy :physiologicalModel_patient1_2019-07-21;
        prov:wasDerivedFrom :ecg_patient1_2019-07-21;
        prov:wasAttributedTo :1dCNN.

:1dCNN a prov:Agent;
        prov:actedOnBehalfOf: doctorX .

:physiologicalModel_patient100_2019-07-21 a prov:Activity;
        prov:used :ecg_patient100_2019-07-21;
        prov:wasAssociatedWith :1dCNN;
        prov:endedAtTime "2019-07-21T17:02:02Z"^^xsd:dateTime.
```

FIGURE 12.13

Example of a semantic representation of derived event.

solution for a possible representation of this type of data. The proposed representation can be found in Fig. 12.12 and contains sequences.

Analytics data set descriptions

The ECG recording produces a data flow in which intermediate datasets can potentially be reused for other purposes, including other analytic methods, or data processing evaluations. The produced datasets in the data pipeline can be systematically annotated, starting from the raw datasets produced by the IoT ECG device, the anomaly detection process, classification as well as a possible complex event processing.

The monitoring result shows how the high level classified events of the CNN model is annotated as a derived dataset from the processed sensor data. The PROV-O7 ontology is used, as recommended by W3C when interchanging and representing provenance information [3]. It contains the following main concepts:

- Entities: Physical or digital entities.
- Activities: Actions that are performed on an entity like transformation or processing.
- Agents: perform or are responsible for the activities upon the entities.

The example in Fig. 12.13 represents a classified event dataset as an entity, which is generated by an activity, described as a physiological model performed by the CNN algorithm.

12.3.3 Issues in the context of semantic enrichment

Some projects have proposed to tackle the interoperability issue from a technological perspective by relying on middleware solutions that promote the interoperability and the manageability of sensors in an IoT system. Although the existing semantic middleware proposals address many challenges and requirements regarding the interoperability in IoT systems, there are still open research challenges related to scalability and real-time reasoning. Using ontologies affects the requirements as parsing, storing, inferencing, and querying over RDF data takes a longer time compared to simple data formats.

Furthermore, do ontologies require domain knowledge and expertise and require a higher computational cost. The complexity is considered to be related to the diversity of libraries to use and the complexity of the programming environment [17]. Another challenge that could be addressed in the research area is related to ontologies for sensors and domain descriptions. Providing a complete ontology that combines the health care domain and sensors in IoT is still an ongoing challenge. Using MOM approaches with semantic descriptions in IoT is still in an early stage.

W3C Web of Things (WoT) [9] can be seen as a major solution for interoperability issues in IoT. It allows an easier way for IoT applications to build upon smart things. The WoT concept relies on the connectivity service of IoT and easy access to sensors data [8]. It can be seen as an evolution of the Internet of things where all components share their information and collaborate to generate and infer advanced knowledge. Using semantic descriptions enables data contextualization for data stream discovery and querying. New research shifts to the semantic web of things [16] where data can be integrated with data and available services. WoT is a open research to improve and investigate several IoT environments, including healthcare.

12.4 **Key features**

In this chapter a practical working procedure and analysis for an ECG dataset is presented.

- ☑ ECG signals may be contaminated with motion noise as the patient is constantly moving. The noisy signal may have a similar morphology to abnormal cardiac signals resulting in false positives.
- ☑ The model training requires a labeled ECG signal. In order to label the ECG data set, trained personnel are needed. In addition, the labeling process is very time-consuming. For example, a 10 s one ECG signal has 2500 data points, and the continuous monitoring usually takes 24–48 h.
- ☑ The ECG heartbeat data is highly imbalanced. Over 99% of the illustrated heartbeat data consists of normal heartbeats, and only 1% presents 35 abnormal cases. Therefore, the highly imbalanced dataset makes it more difficult to adjust the learning step. Several options could be explored to reduce the effect of imbalanced data, such as database re-sampling or using the cost-sensitive method, kernel-based method, or active learning.
- ☑ The HTM algorithm demonstrated that 93% of all the anomalies can be found while reducing the dataload on the eco-system by 57%.
- ☑ Aiming to get insights into scalability in EEG data stream processing and analysis, the extraction and classification of anomalous signals were evaluated on a Faust worker node. Faust is a free Python cluster computing platform for data stream processing.
- ☑ The application of ontologies and annotations to ECG data sets is pointed out as a potentially useful means for ML approaches.
- ☑ Some of the issues that arise in the IoT semantic interoperability and semantic enrichment of data streams are identified and analyzed.

References

[1] MIT-BIH arrhythmia database directory, https://archive.physionet.org/physiobank/database/html/mitdbdir/mitdbdir.htm. (Accessed 5 September 2019).

[2] Saref4health ontology, https://w3id.org/def/saref4health. (Accessed 24 August 2019).

[3] W3c prov-overview, https://www.w3.org/TR/prov-overview/. (Accessed 8 September 2019).

[4] P. Brandt, T. Basten, S. Stuiik, V. Bui, P. de Clercq, L.F. Pires, M. van Sinderen, Semantic interoperability in sensor applications making sense of sensor data, in: 2013 IEEE Symposium on Computational Intelligence in Healthcare and e-Health (CICARE), IEEE, 2013, pp. 34–41.

[5] M. Compton, P. Barnaghi, L. Bermudez, R. García Castro, O. Corcho, S. Cox, J. Graybeal, M. Hauswirth, C. Henson, A. Herzog, V. Huang, K. Janowicz, D. Kelsey, D. Phuoc, L. Lefort, M. Leggieri, H. Neuhaus, A. Nikolov, K. Page, K. Taylor, The SSN ontology of the W3C semantic sensor network incubator group, Web Semantics: Science, Services and Agents on the World Wide Web 17 (2012) 12.

[6] K. Donnelly, SNOMED-CT: the advanced terminology and coding system for eHealth, Studies in Health Technology and Informatics 121 (2006) 279.

[7] B. Gonçalves, G. Guizzardi, J. Pereira Filho, Using an ECG reference ontology for semantic interoperability of ECG data, Journal of Biomedical Informatics 44 (02 2011) 126–136.

[8] D. Guinard, V. Trifa, Towards the web of things: web mashups for embedded devices, in: Workshop on Mashups, Enterprise Mashups and Lightweight Composition on the Web (MEM 2009), in Proceedings of WWW (International World Wide Web Conferences), Madrid, Spain, vol. 15, 2009.

[9] D. Guinard, V. Trifa, F. Mattern, E. Wilde, From the internet of things to the web of things: resource-oriented architecture and best practices, in: Architecting the Internet of Things, Springer, 2011, pp. 97–129.

[10] M.C. Huebscher, J.A. McCann, Adaptive middleware for context-aware applications in smart-homes, in: Proceedings of the 2nd Workshop on Middleware for Pervasive and Ad-Hoc Computing, ACM, 2004, pp. 111–116.

[11] T.J. Jun, M.H. Nguyen, D. Kang, D. Kim, D. Kim, Y.-H. Kim, ECG arrhythmia classification using a 2-D convolutional neural network, arXiv:1804.06812 [abs], 2018.

[12] J. Kim, J.-K. Kim, L. Daesung, K.-Y. Chung, Ontology driven interactive healthcare with wearable sensors, Multimedia Tools and Applications 71 (07 2014).

[13] J. Kim, J. Lee, OpenIoT: an open service framework for the internet of things, in: 2014 IEEE World Forum on Internet of Things (WF-IoT), March 2014, pp. 89–93.

[14] G. Meditskos, S. Dasiopoulou, I. Kompatsiaris, MetaQ: a knowledge-driven framework for context-aware activity recognition combining SPARQL and OWL 2 activity patterns, Pervasive and Mobile Computing 5 (02 2015).

[15] G. Moody, R. Mark, The impact of the MIT-BIH arrhythmia database, IEEE Engineering in Medicine and Biology Magazine: the Quarterly Magazine of the Engineering in Medicine & Biology Society 20 (06 2001) 45–50.

[16] D. Pfisterer, K. Römer, D. Bimschas, O. Kleine, R. Mietz, C. Truong, H. Hasemann, A. Kröller, M. Pagel, M. Hauswirth, et al., SPITFIRE: toward a semantic web of things, IEEE Communications Magazine 49 (11) (2011) 40–48.

[17] R. Zgheib, E. Conchon, R. Bastide, Semantic Middleware Architectures for IoT Healthcare Applications, Springer International Publishing, Cham, 2019, pp. 263–294.

Ethics, emerging research trends, issues and challenges

Protecting patient data

13.1 Ethics and privacy in patient data monitoring

13.1.1 Ethical considerations for machine learning healthcare applications

Development: perpetuation of bias within training data, risk of harm due to group membership, and obtaining training data

An important and acknowledged concern [41,168] in Machine Learning Healthcare Applications (ML-HCAs) development relates to the possibility of bias, particularly whether latent biases in training data may be perpetuated or even amplified. Examples already exist of predictive scores failing both because of poorly composed training data and racially discriminatory outcomes when expanded to broader populations [41,148]. For example, ML programs designed to aid judges in sentencing by predicting an offender's risk for recidivism have shown a disturbing propensity for racial discrimination [69]. In healthcare, when used to predict cardiovascular event risk in nonCaucasian populations, Framingham study data has shown bias both over- and under-estimating risk for different specific populations [74]. Furthermore, any perpetuated biases incorporated into an ML-HCA may subsequently impact clinical decisions and support self-fulfilling prophecies. For instance, suppose clinicians currently routinely de-escalate or withhold interventions in patients with specific severe injuries or progressive conditions. In that case, ML systems may classify such clinical scenarios as nearly always fatal. Any ML-HCA built on such a classification would likely result in an even higher likelihood of de-escalation or withholding, thereby reducing the opportunity to improve outcomes for such conditions [25,68,144,49,196].

Training of ML-HCAs against real-world data, rather than high-quality research-grade data, might be a suboptimal clinical practice, not aligned with the best scientific evidence. On the other side, an algorithm's overreliance on research-grade data alone may miss important clinically relevant sources of knowledge, lowering the quality of care delivered [66]. A related concern is obtaining needed training data and questions of data ownership, pricing and protecting privacy. Machine learning requires large amounts of training data. The aggregation and curation of these large datasets raise not only issues regarding specifying the standards that high-quality reference standard data must achieve but also issues regarding data privacy and data ownership [2,8,49,78,84,97,165,40,206,28].

For diagnostic ML-HCAs, training data will likely be based on data collected from individual patients obtained during routine clinical care (such as laboratory test values, biopsy findings, or diagnostic images) or from individuals enrolled in health insurance plans (such as medical diagnoses from medical encounters or healthcare utilization patterns), along with personal demographic information. Other ML-HCAs may be based on data from nonclinical sources (such as personal devices, social media, financial or legal sources), which may contain potentially controversial data elements or have been collected via novel means that we can not foresee. While privacy laws and regulations are currently in place, open questions need to be addressed regarding who owns the data, the traceability of specific data elements from each patient into the "big" datasets, and whether patient rights to privacy should be extended or curtailed. For example, how should we adjudicate claims regarding the value of the data, the value of each individual's contribution of their data to the aggregate dataset on which an ML-HCA is constructed, and the ML-HCA pricing itself? Most likely, large-scale health systems will have generated and compiled much of this big data, which in turn was paid for by insurance premiums and copays. Many data sets, particularly those involving image or biopsy interpretations, may also reflect the significant intellectual contributions of interpreting clinicians.

The subsequent effort to curate the data and then develop the ML-HCA adds value to the raw data, but certainly not all of the potential value. Just as there are debates regarding drug pricing, when the initial development of a drug was supported by federal or nonprofit funding prior to acquisition and further development by a pharmaceutical company, similar debates are already emerging with ML-HCAs. There has also been ongoing patient activism for inclusion in recognition for specimen contribution to scientific advances [28].

Calibration: accuracy, trading off test characteristics, and calibrated risk of harm

For an ML-HCA to maximize clinical benefits and minimize harm, the application must perform by the cardinal design features of:

- Safety: Preventing injuries and hazards.
- Efficiency: Application effectively solves the problem it was designed for and does so at a reasonable cost, in particular regarding the costs of incorrect classifications, such as false negative or false positive diagnoses.
- Equity: The advantages of the application are shared fairly by all.

Thus, an application has to provide accurate diagnostic or predictive information on the vast majority of patients for whom the ML-HCA is intended to be used, irrespective of subgroups such as age or race. Determining the accuracy of an ML-HCA is, however, not straightforward. Unlike ML designed for other contexts, such as playing games of skill (e.g. chess, go), many medical decisions and diagnoses cannot be perfectly labeled as correct or incorrect, and downstream outcomes cannot always be anticipated [66]. This is a known challenge with a reference "gold standards" in healthcare [71].

While ML accuracy can be higher than that of individual experts in interpreting clinical images such as radiology scans, pathology slides, and photographs of skin lesions [47], the estimated accuracy of an ML-HCA is dependent on the clinical context in which the application is being assessed. Validation studies, therefore, need to be done in the context of managed research trials and general populations of patients. In these settings, endpoints should address patient safety (measured as sensitivity, assuring that patients with the disease or in a designated risk category are not missed), the efficiency of the application to provide an accurate diagnosis (measured as specificity, assuring that patients without the disease are not overdiagnosed, along with corresponding positive and negative predictive values).

A fair ML-HCA will provide equivalent levels of accuracy within the intended-use population across multiple patient subgroups or characteristics and achieve comparable levels of "determinability" or the ability of the HCA to provide a clinically relevant output based on the available inputs. The notion of accuracy in an ML-HCA inherently involves tradeoffs between test characteristics, guided by designer value judgments with consequent ethical implications. For any diagnostic or predictive test, the performance is calibrated to trade off a higher level of one test characteristic (such as more people with the condition being correctly classified as having the condition) with a corresponding lower level of another test characteristic (such as more people who do not have the condition being misclassified as having the condition). Both of these test characteristics will also be influenced by the determinability characteristics of the test. That is, whether the test can use the clinically available information or whether the test cannot determine the disease status or determine a predicted probability.

The determinability test characteristic is also a calibrated tradeoff between returning a result or declaring that the inputted information is insufficient. Even if a specific ML-HCA is found to be superior to an established clinical practice regarding all test characteristics, that specific ML-HCA will have calibrated greater accuracy and particular forms of inaccuracy. The design will predictably generate false positives and false negatives, or indeterminate results, as must be the case with any classification method, whether based on human judgment or machine learning. The key ethical consideration would be whether these inaccuracies and any consequent harms are outweighed by potential benefits and distributed among patients in an equitable manner.

Regulatory issues and policy initiatives

Regulatory issues and policy initiatives in AI systems do more than process information and help officials make decisions. Systems such as the software that controls an airplane on autopilot or a fully driverless car operate direct and physical control over objects in the human environment [36]. Different systems, like medical and radiological devices, provide sensitive services that require training and certification when performed by physicians [110,155,36,174,201]. These applications raise further questions about the AI system standards that are held and the procedures and techniques available to ensure that these standards are met. Questions arise about technologies in development, such as autonomous imaging readers and how to judge systems that give health advice, which requires compliance with complex fiduciary and other duties tied to human judgment.

As unambiguity is one of the cornerstones of any legislation, policy makers need to address the first aspect when regulating new field definitions. This aspect becomes a problem with AI. The lack of a stable, unanimous definition or instantiation of AI complicates efforts to develop an appropriate policy infrastructure. Moreover, one might question the usefulness of the word policy in describing societal efforts to channel AI in the public interest. There are other terms in circulation. For example, governance rather than policy: A new initiative anchored by the Massachusetts Institute of Technology's Media Lab and Harvard University's Berkman Klein Center for Internet and Society calls itself the Ethics and governance of Artificial Intelligence Fund. The policy is needed for the governance of AI in medicine. The second question facing policymakers is whether software used in healthcare should be considered a medical device for legislation. Both the EU and the US have criteria for identifying healthcare and medical devices. However, both definitions share a purpose-based approach. It is interesting to note that not all AI programs used in healthcare are considered medical devices, like AI programs that analyze large amounts of data to develop knowledge about a disease or condition, rather than deciding on treatment options for an individual patient, are not necessarily considered to have a medical purpose and are therefore considered medical devices. This is the fundamental distinction between research programs that advance medical knowledge and those that promote change in healthcare. According to Thierer et al. [198] policymakers can take two main approaches to regulate AI systems. One is the precautionary principle approach, which restricts or sometimes completely bans certain applications due to potential risks, which leads to these applications being never be tested. The other approach is the permissionless innovation approach, where experimentation is free and problems arise as they occur. Scherer [185] instead distinguished between exante and expost regulation. Exante regulation is preventive and tries to anticipate the risks, similar to the precautionary principle [198]. In contrast, expost regulation is retrospective and focuses more on remedying harm that has occurred [119], which is similar to the permissionless innovation approach mentioned above [198]. On the one hand, expost regulation is hindered by the autonomous nature of AI systems, which evolve and constantly change in unpredictable ways according to their experience and learning [112].

On the other hand, exante regulations are hindered by AI applications:

- Discreetness: Development requires little physical infrastructure.
- Discreteness: Components can be designed by different subjects for different purposes without actual coordination.
- Diffuseness: Subjects can be geographically dispersed and still collaborate on the same project.
- Opacity: It can be difficult for outside observers to identify and understand all the features of an AI system [185].

Finally, another problem for policymakers is time. Companies understand the potential of machine learning and are constantly collecting new data to analyze and use [141]. In an ever-changing and unpredictable environment, regulations must be timely. These premises explain why medical device regulation is so contentious and subject to the notions of policy and subjective interpretations. While AI technologies flourished in a permission-free innovation policy environment in the US, policymakers in the EU pursued a different policy for this revolutionary branch of technology [198]. Faster approval of AI medical devices helps manufacturers generate revenue, and doctors can benefit from having more tools at their disposal. However, the ultimate goal of bringing new devices to market should be to improve disease prevention, diagnosis, treatment, and prognosis, with a potentially positive impact on patient outcomes. Hence, systems for approving new medical devices need to provide pathways to market for important innovations while guaranteeing that patients are sufficiently protected.

Challenges of AI in medicine: the case of radiology

Advances in algorithm development combined with easy access to computational resources are currently enabling the use of AI applications in medical decision-making tasks with promising results [111,120]. The use of AI techniques in radiology is a relevant topic for research teams. Deep-learning algorithms are currently being used in mammography for breast cancer detection [55], in CT for colorectal cancer diagnosis [192], in chest radiography for lung nodule detection [44], in MRI for brain tumor segmentation [157] and for the diagnosis of neurological diseases such as Alzheimer's disease [59]. The widespread enthusiasm and momentum regarding the development of AI-based software in radiology are reflected in the increasing evolution of literature over the last decade [158].

Nevertheless, some ethical challenges need to be avoided. One, in particular, is the concern that algorithms may reflect human bias in decision-making. Since healthcare already varies by ethnicity, it is possible that some ethical biases could be inadvertently built into medical algorithms. AI applications used in nonmedical settings have already been shown to make difficult decisions that reflect biases inherent in the data they are trained with [42]. Recently, a program designed to assist judges in sentencing by predicting an offender's risk of recidivism has shown a troubling propensity to discriminate. Likewise, an algorithm created to predict outcomes from genetic findings may be biased if there are no genetic studies in certain populations [42]. The intent behind AI design must also be considered, as some devices can be programmed to work in unethical ways like for example, Uber's algorithm tool "Greyball" which was designed to predict which passengers might be undercover agents, allowing the company to identify and circumvent local laws [42]. In another example, Volkswagen's algorithm enabled vehicles to pass emissions tests by reducing their nitrogen oxide emissions during testing [42]. Similarly, clinical AI algorithm developers might be faced with programming AI systems to guide users to take clinical actions that would yield higher profits for their purchasers (e.g., by recommending drugs, tests, medical devices in which they participate or by changing referral patterns), but not necessarily reflect better care [42]. These examples demonstrate the urgency of serious regulation and policy initiatives on the use of AI, particularly in complicated care practices where the correct diagnosis of a disease and the best management of a patient can be contentious.

Accountability and responsibility: the case of evidence-based medicine

In addition to regulation and data protection itself, there are other legal implications of AI and its use in healthcare. One of these is accountability. As soon as AI starts to make autonomous decisions about diagnoses and treatments and thus goes beyond its role as a tool, the problem arises of whether the developer can be held accountable for its decisions. The first question arises of who gets sued when an AI-based device makes a mistake. Errors in AI occur primarily when mixing factors are correlated with pathological entities in the training datasets rather than actual signs of disease. When AI devices make decisions, their decision is based on the data they have collected, the type of algorithms they are based on, and what they learned since they were created. The reason their decisions are unpredictable is based on two major issues [185].

First, AI devices trying to mimic the neural networks of the human brain think differently than humans. They "think" faster and more accurately [112,115,39]. Usually, there are many possibilities to decide, and people cannot process and weigh all of them to make a decision. The human brain considers the more obvious possibilities, while AI systems can consider every possible scenario and consideration [178,140,110,174,141,115,142]. For this reason, when faced with a decision, we have no common ground with AI devices. Therefore, we cannot predict how AI System will decide in a given situation.

On the other side, AI systems learn from their real experiences, which are inherently unpredictable. Since it is impossible to predict what experiences the system will have, it is also impossible to predict how it will evolve. Suppose something goes wrong because of a decision made by an application; in that case, it is worth considering whether the device itself or its designer/creator is considered at fault. Will the designer be considered negligent for not foreseeing what was described as unpredictable? AI plays an increasingly crucial role in the relationship between clinicians and patients in the coming years [110,198,175,207], and will need to be restrained by core ethical principles such as beneficial care and respect for patients that have guided clinicians throughout the history of medicine [41]. Certainly, a radiologist is much more than an interpreter of images. The responsibilities of a practicing radiologist further include communicating findings, quality assurance, quality improvement, performing interventional radiology procedures, education, setting policy, and many other tasks that computer programs cannot handle. The ability to interpret complex findings, the medical judgment and the wisdom of an experienced radiologist are difficult to quantify or simulate with AI systems [110].

Due to the evolving complexity of AI systems, some of its workings will inevitably look to be a black box to most but the few who can comprehend how it works [39]. This does not mean that the aspect of accountability is solved. In a broader theoretical framework, there should be distinguished between data analysis and complex decision-making. In the context of evidence-based medicine [183], the best external evidence (data from high-quality studies and metaanalyses, guidelines from government agencies and medical societies) must be combined with patient preferences and values, using personal medical expertise. By introducing AI into, for example, radiology, there is also a kind of internal evidence that comes from applying AI to patients' imaging procedures. It can be argued that AI might be able to take over this task instead of doctors in the future. However, if patient preferences and values play a nonnegligible role, human interaction and empathy between doctor and patient will remain a fundamental dimension. Certainly, AI will allow doctors to spend more time communicating with patients and consulting in multidisciplinary teams. Less time will be preoccupied with routine and monotonous tasks that can be effectively done by computers. Accountability for an AI performance can be a simple matter for insurance purposes. The ethical and legal responsibility for decision-making will remain in the hands of the natural intelligence of physicians. From this perspective, in difficult cases, responsibility is likely to be assumed by multidisciplinary boards that consider the information provided by AI to be relevant but not always conclusive.

13.1.2 EU General Data Protection Regulation (GDPR)
Security and privacy challenges in healthcare
Healthcare systems are collaborative due to the high number of users and stakeholders such as physicians, nurses, lab technicians, pathologists, and administrators working together to maximize the effective use of raw and defined healthcare data. Each user/stakeholder generates heterogeneous data such as physical exams, lab reports, diagnostics notes, clinical notes, imaging analysis, patients observations and interviews, and progress and outcomes of the therapies and treatments. The use of emerging technologies, sensors and sharing techniques, and information and communication techniques make it easier to generate and share healthcare data and introduce challenges concerning security and privacy. This is because electronic healthcare data is susceptible to unlawful access, compromise integrity, and unauthorized distribution [172,96,73]. Another major challenge with big data applications in the healthcare sector is healthcare data's complex and distributed nature, diverse schema and standards, and rapid growth of new health terminologies and ontologies. The major challenge here is not the lack of data but the lack of information to support decision-making, planning, and strategy. Following are some of the issues with the adoption of big data in healthcare [130].

Resistance to change
The Healthcare system is traditionally lagging in adopting new technologies compared to the other sectors such as banking or industry. This is because of lack of technical-, administrative support, legislative issues, lack of trust and slow changes to the medical practices, and lack of expertise in the ICT.

Fragmentation of healthcare data
Healthcare data is fragmented and distributed across the healthcare system consisting of legacy and modern equipment with limited interoperability capabilities. It is, therefore, challenging to integrate different data types due to different schema, formats, and standards.

Ethical challenges
Access to complete and comprehensive data related to a patient on time is vital to effective diagnosis and treatment. However, sharing of information among many stakeholders becomes difficult due to

ethical issues, including confidentiality and integrity of the patients' data, control, and extent of access to medical record, ownership, and governance of the healthcare data and commercialization of the healthcare data.

Proliferation of healthcare standards

Standards are agreed-upon specifications that allow different systems, tools, and platforms to work with each other. The Healthcare sector lacks a single central standard for various sources of health data. Due to different layouts and formats of diagnostic reports, examinations, drugs, and decreases, it is challenging to integrate data from various sources and stakeholders into a single entity.

Rules, laws, and regulatory bodies

Other factors that must be considered while using big data analytics for healthcare are rules and laws. Healthcare privacy and security not only concern with the expectations but also with norms involving professional practice, privileges, protected communication, and duty of confidentiality, as well as to data collection, distribution, and retention [150]. In many developed countries, other health acts guide handling healthcare data and setting benchmarks on setting guidelines on how to whom and to what extent of healthcare data be enclosed.

Technological challenges

In today's business environment, many devices, users, and enormous traffic all combine to create a proliferation of data. Security and privacy issues are the center for the optimum use of big data. Traditional tools to handle such data are insufficient. New tools and methods are required to handle the large volume of healthcare data. It can be concluded that the list of issues mentioned above, privacy, and security concerns are vital to the penetration and adoption of big data deployment in the healthcare sector. Trust in the confidentiality and security of the healthcare data results in the level of information a person is willing to share [150]. It is necessary to discuss different types of healthcare data and their unique privacy and security issues to fully understand the problem concerning generating, storing, retrieving, and processing healthcare data.

Security challenges for healthcare data

Although different types of healthcare data are interrelated, they are unique. They thus have individual security and privacy issues based on their source and type of information they possess [117,58,217]. In this section, we present a discussion regarding security and privacy challenges for different healthcare data sources.

GDPR regulations and patients health data

The European Union has agreed with its member countries to employ the General Data Protection Regulation (GDPR) on 25 May 2018. The GDPR is the European Union's new law for ensuring the protection of citizens' private data. It replaces EU existing law, i.e., Data Protection Directive, which has been in effect since 1995. The GDPR imposes a wide range of requirements and regulations on the organizations used to collect and process citizens' personal data. These requirements include transparency, fairness, and lawfulness in handling and processing the personal data of citizens. Furthermore, the law also limits organizations to process personal data with the consent of users and for legitimate purposes. It also requires that organizations must ensure the security, integrity, and confidentiality of personal data by imposing reasonable security measures. In addition, the GDPR empowers the citizen to sue the organizations in the court of law that breach the GDPR. The patient's health data is considered the most sensitive and private data and requires effective security from the insider as well as from the outsider. It is forbidden to share personal data without their consent, even with employees of the health organization. To fulfill the GDPR and effective security of patients' data, we presented a framework for effective data access based on the regulations and rights assigned to the GDPR organization.

Patient generated health data

Patient-generated health data (PGHD) is health-related data created, recorded, or collected from patients to address a specific health problem. PGHD includes, but is not limited to, medical history, treatment history, biometric data, symptoms, or lifestyle choices. PGHD helps collect information that helps improve the quality of care, reduce costs and improve patient safety. PGHD is different from other types of health data, i.e., the patient generates and collects data and later decides with whom to share the data. With the advent of Big Data in healthcare, a problematic cliché is that more data equals more knowledge, which leads to better health outcomes [152]. However, PGHD's success in diagnosis and treatment is based mainly on patients' willingness to share personal data with healthcare providers. This sharing ultimately depends on a patient's trust in the entire sharing mechanism.

With the advent of the Internet, social media, and ever-increasing means of data sharing, the whole phenomenon of healthcare data sharing will be successful only when the elements of privacy, security, trust, and ownership are carefully addressed. The omnipresent Internet and the abundance of wearable online devices have opened a new horizon of healthcare data where an enormous amount of real-time data is being generated, stored, and shared on-demand using mobile applications and Wifi connectivity. While PGHD provides several opportunities, it also introduces many challenges in the healthcare industry. Under poorly designed privacy and security policies, there is a potential to exploit healthcare data by unlawful sharing and retrieving sensitive information. With ever-growing data sources, there is a need to clarify the role of PGHD in the health industry and the commercial sector. For example, the National Institute of Health introduced the Precision Medicine Initiative (PMI), described as a new way of conducting research that promotes open, responsible data sharing with the highest regard for participant privacy and puts engaged participants at the center of research efforts [182,16]. This initiative drew an assumption that in the future, healthcare data will not produce any harmful unintended consequence for the data donors. However, we cannot rely on these assumptions and hope that attacks on privacy will be managed and data handled with responsibility and care. Furthermore, it must be noted that although the healthcare data related to the clinical environment and PGHD are fusing, existing rules and regulations are generally only applicable to the data produced within the boundaries of the healthcare service providers. Furthermore, data produced outside the healthcare sector is not yet fully covered and affected by such regulations.

Mobile technology enables users to generate a large volume of real-time data. Furthermore, with improved methods of collecting, processing, and storing a large amount of data being developed, the conception of the healthcare sector and mobile technologies are evolving. Consequently, it conveys information and conveys medical knowledge and means to understand the detail and processes happening in real-time. However, mobile devices and monitoring tools generating healthcare data outside the boundaries of the healthcare sector are not covered within the rules and regulations in place to protect in-clinic healthcare data. Furthermore, as remote sensors, monitors and devices are becoming more common and cheaper, it is becoming similar and common to use real-time medical data to improve the well-being of the patients. However, data breaches, exploitation, and unlawful exposure create a real threat to the adoption and penetration of this trend in healthcare services.

Security and privacy are growing concerns that are creating a fear of sharing sensitive personal data. It has become obvious that these security and privacy issues must be addressed to allow a smooth penetration of PGHD in the healthcare industry. According to [195], the social norms currently being observed in the society where people are becoming increasingly comfortable with sharing personal information and self-disclosure on social media sites. Mobile application developers and social media sites are assuring users of the safety and privacy of their sensitive data and encouraging users to share their sensitive information without the fear of exploitation. However, do they provide security and confidentiality to the users' data? With data breaches and exploitation of online data is common, it is obvious that not enough is being done, yet more efforts are required to secure online PGHD fully. In summary, there is a dilemma in the whole phenomenon of PGHD where we need to share the data freely to benefit from the offerings of the real-time PGHD data fully, but also this data must be scrutinized to make sure that only limited and necessary sharing of the data to address the privacy and security concerns.

Clinical data

Clinical data is the most important source of healthcare data. Clinical data is either gathered through the treatment of patients by the healthcare service providers during a planned and controlled clinical trial. Clinical data can be divided into six major types:

- Electronic Health Record: This is by far the most abundant form of healthcare data. It is generated in the healthcare service provider facilities and usually not available for external research activities. It is a comprehensive healthcare data set and includes a list of attributes such as personal information, age, address, lab reports, blood and urine tests, X-ray reports, insurance coverage information, medical condition, and treatment history.
- Administrative data: This type mainly contains data related to admission and discharge of a patient from a healthcare facility.
- Claims Data: This is mainly for billing purposes and contains insurance-related information such as coverage type, membership detail, and claims history. It can be obtained from commercial healthcare facilities or government agencies.
- Patient Disease Registry: This contains information related to chronic diseases and helps understand current trends in diseases such as diabetes, heart disease, cancer, HIV, and asthma. It also helps identify any potential outbreak of disease and uses to manage and contain any outbreak. Patient/decease registry also helps draw national healthcare drives and planning the health policy of a nation.
- Health Survey: Health surveys analyze the overall health condition and help identify the most prevalent chronic diseases in a population. It results from national and local level surveys which help in research and development activities. This is one of the few healthcare data types which are primarily used for research purpose.
- Clinical Trial Data: Clinical trial data refers to information collected through publicly and privately supported clinical studies from around the world. Most of the healthcare data produced and generated within the boundaries of a healthcare services provider are considered clinical data. It is either collected during an ongoing treatment of patients or as a part of formal clinical trials. It is by far the most exclusive type of healthcare data, including administrative and demographic information,

diagnosis, treatment, prescription drugs, laboratory tests, physiologic monitoring data, hospitalization, patient insurance, hospital discharge data, claims data, disease registries, health surveys, and clinical trial data [130]. As before, clinical data is of utmost importance when used to aid diagnosis, analysis, and treatment of patients; however, digitization of the healthcare data and sharing and transmission of this sensitive data among healthcare services providers introduces privacy and security challenges.

Security and privacy goals are typically patients' expectations with the healthcare data and its handling. According to the Good Medical Practices, patients have the right to expect that their personal information will not be shared except for the fulfillment of the professional duties of the health services providers, with the consent of the patients. The health service providers must share the clinical data only when needed, and only related information is shared; throughout this process, patients need to be aware of how much and with whom data has been shared. This is particularly important when interpreted within the newly formed regulations within GDPR. Additionally, the integrity and confidentiality of the healthcare data are also important. The Healthcare system handling all clinical data must protect data against any unlawful alteration and be protected against attacks to ensure availability. It is especially challenging to detect data corruption in an electronic database due to malicious actors targeting such datasets and the untrustworthiness of the communication links used for data sharing. Guidelines and regulations such as the Health Insurance Portability and Accountability Act of 1996 (HIPAA) and GDPR cover clinical data, but the integrity of data can not be ensured by these regulations alone. A hardened system capable of defending healthcare data from malicious attacks and data alteration is required to ensure the integrity and availability of the information for lawful use. Consequently, there is a need for an effective security policy to ensure authorized access to critical data.

Pharmacovigilance

Pharmacovigilance is related to data collection, detection, assessment, and monitoring to prevent risks and adverse effects with pharmaceutical products. Information received from patients and healthcare service providers via predefined data sharing agreements and other resources such as medical literature plays a critical role in providing the necessary data for pharmacovigilance. Most countries must make data available to the public before any new drug is introduced in the public domain. This requirement facilitates identifying the hazards associated with pharmaceutical products and minimizes the risk of potential harm to patient health and well-being.

The pharmacovigilance process involves storing, sharing, and accessing information and feedback by patients and health service providers to assess the possible adverse effect of drugs. Pharmacovigilance is a critical part of the healthcare industry, which directly affects the well-being of the general public. This process mainly involves storing, sharing, and accessing appropriate information to identify any unwanted or undesirable effects to minimize the risks. Like any other large data system involved in electronic data sharing, storing, and transferring, this phenomenon is also susceptible to confidentiality and integrity challenges. Technological advancements and the application of Big Data in pharmacovigilance facilitates the possibility to store, transfer and share an enormous amount of data anywhere by increasing the number of patient and healthcare providers. However, confidentiality and integrity of data become an issue as to whom and what type of data is shared. Since this data is being shared between the commercial and health services providers, the result of any data breach, an unlawful exposure, or any manipulation will result in adverse health and financial consequence [153].

Challenges of cloud adaptation in health systems

Cloud computing is a fast-growing area of development in the healthcare sector. The EU's public health objectives are to improve the health and well-being of populations, reduce health inequalities and ensure sustainable and universal people-centered health systems that are equitable, of high quality and guided by skilled intersectoral governance.

Information and communication technology in healthcare plays a key role in expanding access to diagnostic services, improving their quality, improving coordination between providers, improving patient management, and overcoming the physical distance between patients and healthcare professionals. It is more convenient for providers and patients to have cloud-based electronic health record applications and services. Even with all the benefits of cloud technology, its adoption can lead to security challenges that delay the migration of health systems. Many studies in the area of security for cloud computing on health care systems have been conducted. Mehran et al. [137] presented a systematic review of the security challenges in Health-care Cloud Computing. Zriqat et al. [220] showed the Security and Privacy Issues in E-healthcare Systems. Vyawahare et al. [194] elaborated a Survey on Security Challenges and Solutions in Cloud Computing. Johnstone et al. [102] analyzed the challenging task of the integrity of data. When users store and transfer healthcare information, they need the confidence that digital information is uncorrupted and can only be accessed or modified by authorized. Cheng et al. [45], considered other challenges in healthcare Cloud Computing, including fraud considerations.

As an answer to the challenges mentioned above, many researchers and practitioners proposed solutions, in which many of them worked on identifying architectures, developing Cloud-based health applications and systems, presenting frameworks, strategies, and other security solutions [7,161,169,57].

Among various security challenges, particularly faced by the eHealth Cloud SaaS systems, as identified by the related literature, the most important ones are:

- Data and Service Reliability: The use of the cloud for eHealth systems poses the need for high reliability of the provided services. As such services are distributed, the chance of having faulty transmission or incorrect data can increase. The data in the eHealth cloud must be consistent and constantly in a valid state regardless of any software, hardware or network failure.
- Data Management and Control: Data stored in a cloud virtualized environment can be accessed or managed by many people [171]. As such, in a healthcare Cloud environment, the access control mechanisms employed to protect medical records are of vital importance. The data may be replicated at different locations and across large geographic distances. Some of the data could be available locally. Most medical applications require secure, efficient, reliable, and scalable access to medical records. The loss of direct data and applications management can leave users feeling vulnerable to security flaws and theft.
- Cloud security and privacy: Internet-based access is another challenge in healthcare cloud computing. Cloud service providers offer a large number of resources that are collected in a virtualized pool and can be used by healthcare providers. Clouds are on the Internet, and therefore, data can be stolen by hackers for fraudulent purposes. Data security and privacy are major concerns for the healthcare industry - the more distributed the service, the greater the likelihood that the data will be flawed.
- Data breach: The most important thing is to prevent a data breach. Data can be affected in many different ways. A data breach in the cloud is an incident where data is viewed, accessed, or retrieved by a person, application or service without authorization or illegally. The objective is the theft or publication of data in an unsecured or illegal location.

Privacy, security and GDPR requirement analysis in the IoT domain

The vastness and heterogeneity of IoT scenarios require a new challenging vision in interoperability, security and data management. Many IoT frameworks and platforms claim to have solved these problems by fusing different sources of information, combining their data streams in new innovative services, providing robust vulnerability security and respecting the European Commission's GDPR (General Data Protection Regulation). Due to the potentially very sensitive nature of some of this data, privacy and security considerations must be considered both in the design and by default. In addition, an end-to-end secure solution must guarantee a safe environment with end-users for their data in transmission and storage, which must remain under their full control.

This section presents and discusses the key requirements that a platform in the IoT space must meet regarding privacy, security and GDPR. As the GDPR formalizes the aspects related to data protection, it is very difficult to separate the GDPR-related requirements from those related to security. A later subsection will address the verification of GDPR compliance of IoT platforms through related aspects of the GDPR with the following requirements. Therefore, the ideal IoT platform must establish these requirements [21]:

R1: Support for different IoT brokers and thus different IoT devices and IoT edge devices. "Different" means that the platform must be able to support a range of IoT brokers (in the cloud or decentralized on-premises). These can provide different protocols and modalities for authenticating and establishing secure connections with the platform and devices.

R2: Support IoT discovery abstraction for IoT devices. This means that the platform must support the classification and discovery of IoT devices, abstracting from their IoT broker and protocol. Thus, in the activities of searching and subscribing to IoT Devices, it must be possible to identify them by searching for IoT Devices details such as Device ID, Sensor ID, Geoinformation (e.g., near a GPS point, along a path, in an area), Sensor Type (e.g., temperature, humidity), type (environmental, mobility, energy, etc.), value unit (Celsius degree, micrograms per cubic meter), protocol (NGSI, AMQP, COAP, etc.), Broker, etc. The result of the IoT discovery process can be a set of IoT devices or sensors that can be accessed or subscribed to independently of their IoT brokers and protocols.

R3: Ensuring authenticated connections between IoT devices, IoT edge devices, IoT applications, storage in the cloud, dashboards on secure channels. The IoT devices can be in the field and on-premise, others in the cloud and mixed. Authenticated connections need to be established between them, in the best case using mutual authentications. In addition, less secure connection models can be used as a fallback solution, e.g., those based on keys and basic authentication (which can also be used if the IoT devices are not compliant with most secure protocol approaches). Some of the communications between entities are machine-to-machine, M2M, while others are human-to-machine, H2M.

R4: Inform users of the security level at which the solution can operate according to the selected security level (depending on the type of sensitive data managed).

R5: Support developers in managing security. This means that IoT application developers should be supported in creating applications that exploit security as transparently as possible. For example, IoT application developers need to create connections with: Dashboards (for displaying data and collecting actions from users), storage (for accessing historical data or storing additional data, results of some data analytics), and with IoT brokers (for subscribing to the data drive or sending/receiving messages), etc. IoT applications may also invoke and implement data analytics processes that exploit a large data store, e.g., by using machine learning approaches. Therefore, the authentications to establish these M2M connections need to be automated. This means that developers are not forced to use the credentials in the source code to establish authenticated connections (e.g., with the IoT brokers, dashboards, stores).

R6: Ensure secure communication for all types of connections between IoT devices, IoT brokers, IoT applications, dashboards, and storage. In some cases, communication may be in PULL or PUSH. Secure communication must be ensured through an authentication approach using certificates or access tokens and then enabling SSL/TLS connections, supported in the best case by mutual authentication, as described in the previous points. For M2M communications, some user-specific authentication is not provided in the background.

R7: Support developers with open hardware and open-source software to implement secure IoT devices and IoT edge devices. In this context, most platforms use proprietary solutions/devices to ensure secure connections. This requirement is linked to R3, as developers need to create their own security devices to communicate with the rest of the IoT platform in a secure way and with mutual authentications. Adopting an open solution allows users to develop their own devices that can be at the same level of security as the platform provider's native solutions.

R8: Support signed consent to authorize the use, access, and management of the various data types of the platform. The concept of data type is derived from the GDPR and can be considered a category of data. In the context of IoT solutions, the data types can be IoT devices, IoT applications, dashboards, and data units in memory, time series, etc. According to the GDPR, authorization/delegation to manage personal data (types) provided by a user to the IoT platform management must be done through signed consent, rather than informed consent, as was the case previously. For each type of data, there should be a specific signed consent registered on the platform, which the user can revoke at any time.

R9: Register and manage IoT data types that provide, receive, manage, store and retrieve data for personal data and the associated access control. Under GDPR, IoT data types must initially be private to the user, and only after creation can the user decide whether to make them accessible as public or to specific users through delegation. Delegation in accessing data types must be done at the level of (i) IoT data and records (group of IoT devices); (ii) individual IoT devices; (iii) individual sensor/actuator values of an IoT device, (iv) IoT applications, (v) dashboards, (vi) memory values, etc. For example, the owner of an IoT device that collects several personal health parameters (blood pressure, blood sugar, temperature) would be interested in giving a partner access only to the blood sugar level (only for one of the IoT device's sensors) and keeping the others private. Therefore, only the owners or delegated users can access the data. Making a data type public must be the equivalent of making data public anonymously.

R10: Management of IoT data type ownership (allowing change of ownership) and access delegations according to the GDPR. In delegation management, it must be possible to list them (check the permissions granted) and revoke the delegation.

R11: Support for roles, organization, and groups to manage different types of user categories/groups. It must be possible to provide access delegation to data types for user categories to avoid creating thousands of delegations each time a new user joins a group. For example, certain sensors would be directly accessible to all mobility staff in the smart city context. So when a member is added to a group, the delegations for their entities do not need to be created/removed. This requirement arises mainly from Living Lab aspects and multitenancy support on the platform to enable multiple applications and groups on the same platform.

R12: To store personal data encrypted following GDPR to prevent identification of certain individual compromised data in the event of a breach.

R13: Grant users the "right to be forgotten" following the GDPR. A user must manage their data fully and, if necessary, request its deletion from the platform. As a limiting case, the user must have the right to request the deletion of all personal data, including user profile data.

R14: Support auditing for each user to monitor who has accessed their data types. The user must access the auditing data to obtain access to when, where, how, and who accessed the data; the GDPR explicitly requires this feature.

R15: Data breach detection support: Implement automated methods to detect in a short time when some data and data types have been tampered with or leaked (the GDPR requires this feature).

R16: Support accounting for collecting/calculating metrics/indicators about resource consumption. For example, counting the number of IoT devices/data, IoT applications, dashboards, etc. The assessment is the first step to enforce any restrictions according to the user's role or billing. In IoT platforms, billing is very common based on the number of messages exchanged (both H2M and M2M), the amount of data stored, the number of IoT applications created, etc. The billing function is only marginally related to the security and GDPR aspects, while inserting limits on the number of resources each user can request/exploit to/from the platform is a form of security against denial-of-services and penetrations, which in most cases try to abuse the services for resource sharing.

R17: Support data protection (privacy and security) by design and default, building controls into products and services from the earliest stage.

R18: Ensure a level of security through technical and organizational measures appropriate to the risks, including but not limited to pseudo-anonymization, confidentiality, and integrity, and conduct regular penetration testing. The platform must meet this requirement, as many stakeholders may provide multiple types of data with different types of licenses, ranging from highly sensitive data to open data fully.

In addition to the security aspects, it is important to follow a few more nonfunctional requirements, which are valid for Smart City IoT Platforms and may also be for applications in the IoT smart home, Industry 4.0, etc. They are indirectly connected but relevant to privacy and security aspects. A modern IoT platform must:

1. Provides technical and organizational measures to ensure scalability and cloud services for IoT Brokers, IoT devices, and IoT Applications. This means that in most cases, they have to be managed as Virtual Machines or Containers in an architecture supporting vertical and horizontal scaling.
2. Provide technical and organizational measures to ensure availability, resilience, disaster recovery, periodic stress testing, pentest, and workload. This requirement has been identified in the context of Smart City IoT as a nonfunctional requirement related to the reliability and robustness of the platform to guarantee high availability.
3. Provide support for Cloud-Fog data routing and local (on-premise) IoT computation on the IoT Edge, on which the security must be guaranteed as well. This also means that the solution should be installable on the cloud and on-premise, and hybrid solutions may be viable.

4. Provide support for building Dashboards and data presentations, business intelligence, visual analytics with simple visual tools that nonprogrammers can use. Dashboards are the front end of IoT applications, and thus the connection to the rest of the IoT stack has to be performed by using authentications on secure connections, such as via HTTPS or SecureWS.

5. Provide support for registering and managing heterogeneous in/out sensors and actuators on IoT Devices and virtually on Dashboards such as (i) virtual sensor as buttons, dimers, sliders, switches, etc. (which are elements in which the user acts creating data for the platform); (ii) virtual actuators for showing real-time data such as graphic representations of a bulb or an engine, gauge, single content, speedometer, level bars, time trends, etc. (which are elements to show data on the user interface).

State-of-the-art for security and privacy in health-care systems

Data access, storage, and analysis are not unique to healthcare systems. Any large volume of data with stakeholders with different interests and authorities constitutes similar security and privacy challenges, whether online shopping, financial services, defense secrets, or even public service providers. Any measure introduced to protect sensitive data can be applied in all these sectors regardless of the nature of the data or institution. It is an evolutionary process where many security and privacy measures are already in place, being updated to improve the security or counter the newly discovered loopholes.

Access control

The most challenging aspect of a large healthcare data network is the security administration. The Healthcare system is a complex system with diverse data and an ever-increasing number of users with different requirements for types of data and duration. There are many access control models, but Mandatory Access control (MAC), Discretionary Access control (DAC), and Role-Based Access control (RBAC) are the most popular [29][57]. MAC model gives total control to the security policy administrator, and the user has no control or authority to override established policies. Security policy administrator defines the usage and resources and their access policy, and this policy defines who has access to which files. This model is suitable where confidentiality is the main concern, such as defense and national security matters. DAC model gives the authority and control to the end-users where end-users have full control over the resources they own and owners decide who can access their resources. Finally, the RBAC model is based on rights and access to resources according to the membership to predefined groups. RBAC helps in making a mechanism where data is accessed on the need to know basis. It results in less complexity of the system, reduced cost as well as protection of the sensitive data beyond its required and necessary disclosure [138][49].

As mentioned earlier, access control of the resources and information Big Data offers is a key feature of healthcare's overall security and privacy aspects. Healthcare is a dynamic sector where the role is not defined solely by the profession or position of a user in the organization but also depends on the situation [29]. Given the significance and relevance of the above-defined access control models in the healthcare sector, MAC is the strictest and most secure. It is a type of access control model where confidentiality is the main priority and where all control and authority rest with a central administration. It suits the military and defense sectors better as the main priority is to protect the assets from unlawful access. It is static, and the design requires much planning before the implementation. Even after implementation, it requires a huge system management overhead to add new objects, add new users, or modify the rights of existing users. These aspects make this model unsuitable for the healthcare sector due to its dynamic nature. DAC model provides the flexibility needed by the healthcare sector as it rests the authority with the users and makes it more prone to security and privacy risks as users have full control on the assets they created, and a user can set who can access their data. Again, it is obvious that risks associated with this model make it unsuitable for healthcare data. RBAC is currently the most popular mode of access control in the healthcare sector as it defines the privileges and rights of a user based on its membership to a group or groups based on their function in the healthcare sector.

From a healthcare point of view, it means groups like GP, nurses, lab technicians, or X-rays technicians. Lately, some of the drawbacks of this model in the healthcare sector have emerged as there is no way to provide individual users with the rights over and above the privileges assigned to the group they belong to. Since healthcare staff goes through many different situations, their demand for healthcare information can change abruptly.

One of the most critical situations in the healthcare sector is emergency. In the face of an emergency, the roles of the user and the demand for data change. More recently, Attributes Based access control (ABAC) found its way into the healthcare sector as it provides the flexibility needed to handle the situations in the healthcare sector where responsibilities and demand for data change. ABAC is based on user attributes as well as resources, objects, and environmental attributes. It works on the Boolean logic where access to data is based on IF and Then statements. In ABAC, permission to access objects like files, images, and reports is not simply based on the subject but depends on the subject's attributes. Here subject means any user who is accessing the healthcare data. These attributes are static like name, position, and role and dynamics like role, situation, environment, and location. Based on edit and entry, healthcare data can be generalized into two types: Static Data usually stays the same in the normal scenario, and some of the types are patient personal data like name, sex, blood group, allergies, past medical treatment, and records and insurance information. On the other hand, Dynamics Data, such as care plan, progress notes, readings of the vital organs, or medical reports, usually modify, update, or delete regularly. In the healthcare system, diversity is found not only in the data but also in the user and their level of access to the data. The access depends on other stakeholders' consent and input, and it creates a complex web where an entity has some privileges and does other tasks after getting approval from eligible entities within a healthcare system. To understand the complexity of the system, we analyze the mechanism of accessing data from a single patient [64].

The administration has the widest access to healthcare data compared to other stakeholders, and they are mainly responsible for controlling the types of access for the other stakeholders. This data includes medical, personal, and financial information. Nevertheless, again, this access is restricted. They can add past medical records and make medical entries, but it requires the consent and approval of a doctor in the latter case. They are also the only entity that can authorize to delete medical data but must abide by the laws on the data retention period. Doctors usually have full access to their patient's medical records and add medical entries and private notes. Private notes are not visible to the other health workers and administration and are only shared between doctors and their patients. In case of an emergency or a visiting doctor attending other doctors, the patient gets temporary access to the medical record by the patient's consent and notification to the administration. Healthcare workers are required to sign the confidentiality agreement before gaining any access to healthcare data. Normally they have access to the care plan and can add progress notes. As far as emergency data is concerned, crucial data is usually available to all healthcare workers, so they have all the information required to handle an emergency. It must be noted that they normally have access to recent medical records, and historical records are usually not available to them but can be obtained by requesting administration.

Auditing is implemented by having a logging mechanism where any unlawful attempt is recorded, and if a pattern is discovered, the concerned authority is informed for suitable and preventive action. Patients have the right to access their data at any time, including the private notes of doctors. Of course, this access to be only read as they should not be allowed to alter the data. Other users such as volunteer helpers, visiting physiotherapists, social workers, and community service members also require some sort of healthcare data that must be authorized through administration with the time stamp and, in the end, with the consent of the patients. It is obvious from the above discussion of different stakeholders and their requirements for access to the health care data that the RBAC model is most suitable as the roles and requirements are ever-evolving, and the mechanism of accessing healthcare information needs regular reviews and appropriate amendments [100].

Encryption

Encryption is used to ensure security and protects against eavesdropping and skimming. There are many types of encryption currently deployed in healthcare data; some work on the hardware level, and other work on the software level. For best results, it is necessary to deploy encryption on both software and hardware levels. Some encryption is based on symmetric keys while other asymmetric key-based. Again, as there are many solutions available for encryption and are being deployed in the healthcare sector, each has some limitations. In 2009, IBM developed a homomorphic encryption technique that allows the processing of the data without decryption. It gives a huge boost to the processing time as well as the preservation of crucial resources. However, since it is based on an algebraic algorithm, a different ciphertext can be created from a plaintext. Also, homomorphic encryption is not semantically secure and cannot provide any means for verification. Another encryption technique used is ABE—attribute-based encryption [123], used for encryption of data before being shared with others. The data owner has the authority to encrypt the data and allows which entities will have access to the data and, more precisely, which part of the data. The owner will share the keys for decryption with the selected entities, which later will use these keys to decrypt data. The owner of data only retains the privilege to revoke or grant access. The main issue with any encryption technique is key management. Not all users are experienced with keys to managing their keys, and on the other hand, a central key authority will be easily overwhelmed by the number of keys they must manage in the healthcare sector.

Authentication

Authentication techniques are used to verify the source of data to ensure data is coming from the source it claims to be. There are many authentication techniques used in the healthcare sector like password and digital signature, but it can be seen that the most common form of authentication method used in the healthcare sector is an identifier with a password [6]. There is considerable software available to retrieve the passwords, and users usually choose any easier password for convenience. Also, it is common for users to expose their passwords through social engineering and carelessness. One common habit is to write down the password on a piece of paper and keep it in an easily accessible place. A better authentication system is to have a credential system where only those who already possess the legitimate credential can access the system. In a credential system, a user obtains a credential from an organization and later displays possession. A user can perform some cryptographic operation on the credential by digital signing. It is more secure than a password as it cannot be retrieved by guessing.

Policy development

As mentioned earlier, the healthcare sector is undergoing a revolution, and an ever-increasing amount of data is being generated, shared, and stored. A set of fixed policies currently exists in many healthcare services, which are inadequate and threaten security and privacy. There is a need for dynamic and scalable policies on data access and sharing. There must be a mechanism where the rights of all stakeholders to data need to be revised based on their needs without compromising privacy and security. Also, there must be an authority who can monitor and later revise the access to the data with the patients' consent. Most importantly, there is a need to bring awareness about the importance of personal healthcare information and the consequences of any unlawful access or alteration of data. In the end, the mechanism of revising the rights to access type and extent of data cannot be done manually, and automation is required where conditions are set for a change to happen automatically.

Data anonymization

Data mining is a process of analyzing data to identify the pattern and extract information from a large amount of data and thus present a serious security and privacy issue. As mentioned earlier, healthcare data is enormous, heterogeneous and distributed in nature. There is a need to standardize this data for better analysis and extraction of useful information, but any effort in this direction also ensures data exploitation unless proper security and privacy measures are in place [138]. Data anonymization is in place to hide some attributes of a patient like a name, age, gender, and address. However, again, this anonymization is not very effective as still any unlawful extraction and analysis of the data will lead to some sort of pattern and provide sensitive information. Anonymization is a complex phenomenon where anonymization is not an issue, but later the extraction of the information from the anonymized data is a challenge. Due to the diversity of the healthcare data and different stakeholders demanding access to different parts of the whole data, there arises a question of what level of anonymization is suitable for all users. It is understood that data need to be anonymized before it is being shared, but what information needed by entities like doctors and insurance companies is different. Similarly, the level of data mining capabilities required to extract information is diverse. While ethical practices are well defined for the primary users like doctors, patients and nurses, there is still much work that needs to be done for the vast array of disclosures to secondary users like insurance companies and health care evaluators [138].

13.1.3 Machine learning for diagnosis and treatment in the context of data privacy

AI in medicine is rapidly gaining traction as a promising means to deliver significant health benefits with greater efficiency and precision. ML is used in pattern recognition of images, refining and adjusting therapeutic dosages, informing treatment strategies, refining outcome predictions, improving risk assessments, and streamlining research.

ML in diagnostics is already found in one of the earliest applications to diagnose diabetic retinopathy [79], a disease associated with diabetes that leads to blindness. The common method has been the laborious examination of MRI images to detect deceptive abnormalities associated with the onset of the disease. This is an appropriate clinical target for improved diagnosis, as early detection is associated with significantly better outcomes and, in this case, early intervention could prevent the onset of irreversible blindness. With each patient from whom new images are acquired, the machines' ability to accurately detect patterns relevant to diagnosis increases. Being able to process thousands of scanned images and detect even the smallest abnormalities, the potential for this technology to bring significant health benefits is undeniable. However, the health context of ML presents some challenges for data protection, not least because health data is considered sensitive data that exposes individuals to greater vulnerability than nonsensitive personal data. This justifies the heightened protections for health data, a terrain that also requires navigating relevant member state laws beyond the EU GDPR.

Six principles of GDPR in machine learning
Transparency

Transparency is one of the six principles laid down in Article 5 of the GDPR. According to this provision, personal data must be processed "lawful, fair and transparent". Certain applications of ML may give rise to the review of all three dimensions of this principle. In addition, the new provisions of the GDPR regarding profiling and automated decision-making have clear relevance for various applications of ML in healthcare. These provisions crucially support the promotion of transparency and other principles set out in Article 5. ML has been heavily criticized for its apparent lack of transparency, leading to "black box" decision-making. The specific way the ML raises concerns about transparency is useful in assessing the nature and extent of obscurity. Concerns about transparency are often lumped together with general criticisms of ML. This obscures the nature of what is procedurally or substantively non-transparent and whether a particular type of transparency should be a cause for concern. It also reduces opportunities to explore what options are possible to improve transparency and whether mechanisms or practices can be developed to address transparency issues. In what follows, certain ML algorithms are analyzed, potentially used in healthcare and explore the types of issues they raise.

Profiling and automated decision-making

Key provisions supporting the principle of transparency include Article 4(4) on profiling and Article 22 of the GDPR, which relates to automated processing. Like several ML applications in healthcare, MBL can be seen as a form of "profiling". One goal of MBL is to identify the patients that a new patient most resembles, thus creating a "profile" of the patient. This serves as the basis for treatment and related care. Profiling is defined as any form of automated processing of personal data which consists of using such data to evaluate certain personal aspects relating to a natural person, in particular, to analyze or predict aspects relating to that natural person's performance, economic situation, health, personal preferences, interests, reliability, behavior, location or movements.

Working Party 29 (WP 29) discusses the elements of profiling:

- Automated form on processing.
- Carried out on personal data.
- Objective of the profiling is to evaluate personal aspects about a natural person.

Furthermore, WP 29 points out that the objective is central to understanding what constitutes profiling and cites the GDPR's reference to profiling as the automated processing of personal data to evaluate personal aspects, particularly analyzing or making predictions about individuals. According to Article 22(1) of the GDPR, the data subject has the right not to be subject to a decision based only on automated processing, including profiling, which produces legal impacts for him or her or similarly affects him or her.

ML to inform dosing and administration of treatments, where the algorithm generates findings or assessments about a patient, could be quite transparent based on the biological criteria assessed. However, the possibility to challenge an automated treatment decision is practically not contestable and is probably allowed by explicit consent to the use of automated processing if it is not required for the care contract. In the case of ML for health, while there are generally no legal implications, there could be a significant impact on the patient concerned if he or she is denied treatment solely based on an automated decision, e.g., concerning risk prediction or response to treatment, which indicates that this patient should not receive treatment B, for example. This could lead to a significant worsening of the condition or even death. There are three exceptions to this right.

Particularly relevant to the health context is Article 22(2)(b), which provides for such authorization by an EU or Member State law that provides appropriate measures to safeguard the data subject's rights, freedoms, and legitimate interests. This appears to allow the Member States to authorize decision-making based solely on automated processing where appropriate safeguards are in place. These appropriate safeguards include the right to be informed of the logic involved and the significance and nature of the likely consequences (Article 13), and the possibility for the data subject to obtain human intervention, react and challenge the decision. It is important to stress three points about the impact of these exceptions on the prohibition of decisions based solely on automated processing. First, if national laws allow automated decision-making, it may be extremely difficult to make sense of the safeguards in the context of ML for health. Physicians may have little understanding of the underlying logic of algorithmic processes and, therefore, cannot provide much more than vague and generic explanations. The right to human intervention as a meaningful safeguard depends on the nature and scope of that intervention, both of which may be limited by the skills, time and expertise of the doctor or other medical staff. Second, explicit consent as a basis for the exception to the prohibition on relying solely on automated processing suffers from two critical health care considerations.

It should be noted that the inherent vulnerability of patients, especially those suffering from debilitating, serious or potentially fatal diseases, calls into question the voluntary nature of explicit consent. This is above the known power imbalances inherent in the doctor-patient relationship. The first exception set out in Article 22(2)(a), which is required for the contract between the data subject and the processor, seems to facilitate the use of automated decision-making in this situation, but also raises the question of whether the patient has a meaningful choice as to whether to enter into this contract, which in turn raises questions about meaningful alternatives to decisions based solely on automated processing. This suggests the possibility that if there are no meaningful alternatives to automated decisions in a given health context, the prohibited automated processing is necessary for the "contract" to provide the medical treatment.

The possible solutions seem rather unsatisfactory: a patient and his or her clinical team may settle for general or vague explanations that allow decisions based on automated processing, or the clinical team may make nominal inputs into the decision to gain access to useful ML results, or the patient and medical team may abandon the potential benefit of unexplained results generated by automated processing.

Again, Member State laws can address these issues and thus set meaningful parameters, but reliance on this may be problematic if it leads to unequal protection of data subjects or allows unequal access that could lead to medical tourism. Third, the practicability of the safeguard clause allowing the data subject to respond to or challenge the decision is questionable. If transparency has been waived by one of the exceptions allowing automated decision-making, the ability of the data subject - the patient - to respond to or challenge the decision is likely to be significantly limited, as the patient will not know the basis for the decision and the reasons for it. The patient can only express a wish for a different decision, which can be a deeply inadequate remedy for someone who has been denied a particular treatment on a basis they do not understand and which the clinical team cannot explain.

Memory-Based Learning (MBL)

Memory-Based Learning (MBL) is a form of ML algorithm that compares newly collected data to previously collected data to identify how the new data is most similar based on a subset of attributes. The program (unsupervised) can develop these input attributes or use labeled inputs provided by a human (supervised). MBL, an unsupervised type of ML, is useful for creating groups of patients. Subsequent patients are compared to relevant groups identified by the algorithm, but their data is included and used to inform the formation of these groups. These results can be used to inform and refine treatment strategies and risk models. Transparency concerns may arise with this type of ML, as it may not be apparent to the data subject on what basis they are either placed in a particular group or compared to a particular group, as the relevant characteristics that form the basis for the grouping may not be known or explained.

While the GDPR does not define transparency, the language used indicates the need for the data subject to understand the basis for the data relating to them and their decisions. This lack of transparency can affect the use of ML in healthcare in several ways:

1. Lack of transparency is largely overlooked for the sake of deriving the benefit either by providing nominal interpretation and perfunctory explanations by medical personnel.
2. Healthcare is required to forego the benefits of MBL because of the difficulties of complying with principles of transparency. The extent to which other options can be developed technologically, as a matter of regulation, or in practice (e.g., Health Information Counselors) can address these challenges.

Recommender systems

Recommender systems are also a 'Patients-LikeMe' [113] program, a related type of ML. These systems essentially learn what has happened to other patients who are like the current patient. This could include, for example, disease profile, comorbidities, age, and medical history. A clear use case for this type of comparison system identifies which therapeutic interventions are most likely to be effective for a particular patient, given their similarities to others like them. An example of this can be found in the Network of Enigmatic Exceptional Responders (NEER) study. The NEER study aims to understand the behavior and characteristics of exceptional responders to cancer treatments and ultimately prescribe and recommend treatment strategies based on the characteristics of patients with exceptional positive outcomes. This recommender system is also based on grouping patients based on similarities of attributes and characteristics of individuals in the database and concludes the current patient.

Unlike MBL, recommender systems are supervised systems with human-labeled inputs. Nevertheless, to the extent that they generate outputs based on similarities with other patients, they are a form of profiling, as they use automated processing of personal data to analyze or make predictions about an individual. Here, simply predicting that a particular patient will respond to a treatment in a similar way to the patients identified in the database could constitute a form of automated decision-making, insofar as this 'grouping' is deterministic of which treatment strategy will be followed. The degree of transparency of recommendation systems depends in part on the extent to which the relevant behaviors and attributes that serve as the basis for the comparisons are identified and explainable. In addition, these systems may include the ability to weight features as the algorithm learns from both training and new input data. Until it is possible to identify both the relevant features and the weighting of attributes that go into an output for a particular patient, it will be very difficult to explain the basis for the generated recommendation for an individual patient beyond the most general likely descriptors related to disease, stage or age. In recent works, sensitive data collection is comprehensively studied, ranging from biometrics to social media networks to physical activity and more. Based on the idea that more information contributes to the robustness of the recommendation generated by the algorithm, this system illustrates the scenario that data about virtually any aspect of a patient's world can be considered relevant to medical care, diagnosis, or treatment. As a result, the ability to identify what data contributed to the generation of a particular recommendation may be further obscured by the sheer size of the scope and volume of data processed by ML.

Patient clustering

Clustering refers to finding natural groupings of patients based on a large set of data about patients. Such clustering can be very informative for healthcare professionals. As in the NEER study, finding similarities between patients can provide disease management strategies in addition to risk assessments. Transparency in this type of clustering, as with the ML algorithms discussed previously, can be critical for patients, as being placed in one group compared to another may have consequences without understanding or challenging the basis for that grouping or clustering. This lack of transparency could even mask unintended discrimination. For example, if an individual falls into a 'natural grouping' based on a characteristic 'prohibited' under discrimination law, e.g., race, sexual orientation, political or religious affiliation, and these characteristics are weighted by the ML algorithm as highly informative of a relevant outcome, there is a possibility that the ML grouping may unintentionally result in 'unfair' or unequal disease management and potentially produce unequal outcomes on a prohibited basis. Discrimination of this nature is not necessarily outside the scope of the GDPR, as provisions such as those on profiling and automated decision-making, while based on the protection of personal data in these technological contexts, are also intended to serve as important blocks of protection to support antidiscrimination and other forms of unfair treatment. The transparency requirement and the provisions on fully automated decision-making (Article 22) are examples of such provisions. Interestingly, while such attributes may be noted by a physician and incorporated into a treatment strategy, the attribute may merely be a proxy for other factors that can be verified or discarded through human observation. This also illustrates why and how human intervention in the decision-making process can be crucial for optimal outcomes.

Forecasting

Prediction refers to the ability to predict what is likely to happen to a particular patient. This ML program could use neural networks that input past values and predict the next values based on those past values, continuously receiving inputs and generating outputs through multiple layers rather than through a direct input-output correlation. This type of predictive modeling can inform disease management and is likely to be of great interest to healthcare stakeholders interested in risk prediction, such as insurers, providers or hospitals.

Transparency issues arising from predictive modeling or prediction are partly related to the fact that this application falls directly into the category of profiling and, depending on how it is integrated, may raise concerns about automated decision-making. Transparency also depends on the extent to which the inputs and the processing of those inputs are known and understood by clinical staff. The layering of neural networks underlying the algorithm can obscure how ML predictive modeling works, making it virtually impossible to understand the exact basis of the predictions generated by the program. This makes it impossible for the patient to understand or challenge a prediction that they perceive to be unfounded, unsubstantiated, or procedurally or substantively undesirable. This lack of transparency can have significant downstream implications in healthcare, as the consequences of predictions based on forecasts that have not considered a critical aspect of a particular patient can be severe. Even if human intervention is present somewhere in a decision-making process based mainly on ML algorithms, the lack of transparency remains a problem as the learning occurs through interacting layers of neural networks rather than on a direct input-output basis. While this can generate very useful results that can help diagnose, develop treatment strategies, early detection, and predict health outcomes or trajectories, the transparency of the process itself challenges the principle of transparency.

The GDPR's ban on automated decision-making has been noted by authorities tasked with regulating medical devices and support systems, resulting in interim guidelines banning only automated medical decisions. While this furthers the goals of the GDPR, the lack of clarity on the level of human intervention required can be a problem. In addition, any requirement that the data subject can obtain an understandable explanation of the basis for an ML output that affects them is likely to challenge much of the medical staff who are not trained in ML or have a solid understanding of the type of patient data processing that generates these outputs.

Purpose limitation

Purpose limitation is listed in Article 5 of the GDPR. It requires that personal data be collected and specified for explicit and legitimate purposes and not further processed in a way incompatible with those purposes, further adding that scientific research is not considered incompatible (Article 89(1)). The challenges for AI in medicine with purpose limitations have been richly discussed in the literature. Personal data collected in AI processing can be used for an almost infinite number of purposes that cannot be explicitly communicated to the data subject at the time of collection. MBL, prediction and clustering all involve some form of assessment based on comparisons with others, whether to form groups or clusters, to predict treatment responses or health outcomes. While the personal data collected from a particular patient is under the auspices of the data subject's medical care, this data enters a constantly updated database to allow for future comparisons when processed by ML. While this would be defensible under a 'pool' or 'collective' care approach, in the same way a doctor continuously learns from every patient they see, with ML, the personal data collected from patients become part of the database.

An obvious challenge with purpose limitation is that the data entered may be relevant to other uses beyond the original purpose of caring for a particular patient. In this case, the data can be further used in ML systems to refine treatment strategies for other patients, including those with different diseases. Nevertheless, this type of use is not incompatible with the original purpose and may fall under permissible internal use for medical or administrative purposes. National healthcare and health data legislation may ultimately determine the proper parameters for the extended use of sensitive health data, although internal institutional use is generally considered proper protection.

However, as these applications become part of integrated systems, particularly those that involve connections outside the immediate healthcare environment, the potential for concern can be expected to increase. ML for analyzing different types of texts and documents also demonstrates good opportunities for healthcare.

For example, Natural Language Processing (NLP) presents an interesting challenge for earmarking. NLP uses different text processing tools to understand the meaning of a text. For example, it can detect differences in the diagnosis of an individual patient. Both deep learning and text mining provides the opportunity to learn to recognize key features and can be used together to understand both text and context, leading, for example, to a more accurate understanding of conflicting language with diagnoses. NLP implies that databases can be used for unspecified purposes and purposes incompatible with their original use. This is a double dilemma in that while the GDPR aims to support and facilitate research in the public interest and open source, it may encourage the violation of the purpose limitation requirement.

NLP may pose a different kind of challenge to purpose limitation, as these databases are increasingly open source for efficiency reasons and thus facilitate research. Depending on the governance of the database and whether the open-source applies only to the software or includes the database, earmarking may be challenged. However, de-identified, aggregated data is likely to be seen as largely unproblematic.

Storage limitation

The principle of storage limitation requires that data must not be kept in identifiable form for longer than is necessary for the purposes for which the personal data are processed (Article 5(e)). An important exception to this is archiving for the public interest, scientific or historical research (Article 89(1)). Working Party 29 specifically addressed this consideration in the report on automated decision-making, noting that the retention of "collected personal data for extended periods to establish correlations means that organizations will be able to build personal profiles of individuals very comprehensively". ML in the various forms examined here may well retain data beyond the time necessary for its originally collected purpose, but not necessarily in an identifiable form. If this is the case, e.g., NLP or text mining without identification or nonidentifiable image recognition, the storage limit is less of a problem. The risk of re-identification, as generally acknowledged, still exists and increases in integrated systems and the context of BigData.

For ML applications that work optimally with as much personal data as possible, such as MBL, Recommender Systems, or image processing to detect changes and trajectories, the value of the data in this identifiable form is exactly what makes it valuable. Both Recommender Systems and MBL strive to identify patients "like" the patient before them. The more information they have about each patient, the more accurate the comparisons. However, keeping this personal data beyond the time it is useful for treating a data subject patient may technically violate storage limitations. Forecasting or predictive modeling presents an interesting challenge to storage limitations. Predictive modeling, which uses past values to infer likely next values, relies on massive amounts of data over time for optimal accuracy. If the data in this database is removed as soon as the initial patient intake has been achieved, the ML app continuously loses performance and the robustness of the outputs decreases accordingly. The memory limitation is in direct contradiction to the beneficial application of this technology. Furthermore, WP29 points out that this inherent property of ML may conflict with proportionality considerations.

Collapsing of clinical care and research

A fundamental challenge of several applications of ML in healthcare is that it merges clinical care and research activities into one, as the collection and retention of data beyond what is necessary for the care of a patient are no longer under the auspices of medical care for that patient, but rather like research, an activity with its standards, guidelines and regulations.

ML uses the data from each new patient to inform future outcomes, which can be seen as a form of health research. Apart from the demonstrable problem that this is a 'research activity, it circumvents long-standing norms and regulations specifically designed to protect the rights and interests of research participants. This becomes particularly important when reusing data under the scientific research exemption: health research must comply with EU rules and relevant Member State laws. Therefore, the Member States' requirements impose on categories of medical research may also apply to healthcare ML, e.g., with consent (for further research) or the use of patient data collected in the context of clinical care. It could be argued that the scientific research exemption should also apply to extended storage for the development of medical research databases. However, this conflation of clinical and research activities has several implications, not least that these activities are governed by a web of parameters based on national laws that could shape an uneven landscape for the use of ML in research.

ML in context: integrated systems

With a potentially essential link to Big Data and the IoT in healthcare, privacy issues for ML must also be considered when it operates as part of an integrated system. This is a critical step as it addresses the combined power and potential for both benefit and risk of harm that both can independently generate. Potential applications of ML for care and diagnostic assistance can come in many forms. AI robots are being developed specifically to recognize patterns associated with the onset of various types of mental illness. Equipped with a variety of information-gathering mechanisms that detect and relay changes in behavior, these robots monitor movements and activities, perform spatial surveillance, detect indicators of aggression (e.g., cortisol levels), detect aspects of speech patterns, pauses, and articulation, and collect biometric data - weight, consumption, blood pressure or heart rate.

Predictive and behavioral modeling

Conditions such as schizophrenia, dementia, and depression are well-known examples of outbreaks that can harm both the patient and others. The standard healthcare mantra that "earlier interventions lead to better outcomes" is a guiding star in the quest to detect impending health problems at the earliest possible stage. ML technology can be used to identify patterns that could, in principle, indicate the onset of mental illness. Changes in speech, behavior, movement patterns, etc., have long been known to precede outbreaks of schizophrenia and other mental illnesses. With the advent and integration of an ever-growing number of tracking devices, sensors, robots, and other eHealth technologies, the ability to detect patterns before onset is a very attractive intervention for many mental illnesses. 'Digital phenotyping', a method of quantifying individual characteristics by analyzing data generated from a person's use of personal digital devices, such as swiping and scrolling movements, is being used to correlate with the onset of depression.

Therapeutic robotics for patients with mental illness aims to detect and report subtle symptoms, phenomena and biological or behavioral changes based on algorithmically derived predictive indicators. This could include, for example, information on speech patterns, social interactions, gaze characteristics in addition to biological phenomena such as heart rate and blood pressure. In a data-driven approach to disease detection and treatment, little falls outside the rather vague parameters of personal data relating to a natural person's physical or mental health that provides insight into health status. ML is now being deployed to collect virtually any personal data to improve the accuracy and efficiency of early detection of Alzheimer's - a disease notorious for the breadth and scope of personal information potentially relevant to a diagnosis.

Data minimization

It is widely recognized that machine learning for diagnosis and treatment presents an inherent tension with data privacy. In the context of more and more types of data being collected via IoT, mobile health, various forms of eHealth, the ability of machine learning to process and analyze this data, identifying patterns and correlations with health, poses a significant challenge to enforcing and operationalizing the principle of data minimization - the collection and processing of virtually any type of data can be justified as "relevant to health status". In this way, such an expanded scope of data can circumvent the safeguards to reduce the risk that the data minimization principle is designed to ensure. Recital 39, Article 5 (c) of the GDPR states that personal data must be relevant, adequate and limited to what is necessary for the purposes of the processing. This requires ensuring that the period of storage of personal data is kept to a strict minimum. Personal data should only be processed if the purpose of the processing cannot reasonably be fulfilled by other means.

Scientific research exemption and machine learning

The second potential challenge to the ability of the GDPR to ensure adequate protection of data subjects' rights and interests in the integrated context of ML for health is the relaxed restrictions on the further use of data for scientific research. The relevant recitals of the GDPR state that further processing of lawfully collected personal data for scientific research in the public interest is allowed without explicit consent if certain conditions are met. This means that if a Member State requires explicit consent for the use of sensitive data for further use in research, an organization cannot rely on the relaxed restrictions of the GDPR to conduct this research without consent, regardless of the existence of safeguards. The AEGLE project has already produced publications highlighting the extent of the differences between member states regarding the extent to which and how the scientific research exemption can be used. The data protection implications of ML in the health sector alone are difficult enough, but ML can and does involve external processors and other IT services, especially as part of an integrated system. However, an important phenomenon has occurred in the collaboration of healthcare institutions and commercial companies to provide infrastructure services.

In a high-profile agreement, the Royal Free London NHS Foundation Trust entered into a contract with Google DeepMind between July 2015 and October 2016. This agreement involved transferring identifiable patient data from the NHS without explicit consent to develop an app that would provide clinical alerts for kidney injuries. It emerged that data on all patients within the NHS had been obtained from Google DeepMind and not just for patients with kidney problems. It was argued that this would enable research into preventative measures. In a research context, valuable research is being conducted using ML to identify patterns and correlations that could ultimately improve healthcare in treatment, care and drug development. For example, the NEER study, based at the Department of Bioinformatics at Harvard Medical School in the US, collaborates with Amazon, and research participants receive confirmation emails from Amazon. The NEER study aims to understand better those cancer patients who far exceed initial prognoses and expectations and use insights about these exceptional responders to improve cancer patient treatment, care, and counseling to achieve better outcomes for them. Nonetheless, partnering with Amazon or any other commercial company raises serious questions around the data protection rights and interests of data subjects, particularly when collecting and processing sensitive data for reuse without explicit consent. While Cambridge Analytica appears to be a worst-case scenario, the partnership of healthcare entities lawfully processing data for the permitted purposes with commercial entities complicates the risk scenario and potentially the nature of the risk.

Summative analysis

As ML increasingly drives the ability to improve healthcare through greater efficiency and precision in diagnosis and development of treatment strategies, this data-driven technology will and should come under scrutiny in novel ways of processing personal data. It is in the nature of ML that it will lead to a lack of transparency, which may have downstream effects that negatively impact other rights, such as nondiscrimination. In addition, purpose limitation, storage limitation and provisions on automated processing and profiling, if strictly applied, could significantly hinder the ability of ML to deliver on its enormous promise in medicine. The extent to which the GDPR potentially acts as a gatekeeper for medical innovation depends in part on how these principles and provisions are implemented. This points to a key role for data controllers - in assessing risk, providing adequate safeguards and using health data responsibly and prudently. This puts data controllers in the critical position of ensuring compliance with data protection laws and ensuring that trust in medical privacy, central to healthcare, is not compromised. Without the trust that privacy assurances inspire, a healthcare system can fail both its patients and the society it serves. The extent to which the ML can navigate relevant principles and regulations and still fulfill its potential to make important contributions to the treatment, diagnosis and research may well require that the ML engage in the gymnastics necessary to ensure not only privacy compliance but also the maintenance of medical privacy so that trust in the system is not undermined.

13.2 **Noninvasive and personalized solutions for elderly based on IoT technologies**

Noninvasive solutions are becoming a must in medicine. Indeed, invasive solutions not only are difficult and unfriendly to patients. In some cases, such as patients with degenerative solutions (e.g., Alzheimer, Dementia, etc.), the patients may react negatively to invasive solutions of wearable devices. Studies have shown that patients may not want to collaborate with invasive devices, e.g., they do not want to be observed by cameras or to wear all sorts of devices.

As an example, the collection and study of EEG data have experienced a significant change [181, 108]: from traditional EEG helmets to a new generation of EEG sensors, such as EEG headbands Emotiv Insight, Muse InteraXon, Emotiv Epoc+, and Neurosky Mindwave. Moreover, the cost of such new devices has drastically reduced, making thus studies using them more user-friendly and low-cost. Similar examples of a new generation of user-friendly and low-cost devices can be found in many medical applications. Likewise, personalized medicine is being propelled by such devices, many of which allow for real-time monitoring.

We list next examples of platforms oriented towards noninvasive and personalized medicine.

ONDO Systems: ONDO is an IoT cloud platform for senior living and other managed population facilities.[1]

ELLIQ: ELLI Q is a proactive Artificial Intelligence-driven social robot designed to encourage an active and engaged lifestyle by suggesting activities and making it simple to connect With loved ones.[2]

---

[1] H2O official website: https://www.ondosystems.com.
[2] ELLIQ official website: https://elliq.com/.

QORVO Senior Lifestyle: Qorvo's Senior Lifestyle system learns the routine day-to-day activities of the senior resident within a few weeks. It provides intelligent status updates in a dashboard app and sends alerts to designated caregivers if something unexpected happens.[3]

JON: This is a digital pill dispenser that Looks like a regular seven-day model. One type is locked until it is time for medication; the other is unlocked.[4]

Philips Lifeline: Philips Lifeline is a personal aid button for home deployment that is worn around the neck or wrist to detect when the senior has fallen.[5]

GRAND CARE SYSTEMS: GrandCare is a multipurpose system that monitors daily activity, integrates medical monitoring (glucose, weight, oxygen, blood pressure) and can display diets, discharge plans, exercises.[6]

TEMPO: Tempo is a wrist-worn wearable device equipped with an array of sensors that can track a person's activities of daily living and location monitoring.[7]

MOBILEHELP DUO: This company offers a mobile device with GPS satellite tracking and an in-home base station.[8] (MobileHelp, United States, 2014)

SILVER MOTHER: Silver Mother is a smart hub device made of multipurpose tracking sensors that can analyze hundreds of individual daily activities.

SILVERFOX: Silverfox comprises a wearable device for the senior and a caregiver app.

HABITAT: Home Assistance Based on the Internet of Things for the Autonomy of Everybody aims to develop smart devices to support the elderly in their own homes and nursing homes, and to integrate them into everyday life, thus reducing healthcare costs due to the reduced need for personal assistance, and providing a better quality of life for elderly users [30].[9]

13.3 Detection *vs* prediction eHealth solutions at scale

13.3.1 Preventive, predictive, personalized, and participatory (P4) medicine

Chronic diseases are the major global health problem of the 21st century [62,105,106,151]. The major chronic diseases listed by the World Health Organization (WHO) are cardiovascular disease (CVD), cancer, chronic respiratory disease, diabetes mellitus (DM), and neurodegenerative diseases, which are the leading cause of health burden and mortality worldwide and continue to increase in incidence and prevalence [62,151,61]. In addition, chronic diseases are a major cause of poverty and impede economic development [98]. Chronic diseases share common risks, including socioeconomic factors, cluster in comorbidities, and are intertwined with aging [151,60]. The challenge with chronic diseases is their complexity and the often unnoticed change from health to disease with late signs of symptoms.

Fortunately, most chronic diseases can be prevented or delayed until much later in life by, for example, maintaining a healthy lifestyle, resulting in an extended health span [4,177,118,26,1]. Monitoring

---

[3] QORVO official website: https://www.qorvo.com/applications/internet-of-things/lifestyle-systems.

[4] Medminder official website: https://www.medminder.com/news/medminder-locked-pill-dispenser/.

[5] Philips Lifeline official website: https://www.lifeline.philips.com/medical-alert-systems.html.

[6] GrandCare official website: https://www.grandcare.com/.

[7] Carepredict official website: https://www.carepredict.com/.

[8] Mobilehelp official website: https://www.mobilehelp.com.

[9] HABITAT official project page: http://www.eng.habitatproject.info/.

and maintaining normal levels for key health metrics also plays a primary role in reducing the risk for chronic disease [61]. Scientific advances in understanding genomics and the interaction between genomics, lifestyle, personal experience with adversity, and the social and physical environment, further improve the ability to predict risk and prevent chronic disease [32,170,51]. For example, Halfon and Hochstein [80] introduced the concept of lifelong health development (LCD), which describes how health trajectories evolve over an individual's lifetime based on experiences and how this information can guide new strategies to policy and research.

An approach to medicine that is preventive, predictive, personalized, and participatory (P4) [209,18,86,87,90,89,70,85] aims for reducing the burden of chronic disease by leveraging technology and a better understanding of human interaction, evidence-based interventions, and the mechanisms of chronic disease. Current chronic disease management follows interventions and recommendations from the various specialists involved. Minimal interactions between specialists and limited information for the primary care physician and the patient result in a fragmented approach to health, noncoordinated, scattered follow-up, and a suboptimal cost-benefit ratio [17,215]. Combining P4 medicine with other modern concepts and principles has the potential to reinvent health care [116]. Researchers have recently proposed the P4 Health (P4H) continuum model [180], which embraces and extends the concepts of P4 medicine [70] as a framework to promote proactive collaborations with a common language and integrated care model. This framework draws on several concepts that have been previously established [85,139,136,11,33], brought together in a way that increases potential impact.

Stages of health

Chronic disease progression and the transition from health to chronic disease can be into four main stages based on the model of allostatic load [132]. Allostasis is the process of adaptation to daily experiences. Allostatic load and overload refer to the aggregate change in the brain and body when an individual experiences "toxic stress". Toxic stress can be both psychological and physiological when left unchecked, leads to dysregulation of mediators that normally promote adaptation and pathophysiology, resulting in disease. Negative health behaviors associated with a bad lifestyle contribute to allostatic overload. An individual initially moves from healthy (Stage A) to recognizable biological signs (Stage B), where early disease precursors and dysfunction can be detected, but the individual is unaware and has no symptoms. Beginning from Stage B, chronic disease usually progresses slowly where the individual shows symptoms and the traditional reactive health care is initiated (Stage C).

Despite advances in interventions, many individuals with symptoms progress with chronic diseases (stage D), where traditional health care continues and is augmented with pharmacotherapy, surgery, and other interventions to manage the chronic disease. Reaching stage D and confirming a chronic disease, some degree of permanent physiologic dysfunction is likely. For example, a heart attack or stroke, cancer, and other chronic diseases leave permanent damage and dysfunction that typically requires lifelong treatment and care in the current reactive health care system. However, an individual with a chronic disease diagnosis can improve prognosis and quality of life if they seek to improve core components of their health. Type II diabetes is an example of progression through these stages, eventually leading to an irreversible stage. However, with intervention and lifestyle management at stage B or C, the process can be reversed. The following sections describe the stages of health in more detail.

Stage A: apparently healthy and avoiding the accumulation of stressors

Stage A indicates that a person is in apparent good health and well-being. Individuals in Stage A show a healthy lifestyle (i.e., regular physical activity (PA), nutritious diet, no harmful alcohol use) and have key health measures within a normal range (i.e., blood glucose, blood pressure, blood lipids, and body physiques). At this stage, individuals can adapt to potential threats and changes in their environment (often referred to as "stressors") to maintain homeostasis. The term "apparently" healthy is used because there are currently no tools to determine the health beyond the presence of clinical risk factors. Identifying granular risk categories over genomic and other detailed biological, clinical, environmental, and molecular assessments are not currently readily available for assessment by the general public. However, movement in this direction has already begun with precision medicine initiatives [209,32,92,93,188]. Large, dynamic, personalized data clouds, like those generated by the 100K Wellness Project [92], are an example of the shift toward precision medicine. This framework for "scientific wellness" [37] uses millions of data points, including from DNA, blood, saliva, the microbiome, and lifestyle, to exponentially refine the management and optimization of an individual's health.

Chronic diseases share a common set of environmental and lifestyle risk factors or stressors [151, 61,63]. Socioeconomic determinants, particularly poverty, also influence the development, severity, and management of chronic disease [98,83]. It is usually ongoing exposure to these stressors and poor health behaviors that underlie the pathway to allostatic overload and resulting chronic disease. Negative stressors, or distress, are associated in complex ways with persistent local and systemic inflammation and a variety of other dysfunctions [149,156]. The reason of a complex set of disorders such as chronic disease can often not be traced to a single cause and underlies more likely a highly complex, interacting network of many mediators and factors involved, interacting at multiple levels across time and space [90,156,20,19]. In addition, it is important to note that biological systems function nonlinearly, with the brain being the central organ of adaptation or maladaptation [133]. Furthermore, progression along chronic disease trajectories, which is cumulative and does not follow a specific time frame, becomes a unique personalized experience for each individual, requiring personalized care [134]. Certain factors can increase resilience to stressors and keep an individual in Stage A. With the right data and interpretive tools, such preventive activities can be effectively tailored to the individual (e.g., feedback through monitoring) [91]. Beyond healthy lifestyles, much to be done about how pharmaceutical or other interventions might increase resilience to external stressors and prevent disease. It is important to remember that some level of positive stress (i.e., eustress) is necessary to maintain health; physical activity and calorie reduction lead to eustress, which leads to positive biological adaptations [156,127,125]. The transition from Stage A (i.e., allostasis) to the onset of a prechronic disease state [61], stage B (i.e., allostatic load) is usually of slow progression and is often unnoticed by the individual experiencing this transition. As stressors accumulate and individuals exhibit more unhealthy lifestyle characteristics, the signs of chronic disease risk, which defines Stage B, become next. This accumulation of stressors and failures of biological resilience, or allostatic load, can be defined as transitioning from Stage A to B.

Stage B: the emergence of chronic disease signs

The intertwined accumulation of stressors to which most individuals have exposed in stage A results in complex situations that eventually manifest as biological signs [33]. Stage B signifies the onset of observable phenomena associated with increased chronic disease risk. Traditional signs include elevated blood pressure, dyslipidemia, and elevated blood glucose [60]. Measures of chronic inflammation have also emerged as important signs of chronic disease risk, and the allostatic load, which has predictive value for later disease, combines measures of primary and secondary mediators of allostasis that can be assessed and represented in several ways [213,187,135]. The fields of genomics, epigenetics, transcriptomics, metabolomics, proteomics, and analyses of the gut microbiome in the context of predicting chronic disease risk continue to evolve, and future discoveries will refine the identification of individuals at stage B [188,145]. It is important to note that "-omics" are usually considered to provide a disease signature, but maybe even more important in the transition from stage A to stage B before there is clear evidence of allostatic load and clinical biomarkers of disease. In addition, the importance of a deeper insight level of cardiorespiratory fitness and muscle strength/endurance is a powerful predictor of future risk for chronic disease and adverse events [52,53,159,160,15,122]. A too high body mass, particularly visceral fat, is also a significant predictor of the risk of chronic disease and associated adverse events [61,9,214,203].

Nevertheless, physical fitness and body physiques, although recognized as important markers of health and prognosis, have not traditionally been considered "signs" of chronic disease risk. A paradigm shift was proposed in this way of thinking that recommends that below-average physical performance and excessive body mass be treated as signs of increased chronic disease risk and, when present, allows for classification as stage B. This list of signs is broad and does not purport to be exhaustive but rather represents a presentation of general issues as research on the optimal combination of signs to identify risk continues to evolve. With constraints on resources, health care professionals may not be able to perform an exhaustive assessment of signs, and in such cases, they should perform assessments with the resources available to them. Much information related to an individual's health, the risk for chronic disease, and prognosis can be discovered from signs linked with traditional health behaviors and fundamental metrics like physical activity, dietary patterns, blood pressure, lipids, or blood glucose. Early dysfunction and precursors to chronic disease as signs of allostatic load are often overlooked. Individuals with the classic early signs of chronic disease risk, such as high blood pressure, blood glucose, dyslipidemia, and newly discovered signs such as telomere length shortening and changes in the gut microbiome, are not usually associated with functional impairment in daily life. Furthermore, decreased physical performance often goes undetected even in the general population. This inadequate exercise performance is partly because a large percentage of the population, particularly the part at greatest risk for chronic diseases, leads inactive lifestyles and avoids exercise that would likely be a sign of Stage B (e.g., decreased cardio-respiratory fitness and muscle strength/endurance). Complex systems, such as humans, have tipping points, which are currently difficult to predict. Work in several scientific fields focusing on finding those critical points before they are reached now suggests the existence of generic early-warning signals [184,43,202]. Dynamic network biomarker theory (e.g., driver networks) has recently been used to describe upstream, tissue-specific, critical transitions in the liver, adipose tissue, and muscle that lead to the development and progression of type 2 Diabetes [124]. Monitoring such early warning signs may help predict the stage of disease progression and the occurrence of abrupt transitions to deteriorating health.

In stage B, individuals would benefit greatly from a proactive, preventive approach to address the signs and return an individual to stage A. At this stage, a particularly important opportunity arises for the health care professional to assess the person's understanding of health information and identify barriers or motivations for the patient to make lifestyle changes. Open-ended questions leading to discourse analysis can illuminate and enhance the individual's critical thinking skills. Simply collecting narratives will shed light on the individual's motivations and goals for their health. Because most people are either unaware that their health is going downhill and approaching chronic disease or are unwilling to take steps to reverse this trend, they are unlikely to take preventive, proactive measures, such as lifestyle changes or biological or pharmaceutical interventions [92]. New efforts are aimed at providing people with the knowledge to optimize their well-being and reverse this trend. It is necessary to view this early health surveillance and counseling as critically as early immunizations. Knowledge and motivation can prevent people from continuing down the silent path of chronic disease. When this is not the case, individuals continue to move along the Stage B portion of the continuum; a group of signs that are both silent and increasingly evident worsen in severity. After a variable period that may last decades, the stage B signs give way to Stage C symptoms.

Stage C: emergence of chronic disease symptoms

The chronic disease symptoms manifestation is a typical entry point for individuals into the traditional reactive healthcare system today. For example, shortness of breath that occurs in activities of daily living (e.g., climbing stairs) is a Stage C symptom. Persistent depression should also be considered a symptom that increases the risk of chronic disease [54,131]. Although a formal diagnosis of chronic disease has not yet been established, significant pathophysiologic dysfunction is likely already established. In addition, unhealthy lifestyle characteristics and abnormalities in important health measures are well established in most cases, even in Stage C, and are now reinforced by clear symptoms. In the traditional reactive health care system, symptoms are often treated without addressing the poorly understood causes and mechanisms at the root of dysfunction, much of which consists of unhealthy lifestyle behaviors. In this sense, this approach to health care continues the reactive cycle. Symptoms are temporarily relieved while the level of dysfunction persists and becomes progressively worse, as do unhealthy lifestyle habits, leading to further symptomatic episodes and progressive biological damage. At this point, the risk for an eventual diagnosis of chronic disease and transition to stage D (i.e., allostatic overload) is extremely high.

Stage D: confirmed chronic disease diagnosis

Once diagnosing a chronic disease, the treatment procedure becomes more aggressive and is the defining moment of the reactive health model. Treatment of chronic diseases, such as coronary artery disease, requires expensive and often invasive interventions. As in Stage C, the underlying causes and mechanisms of the chronic disease are often not addressed. The reactive model of health care focuses on stabilizing the individual and alleviating acutely elevated symptoms. In recent decades, this model has proven to be very effective, as evidenced by the decline in annual cardiovascular disease mortality rates [61]. However, little is being done to address the root cause of these diseases. At this stage, lifestyle and environmental risk factors that, if changed, significantly improve prognosis and quality of life are not usually addressed [13]. Thus, dysfunction continues in a downward spiral, and symptoms worsen with morbidity and premature mortality and rising health care costs as a consequence. Although this need not be the case, once people reach Stage D, they typically remain in that stage, with a coexisting and worsening accumulation of stage B and C signs and symptoms. In addition, many people are diagnosed with more than one chronic disease (i.e., multimorbidity). Multiple chronic diseases may be able to revert from stage D (or even stage C) to stage A (or B) again [180].

Health stages progression

Health stages A-D should not be considered as one-directional or stationary. It was shown in the past that improving health behaviors and key health indicators significantly improve a person's future health [13,10,121]. For example, a person diagnosed with a chronic disease but who highly improves his or her health metrics and lifestyle behaviors may improve all stage C symptoms and stage B signs. Looking at health stages allows individuals to understand the importance of improving health metrics and lifestyle behaviors. P4 medicine aims to prevent the first event/diagnosis and subsequent events when a personalized diagnosis has already been made. Both goals are important in the P4H continuum to ensure that individuals at all stages of health receive appropriate care.

Levels of intervention

By moving forward to a proactive health care system, different levels of intervention are defined and expand the list of stakeholders invested in implementing the P4H continuum model [180]. Health and well-being depend on complex systems that constantly interact and shape human biology, behavior, and environment, particularly concerning lifestyle characteristics and chronic disease. In the following, the four levels of intervention in the P4H continuum model are described.

Level I: global and country-based interventions

Global and country population health strategies, known as public health, aim to improve the health of a large population and reduce the burden of chronic disease. The World Health Organization (WHO) is the main example of an organization with a strong focus in this area, as evidenced by its initiatives, publications on chronic diseases, and targets for improvement [151]. National governments also focus on strategies to improve the health of their populations [106,31,128,50,199]. Global and multi-country public health organizations and national/state governments play an important role in Level I interventions through health-promoting legislative measures, financial investments in health-promoting initiatives and research, and policy reports and recommendations. For example, WHO has launched the health in all policies initiative, calling on governments to consider population health impacts in all legislative proposals. This framework is defined as "an approach to public policies across sectors that systematically takes into account the health implications of decisions, seeks synergies, and avoids harmful health impacts, in order to improve population health and health equity" [23,219]. Such an approach helps governments consider Level I health interventions in all actions they take.

Level II: community-based interventions

Despite public health efforts and legislation, health-changing behaviors are primarily prevalent in local communities and their settings. Although categorized as chronic diseases, they follow a network pattern to some degree. This has been demonstrated for chronic disease risk behaviors related to obesity and lifestyle. Communities influence lifestyle patterns and behaviors in significant ways [37,95,48,219, 200]. Level II interventions aim at creating an environment in which individuals are involved in a healthy lifestyle environment and have easy access to nutritious and affordable foods, opportunities for PA and contemplative practices, a smoke-free environment, information and resources to maintain health and prevent chronic disease, and health systems that encourage preventive medicine and healthy lifestyle practices. There are also numerous opportunities for health systems within a community to practice preventive medicine and adopt healthy lifestyle interventions [12].

Level III: individual and family unit interventions

The individual must embrace preventive medicine and healthy lifestyle interventions in a participatory manner [86]. In addition to the higher goal of Level I and II interventions reaching the individual, Level III interventions continue the P4H care plan through face-to-face interactions with health professionals. Level III interventions address the individual as a whole and thus focus on healthy lifestyle interventions. To effectively deliver Level III healthy lifestyle interventions, there is a need to rethink health professions' education to ensure that all disciplines receive the education and training necessary to deliver care plans effectively [14]. Health professionals delivering Level III interventions benefit greatly from effective Level I and II interventions. Level III interventions, delivered by a broad range of health professionals, need to be expanded beyond the healthcare system's traditional borders (i.e., hospital and outpatient clinics). To best prevent chronic disease, there a focus needs to be directed on delivering Level III interventions in community settings, in addition to traditional outpatient clinics and hospitals [11,13,176]. In this manner, Level III interventions reach individuals at all stages of health, where the main "clinic" of Level III interventions is in the person's home.

Level IV: system-specific interventions

Level I-III interventions focus on the whole individual and encourage participation in a healthy lifestyle. Finally, level IV interventions are system-specific and target a specific physiological system within an individual with abnormal function or chronic disease. Examples include pharmacologic interventions for hypertension, dyslipidemia, elevated blood glucose, and surgical interventions for cancer or CVD.

Level IV interventions account for the majority of care in the current responsive health care system. Most individuals receiving Level IV interventions are in Stage C and D health states and receive generalized care based on current scientific evidence. This generalized, downstream approach (i.e., Levels C and D) is not optimal [180]. Precision medicine can be described as treatment and prevention that considers the individual variability of genes, environment, and lifestyle for each person. As precision medicine advances, the ability to deliver Stage IV interventions to individuals in Stage A and B health will evolve, and the ability to deliver P4 medicine will improve [32,209,126].

All levels of intervention for all stages of health

All levels of intervention are essential for all health stages. Regardless of the health stage at which a person enters the P4H continuum model, the primary goal is to prevent future chronic disease diagnoses and adverse events, improve symptoms and signs when present, and improve lifestyle behaviors. In this context, all levels of intervention should be implemented at all stages of health.

Leveraging technology

The use of technology to continuously engage people in preventive medicine and to communicate healthy lifestyle information and interventions is critical for the future. More health-focused platforms are emerging, and evidence of the meaningful impact of technology-based healthy lifestyle interventions is growing [35,24,81]. There is particular potential value in using the IoT platform for ongoing engagement in preventive medicine and delivery of healthy lifestyle information and interventions [163]. In addition, the use of well-designed technological platforms has the potential to create customized public health messages. All stakeholders in the P4H continuum model should leverage technology to increase the reach and impact of initiatives and interventions. With advances in technology, an idea for a role was proposed for characterizing levels of robust health (opposed to disease risk) in

Stage A, which adds a motivational goal to strive for and further promotes the ability to measure and prevention [180].

Systems medicine and the complexity of chronic diseases

Understanding a system as complex as the human body requires the interactive collaboration of specialists from different fields. Biologists have extensively studied specific proteins and molecular networks individually and described local interactions in detail. While understanding the individual components is an important first step, an integrated approach must fully understand complex biological systems. A common, orchestrated language that allows health specialists to talk and communicate with each other should be standard. In addition, a variety of data at all relevant levels of a cellular organization need to be integrated with clinical and individually reported disease markers, using the advanced computational and mathematical modeling to enable understanding of the mechanisms, prediction, prevention, and treatment of disease [34].

P4 and systems medicine are taking global, integrated, and quantified approaches to address the challenge of biological complexity. Systems medicine uses high-throughput technologies such as DNA and RNA sequencing to generate global data sets that track multiple dimensions of dynamic network interactions to predict better and prevent chronic disease [170,145]. Large amounts of data obtained by tracking multiple biological networks are integrated to create a comprehensive understanding of human biology. With this information, scientists infer knowledge of, for example, how an individual's genetic makeup and the environment combine to produce health and disease [51,93,92,125,104]. Modern medicine requires new infrastructure, described as the "five pillars" [72] of systems-based P4 medicine:

Pillar 1 - cutting-edge technologies for generating data regarding multiple dimensions of each person's experience of health and disease.

Pillar 2 - a digital infrastructure linking participating discovery science and clinical institutions, as well as patients/consumers.

Pillar 3 - Personalized data clouds providing information about multiple dimensions of each individual's unique dynamic experience of health and disease ranging from the molecular to the social. These data will include genetic and phenotypic characteristics, medical history, demographics, and other sociometric.

Pillar 4 - new analytic techniques and technologies from deriving actionable knowledge from the data.

Pillar 5 - systems biology models for understanding the unique health status of each individual in terms of dynamic network states.

13.3.2 Predictive, personalized, preventive and participatory (P4) medicine applied to telemedicine and eHealth

P4 medicine describes a focus on systems containing predictive, personalized, preventive, and participatory aspects [99]. It proposes the integration of multiple points of biological data that include longitudinal molecular, cellular, and phenotypic measurements, as well as individual genome sequences, to better define each person's health or well-being, predict transitions to disease, and spot medical interventions [109,129]. The implementation of P4 medicine from a clinical perspective will create predictive and personalized models that represent the well-being of each patient, enabling the design of new pharmacological tests [164,89].

Computational technology and advanced analytics have been applied in various fields to achieve greater improvements in healthcare. Building a software system in combination with IoT wearable devices is a promising solution to promote preventive medicine in terms of continuous monitoring and early warning [107,179]. The future of healthcare revolves around providing people with a complete picture of the many factors that affect their health. Real-time analytics will enable physicians, researchers, and other interested parties to make better decisions while providing patients with greater control over their medical care [77,167]. Artificial intelligence and signal processing represents a new paradigm of systems, hypothesis generation and evaluation, and dynamic learning. Advances in data availability, connectivity, artificial intelligence, and signal processing are enabling physicians, researchers, and other health professionals to personalize their service with greater diagnostic confidence [3].

P4 medicine currently promises an innovative new biomedical direction that is holistic rather than reductionist [209,197]. With the rapid development of high-performance technology, there is a high accumulation of biological information at multiple levels of biological processes. Implementing integrative analysis of diverse "-omic" and clinical data is the best way to obtain systematic and complete views, better understand disease mechanisms, and find personalized and applicable health treatments [218].

The following studies were identified supporting the field of predictive, personalized, preventive, and participatory medicine in telemedicine and eHealth:

- [180] provides an overview of state of the art in 4P in telemedicine and eHealth to provide a better overview of the field and propose new lines of research with personalized medicine applications in healthcare.
- [88] discusses the emergence of P4 medicine, the impact on society, including the ability to access the growing cost of medical care.
- [190] presented an overview that establishes the basic conceptual foundations and discusses the most important aspects of P4 medicine.
- [147] provides an overview of the potential of P4 medicine to predict and prevent disease in a revolution that will be personalized in nature, essentially probabilistic, and participatory.

Outlook

With an aging population, the prevalence of chronic diseases and rising costs have created unique health challenges for our global society. In response to these health needs, researchers actively seek innovative solutions focused on prevention, personalized diagnosis, and treatment. It is predicted that taking preventive measures to control health and diagnosing and treating patients with a personalized focus in the early stages of the disease will make care more successful [162]. The development and application of P4 medicine for biology and disease is transforming medical research and clinical practice at an unprecedented pace. The convergence of these new practices will enable accurate prediction of disease and early diagnosis for a preventive health approach, as well as personalized treatment tailored to each individual [94]. The challenges for today's medical care scenarios are the heterogeneous collection of users in different locations, the distribution of large and heterogeneous data sources, distributed computing environments, and the complex process chains for analysis [211]. Medical genetics and the study of genetic variation are fundamentally related to health and human disease. Awareness and capabilities in DNA, genome sequencing, together with continuous monitoring of clinical data development, make it possible to deeper study underlying human disease mechanisms to predict, personalize, prevent, or treat various diseases.

Predictive medicine

Predictive diagnoses for early treatment of complex diseases such as Alzheimer's disease, cancer, cerebrovascular accidents, chronic kidney and heart disease represent clinical heterogeneity. The methods of conventional diagnostics, based on the measurement of only one parameter, encounter the danger of low sensitivity for the precise differentiation of patients with very heterogeneous clinical manifestations [216]. Although genome-based methods and tests conventionally represent predictive diagnoses, biomarkers form an integral part of medical diagnosis, especially diagnosing neurological diseases.

Preventive medicine

The main goal of the preventive measures against complex diseases is to identify the individuals at risk long before developing the disease symptoms to plan preventive treatments. Consequently, the preventive biomarkers aim to detect a population and stratify the individuals at high risk of developing a disease by measuring the association between their molecular profile and disease phenotype [216].

Personalized medicine

Personalized medicine is a rapidly growing area of healthcare. Its advantage is the availability of clinical, genetic, genomic, and environmental information unique to each patient [101,65]. Medical care that incorporates personalized medicine provides a coordinated, continuous service based on the patient's data [204]. Personalized medicine aims to promote health, well-being, satisfaction, and a sense of security and increase the possibility of successful prevention, detection, and treatment of a disease [38]. This form of medicine uses genomic information data, in addition to patient data and biological measures of medicine, to understand the molecular structure of disease and optimize care strategies and pharmacological treatment [114,212]. In areas such as oncology, the linkage between clinical data and genomic information could lead to the development of clinical-molecular profiles that further enhance personalized oncology health care [75,208].

Participatory medicine

Patient-centered medicine based on patient-oriented research is being developed to identify the best treatment strategy based on a diagnosis of the heterogeneity of the disease [86]. The Internet has facilitated the participation of individual patients in health care when they share their experiences on blogs and other social media. Patient communities are a driving model for participatory medicine [216]. Asthma is a good candidate for participatory medicine focus within health disorders, as current medical guidelines provide for self-monitoring of the disease. In [205], their work focuses on health for patients with asthma and decentralized air quality monitoring by the patients themselves using accessible and available hardware platforms based on Arduino. The results show creating a lightweight and accessible air quality sensor that uses a cloud-based architecture to add and analyze the readings.

Summative analysis

The antiquated focus of medicine, which was based on disease, will change in the next decade to personalized medicine, in which the genetic composition, molecular characteristics combined with clinical and environmental data will determine the focus for treating the disease [143]. Modern medicine lacks precision in diagnosis and treatment. Personalized medicine will transform modern medicine by focusing on the patient, their genes, their environment, their response to treatments, and their involvement in their care. The ubiquitous convergence of mobile applications, smart sensors, and artificial intelligence methods will enable the creation of automatic detection systems and pathology recognition in the healthcare of a new generation [146]. These systems will help create more effective and adaptive treatment platforms for humans, which they see as the future medicine.

Clinical research that generates hypotheses has the potential to provide data that illuminate the full spectrum of health and eliminate the biases that have limited this understanding in the past [27]. Applying these principles to clinical medicine may open new avenues for diagnosis and provide the theoretical basis for predictive medicine that can identify susceptibility to disease and enable health maintenance rather than focusing solely on treating the obvious disease. The use of personalized medicine will make clinical trials more efficient by reducing the costs incurred from adverse drug reactions and prescribing drugs that are ineffective for certain genotypes or health progressions. Through personalized medicine, patients can receive early monitoring of the signs and symptoms of a disease, receive preventive treatment that has benefited other patients like them, or receive treatment that is customized to their characteristics.

The focus on P4 medicine will enable scientists and medical professionals to find better treatment targets for different types of complex diseases at different stages [85]. An important step in such efforts would be discovering dynamic biomarkers, establishing continuous health observation and alert systems for presymptomatic diagnosis and prognosis to help predict and prevent diseases at different stages.

In summary, P4 medicine will improve health care, reduce health care costs, and stimulate innovation and new businesses.

13.3.3 Towards interpretable modeling approaches
Causal models
(Deep) machine learning models are nonlinear correlations between predictor variables and clinical outcomes and are often criticized as black boxes. The advantage of these methods is that they do not require a detailed prior understanding of cause-effect relationships or detailed mechanisms. The main limitation is the difficulty of interpreting them. An important question is to which extend machine learning methods might evolve into causal models in the future.

Causal graphical models (in particular, causal Bayesian networks) provide an established framework for causal reasoning. They provide a mathematical and visual representation of a multivariate distribution and allow predictions over unseen interventions (e.g., a new treatment). Causal graphical models can be trained over observational data [191,46,189]. It is possible to include background knowledge or to account for hidden or unmeasured confounders.

Causal graph learning methods may experience increasing importance in identifying appropriate predictor variables with causal influence on clinical outcomes in the future [173] to help move toward causal interpretation of predictor variables for machine learning models [5]. Challenges that need to be addressed are dealing with assumption violations and nonlinear relationships, high computational costs [193].

13.3.4 Hybrid machine learning and mechanistic models

The predictive power of most available disease models still does not meet the requirements of clinical practice. One reason is that predictive disease models should cover all relevant biotic and abiotic mechanisms that accelerate disease progression in patients. Although the primary disease-driving mechanisms are often molecular-level irregularities, such as mutations in the genome, disease progression is influenced by the robustness of the overall system. However, biological systems have many repair mechanisms to compensate for the effects of molecular aberrations, introducing feedback loops and nonlinear interactions into the system [82]. Overall, disease progression is influenced by many highly diverse mechanisms across biological hierarchies that vary in every patient.

Therefore, a disease model designed for precision medicine applications should integrate three conceptual levels:

- A core disease model (CDM) represents only the known intra- and intercellular processes that are the main drivers of disease in an average patient.
- The CDM must be adapted to the individual patient and their specific disease history and environment, such as genetic variations, comorbidities, or physiology, through environmental adaptation models (EAM). The EAM must provide individualization of the parameters controlling CDM, possibly combined with an individualized restructuring of CDM, e.g., by adding or excluding biological mechanisms that are relevant only in specific patient populations.
- Monitoring models need to be developed to describe how clinically accessible outcome measures representing disease progression are linked to CDM.

Fully mechanistic models exist for a range of core disease-driving processes at the molecular and cell population levels [56]. However, the broader application of mechanistic modeling to implement CDM for complex diseases is hampered by insufficient knowledge of the interplay of disease-driving core mechanisms across scales.

Furthermore, the relevant mechanisms for EAM and monitoring models are rarely fully known. Therefore, it seems unlikely that fully mechanistic models will soon play a dominant role in personalized medicine. Although machine learning models are not affected by insufficient biomedical knowledge, they are, as previously stated, often criticized for their black-box nature. Hybrid modeling, also called gray-box or semiparametric modeling, is an approach that combines available mechanistic and machine learning-based submodels into a collaborative computational network. The nodes in the network represent model components and the edges their interaction. Initial combinations of mechanistic and data-driven models were developed for chemical and biotechnological process modeling [210].

Neural networks were previously used to compensate for the systematic errors of inadequate mechanistic models, to approximate unobservable parameters in mechanistic models from observable data, or to determine the interaction between different mechanistic submodels [166,67].

Another example of hybrid modeling is learning the drug's mechanism of action from data [186,22]. Hybrid models can be a way to combine the positive aspects of fully mechanistic and purely data-driven machine learning models. The potential has been demonstrated, but more successful applications are needed, and a deeper knowledge of the capabilities of hybrid models and their limitations.

13.3.5 Controlling critical transitions in patient trajectories

One main goal of personalized medicine is to predict a person's risk of developing a particular disease or at the onset of the disease to predict the most appropriate therapy. This includes determining the probable course of the disease. Modeling disease trajectories is not completely different from attempts to model and simulate other complex systems, such as climatological, ecological, economic, or social systems. In many highly nonlinear, complex systems with thousands or millions of components that exhibit redundant and intertwined feedback relationships, so-called critical transitions or catastrophic shifts can be observed. Critical thresholds that define such transitions are sometimes referred to as tipping points, where a system abruptly transitions from one state to another. However, critical transitions are often extremely difficult to determine in advance.

For diseases, there exists the belief that the concept of critical transitions may also be applicable in personalized medicine. Tipping points are often observed during acute and chronic disease progression. To predict a critical transition of an evolving disease before it occurs is highly desirable and would provide valuable biomarkers for the period prior to the disease.

From a broader perspective, evolutionary principles could help improve our understanding of human diseases [76]. Evolutionarily conserved control genes are likely to be of great importance for the proper functioning of molecular signaling pathways [103], and the evolutionary history of human disease genes reveals phenotypic correlations and comorbidities among some diseases [154]. Next-generation sequencing of the entire genomes of soon millions of patients with common and rare diseases provides us with a rich genotype-phenotype landscape underlying the development and manifestation of human diseases. Such data offer exciting opportunities to understand better the impact of genomic variants on evolutionary conserved genomic regions and molecular networks associated with human disease.

Evolutionary conservation could be relevant for constraining models and simulating human disease. Biologically possible and plausible disease trajectories are likely to be constrained by the topological and dynamic upper and lower limits set by the evolutionary history of the disease network. A key challenge for personalized medicine is to develop a mechanistic explanation for an individual's disease evolution.

13.4 Key features

In this last chapter of the book, we have analyzed important issues related to the new generation of healthcare solutions. Such issues include ethics, privacy, data protection, data anonymization, etc. Also, the role of eHealth systems, particularly IoT systems, to noninvasive and predictive medicine is highlighted and discussed.

- ☑ Ethical considerations for Machine Learning Healthcare Applications are given with the aim to stress for inclusive and integral eHealth solutions for all groups of populations.
- ☑ Regulatory issues and policy initiatives in AI systems are envisaged as crucial to eHealth systems as they do more than process information and assist officials to make decisions of consequence; they exert direct and physical control over objects in the human environment.
- ☑ Various challenges of AI in medicine are briefly analyzed and exemplified using AI in radiology and evidence-based medicine.

☑ The security and privacy challenges in healthcare are analyzed in the context of the EU General Data Protection Regulation (EU GDPR), including the GDPR requirements analysis in the IoT Domain.

☑ The limitations of Machine Learning for diagnosis and treatment in the context of data privacy are highlighted. The core six principles of the GDPR in Machine learning are described.

☑ Finally, the role of Cloud digital ecosystems (Cloud-to-thing continuum) is analyzed as a cornerstone to Preventive, Predictive, Personalized, and Participatory (P4) Medicine.

References

[1] Increasing healthspan: prosper and live long, EBioMedicine 2 (2015) 1559.

[2] S. Aboueid, R.H. Liu, B. Desta, A. Chaurasia, S. Ebrahim, The use of artificially intelligent self-diagnosing digital platforms by the general public: scoping review, JMIR Medical Informatics 7 (2019).

[3] M.N. Ahmed, A.S. Toor, K. O'Neil, D. Friedland, Cognitive computing and the future of health care cognitive computing and the future of healthcare: the cognitive power of IBM Watson has the potential to transform global personalized medicine, IEEE Pulse 8 (2017) 4–9.

[4] A. Åkesson, S. Larsson, A. Discacciati, A. Wolk, Low-risk diet and lifestyle habits in the primary prevention of myocardial infarction in men: a population-based prospective cohort study, Journal of the American College of Cardiology 64 (13) (2014) 1299–1306.

[5] C. Aliferis, A. Statnikov, I. Tsamardinos, S. Mani, X. Koutsoukos, Local causal and Markov blanket induction for causal discovery and feature selection for classification part I: algorithms and empirical evaluation, Journal of Machine Learning Research 11 (2010) 171–234.

[6] F. Allaert, G. Teuff, C. Quantin, B. Barber, The legal acknowledgement of the electronic signature: a key for a secure direct access of patients to their computerised medical record, International Journal of Medical Informatics 73 (3) (2004) 239–242.

[7] A.-R. Alzoubaidi, Cloud computing national e-health services: Data center solution architecture, 2016.

[8] R. Amarasingham, A. Audet, D. Bates, I.G. Cohen, M. Entwistle, G. Escobar, V. Liu, L. Etheredge, B. Lo, L. Ohno-Machado, S. Ram, S. Saria, L. Schilling, A. Shahi, W. Stewart, E. Steyerberg, B. Xie, Consensus statement on electronic health predictive analytics: a guiding framework to address challenges, eGEMs 4 (2016).

[9] S.S. Anand, S. Yusuf, Stemming the global tsunami of cardiovascular disease, The Lancet 377 (2011) 529–532.

[10] L. Anderson, R. Taylor, Cardiac rehabilitation for people with heart disease: an overview of Cochrane systematic reviews, International Journal of Cardiology 177 (2) (2014) 348–361.

[11] R. Arena, M. Guazzi, L. Lianov, L. Whitsel, K. Berra, C. Lavie, L. Kaminsky, M. Williams, M. Hivert, N.C. Franklin, J. Myers, D. Dengel, D. Lloyd-Jones, F. Pinto, F. Cosentino, M. Halle, S. Gielen, P. Dendale, J. Niebauer, A. Pelliccia, P. Giannuzzi, U. Corrá, M. Piepoli, G. Guthrie, D. Shurney, N. Franklin, Healthy lifestyle interventions to combat noncommunicable disease-a novel nonhierarchical connectivity model for key stakeholders: a policy statement from the American Heart Association, European Society of Cardiology, European Association for Cardiovascular Prevention and Rehabilitation, and American College of Preventive Medicine, European Heart Journal 36 (31) (2015) 2097–2109.

[12] R. Arena, C. Lavie, The healthy lifestyle team is central to the success of accountable care organizations, Mayo Clinic Proceedings 90 (5) (2015) 572–576.

[13] R. Arena, C. Lavie, L. Cahalin, P.D. Briggs, S. Guizilini, J. Daugherty, W.-M. Chan, A. Borghi-Silva, Transforming cardiac rehabilitation into broad-based healthy lifestyle programs to combat noncommunicable disease, Expert Review of Cardiovascular Therapy 14 (2016) 23–36.

[14] R. Arena, C. Lavie, M. Hivert, M. Williams, P.D. Briggs, M. Guazzi, Who will deliver comprehensive healthy lifestyle interventions to combat non-communicable disease? Introducing the healthy lifestyle practitioner discipline, Expert Review of Cardiovascular Therapy 14 (2016) 15–22.

[15] R. Arena, J. Myers, M. Guazzi, The future of aerobic exercise testing in clinical practice: is it the ultimate vital sign?, Future Cardiology 6 (3) (2010) 325–342.

[16] S. Arora, M. Kumar, P. Johri, S. Das, Big heterogeneous data and its security: a survey, in: 2016 International Conference on Computing, Communication and Automation (ICCCA), 2016, pp. 37–40.

[17] A. Auerbach, S. Kripalani, E. Vasilevskis, N. Sehgal, P. Lindenauer, J. Metlay, G.S. Fletcher, G. Ruhnke, S. Flanders, C. Kim, M. Williams, L. Thomas, V. Giang, S. Herzig, K. Patel, W.J. Boscardin, E.J. Robinson, J. Schnipper, Preventability and causes of readmissions in a national cohort of general medicine patients, JAMA Internal Medicine 176 (4) (2016) 484–493.

[18] C. Auffray, D. Charron, L. Hood, Predictive, preventive, personalized and participatory medicine: back to the future, Genome Medicine 2 (2010) 57.

[19] C. Auffray, S. Imbeaud, M. Roux-Rouquié, L. Hood, Self–organized living systems: conjunction of a stable organization with chaotic fluctuations in biological space–time, Philosophical Transactions of the Royal Society of London. Series A: Mathematical, Physical and Engineering Sciences 361 (2003) 1125–1139.

[20] N. Auffray, R. Bouchet, Y. Bréchet, Class-jump phenomenon for physical symmetries in bi-dimensional space, 2009.

[21] C. Badii, P. Bellini, A. Difino, P. Nesi, Smart city IoT platform respecting GDPR privacy and security aspects, IEEE Access 8 (2020) 23601–23623.

[22] S. Balabanov, T. Wilhelm, S. Venz, G. Keller, C. Scharf, H. Pospisil, M. Braig, C. Barett, C. Bokemeyer, R. Walther, et al., Combination of a proteomics approach and reengineering of meso scale network models for prediction of mode-of-action for tyrosine kinase inhibitors, PLoS ONE 8 (1) (2013) e53668.

[23] F. Baum, A. Lawless, T. Delany, C. MacDougall, C. Williams, D. Broderick, D. Wildgoose, E. Harris, D. Mcdermott, I. Kickbusch, J. Popay, M. Marmot, Evaluation of health in all policies: concept, theory and application, Health Promotion International 29 (Suppl 1) (2014) i130–i142.

[24] A.L. Beatty, Y. Fukuoka, M. Whooley, Using mobile technology for cardiac rehabilitation: a review and framework for development and evaluation, Journal of the American Heart Association: Cardiovascular and Cerebrovascular Disease 2 (2013).

[25] E. Begoli, T. Bhattacharya, D. Kusnezov, The need for uncertainty quantification in machine-assisted medical decision making, Nature Machine Intelligence 1 (2019) 20–23.

[26] D. Belsky, A. Caspi, R. Houts, H. Cohen, D. Corcoran, A. Danese, H. Harrington, S. Israel, M. Levine, J. Schaefer, K. Sugden, B.H. Williams, A. Yashin, R. Poulton, T. Moffitt, Quantification of biological aging in young adults, Proceedings of the National Academy of Sciences 112 (2015) E4104–E4110.

[27] L. Biesecker, Hypothesis-generating research and predictive medicine, Genome Research 23 (7) (2013) 1051–1053.

[28] M. Bledsoe, W. Grizzle, Use of human specimens in research: the evolving United States regulatory, policy, and scientific landscape, Diagnostic Histopathology 19 (9) (2013) 322–330.

[29] D. Bokefode Jayant, A. Ubale Swapnaja, S. Apte Sulabha, G. Modani Dattatray, Analysis of DAC MAC RBAC access control based models for security, International Journal of Computer Applications 104 (2014) 6–13.

[30] E. Borelli, G. Paolini, F. Antoniazzi, M. Barbiroli, F. Benassi, F. Chesani, L. Chiari, M. Fantini, F. Fuschini, A. Galassi, G.A. Giacobone, S. Imbesi, M. Licciardello, D. Loreti, M. Marchi, D. Masotti, P. Mello, S. Mellone, G. Mincolelli, C. Raffaelli, L. Roffia, T.S. Cinotti, C. Tacconi, P. Tamburini, M. Zoli, A. Costanzo, HABITAT: an IoT solution for independent elderly, Sensors (Basel, Switzerland) 19 (2019).

[31] D. Bornstein, R. Pate, D. Buchner, Development of a national physical activity plan for the United States, Journal of Physical Activity & Health 11 (3) (2014) 463–469.

[32] C. Bouchard, L.M. Antunes-Correa, E. Ashley, N. Franklin, P.M. Hwang, C. Mattsson, C. Negrão, S. Phillips, M. Sarzynski, P. Wang, M. Wheeler, Personalized preventive medicine: genetics and the response to regular exercise in preventive interventions, Progress in Cardiovascular Diseases 57 (4) (2015) 337–346.

[33] J. Bousquet, J. Antó, P. Sterk, I. Adcock, K. Chung, J. Roca, A. Agustí, C. Brightling, A. Cambon-Thomsen, A. Cesario, S. Abdelhak, S. Antonarakis, A. Avignon, A. Ballabio, E. Baraldi, A. Baranov, T. Bieber, J. Bockaert, S. Brahmachari, C. Brambilla, J. Bringer, M. Dauzat, I. Ernberg, L. Fabbri, P. Froguel, D. Galas, T. Gojobori, P. Hunter, C. Jorgensen, F. Kauffmann, P. Kourilsky, M. Kowalski, D. Lancet, C. Pen, J. Mallet, B. Mayosi, J. Mercier, A. Metspalu, J. Nadeau, G. Ninot, D. Noble, M. Öztürk, S. Palkonen, C. Préfaut, K. Rabe, E. Renard, R. Roberts, B. Samolinski, H. Schünemann, H. Simon, M. Soares, G. Superti-Furga, J. Tegnér, S. Verjovski-Almeida, P. Wellstead, O. Wolkenhauer, E. Wouters, R. Balling, A. Brookes, D. Charron, C. Pison, Z. Chen, L. Hood, C. Auffray, Systems medicine and integrated care to combat chronic noncommunicable diseases, Genome Medicine 3 (2011) 43.

[34] J. Bousquet, C. Jorgensen, M. Dauzat, A. Cesario, T. Camuzat, R. Bourret, N. Best, J. Antó, F. Abécassis, P. Aubas, A. Avignon, M. Badin, A. Bedbrook, H. Blain, A. Bourdin, J. Bringer, W. Camu, G. Cayla, D. Costa, P. Courtet, J. Cristol, P. Demoly, J.E. de la Coussaye, P. Fesler, F. Gouzi, J. Gris, B. Guillot, M. Hayot, C. Jeandel, O. Jonquet, L. Journot, S. Lehmann, G. Mathieu, J. Morel, G. Ninot, J. Pélissier, M. Picot, F. Radier-Pontal, J. Robine, M. Rodier, F. Roubille, A. Sultan, A. Wojtusciszyn, C. Auffray, R. Balling, C. Bárbara, A. Cambon-Thomsen, N. Chavannes, A. Chuchalin, G. Crooks, A. Dedeu, L. Fabbri, J. Garcia-Aymerich, J. Hajjam, E.M. Gomes, S. Palkonen, F. Piette, C. Pison, D.H. Price, B. Samolinski, H. Schunemann, P. Sterk, P. Yiallouros, J. Roca, P.V. de Perre, J. Mercier, Systems medicine approaches for the definition of complex phenotypes in chronic diseases and ageing. From concept to implementation and policies, Current Pharmaceutical Design 20 (38) (2014) 5928–5944.

[35] L. Burke, J. Ma, K. Azar, G. Bennett, E. Peterson, Y. Zheng, W. Riley, J.D. Stephens, S.H. Shah, B. Suffoletto, T. Turan, B. Spring, J. Steinberger, C. Quinn, Current science on consumer use of mobile health for cardiovascular disease prevention: a scientific statement from the American Heart Association, Circulation 132 (12) (2015) 1157–1213.

[36] R. Calo, Artificial intelligence policy: a primer and roadmap, University of Bologna Law Review 3 (2017) 180–218.

[37] K. Campbell, D. Crawford, J. Salmon, A. Carver, S. Garnett, L. Baur, Associations between the home food environment and obesity-promoting eating behaviors in adolescence, Obesity 15 (2007).

[38] C. Carlsten, M. Brauer, F. Brinkman, J. Brook, D. Daley, K. Mcnagny, M. Pui, D. Royce, T. Takaro, J. Denburg, Genes, the environment and personalized medicine: we need to harness both environmental and genetic data to maximize personal and population health, EMBO Reports 15 (06 2014).

[39] D. Castelvecchi, Can we open the black box of AI?, Nature News 538 (7623) (2016) 20.

[40] Cerf and F. Community, Artificial intelligence and medical imaging 2018: French radiology community white paper, Diagnostic and Interventional Imaging 99 (11) (2018) 727–742.

[41] D. Char, N. Shah, D. Magnus, Implementing machine learning in health care - addressing ethical challenges, The New England Journal of Medicine 378 (11) (2018) 981–983.

[42] D.S. Char, N.H. Shah, D. Magnus, Implementing machine learning in health care—addressing ethical challenges, The New England Journal of Medicine 378 (11) (2018) 981.

[43] L. Chen, R. Liu, Z.-P. Liu, M. Li, K. Aihara, Detecting early-warning signals for sudden deterioration of complex diseases by dynamical network biomarkers, Scientific Reports 2 (2012).

[44] S. Chen, K. Suzuki, H. MacMahon, Development and evaluation of a computer-aided diagnostic scheme for lung nodule detection in chest radiographs by means of two-stage nodule enhancement with support vector classification, Medical Physics 38 (4) (2011) 1844–1858.

[45] F.-C. Cheng, W.-H. Lai, The impact of cloud computing technology on legal infrastructure within internet— focusing on the protection of information privacy, Procedia Engineering 29 (2012) 241–251.

[46] D.M. Chickering, Learning equivalence classes of Bayesian-network structures, Journal of Machine Learning Research 2 (2002) 445–498.

[47] T. Ching, D.S. Himmelstein, B. Beaulieu-Jones, A. Kalinin, B.T. Do, G.P. Way, E. Ferrero, P. Agapow, M. Zietz, M.M. Hoffman, W. Xie, G. Rosen, B.J. Lengerich, J. Israeli, J. Lanchantin, S. Woloszynek, A. Carpenter, A. Shrikumar, J. Xu, E.M. Cofer, C.A. Lavender, S.C. Turaga, A. Alexandari, Z. Lu, D.J. Harris, D. DeCaprio, Y. Qi, A. Kundaje, Y. Peng, L.K. Wiley, M.H.S. Segler, S. Boca, S.J.J. Swamidass, A. Huang, A. Gitter, C. Greene, Opportunities and obstacles for deep learning in biology and medicine, Journal of the Royal Society Interface 15 (2018).

[48] N. Christakis, J. Fowler, Social contagion theory: examining dynamic social networks and human behavior, Statistics in Medicine 32 (4) (2013) 556–577.

[49] I.G. Cohen, R. Amarasingham, A. Shah, B. Xie, B. Lo, The legal and ethical concerns that arise from using complex predictive analytics in health care, Health Affairs 33 (7) (2014) 1139–1147.

[50] M.A. Colchero, B. Popkin, J. Rivera, S. Ng, Beverage purchases from stores in Mexico under the excise tax on sugar sweetened beverages: observational study, The BMJ 352 (2016).

[51] D. Corella, J. Ordovas, Aging and cardiovascular diseases: the role of gene–diet interactions, Ageing Research Reviews 18 (2014) 53–73.

[52] C. Crump, J. Sundquist, M. Winkleby, W. Sieh, K. Sundquist, Physical fitness among Swedish military conscripts and long-term risk for type 2 diabetes mellitus, Annals of Internal Medicine 164 (2016) 577–584.

[53] C. Crump, J. Sundquist, M. Winkleby, K. Sundquist, Interactive effects of physical fitness and body mass index on the risk of hypertension, JAMA Internal Medicine 176 (2) (2016) 210–216.

[54] A.K. Dhar, D. Barton, Depression and the link with cardiovascular disease, Frontiers in Psychiatry 7 (2016).

[55] J. Dheeba, N.A. Singh, S.T. Selvi, Computer-aided detection of breast cancer on mammograms: a swarm intelligence optimized wavelet neural network approach, Journal of Biomedical Informatics 49 (2014) 45–52.

[56] D. Dingli, F. Michor, Successful therapy must eradicate cancer stem cells, Stem Cells 24 (12) (2006) 2603–2610.

[57] N. Dong, H. Jonker, J. Pang, Challenges in ehealth: from enabling to enforcing privacy, in: FHIES, 2011.

[58] M. Elhoseny, G. Ramírez-González, O. Abu-Elnasr, S.A. Shawkat, N. Arunkumar, A. Farouk, Secure medical data transmission model for IoT-based healthcare systems, IEEE Access 6 (2018) 20596–20608.

[59] B.J. Erickson, P. Korfiatis, Z. Akkus, T.L. Kline, Machine learning for medical imaging, Radiographics 37 (2) (2017) 505–515.

[60] D. Lloyd-Jones, et al., Defining and setting national goals for cardiovascular health promotion and disease reduction: the American Heart Association's strategic impact goal through 2020 and beyond, Circulation 121 (2010) 586–613.

[61] D. Mozaffarian, et al., Heart disease and stroke statistics—2016 update: a report from the American Heart Association, Circulation 133 (2016) e38–e360.

[62] M. Naghavi, et al., Global, regional, and national age-sex specific all-cause and cause-specific mortality for 240 causes of death, 1990-2013: a systematic analysis for the global burden of disease study 2013, The Lancet 385 (2015) 117–171.

[63] S.S. Lim, et al., A comparative risk assessment of burden of disease and injury attributable to 67 risk factors and risk factor clusters in 21 regions, 1990–2010: a systematic analysis for the global burden of disease study 2010, The Lancet 380 (2013) 2224–2260.

[64] M. Evered, S. Bögeholz, A case study in access control requirements for a health information system, in: ACSW, 2004.

[65] A. Evers, M. Rovers, J. Kremer, J. Veltman, J. Schalken, B. Bloem, A.V. van Gool, An integrated framework of personalized medicine: from individual genomes to participatory health care, Croatian Medical Journal 53 (2012) 301–303.

[66] J. Fenton, S. Taplin, P. Carney, L. Abraham, E. Sickles, C. D'Orsi, E. Berns, G. Cutter, R. Hendrick, W. Barlow, J. Elmore, Influence of computer-aided detection on performance of screening mammography, The New England Journal of Medicine 356 (14) (2007) 1399–1409.

[67] B. Fiedler, A. Schuppert, Local identification of scalar hybrid models with tree structure, IMA Journal of Applied Mathematics 73 (3) (2008) 449–476.

[68] A. Fiske, P. Henningsen, A. Buyx, Your robot therapist will see you now: ethical implications of embodied artificial intelligence in psychiatry, psychology, and psychotherapy, Journal of Medical Internet Research 21 (2019).

[69] A.W. Flores, K. Bechtel, C.T. Lowenkamp, False positives, false negatives, and false analyses: a rejoinder to "machine bias: there's software used across the country to predict future criminals. And it's biased against blacks", Federal Probation 80 (2016) 38.

[70] M. Flores, G. Glusman, K. Brogaard, N. Price, L. Hood, P4 medicine: how systems medicine will transform the healthcare sector and society, Personalized Medicine 10 (6) (2013) 565–576.

[71] T. Frieden, Evidence for health decision making — beyond randomized, controlled trials: the changing face of clinical trials, The New England Journal of Medicine 377 (2017) 465–475.

[72] H. Fröhlich, R. Balling, N. Beerenwinkel, O. Kohlbacher, S. Kumar, T. Lengauer, M. Maathuis, Y. Moreau, S. Murphy, T. Przytycka, M. Rebhan, H.L. Röst, A. Schuppert, M. Schwab, R. Spang, D. Stekhoven, J. Sun, A. Weber, D. Ziemek, B. Zupan, From hype to reality: data science enabling personalized medicine, BMC Medicine 16 (2018).

[73] Y. Gahi, M. Guennoun, H. Mouftah, Big data analytics: security and privacy challenges, in: 2016 IEEE Symposium on Computers and Communication (ISCC), 2016, pp. 952–957.

[74] C.M. Gijsberts, K. Groenewegen, I. Hoefer, M. Eijkemans, F. Asselbergs, T. Anderson, A. Britton, J. Dekker, G. Engström, G. Evans, J. de Graaf, D. Grobbee, B. Hedblad, S. Holewijn, A. Ikeda, K. Kitagawa, A. Kitamura, D.D. de Kleijn, E. Lonn, M. Lorenz, E. Mathiesen, G. Nijpels, S. Okazaki, D. O'leary, G. Pasterkamp, S. Peters, J. Polak, J. Price, C. Robertson, C. Rembold, M. Rosvall, T. Rundek, J. Salonen, M. Sitzer, C. Stehouwer, M. Bots, H.D. den Ruijter, Race/ethnic differences in the associations of the framingham risk factors with carotid IMT and cardiovascular events, PLoS ONE 10 (2015).

[75] G. Ginsburg, N. Kuderer, Comparative effectiveness research, genomics-enabled personalized medicine, and rapid learning health care: a common bond, Journal of Clinical Oncology: Official Journal of the American Society of Clinical Oncology 30 (34) (2012) 4233–4242.

[76] P.D. Gluckman, F.M. Low, T. Buklijas, M.A. Hanson, A.S. Beedle, How evolutionary principles improve the understanding of human health and disease, Evolutionary Applications 4 (2) (2011) 249–263.

[77] S. Green, H. Vogt, Personalizing medicine: disease prevention in silico and in socio, Humana.Mente 9 (2016) 105–145.

[78] D. Gruson, J. Petrelluzzi, J. Mehl, A. Burgun, N. Garcelon, [Ethical, legal and operational issues of artificial intelligence], La Revue du praticien 68 (10) (2018) 1145–1148.

[79] V. Gulshan, L. Peng, M. Coram, M.C. Stumpe, D. Wu, A. Narayanaswamy, S. Venugopalan, K. Widner, T. Madams, J.A. Cuadros, R. Kim, R. Raman, P. Nelson, J. Mega, D.R. Webster, Development and validation of a deep learning algorithm for detection of diabetic retinopathy in retinal fundus photographs, JAMA 316 (22) (2016) 2402–2410.

[80] N. Halfon, M. Hochstein, Life course health development: an integrated framework for developing health, policy, and research, Milbank Quarterly 80 (3) (2002) 433–479, iii.

[81] C.S. Hall, E. Fottrell, S. Wilkinson, P. Byass, Assessing the impact of mhealth interventions in low- and middle-income countries – what has been shown to work?, Global Health Action 7 (2014).

[82] D. Hanahan, R.A. Weinberg, Hallmarks of cancer: the next generation, Cell 144 (5) (2011) 646–674.

[83] E. Havranek, M. Mujahid, D. Barr, I. Blair, M.S. Cohen, S. Cruz-Flores, G. Davey-Smith, C. Dennison-Himmelfarb, M. Lauer, D.W. Lockwood, M. Rosal, C. Yancy, Social determinants of risk and outcomes for cardiovascular disease: a scientific statement from the American Heart Association, Circulation 132 (2015) 873–898.

[84] C. Henshall, L. Marzano, K. Smith, M. Attenburrow, S. Puntis, J. Zlodre, K. Kelly, M. Broome, S. Shaw, A. Barrera, A. Molodynski, A. Reid, J. Geddes, A. Cipriani, A web-based clinical decision tool to support treatment decision-making in psychiatry: a pilot focus group study with clinicians, patients and carers, BMC Psychiatry 17 (2017).

[85] L. Hood, Systems biology and p4 medicine: past, present, and future, Rambam Maimonides Medical Journal 4 (2013).

[86] L. Hood, C. Auffray, Participatory medicine: a driving force for revolutionizing healthcare, Genome Medicine 5 (2013) 110.

[87] L. Hood, R. Balling, C. Auffray, Revolutionizing medicine in the 21st century through systems approaches, Biotechnology Journal 7 (8) (2012) 992–1001.

[88] L. Hood, M. Flores, A personal view on systems medicine and the emergence of proactive p4 medicine: predictive, preventive, personalized and participatory, New Biotechnology 29 (6) (2012) 613–624.

[89] L. Hood, S. Friend, Predictive, personalized, preventive, participatory (p4) cancer medicine, Nature Reviews Clinical Oncology 8 (2011) 184–187.

[90] L. Hood, J. Heath, M. Phelps, B. Lin, Systems biology and new technologies enable predictive and preventative medicine, Science 306 (2004) 640–643.

[91] L. Hood, J. Lovejoy, N. Price, Integrating big data and actionable health coaching to optimize wellness, BMC Medicine 13 (2015).

[92] L. Hood, N. Price, Demystifying disease, democratizing health care, Science Translational Medicine 6 (2014) 225ed5.

[93] L. Hood, N. Price, Promoting wellness & demystifying disease: the 100k project, Clinical OMICs 1 (2014) 20–23.

[94] L. Hood, Q. Tian, Systems approaches to biology and disease enable translational systems medicine, Genomics, Proteomics & Bioinformatics 10 (2012) 181–185.

[95] S. Jackson, A. Steptoe, J. Wardle, The influence of partner's behavior on health behavior change: the English longitudinal study of ageing, JAMA Internal Medicine 175 (3) (2015) 385–392.

[96] P. Jain, M. Gyanchandani, N. Khare, Big data privacy: a technological perspective and review, Journal of Big Data 3 (2016) 1–25.

[97] J. Jaremko, M. Azar, R. Bromwich, A. Lum, L.H.A. Cheong, M. Gibert, F. Laviolette, B.G. Gray, C. Reinhold, M. Cicero, J. Chong, J. Shaw, F. Rybicki, C. Hurrell, E. Lee, A. Tang, Canadian association of radiologists white paper on ethical and legal issues related to artificial intelligence in radiology, Canadian Association of Radiologists Journal 70 (2019) 107–118.

[98] L. Jaspers, V. Colpani, L. Chaker, S.V.D. Lee, T. Muka, D. Imo, S. Mendis, R. Chowdhury, W. Bramer, A. Falla, R. Pazoki, O. Franco, The global impact of non-communicable diseases on households and impoverishment: a systematic review, European Journal of Epidemiology 30 (2014) 163–188.

[99] S.L. Jenkins, A. Ma'ayan, Systems pharmacology meets predictive, preventive, personalized and participatory medicine, Pharmacogenomics 14 (2) (2013) 119–122.

[100] X. Jin, R. Krishnan, R. Sandhu, A unified attribute-based access control model covering DAC, MAC and RBAC, in: DBSec, 2012.

[101] John C. O'Donnell, Personalized medicine and the role of health economics and outcomes research: Issues, applications, emerging trends, and future research, 2015.

[102] M.N. Johnstone, Cloud security: a case study in telemedicine, 2012.

[103] I.K. Jordan, I.B. Rogozin, Y.I. Wolf, E.V. Koonin, Essential genes are more evolutionarily conserved than are nonessential genes in bacteria, Genome Research 12 (6) (2002) 962–968.

[104] S. Karaca, S. Erge, T. Cesuroğlu, R. Polimanti, Nutritional habits, lifestyle, and genetic predisposition in cardiovascular and metabolic traits in Turkish population, Nutrition 32 (6) (2016) 693–701.

[105] B.B. Kelly, J. Narula, V. Fuster, Recognizing global burden of cardiovascular disease and related chronic diseases, The Mount Sinai Journal of Medicine, New York 79 (6) (2012) 632–640.

[106] Y. Khang, Burden of noncommunicable diseases and national strategies to control them in Korea, Journal of Preventive Medicine and Public Health 46 (2013) 155–164.

[107] I. Khemapech, W. Sansrimahachai, M. Toahchoodee, A real-time health monitoring and warning system for bridge structures, in: 2016 IEEE Region 10 Conference (TENCON), 2016, pp. 3010–3013.

[108] K.H. Khng, R. Mane, Beyond BCI—validating a wireless, consumer-grade EEG headset against a medical-grade system for evaluating EEG effects of a test anxiety intervention in school, Advanced Engineering Informatics 45 (2020) 101106.

[109] M. Khoury, M. Gwinn, M. Bowen, W.D. Dotson, Beyond base pairs to bedside: a population perspective on how genomics can improve health, American Journal of Public Health 102 (1) (2012) 34–37.

[110] B.F. King, Artificial intelligence and radiology: what will the future hold?, Journal of the American College of Radiology 15 (3) (2018) 501–503.

[111] B.F. King Jr., Guest editorial: discovery and artificial intelligence, 2017.

[112] M. Kohli, L.M. Prevedello, R.W. Filice, J.R. Geis, Implementing machine learning in radiology practice and research, American Journal of Roentgenology 208 (4) (2017) 754–760.

[113] G. Koren, D. Souroujon, R. Shaul, A. Bloch, A. Leventhal, J. Lockett, V. Shalev, "A patient like me" – an algorithm-based program to inform patients on the likely conditions people with symptoms like theirs have, Medicine 98 (2019).

[114] I. Kouris, C. Tsirmpas, S. Mougiakakou, D. Iliopoulou, D. Koutsouris, E-health towards ecumenical framework for personalized medicine via decision support system, in: 2010 Annual International Conference of the IEEE Engineering in Medicine and Biology, 2010, pp. 2881–2885.

[115] C. Krittanawong, The rise of artificial intelligence and the uncertain future for physicians, European Journal of Internal Medicine 48 (2018) e13–e14.

[116] D. Kufe, R. Pollock, R. Weichselbaum, R. Bast, T. Gansler, J. Holland, E. Frei, Holland-Frei Cancer Medicine, 2016.

[117] P. Kumar, H. Lee, Security issues in healthcare applications using wireless medical sensor networks: a survey, Sensors (Basel, Switzerland) 12 (2012) 55–91.

[118] S. Larsson, A. Åkesson, A. Wolk, Primary prevention of stroke by a healthy lifestyle in a high-risk group, Neurology 84 (2015) 2224–2228.

[119] J. Law, A Dictionary of Law, OUP, Oxford, 2015.

[120] Y. LeCun, Y. Bengio, G. Hinton, Deep learning, Nature 521 (7553) (2015) 436–444.

[121] A. Leon, B. Franklin, F. Costa, G. Balady, K. Berra, K. Stewart, P. Thompson, M. Williams, M. Lauer, Cardiac rehabilitation and secondary prevention of coronary heart disease: an American Heart Association scientific statement from the Council on Clinical Cardiology (Subcommittee on Exercise, Cardiac Rehabilitation, and Prevention) and the Council on Nutrition, Physical Activity, and Metabolism (Subcommittee on Physical Activity), in collaboration with the American association of Cardiovascular and Pulmonary Rehabilitation, Circulation 111 (3) (2005) 369–376.

[122] D. Leong, K. Teo, S. Rangarajan, P. López-Jaramillo, A. Avezum, A. Orlandini, P. Serón, S.H. Ahmed, A. Rosengren, R. Kelishadi, O. Rahman, S. Swaminathan, R. Iqbal, R. Gupta, S. Lear, A. Oğuz, K. Yusoff, K. Zatońska, J. Chifamba, E. Igumbor, V. Mohan, R. Anjana, H. Gu, W. Li, S. Yusuf, Prognostic value of grip strength: findings from the prospective urban rural epidemiology (pure) study, The Lancet 386 (2015) 266–273.

[123] M. Li, S. Yu, Y. Zheng, K. Ren, W. Lou, Scalable and secure sharing of personal health records in cloud computing using attribute-based encryption, IEEE Transactions on Parallel and Distributed Systems 24 (2013) 131–143.

[124] M. Li, T. Zeng, R. Liu, L. Chen, Detecting tissue-specific early warning signals for complex diseases based on dynamical network biomarkers: study of type 2 diabetes by cross-tissue analysis, Briefings in Bioinformatics 15 (2) (2014) 229–243.

[125] C. Ling, T. Rönn, Epigenetic adaptation to regular exercise in humans, Drug Discovery Today 19 (7) (2014) 1015–1018.

[126] J. Loscalzo, A. Barabasi, Systems biology and the future of medicine, Wiley Interdisciplinary Reviews: Systems Biology and Medicine 3 (2011).

[127] F. Madeo, F. Pietrocola, T. Eisenberg, G. Kroemer, Caloric restriction mimetics: towards a molecular definition, Nature Reviews Drug Discovery 13 (2014) 727–740.

[128] R. Magnusson, D. Patterson, The role of law and governance reform in the global response to non-communicable diseases, Globalization and Health 10 (2014) 44.

[129] M. Maier, T. Takano, R. Sapir-Pichhadze, Changing paradigms in the management of rejection in kidney transplantation: evolving from protocol-based care to the era of p4 medicine, Canadian Journal of Kidney Health and Disease 4 (01 2017) 205435811668822.

[130] C. Maloy, Library guides: data resources in the health sciences: clinical data, 2012.

[131] K. Matthews, Y. Chang, K. Sutton-Tyrrell, D. Edmundowicz, J. Bromberger, Recurrent major depression predicts progression of coronary calcification in healthy women: study of women's health across the nation, Psychosomatic Medicine 72 (2010) 742–747.

[132] B. McEwen, Protective and damaging effects of stress mediators, The New England Journal of Medicine 338 (3) (1998) 171–179.

[133] B. McEwen, Protective and damaging effects of stress mediators: central role of the brain, Dialogues in Clinical Neuroscience 8 (2006) 367–381.

[134] B. McEwen, L. Getz, Lifetime experiences, the brain and personalized medicine: an integrative perspective, Metabolism: Clinical and Experimental 62 (Suppl 1) (2013) S20–S26.

[135] B. McEwen, T. Seeman, Protective and damaging effects of mediators of stress: elaborating and testing the concepts of allostasis and allostatic load, Annals of the New York Academy of Sciences 896 (1999).

[136] B.S. McEwen, E. Stellar, Stress and the individual: mechanisms leading to disease, Archives of Internal Medicine 153 (18) (09 1993) 2093–2101.

[137] E. Mehraeen, M. Ghazisaeedi, J. Farzi, S. Mirshekari, Security challenges in healthcare cloud computing: a systematic review, Global Journal of Health Science 9 (3) (2016) 59729.

[138] M. Meingast, T. Roosta, S. Sastry, Security and privacy issues with health care information technology, in: 2006 International Conference of the IEEE Engineering in Medicine and Biology Society, 2006, pp. 5453–5458.

[139] S. Melov, Geroscience approaches to increase healthspan and slow aging, F1000Research 5 (2016).

[140] D.D. Miller, E.W. Brown, Artificial intelligence in medical practice: the question to the answer?, The American Journal of Medicine 131 (2) (2018) 129–133.

[141] T. Mitchell, E. Brynjolfsson, Track how technology is transforming work, Nature News 544 (7650) (2017) 290.

[142] V. Mnih, K. Kavukcuoglu, D. Silver, A.A. Rusu, J. Veness, M.G. Bellemare, A. Graves, M. Riedmiller, A.K. Fidjeland, G. Ostrovski, et al., Human-level control through deep reinforcement learning, Nature 518 (7540) (2015) 529–533.

[143] J. Morley, S. Anker, Myopenia and precision (p4) medicine, Journal of Cachexia, Sarcopenia and Muscle 8 (2017) 857–863.

[144] J. Nabi, How bioethics can shape artificial intelligence and machine learning, The Hastings Center Report 48 (5) (2018) 10–13.

[145] T. Niiranen, R. Vasan, Epidemiology of cardiovascular disease: recent novel outlooks on risk factors and clinical approaches, Expert Review of Cardiovascular Therapy 14 (2016) 855–869.

[146] S. Nikolaiev, Y. Timoshenko, Reinvention of the cardiovascular diseases prevention and prediction due to ubiquitous convergence of mobile apps and machine learning, in: 2015 Information Technologies in Innovation Business Conference (ITIB), 2015, pp. 23–26.

[147] G. Noell, R. Faner, A. Agustí, From systems biology to p4 medicine: applications in respiratory medicine, European Respiratory Review 27 (2018).

[148] Z. Obermeyer, B.W. Powers, C. Vogeli, S. Mullainathan, Dissecting racial bias in an algorithm used to manage the health of populations, Science 366 (2019) 447–453.

[149] J. Odegaard, A. Chawla, Pleiotropic actions of insulin resistance and inflammation in metabolic homeostasis, Science 339 (2013) 172–177.

[150] I. Olaronke, O. Oluwaseun, Big data in healthcare: prospects, challenges and resolutions, in: 2016 Future Technologies Conference (FTC), 2016, pp. 1152–1157.

[151] W. H. Organization, et al., Global Action Plan for the Prevention and Control of Noncommunicable Diseases 2013-2020, World Health Organization, 2013.
[152] K. Ostherr, S. Borodina, R.C. Bracken, C. Lotterman, E. Storer, B. Williams, Trust and privacy in the context of user-generated health data, Big Data & Society 4 (2017).
[153] J.L. Painter, Containing the cloud: security issues in a large scale observational pharmacovigilance research project, in: Security and Management, 2010.
[154] S. Park, J.-S. Yang, J. Kim, Y.-E. Shin, J. Hwang, J. Park, S.K. Jang, S. Kim, Evolutionary history of human disease genes reveals phenotypic connections and comorbidity among genetic diseases, Scientific Reports 2 (1) (2012) 1–7.
[155] H.Y. Paul, F.K. Hui, D.S. Ting, Artificial intelligence and radiology: collaboration is key, Journal of the American College of Radiology 15 (5) (2018) 781–783.
[156] B. Pedersen, The diseasome of physical inactivity – and the role of myokines in muscle–fat cross talk, The Journal of Physiology 587 (2009).
[157] Ú. Pérez-Ramírez, E. Arana, D. Moratal, Computer-aided detection of brain metastases using a three-dimensional template-based matching algorithm, in: 2014 36th Annual International Conference of the IEEE Engineering in Medicine and Biology Society, IEEE, 2014, pp. 2384–2387.
[158] F. Pesapane, M. Codari, F. Sardanelli, Artificial intelligence in medical imaging: threat or opportunity? Radiologists again at the forefront of innovation in medicine, European Radiology Experimental 2 (2018).
[159] M. Peterson, P. Zhang, P. Choksi, K. Markides, S.A. Snih, Muscle weakness thresholds for prediction of diabetes in adults, Sports Medicine 46 (2016) 619–628.
[160] M. Peterson, P. Zhang, W. Saltarelli, P. Visich, P. Gordon, Low muscle strength thresholds for the detection of cardiometabolic risk in adolescents, American Journal of Preventive Medicine 50 (5) (2016) 593–599.
[161] M. Plachkinova, A. Alluhaidan, S. Chatterjee, Health records on the cloud: a security framework, 2015.
[162] C. Poon, M.D. Wang, P. Bonato, D. Fenstermacher, Editorial: special issue on health informatics and personalized medicine, IEEE Transactions on Biomedical Engineering 60 (2013) 143–146.
[163] M. Pratt, O. Sarmiento, F. Montes, D. Ogilvie, B. Marcus, L. Perez, R. Brownson, The implications of megatrends in information and communication technology and transportation for changes in global physical activity, The Lancet 380 (2012) 282–293.
[164] G. Pravettoni, A. Gorini, A p5 cancer medicine approach: why personalized medicine cannot ignore psychology, Journal of Evaluation in Clinical Practice 17 (4) (2011) 594–596.
[165] W. Price, I.G. Cohen, Privacy in the age of medical big data, Nature Medicine 25 (2019) 37–43.
[166] D.C. Psichogios, L.H. Ungar, A hybrid neural network-first principles approach to process modeling, AIChE Journal 38 (10) (1992) 1499–1511.
[167] S. Pulciani, A.D. Lonardo, C. Fagnani, D. Taruscio, P4 medicine versus hippocrates, Annali dell'Istituto superiore di sanita 53 (3) (2017) 185–191.
[168] A. Rajkomar, J. Dean, I. Kohane, Machine learning in medicine, The New England Journal of Medicine 380 (2019) 1347–1358.
[169] A. Rani, E. Baburaj, An efficient secure authentication on cloud based e-health care system in WBAN, Biomedical Research-Tokyo (2016) 53–59.
[170] T. Rankinen, M. Sarzynski, S. Ghosh, C. Bouchard, Are there genetic paths common to obesity, cardiovascular disease outcomes, and cardiovascular risk factors?, Circulation Research 116 (5) (2015) 909–922.
[171] R.V. Rao, K. Selvamani, Data security challenges and its solutions in cloud computing, Procedia Computer Science 48 (2015) 204–209.
[172] S. Rao, S. Suma, M. Sunitha, Security solutions for big data analytics in healthcare, in: 2015 Second International Conference on Advances in Computing and Communication Engineering, 2015, pp. 510–514.
[173] C. Rathnam, S. Lee, X. Jiang, An algorithm for direct causal learning of influences on patient outcomes, Artificial Intelligence in Medicine 75 (2017) 1–15.
[174] D. Ravì, C. Wong, F. Deligianni, M. Berthelot, J. Andreu-Perez, B. Lo, G.-Z. Yang, Deep learning for health informatics, IEEE Journal of Biomedical and Health Informatics 21 (1) (2016) 4–21.

[175] M. Recht, R.N. Bryan, Artificial intelligence: threat or boon to radiologists?, Journal of the American College of Radiology 14 (11) (2017) 1476–1480.

[176] N. Record, D.K. Onion, R. Prior, D.C. Dixon, S. Record, F.L. Fowler, G.R. Cayer, C. Amos, T. Pearson, Community-wide cardiovascular disease prevention programs and health outcomes in a rural county, 1970-2010, JAMA 313 (2) (2015) 147–155.

[177] L.C. Roura, S. Arulkumaran, Facing the noncommunicable disease (NCD) global epidemic–the battle of prevention starts in utero–the FIGO challenge, Best Practice & Research. Clinical Obstetrics & Gynaecology 29 (1) (2015) 5–14.

[178] S. Russell, J. Bohannon, Artificial intelligence. Fears of an AI pioneer, Science (New York, NY) 349 (6245) (2015) 252.

[179] S. Sabra, M. Alobaidi, K. Malik, V. Sabeeh, Performance evaluation for semantic-based risk factors extraction from clinical narratives, in: 2018 IEEE 8th Annual Computing and Communication Workshop and Conference (CCWC), 2018, pp. 695–701.

[180] M. Sagner, A. McNeil, P. Puska, C. Auffray, N. Price, L. Hood, C. Lavie, Z.G. Han, Z. Chen, S. Brahmachari, B. McEwen, M. Soares, R. Balling, E. Epel, R. Arena, The p4 health spectrum - a predictive, preventive, personalized and participatory continuum for promoting healthspan, Progress in Cardiovascular Diseases 59 (5) (2017) 506–521.

[181] A. Salehzadeh, A.P. Calitz, J. Greyling, Human activity recognition using deep electroencephalography learning, Biomedical Signal Processing and Control 62 (2020) 102094.

[182] K.A. Salleh, L. Janczewski, Technological, organizational and environmental security and privacy issues of big data: a literature review, Procedia Computer Science 100 (2016) 19–28.

[183] F. Sardanelli, M.G. Hunink, F.J. Gilbert, G. Di Leo, G.P. Krestin, Evidence-based radiology: why and how?, European Radiology 20 (1) (2010) 1–15.

[184] M. Scheffer, J. Bascompte, W. Brock, V. Brovkin, S. Carpenter, V. Dakos, H. Held, E.V. Nes, M. Rietkerk, G. Sugihara, Early-warning signals for critical transitions, Nature 461 (2009) 53–59.

[185] M.U. Scherer, Regulating artificial intelligence systems: risks, challenges, competencies, and strategies, Harvard Journal of Law & Technology 29 (2015) 353.

[186] A.A. Schuppert, Efficient reengineering of meso-scale topologies for functional networks in biomedical applications, Journal of Mathematics in Industry 1 (1) (2011) 1–20.

[187] T. Seeman, T. Gruenewald, A. Karlamangla, S. Sidney, K. Liu, B. McEwen, J. Schwartz, Modeling multisystem biological risk in young adults: the coronary artery risk development in young adults study, American Journal of Human Biology 22 (2010).

[188] S.H. Shah, D. Arnett, S. Houser, G. Ginsburg, C. Macrae, S. Mital, J. Loscalzo, J. Hall, Opportunities for the cardiovascular community in the precision medicine initiative, Circulation 133 (2016) 226–231.

[189] S. Shimizu, P. Hoyer, A. Hyvärinen, A.J. Kerminen, A linear non-Gaussian acyclic model for causal discovery, Journal of Machine Learning Research 7 (2006) 2003–2030.

[190] P. Sobradillo, F. Pozo, A. Agustí, P4 medicine: the future around the corner, Archivos De Bronconeumologia 47 (2011) 35–40.

[191] P. Spirtes, C. Glymour, R. Scheines, Causation, Prediction, and Search, 2nd edition, 2001.

[192] R.M. Summers, C.F. Beaulieu, L.M. Pusanik, J.D. Malley, R.B. Jeffrey Jr, D.I. Glazer, S. Napel, Automated polyp detector for ct colonography: feasibility study, Radiology 216 (1) (2000) 284–290.

[193] X. Sun, D. Janzing, B. Schölkopf, K. Fukumizu, A kernel-based causal learning algorithm, in: Proceedings of the 24th International Conference on Machine Learning, 2007, pp. 855–862.

[194] H. Tabrizchi, M.K. Rafsanjani, A survey on security challenges in cloud computing: issues, threats, and solutions, The Journal of Supercomputing (2020) 1–40.

[195] N. Talebi, C. Hallam, G. Zanella, The new wave of privacy concerns in the wearable devices era, in: 2016 Portland International Conference on Management of Engineering and Technology (PICMET), 2016, pp. 3208–3214.

[196] M. Taljaard, M. Tuna, C. Bennett, R. Perez, L. Rosella, J. Tu, C. Sanmartin, D. Hennessy, P. Tanuseputro, M. Lebenbaum, D. Manuel, Cardiovascular disease population risk tool (CVDPoRT): predictive algorithm for assessing CVD risk in the community setting. A study protocol, BMJ Open 4 (2014).

[197] A. Talukder, M. Chaitanya, D. Arnold, K. Sakurai, Proof of disease: a blockchain consensus protocol for accurate medical decisions and reducing the disease burden, in: 2018 IEEE SmartWorld, Ubiquitous Intelligence & Computing, Advanced & Trusted Computing, Scalable Computing & Communications, Cloud & Big Data Computing, Internet of People and Smart City Innovation (SmartWorld/SCALCOM/UIC/ATC/CBDCom/IOP/SCI), 2018, pp. 257–262.

[198] A. Thierer, A.C. O'Sullivan, R. Russell, Artificial intelligence and public policy, Innovation Law & Policy eJournal (2017).

[199] B. Thomas, L. Gostin, Tackling the global NCD crisis: innovations in law and governance, The Journal of Law, Medicine & Ethics 41 (2013) 16–27.

[200] H. Thomson, S. Thomas, E. Sellstrom, M. Petticrew, Housing improvements for health and associated socioeconomic outcomes, The Cochrane Database of Systematic Reviews 2 (2013) CD008657.

[201] J.H. Thrall, X. Li, Q. Li, C. Cruz, S. Do, K. Dreyer, J. Brink, Artificial intelligence and machine learning in radiology: opportunities, challenges, pitfalls, and criteria for success, Journal of the American College of Radiology 15 (3) (2018) 504–508.

[202] C. Trefois, P. Antony, J. Gonçalves, A. Skupin, R. Balling, Critical transitions in chronic disease: transferring concepts from ecology to systems medicine, Current Opinion in Biotechnology 34 (2015) 48–55.

[203] G. Twig, G. Yaniv, H. Levine, A. Leiba, N. Goldberger, E. Derazne, D.B.-A. Shor, D. Tzur, A. Afek, A. Shamiss, Z. Haklai, J.D. Kark, Body-mass index in 2.3 million adolescents and cardiovascular death in adulthood, The New England Journal of Medicine 374 (25) (2016) 2430–2440.

[204] M. Ullman-Cullere, J. Mathew, Emerging landscape of genomics in the electronic health record for personalized medicine, Human Mutation 32 (2011).

[205] A. Vasilateanu, I. Radu, A. Buga, Environment crowd-sensing for asthma management, in: 2015 e-Health and Bioengineering Conference (EHB), 2015, pp. 1–4.

[206] E. Vayena, A. Blasimme, Health research with big data: time for systemic oversight, The Journal of Law, Medicine & Ethics 46 (2018) 119–129.

[207] A. Verghese, N.H. Shah, R.A. Harrington, What this computer needs is a physician: humanism and artificial intelligence, JAMA 319 (1) (2018) 19–20.

[208] E. Vieta, Personalized medicine applied to mental health: precision psychiatry, Revista de Psiquiatría y Salud Mental 8 (2015) 117–118.

[209] H. Vogt, B. Hofmann, L. Getz, The new holism: P4 systems medicine and the medicalization of health and life itself, Medicine, Health Care, and Philosophy 19 (2016) 307–323.

[210] M. Von Stosch, R. Oliveira, J. Peres, S.F. de Azevedo, Hybrid semi-parametric modeling in process systems engineering: past, present and future, Computers & Chemical Engineering 60 (2014) 86–101.

[211] D. Wegener, S. Rossi, F. Buffa, M. Delorenzi, S. Rüping, Towards an environment for data mining based analysis processes in bioinformatics and personalized medicine, Network Modeling Analysis in Health Informatics and Bioinformatics 2 (2013) 29–44.

[212] S. Weiss, Implementing personalized medicine in the academic health center, Journal of Personalized Medicine 6 (2016).

[213] J. Wiley, T. Gruenewald, A. Karlamangla, T. Seeman, Modeling multisystem physiological dysregulation, Psychosomatic Medicine 78 (2016) 290–301.

[214] J. Wise, "Tsunami of obesity" threatens all regions of world, researchers find, 2011.

[215] C. Yam, E.L. Wong, F.W. Chan, M. Leung, F. Wong, A. Cheung, E. Yeoh, Avoidable readmission in Hong Kong - system, clinician, patient or social factor?, BMC Health Services Research 10 (2010) 311.

[216] E. Younesi, M. Hofmann-Apitius, From integrative disease modeling to predictive, preventive, personalized and participatory (p4) medicine, The EPMA Journal 4 (2013) 23.

[217] B. Yüksel, A. Küpçü, Ö. Özkasap, Research issues for privacy and security of electronic health services, Future Generations Computer Systems 68 (2017) 1–13.

[218] Y. Zhang, Y. Cheng, K. Jia, A. Zhang, Opportunities for computational techniques for multi-omics integrated personalized medicine, Tsinghua Science & Technology 19 (2014) 545–558.

[219] S. Zieff, J. Hipp, A. Eyler, M. sook Kim, Ciclovía initiatives: engaging communities, partners, and policy makers along the route to success, Journal of Public Health Management and Practice: JPHMP 19 (3 Suppl 1) (2013) S74–S82.

[220] I.A. Zriqat, A. Altamimi, Security and privacy issues in ehealthcare systems: towards trusted services, International Journal of Advanced Computer Science and Applications 7 (2016).

Index

Printed in the United States
by Baker & Taylor Publisher Services